LAW AND SOCIOLOGY

CURRENT LEGAL ISSUES 2005

VOLUME 8

CURRENT LEGAL PUBLICATIONS

Law and Sociology

Current Legal Issues 2005

VOLUME 8

Edited by
MICHAEL FREEMAN
Professor of English Law
University College London

UNIVERSITY PRESS

OXFORD
UNIVERSITY PRESS

Great Clarendon Street, Oxford OX2 6DP

Oxford University Press is a department of the University of Oxford.
It furthers the University's objective of excellence in research, scholarship,
and education by publishing worldwide in

Oxford New York

Auckland Cape Town Dar es Salaam Hong Kong Karachi
Kuala Lumpur Madrid Melbourne Mexico City Nairobi
New Delhi Shanghai Taipei Toronto

With offices in

Argentina Austria Brazil Chile Czech Republic France Greece
Guatemala Hungary Italy Japan Poland Portugal Singapore
South Korea Switzerland Thailand Turkey Ukraine Vietnam

Published in the United States
by Oxford University Press Inc., New York

First published 2006

British Library Cataloguing in Publication Data
Data available

Library of Congress Cataloging in Publication Data

Law and sociology / edited by Michael Freeman.
p. cm.—(Current legal issues ; 2005, v. 8)
Includes bibliographical references and index.
ISBN-13: 978–0–19–928254–8
ISBN-10: 0–19–928254–4
1. Sociological jurisprudence I. Freeman, Michael D. A.
II. Current legal issues ; v. 8.
K370.L3865 2006
340′.115—dc22 2005034738

Typeset by Newgen Imaging Systems (P) Ltd., Chennai, India
Printed in Great Britain
on acid-free paper by
Biddles Ltd., King's Lynn, Norfolk

ISBN 0–19–928254–4 978–0–19–928254–8

1 3 5 7 9 10 8 6 4 2

General Editor's Preface

UCL Law School held its eighth international interdisciplinary colloquium in September 2004. This book is the product of the colloquium. My thanks are to Professor Hazel Genn who helped to co-convene the colloquium, to Lisa Penfold who ably administered it and to Laura Smith and Priscilla Saporu without whose administrative and secretarial assistance the book would not have seen the light of day.

The next volume in this series, to be published later in 2006, is on 'Law and Psychology'.

The next colloquium on 'Law and Philosophy' will take place on 6 and 7 July 2006. Enquiries about this may be addressed to Lisa Penfold at (**lisa.penfold@ucl.ac.uk**). One is planned on 'Law and Bioethics', for July 2007.

Professor Michael Freeman

Contents

Notes on Contributors

Michael Freeman is Professor of English Law at University College London. He conceived this series of ongoing international inter-disciplinary colloquia and has edited previous books in the series including *Law and Literature, Law and Medicine*, and *Law and Popular Culture*. He is the author of Lloyd's *Introduction To Jurisprudence*, the eighth edition of which is being prepared currently.

Roger Cotterrell is Professor of Legal Theory at Queen Mary, University of London. He is the author of *The Politics of Jurisprudence* (Butterworths, 1989), *The Sociology of Law* (Butterworths, 1992), and *Emile Durkheim: Law in a Moral Domain* (Edinburgh University Press, 1999).

Richard Nobles and David Schiff are Readers in Law at the London School of Economics. With James Penner, they edited and wrote many of the chapters in the book *Introduction to Jurisprudence and Legal Theory: Commentary and Materials* (Butterworths, 2002). They have written extensively on criminal appeals and mis-carriages of justice, including *Understanding Miscarriages of Justice: Law, the Media, and the Inevitability of Crisis* (Oxford University Press, 2000). They recently edited and wrote the Introduction to a translation of Niklas Luhmann's major work on law, *Law as a Social System* (Oxford University Press, 2004).

John Griffiths is Professor of Sociology of Law at the University of Groningen, the Netherlands. He studied philosophy (University of California) and law (Yale University) and taught law in the United States and Ghana before joining the Faculty of Law in Groningen in 1977. Over the years, his theoretical writings have been concerned with the (empirical) concept of law, legal pluralism, disputing, and the effectiveness of legal rules. In recent years, his legal and empirical research has been largely devoted to problems of the regulation of euthanasia and other socially problematic medical behaviour.

Hamish Ross is a Lecturer in Law at the Robert Gordon University of Aberdeen in Scotland and is the author of *Law as a Social Institution* (Hart Publishing, 2001).

Julian Webb is Professor of Law at the University of Westminster, London, England and Visiting Professor of Legal Education at Southampton Solent University. He is co-author with Donald Nicolson of *Professional Legal Ethics: Critical Interrogations* (Oxford University Press, 1999), and his latest book, *Law, Complexity and Globalization* is due to be published by UCL Press in 2006.

Tim Murphy is Professor of Law at London School of Economics, and is the author of *The Oldest Social Science* (Oxford University Press, 1997).

Krzysztof Motyka is a Lecturer at the Catholic University of Lublin and a part-time Assistant Professor at Warsaw University in Poland, where his teaching includes courses in Legal Philosophy, Human Rights and Introduction to Sociology of Law. Since 2005 he has been Head of the Department of Theory and Sociology of Law, University of Information Technology and Management in Rzeszów. He recently published a monograph on American debates over the right to privacy (in Polish) and is currently preparing an English translation of his Ph.D. thesis entitled *Challenging Legal Orthodoxy: Petrażycki, Polish Jurisprudence and the Quest for the Nature of Law*, to be published by Springer.

Bettina Lange is a Lecturer in the Law School at Keele University in England. She was a Jean-Monnet Fellow at the European University Institute, Florence, Italy in 2004–5. She has published works in the fields of environmental regulation, regulation theory and socio-legal research methods.

Daphne Barak-Erez is a Professor at the Faculty of Law of Tel-Aviv University. Her fields of interest include administrative and constitutional law, human rights law, law and society and legal history. Previously, she served as the Director of the Minerva Center for Human Rights at Tel-Aviv University and as the Deputy Dean of the Faculty of Law at Tel-Aviv University. She has published several books and many articles in Israel, England, the United States, and Canada.

Lawrence M. Friedman is the Marion Rice Kirkwood Professor at the Stanford Law School, California, USA. He has written extensively on the sociology and history of law, and is current President of the Research Committee on the Sociology of Law of the International Sociological Association.

David Nelken is Distinguished Professor of Sociology, University of Macerata, Italy, Distinguished Research Professor of Law, University of Wales, Cardiff, and Visiting Professor of Law, London School of Economics. He has received a Distinguished Scholar award from American Sociological Association and has been a Trustee of the Law and Society Association. He is Vice President of the RCSL and on the Board of Governors of the Onati International Institute. He writes in the fields of sociology of law, criminology, and comparative law.

Issachar Rosen-Zvi is a Lecturer in Law at Tel-Aviv University in Israel. His fields of interest include legal pluralism, law and geography, local government law and environmental law. His latest book, *Taking Space Seriously* (Ashgate, 2004) explores the different ways in which a multicultural state deals with various social groups through the mechanism of space.

Robert Fine is Professor of Sociology at the University of Warwick in England. He is author of *Democracy and the Rule of Law: Marx's Critique of the Legal Form* (Blackburn, 2002) and *Political Investigations: Hegel, Marx, Arendt* (Routledge, 2001). He is currently researching into cosmopolitan social theory, and his latest book, *Cosmopolitanism*, is due to be published by Routledge in 2006–7. He is currently Convenor MA Social and Political Thought and Head of Department.

Rolando Vázquez is Visiting Fellow at the Sociology Department, University of Warwick, England and at the Sociology Department, Göteborgs University in Sweden. He has done research linking the thought of Walter Benjamin and Hannah Arendt, particularly in relation to the modern ideas of history and time. He is currently researching the temporality of globalization discourses in current social theory.

Dennis M. Patterson writes in the fields of international trade law, commercial law, and legal philosophy. He is Co-Director of the Rutgers (Camden) Institute for Law and Philosophy and holds the rank of Distinguished Professor of Law (Camden) and Philosophy (New Brunswick, Affiliated Faculty) at Rutgers University in New Jersey. He is the author of *Law and Truth* (Oxford University Press, 1996) and editor of the *Blackwell Anthology to the Philosophy of Law and Legal Theory* (Blackwell, 2003).

Iain Stewart is a Senior Lecturer in Law at Macquarie University, Sydney, Australia.

James Marshall is a Lecturer in Law at the University of Lancaster in England. He is also a solicitor.

Joseph Sanders is Professor of Law at the Law School, University of Houston, Texas, USA.

Katerina Sideri is Lecturer in Law at the University of Exeter, England.

Mohamed S. Abdel Wahab is a Lecturer at the Faculty of Law, Cairo University, Egypt and Assistant Director of the Human Rights Centre at Cairo University. He holds a number of visiting posts and has been appointed as a Fellow of the Centre for Information Technology and Dispute Resolution at the University of Massachusetts, Amherst, USA. He is a member of the UN Expert Group on Online Dispute Resolution, vice-president of the Cairo branch of the Chartered Institute of Arbitrators, and an Of Counsel at Shalakany Law Office Cairo. He holds a number of prizes for academic achievement, and has published several articles in learned international journals and is regular speaker at international conferences on Globalization, Socio-Legal Studies, Private International Law, Alternative Dispute Resolution, Online Dispute Resolution and E-commerce and IT Law.

David Hirsh is a Lecturer in the Sociology Department at Goldsmiths College, London University. His book, *Law against Genocide: Cosmopolitan Trials* (Glasshouse Press, 2003) won the British Sociological Association Philip Abrams Prize in 2004. He is currently working on cosmopolitanism, cosmopolitan law, Zionism, anti-Zionism and anti-Semitism.

Janne Pölönen is a Ph.D candidate in history and civilizations at the Ecole de Hautes Etudes en Sciences Sociales, Paris.

Bogusia Puchalska is a Senior Lecturer in Law at the Lancashire Law School, University of Central Lancashire, Preston. Her research interests are comparative law; socio-legal and political studies of transitions countries, particularly Poland; and the EU.

Vincenzo Ferrari is Professor of Sociology of Law and currently Dean of the Law Faculty at the University of Milan, Italy. He has been Visiting Professor at a number of Italian and foreign universities, and is a Former President ISA Research Committee on Sociology of Law. Among his most recent publications are *Lineamenti di sociologia del diritto. Azione giuridica e sistema normativo* (Roma-Bari, 1997) and *Diritto e società* (Roma-Bari, 1997).

Robert van Krieken is Associate Professor of Sociology at the University of Sydney, Australia.

Helen Reece is a Reader in Law at Birkbeck College, University of London and the author of *Divorcing Responsibly* (Hart Publishing, 2003).

1

Law and Sociology

Michael Freeman

One of the most characteristic features of twentieth-century jurisprudence was the development of sociological approaches to law.[1] The social sciences had an influence almost comparable to that of religion in earlier periods.[2] And legal thought has tended to reflect the trends to be found in sociology.

There are different approaches but one can pinpoint a number of ideas in the thinking of those who adopt a sociological approach to the legal order. There is a belief in the non-uniqueness of law: a vision of law as but one method of social control.[3] There is also a rejection of a 'jurisprudence of concepts', the view of law as a closed logical order.[4] Further, sociological jurists tend to be sceptical of the rules presented in the textbooks and concerned to see what really happens, the 'law in action'.[5] It is common to see reality as socially constructed, so that there is no natural guide to the solution of many conflicts.[6] Sociological jurists have believed also in the importance of harnessing the techniques of the social sciences, as well as the knowledge culled from sociological research, towards the erection of a more effective science of law. There is also a concern with social justice, though in what this consists, and how it is to be attained, views differ.[7]

1 See R. Cotterrell, 'Why Must Legal Ideas Be Interpreted Sociologically?' (1998) 25 *Journal of Law and Society* 171.

2 Auguste Comte (1798–1857) of course, who invented the term 'sociology', though not the discipline, put forward a new Religion of Humanity, with an elaborate ritual aimed at achieving an effective means of social cohesion. See M. Pickering, *Auguste Comte* (London, 1993).

3 On Eugen Ehrlich (1862–1922) see N. Littlefield, 'Eugen Ehrlich's Fundamental Principles of the Sociology of Law' (1967) 19 *Maine Law Review* 1–27. See also S. Henry, *Private Justice* (London, 1983). Cotterrell, below p. 19 discusses Ehrlich.

4 Exemplified in the work of F. Gény, *Méthode d'Interprétation et Sources en Droit Privé Positif* (Paris, 2nd edn., 1932).

5 And note K. Llewellyn's programme of 'Realism': 'Some Realism About Realism' (1931) 44 *Harvard Law Review* 1222. See, further, N.E.H. Hull, *Roscoe Pound and Karl Llewellyn: Searching for An American Jurisprudence* (Chicago, 1997).

6 *Cf.* P. Berger and T. Luckmann, *The Social Construction of Reality* (Harmondsworth, 1966) and I. Hacking, *The Social Construction of What?* (Cambridge, Mass., 1999). Social order has been described as where 'the struggle between individuals was halted and truce lines were drawn up' (*per* A. Hutchinson and P. Monahan (1984) 36 *Stanford Law Review* 199, 216).

7 Contrast the views of the social engineer Roscoe Pound (1870–1964) (on whom see D. Wigdor, *Roscoe Pound: Philosopher of Law* (Westport, Conn., 1974)) with today's Rational Action Theory, discussed by Cotterrell at p. 26.

For much of the twentieth century the sociology of law was eclipsed by sociological jurisprudence. It was Pound, rather than Weber or Durkheim, who was the dominant figure, despite the 'vagueness of his conceptual thinking'.[8] From the 1960s the term 'sociological jurisprudence' was used less frequently, and what came to be known as 'socio-legal studies' took root. Advocates of socio-legal studies[9] emphasize the importance of placing law in its social context, of using social-scientific research methods, of recognizing that many traditional jurisprudential questions are empirical in nature and not just conceptual.[10] Socio-legal studies have been described by Cotterrell as a 'transition phase'.[11] It had a considerable impact: on the law, on legal education, on legal research, on law publishing. It also had shortcomings, well identified by Lawrence Friedman.

> To many observers, the work done so far amounts to very little: an incoherent or inconclusive jumble of case studies. There is (it seems) no foundation; some work merely proves the obvious, some is poorly designed; there are no axioms, no 'laws' of legal behavior, nothing cumulates. The studies are at times interesting and are sporadically useful. But there is no 'science', nothing adds up . . . Grand theories do appear from time to time, but they have no survival power; they are nibbled to death by case studies. There is no central core.[12]

Socio-legal studies was largely lacking in any theoretical underpinning.[13] The law—and this was often defined narrowly[14]—and the legal system were treated as discrete entities, as unproblematic, and as occupying a central hegemonic position.[15] There was rarely any attempt to relate the legal system to the wider social order or to the state. When reforms were proposed, they were to make the legal system operate more efficiently or effectively. And the emphasis was more on the 'behaviour'[16] of institutions, than on trying to understand legal doctrine.

This is not what the sociology of law is about, as those who remember the writings of Weber, Durkheim, or Ehrlich were able to point out. For the sociology of law, as Campbell and Wiles pointed out thirty years ago, focuses on 'understanding the nature of social order through a study of law'.[17]

Much of the focus in contemporary writing, as this book simply demonstrates, is on what is involved in this understanding. Should legal definitions be transformed into sociological categories, or sociological insights into legal concepts? Can the

[8] As Cotterrell, at p. 19, notes.

[9] For example, Hazel Genn.

[10] *Cf.* J. P. Gibbs, 'Definitions of Law and Empirical Questions' (1968) 2 *Law and Society Review* 429.

[11] *Law's Community* (Oxford, 1995), 296.

[12] 'The Law and Society Movement' (1986) 38 *Stanford Law Review* 763, 779.

[13] And see A. Hunt, 'Dichotomy and Contradiction In The Sociology of Law' (1981) 8 *British Journal of Law and Society* 47.

[14] See Cotterrell, n.11, above.

[15] This was also the common juristic position, exemplified in the classic by H.L.A. Hart, *The Concept of Law* (Oxford, 1961; 2nd edn., 1994). He, of course, purported to be writing 'descriptive sociology'. And see N. Lacey, *HLA Hart* (Oxford, 2004), and H. Ross, *Law As a Social Institution* (Oxford, 2001).

[16] See also D. Black, *The Behavior of Law* (New York, 1976). A defence of Black is M.P. Baumgartner in D. Patterson (ed.), *A Companion to Philosophy of Law and Legal Theory* (Oxford, 1996), ch. 28.

[17] 'The Study of Law in Society in Britain' (1976) 10 *Law and Society Review* 547, 578, 553.

two approaches be combined? If the law has a limited sociological understanding of the world, does sociology have anything to offer the jurist to enable him/her better to appreciate it? As David Nelken has pointed out, there are dangers.[18] He, following Sarat and Silbey,[19] notes the concern of sociologists of law that they will be used ('the pull of the policy audience'), compromising academic social science and blunting the edge of political critique. Nelken's own concern is that 'the introduction of different styles of reasoning can have ill effects for legal practice by misunderstanding and thus threatening the integrity of legal processes or the values they embody'.[20]

For Cotterrell, on the other hand, the sociology of law is a 'transdisciplinary enterprise and aspiration to broaden understanding of law as a social phenomenon.'[21] He emphasizes the centrality of the sociology of law for legal education and legal practice: 'the methodology of sociological understanding of legal ideas is the deliberate *extension* in carefully specified directions of the diverse ways in which legal participants themselves think about the social world in legal terms'.[22] Sociology, Cotterrell argued, offers insights into legal thinking, and can transform legal ideas by re-interpreting them.

But can sociology 'climb out of its own skin and get inside the law to understand and explain the law's "truth"?'[23] That it has difficulties in so doing are attributable only in part to its limitations. As Banakar demonstrates, 'the fact that law secures its domination and authority through normative closure ... denies the commonality of discourses of sociology and the law, posing unique methodological problems for the sociology of law. The sheer institutional strength of the law hampers access to empirical material, questions the relevance of sociological insights into legal reasoning and ... raises doubts on the adequacy of sociology to produce a knowledge which transcends its own reality'.[24]

Nelken's response is that if we are 'to bring sociology of law up against its limits',[25] its dependence on sociology must be recognized. It then becomes necessary to 'examine more carefully how its reflexivity and that of law relate'.[26] He points to a range of writing in legal and social theory which sets out to analyse differences, and similarities, between sociological reflexivity and legal closure: Lyotard's 'phrases in difference',[27] Luhmann's autopoiesis,[28] Murphy's law's estrangement.[29]

[18] 'Blinding Insights?', 'The Limits of a Reflexive Sociology of Law' (1998) 25 *Journal of Law and Society* 407.

[19] 'The Pull of the Policy Audience' (1988) 10 *Law and Policy* 97.

[20] n.18, above, 408.

[21] 'Why Must Legal Ideas Be Interpreted Sociologically?' (1998) 25 *Journal of Law and Society* 171, 187.

[22] *Ibid*, 190.

[23] This question was posed by R. Banakar, 'Reflections on the Methodological Issues of the Sociology of Law', (2000) 27 *Journal of Law and Society* 273, 274. See further, R. Banakar, *Merging Law and Sociology: Beyond The Dichotomies in Socio-Legal Research* (Berlin, 2003).

[24] *Ibid*, 284.

[25] n.18, above, 415.

[26] *Ibid*, 417.

[27] *The Differend, Phrases in Dispute* (Minneapolis, Minn., 1988).

[28] See further M. King and C. Thornhill, *Niklas Luhmann's Theory of Politics and Law* (Basingstoke, 2003).

[29] *The Oldest Social Science* (Oxford, 1997).

Cotterrell believes that the law can profit from sociologically-inspired resolutions, particularly when legal doctrine is rift by conflicting precedents. This is undeniably true, and it would be foolish for the lawyer to ignore social insights. However, as Nelken points out, the institution of such insights has 'the potential to distort or at least change . . . legal practices rather than simply help them to sort out self-induced muddles'.[30] If only we knew when social science could guide us to the answer, and convince us it was the right one. Nelken may well be right that social insights function differently when they prise open legal closure (he cites Downs's discussion of the so-called 'battered women's syndrome' as a method of displacing law's myths about women battering[31]), than when they are used to provide closure.[32] But, as Trubek points out, 'whatever social sciences can do for the law, it *cannot* offer . . . objectivist grounding for legal policy'.[33] This is not the view of all legal sociologists.

Donald Black, notably, predicts the development of 'sociological law', when lawyers reflexively internalize the conclusion that sociology is the best guide to legal outcomes.[34] According to Black, the sociology of law entails the adoption of an observer's perspective:[35] this requires detachment (in striking contrast to what Cotterrell advocates). Black, however, claims that its findings are of great relevance to participants in the legal system. It may challenge long-standing conceptions about law: 'official versions' of the intentions and purposes of particular statutes are not, as a result, granted automatic respect, but are instead subjected to critical scrutiny.[36] So too are the 'conventional justifications of court procedures, and the legal representation of clients'. The sociology of law 'even suggests new possibilities for manipulating legal systems deliberately in order to bring about desired results, techniques of social engineering likely to become highly controversial as well as highly effective'.[37]

In the late 1990s a new form of sociological jurisprudence was proclaimed: realistic socio-legal theory. To Brian Tamanaha, this identifies and develops foundations for the social scientific study of law.[38] He draws on philosophical pragmatism to establish an epistemological foundation which specifies the nature of social science and its knowledge claims, and a methodological foundation which uses both behaviourism and interpretivism. Like Cotterrell, but for very different reasons, Tamanaha believes that legal theory and socio-legal studies have a lot to learn from one another. Unlike many sociologists of law, who took

[30] n.18, above, 422.

[31] See D. Downs, *More Than Victims: Battered Women, the Syndrome Society, and the Law* (Chicago, 1996).

[32] n.18 above, 422.

[33] 'Back To The Future: The Short Happy Life of the Law and Society Movement' (1990) 18 *Florida State University Law Review* 1.

[34] *Sociological Justice* (New York, 1989).

[35] *Ibid*, 19–22.

[36] An excellent example is M.J. Lindsay, 'Reproducing a Fit Citizenry: Dependency, Eugenics and the Law of Marriage in the United States, 1860–1920' (1998) 23 *Law and Social Inquiry* 541–85.

[37] *Per* Baumgartner, n.16, above, 413.

[38] *Realistic Socio-Legal Theory* (Oxford, 1997).

a definition of law from within jurisprudence,[39] Tamanaha insists that law should not be defined in ways that assume sociological connections, but should be subject to investigation and proof.

In a riposte to standard conceptual jurisprudence he maintains that

> what law is and what law does cannot be captured in any single scientific concept. The project to devise a scientific concept of law was based upon a misguided belief that law comprises a fundamental category. To the contrary law is thoroughly a cultural construct, lacking any universal essential nature. Law *is* whatever we attach the label *law* to.[40]

This is to confront conceptual jurisprudence face-on by denying that there is a concept of law. That he does not go this far is apparent from later work,[41] and from a response to this very criticism[42] in his Symposium on the book.[43] There he says of theorizing about the concept of law that 'we do it because law is a key social phenomenon that must be understood, analysed and discussed, which could not begin nor be carried far without conceptual analysis.'[44]

It is rather a recognition—of course, not novel[45]—that different phenomena fall under the concept 'law'. Law is a concept conventionally applied to a 'variety of multifaceted, multifunctional phenomena: natural law, international law, people's law, and indigenous law . . .'.[46] Tamanaha insists that there is not a 'central case of law':[47] he cites the example of international law which has its own integrity and has been functioning as a form of law for at least two centuries but which remains, under traditional and conceptual analysis, 'a borderline form of law'.[48] He is concerned that the central case approach to the concept of law fits, and was the product of, the ascendancy of state law that accompanied the rise of the state. His alternative conceptualization of law is, he believes, 'better able to account for the proliferation of different kinds of law than the traditional monotypical view of *the* concept of law'.[49]

On the question as to how one can evaluate whether one concept of law is better than another, Tamanaha offers the following evaluative criteria:

> First, the concept must be coherent, or analytically . . . sound, in the sense that, for example, it should not contain internal contradictions, or have gaps in crucial spots. Second, the concept must be consistent with, or 'fit', or be adequate to, the reality, phenomenon, or

[39] For example, Max Weber. [40] n.38, above, 128.

[41] 'A Non-Essentialist Version of Legal Pluralism' (2000) 27 *Journal of Law and Society* 296–321.

[42] By Brian Bix, 'Conceptual Jurisprudence and Socio-Legal Studies' (2000) 32 *Rutgers Law Journal* 227–39, 229–30.

[43] 'Conceptual Analysis, Continental Social Theory, and CLS' (2000) 32 *Rutgers Law Journal* 281–306. [44] *Ibid*, 283.

[45] John Austin recognized it: so do H.L.A Hart and John Finnis (note his emphasis on the 'focal' meaning of law). [46] n.38, above, 128.

[47] n.43, above, 284. [48] *Ibid.*

[49] n.43, above, He does not include within this the implications of cyberspace, on which see M.J. Radin and R.P. Wagner, 'The Myth of Private Ordering: Rediscovering Legal Realism in Cyberspace' (1998) 73 *Chicago and Kent Law Review* 1295–317.

idea it purports to represent, describe, or define.... Third, the concept must have use value in the sense that it will enhance our understanding or help us achieve our objective.[50]

Hart, as indicated above,[51] purported to be writing 'an essay in descriptive sociology', but it contains no description of social practices drawn from any legal system. Can conceptual jurisprudence have autonomy, or at least relative autonomy, from empirical reality? For Tamanaha, it cannot. Thus, one of the overriding objectives of his *Realistic Socio-Legal Theory* is to 'bring into legal theory an infusion of insights from the social scientific study of law. Socio-legal theory is a practice of theorizing about law that incorporates aspects of both (conceptual and socio-legal) approaches to legal phenomena.'[52] Sociological inquiries into 'the practices that legal theories purports to analyse and explain (and describe and prescribe) are essential to the enterprise of legal theory, or at least to a legal theory that wants to be good at what it does'.[53] But legal theory can neither be 'subsumed within nor dictated to' by legal sociology.[54]

Much of interest emerges from Tamanaha's realistic socio-legal theory. Most significantly, that law is a social practice amenable to social scientific study, and that legal theory and socio-legal theory have a lot to learn from each other.[55] It has long been recognized that sociological thinking about law would be considerably hampered without the insights of analytical jurisprudence. But analytical jurisprudence can look to sociology as well, and has much to gain, provided it uses the data appropriately. Thus, it is important for those studying the concept of law to know why people obey—or don't obey—the law,[56] why people use extra-legal norms[57] and procedures to resolve disputes,[58] how other societies (not those in Hart's central case, for example) deal with disputes. So long as it is recognized that analytical jurisprudence is not making empirical claims.

In the first essay in the volume Cotterrell asks what legal theory can learn from sociology, in particular from sociology's disciplinary debates. And his answer applies to all legal theory, not just that which ties itself to sociology. As he points out, any juristic study is 'a social practice, an intervention in the social world and a way of interpreting that world'.[59] The very diversity of legal theory may, he argues, be understood in terms of four categories of sociological practice described by the French sociologist Boudon.[60] Boudon distinguishes policy-oriented sociology

[50] n.43, above, 285. [51] At p. 2. [52] n.43, above, 287.

[53] *Ibid.* [54] *Ibid*, 288.

[55] One of Tamanaha's best chapters is on the internal/external distinction, throwing light on a central problem in contemporary analytical jurisprudence. See also 'The Internal/External Distinction and the Notion of a Practice in Legal Theory and Sociological Studies' (1996) 30 *Law and Society Review* 163–204.

[56] On which see T. Tyler, *Why People Obey the Law* (New Haven, 1990).

[57] On which see R. Ellickson, *Order Without Law: How Neighbors Settle Disputes* (Cambridge, Mass., 1991).

[58] A good example of which is B. Tamanaha, *Understanding Law in Micronesia: An Interpretive Approach To Transplanted Law* (Leiden, 1993). [59] See p. 30. [60] Post, p. 28.

('cameral/descriptive') from cognitive/scientific sociology which is driven by a disinterested search for knowledge, and from expressive sociology and critical sociology. Each has its parallel in legal theory, which can be policy-oriented, expressive, or critical (this reflected in radical movements like critical race theory[61] or Lat-Crit[62]), and can also be cognitive/scientific though, as Cotterrell concedes, this is 'as vague for legal theory as for sociology',[63] challenging us, as it does, to examine methods, aims, and objects.

Nobles and Schiff examine the implications of Luhmann's systems theory for jurisprudence, in particular for some of Ronald Dworkin's thinking. Luhmann's theory offers, they argue, a sociological explanation for the long-running debates within jurisprudence over such questions as the source of law, its determinacy/indeterminacy, and the role of justice. His systems theory is projected as a response to the 'paradox consequential to the tautology that the law decides what is and can be law . . . it is the legal system that identifies its own boundaries'. Dworkin, it may be argued, achieves this, but Nobles and Schiff maintain that 'Hercules',[64] whether in human or ideal form, provides a poor description of law 'or at least one that might appeal to a sociologist concerned to accommodate the given world of law's vast numbers of operations within their descriptions'.[65]

For Griffiths it is 'social control', and not 'law' that is the proper subject of sociology of law. The sociology of law is, in his view, not just one sociology among many, but that part of sociology which concerns itself with the 'social element' presupposed by all social life. It is not just one of the many sub-disciplines of sociology but it 'deals with the *sine qua non* of all sociology. The rest is derivative.'[66] Among the subjects discussed within this framework are its implications for legal pluralism.

There seems little doubt that, despite his protestations to the contrary,[67] Hart was influenced by Max Weber. But was the arch-positivist (or normativist[68]) Hans Kelsen also so influenced? This is explored in Hamish Ross's essay. Is, as Tur argued,[69] Kelsen's theory a model for 'a collectivist *verstehende* sociology'? Ross argues that Kelsen's concept of *Rechtssatz* and his concept of legal meaning (*rechtliche Bedeutung*) 'gravitate' towards Weberian interpretive sociology. Ross believes this is in spite of Kelsenian devices like imputation,[70] which, it may be

61 See K. Crenshaw, N. Gotanda, G. Pellar and K. Thomas, *Critical Race Theory—The Key Writings That Formed The Movement* (New York, 1995).

62 On which see B. Esperanza Hernández-Truyol, 'Borders (En) Gendered: Normativities, Latinas and a LatCrit Paradigm' (1997) 72 *New York University Law Review* 882.

63 See p. 30

64 First discussed by Dworkin in *Taking Rights Seriously* (London, 1977), 105–30.

65 See p. 37.

66 See p. 52. There are, as Griffiths notes, similarities with Durkheim's thesis that law reproduces the principal forms of social solidarity (*The Division of Labour in Society* (London, 1984), 68).

67 As discussed by Nicola Lacey, n.15, above, 230.

68 See, e.g. J. Raz, 'The Purity of the Pure Theory' (1983) *Revue International de Philosophie* 442–59.

69 'The Kelsenian Enterprise' in R. Tur and W. Twining, *Essays on Kelsen* (Oxford, 1980), 149.

70 Though Ross does not so indicate, the fullest discussion of this is in H. Kelsen, *What is Justice?* (Berkeley, California, 1957), 324. See also W. Ebenstein 'The Pure Theory of Law: Demythologizing Legal Thought' (1971) 59 *California Law Review* 617–52, 635–7.

remembered, was scorned by the Scandinavian Realist Karl Olivecrona.[71] But can a case be made, despite Kelsen's protestations, for Kelsen as an example of interdisciplinary? Or does this stretch credence too far? In Kelsen's view a science of law constructs its own objects and presents legal reasoning as a realm of thought and understanding wholly apart from sociological observation. To quote Kelsen: 'in so far as it is the method or form of understanding through which the object is determined, the antithesis of causal and normative sciences rests just as much on a difference in the direction of understanding as in a difference in the object of understanding.'[72]

For Webb it is a trans-disciplinary worldview that needs to be adopted to deal with trans-legal problems. He concedes, however, that neither the epistemological nor the ontological assumptions of transdisciplinarity are settled. It is, he argues, 'complexity itself' that contributes the greatest challenge to traditional disciplinarity, so that what is required is 'a theory of knowledge that takes complexity seriously.'[73] Following Gibbons and his colleagues he looks to, what is called, 'mode 2' knowledge production as the purposeful direction. But he goes further and suggests that a '"truly" better transdisciplinary system is likely to be based on "a mode-2 epistemology", not just mode-2 knowledge production'.[74] He concludes that mode 2 will be pushed by the agendas of universities, funding bodies and the state 'to a narrow, technocratic and scientistic means-end rationality.'[75]

The next chapter in this collection, by Murphy, is entitled, intriguingly, 'Durkheim in China'. Weber, of course, took great interest in China, and his views on China and rationality remain of controversy even today.[76] But Durkheim was not so interested. Murphy chooses to examine some trends in China seeing it as a 'society and governmental system (and "tradition") which has been claimed to illustrate and exemplify Durkheimianism at the level of social and political practices'.[77] Confucius, the fount of traditional Chinese wisdom, believed that societal cohesion was furthered by example and established morality, not by regulation and punishment.[78] A distinction was drawn in Chinese culture between *Li* and *Fa: Fa* (law) is an unpleasant necessity; *Li* (an ethical system of proper behaviour) is the more worthy and more useful method of social control.[79] But what of contemporary

[71] In *Law As Fact* (Copenhagen, 1939) who said of Kelsen's use of imputation to connect delict and punishment: 'A mystery it is and a mystery it will remain for ever' (21).

[72] Quoted by A. Wilson in n.69 above, 53.

[73] See p. 99.

[74] See p. 101. 'Mode 1' is mono-disciplinary and homogeneous: mode 2 is 'applied, transdisciplinary and heterogeneous'.

[75] See p. 105.

[76] See M. Weber, *Reading and Commentary on Modernity* (Oxford, 2005).

[77] See pp. 107–8.

[78] On the Confucian attitude to law see B. Schwartz in J.A. Cohen, *The Criminal Process in the Peoples Republic of China 1949–1963* (Berkeley, California, 1968), 62–70.

[79] See Y. Liu, *Origins of Chinese Law: Penal and Administrative Law in its Early Development* (Hong Kong, 1998) and X. Ren, *Tradition of The Law and Law of the Tradition* (Westport, Conn., 1997).

China? Does Durkheimian sociology cast any light on how it functions? Or, as Murphy insinuates, is Tarde more likely to provide such an explanation? Certainly, the idea of government by example may be traced to Tarde's long-ignored writing. But, as Murphy points out, exemplarity is only part of the cement that holds Chinese society together. There is also *guanxi*.[80] Do either Durkheim or Tarde explain this? Indeed, can any Western sociology? Do Chinese law and sociology scholars have any insights? Perhaps in time we shall discover these.

Murphy alludes to the rediscovery of Tarde. Another theorist awaiting rediscovery is Leon Petrażycki.[81] Motyka's essay offers a distinctively Petrażyckian perspective on law and sociology. There are similarities with Ehrlich.[82] Significantly, Petrażycki saw law as including unofficial as well as official, and intuitive as well as positive forms. The importance of Petrażycki is that he placed law in the realm of the sociologist. It was of course the province of sociology of Petrażycki's era and so is unsurprisingly functionalist. It would be all too easy for contemporary law and sociology scholars to dismiss his contribution, but there are insights of value, particularly on legal socialization.[83]

It is Lange's argument that the 'social' still matters for analysing legal regulation. She explores three sociological perspectives which helps to 'imagine' the social in legal regulation in new ways. These are the sociological analysis of emotions—a very different picture of which can be found in Motyka's examination of Petrażycki[84]—actor-network theory and economic sociology. Together these raise questions about such issues as the nature of bureaucratic organizations, the relationship between structure and agency and between legal and economic normativity.

Barak-Erez returns us to Durkheim's social solidarity thesis and examines through the prism of a case study of Israel the part which law, in particular court decisions, can play in constructing this. As she indicates, Israel offers an interesting test case given the ways its society is divided by culture and conflict (one of these conflicts is at the root of Rosen-Zvi's paper discussed later in this introduction[85]). The judicial system, with the Supreme Court in the vanguard, has become increasingly involved in normative decisions which claim to express shared basic

[80] Translated as 'relations'. See W. de Bary, 'Neo-Confuciannism and Human Rights' in L. Rouner (ed.), *Human Rights and the World's Religions* (Notre Dame, Indiana, 1998), 183. On notions of *guanxi* in western societies see J.M. Ghéhenno, *The End of The Nation State* (transl by V. Elliott) (Minneapolis, 1995).

[81] See further K. Motyka, *Challenging Legal Orthodoxy: Petrażycki, Polish Jurisprudence and the Quest for the Nature of Law* (forthcoming).

[82] On which see K.A. Ziegert, 'The Sociology Behind Eugen Ehrlich's Sociology of Law' (1979) 7 *International Journal of the Sociology of Law* 225–73.

[83] See, generally, J.L. Tapp and F. J. Levine, *Law, Justice and the Individual in Society: Psychological and Legal Issues* (New York, 1977).

[84] See p. 119.

[85] See p. 11.

values. And, not surprisingly, it has been frequently criticized for its activism. But the court finds itself having to step into the breach when the legislature fails to act. In doing so, does it assist the creation of social cohesion or further undermine it? The question can be asked in the context of other legal systems too. What has been the effect in the United States of the Supreme Court decision in *Roe* v. *Wade*?[86] That controversial court decisions catalyse public discussion of issues by supplying a discursive framework that would otherwise not exist may well be true. But they may also exacerbate conflict. Or conflict may relocate: in the United States one of the consequences of *Roe* v. *Wade* is the politicization of appointments to the Supreme Court.[87]

Culture is the key to the next contributions to this book. 'Legal culture', Friedman acknowledges, is a 'troublesome concept'.[88] His main argument hinges on its centrality in the social study of law. But legal structure[89] is also important, and the relationship between the two is difficult to unpick. Which is the primary force? There is no agreement.[90] There may be differences also on what belongs to each category. Where, for example, do religion and history fit? The role that religion plays in the development of family law or the laws on embryo research or cloning cannot be underestimated. Is the reception of Roman law in continental Europe explained by structure or culture or both, and can we explain the English failure to receive Roman law in the same way?[91]

Nelken's paper asks how the concept of 'legal culture' can be put to good use even by those who do not share Friedman's premises or conclusions. There are, and he catalogues them, alternatives such as 'legal tradition'[92] and 'legal ideology'.[93] The promise of the term 'legal culture' lies in its ability, if it can be shown to have this, to make comparisons of legal systems 'more sociologically meaningful'.[94] But, as Nelken argues, there is a tendency for the term to be applied 'both to elements within a society and to whole societies composed of these elements' and so to end up 'as an explanation of itself'.[95] Can this be avoided? Nelken shows that there are occasions when we want to explain this legal culture (or consciousness) and others when we think it can help us explain something else. The reference to 'legal consciousness' is significant. As Nelken points out: 'Students of legal consciousness seek to understand how and how far people come to think of themselves as rights-bearing subjects and to describe "legality" as a structure of action and meaning'.[96] Such concerns are prior to the question of why people use

86 410 US 113 (1973). And see D. Garrow, *Liberty and Sexuality* (New York, 1994).

87 As witness the preliminary skirmishes following the resignation of Sandra Day O'Connor in July 2005. For an earlier example see R. Bork, *The Tempting of America* (New York, 1990).

88 See p. 188.

89 See M.D.A. Freeman, *The Legal Structure* (Harlow, 1974).

90 The work of E. Blankenburg is often cited (see, e.g. 'Civil Litigation Rates as Indications for Legal Culture' in D. Nelken (ed.), *Comparing Legal Cultures* (Aldershot, 1997)).

91 See R.C. van Caenegem, *The Birth of The English Common Law* (Cambridge, 2nd edn., 1988).

92 H. Patrick Glenn, *Legal Traditions of the World* (Oxford, 2nd edn., 2004).

93 See R. Cotterrell, 'The Concept of Legal Culture' in Nelken (ed.), n. 90 above, 13–32.

94 See p. 200.

95 See p. 201.

96 See p. 217.

the law. Legal culture can be seen as a specific pattern of attitudes, uses and discourses about law. But it can be made to work as an explanatory variable in other ways too: for example, the decision to introduce a rule, a practice, an institution may result from legal culture elsewhere: the ombudsman concept from Sweden[97] or restorative justice from New Zealand.[98]

Rosen-Zvi tries to find an approach to the intractable problem of culture conflict. His starting point is an Israeli Supreme Court decision which sought a solution to the conflict between those who would ban the sale of pork and those who wished to eat it.[99] Rejecting the Court's solution as an essay in the 'ethics of provincialism', and finding no real answer in liberalism, multiculturalism or civil republicanism, Rosen-Zvi advocates an alternative vision based on Cass Sunstein's neo-republicanism[100] and Richard Ford's civic pluralism.[101] He looks for the politics of difference to be replaced by political dialogue, negotiation, and compromise.

Fine and Vázquez offer an interpretation of Hegel's classic text for the social theory of law *Elements of The Philosophy of Right*.[102] They explore the contrast between Hegel's recognition of subjective freedom as the great achievement of modern society, and his critique of subjectivism as its foremost pathology. Hegel, though he was the first to separate civil society from the state,[103] is neglected by law and sociology scholars. This essay may go some way towards addressing the balance.

If it helps to bring legal philosophy and legal sociology closer together—the adjustment has always been closer on continental Europe than it is in Anglophone countries—it will be grist to Patterson's mill. Patterson's note is an invitation to contemporary sociologists to engage with pragmatic philosophy.

Stewart is puzzled. Why, he asks, should generations of jurists have expended so much energy on the meaning of the word 'law' (as, of course, they have) when it is a meaning they need to keep obscure? The explanation then lies in legal ideology and in 'dark perfomatives'.[104] He proceeds to ask questions about the use of law, how one uses the word 'law'.

There is much about positivism in Stewart's pages. Marshall is also interested in positivism, in particular the positivist approach taken to law by small-town solicitors who were the subject of his empirical investigation. His research is derived from the conceptual framework of Bourdieu,[105] for whom the predictability of the

[97] See G. Drewry, 'The Ombudsman: Parochial Stopgap or Global Panacea?' in P. Leyland and T. Woods, *Administrative Law: Facing The Future* (London, 1997), 98.

[98] See A. Ashworth, 'Is Restorative Justice The Way Forward for Criminal Justice?' (2002) 54 *Current Legal Problems* 347–76; T. F. Marshall, *Restorative Justice: An Overview* (London, 1999).

[99] *Solodkin* v. *City of Beit Shemesh* H.C. 953/01 (2004).

[100] See C. Sunstein, *Free Markets and Social Justice* (Oxford, 1997), ch. 13.

[101] R.T. Ford, 'Geography and Sovereignty: Jurisdictional Formation and Racial Segregation' (1997) 49 *Stanford Law Review* 1365.

[102] And see. G.W.F. Hegel, *Elements of the Philosophy of Right* (ed. A.W. Wood) (Cambridge, 1991).

[103] See S. Avineri, *Hegel's Theory of The Modern State* (Cambridge, 1972). See also F. Dallmayr, 'Rethinking The Hegelian State' (1989) 10 *Cardozo Law Review* 1337.

[104] See p. 271.

[105] P. Bourdieu, 'The Force of Law: Toward a Sociology of the Juridical Field' (1987) 38 *Hastings Law Journal* 805.

law arises not from precedent but from the 'consistency and homogeneity of the legal habitus,'[106] though it goes beyond Bourdieu's conceptual perspective. Marshall's findings are broadly what one might expect. Perhaps his most interesting finding is the contrast between legal outsiders who tended to be rather more positivistic and those who were part of the local legal community and thus able to rely on informal relationships and practices. There are further insights here into the meaning of law and into legal culture.

As there are in Sanders' essay. The jury may be under attack in England[107] but there is a resurgence of interest in it in countries as diverse as Japan, Russia, and Spain.[108] Of course, the existence of various types of lay tribunals focuses our attention on the role of norms in society, and how norms and law interact to produce social order. One of the main justifications for the jury is the opportunity it offers for lay participation and hence the injection of community norms.[109] Juries have often acted as catalysts for law reform.[110] The revived interest in norms has come from law and economics.[111] Law and economics scholars have begun to examine the relationship between norms and legal rules and how norms influence an individual's decision whether to comply with or avoid a legal prescription. But there are factors in the law and economics discussion of norms which are under-emphasized. Sanders draws attention to three of these: power, role, and organization. He goes on to demonstrate how these factors are beneficial to our understanding of norms within the context of decision making of lay tribunals.

Sideri focuses on decentralized regulatory measures relating to the control of information in the European Union. She examines the ways modern governance techniques empower (or fail to empower) communities to participate in the decision-making process. Communication and co-operation are central and it would seem in this area they have failed. There are various ways of explaining this through relational actor-based theories or through using a Durkheimian approach. But these are not satisfactory, Sideri argues. She points instead to the importance of tacit knowledge 'encapsulated in practice and operating beyond the conscious level' (*phronesis* in Aristotle's language).[112]

The impact of globalization on the invocation of public policy is investigated by Wahab. It, or its civilian counterpart (*ordre public*) is the classical filter to

[106] See p. 282. [107] It has been the case since the 1960s.

[108] See S. Thaman, 'Europe's New Jury Systems: The Cases of Spain and Russia' in N. Vidmar (ed.), *World Jury Systems* (Oxford, 2000), 319, J. Kodner, 'Re-Introducing Lay Participation to Japanese Criminal Cases: An Awkward Yet Necessary Step' (2003) 2 *Washington University Global Studies Law Review* 569.

[109] See M.D.A. Freeman, 'The Jury On Trial' (1981) 34 *Current Legal Problems* 65–111.

[110] The introduction (in England) of the crimes of death by dangerous driving and infanticide are usually attributed to the refusal by juries to convict of more serious offences.

[111] For example, E. Posner, *Law and Social Norms* (Cambridge, Mass., 2000) and R.B. Korobkin and T.S. Ulen, 'Law and Behavioral Science: Removing The Rationality Assumption from Law and Economics' (2000) 88 *California Law Review* 1051. [112] See p. 337.

protect the forum against offensive laws or institutions.[113] But, Wahab points out, it is no longer an inherently exclusive national conception. Under the impact of globalization it has acquired transnational dimensions.[114] Nevertheless, it remains a last defence, and in extreme circumstances national courts will resort to it. It is, for example, preserved within the Rome Convention on contract[115] and the Brussels Regulation on Jurisdiction and Judgments,[116] and these are documents which are the products of a close European family.[117]

The subject of international law is also at the heart of Hirsh's paper. It is a new form of international law (or rather law) that he calls, following Kant, 'cosmopolitan law'.[118] It represents a break from international law 'because it does not put the rights of states above the rights of the people'. But cosmopolitan law could not emerge without the development of a cosmopolitan social collective memory. Hirsh points to the way that: 'Cosmopolitan courts receive nationally particularistic narratives as testimony that they transform into an authoritative cosmopolitan social memory'.[119]

Pölönen invites us to take a sociology of Roman law more seriously. I've studied (indeed, briefly, taught) Roman law and there was little sociology in the discipline then (the 1960s). UCL's last Professor of Roman Law, J.A.C.Thomas, would have reacted rather as Goering (or Hanns Johst) did to 'culture',[120] if encouraged to explore the sociology of his subject! And yet, as Pölönen points out, Rome and its law inspired many of the founding fathers of legal sociology. That it does not resonate with contemporary legal sociologists is hardly surprising, since very few of them will have any familiarity with Roman law. But Pölönen certainly makes out a case, and his detailed references point to much work that is being done and to leads that could be followed up. Indeed, he suggests insights which might enhance contemporary studies of law and sociology. He offers the challenge of Roman law as a test-case for modern sociological theories about law.

Puchalska's essay explains the Polish peoples' disillusionment with state institutions and the law in terms of Polish history, tradition, and character. A decade and a

113 See P.B. Carter. 'Transnational Recognition and Enforcement of Foreign Public Laws' (1989) 48 *Cambridge Law Journal* 417–35, and P. B. Carter, 'The Role of Public Policy in English Private International Law' (1993) 42 *International and Comparative Law Quarterly* 1–10.

114 See, e.g. *The Kribi* [2001] 1 Lloyd's Rep 76.

115 See Article 16.

116 Council Regulation 44/2001 Article 34(1). See *Maronier* v. *Larmer* [2002] 3 WLR 1060.

117 And thus in both public policy should only be invoked if the offensive law or judgment is manifestly contrary to public policy.

118 See M. Nussbaum, 'Kant and Cosmopolitanism' in J. Bohman and M. Lutz-Bachmann (eds.), *Perpetual Peace: Essays on Kant's Cosmopolitan Ideal* (Cambridge, Mass., 1997).

119 See p. 389. See more fully D. Hirsh, *Law Against Genocide: Cosmopolitan Trials* (London, 2003).

120 That 'he would reach for his revolver'. Though usually attributed to Hermann Goering, the Penguin *Dictionary of Modern Quotations* now says it was Hanns Johst who said this (Harmondsworth, 1980, 175). J.J. Good's response (also in the *Dictionary*, 135) is apposite: 'When I hear the word "gun" I reach for my culture'.

half after the collapse of Communism there has been no significant change in the perception of law. There is a crisis of legitimacy with social norms filling gaps. Economic and political changes of major proportions seem unable to shift a *Volksgeist*.[121] Is this the same in other countries with similar histories? Or is Poland a unique case? If so are there features of its history (the Partitions, the Nazi occupation, its Catholicism) which explains this? Puchalska offers us insights into these, but we need explorations of other post-Communist countries to get a fuller picture.

Ferrari's article is the only one in this collection which looks at the implications of students studying the sociology of law. It concentrates on Italian experiences, appropriately so, not only because the author is a leading Italian thinker in the area, but also because the study of the sociology of law is arguably more firmly entrenched in Italy than elsewhere, and certainly more so than in England. The doyen of Italian sociology of law, Renato Treves,[122] set out these approaches: grand theorizing; contributions to the general theory of law; and empirical research (which he thought the most promising and fertile, in view of the need to measure 'the distance between normative structures that are often obsolete and social contexts in endless development'[123]). In fact, as Ferrari points out, the centre of gravity of Italian sociology of law has not lain in socio-legal studies, as Treves hoped, but in grand theorizing, with Marxism and then the writings of Luhmann the dominant influences.

The final two papers in this book look at aspects of family law. Van Krieken examines the relationship between law and sociology in family law against the background of a discussion of Luhmann's analysis of law's combined operational closure and cognitive openness. He relates these theoretical concerns to the particular empirical example of debates within family law about the socio-legal construction of the post-separation custody of children. Both sociological research and theoretical debate have played a significant role in this. He uses the empirical example to identify ways in which the theoretical conception of law's relationship to challenges to its epistemic authority might be developed, including an improved understanding of the highly fragmented character of the social sciences, as well as of the importance of a range of 'mediating' agencies on the border of law and science, and of the significance of 'lay' forms of knowledge-construction, and of the role of political bodies that are neither legal nor scientific.

Reece follows her examination of responsible divorce[124] by looking at current English policies on parental responsibility. Earlier changes in the meaning of the

[121] To use the term we identify with F.K. von Savigny. See his *System of Roman Law* (1840) (English translation by W. Holloway, 1867) (the relevant passage is in M.D.A. Freeman, *Lloyd's Introduction To Jurisprudence* (London, 7th edn., 2001), 921–5).

[122] See R. Treves, 'Co-operation Between Lawyers and Sociologists: A Comparative Comment' (1974) 1 *British Journal of Law and Society* 200–4.

[123] R. Treves, 'Tre Concezioni e Una Proposta' (1974) 1 *Sociologia del Diritto* 1.

[124] H. Reece, *Divorcing Responsibly* (Oxford, 2003).

concept of parental responsibility have been traced by others.[125] Reece looks at the way the concept has shifted from one which emphasized parental authority to one which stresses parental accountability. And she points out that whilst parental responsibility as authority was clear-cut, now 'responsibility has become an attitude for which the parent is held to account . . . [and] he or she is no longer able to be fully responsible or fully irresponsible, because there is no action that he or she must take or refrain from taking in order to be responsible . . . Responsibility now extends infinitely; it is therefore impossible to define, impossible to fulfil and, crucially, virtually impossible to regulate'.[126] It is, of course, a New Labour policy and, therefore, it sounds good—and, perhaps, this is all that matters.

125 For example, J. Eekelaar 'Parental Responsibility: State of Nature or Nature of the State?' (1991) 13 *Journal of Social Welfare and Family Law* 37; S. Edwards and A. Halpern 'Parental Responsibility: An Instrument of Social Policy' (1992) 22 *Family Law* 113.

126 See p. 483.

2

From 'Living Law' to the 'Death of the Social'—Sociology in Legal Theory

Roger Cotterrell

Theoretically-minded lawyers—jurists—have actively reflected on sociology's potential throughout much of its modern history. They have often wondered whether sociology can be a resource to aid their inquiries about the nature and functions of law, or a competitor in these inquiries. The relations of juristic legal theory, in this sense, and sociology have been debated over many decades, at least by legal scholars.

A century ago sociology was in the process of becoming institutionalized as a modern discipline. Around that time, the vast diversity of possible attitudes of jurists to sociology was first clearly signalled. Eugen Ehrlich proclaimed in 1913 that legal theory *is* sociology of law. 'Since the law is a social phenomenon, every kind of legal science is a social science; but legal science in the proper sense of the term [as a theoretical study] is part of the theoretical science of society, of sociology. The sociology of law is the theoretical science of law.'[1] Hans Kelsen answered by bluntly declaring sociology irrelevant to a genuine science of law, which studies not social activity but norms governed by a specific coercive technique.[2] In sharp contrast, around the same time, Roscoe Pound attached the label 'sociological' to his entire legal philosophy to suggest its progressive outlook.[3]

In these and all later juristic engagements with sociology, the latter is usually taken as a given, its nature assumed to be well-understood. For Kelsen, Ehrlich's writings (and related work by Hermann Kantorowicz) were sufficient initially to represent sociology in its relation to law and allow an assessment of its prospects;[4] for Pound, early influences especially from the sociologists Edward Ross and Albion Small[5] gave

[1] E. Ehrlich, *Fundamental Principles of the Sociology of Law* (New Brunswick, 2002), 25.

[2] H. Kelsen, *General Theory of Law and State* (New York, 1945), 24–8.

[3] N.E.H. Hull, *Roscoe Pound and Karl Llewellyn: Searching for an American Jurisprudence* (Chicago, 1997), 84–5.

[4] See generally, R. Treves, 'Hans Kelsen et la sociologie du droit' (1985) 1 *Droit et Société* 15.

[5] Hull, n.3, above, 55; R. Pound, 'Sociology of Law' in G. Gurvitch and W.E. Moore (eds), *Twentieth Century Sociology* (New York, 1945), 297, 335.

sufficient indications to make the 'sociological' label initially meaningful for him; it was a term that was 'in the air' early in the twentieth century.[6] Matters have changed little since: the nature of sociology as a knowledge-field has remained largely unexamined in detail by jurists.

My chapter seeks to address this topic. It asks: what is sociology for legal theorists, especially for jurists pursuing theoretical inquiries about the nature of law as doctrine, ideas and reasoning? And, by contrast, what is sociology for sociologists? Can an inquiry into the awareness which sociology's practitioners have of its nature as a scholarly practice and field help to clarify relationships between legal theory and sociology? I think that it can, if only by raising issues about the nature of the kinds of social inquiry to which legal studies might relate.

Law as a scholarly field of juristic studies undoubtedly has important internal debates on methods and aims. But these usually seem very limited compared with the anguished self-examination which sociology regularly undergoes. From some standpoints, this is undoubtedly a weakness of sociology, raising doubts about its disciplinary status, its coherence and unity as a scholarly field, its usefulness (for what? to whom?), its scientific credentials and its identity and demarcation from other fields of knowledge. From another standpoint, however, sociology's incessant navel-gazing and its radical debates on methods, theory, aims and achievements are far from counter-productive. They are instructive—and not just for sociologists. In what follows I shall try to show that they can even help to clarify the very nature of theoretical legal studies.

Conceptualizing Sociology in Relation to Legal Theory

Sociology's intellectual discomforts suggest not its weakness but its inherently reflexive character. The aim of sociology is to study systematically and empirically the nature of the social (however much debate there is about how to do this). Consequently, it cannot help but reflect on its *own* research practices as social practices. So there is nothing paradoxical about the idea of a sociology of sociology.[7] The implication of it is that sociology seeks methods of critically examining its

[6] *Cf.* Benjamin Cardozo's use of the phrase 'the method of sociology' (the term 'sociology' remaining unexplained) in his *Nature of the Judicial Process* (New Haven, 1921) to suggest purposive, policy-oriented shaping of law.

[7] See, e.g. A.W. Gouldner, *The Coming Crisis of Western Sociology* (London, 1971), ch. 2. The idea of a law of law is not paradoxical either. Natural law can be seen as a (moral) law of (positive) law. Yet it is surely significant that law's reflexivity in the form of natural law theory is now pushed to the margins of legal scholarship, having little impact on much of it, while, as will be discussed below, sociology's self-critique seems never far from the centre of sociologists' concerns. The idea of sociology's reflexivity which is central to Pierre Bourdieu's influential work is treated by him as compatible with a strong sense of disciplinarity. See P. Bourdieu and L.J.D. Wacquant, *An Introduction to Reflexive Sociology* (Cambridge, 1992). I argue in this chapter that the full implications of reflexivity make that compatibility doubtful.

own methods; theory to explain its own theory; paradigms to upset the rigidities of its existing paradigms. This is not a recipe for comfortable existence. But it might be a necessary prescription for permanently reflexive practice in social research: practice that seeks to understand its own ambiguities, problems, and limits at any given time, but also is engaged in a continuous, never-ending effort to transcend them.[8]

These features of sociology will be illustrated later by considering aspects of sociologists' contemporary debates about the nature of their scholarly enterprise. But how could such matters be relevant to juristic concerns? I think jurists have often failed to consider sociology's complex nature sufficiently and so may have sometimes over-estimated and sometimes under-estimated possibilities for engaging with it, or failed to see problems. In particular, if sociology embraces (i) well-recognized common methods, theories and research traditions but also (ii) a permanent tendency to reject confinement within these, it can be conveniently seen for the purposes of legal theoretical inquiries in two contrasting yet related ways.

On the one hand, 'sociology' means the established products of sociology-as-discipline: the methods, theories, research, and writings of self-professed sociologists, accredited members of a distinct discipline. This is *professionalized sociology*—sociology as a self-consciously organized academic field and professional practice.

On the other hand, sociology's reflexive character, which often disturbs its self-perceptions as a discipline, suggests that its intellectual boundaries are often open and largely unpoliced. This situation makes it plausible to consider sociology as something beyond a specialized discipline or professional practice. It can be understood as any systematic, empirically-oriented study of the social (the human relations that make up social life), whether or not conducted by scholars who are identified or identify themselves in any way with sociology as a discipline, science, or profession.[9] Stjepan Meštrović described sociology as a 'wild discipline', that bursts free of attempts to contain it through agreed disciplinary protocols, resists organization, is the focus of work for scholars of any discipline or none, and draws on any knowledge-fields (including the humanities, and the natural and social sciences) that may be helpful.[10] Sociology in this second, wider sense, might be called *transdisciplinary sociology*—sociology as an aspiration and resource, unconstrained by and often oblivious to demarcations of academic fields and formal divisions of professional accreditation.

I suggest that both of these conceptions of sociology are relevant to legal theory. Because the nature and problems of sociology as an organized discipline have

[8] See generally R. Cotterrell, *Law's Community: Legal Theory in Sociological Perspective* (Oxford, 1995), ch. 3, and for further discussion and critique, D. Nelken, 'Can There Be a Sociology of Legal Meaning?', in Nelken (ed.) *Law as Communication* (Aldershot, 1996); D. Nelken, 'Blinding Insights? The Limits of a Reflexive Sociology of Law' (1998) 25 *Journal of Law and Society* 407.

[9] R. Cotterrell, 'Why Must Legal Ideas Be Understood Sociologically?' (1998) 25 *Journal of Law and Society* 171.

[10] S. Meštrović, Anthony Giddens: The Last Modernist (London, 1998), 209–11.

seldom been examined by legal scholars (and seldom been of much interest to them), legal scholarship has rarely sought a place in the concerns of professionalized sociology, or a means of integrating juristic viewpoints with them. But it has often allied itself with various kinds of transdisciplinary sociology, drawing on it, contributing to it, and even becoming integrated in some aspects with it.

Correspondingly, juristic issues (questions about the nature of legal doctrine and its interpretation, legal values, and concepts, relations of legal and moral ideas, etc) have rarely been a concern for social scientists. A few leading sociological theorists (notably Philip Selznick and Niklas Luhmann recently, and Emile Durkheim, Max Weber, and Georges Gurvitch among classical sociological theorists) have had a sufficient interest in juristic concerns to define a clear, prominent place for them in relation to sociology. But the primary link of professionalized sociology to law has been through empirical sociolegal studies using categories that social scientists, not jurists, have defined as research foci.

What seems clear is that when jurists first began to appeal in a sustained way to sociology or social psychology for enlightenment they saw primarily a transdisciplinary sociology of some kind, if only because professionalized sociology then hardly existed. Ehrlich's sociology of law is clearly a jurist's homespun (but insightful) sociology, largely unrelated to any sense of sociology as an organized discipline.[11] But his *Fundamental Principles of the Sociology of Law* does not need re-labelling as a work of sociological jurisprudence.[12] Pound, for all the vagueness of his conceptual thinking, recognized that scholars such as Ehrlich aimed to contribute to a science of social life in a way that Pound's own sociological jurisprudence ultimately did not.[13] If Ehrlich's sociology of law is a jurist's sociology, it is sociology none the less. His concept of 'living law' was intended to identify normative structures of social life—that is, to pursue a sociological project of systematic empirical study of the social. But Ehrlich's sociology sought to wake lawyers up to their failure (as he saw it) in understanding social conditions that give law its substance.[14] Sociology could reveal and define social norms that lawyers should accept as part of the regulatory field their work addressed.

Half a century after Ehrlich wrote his great book on sociology of law, a strongly contrasting juristic invocation of sociology was made when H.L.A. Hart described his *Concept of Law* as 'an essay in descriptive sociology'.[15] Sociolegal

[11] Ehrlich (n.1, above, 25), explicitly denies that sociology is a unitary field distinct from 'the social sciences as a whole'.

[12] *Cf.* R. Banakar, *Merging Law and Sociology: Beyond the Dichotomies in Socio-Legal Research* (Glienicke, Berlin, 2003), ch. 7; R. Banakar, 'Sociological Jurisprudence' in R. Banakar and M. Travers (eds), *An Introduction to Law and Social Theory* (Oxford, 2002).

[13] R. Pound, 'Preface' to G. Gurvitch, *Sociology of Law* (London, 1947), ix, x, xv; Pound, 'Sociology of Law' (n.5, above), 297, 301–2. D. Nelken, 'Law in Action or Living Law? Back to the Beginning in Sociology of Law' (1984) 4 *Legal Studies* 157 carefully highlights the differences between Pound's and Ehrlich's projects.

[14] K.A. Ziegert, 'The Sociology behind Eugen Ehrlich's Sociology of Law' (1979) 7 *International Journal of the Sociology of Law* 225.

[15] H.L.A. Hart, *The Concept of Law*, 2nd edn. (Oxford, 1994), vi.

scholars have often treated Hart's claim as a simple category mistake, noting that his essay in legal philosophy lacks systematic sociology.[16] The elements most obviously missing are those associated with professionalized sociology, such as established social scientific methods, concepts, or theories. Yet the reason why Hart's claim to have written sociologically was mistaken is surely not that legal philosophy and sociology are *inherently* different enterprises or that legal philosophy cannot be sociological in some respects. It is that *The Concept of Law* is not seriously concerned with systematic empirical inquiry about the diversity—what Selznick calls 'variation'[17]—of the social (and, one might add, insufficiently reflexive about its own social practices of juristic speculation).

Shortly before Hart's book was published, Ernest Gellner labelled its main intellectual inspiration—Oxford linguistic philosophy—as 'pseudo-sociology' because its speculation on linguistic usage was claimed to be able to reveal features of social life. Gellner thought that 'some of its insights logically call for sociological inquiry, if indeed they do not imply that sociology should replace philosophy.'[18] Linguistic philosophy 'calls for sociology. If the meaning of terms is their use and context, then those contexts and the activities therein should be investigated seriously—and without making the mistaken assumption that we already know enough about the world and about society to identify the actual functioning of our use of words.'[19] Linguistic philosophy (including its juristic branch) might be empirically-oriented in its concern with 'ordinary usage'. But what particular part of the social world does this philosophy reflect? Whose ordinary usage is assumed? For Gellner, it was that of 'the [academic] folk of North Oxford, roughly.'[20]

There is no need here to pursue further Gellner's fascinating polemic. The point is to note how different senses of 'sociology' are invoked. Hart and some other philosophers claim to be doing a kind of social analysis—even sociology—by analysing certain social practices (of language use). Gellner, however, implies that a real sociology would show the emptiness of the philosophers' 'pseudo-sociology'. He appeals not necessarily to professionalized sociology but surely to methods and theories associated with it: these would be criteria of real rather than pseudo-sociology. But what if, today, sociologists themselves do not agree on what is real or pseudo-sociology? And if they adopt disciplinary definitions, why must these be accepted by jurists? If the idea of a transdisciplinary sociology is accepted, the criticism of Hart is not that his legal philosophy is pseudo-sociology, but that as sociology (systematic empirical study of the social) it is demonstrably weak, even if

[16] See, e.g. J.P. Gibbs, 'Definitions of Law and Empirical Questions' (1968) 2 *Law and Society Review* 429; S. Roberts, *Order and Dispute: An Introduction to Legal Anthropology* (Harmondsworth, 1979), 24–5; M. Krygier, '*The Concept of Law* and Social Theory' (1982) 2 *Oxford Journal of Legal Studies* 155; P. Fitzpatrick, *Modernism and the Grounds of Law* (Cambridge, 2001), 97–9.

[17] R. Cotterrell and P. Selznick, 'Selznick Interviewed' (2004) 31 *Journal of Law and Society* 291, 296.

[18] E. Gellner, *Words and Things* (Harmondsworth, 1968), 255–6. [19] *Ibid*, 257.

[20] *Ibid*, 265.

its conceptual analysis may be useful in structuring certain kinds of sociological inquiry.[21]

Jurists and Sociologists

Some jurists have taken methods, theories, or traditions of professionalized sociology very seriously, adopting them directly in their work. Some of Lon Fuller's writings on the forms and functions of legal processes, the use by French jurists such as Léon Duguit, Paul Huvelin, and Emmanuel Lévy of Durkheim's sociology, and Gunther Teubner's developments of Niklas Luhmann's social theory, are varied illustrations of this.[22]

Indeed, relations between juristic study and sociology have occasionally been described—at least rhetorically—as relations of dependence, and not just of the former on the latter. Celestin Bouglé, a follower of Durkheim, proclaimed the study of laws and customs as essential to sociology, which 'must inscribe on the mansion it seeks to build: "No-one may enter here who is not a jurist."'[23] Such a claim now seems very strange, but it represents a particular sociological view that the theoretical study of law could be detached from its pragmatic ties to the concerns of lawyers and treated as an important, perhaps foundational social study in its own right, even where it was built on the work of jurists.[24] Conversely Ehrlich's and Pound's claims that legal theory relies on sociology presuppose a transdisciplinary sociology. Claims of dependence usually seem to presuppose a view that largely rejects the disciplinary distinctiveness of either sociology or legal studies.

Where, however, juristic study and sociology are seen in terms of strong disciplinary or scientific identities of some kind, the relation between them may often be simply one of indifference or, at most, mutual observation. Weber presented his sociology of law as essentially distinct from juristic studies,[25] and focused

[21] See, e.g. H. Ross, *Law as a Social Institution* (Oxford, 2001); E. Colvin, 'The Sociology of Secondary Rules' (1978) 28 *University of Toronto Law Journal* 195; Cotterrell and Selznick, n.17, above, 303–4, 305.

[22] See, e.g. W.J. Witteveen and W. van der Burg, *Rediscovering Fuller: Essays on Implicit Law and Institutional Design* (Amsterdam, 1999); E. Pisier-Kouchner, 'La sociologie durkheimienne dans l'oeuvre de Duguit' (1977) 28 *Année Sociologique*, new series 95; R. Cotterrell, 'Emmanuel Lévy and Legal Studies: A View from Abroad' (2004) 56/57 *Droit et Société* 131; R. Cotterrell, 'Durkheim's Loyal Jurist? The Sociolegal Theory of Paul Huvelin' (2005) 18 *Ratio Juris* 504; G. Teubuer, *Law as an Autopoietic System* (Oxford, 1993).

[23] C. Bouglé, *Bilan de la sociologie française contemporaine* (Paris, 1935), 96. See also W. Schluchter, 'The Sociology of Law as an Empirical Theory of Validity' (2003) 19 *European Sociological Review* 537, 538, claiming that, for Durkheim, sociology 'is first of all a comparative sociology of law' focused on the comparative study of (primarily legal) rules.

[24] Kelsen (n.2, above, 175–7) claims that sociology of law depends on juristic legal science to specify its object 'law', but this seems incorrect unless sociology of law has to be restricted to the study of law as jurists define it. Kelsen gives no reason why it must be.

[25] M. Weber, *Economy and Society* (Berkeley, 1978), Part 2, ch. 1, and see Weber, *Critique of Stammler* (New York, 1977), 126–43 (distinguishing normative justification and empirical regularity). Kelsen (n.2, above, 175–7) essentially follows Weber in this respect.

mainly on the development and consequences of law's professional organization in different historical contexts. Luhmann stresses even more forcefully the separate discursive spheres of law and sociology and enshrines these in the terms of his systems theory.[26]

Sometimes more than indifference is involved. Nicholas Timasheff claimed (referring to Auguste Comte's writings) that the discipline of sociology 'was born in the state of hostility to law'.[27] The sense of disciplinary power may sometimes become imperialistic. 'Law is entering an age of sociology,' writes the sociologist Donald Black[28] and 'sociological justice' is now feasible: sociology will reveal the myths that pervade legal thought and how to reorganize legal practice realistically. Black even envisages sociology, as a way of thinking, replacing juristic ways.[29] Early in sociology's disciplinary career, Durkheim gave at least rhetorical support to some such imperialism: 'My aim has been precisely to introduce . . . [the sociological idea] into those disciplines from which it was absent and thereby to make them branches of sociology.'[30] Durkheim's fierce advocacy of sociology as a distinct discipline (like Black's, many decades later) no doubt encouraged the widespread opposition to such imperialism among the jurists of his time. By contrast, Ehrlich's idea of 'sociologizing' law seemed to appeal to many progressive jurists, perhaps in part because he invoked a transdisciplinary, not a professionalized sociology—a cooperative, open effort in building knowledge of law.

The time of Ehrlich was one in which some progressive legal scholars could look to sociology with unlimited and, seen from today's perspectives, naive optimism; with a sense that anything might be possible in social research on law, even if the new territories opened up were vast. Reading Ehrlich one could be, as Karl Llewellyn noted, 'somewhat crushed in spirit, because he had seen so much'.[31] But optimism was encouraged by sociology's aura of a promise still to be realized.

Early sociology in the United States, where the subject first began to flourish as an organized discipline, had three particular elements that could appeal to legal scholars. Each of them contrasts with those primarily associated with American sociology as a discipline today. First was a strong social reform orientation which might relate to studies of law's social functions and of legal reform. Practical social reform foci (the concerns of 'damned do-gooders') tended to be much less prominent in sociology as it became a distinct, professionalized academic field, though they have never been

[26] See, e.g. N. Luhmann, 'Operational Closure and Structural Coupling: The Differentiation of the Legal System' (1992) 13 *Cardozo Law Review* 1419.

[27] N.S. Timasheff, *An Introduction to the Sociology of Law* (Cambridge, Mass., 1939), 45.

[28] D. Black, *Sociological Justice* (New York, 1989), 4.

[29] *Cf.* Cotterrell, n.8, above, 183–93.

[30] E. Durkheim, *The Rules of Sociological Method and Selected Texts on Sociology and Its Method* (London, 1982), 260.

[31] Quoted in Hull, n.3, above, 291; and *cf.* C.K. Allen's *Law in the Making*, 7th edn. (Oxford, 1964), 30–2, famously despairing of the unlimited range of Ehrlich's 'megalomaniac jurisprudence'.

excluded.[32] Second was an emphasis, notably in influential early Chicago-school sociology, on empirical social description which, while not atheoretical, avoided 'the inhibiting consequences of doctrines, schools of thought, and authoritative leaders'.[33] Correspondingly, 'fact research'—gathering data about social life—could appear as an aid to understanding law's effects; pursued or adopted by jurists it could readily inspire 'legal realism' or the study of 'living law' or 'law in action'.[34] Third was sociology's early professional catholicity including scholars from groups outside the academic establishment (e.g. women, black scholars, social and political campaigners and reformers).[35] Early sociology suggests an open club in which jurists might not feel complete outsiders if they sought some association with it.

A very different situation obtains in today's highly developed academic discipline of sociology, with its sophisticated research methods, elaborate theoretical traditions, distinctive professional training, qualifications and career paths, and numerous disciplinary specialisms. Nevertheless, certain factors limit the tendencies towards professionalization (and associated specialization and technicality) that have made it harder for sociology to appear as a general resource and locus of aspiration for legal scholars and others.

One is the enduring idea of a public sociology—the idea that sociologists should, to some extent, use their work to hold up a mirror to their society and explain it to itself, addressing its broadest, most widely-felt social concerns. Books such as David Riesman's million-selling *The Lonely Crowd* and, recently, Robert Putnam's *Bowling Alone*[36] exemplify writing that has achieved this in some way. Here sociology remains a resource for general reflection on the social. Yet some of this writing has been called 'expressive' rather than 'scientific' sociology[37] because of its popular, non-technical, non-specialist appeal as a kind of evocation, in arresting terms, of the widely-felt and the familiar.

The other phenomenon that has limited sociology's tendencies towards professionalism has been its already-mentioned insecurity about its character as a knowledge-field and research practice. A closer view of this matter is needed so as to be able to move towards some conclusions about relations of legal theory and sociology today.

[32] J.R. Feagin, 'Social Justice and Sociology: Agendas for the Twenty-First Century' (2001) 66 *American Sociological Review* 1, 6–10. The quoted words are Robert Park's: see *ibid* 8.

[33] J.F. Short Jr.,'Introduction', in Short (ed.) *The Social Fabric of the Metropolis: Contributions of the Chicago School of Urban Sociology* (Chicago, 1971), xi, xiv (quoting Albion Small).

[34] A. Nussbaum, 'Fact Research in Law' (1940) 40 *Columbia Law Review* 189; M. Rehbinder, 'The Development and Present State of Fact Research in the United States' (1972) 24 *Journal of Legal Education* 567; J.H. Schlegel, *American Legal Realism and Empirical Social Science* (Chapel Hill, N. Carolina, 1995).

[35] Feagin, n.32, above, 6–8; C. Lemert, 'Representations of the Sociologist: Getting over the Crisis' (1996) 11 *Sociological Forum* 379, 386 (emphasizing the institutional outsider status of many early sociologists).

[36] D. Riesman with N. Glazer and R. Denney, *The Lonely Crowd: A Study of the Changing American Character* (New Haven, 1950); R. Putnam, *Bowling Alone: The Collapse and Revival of American Community* (New York, 2000).

[37] R. Boudon, 'Sociology That Really Matters' (2002) 18 *European Sociological Review* 371, 372.

Sociology as Discipline

Professionalized sociology's self-examinations are, no doubt, partly fuelled by external perceptions. In Britain in 1989, A.H. Halsey noted 'the remorseless chill of received opinion about sociology'.[38] A mid-1990s commentator declared that 'sociologists have nothing worth saying about things that matter, in the here and now of contemporary politics, in the national conversation about identity and purpose.'[39] Paul Wiles has recently suggested that 'the reputation of sociology for practical utility is at an historical low and sociology is regarded as the least developed of the social sciences in terms of the rigour of its methods.'[40] In America in the 1980s sociology fell into a 'terrible reputational state'[41] and in 1994 Seymour Martin Lipset called it 'an endangered discipline'.[42] Yet it *continues to thrive*. There are more than 13,000 career sociologists in the United States.[43] The Paris-based sociologist Raymond Boudon claims that sociology has an 'identity crisis' but 'seems more solidly institutionalized than ever'.[44] In Britain, Ray Pahl notes, hostile political currents in the 1980s 'did no harm to sociology: staff, students and research all expanded rapidly.'[45] The image is of an insecure, embattled, yet flourishing research field; exactly what we should expect if sociology's reflexiveness, far from undermining it, helps to make it vibrant and rich, though always controversial.

One main theme of sociologists' current debates about their enterprise is about disciplinarity. A recent presidential address to the American Sociological Association called sociology 'a broad *interdisciplinary* field that draws on ideas from other social sciences, the humanities, and the physical sciences. Our intellectual and methodological pluralism, as well as our diversity of practitioners, are major virtues.'[46] Some writers stress sociology's 'disciplinary openness'.[47] But worries are expressed that social research training not anchored in any specific discipline may produce 'technologists ... equipped only with investigative skills',[48] and some sociologists are embarrassed to profess a discipline that is 'something of a rickety shed'.[49]

[38] Quoted in D. Walker, 'All Quiet on the Home Front' *Times Higher Education Supplement*, 17 March 1995, 21.

[39] *Ibid.*

[40] P. Wiles, 'Policy and Sociology' (2004) 55 *British Journal of Sociology* 31.

[41] Charles Lemert, quoted in R. Pahl, Book review, *Times Higher Education Supplement*, 23 August 1996. See also Lemert's (n.35, above) excellent critical discussion of sociologists' concerns about their field.

[42] Quoted in I. Deutscher, 'Sociological Practice: The Politics of Identities and Futures' (1998) 3 *Sociological Research Online*, No. 1, para 5.5 *http://www.socresonline.org.uk/socresonline/3/1/3.html*.

[43] J. Steele, 'Four Days in California' *Guardian*, 24 August 2004.

[44] Boudon, n.37, above, 371.

[45] Pahl, n.41, above.

[46] Feagin, n.32, above, 6 (my emphasis).

[47] H. Lauder, P. Brown and A.H. Halsey, 'Sociology and Political Arithmetic: Some Principles of a New Policy Science' (2004) 55 *British Journal of Sociology* 3, 6, 8.

[48] M. Williams, quoted in Lauder et al., n.47, above, 5.

[49] D. Voas, 'The So-So Construction of Sociology' (2003) 54 *British Journal of Sociology* 129.

There is also, however, a tendency to reject fixations with disciplinarity. For Paul Wiles, 'disciplines are simply the social organisation of the knowledge produced in response to yesterday's problems (usually for the purpose of teaching that knowledge to neophytes).'[50] It follows that cutting-edge work will often escape disciplinary bounds. Craig Calhoun argues that sociology's future will be stronger if 'we embrace rather than marginalize interdisciplinary projects'; disciplines, like nations, are committed to defending their turf and boundaries, 'promulgating myths about their essential internal unity and character and literally disciplining the individualistic and dissentient opinions and behaviours of their members.'[51] Disciplines 'exalt into matters of principle what are in fact matters of historical accident, gradual cultural change, networks of personal relationships, particular combinations of styles and . . . a never fully articulated system of socially constituted dispositions that guides agents in their perception and action. It is always and in every case impossible to identify a principle of belonging that unifies everyone in the discipline without also including others one intuitively thinks don't fit. Likewise, most of the disciplinary "principles" that matter most to us actually unify only some of the members of the discipline.'[52] Calhoun's observations suggest a sociology of sociology: a *transdisciplinary* sociology of *professionalized* sociology, but also of professional disciplinary organization in general.

But what follows from such disciplinary ambivalence? Certainly, one might hesitate to call sociology of law a sub-discipline of sociology when sociology debates its own disciplinarity in this way. But, of course, such debates in no way prevent a vast amount of research being pursued by sociologists in well-recognized fields, according to settled methods and by reference to familiar canons of established theory. This situation does, however, suggest that an important distinction is to be drawn between, on the one hand, recognizing the existence of relatively coherent sets of methods, theories, and research traditions (which is as easy to do for sociolegal studies or sociology of law as for sociology) and, on the other, making any strong claims about disciplinary identity, unity, or integrity.

Sociology as Science

Often debates about sociology focus on the idea of science. A leading British sociologist, John Goldthorpe, sees much sociology as 'pretend social science', more like 'social revelation' or 'social poetry' than science.[53] Another commentator

[50] Wiles, n.40, above, 33.

[51] C. Calhoun, 'The Future of Sociology: Interdisciplinarity and Internationalization', paper presented to the University of Minnesota Sociology Department at its Centennial celebration, 29–30 March 2002, pp. 1, 2 *http://www.src.org/programs/calhoun/publications/futureofsoc.pdf.*

[52] *Ibid*, 1, 2, 3–4.

[53] J. Goldthorpe, 'Book Review Symposium: The Scientific Study of Society' (2004) 55 *British Journal of Sociology* 123, 125.

sees 'the path of testable theory and empirical investigation' as the 'homeward route' for a discipline that has lost its way; scientific laws and value-free research in sociology are possible, he claims, but sociologists reject the 'scientific' label because of 'the dread' that they 'might then commit the sin of prediction'.[54] A natural science model is clearly being invoked here as the guarantor of scientific status and integrity. Other sociologists insist that scientific method or at least 'some special expertise' is needed to distinguish sociology from journalism or even novel-writing.[55]

Fears for sociology's scientific status were an important impetus for sociologists' efforts to separate it professionally from social reform activity so as to pursue 'the pure-science ideal' or 'a detached-science perspective'.[56] Both Weber and Durkheim devoted much attention to specifying scientific methods for social research. Later, functionalism was, for a time, advocated as sociology's distinctive scientific approach,[57] though it was always shared with other social studies. Today much argument centres on the merits of rational action theory (RAT) derived from rational choice theory in economics and advocated as a general sociological approach. The sense that sociology should learn from economics is no doubt encouraged by the relatively high status of the latter as a discipline of social explanation.

Goldthorpe defines RAT as any 'theoretical approach that seeks to explain social phenomena as the outcome of individual action that is construed as rational, given individuals' goals and conditions of action, and in this way made intelligible.'[58] Boudon identifies a range of postulates underlying various rational choice or rational action approaches. The most basic of these characterize methodological individualism, a sociological approach derived from Weber. They are: the centrality of the individual, an emphasis on understanding the meaning for individuals of their social actions, and a claim that that meaning explains why they act. Beyond this, other postulates can be added: consequentialism (actors' reasons always concern the effects of their actions), egoism (relevant effects for actors are those that impact on themselves), and cost-benefit balance (actors always choose alternatives with the optimum cost-benefit balance). Boudon suggests that these postulates are the basis of rational choice theory. But RAT adds yet other postulates because choice is sociologically too simple an idea unless social or psychological restrictions shaping choice are added. These postulated restrictions vary depending on the kind of RAT adopted.[59]

What may be of most interest here is the fact that, in both sociology and juristic studies, rational choice or rational action ideas have been advocated to address

[54] Voas, n.49, above, 130, 132.

[55] T. Tam, 'The Industrial Organization of Sociology' (1998) 3 *Sociological Research Online*, No. 1, para 3:6 *http://www.socresonline.org.uk/socresonline/3/1/4.html*; Wiles, n.40, above, 34.

[56] Feagin, n.32, above, 9, 10; Calhoun, n.51, above, 19.

[57] K. Davis, 'The Myth of Functional Analysis as a Special Method in Sociology and Anthropology' (1959) 24 *American Sociological Review* 757.

[58] J. Goldthorpe, 'The Quantitative Analysis of Large-Scale Data Sets and Rational Action Theory: For a Sociological Alliance' (1996) 12 *European Sociological Review* 109.

[59] R. Boudon, Book Review (2001) 17 *European Sociological Review* 451, 451–2.

perceived defects in the scientific, practical, or predictive power of traditional scholarship. But rational action scholarship in sociology is only 'a niche operation'[60] and, in legal studies, research models derived from economics have been very influential in some locations (especially in the United States) but so far much less so in Britain. Since much law is concerned to regulate instrumental relations and presupposes instrumental (means-ends) rationality it is unsurprising that rational action approaches in legal theory have an appeal.

Yet most jurists have tended to assume that there is more to the social world which law attempts to regulate than means-ends rationality. Debates in sociology make explicit the kind of problems that may induce juristic caution. Both Goldthorpe and Boudon stress the variety of forms of rationality but some sociological critics of rational choice theory note that it 'leaves little place for affect or emotional attachments'.[61] Weber's sociology, after all, not only postulated categories of what he considered non-rational action (action driven by blind habit or pure emotion) alongside (potentially conflicting) categories of rational action, but assumed that non-rational action was more socially pervasive than rational.[62] For one recent sociological commentator on RAT, economists 'assume away preferences and utility whereas sociologists ... want to know something about desires, preferences, beliefs, evaluations, expectations, and intentions when these are central in their explanations.'[63]

It is not hard to see a direct relevance for theoretical legal inquiries in controversies around RAT. Sociologists (like lawyers) usually accept the great significance of the kind of rational action on which RAT focuses. But many see the social as much wider and more diverse than rational choice approaches can grasp. And implicit in the resistance of many legal scholars to economic analysis of law may be a conviction that the social for law is better seen in the untidy, empirically complex way sociology usually presents it—in terms of combinations of many kinds of rational and non-rational action (judged as such from numerous perspectives)—than in terms of the rational structures through which economists tend to portray it.

Advocates of RAT tend to admit that it is only one method, which cannot address all sociological inquiries. Yet it often carries for them the hopes of 'scientific' sociology. Perhaps an appropriate conclusion is that no universal methods can cover the vast diversity of social inquiries. Science is an aim and aspiration to question all received assumptions and continually, systematically, to broaden perspectives on experience. But a search for absolute protocols for doing this is doomed to failure.

60 D.B. Grusky and M. Di Carlo, Book Review (2001) 17 *European Sociological Review* 457.

61 N. Smelser, 'The Rational and the Ambivalent in the Social Sciences' (1998) 63 *American Sociological Review* 1, 4.

62 R. Brubaker, *The Limits of Rationality: An Essay on the Social and Moral Thought of Max Weber* (London, 1984), ch. 2.

63 B. Laplante, Book Review (2002) 18 *European Sociological Review* 121, 122.

Sociology's Aims and Object

Other debates focus on sociology's aims. How far should it seek to be useful to policy-makers? Does a concentration on theory drive research away from practicality and towards useless abstraction? Boudon sees risks in policy-oriented or, as he calls it, cameral/descriptive sociology, which he contrasts with cognitive/scientific sociology driven by a disinterested search for knowledge: 'Once the cameral orientation becomes dominant, the cumulative character of sociology is weakened. Sociology of the cognitive type is internally driven, but cameral sociology is externally driven.'[64] Goldthorpe, however, sees no necessary tension between these types of sociology. Both 'share . . . a commitment to the same logic of inference or understanding of the relation of evidence and argument'.[65] Can theory in sociology progress? Goldthorpe has doubts because of 'the relatively high degree of mutability of social phenomena'.[66] He advocates studying the causes of specific social phenomena. But other sociologists suggest that sociology lost its way by devaluing its past agenda of social description in favour of attempts to explain the causes of what was described. Thus, endless debates were opened about the nature of social causality.[67]

Sociology's aims are thus varied and contested. Boudon distinguishes not only cognitive/scientific and cameral/descriptive sociology but also two other kinds.[68] Expressive sociology, as mentioned earlier, is writing that vividly expresses the widely-felt and the familiar in social life; for Boudon it is more art (literature) than science. Critical sociology, by contrast, aims at critiquing or changing society. Sociology is, on this view, not a single enterprise. It is many things and sociologists differ as to which of them is central. One can see the ghosts of early sociology as mentioned earlier (social reform, descriptive fact-gathering, professional diversity) refracted through contrasting categories of sociological work and views of sociology's aims.

One final theme from contemporary debates deserves mention. What object does sociology study? Traditionally the discipline has been called the science of 'society' but the concept of society is now widely seen as problematic. As Craig Calhoun notes, sociologists have imagined society primarily on the model of the nation-state; as, for example, British society or French society. The notion of society 'had largely to do with the idea that legitimate rule ought to reflect the interests of a more or less integrated population called a people' but we 'should ask when integration at any scale involves boundaries and some overall sort of order, and how that is achieved and . . . not assume that the nation-state provides us with the image of the "whole" society.' The tendency to equate society and nation 'encouraged

[64] Boudon, n.37, above, 375.

[65] J. Goldthorpe, 'Sociology as Social Science and Cameral Sociology: Some Further Thoughts' (2004) 20 *European Sociological Review* 97, 100.

[66] *Ibid*, 102.

[67] Grusky and Di Carlo, n.60, above, 458.

[68] Boudon, n.37, above.

sociologists to think of whole and individual societies in a way at odds with manifest transnational relations and intranational divisions.'[69] An important question is thus: What is sociology's object? And the issue is no less acute for sociolegal studies and sociology of law, which have taken as their field the study of 'law and society' or 'law in society'. What exactly is it that law must be related to? What is the social? How should it be conceptualized? What are its boundaries and components?

Can sociology conceptualize Europe, for example, as a social entity and offer a means of studying this?[70] More prosaically, can it adjust to the decline of various expressions of a general society-wide social realm, such as social work, social welfare, social solidarity, and socialism?[71]

In a widely cited article, 'The Death of the Social?', Nikolas Rose notes the decline of a sense of the social where this refers to society-wide relations, activities, and policies such as those linked to the welfare state. He sees the social as losing importance as a specific primary field of government intervention, fragmenting into many localized sites where intervention and control take diverse forms.[72] For sociology the danger is of losing its focus if it can no longer identify a well-defined field of social relations distinct from (or more general than), for example, economic or political relations. Perhaps the answer is to associate the social not with society as a kind of unity, but with fundamental types of structured human relations (or community) that can exist on any scale (within or beyond nation-states) and in innumerable empirically observable combinations.

Legal Theory in the Mirror of Sociology

How do these debates about sociology bear on the nature and tasks of legal theory? This chapter began by noting Ehrlich's equation of legal theory with sociology of law. One might say he equates it with *sociology*, since his view of law, including 'living law' or social norms, is so broad. Certainly, he treats the theoretical science of law as the systematic empirical study of law as an aspect of social experience. Legal theory can still be seen in this way and, for the present writer, it is the most attractive way to see it. On such a view, sociology's disciplinary debates bear directly on the nature and tasks of legal theory. They suggest (i) that the theoretical study of law can be governed by established disciplinary protocols, conceptions of science and understandings of the nature of the social, but at the same time

[69] Calhoun, n.51, above, 2, 6, 10. See generally Z. Bauman, *Society Under Siege* (Cambridge, 2002).

[70] G. Delanty, 'Social Theory and European Transformation: Is There a European Society?' (1998) 3 *Sociological Research Online*, No. 1 *http://www.socresonline.org.uk/socresonline/3.1.1.html.*

[71] *Cf.* J. Simon, 'Law After Society' (1999) 24 *Law and Social Inquiry* 143, 144–7.

[72] N. Rose, 'The Death of the Social? Re-Figuring the Territory of Government' (1996) 25 *Economy and Society* 327. Like many others, Rose links this development with a growing importance of the concept of community (rather than society): see also Z. Bauman, *Intimations of Postmodernity* (London, 1992), 36–7.

(ii) all of these can be challenged in the name of a transdisciplinary sociology to which legal inquiry must relate.

A vital lesson from sociology's disciplinary debates is, however, that sociological approaches to legal study are not unified by fundamental aims. This is the message of Boudon's fourfold categorization of the uses of sociology, as of earlier ones.[73] We should not expect to find unifying objectives of sociology of law or sociolegal theory. Sociology is irreducibly diverse in its very nature.

Is this diversity a feature of legal theory? It seems that it must be for any legal theory that, like Ehrlich's, ties itself to sociology. It will benefit from the characteristics of sociology that point towards open, transdisciplinary social inquiry. But what of other kinds of legal theory? Surely there are many kinds of juristic studies that need no relation with sociology? Their concern is not with 'living law' but with the positive law that lawyers identify as such. And debates on the 'death of the social' or other forms of sociology's self-questioning have little bearing on juristic researches that treat the social as merely whatever legal doctrine declares it to be.

Any juristic study is, however, a social practice, an intervention in the social world and a way of interpreting that world. So is sociology, but, as has been seen, sociology reflects in radical ways on its own social practice. As such it provides a model of reflexivity. When (juristic) legal theory asks interminably 'What is law?', it implies (but rarely answers adequately) a need to address fundamental questions about the nature of law as discipline, science and object: questions that parallel exactly those we considered earlier about sociology's character, aims, and object. And if legal theory is a highly diverse enterprise, Boudon's four categories of sociological practice suggest how legal theory might understand its own diversity. First, legal theory may be cameral, instrumental or policy-oriented in some way; it may aim at helping lawyers, administrators, or others to do their work better. Secondly, it may be expressive, perhaps presenting in a striking, reassuring or vivid way what is familiar about law to lawyers or citizens. Boudon's disparagement of 'expressive' literature which appeals to the emotions is paralleled memorably by, for example, Karl Llewellyn's scornful criticism of Pound for offering 'bed-time stories for the tired bar',[74] a kind of after-dinner-speech jurisprudence. Boudon's third 'critical' category is well represented in legal theory in, for example, much Marxist, feminist and postmodernist writing and critical race theory.

Finally, Boudon's cognitive/scientific category remains as vague for legal theory as for sociology because it raises all the issues discussed earlier about the methods, aims, and objects of science. It points simply to the inevitability of endless critical reflection on these matters. What David Nelken strikingly terms 'sociological blindness'[75] (the inherent limits of sociology's understanding) is, I think, simply

[73] See especially P. Abrams, 'The Uses of British Sociology, 1831–1981', in M. Bulmer (ed.), *Essays on the History of British Sociological Research* (Cambridge, 1985).

[74] K.N. Llewellyn, 'A Realistic Jurisprudence—The Next Step' (1930) 30 *Columbia Law Review* 431, 435.

[75] Nelken, 'Can There Be a Sociology of Legal Meaning?' (n.8, above) 118.

the impossibility of this process of reflection ever ending. Boudon's specification of good scientific theory (which might be adopted by some jurists also for legal theory) is that it 'explains a given phenomenon by making it the consequence of a set of statements compatible with one another and individually acceptable either because they are congruent with observation, or for all kinds of other reasons variable from one case to the other.'[76] The vagueness of this formulation merely illustrates that for all studies of the social (including the study of law) the worth of theory and research methods cannot be judged at an abstract level. They depend on the aims of research and the specific contexts of intellectual debate in which it takes place.

Legal theory is primarily the concern of jurists and sociolegal scholars who may occupy different positions in relation to the debates considered in this chapter. Legal studies, as social studies of a kind, may have all of the problems that are addressed in sociology's disciplinary debates. But whereas sociology pursues its self-analyses in a context in which official support is not guaranteed, law remains secure as a legitimated practice because of its connections with government, politics, and power. Legal studies are being increasingly freed from disciplinary demarcation disputes. Social theory, empirical sociolegal studies, and (to some extent) the indirect influence of sociology's disciplinary debates have greatly enriched the field of theoretical legal inquiries. Yet jurists inevitably remain tied, to some extent, to law's cocoon-like official existence, relatively secure from the kind of self-questioning that sociology reveals. Law achieves its discipline-effect and its status as juristic knowledge as much from its location in the power-knowledge complexes of the nation-state as from its own intellectual self-awareness. In my view, sociology, with its permanent self-doubts as well as its remarkable professional achievements, continues to offer important lessons for all legal theorists, whether or not they see their interests as allied to the agendas of sociolegal research.

[76] Boudon, n.37, above, 372–3.

3

A Sociology of Jurisprudence

Richard Nobles and David Schiff *

In what follows we examine the implications of a sociological theory, systems theory, most particularly as set out in the writings of Niklas Luhmann, for jurisprudence. This theory provides a sociological explanation for the interminable[1] debates amongst and between different schools of jurisprudence on topics such as the origin and/or source of law, the nature of law's determinacy or indeterminacy, and the role of justice. Our project is to continue the work begun by Luhmann in his book, *Das Recht der Gesellschaft*.[2]

Jurisprudential theories typically take as their object the unity or identity of law.[3] What is it that unites law, and distinguishes it from other aspects of social life? Even the most critical of theories accept that law is something different from other things that it is not, although answers as to this difference vary between the respective theories.[4] Although it is not possible here to set out in any detail the modification that systems theory could make to our understanding of all the answers given by diverse theories, what we will seek to demonstrate is the explanatory power and sociological enterprise of systems theory by applying it to the writings of Ronald Dworkin, in the context of his debate with analytical positivists, most notably Joseph Raz, on the nature or basis of the unity or identity[5] of law.

* We wish to thank our colleague James Penner for his astute comments on a draft of this chapter.

[1] In *The Argument from Injustice: A Reply to Legal Positivism*, R. Alexy suggests that the possible points of disagreement between Natural Law theorists and Legal Positivists can be represented in sixty-four separate theses (Oxford, 2002, translated by B.L. and S.L. Paulson). However, his estimation reflects his rather generalized analysis, and only relates to those two principal types of theorist. At a more particular level, when including other theorists, the possibilities indeed become interminable.

[2] Frankfurt am Main, 1993; translated by K.A. Ziegert as *Law as a Social System* (Oxford, 2004).

[3] Even when, as with the critical legal theorists (see H. Collins, 'Law as Politics: Progressive American Perspectives' in J.E. Penner, D. Schiff and R. Nobles (eds), *Jurisprudence and Legal Theory* (London, 2002), ch. 7) the focus results in a sustained attempt to show its disunity. Luhmann describes these presentations of 'the unity of the system in the system' as 'self-description' (n.2, above, 424).

[4] Thus even if 'law is politics', this still presupposes that this composite can be distinguished from other things that are not politics.

[5] Hereafter we will refer to 'unity' as an entity that represents unity as identity (rather than refer to 'unity or identity' each time we use the word 'unity'). This is the way that Luhmann seems to use the word 'Einheit', which tends to be translated as 'unity'. The idea of unity as identity can be distinguished from the idea of unity as completeness, perfection, or sum total.

A Sociology of the Object of Jurisprudence

Law occurs. In any twenty-four-hour period billions of things happen that have legal significance. And such things have been happening for quite some time. However, by definition, law only exists in the present, even though it has existed in the past. In law's past it had forms, institutions, and practices that are different from what they are today. And the obvious lesson that can be drawn from the differences in law between past, present, and future is that it will evolve: that it has a different existence from its past and will have a different existence in the future. If one accepts these conditions, one must also accept the inevitable contingency of law. It has, and has always had, endless possibilities of being other than what it is now. But the nature of law's contingency is not sufficient to prevent its existence. Indeed, recognition of the legal significance of social events takes place with sufficient stability and regularity, that not only can it become the subject of academic analysis and occupy an individual for years,[6] but, to repeat what is the character of the social reality that has to be described, incalculably numerous acts and decisions with acknowledged legal significance occur within fractions of each second. Jurisprudential theories on the nature of law, or law's unity, can be assessed by reference to their ability to account for law's vast but at the same time limited possibilities.

If one recognizes the contingency of law, there immediately arises a problem in attempting to describe its unity. Law is never in a steady state. It constantly selects. Within the range of possibilities of what can have legal significance at any moment, there are selections of what that significance will be, and the range of possibilities of legal significance changes over time: law evolves. Jurisprudential theories that seek to describe the unity of law have to account for this contingency and evolution. In so doing, they seek to identify structures that account for both stability and change. However, many of their descriptions of these structures might be found wanting, in that they may appear too far removed from the actual happenings of law's operations. As Luhmann, ironically remarks, quoting Powell: 'This does not mean necessarily that the texts of self-description guide the everyday practice of the system, as statutes do. This is rather unlikely "and it is hard to imagine many JPs thumbing through the *Summa Theologiae* after a hard day at the sessions."'[7] What then is the relationship between such 'texts of self-description' (jurisprudence) and law's operations? We assume here that any developed sociological understanding of such happenings must take into account lawyers' self-understandings of what they do and what law is. And here jurisprudence offers one possible route to such self-understanding, but the problem with its discussion of 'justice' or 'due process and fairness', or other values that try to express law's

[6] Or even a lifetime, as with Hans Kelsen and his Pure Theory!

[7] Luhmann, n.2, above, 425.

unity, is that such talk might seem to bear only the most tangential relationship to concrete practices, namely the everyday legal practices that they are somehow meant to reflect. While, another route to self-understanding, the talk of practising lawyers in the course of their practices, which might include reference to the same values as those referred to above, could arouse suspicions that what is being represented is primarily no more than some self-serving gloss adopted for professional interest purposes.

Luhmann's systems theory offers a way to take practising lawyers' self-understandings seriously and to investigate the relationship between these self-understandings and those offered within jurisprudence. Further, it attempts to do so while accounting for the detail and practical manifestation of law's operations. Indeed, through the analysis offered by systems theory, both the evolution of legal doctrines (the generalization of particular legal rules and decisions) and the even more general theories offered within jurisprudence, can be understood as attempts by both practising lawyers as much as by legal theorists to disguise and avoid what appears as a tautology[8] at the heart of law's supposed or assumed unity.[9] A systems theory approach to this task would acknowledge and thereby respond to what amounts to a paradox[10] resulting from law's autonomic form, namely the paradox consequential to the tautology that the law decides what is and can be law at any and every moment; it is the legal system itself that identifies its own boundaries. This way of thinking about the law starts with the simple logical tautology: the law is what the law says it is; the law determines itself, both what is legal and illegal. The theory works from the premise that there is nothing outside of law that can establish the identity and existence of law. But, despite that, the theory does not presume that systems operate with a self-conscious (or system self-conscious) awareness of such tautologies. Indeed, on the contrary, the need to make meaningful distinctions despite the absence of any value or interest that can determine what is legal, generates structures within law that hide and displace its tautological form.[11] And theories that take these structures seriously, most notably

[8] We use the word tautology not to represent the fault of saying the same thing twice (what might be understood as a verbal tautology), but rather the idea of a statement that is necessarily true within itself (what might be understood as a logical tautology).

[9] 'But it can be assumed that legal practice presupposes that the fundamental questions of the meaning of the system can be answered and it bases its decision-making on that in the form of a presupposition (rather than on information).' (Luhmann, n.2, above, 425).

[10] We recognize that this might appear to be a paradox, rather than actually be a paradox. But, as with many 'supposed' paradoxes (a statement that might be anathema to logicians) the puzzle represented by the paradox 'has been the occasion for major reconstruction at the foundation of thought.' (Quine, quoted in M. Clark, *Paradoxes from A to Z* (London, 2002), ix. See n.14 below for a fuller statement of Luhmann's characterization of law's paradox. For Luhmann, while 'The unity of a system operating a binary code can be described only as existing in the form of a paradox', this paradox is extremely productive: 'The paradox of the system—in law as, in a different way, in logic—is its blind spot, one that renders the operation of observing possible in the first place' (n.2, above, 182).

[11] On the complications associated with the internal/external character of descriptions of self-descriptions of law (this sociology of jurisprudence), see Luhmann, *ibid*, 426–31.

jurisprudential theories, will seek, and fail to find answers to the nature of law's existence and evolution that are not themselves tautological.[12] Systems theory, on the other hand, recognizes and delves into law's autonomic character, and it does so by exploring the apparent paradox associated with law's tautology,[13] how it establishes itself and evolves through its own circular self-reference.[14]

Dworkin's Attempt to Defuse the Tautology and Unfold the Paradox of Law

Dworkin's writings can be viewed as a sustained attempt to describe the unity of law in a manner that accounts for both its stability and its capacity to evolve. His discussion of conventionalism is premised on the impossibility of law continuing to be what it has always been.[15] There must be a mechanism for change. This is a particularly acute problem for jurists of a legal system such as the United States, where their constitution prevents the mechanism for change being exhaustively exported into the politics of legislatures. Having rejected conventionalism, for failing to account for change, Dworkin rejects pragmatism for failing to account for what remains stable.[16] In doing so he rejects the suggestion that law's ability to change lies solely in structures outside of law: in politics. For, if politics determines what changes in law, it must also determine what remains the same.[17] Dworkin's

[12] Thus, in discussing economic theories of law, as with other jurisprudential theories, Luhmann states: 'Like all attempts at introducing the unity of law in any form (and, that is, through a relevant distinction) into law, this attempt also rests on the dissolution (unfolding, making invisible, civilizing, making asymmetrical) of a paradox.' (*ibid*, 64) Or, in one of Luhmann's most succinct statements: 'The unity of the binary code, therefore, can only be understood as a paradox ... The paradox is rendered invisible through the process of its unfolding and determination' (*ibid*, 212).

[13] 'There is no supreme norm which guarantees that coding represents the unity of the system within the system ... Coding legal/illegal cannot be applied to itself without running into a paradox that blocks further observations' (*ibid*, 101–2).

[14] Luhmann uses the term paradox to describe the following propositions: 1. Only the law can decide what can be law; 2. Law is the application by law of a distinction particular to law: legal/illegal; 3. The distinction has no meaning outside of law, and no meaning inside of law other than the history of its application; 4. Whilst the law decides what is law (nothing else can) law cannot decide in a deterministic manner, as there is nothing which law can use to determine (code) the application of the distinction legal/illegal other than its own past applications. Thus 'One has to apply this distinction even though one can neither ask nor answer the question (because it would lead to a paradox) as to whether the distinction between legal and illegal itself is legal or illegal. The paradox itself turns unwittingly into a creative principle because one has to try so hard to avoid and to conceal it' (*ibid*, 177).

[15] 'We tested conventionalism against two perspectives on our practice: in cross-section, as an account of what particular judges do about particular cases, and over time, as a story about how legal culture develops and changes as a whole. Conventionalism failed from the latter perspective.' (*Law's Empire* (London, 1986), 157.) Others have, subject to redefining the character of conventionalism, reached the conclusion that it should not be rejected: see N. Simmonds, 'Why Conventionalism does not Collapse into Pragmatism' (1990) 49 *Cambridge Law Journal* 63–79.

[16] Dworkin, n.15, above, 159–64.

[17] Of course, attempts to export the source of law into politics presuppose that tautology will not simply reappear within politics. What, other than the political system, determines what has political

own answer is a combination of things external and internal to the legal system. Law as integrity,[18] based on a commitment to consistency and justice, allows law to be interpreted in a manner compatible with its evolution: law is stable, yet has the capacity to change. The capacity to change arises from the changing possibilities of attempts to justify existing legal material: statutes, the constitution, and legal decisions. The legal material is internal to law, but the plausibility of justification depends on developments outside of law, in particular, within political philosophy, rather than the political system. There is however, although the account is never quite clear, an input from the political system qua system. Statutes represent material likely to be introduced for reasons which have no connection with the application of principle, as it would be understood by a moral philosopher but which can be used in the interpretive process as if they were.[19]

Dworkin's attempt to steer his description so as to avoid 'the paradox of law'[20] by attributing the unity of law to the interpretive processes of judges, and insisting that these processes involve a significant use of political and perhaps moral philosophy, has been subjected to numerous criticisms, particularly from analytical positivists like Raz. In response, Dworkin has repeatedly attempted to restate his position. Many of these criticisms, and Dworkin's reactions to them, can be reformulated using systems theory. The earlier writings of Dworkin utilized the figure of Hercules, a personification of legal rationality, who had infinite time and resources to devise a holistic theory of law, which gave the best interpretation at every level of the legal system, and a right answer to every difficult situation.[21] Crucial to the work of this figure, and reformulations of the theory, is the ability to declare earlier institutional history (earlier authoritative interpretations) to be mistakes.[22] This description of the judicial process provided no basis for the stability of the interpretation of legal materials other than the stability provided through political or moral philosophy. Legal materials had no authority in and of themselves, only that provided through the principles which justified their interpretation as

significance within society? Dworkin seems to have some awareness of this when he re-exports this tautology into moral philosophy, by attributing a doctrine of political responsibility to both political and legal actors, which doctrine restrains their actions by requiring consistency. Thus, in his early writing, he relies on the claim that 'Judges, like all political officials, are subject to the doctrine of political responsibility.' *Taking Rights Seriously* (London, 1977), 87. However, his attempts to identify what could stabilize politics are even less sociologically informed than those addressed to law. His definition of politics as policy resembles act utilitarianism without even the consistent commitment to general happiness: acts that maximize goals (see, as a stark example, *ibid*, 113–14).

18 The whole of *Law's Empire*, n.15, above, develops this interpretation. A short summary of the substantive argument of 'law as integrity' can be found at 216–24.

19 Dworkin's presentation of the doctrine of political responsibility within politics acknowledges the gap between philosophy and the likely behaviour of a senator in a manner likely to lead to idealism (senators do or ought to vote consistently), or cynicism (senators fail to take account of principles). As such it fails to reflect the manner in which principles operate constantly, within politics. Principles, it may be suggested, have a meaning within, and are constructed by, politics as a system, that is not the same as their construction within either moral philosophy or law.

20 See n.14 above.

21 Dworkin, n.17, above, 105–30.

22 *Ibid*, 118–23.

authorities. Thus, in its most extreme formulation, Dworkin's attempt to defuse any tautology in law by attributing stability and change to a combination of matters that were internal and external to law actually relied on external factors alone.

Whilst avoiding paradox, the figure of Hercules provides a poor description of law, or at least one that might appeal to a sociologist concerned to accommodate the given world of law's vast numbers of operations within their descriptions. Although there are moments in the judicial process where thousands of hours go into a single judgment, and that judgment includes statements that appear to come from political or moral philosophy, any attempt to ascribe to these moments the unity of the legal system and its capacity for stability and change, is patently implausible. Decisions have to be made in an instant in huge numbers of situations. And the fact that these decisions are made, and closure achieved for so many legal questions all of the time, cannot be explained through the work of Hercules or Herculean actors. Later Dworkin modified his position, by arguing that Hercules is only an ideal figure, to which judges should (and if his theory is descriptively accurate, will) approximate.[23] He also sought to reduce the burden of holistic reasoning by arguing that judges would seek to provide consistent explanations of local areas of doctrine, only moving outwards to check if their explanations of one area of doctrine were compatible with consistent explanations of surrounding areas of doctrine. Provided surrounding areas confirmed the correctness of the principles and rights found to explain the original area of doctrine, there was no need to go further.[24] While these concessions increase the plausibility of his thesis in some respects, it still fails to account for the unity of law. Unity, with these concessions, is the restriction of contingency resulting from the consensus of political or moral justifications for the whole or significant parts of the legal system. Dworkin's theory cannot operate if it can be shown that not only are there contradictory rationales for particular areas of doctrine, but that such contradictions occur right across doctrine as a whole.[25]

Reconsidering Dworkin from a Systems Theory Perspective

The Local Nature of connecting Legal Communications

Luhmann, in chapter 7 of *Law as a Social System,* places judges in a central position in the legal system. But they are not in a hierarchical position; indeed, unlike Hercules they do not determine the content of what can be legal. Judges, and their interpretive practices, are a structure within the legal system, which system comprises the totality of legal communications. Huge numbers of legal communications occur within the system. Membership of that system is established by the

[23] Dworkin, n.15, above, 245–50. [24] *Ibid*, 250–4.

[25] As illustrated convincingly by the critical legal theorists, see Collins, n.3, above, especially 287–320.

connection between legal communications, and what they have in common as legal communications is their coding; they code the world into what is legal and what illegal.[26] And in this process of coding, the legal system establishes both itself, and its environment (what it considers it is not). This is not the work of a supra individual like Hercules, or the distribution, within judges, of the ideal form of rationality he represents. It is, inevitably, the outcome of itself. The possibilities of what can be coded legal or illegal at any moment are the consequence at that moment of the state of the legal system. It is both total and local. Total, in the sense just stated—it is the outcome of all that currently exists. It is also local in that, at any moment, what a single legal communication can connect to is limited to material to which it has a limited proximity.

An example may assist to understand how this way of viewing the legal system differs from Dworkin's analysis. Consider a demand to pay a parking fine. For Dworkin, using Hercules, the validity of this parking fine requires a systematic assessment of the totality of the legal system. The starting point for this assessment is pre-interpretive[27] (so we have an idea of what needs to be put into a best moral light prior to carrying out that assessment). In making that assessment we need to declare some part of our existing legal material to be mistakes at the outset, i.e. that these are not law after all. Under Dworkin's original formulation of his theory, our assessment needs to take account of every level in the legal system. Using his more modest theory, the assessment has a stopping point provided that the analysis of one area of doctrine can be confirmed by its ability to provide an equally appropriate explanation of surrounding areas of doctrine.

Within systems theory the account would be very different. There is no possibility, at one moment in the legal system, to connect to every other part of that system. This does not alter the fact that the possibilities of connection at any moment are a consequence of the state of the legal system at that moment. But actual connections are, invariably, local. In the case of our parking fine, the first order of connection (or communication which is the form of this connection) is that it conveys information on legality and illegality: your parking was illegal. Thus it is coding, rather than the view of a hypothetical supra individual on the validity of the fine, which makes this a legal communication. All such coding can be re-coded, as a result of secondary observation. We can make communications about the validity of the parking fine. This re-coding does not make the original meaning of the parking fine anything other than a legal communication, even if a person making such a re-coding might describe the earlier coding as 'not law'.

[26] On the nature of this binary coding, its exclusion of third values (which would be included with any attempt to add any ingredient such as legally significant/legally insignificant), its institutionalization, and its ability to respond to its complex environment (society), see Luhmann, n.2, above, ch. 4, part II. The exclusion of third values has been strongly criticized, but that criticism rejected by Luhmann (see H. Rottleuthner, 'A Purified Theory of Law: Niklas Luhmann on the Autonomy of the Legal System' (1989) *Law and Society Review* 779–97).

[27] Dworkin, n.15, above, 65–6.

However, such re-coding, if applied within structures such as a judiciary, will stabilize communications about parking fines, creating a sense of coherence. It is conceivable that a parking fine arises in situations that generate a massive judgment by the highest court in the land on a major constitutional issue. Such a judgment may be the consequence of connections between a large number of earlier legal communications but, however large, it cannot be a consequence of connection between all of the legal system. There is not the time, the connections are not established by logic but from the fact of connection (as in all successful uses of language) so they lie outside the capacity of even a supra-human individual and, in any case, by the time such connections could be made things have moved on (there are millions more communications). So the best that can be achieved, even in significant legal cases, is widespread connections. And these secondary observations do not determine the existence, as legal statements, of even the first order communication. They only stabilize the making of such communications: they limit what is likely to be communicated as legal and illegal, and reinforce the institutional arrangements from which one expects such stable communications.

So what is the status of the procedures that Dworkin describes? Courts are structures, and structures stabilize the making of communications within and by a system, but they must not be understood as the unity of that system, or the cause of its unity. Courts are important for stabilizing the making of communications about what is legal and illegal, but the unity of the legal system lies in the possibilities for connection contained within the totality of legal communications, not just in the communications of courts, and certainly not in the hypothetical possibilities of a supra individual judge such as Hercules.

What is Hercules doing?

So far our systems theory analysis may be considered to do no more than present a criticism that can be made in far more straightforward terms: Dworkin attempts to present the interpretive practices of judges, which can only be one aspect of the legal system, as if they were the whole.[28] But the theory has more potential yet. Let us consider the debate between Dworkin and the positivists on the nature of the material used by judges to make their decisions. For Dworkin moral philosophy, because judges use it in the form of principles, *is* part of law.[29] For positivists such

[28] See, e.g. Raz's defence of Hart as set out in J. Raz, 'Dworkin: A New Link in the Chain' (1986) 74 *California Law Review* 1103–19.

[29] Kelsen recognized the errors of this position in his debate with Esser who, in 1956, offered a transformation theory that claimed that law is established through the input of moral principles. (See H. Kelsen, *General Theory of Norms*, (translated by M. Hartney, Oxford, 1991), ch. 28.) Kelsen argued that any claim that law transformed morality into itself was a confusion resulting from a mistaken metaphor. Craftsmen transform their material (wood, etc) into objects. Law cannot transform moral principles into legal principles. Law can only select principles, and the basis of selection remains with the law. Kelsen's critique of 'principles' as law was, of course, formulated without reference to

as Raz, moral philosophy is not law just because judges use it to make decisions. If it were, then science, aesthetics, even language would be law, because they share this feature of being used by judges to make decisions. Dworkin can only justify the use of moral philosophy as something legal if the manner in which that philosophy is used is peculiar to law. For the positivists, the legal part of a judge's decision is established by reference to authoritative sources. It is these sources that restrict what can be considered as part of a legal decision. In this way the reasoning processes of judges are only peculiar to law because law has institutional means of treating matters as having been decided.[30]

Systems theory throws light on this debate between Dworkin and the positivists. It starts, as mentioned above, from the premise that the law decides what can be law. This assertion is further explored through the logic of forms.[31] The distinction between legal and illegal is simply a distinction. This can be understood through the following question: 'If I told you that an unknown fact "X" was legal, what would this tell you other than that it was not illegal, and vice versa?' If legal cannot universally be equated with a third value, such as 'good' or 'politically acceptable', etc, then it can only be a distinction. As a distinction, there is nothing to distinguish what is put on either side of the distinction: the legal is illegal, and vice versa.[32] The legal system avoids or unfolds this 'paradox' through its logical tautology: the law decides what is legal and what is illegal. And it does so endlessly. In so doing it builds up structures. These can be described as conditioning programmes: 'in the case of X, Y is legal.' These structures can (only 'can', it is all contingent) include courts: 'If a person appointed as a high court judge decides this matter, it is legal'.[33] These courts have a central role within the legal system as they have a duty to decide (they cannot decide not to decide). And this role makes the unfolding of the paradox of law central to their operation:[34] there is no third value that decides what is legal or illegal. What the courts do is decide, and in so deciding they carry out secondary observation: they observe what has been decided before. In this role, they cannot avoid hard cases: whatever has been

Dworkin's analysis of principles. But as a critique of 'principles' Kelsen's work has much in common with the systems theory approach presented here, with one key difference, namely Kelsen's reliance on acts of will (and their objective meaning) as law forming acts.

[30] Principally it relies on the programmes associated with 'res judicata' and equality (see later discussion of equality, as a legal communication).

[31] See Luhmann, n.2, above, ch. 4, Part II. In presenting his arguments he relies in particular on G.S. Brown, *Laws of Form* (London, 1969).

[32] Luhmann, n.2, above, ch. 4, Part I, 175–7.

[33] Such a communication is, of course, closely analogous to Hart's characterization of a rule of adjudication: see H.L.A. Hart, *The Concept of Law* (Oxford, 1961), 94–6.

[34] To clarify the importance of paradox in relation to the duty of courts to decide, see Luhmann, n.2, above, 292–3. 'The paradox, however, is the holy shrine of the system. It is a deity in many forms: as *unitas multiplex* and as re-entry of the form into the form, as the sameness of difference, as the determinacy of indeterminacy, as self-legitimation. The unity of the system can be expressed in the system as distinctions, which turn into guiding distinctions in this function because they hide from view what they reveal . . . courts are in charge of the task of unfolding the paradox of the legal system—as is required by and, at the same time, veiled by the prohibition of the denial of justice . . .' (292).

decided will not decide all that could be decided. It also means that there is no single way (no single structure) for describing how courts decide. The duty to decide forces courts to find reasons for deciding. And there is no way of deciding how 'successful' such reasons are except for the fact of their (or something they lead to) being re-used. This has a stabilizing bias. The reasons that are more obviously appropriate to justify decisions, are those that have been used before. These are reasons that are likely to provide stable structures for dealing with contingency. Positivists present this stabilizing bias as the whole process. Thus judicial decisions are seen as authoritative sources, for one of the most common bases for justifying a decision is to claim that judges have decided this way before. Other sources, which provide structures to stabilize, and thus unfold the paradox that lies behind the legal/illegal distinction, include the constitution (particularly in the USA) and the sovereignty of Parliament (particularly in the UK).

The debate between Dworkin and positivists can be reconsidered from the perspective of the duty to decide.[35] Whatever structures are developed to avoid the paradox of law's tautology will inevitably be used in some situations where they are not as successful as others. For example, the doctrine of sovereignty suffers not only from its patent fictional quality when considered by reference to the complexities of the political system (it is a construct of the legal system),[36] but its use within the legal system generates cases where it adds little (to secondary observers) to the fact that the relevant court decided the matter. The damage (to stability) done by such cases is further reduced, however, if that decision is treated as a good reason to decide the same way in future. But this means that the assumed hierarchy of Parliament and courts is also paradoxical because, in this situation, the will of Parliament is only expressed though fidelity to the decisions of the courts.[37]

In this situation, positivists and Dworkin are trying to establish rival hierarchies for the structures that stabilize legal communications and determine their evolution. For positivists such as Hart and Raz, the reasons that 'best' explain legal decisions are the sources of law. The paradox of law's tautology, that law decides what is law, is avoided by them through treating judicial commitment to these sources as a social fact established and maintained outside of the legal system. For Dworkin the inability of such structures to explain all of the decisions made by courts leads him to look for alternative bases for stability and change. He finds

35 Or, as Luhmann describes it, 'the prohibition of the denial of justice': *ibid*, ch. 7, Part IV.

36 Hence the usual critique within jurisprudence of Austin's notion of sovereignty as descriptively inaccurate (see Hart, n.33, above, ch. 4). Of course Austin simplifies two sovereignties, and then conflates them. His account does not adequately describe the role of legislatures within politics or law.

37 Thus, within this description, lies an explanation for the interminable debates about the relationship between courts and legislative bodies between jurisprudential theories. See, as a straightforward example, Hart's denunciation of the overly court-centred approach of American Realists, in Hart, n.33, above, ch. 7, and his 'Postscript' reply to his critics, in *The Concept of Law* (2nd edn., Oxford, 1994). See, for a more extensive argument, J.L. Coleman, *The Practice of Principle: In Defence of a Pragmatist Approach to Legal Theory* (Oxford, 2001). And, to continue the theme of the interminability of such debates, see Dworkin's review of Coleman, 'Thirty Years On: A Review of Jules Coleman, *The Practice of Principle*' (2002) 115 *Harvard Law Review* 1655–87.

these in moral philosophy, and moral principles. For him, principles establish the weight to be given to authoritative sources, and the decision to be reached when such sources do not by themselves indicate a particular result. Because authoritative sources are not always good reasons for decisions, principles (which operate most clearly when authoritative sources most clearly do not) are considered by him to be the superior structure. In addition, because his principles are weighted (at least partially) through their connection to morality, the stability and change of the legal system does not depend entirely on what is already law. The tautology is defused.[38]

Systems theory treats both Dworkin and positivists as operating at a third level of observation, which can also be called self-description.[39] The need to decide without any third value determining what is legal or illegal generates, at the first level, decisions. Secondary observation of such decisions generates structures that stabilize those decisions. At a third level, observations of those structures lead to attempts to present particular structures in a hierarchical manner, as if they represented or accounted for the unity and totality of the legal system: self-descriptions (the substance of so much jurisprudence).

Systems theory leads one to accept that all self-descriptions are partial, because the structures that they seek to arrange in hierarchical order cannot, in practice, maintain a hierarchical order. This occurs most fundamentally at the level of language: structures, which order communications, are generated by communications, so that which they order can change them. Within the Dworkin–positivist debate, the structures, which are given central focus, are those that stabilize judicial decisions. There are reasons, set out above in the section. 'The local nature of connecting legal communications' why judicial decisions should not be presented as representing the unity of law. But even if legal decisions could represent the unity of law, the structures that stabilize those decisions could not. What they seek to stabilize will escape them, and can change them. And, attempts to present a constant hierarchy of structures are doomed to failure. Just as parliamentary sovereignty exists alongside the courts' duty to decide what is law (constantly threatening to reduce the hierarchy of Parliament and politics over the courts and law to a rhetorical device), so too, principles constantly threaten to subvert the supremacy of rules and authoritative sources.

Adjudicating on Dworkin and the Positivists

The debate between Dworkin and his positivist critics has resulted in concessions on both sides that considerably narrow the differences between them. Hart's

[38] But defusing tautology by attributing the unity of law to inputs from outside, such as morality, has a cost in terms of failing to recognize the identity of law as something different from its inputs: see n.29 above.

[39] See R. Nobles and D. Schiff, 'Introduction' to Luhmann, n.2, above, 12–13 and 44–8. Understanding jurisprudence as self-description is the subject of our forthcoming book, *A Sociology of Jurisprudence* (Oxford, 2006).

formulation of law as a matter of rules, and Dworkin's criticism of his omission of principles, has led to Raz and his concession that the legal system is made up of standards that consist of both, and that even the rule of recognition is not simply a rule but consists of 'all the customary rules and principles of the law enforcing agencies [that identify] . . . all the laws recognized by them'.[40] But important differences remain. Dworkin denies the possibility of a general explanation of what counts as adequate institutional support for a legal principle: there is no measure or yardstick for the amount of institutional recognition required for a principle used by or presented to a court to count as a legal principle. Dworkin thus maintains the claim that one looks outside the legal system, to moral philosophy, to account for the legal system's ability to find weight in principles other than in some empirical relationship to the frequency of their citation or implied use by courts. For Raz, the inability to provide a general explanation of what counts as adequate institutional support would dissolve the border between law and non-law standards, and with it the distinctive feature that distinguishes a legal system from the wider social system. He looks for an adequate explanation of the concept of a customary norm, so that one can make a complete statement of judicial custom and thus have a complete criterion of identity.[41]

While this exchange has sharpened our awareness of the many different kinds of standards used by judges when adjudicating on legal issues, the protagonists still leave us with two different ways to defuse the tautology that systems theory accepts. For Dworkin, law is not simply determined by law because there is a residual element of moral philosophy, or justice, that provides the relative commitment to stability and change. For Raz, the standards that are law do not determine themselves, because there is a sociological condition, the customary norms of judges as a group, which provide this commitment. Systems theory offers an alternative to both positions.

The ability of judges to find standards or reasons to determine every issue which comes before them is a process limited by the same process by which all communications are made: the ability to communicate is determined by the system to which any new communication seeks to connect. These are not processes for which one can substitute any other factor and have it stand in place of the process of communication. So the psychological or normative commitments of the participants (judicial customs) do not determine the possibilities of communication. It is the existing state of communication that determines what can be connected. Thus, (as Fish would acknowledge)[42] communicating law requires the

[40] J. Raz, 'Legal Principles and the Limits of Law' (1972) 81 *Yale Law Journal* 823, 853, responding to Dworkin's early critique of Hart, 'The Model of Rules' (1967) 35 *University of Chicago Law Review* 14–46, reprinted as 'Is Law a System of Rules' in R.S. Summers (ed.), *Essays in Legal Philosophy* (Oxford, 1968), 25–60, and later as 'The Model of Rules I', n.17, above, ch. 2.

[41] However, at a later stage, Raz concedes that the standards binding upon judges may be supplemented by standards that they can only reach through processes that are so indeterminate that they could best be described as exercises of discretion. (n.28, above, 1115–18.)

[42] S. Fish, 'Working on the Chain Gang: Interpretation in Law and Literature' (1982) 60 *Texas Law Review* 551–67.

participants to have regard to the existing structures of communication. In the case of law, at this moment, in most legal systems, these are constitutions, cases, and statutes: forms that generate and support innumerable rules and principles. These structures are used in making communications not simply because the participants are committed to them in a normative sense, but because utilizing them to make communications increases the chances of successful[43] communication. Change is restricted by the same factors that encourage stability. Jettisoning an important structure (such as parliamentary sovereignty) is not difficult because of an internal (psychological) or external (universal moral value) commitment to democracy. It is first and foremost difficult because massive amounts of law would not be possible. An all-out attack on this structure would require vast numbers of laws to be re-configured. Whatever the weaknesses of this structure, and however many times its nakedness is exposed, its abandonment would require a substitute structure that allowed similar communications to be made. From the point of view of the courts, one would need a structure that has a similar ability to provide reasons for decisions. To express this in systems theory terms: evolution requires the variation of an element, which results in the selection of a structure that is capable of stable reproduction. Variations that do not amount to new structures do not lead to evolution, and new structures that do not stabilize and reproduce themselves also do not result in evolution.[44]

The judiciary is a sub-system of the legal system that carries out secondary observation of legal communications and develops structures that stabilize the application of the code legal/illegal. It puts into operation a value that is commonly thought to be external to the legal system: equality. The value remains internal because the equality required is to 'treat like cases alike'. This is an eigenvalue—a value that has no existence outside of the operations that express it. The courts observe what has been coded, and seek to account for that coding. These accounts have the possibility, if reproduced, to become structures. Consistent accounts of coding are (in *whatever* form they develop) treating like cases alike. Equality is consistency, and consistency is the only equality the law intrinsically expresses. This process is partial, and local, but has the capacity to be dynamic. The configurations of what can be compared are not given from outside the legal system but from within. Only the legal system can construct a 'case' that needs to be compared with another 'case'. This means that the issue decided by a judicial decision is never the issue that would arise if a decision were taken in another area of social life. (The legality of a particular abortion never determines, even to an incremental degree, the moral right to life.)

The dynamics of this basis for decisions cannot be captured by a meta-structure, such as a criterion of identity. Fortunately this does not have the outcome, as

[43] Success here only refers to (a) the likelihood of a statement having meaning in terms of legal coding, and (b) the likelihood of it providing a basis for the generation of further legal communications.

[44] For more detail see Luhmann, n.2, above, ch. 6 'The Evolution of Law', and particularly Part I.

Raz supposes, of a conflation of legal and non-legal standards that results in the legal system having no separate identity from the rest of society. The separation is simply not reducible to a philosophical distinction between the standards appropriate to law and elsewhere. The uniqueness of law is found in what it does and how it does it. It codes in terms of what is legal as opposed to, and dependent on, what is illegal, and it constructs, through its own programmes, what (such as cases) it codes. The application of a standard such as 'no one shall be permitted . . . to take advantage of his own wrong'[45] does not result in the dissolution of law into morality for so many reasons. First, the standard is being used to apply a label that is not moral: to decide what is legal. Secondly, the 'wrongdoing' and the 'benefit' will be identified through legal categories (in the case of *Riggs* v. *Palmer* that of being convicted of murder and inheriting through a properly executed will). Thirdly, the arrival of this issue for decision is a moment established by the legal system through writs, conviction, evidence, judgment and appeals. Fourthly, the legal system has developed structures (precedent) that routinely replace reasons for decisions with decisions as reasons for decisions. In consequence of all of this, how (except within an exercise in self-description) could the application of a moral value without a meta-criterion assigning it definite weight on all future instances of its usage be treated as the superiority of moral values over legal ones, or the collapse of legal standards into social ones?

The morality identified by Dworkin within legal reasoning is not the morality of moral philosophy, or the principles of political theory. Justice, as the treating of like cases alike, is a mechanism for the evolution of law. The general norm to 'be just' is simply the process of justification involved in secondary observation. The evolutionary capacity of this process can generate rules, exceptions, and principles. What has been decided can be described in terms of rules. Distinctions based on rules allow for further distinctions in terms of exceptions. Distinctions that cannot be accommodated through rules and exceptions (and exceptions as rules with exceptions in turn) can be articulated in terms of principles: matters that need to be considered prior to the application of the code. Such non-rule restrictions on the basis for decisions can be termed 'discretion'. And the existence of such discretion, constructed through standards of what needs to be considered in order to decide, does not result in either subjectivity (a judge can communicate as law whatever she/he wants law to be) or morality. Discretion, and the standards which restrict its exercise, do not lie outside the legal system. Rather, they are structures for generating a more complex legal system with more capacity to precipitate productive interactions with other functioning sub-systems of society than could ever be achieved through rules alone.

The values generated by this process of secondary observation are not the input of morality into the legal system from outside. This is not an input–output

[45] The principle that Dworkin relies on (n.17 above, 23) from the case of *Riggs* v. *Palmer* to develop his argument.

relationship.[46] Justice, understood by the legal system as something beyond and outside of itself, is more than the application of rules, because legal decisions are more than the application of rules. It is something always beyond what currently exists. But this 'justice' is still a value whose existence still lies in the operations of the legal system: the search for reasons for decisions, most particularly located within the courts that have the duty to decide (and cannot deny justice).[47] This search is not resolvable in terms of a rational schema, and certainly not one that would be recognized by moral philosophy. The process of secondary observation undertaken by courts assesses the 'equality' of its own deliberations by asking what are the consequences in terms of the re-configurations of legal relationships, of alternative descriptions of what has already been decided. These re-configurations are accessible to the legal imagination. One can say 'If you decide this case in this way, you would have to decide all these other cases in a similar/different way.' In some cases, the equality represented by treating like cases alike can be understood as the application of rules. But in other situations, it can result in comparisons between areas of doctrine, requiring for example, the treatment of 'residence' for political rights to be the same, or different (for a reason) as that for housing rights. Here, provided that the difficulties for communication created by such 'equalities' can be stabilized, one has a fruitful basis from which to reach new legal conclusions: make novel legal communications.

Another reason why judicial reasoning cannot be described solely by reference to moral values is that the values utilized in secondary observation are not only moral ones. The rules and principles generated by secondary observation are conditional programmes for the application of the code legal/illegal. At the moments of their generation they allow all kinds of values generated within other systems to form part of what is regarded as equal or unequal about different constellations of legal relationships. For example, in criminal law the legal system can assess the consequences of different combinations of defence rights for the likelihood that evidence will reveal the truth of what has occurred. But this momentary consideration of matters pertaining to truth will not make the criminal justice process into an expression of scientific, or other expressions, of the values of truth. And in contract law, a decision on the concept of duress may make reference to 'fair competition', but this will not make contract law an expression of morality (fairness) or economics (competition). Nor will law be troubled by philosophical arguments on the incommensurability of fairness and competition, or of either with truth.[48]

While conditioning programmes may be constructed by reference to every kind of value communicated within society, they never impose a value that

[46] Such a statement goes to the basics of autopoietic systems theory in the writings of H.R. Maturana and F.J. Varela, *Autopoiesis and Cognition* (Boston, 1980); *Tree of Knowledge: Biological Roots of Human Understanding* (Boston, 1988).

[47] See Luhmann, n.2, above, ch. 5 'Justice, a Formula for Contingency', particularly Part II.

[48] This aspect of legal reasoning has been recognized by Sunstein, who refers to it as 'incompletely theorised agreements'; see C.R. Sunstein, *Legal Reasoning and Political Conflict* (New York, 1996), ch. 2.

determines, for the system as a whole, what is legal and illegal. Not only are too many values utilized for them ever to be reduced to a single value (or rationalized within one meta-moral schema), but also no value utilized within a conditional programme is applied in the same manner as it exists in the system from which it originated. To re-use one of the above examples, law has regard to fairness and competition only for the purposes of deciding whether a contract should be coded as legal or illegal, i.e. to determine what other legal communications can be generated in turn. The alternative possibilities remain legal, even though the legal system has constructed something outside itself (fairness and competition) for the purposes of determining which coding on this occasion is a more consistent application of its coding: legal/illegal.

Conclusion

Systems theory allows us to agree with Raz that by demonstrating that judges have regard to morality in their decisions, Dworkin has not shown that morality is part of law. However, within systems theory, this is not achieved by taking particular structures, such as sources, or the ability of law to limit what counts as a reason for a decision, and treating these as the basis of the unity of law while casting morality and other 'values' into the category of non-law. Law not only constructs itself, but also constructs its environment. Law constructs the things that it identifies as different from itself. Thus references to morality in law are legal, even on those occasions when their use cannot be accounted for through a theory of sources, or an adequate comprehensive statement of judicial custom. They are legal, not because they are identified as such by legal sources, but because they are selected by the law, from the system where they occur in a manner that gives them a quite different meaning from that given by their original generating system. Morality within law is not morality, just as truth within law is not scientific or any other expression of truth. Law selects and reconstructs communications from other systems as it endlessly develops programmes that apply the code legal/illegal.

Moral communications are only one of the communications which law can select as something different from itself in order to explain, to itself, how it decides what is to be legal and illegal. It can also use economic and political communications. However, law appears to have more to do with morality than other aspects of society and its functioning sub-systems because the function of law (the major consequence of its operations) is the stabilization of normative expectations.[49] This is a consequence of the operations (secondary observation) that provide structures to stabilize the application of the code. And this stabilization (consistency) is primarily organized by reference to justice as equality. It is this commitment to consistency

[49] See particularly, Luhmann, n.2, above, ch. 2, Part VI.

(justice as equality) that Dworkin attempts to capture within his writings. But his attempt to attribute it to moral or political philosophy, and to attribute the evolution of law to a process of constant approximation to such moral or political philosophy is sociologically inadequate. The use of morality in law requires a description of the processes by which law identifies itself and its environment through a fact/norm distinction, and controls for itself the processes by which this border is constantly developed and articulated. Law (the existing state of the legal system) controls not only what counts as a relevant fact (selected by law's norms) but also when and how communications about values can be utilized by law for the application of the code legal/illegal. But the overlapping use of terminology and syntax from science, religion, accountancy, economics, politics or morality cannot retain the meaning of such communications within their own systems. And it is in this sense that, ultimately, law remains tautological: it is the legal system, which determines what is and can be law. As such, systems theory's answer to the 'great jurisprudential debate' is a quiet and subtle answer. Law borrows whatever it attributes as law from whatever environmental sources it understands as part of its own communications. There is no answer to the source or determinacy of law except that which operates within law. There is no structure outside of law that determines the possibilities of what can be law, since law cannot be external to itself.

4

The Idea of Sociology of Law and its Relation to Law and to Sociology

John Griffiths

Prologue

In the beginning there should always be a problem. Mine concerns what might be called 'One Hundred Years of Confusion'. Confusion about what sociology of law is, and in particular about its relationship to law and to sociology. I am not going to address the confusion itself and provide a sort of intellectual history, citing all of the chapters and verses where it can be observed. Everyone with any acquaintance with sociology of law will recognize at once what I have in mind and I doubt that spending the limited space available here belabouring the obvious would prove very entertaining. What I shall address is not the confusion but its solution.

I shall formulate the solution at which I have arrived over the past couple of decades in three related, non-obvious, and I hope in their inter-relationship radical, propositions. The first is that social control is constitutive of every kind of social group and is therefore the foundational concept of sociology. The second is that social control—not 'law'—is the proper subject of sociology of law. And the third is that the sociology of law is not just one of the many sub-disciplines of sociology but that part of sociology that concerns itself with the elementary 'social cement' presupposed by all social life.[1] I shall end with a short homily on the importance of sociology of law to a legal scholarship that aspires to more than the exegesis of legal texts.

There is obviously nothing modest about such an undertaking. Coming from a sociologist of law, the endeavour might be considered imperialist or even megalomaniac. 'Sociology', 'social control' and the concept of 'law' are subjects on which many books could be, and have been, written. One who proposes to polish them all off at once in a few pages cannot be denied a certain temerity even if he pretends to offer no more than the sketch of an argument.

[1] Compare J. Elster, *The Cement of Society. A Study of Social Order* (Cambridge, 1989).

What is Sociology of Law?

Let us begin with the seemingly simple question: 'What is sociology of law?' Anyone who like me earns his living doing it is regularly confronted with this sort of naive curiosity. The 'sociologist of law' apparently enjoys a less well-defined social image than the farmer or the lawyer. But however simple the question sounds, giving a reasonably satisfactory answer is not simple at all and turns out to have interesting ramifications.

Obviously, there is more than one possible idea of 'sociology of law' and therefore more than one answer to the question what it is. None of them is the 'right' one, though some may be more right than others. Insofar as they are mutually exclusive, only the results of competition will ultimately permit a choice between them: the proof of the intellectual pudding is in the eating.[2] I take the position that sociology of law is an *empirical social science* about an *observable social phenomenon commonly called 'law'* and that the ultimate objective of the enterprise is the *formulation and testing of explanatory theory*.[3] I shall not address attention to other possible approaches, which can undoubtedly be better presented by those who hold them.[4]

In my view, the shortest and at the same time complete and correct answer to the question what sociology of law is, is that it is the *sociological study of law*. The only problem with this is that whoever asked the question won't find such an answer very enlightening. But the answer contains more than one might think, including one proposition that is not at all self-evident at all: sociology of law is a part of sociology, not a sort or a part of legal scholarship.[5] We will see shortly how important this is for the fundamental nature of sociology of law.

[2] As far as I am concerned, the 'eating' in this case consists of the cumulation of useful knowledge: of theoretical propositions that are empirically testable and have proven to be robust. I am in this regard an unrepentant adherent of Karl Popper.

[3] I have written elsewhere on the sociological point of view in sociology of law: J. Griffiths, 'Wat is rechtssociologie?' [What is sociology of law?], in J. Griffiths (ed.), *De Sociale Werking van Recht* [The Social Working of Law] (Nijmegen, 1996), 1. I hope to return to that theme in the near future. In the meantime, I shall simply take that point of view for granted in this chapter.

[4] I should perhaps emphasize that while I take a rather relaxed, eclectic approach to the what and the how of observation, I do regard a social science as limited to observable phenomena, ultimately to human behaviour. To the extent the oft-heard claim that 'because law is about values and interpretations', the sociology of law must therefore be about such things too, is meant to go beyond observable phenomena (including positive morality), I reject the claim, at least in the sense that I myself use the expression 'sociology of law' in a different way. The point of the enterprise, as I see it, is not to 'grasp' or to 'interpret' law, but to be able to *explain* it.

[5] This is of course not meant to deny the fact that to an important extent the intellectual roots of the sociology of law lie historically, and still lie, in the interest that socially engaged lawyers have in the social origins and the social effects of law. The importance of these roots reflects itself in the fact that sociologists of law have generally directed their attention to the sorts of questions about law that interest such lawyers, with as a consequence that sociology of law often in practice seems little more than a para-legal endeavour. A. Hunt (*The Sociological Movement in Law* (London, 1978)) calls the interest of lawyers in the social effects of law the 'sociological movement in law' to distinguish it from sociology of law in the sense of a social science of law. Compare C.M. Campbell and P. Wiles ('The Study of Law and Society in Britain' (1976) 10 *Law and Society Review* 547) for a similar distinction

The expression 'sociological study of law' contains two concepts: 'sociology' and 'law'. We will know what sociology of law is when we have examined these two concepts and the relationship between them.[6]

Sociology

Sociology is the scientific study of human social life. It deals with everything that makes a *human social group* more than an accidental collection of individuals. Without some sort of social order, a group simply does not exist. Its particular social order determines the nature and composition of a group and governs its internal and external relationships. The behaviour of human beings has a social aspect—and is hence the subject of sociology—insofar as it is not left up to individuals how to behave—insofar as their behaviour is the subject of what is commonly called 'social control'.[7]

There have been attempts to found sociology not in a group-level phenomenon such as social control but in the individual-level choices made by so-called 'rational actors'. All such attempts ultimately fail. Hobbes' effort to derive social order from individual commitment to a social contract forced him to accept a pre-existing 'natural' obligation to keep one's promises.[8] Coleman sought to show that social norms can be derived from self-interested choices, but like Hobbes he had to assume as part of his analysis the very thing he sought to explain: the existence of social norms.[9] The intellectual history of such repeated failures to derive collective goods from private choices leads me to the conclusion that the attempt to argue one's way out of a pre-social state of nature and into social life is a prime example of the Baron von Münchhausen fallacy: trying to lift oneself out of a swamp by pulling on one's own hair. I assume—on the contrary—that, historically speaking, human beings have always lived in social groups, and that for sociology the existence of social order—of social control—can be taken as given.[10]

(applied to the specific situation in Great Britain) between 'socio-legal studies' and 'sociology of law'. *Cf.* R. Cotterrell, *Law's Community* (Oxford, 1995), 74–7.

[6] A few words about the relationship between sociology of law and some adjacent social scientific disciplines. As far as the *anthropology of law* is concerned the situation is, in principle, simple: the two terms derive from different intellectual histories but are ultimately simply two names for the same thing. In this chapter I use the term sociology of law to refer to both. To the extent that other social sciences, such as criminology, law and economics, legal history, psychology of law, and administrative science deal in an empirical way with the legal aspect of social behaviour, they fall within the scope of sociology of law as I conceive it. Considering the matter purely from the scientific perspective, there is but one general social science of law and there seems to me good reason to call this the sociology of law. In daily life, of course, scientific considerations are often crowded out by a host of accidental traditions and institutional arrangements.

[7] Being subject to social control does not imply that behaviour is thereby completely determined. Like law, social control is often not very effective and usually leaves considerable room for behavioural choice.

[8] T. Hobbes, *Leviathan* (London, 1651), ch. xv.

[9] See J.S. Coleman, *The Foundations of Social Theory* (Cambridge, MA, 1988). See also n.14 below.

[10] This does not mean that social order cannot be explained, just that it cannot be explained within sociology. It is presumably possible to give a socio-biological account of the emergence of social life among the evolutionary ancestors of human beings. In such an account, not 'rational choice' but reproductive success would play the key role.

Social Control

Social control is not an 'extra' substance that, when added to a collection of individuals, creates social order and turns them into a group. Nor does the concept carry any top-down implication that one person or group 'controls' the behaviour of others, although obviously such a state of affairs is possible, especially in large and highly differentiated groups. The concept of social control as used here refers to the fact that the behaviour of the members of a group in relation to one another is *regulated.* The regulation resides largely and ultimately in the *mutual relationships and interactions of the members.* Behaviour that is regulated in this way can be called *social behaviour.* Sociology is thus the study of the mutually regulated behaviour of human beings as members of groups.[11]

Social control understood in this way is constitutive of every human group and every social activity and therefore the foundational concept of sociology. All other characteristics and activities of groups and all of the consequences that groups have for human life are structured by and dependent on social control. The various distinguishable aspects of group life that are subject to social control are the domains of specialties within sociology such as the sociology of medicine, of knowledge and of science, of religion, of sport, of cooking, and so forth. Common to and constitutive of all such aspects of group life is social control.

These considerations lead ineluctably to the conclusion that social control is the most fundamental object of study in sociology. The term 'law' should, as we will see shortly, be taken for sociological purposes to refer in a broad sense to social control. In short, sociology of law is not just one of the many sub-disciplines of sociology, addressed to social behaviour on a particular terrain of social life. Sociology of law—the study of social control—deals with the *sine qua non* of all sociology. The rest is derivative. A few of the great sociologists (in particular, Durkheim and Homans) were more or less explicitly aware of this. But in light of the above argument it is peculiar that sociology of law is mostly institutionalized in faculties of law, where it is a marginal subject welcomed, if at all, as a source of information that can be incorporated into legal arguments. There where it belongs to the very core of the discipline, in sociology departments, it is almost never present and there seems generally to be very little awareness of what it is about.[12]

This chapter is not about social control itself, but in light of the central place the concept occupies in my argument, I do feel obliged to address a few words to what it is I have in mind. I begin, as sociology classically does, with the 'problem of

[11] This conception of sociology owes much to G.F. Homans, *The Human Group* (New York, 1950). In the modern sociology of law the technical term 'semi-autonomous social field' is often used to denote the groups within which the regulation of behaviour (social control) takes place (see J. Griffiths, 'The Social Working of Legal Rules' (2003) 48 *Journal of Legal Pluralism* 1); the term derives from S.F. Moore, 'Law and Social Change. The Semi-Autonomous Social Field as an Appropriate Subject of Study' (1973) 7 *Law and Society Review* 719.

[12] Historically, the situation has perhaps been better among anthropologists, many of whom have understood why social control/law is crucial to most of what they are interested in.

social order': how is human social behaviour possible? If the world were in a state of nature and human beings were 'rational actors' each pursuing his own immediate preferences, life would indeed be 'solitary, poor, nasty, brutish and short'.[13] Individual choice must be limited if the coordinated behaviour necessary to social life is to be possible.[14] The characteristically human way of producing order in social behaviour is by subjecting it to rules. Social control is 'the enterprise of subjecting human behaviour to the governance of rules'.[15] But to avoid misunderstanding I emphasize once again that in all but the most extreme of situations it is mostly an enterprise of, by and for the members of a group, largely undifferentiated from their interactions with one another in the course of the affairs of group life.

As Moore argues,[16] it is social groups that are the social locus of rule-creation, rule-learning, rule-following, and of the social disapprobation required to support rule-following. Some of these social groups are known as 'states' and their rules as 'law', a form of social control so elaborated that it consists not only of rules, but also of rules about rules,[17] and even of rules about rules about rules (as in the case of a constitutional rule that limits the authority of a legislature to create or modify rules).

Law

We have now arrived at the second of the two concepts that the expression 'sociology of law' conjoins, namely 'law'.

The Relationship between 'Law' and Social Control

The ladder of law has no top and no bottom.[18]

The common element in the various manifestations of law—rules, institutions, processes, and so forth—is that there is something 'legal' about all of them. From the simplest rule to the most complex institution and the 'legal system' as a whole, they apparently share something that distinguishes them from related but non-'legal' forms of social control. The internal perspective of the lawyer has no problem here. With the ease of Baron von Münchhausen legal scholarship raises 'law' up out of the dismal swamp of social control by pulling on its own hair: law is

13 Hobbes, n.8, above, 82.

14 The problem of social order has a long and distinguished history in social thought, from Hobbes (*ibid*, 87) to Homans (n.11, above). The impossibility that social goods can be accounted for in terms of self-interested 'rational choice' was famously demonstrated by G. Hardin, 'The Tragedy of the Commons' (1968) 162 *Science* 1243. See also J. Griffiths, 'Normative and Rational Choice Accounts of Human Social Behavior' (1995) 2 *European Journal of Law and Economics* 285 (criticism of Coleman's idea that norms can arise out of rational choice).

15 Paraphrasing L. Fuller, *The Morality of Law* (New Haven, 1964), 91 (referring specifically to 'law').

16 Moore, n.11, above.

17 See H.L.A. Hart, *The Concept of Law* (Oxford, 1961); *cf.* P. Bohannan, 'The Differing Realms of the Law' (1965) 67 *American Anthropologist* (No. 6, Part 2, special publication) 33.

18 Bob Dylan, 'The lonesome death of Hattie Carroll'.

what lawyers, and in particular the most authoritative among them, and derivatively and to a variable degree, other members of society, consider to be law.[19] For the internal, normative purposes of lawyers and other participants in legal discourse, there is nothing wrong with this: what lawyers consider to be 'law' fixes—for the time being—the boundaries of a category that is the keystone of an important social practice. But the concept of law, so conceived, is not descriptive of social reality. It reflects a particular political consensus that is highly contingent, a fact that reveals itself anew after every *coup d'état* or revolution.[20]

Sociology of law has known a long tradition of attempts to define law in terms that are not reflective of the moral and political preoccupations of lawyers and that can meet the demands of sociological theory. In the box below I list a few of the better-known products of this tradition.[21] None of them is satisfactory, and the whole enterprise has long since come to seem like a wild-goose chase. A quarter of a century ago Richard Abel drew from this conceptual history the pessimistic conclusion that 'for the time being, at least, it seems clear that we must displace law from the centre of our conceptual focus as we attempt to build social theory'.[22] His despair is a good place to begin, but I intend to come to precisely the opposite conclusion.

[19] *Cf.* T. Eckhoff and N. Christie, 'Studieorganisasjon og sosial integrering' *Jussens Venner* (1967) No. 4, 89, for an account of how the Baron von Münchhausen operation works in legal education. H.L.A. Hart's 'sociological' approach to the concept of law (n.17, above) treats 'law' as what the 'rule of recognition' accepted among legal officials identifies as law.

[20] Despite all the efforts of legal positivists in the tradition of John Austin to define 'law' as a descriptive concept, even legal practice is forced from time to time to confront the essentially political/normative character of the internal concept of law, for example in the case of the Unilateral Declaration of Independence by Ian Smith's regime in Southern Rhodesia (see *Reg.* v. *Ndhlovu*, 1968 (4) S.A. 515 (Rhodesia, Appellate Division). The debate among legal philosophers on the question whether Nazi law was 'really' law (see H.L.A. Hart, 'Positivism and the Separation of Law and Morals' (1958) 71 *Harvard Law Review* 593; L. Fuller, 'Positivism and Fidelity to Law—A Reply to Professor Hart' (1958) 71 *Harvard Law Review* 630) derives its enduring attraction from the failure to distinguish the descriptive and the evaluative uses of the word law.

[21] Sources for the examples in the box: E. Ehrlich, *Fundamental Principles of the Sociology of Law* (transl. W.L. Moll, Cambridge, MA, 1936), 24; M. Weber, *Max Weber on Economy and Society* (transl. E. Shils and M. Rheinstein, New York, 1954), 5; B. Malinowski, *Crime and Custom in Savage Society* (London, 1926), 55; A.R. Radcliffe-Brown, 'Primitive Law', in A.R. Radcliffe-Brown, *Structure and Function in Primitive Society* (New York, 1933), 212); K.N. Llewellyn and E.A. Hoebel, *The Cheyenne Way: Conflict and Case Law in Primitive Jurisprudence* (Norman, OK, 1941), 23, 283–5; R. Pound, *Social Control Through Law* (Camden, NJ, 1942), 25; Hoebel, n.12, above, 28; R. Schwartz, 'Social Factors in the Development of Legal Control: a Case Study of Two Israeli Settlements' (1954) 63 *Yale Law Journal* 471; Hart, n.17, above, 91–2; P. Bohannan 'The Differing Realms of the Law', in L. Nader (ed.), *The Ethnography of Law* (supplement to 67 *American Anthropologist*, 1965), 33, 36; P. Selznick, *Law, Society and Industrial Justice* (New York, 1969), 7; Pospisil, n.12, above; D. Black, *The Behavior of Law* (New York, 1976).

Social scientific conceptions of law often track those of legal philosophers. Thus Hoebel's definition resembles the classic legal positivist definition of John Austin (*cf.* Hart, n.17, above, 25): a rule of law is a general command, given by a sovereign (a person who is habitually obeyed but does not habitually obey another) and supported with threats of sanction. Bohannan's definition resembles that of H.L.A. Hart. And Pospisil's definition resembles Holmes' classic 'realist' definition of law: 'The prophecies of what the courts will do in fact, and nothing more pretentious, is what I mean by the law' ('The Path of the Law' (1897) in *Collected Legal Papers* (Boston, 1920), 173).

[22] R. Abel, 'A Comparative Theory of Dispute Institutions in Society' (1974) 8 *Law and Society Review* 218, 224.

THE SEARCH FOR AN EMPIRICAL CONCEPT OF LAW

a small chronological survey of diverse proposals

1913 ***Ehrlich***	A rule of law is an 'ordering' of social relationships in a group ('association'): 'a rule which assigns to each and every member of the association his position in the community . . . and his duties'.
1922 ***Weber***	Law is 'order [that is] externally guaranteed by the probability that coercion (physical or psychological), to bring about conformity or avenge violation, will be applied by a *staff* of people holding themselves specially ready for that purpose' (emphasis added).
1926 ***Malinowski***	'The rules of law stand out from the rest in that they are felt and regarded as the obligations of one person and the rightful claims of another. They are sanctioned not by a mere psychological motive, but by a definite social machinery of binding force . . .'
1933 ***Radcliffe-Brown***	Law is 'social control through the systematic application of the force of politically organized society'.
1941 ***Llewellyn & Hoebel***	'[T]he *legal* is best seen as that which is marked by authority—which is recognized as imperative . . .' (emphasis added)
1942 ***Pound***	Law is social control by the state—'the systematic and orderly application of force by the appointed agents.'
1954 ***Hoebel***	'A social norm is legal if its neglect or infraction is regularly met, in threat or in fact, by the application of physical force by an individual or group possessing the socially recognized privilege of so acting.'
1954 ***Schwartz***	Legal control is 'social control delegated to specialized functionaries'.
1961 ***Hart***	Law is the 'union of primary rules of behaviour with . . . secondary rules . . . [which] specify the ways in which the primary rules may be conclusively ascertained, introduced, eliminated, varied, and the fact of their violation conclusively determined'.
1965 ***Bohannan***	Law is '"a body of binding obligations regarded as a right by one party and acknowledged as a duty by the other" [Malinowski 1926: 58] which has been reinstitutionalized within the legal institution so that society can continue to function in an orderly manner on the basis of rules so maintained'.
1969 ***Selznick***	Law is 'endemic in all institutions *that rely for social control on formal authority and rule-making*' (emphasis in original).
1971 ***Pospisil***	Law consists of those rules that (implicitly) underlie the decisions of persons whose authority enjoys general recognition.
1976 ***Black***	'Law is governmental social control.'

Among other things, the examples in the box show that law is generally looked upon, for empirical purposes, as a sub-set of a more general and fundamental social phenomenon: a *species* of a more encompassing *genus*.[23] All such conceptions of law as a particular species of an encompassing genus we can call *'taxonomic'* conceptions: they mimic the way living things are grouped and distinguished in taxonomic biology.

Although other genuses are conceivable, most taxonomic definitions of law for empirical purposes treat it as a sub-set of social control.[24] Within that encompassing genus, 'law' is identified by means of one or another distinguishing characteristic: the state, power, authority, and so forth. For Black, law is governmental social control. For Schwartz, legal control is 'specialized' social control. For Hart, a social group has 'law' if its primary rules of social control are combined with secondary 'rules about rules'. In what follows I shall limit the discussion of taxonomic definitions of law to the social control variant. This is because, in light of what I said earlier about the constitutive importance of social control for sociology, social control seems to me the most promising general category within which to try to locate law for sociological purposes. If I succeed in doing so, I will have located the sociology of law in the very heartland of sociology.

But first I have to dispose of the whole taxonomic approach. The defects of Schwartz's concept of law are characteristic of that approach, so I will use his deservedly famous article on social control in two Israeli agricultural settlements[25] to make my point. For Schwartz, 'law' is social control delegated to specialists. Schwartz seeks to understand why such delegated social control emerged in one of the two settlements and not in the other. The core of his argument can be summarized in terms of the idea of relational distance: delegated social control—'law'—is associated with increasing relational distance. The fact that one settlement had 'law' can be explained as the result of the fact that its socio-economic organization was such that the inhabitants had fewer overlapping social relationships with, and were generally less dependent on, one another than in the settlement that did not have 'law'. Schwartz's analysis is convincing and made especially plausible by the fact that many other researchers, in widely varying contexts, and with regard to different manifestations of law, have come to essentially the same conclusion. For present purposes it is enough to refer to but one example: Macaulay's equally famous study of the extent to which business interactions are regulated by law or by informal social control.[26] Here, too, relational distance seems to be the critical variable.

[23] *Cf.* Hart, n.17, above.

[24] Other overall categories suggested from time to time in the literature are rules, morality, and politics. The distinguishing criteria are more or less the same as in the case of social control. Thus someone might define law as morality enforced by the state. Someone else might define it as political decisions made by applying rules. Treating law as a species of social control has the advantage over these other possibilities that all of the manifestations of law are covered.

[25] Schwartz, n.21, above.

[26] S. Macaulay, 'Non-contractual Relations in Business: a Preliminary Study' (1963) 28 *American Sociological Review* 55. *Cf.* also H. Todd, 'Litigious Marginals. Character and Disputing in a Bavarian Village', in L. Nader and H. Todd (eds), *The Disputing Process—Law in Ten Societies* (New York, 1978), 86.

Nevertheless, there is a serious problem at the heart of Schwartz's analysis and it derives from his taxonomic conception of law. It is simply not true that what Schwartz calls 'specialization'[27] in social control only existed in the settlement he characterizes as having 'law'. That settlement did possess the differentiated adjudicatory institution that had particularly attracted his attention—a Judicial Committee charged with settling disputes—but Schwartz's own account makes plain that the other settlement also knew considerable differentiation in social control. It may have been less highly visible than in the first settlement, but there was differentiation in legislation, adjudication and sanctioning. On Schwartz's own definition there was thus 'law' in both settlements. The difference for which he sought an explanation was, in Schwartz's conceptual terms, non-existent.

For anyone who is familiar with Schwartz's article, such a conclusion—that the difference that he observed between the two settlements, and for which he offered a plausible explanation, did not exist—will seem absurd. The problem is that Schwartz was unwittingly imprisoned in the fundamental assumption of the taxonomic approach, namely that the relationship between law and social control is one of sub-set to set and that the characteristic which defines the sub-set has a distinct number of values, in this case two:[28] differentiated or not-differentiated. In fact, however, differentiation—like most (if not all) social variables[29]—varies *continuously*. It is like temperature (and not like sex): physical objects do not fall into two categories, 'hot' or 'cold', depending on whether they possess some characteristic that is either present or not; they can be continuously warmer or colder. Schwartz should have tried to explain why social control was *more* differentiated in one settlement than in the other. It might seem a mere quibble, but in fact the choice for a *continuous variable* to describe the relationship between law

[27] 'Differentiation' is a better term and I shall use it from here on. It is better because it refers to the institutionalization of distinct social roles and not to the allocation of natural persons over those roles (nor to the capacities required for performing them). A role, such as member of the general assembly of one of Schwartz's settlements, can be highly differentiated (as in fact it was, no one being able to carry it out except in narrowly defined circumstances) but not specialized at all (every member of the group being entitled to perform it together with all the others).

[28] All taxonomic concepts of law of which I am aware assume two. It would make little difference to my argument if there were more than two.

[29] The formulation of theoretical propositions in terms of discontinuous variables (taxonomically-defined concepts, typologies, Weberian 'ideal types') has a long and I believe dismal history in the social sciences, among them sociology of law. It leads in general to feeble or untenable theory. (I have long intended to write an article that in this respect it is Durkheim and not Weber who should be taken as the patron saint of sociology of law.) Thus Black (n.21, above), whose independent variables (stratification, relational distance, etc) are all admirably continuous, defines his dependent variable 'law' in taxonomic terms (social control by the state) and goes on to distinguish four distinct 'styles' of law. Macaulay (n.26, above), who makes an important contribution to empirical theory by abandoning the taxonomic distinction between 'contractual' and 'non-contractual' obligations nevertheless falls into the taxonomic trap by distinguishing 'legal' from 'non-legal' sanctions. The social relations that affect the mobilization of law were for a long time conceived taxonomically ('simplex' and 'multiplex' relations—see L. Nader and H.F. Todd, 'Introduction', in *The Disputing Process—Law in Ten Societies* (New York, 1978) until Black introduced the continuous variable 'relational distance'. And so forth. The problems that a taxonomic concept of law poses for the formulation of good theory plague these other cases as well.

and the rest of social control has profound consequences in both theory and research.[30]

The relationship between law and social control can be conceptualized in a better way. All the distinguishing criteria that the taxonomic approach to the concept of law has produced suffer from the same problem: they do not define sub-sets of social control but roughly indicate various points on a continuous dimension of differentiation in social control (see the figure on the following page). The authors concerned call social control 'law' if it is at least as differentiated as the point on the continuum that their conception of law requires.[31] But instead of asking 'When is there enough differentiation to call social control "legal"?' it would be better to be satisfied with noting the fact that all social control is *more or less* differentiated. On a scale between two analytic poles—the absolute-zero point of differentiation and the point of infinitely great differentiation—we can locate any particular observed situation.[32] We will seek then to understand, not what it is that produces supposedly theoretically different sorts of social control, but *what accounts for different positions on a dimension of continuous variation in social control.*[33]

[30] Some further objections to 'taxonomic' definitions of law are:

1. After more than a century of effort, there is still no sign of any consensus on what the proper taxonomic criterion might be.

2. On the continuum of increasing differentiation there are no inherent break-points (comparable to the freezing and boiling points of water) that one could choose to distinguish law from the rest of social control. The choice of any particular point is thus arbitrary. In practice, what is concealed behind an apparently arbitrary choice for a particular level of differentiation is an author's ethnocentric preference for what is called 'law' in his own society. (Herein undoubtedly lies the key to the question why so many sociologists of law seem incapable of relinquishing a taxonomic concept of law, or even of recognizing the problems to which it gives rise. On the ideologically sensitive matter of 'law' they remain unreflectingly trapped within the internal perspective and its fundamental need to distinguish that which in their culture is considered 'law' from 'morality', 'politics', 'social control', and so forth.)

3. All taxonomic conceptions of law are at once over- and under-inclusive. Observations close to but on opposite sides of the line that separates 'law' from the rest of social control have more in common with each other than either of them has with observations that lie on the same side but much farther apart. Using Schwartz's conception of law, one of his settlements shared 'law' with the Israeli state whereas the other shared 'informal social control' with the family and all sorts of fleeting or amorphous social groups. But everyone who has read Schwartz will protest that the two settlements had much more in common in their social control than either of them had with such distant relatives that happen to fall on the same side of an arbitrary taxonomic dividing line. Introduction of such an arbitrary dichotomy into the fundamental conceptual apparatus of sociology of law dooms powerful theorizing from the start.

[31] The fact that we can construct such a scale means it is in principle possible to reinterpret the work of sociologists of law who have used differing taxonomic conceptions of law in a way that makes their theories compatible and their findings commensurable. In this way, the ideal of cumulation of knowledge comes within reach.

[32] Such a continuous scale also makes it easier to recognize that not all social control commonly associated with a particular point on the scale—for example, the state—is in fact at the same level of differentiation. Nor is all social control by the state more differentiated than some forms of non-state social control. There is of course no reason at all why all of the social control of the state should be equally differentiated and occupy a unique point on the scale, but the taxonomic approach makes it difficult to acknowledge and to deal theoretically with such an idea. See, for example, Macaulay (n.26, above), who despite his admirably non-taxonomic approach to the concept of 'contract' nevertheless seems to assume that 'legal sanctions' for breach refers to some theoretically distinct type of sanction.

[33] I first developed this idea in J. Griffiths, 'The Division of Labor in Social Control', in D. Black (ed.), *Toward a General Theory of Social Control*, Vol. I (Orlando, FL, 1984), 37.

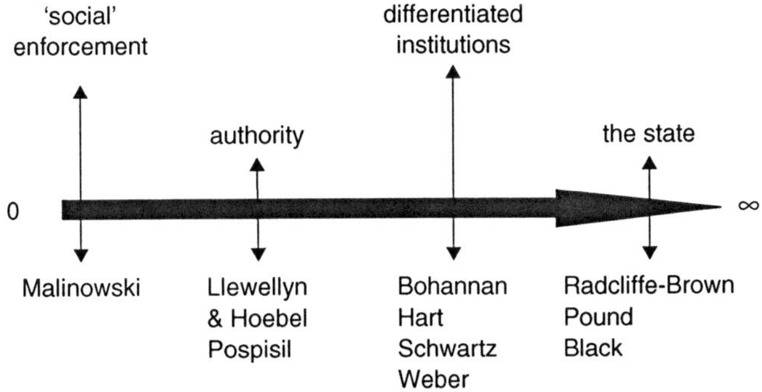

Taxonomic conceptions of law on a scale of increasing differentiation in social control

The most important conclusion of this discussion is that for purposes of the sociology of law we should not try to define 'law' as a distinct type of social control. 'Law' so conceived is a concept that belongs to the internal point of view—the point of view of lawyers who to do their work must distinguish 'legal' from other considerations such as morality and politics. For external, empirical purposes it is more useful to treat social control as the fundamental object of study, with continuous variation in the extent of differentiation therein as a key variable. Sociology of law is, hence, the study of social control and of differentiation therein and in particular—if one likes—of the more highly differentiated forms of social control.[34]

The foregoing exercise is not merely, in the pejorative sense of the word, 'theoretical'. An empirical concept of law that assumes that the relationship between law and the rest of social control is a continuous one does not do the violence to social reality involved, as the example of Schwartz shows, in the use of discontinuous typologies. It therefore opens the way to the formulation of powerful empirical theory that does not require *ad hoc* (hence theoretically arbitrary) exceptions for all of the myriad 'special', 'exceptional' cases that clutter the literature in legal philosophy and in sociology and anthropology of law. It permits us to formulate the 'relational distance' proposition—latent, at least, in a great deal of the literature in sociology of law—as one between two continuous variables: relational distance on the one hand, and the degree of differentiation in social control on the

[34] The emphasis here on differentiation corresponds to the central idea in H.L.A. Hart's (n.17, above) philosophical analysis of the concept of law: that law can be distinguished from the rest of social control by the fact that it consists both of 'primary rules' that regualte social behaviour and of 'secondary rules' that prescribe how to do things with rules (recognition, creation and change, interpretation and application). The secondary rules—and in particular the 'rule of recognition', which determines what counts as 'law'—constitute and regulate the behaviour of social-control specialists. The only change needed in H.L.A. Hart's theory to accommodate it to the argument here is the idea that differentiation is a matter of continuous variation. In that case, the object of his theory would have to be called, in non-taxonomic terms, not the 'concept of law' but the 'concept of the (continuously variable) legal'. The greater the differentiation constituted by secondary rules, the more 'legal' the social control.

other. That proposition then explains not just one supposedly fundamental dichotomy (between 'law' and the rest of social control) but a whole range of gradual differences in the degree of differentiation in social control—differences that are equally present on both sides of the taxonomic line between 'law' and the rest. In short, the generality, and hence the force, of the 'relational distance' proposition is far greater when 'law' is conceived in non-taxonomic terms.

Legal Pluralism[35]

The foregoing considerations permit us to consider the idea of 'legal pluralism' in a new light. The term refers to the fact that the law of the state is only one of the forms of binding regulation in society, that behaviour is often subject to regulation by more than one source of rules. More precisely, 'legal pluralism' designates the situation in which an actor's behaviour is subject to the social control of more than one semi-autonomous social field. In this sense, legal pluralism is a normal characteristic of social life, present in all but the most simple of social situations. Since the fact of overlapping and often divergent regulation has far-reaching consequences for the system of social control as a whole,[36] legal pluralism necessarily plays a central role in the sociology of law.

Nevertheless, perhaps because legal positivism remains such a powerful force in legal theory, both lawyers and social scientists (often unwittingly under its spell) remain reluctant to recognize as 'law' anything other than the law of the state.[37] An important part of the ideological heritage of the bourgeois revolutions that gave rise to the modern state consists of a complex of ideas concerning the nature of law and its place in social organization. This complex, often called 'legal centralism', includes the belief that the law of the state is exclusive of all other law. With minor, partial exceptions—canon law and international law are the most important—nothing else that can properly be described as 'law' is taken to exist. This law-properly-so-called is supposed to be uniform for all persons and administered by a single structure of state institutions. To the extent other normative orders—the internal rules of religious groups, voluntary associations and so forth—are conceded to exist, this is assumed to be thanks to the approval or at least the toleration of the state and subject to the general law.

[35] 'Legal pluralism' is used here in the sociological sense. The term can also be used in a specifically legal sense to describe a particular state of affairs in positive law: law is 'pluralistic' if it provides different rules for different groups in the population (based, for example, on ethnicity, religion, nationality, trade, and so forth) (*cf.* M.B. Hooker, *Legal Pluralism. An Introduction to Colonial and Neo-Colonial Laws* (Oxford, 1975)). In the sociological sense, by contrast, 'legal pluralism' refers to a *factual* situation of multiple sources of binding rules. See generally J. Griffiths, 'What is legal pluralism?' (1986) 24 *Journal of Legal Pluralism* 1, and 'Legal Pluralism', in *International Encyclopedia of the Social and Behavioural Sciences* (Oxford, 2001), 8650.

[36] See for an extensive discussion of these consequences, Griffiths, n.11, above.

[37] E.g. B. Tamanaha, 'The Folly of the Social Scientific Concept of Legal Pluralism' (1993) 20 *Journal of Law and Society* 192.

'Legal centralist' beliefs of this sort are not just a normative ideal. Legal centralism pretends to *describe* legal reality, and in that sense it is an illusion. Not only lawyers but also social scientists have been influenced by this illusion and have limited their attention to that aspect of legal reality that lawyers call 'law'. If they have taken account at all of other sources of regulation, they have generally supposed these to be vestigial remnants of earlier social organization, or less 'legitimate' and therefore less powerful influences on social behaviour than 'law', and hence marginal to the descriptive and explanatory concerns of sociology of law.

A key example of the hold of legal centralism not only on the legal, but also on the sociological mind, will suffice to illustrate my point: The state (and hence its law) is widely credited with the possession of a 'monopoly of force', a peculiar illusion that one finds uncritically repeated throughout the social scientific literature, despite its evident falsehood.[38] In the anthropological literature one found in an earlier generation the same idea expressed in terms of the 'irresistible force' that—by contrast with the rules of custom, morality and so forth—is supposedly characteristic of law 'in the strict sense'.[39]

Weber protested against this illusion as early as 1922:[40]

[W]e categorically deny that 'law' exists only where legal coercion is guaranteed by the political authority ... The possession of ... an apparatus for the exercise of physical coercion has not always been the monopoly of the political community ... [C]onflict between the means of coercion of the various corporate groups is as old as the law itself. In the past it has not always ended with the triumph of the coercive means of the political body, and even today this has not always been the outcome.

But Weber's warning has not helped very much. The formulation of theory in sociology of law still regularly gets stuck in the mud of the unarticulated, normatively based assumption about law against which he protested. As Galanter has observed, sociologists of law seem doomed continually to have to rediscover to their surprise 'the other side of the legal world':

[the fact] that law in modern society is plural rather than monolithic, that it is private as well as public in character and that the national (public, official) legal system is often a secondary rather than a primary locus of regulation.[41]

[38] There are of course those who seek an escape from this empirical objection by moving to the other horn of the dilemma: for them, the state has a monopoly of 'legitimate' force. Here we encounter Baron von Münchhausen again. Law is what the state commands, and the state is anyone who (for the time being) successfully proclaims that whatever he commands is law.

[39] See M. Fortes, 'The Political System of the Tallensi of the Northern Territories of the Gold Coast', in M. Fortes and E.E. Evans-Pritchard (eds), *African Political Systems* (Oxford, 1940), 271; E.E. Evans-Pritchard, 'The Nuer of the Southern Sudan,' in Fortes and Evans-Pritchard (eds), op cit., 293.

[40] M. Weber, *Max Weber on Law in Economy and Society* (transl. E. Shils and M. Rheinstein) (New York, 1954; original German edition 1922), 16, 19.

[41] M. Galanter, 'Justice in Many Rooms: Courts, Private Ordering and Indigenous Law' (1981) 19 *Journal of Legal Pluralism* 1. Writers like M.G. Smith (*Corporations and Society* (London, 1974), 114–26) and G. van den Bergh ('The concept of folk law in historical context: a brief outline', in

The normative heterogeneity so prominently characteristic of the complex societies of the modern world has long been apparent to anthropologists of law. They have assumed that one cannot understand any of the varieties of legal behaviour unless one takes account of the legally pluralistic context within which it occurs. This applies to the emergence and life histories of disputes, the commission and reporting of 'crimes', the use made of legal facilities such as those of the welfare state, the social working of legislation, and so forth. This theoretical insight from legal anthropology has in recent years gradually begun to influence sociology of law, for example in connection with the study of legal effectiveness.[42]

However, while appreciating the importance of legal heterogeneity, the study of legal pluralism remained for a long time taxonomic in its approach. 'State law' was contrasted with 'customary' or 'tribal' or 'local' or 'traditional' or 'folk' law, and conceived of as a different, if related, sort of thing. In recent years it has become widely accepted that distinctions between supposedly different types of law can be important for lawyers and sometimes afford a convenient descriptive vocabulary, but that they serve no useful theoretical purpose.

What's in a Name?

Law is only law if it is labelled law.[43]

The considerations we have been exploring—the objections for sociological purposes to a taxonomic concept of law, and the importance in sociology of law of the related idea of legal pluralism—lead to the conclusion that the word 'law' as commonly defined is a folk concept of lawyers, belonging to their internal point of view, and, because of its connections to the normative preoccupations of lawyers, unsuitable for empirical purposes.[44]

In principle one could react with Humpty Dumpty to the problem of definition: '*When **I** use a word, it means just what I choose it to mean—neither*

K. von Benda-Beckmann and F. Strijbosch (eds), *Anthropology of Law in the Netherlands: Essays on Legal Pluralism* (Dordrecht, 1986), 67–89) have similarly called attention to the fact that legal centralism stands in the way of the development of a sociological approach to law.

[42] See Griffiths, n.11, above. See also J. Griffiths, 'The General Theory of Litigation—A First Step' (1983) 5 *Zeitschrift für Rechtssoziologie* 145, on the study of dispute processes.

[43] 'Recht is alleen recht als er recht op staat' (R. Pieterman, 'Contextuele Rechtsgeschiedenis van de Negentiende Eeuw' [Contextual Legal History of the Nineteenth Century], in C.H.J. Jansen, E. Poortinga and T.J. Veen (eds), *Twaalf Bijdragen tot de Studie van de Rechtsgeschiedenis van de Negentiende Eeuw* [Twelve Contributions to the Study of the Legal History of the Nineteenth Century] (Amsterdam, 1993), 132)—borrowed from the advertisement for Rang (a sort of candy sold in a roll, like life-savers): 'Rang is alleen Rang als er Rang op staat'. Compare Baron von Münchhausen's approach to the concept of law (see text at n.19 above).

[44] Considered from Hart's 'moderate external perspective', it is an important *fact* of their social control system that participants call certain forms of social control 'law' and attach special significance to that label. This does not justify the conclusion—on the contrary, it excludes the conclusion—that their internal concept 'law' is suitable for the external, empirical, and comparative purposes of sociology of law.

more nor less.'[45] If Black, for example, chooses to define 'law' as 'governmental social control', then it is just silly to criticize his theory of law because it does not apply to the things that dictionaries, lawyers, and the man in the street think of as 'law'. A few years ago I decided to take advantage of the freedom to define. In light of the considerations discussed above, I proposed that 'law' should be considered the name of a dimension of variation in social control: depending on the degree of differentiation, social control would be described as more or less 'legal'.[46] The proposal required the use of ungainly expressions such as 'legalness'. But more importantly, it encountered the withering criticism of my late colleague Govaert van den Bergh that the words 'law' and 'legal' cannot be stipulatively purged of their associations with normative ideas about justice and legality.[47] To borrow an expression from the philosopher John Austin, 'law' is a word that comes 'trailing clouds of etymology'. Its associative history cannot be shucked off merely by giving the word a different formal definition.

In the intervening years, further reflection on the concept of law[48] has led me to the conclusion that the word 'law' could better be abandoned altogether for purposes of theory formation in sociology of law.[49] Sociology of law can best be simply considered the study of social control, with differentiation a key variable.

Nevertheless, one must make concessions to practicality. A sociologist of law who seeks to communicate with lawyers and lay people about what he is doing cannot easily avoid using words like 'law', 'legal' and 'legal pluralism'.[50] Nor is there anything wrong with paying special attention to phenomena that are at roughly the same level of differentiation in social control, nor with referring to these phenomena collectively as 'law' or even using the word 'law' as *pars pro toto* for social control at all different levels of differentiation (as in the expressions 'sociology of law' and 'legal pluralism'). The argument here is not about linguistic purity. A certain amount of opportunistic sloppiness from time to time can be unavoidable and even refreshing, but when one chooses for good reasons to express oneself sloppily, one should be aware of what one is doing and of the risks involved. And misleading terms should be resolutely banned from the professional core of sociology of law: theory formation.

Conclusion: The age-old problem of a concept of law suitable for empirical purposes can be solved by no longer considering 'law' the theoretical object of the

[45] L. Carroll, *Through the Looking-Glass and What Alice Found There* (London, 1871), ch. 6.

[46] Griffiths, n.33, above.

[47] G. van den Bergh, 'Over een Theorie van Sociale Controle en het Meten van Recht' [About a Theory of Social Control and the Measuring of Law]' (1986) 1986/4 *Recht en Kritiek* 374. See also B. Tamanaha, 'An Analytical Map of Social Scientific Approaches to the Concept of Law' (1995) 15 *Oxford Journal of Legal Studies* 501.

[48] And on the related concept of 'legal pluralism', which had attracted from Tamanaha criticism similar to Van den Bergh's. See Tamanaha, n.37, above.

[49] Van den Bergh chose another solution: retaining the inevitably normative concept 'law' and abandoning the ambition to study law as an empirical social phenomenon.

[50] Compare Moore, n.11, above.

sociology of law. The theoretical object of sociology of law is social control. It also follows from the above considerations that the expression 'legal pluralism' can and should be reconceptualized as 'normative pluralism' or 'pluralism in social control'. 'Law' is not a theoretical concept in the sociology law.

Sociology of Law

The various considerations I have been exploring lead me to the conclusion that the answer to the question with which I began this chapter—'what is sociology of law?'—is as follows:

Sociology of law is the empirical social science whose object is social control.

Such a definition determines for sociology of law the criteria applicable to the formulation of research questions, the concepts deployed, the research methods used and the relevance and weighing of evidence. In short, it establishes the fundamental nature of the discipline.

Law as Dependent and Independent Variable in the Sociology of Law

One can group theories in sociology of law into those in which social control is the dependent or the independent variable. In the first sort of theory the object is to explain the differences between social control under differing social circumstances. If, for example, we are interested in rules of behaviour, such a theory is one of normative change: when and how do rules come into being, change, and pass away? Other manifestations of social control—dispute processes, normative decision-making, institutions, and so forth—have also been the dependent variables in theoretical propositions. Black's 'theory of law', for example, seeks to explain the quantity of social control in all of its manifestations.[51]

In the second group of theories social control is an independent variable and the question is, what are the social consequences of one or another of its manifestations (rules, decision-making, etc)? To what extent is social control the *cause* of a given social state of affairs, and of stability or change therein? The theory of the 'social working of rules', for example, addresses the question when, why and how people follow rules.[52]

Most sociologists of law choose one or the other of the two approaches without articulating their reasons for the choice, or they swing back and forth between the one and the other without giving any sign of having reflected on what they are

[51] Black, n.21, above. Classic studies in which social control/law is the dependent variable are, for example, Macaulay, n.26, above; Schwartz, n.21, above.

[52] See Griffiths, n.11, above. A classic study in which social control is the independent variable is, for example, V. Aubert, 'Some Social Functions of Legislation' (1966) 10 *Acta Sociologica* 99–110. *Cf.* also Moore, n.11, above.

doing. Some study the process of normative/legal development surrounding euthanasia and try to explain where and when change has taken place, others address themselves to the question whether 'legal' or other rules have an influence on medical practice, and still others attempt both. It is rare that anyone considers whether and how these two questions are related to each other. It is worth wondering whether the result of so much indifference is that the sociology of law is a sort of hotchpotch of incompatible ingredients, comparable to a textbook of geology in which theories about the origins of coal and oil are mixed up with theories about the influence of hydrocarbons on social life, including not only heating and transportation but also such matters as environmental pollution, wars, and so forth.

Black is of the opinion that sociology of law is indeed in such a state. His view is that every science is defined by its dependent variable: what the practitioners of that science seek to explain. Sociology of law is, in his view, the science that seeks to explain variation in law and social control. The influence that social control may have on other things has no more place in such a science than the uses people make of coal and oil have in geology.[53]

Nevertheless, despite an undeniable initial appeal, I believe Black's position is untenable. A concept of social control that takes no account of its effects is impossible. A rule of behaviour without any effects on behaviour would be nothing more than a bit of talk, a legal rule without effects nothing more than words on paper. The situation is even worse than that, since language itself is rule-governed behaviour that only exists as language because the rules concerned have effects and produce meaning. In other words, if one takes no account whatever of the effects of rules, then the rules themselves will be nothing more than unintelligible noise, and social control—the subjection of behaviour to the governance of rules—will not be an identifiable subject of study.[54]

[53] In Black's writings, this position is not always made explicit. In a letter dated 14 February 1996, reacting to an early version of an article of mine (Griffiths, n.11, above), he writes as follows:

> I do not believe the effects of law fall within the jurisdiction of the sociology of law . . .
> I believe that each field of sociology should be defined by the range of variation it seeks to order, i.e., its cluster of dependent variables . . .
>
> [Y]our effort to include the effects of law in the sociology of law [requires you] to take responsibility for everything on which law has an effect and for everything else that might have effects on the same elements of human behaviour [such as religion, politics, recreation, etc]. This would quickly expand your subject in a way that would seem to me unmanageable. It would, among other things, take you into the study of deviant behaviour and conformity. Hardly anyone now tries to understand the sources of conformity, perhaps because they realize it would entail an understanding of virtually everything people do.
>
> For these reasons, I would not venture to comment on your paper. I would regard the likely effect of anything I might say as a case of spitting in the ocean.

[54] On the other hand, rules are not reducible to their effects on behaviour, since it is always possible to break a rule (whether it be a rule of language or of other behaviour) without thereby calling the existence of the rule into question.

In short, Black's tidy solution will not work. To understand it, social control must be studied both as a dependent and as an independent variable. The relationship between rules and their effects is a complex and reciprocal one that should form the heart of theory-formation in sociology of law.

The Position of Sociology of Law in Relation to Sociology

All collective human life is directly or indirectly shaped by law. Law is, like knowledge, an essential and all-pervasive fact of the human condition.[55]

Given my point of departure, that sociology is the study of human social life—that is, of groups—and social control the constitutive element of every group, it follows as I have argued earlier that the study of social control is the fundament on which the whole of sociology necessarily rests. General sociology and medical sociology, the sociology of labour, of knowledge, of religion, and every other sort of sociology: all of them are unthinkable without the internal social control of human groups. This explains the key role of social control ('law') in the work of classical sociologists like Weber, Durkheim, Malinowski, and Homans.

It follows that the relationship of the sociology of law (conceived of as the study of social control) to general sociology is not one of one sub-discipline among many to its mother discipline, as is generally supposed, but rather that of the foundation to a building. Even that metaphor is not strong enough, since social control is not merely the foundation on which the building of sociology rests; it is the essential cement of every bit of the whole edifice. Human social life—it cannot be said often enough—is constituted by social control, which penetrates its every nook and cranny and makes possible its every manifestation.

The Relation of Sociology of Law to Legal Scholarship

A little sociology leads away from the law but much sociology leads back to it.[56]

Having dealt extensively with what sociology of law is and with its relation to sociology, let me now finish off with a few words on its relationship to legal scholarship.

There are a number of important differences between legal scholarship and an empirical social science of law. Of these, most important is the fact that, as Maitland observed, the first is driven by the 'logic of authority' and the second by the 'logic of evidence'.[57] The *validity of a legal proposition* is the *result of a social*

[55] N. Luhmann, *A Sociological Theory of Law* (Boston, 1985), 1.

[56] M. Hauriou, cited in G. Gurvitch, *Sociology of Law* (London, 1947), 2.

[57] *The Collected Papers of Frederic William Maitland* (Cambridge, 1911), Part I, 491.

process—called 'legal reasoning'—in which authority, power and procedures play key roles and which results in *normative agreement* (or at least acceptance, acquiescence). The validity of a legal rule is ultimately dependent on the fact that the members of a legal community accept it as valid.[58]

By contrast, the *truth of a scientific statement* is not dependent on its acceptance by any group of scientists. Truth is not the outcome but the *guiding criterion* of the social process we call science.[59]

The distinction between *legal scholarship* and a *social science* with social control/law as its subject is not meant to imply disqualification of the work of academic lawyers. After all, a great deal of what is done by other academic researchers and teachers is not 'science' either. If we want to call everything that academic researchers and teachers do and that meets minimal standards of coherence and cumulation, 'science', then we will simply need another word to make the distinction I am insisting upon. The discipline I am discussing in this chapter we might then describe as an '*empirical* science'.

The words are not important. What is important is that the point of view—the nature—of sociology of law is fundamentally different from that of legal scholarship. On the other hand, ultimately the two disciplines concern themselves with the same object (although they conceptualize it differently). They ought to be able to learn from each other. I will not concern myself here with what social scientists can learn from lawyers—in my opinion, they have a great deal to learn, if only they are careful not to let their point of view be corrupted by the acquaintanceship. But I do want just to mention what it is in my view that lawyers can learn from the sociology of law.

It is in the lawyer's ability to adopt different points of view in thinking about law that the continual enrichment of legal thought resides. Among other sources of such enrichment is the rediscovery by every generation of lawyers of the importance of an interdisciplinary approach to law, of giving empirical substance to normative reasoning.[60] Between the periods of periodic rediscovery of sociology of law lie periods in which legal scholars withdraw into dry, formalistic legal positivism—what William Twining calls the 'expository' style of legal scholarship[61] and Ehrlich caricatured as 'a more emphatic form of publication of statutes'.[62] Fortunately for legal scholarship, such periods never seem to last very long. Thinking about law without thinking about where it comes from and about all of

[58] *Cf.* Hart (n.17, above); Eckhoff and Christie (n.19, above).

[59] This is why the so-called 'forum theory' of scientific truth propagated by A.D. de Groot (for an early formulation see his *Methodology. Foundations of Inference and Research in the Behavioral Sciences* (The Hague, 1969)) is, as an epistemological theory, untenable, whereas as an empirical theory (what scientists in practice take to be the truth) there is much to be said for it. Similarly, Kuhn's (*The Structure of Scientific Revolutions* (Chicago, 1962)) famous distinction between 'normal' and 'revolutionary' science is only tenable when taken as a contribution to the sociology and not to the logic of science.

[60] *Cf.* the writings of W. Twining, *Karl Llewellyn and the Realist Movement* (London, 1973); *Law in Context* (Oxford, 1997).

[61] Twining (1997), n.60, above.

[62] Ehrlich, n.21, above, 19.

the things that make it important and interesting, is dreadfully dull. Legal reasoning as caricatured in the old legal-realist jibe—'Thinking about something that only has meaning in relation to something else, without thinking about the something else'—is too sterile to keep the mind awake for long. What lawyers can learn from serious sociology of law—from sociology of law that does not disqualify itself for interdisciplinary co-operation by snuggling up to lawyers and adopting their internal point of view—is how to think in a responsible and disciplined way about the relationships between 'law' and all of the 'something else' that gives it meaning.

5

The *Pure Theory of Law* and Interpretive Sociology—A Basis for Interdisciplinarity?*

Hamish Ross

Introduction

This chapter considers aspects of the relationship between academic disciplines that have rarely been thought to be mutually compatible—on one hand the academic study of law (specifically, the theoretical part of jurisprudence, exemplified by Hans Kelsen's *Pure Theory of Law*) and on the other hand the academic study of human behaviour and society (specifically, interpretive sociology, exemplified by writings of Max Weber). A passage from Nicola Lacey's recent biography of H.L.A Hart, *A Life of H.L.A. Hart: The Nightmare and the Noble Dream*, sets the scene whilst prefacing lines of discussion to be pursued further here. The passage concerns the occasionally disputed question of whether Hart read, and was influenced by, the work of Max Weber.

> [T]here is an interesting question here about the influence of sociological thought on Herbert's [Hart's] work. On one occasion, John Finnis consulted one of Herbert's volumes of Max Weber and found it heavily annotated (as was the case with most of the books which Herbert read closely). Finnis later asked him on two separate occasions about Weber's influence on his account of the 'internal aspect of rules'. Herbert denied that any such influence existed, ascribing the origins of the idea instead to Peter Winch's *The Idea of a Social Science*. Finnis felt unable to respond to his denial by saying that he had seen the counter-evidence in his copy. . . .Weber's discussion of the variety of ways in which conduct may be orientated towards certain maxims within an order is marked [on Hart's copy of *Max Weber on Law in Economy and Society*] "Good, like it, likely to be useful".'[1]

Lacey suggests that Hart's seeming reluctance to acknowledge any intellectual debt to Weber may have originated in the fact that in the predominantly philosophical

* I am grateful to Iain Stewart for commenting on an earlier version of this chapter.

[1] *A Life of H.L.A. Hart: The Nightmare and the Noble Dream* (Oxford, 2004), 230.

world that Hart inhabited, any indebtedness to Weber would have been unlikely to win Hart much praise. Hart may thus have been disinclined to be seen to have grounded key aspects of *The Concept of Law*—for instance, the 'internal aspect of rules'—on the work of a 'mere' sociologist, even if the sociologist in question, Max Weber, happened to be a towering figure in the development of sociology as an academic discipline as well as a renowned jurist in his own right. Indeed, Hart once commented with little sympathy on the—as he perceived it—apparent lack of intellectual and analytical rigour attending 'average' books on sociology:

> ... I think that no candid student of sociology could deny that, valuable as the insights have been which it has provided, the average book written in the sociological vein ... is full of unanalyzed concepts and ambiguities ... Both psychology and sociology are relatively young sciences with an unstable framework of concepts and a correspondingly uncertain and fluctuating terminology.[2]

It is beyond the scope of this chapter to consider, or revisit, the question of whether Hart may have been influenced by Weber when writing *The Concept of Law*.[3] My primary aim is instead to examine a few unexplored issues arising from possible 'resonances' between the writings of Kelsen and Weber. But the attitude of seeming mutual antipathy between leading analytical jurists and sociologists during the twentieth century—weighing, more often than not, against sociology—is an instructive point of departure for an assessment of a few aspects of the autonomous domain that Kelsen claimed to have created for his *Pure Theory of Law*. Kelsen's theory aspired to the possibility of severing legal theory from the influence of 'foreign' disciplines such as sociology, biology, or ethics. Any attempt to 'mix' disciplines was 'syncretism'—without doubt, for Kelsen, a malign and futile undertaking.[4]

Yet the enduring question of whether the *Pure Theory of Law*—ostensibly purged of any 'syncretic' tendency—achieved the theoretical independence that Kelsen claimed for it assumed a paradoxical turn with Richard Tur's observation that Kelsen's theory is in fact a model for 'a collectivist *verstehende* sociology'.[5] Could such a paradigm of theoretical purity—on the face of it, perhaps, as far removed as it is possible to be from the spectre of interdisciplinarity or 'syncretism', to use Kelsen's more pejorative expression—possibly serve as a blueprint for an approach to theoretical jurisprudence embedded in interpretive sociology? That is a question the beginnings of which I will take up in this chapter: without, however, engaging

[2] H.L.A. Hart, 'Analytical Jurisprudence in Mid-Twentieth Century: A Reply to Professor Bodenheimer' (1957) 105 *University of Pennsylvania Law Review* 953, 974.

[3] This is, however, examined at greater length in H. Ross, *Law as a Social Institution* (Oxford, 2001).

[4] See generally Hans Kelsen, *Pure Theory of Law* (otherwise Hans Kelsen, *Introduction to the Problems of Legal Theory* (trans. and eds Bonnie Litschewski Paulson and Stanley L. Paulson) (Oxford, 1992) (hereinafter 'PTL') at xxi and at n.14. For usage of the expression 'syncretism' see *The Encyclopedia of Religion* Vol. 14 (New York, 1987), 218 ff.

[5] Richard Tur, 'The Kelsenian Enterprise' in Richard Tur and William Twining (eds), *Essays on Kelsen* (Oxford, 1986), 149 ff. See also 178 and 182, n.4.

in extensive critical engagement with Kelsen's pure theory as such. Tur's challenging observation will frame a discussion that seeks to develop that question from aspects of Kelsen's theory that are merely *suggestive* of areas for sociological theoretical development. So while the discussion will not pretend to 'dispose' of the question, some remarks will be made as to what might be learnt from the exercise of viewing some aspects of Kelsen's pure theory, albeit 'sociologically repositioned', as a model for 'a collectivist *verstehende* sociology'.

Kelsen's Reconstructed Legal Norm (*Rechtssatz*)

For reasons to be clarified, I propose to consider Tur's observation in the context of Kelsen's concept of the Reconstructed Legal Norm (*Rechtssatz*).[6] In the *Pure Theory of Law* the Reconstructed Legal Norm is a 'legal category' that is 'cognitively and theoretically transcendental in terms of the Kantian philosophy'. Kelsen uses this device in part to assist in the task of separating the 'legal world' from the 'moral world' and the 'natural world'.[7] Yet, more significantly for the present discussion, its status in the pure theory as 'hypothetical judgment'—and (thus, as I will argue) as the hypothesized outcome of the judicial interpretive process of conferring legal meaning on legally relevant facts and events—raises the question of whether, and how far, it can be regarded as capable of rendition as an 'artefact' of interpretive or *verstehende* sociology.

For Kelsen, the Reconstructed Legal Norm—the 'quasi-technical' *Rechtssatz* of the pure theory—represents a hypothetical judgment expressing the linking of a conditioning material fact with a conditioned legal consequence. This feature serves to distinguish legal norms from moral norms—facilitating Kelsen's project of carving out an autonomous domain for legal theory. Kelsen suggests that the notion that both legal and moral norms assume an imperative form—for instance, 'thou shalt not . . .'—had led 'traditional theory' into the error of assimilating one with the other.[8] As these were imperatives the question could be asked

6 As the Paulsons observe, the expression 'Reconstructed Legal Norm' ('*Rechtssatz*') is Eugenio Bulygin's terminology for Kelsen's hypothetically formulated legal norm: see PTL, 23 n.20. See also PTL, 132–4. The Paulsons comment that the Reconstructed Legal Norm has a 'quasi-technical use' in the pure theory: PTL, Supplementary Notes, 133. In other words, in Kelsen's usage in the specific context of the pure theory it is not (as is seemingly the case with other jurists and indeed with Kelsen in the context of other writings) a synonym for '*Rechtsnorm*' or 'legal norm'. It would appear to represent a theoretically conceived or 'ideal form' of the legal norm posited by legal science, as opposed to any instance of an actual legal norm existing in some enacted form or capable of extrapolation as a principle or doctrine from an authoritative source such as a judicial precedent. Bulygin had rendered the *Rechtssatz* as one type of 'reconstruction of a norm'. (PTL, 133.)

7 See generally PTL, 22–5.

8 PTL, 23 and, generally, Supplementary Notes at 133 where the Paulsons observe: 'Kelsen enquires into the "ideal form" of the legal norm as part of his effort to distinguish legal norms from norms of morality. Earlier theorists had argued that both legal and moral norms have the same imperative form, a view Kelsen believes to be mistaken and a source of confusion generally about the law and morality.'

whether it was appropriate, or at least tenable, to regard them as the 'same thing'. Kelsen's Reconstructed Legal Norm rendered that assimilation impossible because unlike the moral world a legal consequence—for instance, a criminal penalty imposed by a court—is linked to a legal condition, for example, the commission of a crime. In the pure theory the legal norm is understood 'as a hypothetical judgment that expresses the specific linking of a conditioning material fact with a conditioned consequence':[9] 'If A commits an unlawful act, A ought to be punished'.[10] Such a linkage could not realistically be made in the moral world because—whatever the 'consequence' of a course of behaviour adjudged 'immoral' might be (manifested, for example, in outrage, criticism, censure, and so on)—that response is nowhere specifically predetermined as an outcome in the same sense that legal consequences would be in the legal world.

For Kelsen the conceptual act of linking a perceived act with the consequence that in law ought to follow it is an act of 'imputation'. In the pure theory this further differentiates the legal from the natural world: separating the 'is' from the 'ought'. According to this view, in the natural world *causality* is the linking principle between one natural event and another. Thus laws of nature take the form: 'if A is, then B [causally] must be'. Laws of the legal world take the form: 'if A is, then B [normatively] ought to be'. Kelsen's doctrine of the Reconstructed Legal Norm allows him to connect 'legal condition and legal consequence' through the medium of the 'ought' as a (Kantian) 'category of the law' without reliance upon the linking principle of causality.[11]

Kelsen additionally places the legal norm—theoretically refashioned in the Reconstructed Legal Norm—in an institutional context. In that setting the legal norm has the additional property of being *coercive* in nature. It is a norm 'providing for coercion'.[12] The consequence attaching to a certain condition is 'the coercive act of the state—comprising punishment and the civil or administrative use of coercion'.[13] The behaviour constituting (say) a delict is set in the Reconstructed Legal Norm as the condition of a specified consequence. The positive legal system, as Kelsen observes, responds to this behaviour with a coercive act. The role of coercion in the law is to induce human beings to behave in a legally prescribed manner by means of the technique of visiting an 'evil' upon anyone who fails so to behave. Human beings thus treat this coercive act as an evil to be avoided. The 'efficacy' of the legal system lies in its potential to *motivate* behaviour towards the avoidance of relevant sanctions.[14]

[9] PTL, 23.

[10] As Kelsen notes: 'Positive laws say: "if *A* is, then *B* ought to be".' See PTL, 24.

[11] PTL, 25.

[12] As nineteenth-century positivist legal theory had held. See PTL, 26.

[13] *Ibid.*

[14] Kelsen, however, concedes a degree of uncertainty as to the motivational force of legal coercion and sanctions: 'It is difficult to decide whether human behaviour that conforms to the legal system is actually an effect of the notion engendered by the threat of a coercive act. ... The motive is by no means always fear of sanction or of the coercive act being carried out; there are religious and moral reasons for doing this or that, there is regard for social custom, concern about social ostracism, and very often there is simply no stimulus to behave contrary to law....' (see PTL, 31). Weber similarly

Two strands of analysis in Kelsen's pure theory, each gravitating around the concept of the Reconstructed Legal Norm, are suggestive of the possibility of a sociological repositioning of that concept towards the *interdisciplinary* approach to theoretical jurisprudence alluded to at p. 70 above.[15]

First, the Reconstructed Legal Norm as the 'hypothetical judgment' of a court of law can be taken to represent the hypothesized outcome of the judicial interpretive process of conferring legal meaning on legally relevant facts and events. Put another way, for a judge to conclude—from a determination of the fact that 'A is'—that 'B [legally] ought to be' is an interpretive act, i.e. an act of interpretation of the legal signification of fact A, or the legal consequences that should flow from a situation involving fact A. In other words, it is an act of conferring legal meaning or sense upon fact A. Just as importantly, it is 'social action' in Weber's sense, and for Weber, social action is the key concept, and the very object, of interpretive sociology.[16] (The connection with Kelsen's concept of 'legal meaning' (*rechtliche Bedeutung*) is briefly outlined at p. 76 below.)

Secondly, Kelsen's acceptance of the *motivational* dimension of the legal norm prevents the legal norm from being viewed as some kind of 'causative force'—i.e. a 'cause' that *impels* an 'effect' such as in the case of (e.g.) a transfer of energy in the natural world. Instead—to the extent that the legal norm functions to motivate human behaviour—the norm comes to be incorporated into the meaningful (mental) processes of the actor so motivated. It does not, in other words, directly 'enact' behaviour in the sense (say) that a red billiard ball striking a green billiard ball causes the latter to move towards a side pocket.

Both of these strands of analysis run in parallel with comparable analyses in mainstream sociological writings. In particular, Kelsen appears to acknowledge subjective meaning (*Sinn*)—in the sense that Weber conceives this—as a component, and the meaningful content, of human behaviour (or *legally directed* human behaviour, to be more specific): 'only the human being, endowed with reason and will, can be motivated by the notion of a norm, motivated to behave in conformity with

concedes uncertainty. A legal norm may be seen as merely *one* determinant of human behaviour in a given instance. There may be a range of degrees of consciousness of the influence exerted on action by determinants such as legal norms. See Max Weber, 'The Concept of "Following a Rule"' in W.G. Runciman (ed.), *Max Weber, Selections in Translation* (Cambridge, 1978), ch. 5, especially at 105.

[15] Such an approach—doubtless amounting to Kelsenian 'syncretism'—would surely be anathema to Kelsen. It is not, of course, suggested that the 'sociological repositioning' to be proposed here is anything other than an 'inventive step' or extrapolation from a Kelsenian point of departure towards a decisively *non-Kelsenian* theoretical end. Kelsen's pure theory by no means endorses, nor indeed does it necessarily imply, that proposed end. The expression 'interdisciplinary' suggests, on one hand, theoretical jurisprudence in the specific sense of Kelsen's *Pure Theory of Law*, and on the other hand, interpretive sociology in the sense of the sociological writings of Weber. For the latter, see generally, Max Weber, *The Theory of Social and Economic Organization* (trans. A.M. Henderson and Talcott Parsons) (New York, 1947); Max Weber, *Economy and Society: An Outline of Interpretive Sociology* (eds and trans. Guenther Roth, Claus Wittich and others), (New York, 1968); and Max Weber, '"Objectivity" in Social Science and Social Policy' in Max Weber, *The Methodology of the Social Sciences* (New York, 1949).

[16] See nn.31 and 38 below.

that norm'.[17] Where law is viewed causally, lawmaking acts are looked upon as causes of certain effects, manifested in the regularity of patterns of human behaviour. But Kelsen holds that that ignores the normative nature of law. It deprives law of its normative *meaning*.

Subjective Meaning—*Sinn*

I have alluded to the possibility that subjective meaning—as the ideative component of human behaviour in the sense developed by Weber (i.e. *Sinn*)—resonates with aspects of Kelsen's pure theory. In particular, the concept of the Reconstructed Legal Norm or *Rechtssatz*—which along with other concepts such as the *Grundnorm*, lies at the centre of the Kelsenian enterprise of attaining a 'pure' legal science—when viewed as a 'hypothetical judgment' of a court of law, incorporates an interpretive element. Its function is as a kind of theoretical reconstitution of the acts of interpretation brought to bear by a judge on facts presented to a court in the context of a legal process. That interpretive element can be positioned within the wider frame of reference of Weberian interpretive sociology as a step towards the sociological repositioning of the Reconstructed Legal Norm attempted later in this chapter. As Julien Freund observes:

> Weber introduced the interpretive method. Some historians of sociology even refer to it as his 'interpretive sociology'. [Weber] was not the inventor of the interpretive method, nor even of the distinction between explaining (*erklären*) and understanding (*verstehen*). Droysen before him had tried to apply it to history, and Dilthey had made of it the cornerstone of the general methodology of the human sciences (*Geisteswissenschaften*). Weber's merit is to have elaborated this method conceptually with more rigor, applying it to sociology.[18]

Human beings act 'meaningfully' in reflecting upon and interpreting their *own* behaviour, for instance pursuing goals, acting evaluatively or conscientiously, participating in rule-following behaviour, engaging in political activity, and so on. Furthermore, they reflect upon and interpret the behaviour of *others*, often as a basis for their own behaviour.[19] Knowledge of these meaningful processes—the

[17] PTL, 29. See also Iain Stewart, 'The Critical Legal Science of Hans Kelsen' (1990) 17(3) *Journal of Law and Society* 273, 283 (and articles cited at n.76). The 'paralleling' of analyses referred to here is considered by H. Ross, 'Hans Kelsen and the Utopia of Theoretical Purism' (2001) 12 *King's College Law Journal* 174, 180–4.

[18] Julien Freund, 'German Sociology in the Time of Max Weber', in Tom Bottomore and Robert Nisbet (eds), *A History of Sociological Analysis* (London, 1978), 167.

[19] As Freund further comments (*ibid*, 167): 'Unlike the naturalist, the sociologist does not work on inert matter, analyzing instead social relations and an activity (*Handeln*), that is to say forms of social behavior which are always evolving with the constant development of circumstances. Since man's activity never ceases, he is not a passive object. Now, human activities, which produce social relations, are affected by a quality absent in natural phenomena *meaning*. To act socially is, on the one hand, to take part in a conventional context of institutions, customs, rules and laws, created by men with certain ends in mind; second, to give oneself a goal or an end which justifies the activity, and finally, to appeal to certain values, aspirations, or ideals as motives for activity. Meaning plays a role on all three of these levels.'

science of the mental component of human behaviour or 'human sciences' (*Geisteswissenschaften*)—was achievable through experience and understanding, using techniques that included re-experiencing, re-living, and empathy. The empathic technique, in particular, involved the investigator in an introspective process, drawing on the investigator's own reservoir of experience, and bridging the gap between that and the subjective states of the actor under investigation by a kind of 'projection' into the 'expressions' of that actor. The greater the correspondence between the investigator's experiences and those of the actor under investigation, the more exhaustive and enlightened would be the investigator's understanding.[20]

Critically for Dilthey, *as for Weber*, knowledge of human behaviour—*scientific* knowledge, to be sure—proceeded from the attainment of a grasp of mental processes. It was legitimate to make mental processes, or 'objects' of the mind, possible candidates for theoretical discussion and ultimately *scientifically* valid knowledge. Thus the 'acquired structure of mental life', as Dilthey called it—which included valuations and purposes affecting behaviour, influencing ideas, organizing impressions and controlling emotional states—could be abstracted from the pattern of experience and subjected to scientific scrutiny.[21]

Unlike Dilthey—indeed, *contrary* to Dilthey—Weber held that 'positivistic' methods—i.e. those appropriate to the natural sciences or *Naturwissenschaften*—still had to be brought to bear in the study of human behaviour as a critical *verifying* procedure so that the knowledge thus acquired could attain the 'dignity' of 'scientific' knowledge.[22] For his part, indeed, Kelsen exalted the value of 'purity' as a scientific aspiration. The detachment and objectivity implied by the notion of scientific 'purity' not only seemingly endowed Kelsen's theory with the 'prestige' of a 'natural science' such as pure physics, pure mathematics, and such like, but proclaimed legal science as a discipline *no less* detached, objective, and prestigious than the sciences of the natural world. I have observed elsewhere, however, that in the *Pure Theory of Law* Kelsen, if merely by implication and omission, appeared to exaggerate the dependence of sociology on 'positivistic' methods thereby de-emphasizing the hermeneutic or *verstehende* dimension of (specifically) Weberian

20 See generally H.P. Rickman (ed. and trans.), *W. Dilthey Selected Writings* (Cambridge, 1976), 172. For Dilthey, an 'expression' was any manifestation of mental content, foremost among these being basic modes of human communication such as language, gestures, facial expressions, and so on. So far as understanding (*verstehen*) is concerned, Dilthey comments as follows (*ibid*, 170–1): 'The approach of higher understanding to its object is determined by its task of discovering a vital connection in what is given. This is only possible if the context which exists in one's own experience and has been encountered in innumerable cases is always—and with all the potentialities contained in it—present and ready. This state of mind involved in the task of understanding we call empathy, be it with a man or a work .... If, therefore, understanding requires the presence of one's own mental experience this can be described as a projection of the self into some given expression.'

21 *Ibid*, 170–1.

22 See Lewis A. Coser, *Masters of Sociological Thought: Ideas in Historical and Social Context* (2nd edn., London, 1977), 220–1.

interpretive sociology.[23] (We might legitimately ask this: Is the Kelsenian argument in support of 'purity' and against 'syncretism'—e.g. in the sense of the 'uncritical mixing' of (say) sociology with the legal conceptual analysis characteristic of jurisprudence—somehow reinforced or fortified if a Comteian 'positivistic' sociology is presented as being characteristic of *sociology in general*?[24])

So it was that in Weberian sociology the observation of regular relations—such as of 'cause' and 'effect'—between external events necessarily *complemented* the essentially hermeneutic task of discerning and interpretively understanding the subjective meanings underlying the behaviour of actors under investigation. For Weber: 'Immediate intuitions of meaning can be transformed into valid knowledge only if they can be incorporated into theoretical structures that aim at causal explanation'.[25]

Rechtliche Bedeutung and *Rechtssatz*

Remarkably—for a jurist espousing an approach to the scientific analysis of the legal world that sought to eschew anything 'sociological' in character—one of Kelsen's key insights into the workings of the legal world resonates quite consonantly with one of the key aims of Weberian interpretive sociology—attaining an understanding (and explanation) of the meaningful subjective states underlying human behaviour. For Kelsen a critical factor differentiating the domain of law from that of objects in the 'natural world' was that of *legal meaning* (*rechtliche Bedeutung*). In the legal world, as elsewhere, there are acts and events capable of being perceived by the senses and existing in time and space. But those same acts

[23] See H. Ross, 'Hans Kelsen and the Utopia of Theoretical Purism' (2001) 12 *King's College Law Journal* 174, 177–8. And see especially PTL, 13–4: '[C]ognition in legal sociology is not concerned with the legal norm *qua* specific meaning; rather, it is directed to certain events quite apart from their connection to norms that are recognized or presupposed as valid. Legal sociology does not relate the material facts in question to valid norms; rather, it relates these material facts to still other material facts as causes and effects.' The fact that this portrayal of legal sociology does not hold for *Weber's* sociology of law is recognized by Kelsen in his *General Theory of Law and State*. (See n.24 below.)

[24] Elsewhere Kelsen presents a more balanced perspective on (Weberian) social theory. Kelsen argues in effect that to be fully intelligible 'sociological jurisprudence' is dependent upon and must, of necessity, incorporate the conceptual apparatus of 'normative jurisprudence'. But this concession requires some acknowledgment of the *ideative* dimension of sociology—doubtless, however, the sociology more characteristic of a Weber than of a Comte. See Hans Kelsen, *General Theory of Law and State* (trans. Anders Wedberg) (Cambridge, Massachusetts, 1945). See particularly at 177 where Kelsen observes: 'Sociology of law, as defined by Max Weber, is possible only by referring the human behavior which is its object to the law as it exists in the minds of men as contents of their ideas. In men's minds, law exists, as a matter of fact, as a body of valid norms, as a normative system. Only by referring the human behavior to law as a system of valid norms, to law as defined by normative jurisprudence, is sociological jurisprudence able to delimit its specific object from that of general sociology.... ' For discussion of the historical context of sociological positivism in the sense of Auguste Comte see Anthony Giddens, 'Positivism and its Critics', ch. 7 of Bottomore and Nisbet (eds), n.18, above, 237 ff.

[25] Coser, n.22, above, 220–1.

and events may also possess the quality of being endowed with immanent 'legal sense' or significance. Kelsen gives the example of the enactment of a statute:

People assemble in a hall, they give speeches, some rise, others remain seated—this is the external event. Its meaning: that a statute is enacted.[26]

For Kelsen, meanings could be either subjective or objective and those meanings could coincide—though they did not need necessarily to coincide. Legal meaning had 'objective', as opposed to 'subjective', status. Kelsen gives the example of a secret society acting outside the law but in accordance with its own norms. If the society condemns to death and then executes a traitor the 'subjective' meaning of this act *to the society members* (interpreted by reference to the society's norms) is 'lawful' execution. But the same act also carries an 'objective' meaning—its *legal* meaning—which is that it constitutes *murder*, not the carrying out of a death penalty in the conventional legal sense. Legal meaning thus derives from a legal norm whose content, according to Kelsen, refers to a relevant act or event and 'confers' legal meaning upon it. According to this view acts are to be perceived as either 'legal' or 'illegal' to the extent that they correspond (or fail to correspond) to the relevant content of a valid legal norm. In the judicial setting when, in Kelsen's view, a judge establishes a material fact or concrete event as (for example) a *delict* his cognition is first directed towards the fact as an event in the 'natural' world. But the cognition becomes 'legal' through the application of a legal norm to the established material fact when the fact is interpreted *as* a delict: for example, as theft or fraud:

The specifically legal sense of the event in question, its own peculiarly legal meaning, comes by way of a norm whose content refers to the event and confers legal meaning on it; the act can be interpreted, then, according to this norm. The norm functions as a scheme of interpretation.[27]

In his analysis of legal meaning in the *Pure Theory of Law* Kelsen uses strikingly similar imagery to that used by Weber. For instance Weber argues that we cannot 'understand' the behaviour of cells in the same way that we might 'understand' meaningful human behaviour. All we can hope for is to observe the relevant functional relationships and generalize on the basis of these observations.[28] Similarly, in differentiating the legal realm from the natural realm Kelsen notes that human behaviour can declare its own sense if expressed verbally, this being 'a special characteristic of the material dealt with in social and in particular in juristic knowledge'. However:

A plant can convey nothing about itself to the research worker who is trying to define it. It makes no attempt to explain itself scientifically. But a social act can very well carry with it an indication of its own meaning.[29]

[26] PTL, 8. [27] PTL, 10.

[28] Max Weber, *The Theory of Social and Economic Organization* (trans. A.M. Henderson and Talcott Parsons) (New York, 1947), 94.

[29] See Hans Kelsen, 'The Pure Theory of Law' (1934) 50 *Law Quarterly Review* 478, 480–1. See also Hans Kelsen, *Pure Theory of Law* (trans. Max Knight, of *Reine Rechtslehre*, 2nd edn., 1960) (Berkeley and Los Angeles, 1967), 2–3.

Kelsen's notion of legal meaning is more than anything the key to what might be loosely described as his '*Geisteswissenschaft* tendency' or, more specifically, his tendency to be drawn by the 'gravitational pull' of elements of Weberian interpretive sociology.[30] The act of bringing a vehicle to a halt at red traffic lights may have 'meaning' on many different levels: for instance, *safety* (as perceived by the driver and other road users), *utility* (as perceived by traffic-flow planners), *convenience* (as perceived by pedestrians who cross the road when traffic is halted). The specifically legal meaning of the act as perceived by (say) an *institutional* actor—for example, traffic police, judges, prosecutors—may be in terms of legal *necessity*: what is prescribed by law and is thereby rendered non-optional. The act is perceived as a legal duty or obligation. If it is a requirement of the law that drivers comply with a relevant legal norm then, in the view of law enforcement officials, they have no option but to comply. The legal meaning of the act of *stopping* at red lights is an act in compliance with the law. The legal meaning of the act of driving through the red lights *without stopping* is an act in violation of the law, an offence; a crime.

Whilst the Kelsenian idea of legal meaning or *rechtliche Bedeutung* appears to resonate with (e.g.) the 'Diltheian' assumptions underlying human sciences or *Geisteswissenschaften* and the Weberian idea of subjective meaning or *Sinn*, it generally lacks the explicit behavioural context of *Sinn*. For Weber *Sinn* is the ideative component of socially directed human behaviour (social action). It is the mental component of social action and includes anything that motivates the individual or makes a particular course of action meaningful.[31] Kelsen does not explicitly identify legal meaning as the exclusive preserve of *any specific actor* though, of course, he does refer to what is cognized by a *judge* when an event is interpreted in legal terms:

> His [a judge's] cognition becomes legal at the point at which he brings together the material fact he has established and the statute he is to apply; that is to say, his cognition becomes legal when he interprets the material fact as 'theft' or 'fraud'.[32]

[30] Note that Kelsen at PTL, 15, explicitly maintains that legal science is a human science in the sense of *Geisteswissenschaft*: 'In marking off the law from nature, the Pure Theory of Law seeks the boundary between the natural and the ideal. Legal science belongs not to the natural sciences, but to the human sciences.' (*'Indem die Reine Rechtslehre das Recht gegen die Natur abgrenzt, sucht sie die Schranke, die die Natur vom Geist trennt. Rechtswissenschaft ist Geistes-, nicht Naturwissenschaft.*') On the other hand, as the Paulsons observe (PTL, 131): 'Kelsen himself... had never been content with the notion of *Geisteswissenschaft* either, and he in fact rarely appeals to it.... He prefers a distinction between *normative sciences* and *natural sciences*....' The Paulsons also point out that Kelsen's appeal to *Geisteswissenschaft* at PTL, 15, is 'one such rarity'. In H. Ross, 'Hans Kelsen and the Utopia of Theoretical Purism' (2001) 12 *King's College Law Journal* 174 there is fuller discussion of *other* ways (i.e. beyond resonances of *Geisteswissenschaften*) in which Kelsen's *Pure Theory of Law* appears to run analytically parallel to the sociological writings of, and the scientific approach adopted by, Max Weber.

[31] According to Weber: 'Action [in the general sense of human behaviour] is social in so far as, by virtue of the subjective meaning attached to it by the acting individual (or individuals), it takes account of the behaviour of others and is thereby oriented in its course.' (See Max Weber, *The Theory of Social and Economic Organization*, n.28, above, 88.)

[32] PTL, 11. This cognitive dimension of the judicial role has greater significance in the context of the line of argument to be pursued later in this chapter. From the point of view of Kelsen's pure theory, however, the act of a judge's cognizing material facts legally—for example, interpreting a factual

Arguably lying behind legal meaning is a set of 'behavioural' assumptions which, if not made, would render the notion unintelligible. Yet paradoxically for Kelsen legal meaning is seemingly taken to be 'conferred' upon a human act or other event '*by*' a legal norm, the norm being thereby severed from human agency:

> The specifically ... legal meaning [of an event], comes by way of a norm whose content refers to the event and confers legal meaning on it....[33]

Taking this as a mere curiosity of expression arguably *could* allow it to be lightly disregarded because no one really believes that legal norms as such actually 'do' things: literally 'confer', truly 'interpret', and so on. But if the point is pressed further it becomes possible to discern a genuine substantive objection to Kelsen's approach: an objection that, ultimately, finds its expression in the idea that the pure theory engages in a kind of 'reductionism' of human behaviour *to* legal norms. On that basis legal norms virtually take on the role of 'protagonist', to use Donald Galloway's expression.[34] This manipulation arguably retards the pure theory's slide wholesale towards (say) a sociology of judicial action. But it creates a distortion that is scarcely compensated for in terms of the 'payoff' that comes from the idea that the pure theory defines an autonomous realm for legal science, entirely independent of 'foreign', non-law disciplines. Seen literally, Kelsen almost assigns *to* legal norms the task of 'conferring' legal meaning upon acts or events. The norm is 'made flesh', so to speak, and dwells among those who inhabit that autonomous legal universe that Kelsen strives diligently to construct in the *Pure Theory of Law*. The interpretive act of conferring legal meaning—which would ordinarily be seen as a task capable of performance only *by a human being* (e.g. by a judge)—is virtually usurped by the legal norm itself. By that reckoning Kelsenian legal meaning appears *not* to reside with a human being, remaining in some unspecified or metaphorical sense, bound up with the very material of the legal norm itself and analytically disjoined from human agency. The Reconstructed Legal Norm, as a *legal norm*, sits uncomfortably with this scenario becoming merely the *outcome* of

scenario as 'theft' or 'murder', and so on—is seemingly offered by Kelsen as merely one, albeit a particularly characteristic, instance of legal cognition. Arguably Kelsen could have maintained that a lawyer (*any* lawyer) arguing his or her case before a court of law, or giving legal advice to his or her client, engages in no less characteristic an act of legal cognition. Indeed *anyone* 'applying' a law to a factual situation engages in such legal cognitive acts. The main point of departure of the argument pursued below, however, is that certain judicial cognitive acts—specifically those of judges sitting in the hierarchically supreme court of a given jurisdiction—have a special status as authoritative and final acts of legal cognition: in other words, authoritative and final acts of conferring legal meaning upon relevant facts established in evidence. More significantly, the hierarchically supreme court (embodied in the conceptual device referred to as *Iudex*—for which, see further below) becomes a special repository of final, authoritative legal meaning for the legal system in question.

33 PTL, 10. And see the entire passage from PTL cited at n.27 above.

34 See Donald Galloway, 'The Axiology of Analytical Jurisprudence: A Study of the Underlying Sociological Assumptions and Ideological Predilections' in Thomas W. Bechtler (ed.), *Law in a Social Context: Liber Amicorum Honouring Professor Lon L. Fuller* (The Netherlands, 1978), 84. Roger Cotterrell makes an essentially similar point in *The Politics of Jurisprudence: A Critical Introduction to Legal Philosophy* (London, 1989), 112.

a humanly mediated process, with the process itself and its human agent receding into the background. Just as legal norms in general 'confer' legal meaning (per Kelsen), so the Reconstructed Legal Norm 'confers' legal meaning, albeit (one assumes) as a mere end result of a human interpretive process.

On the other hand, and quite significantly (as has been noted[35]), Kelsen's pure theory does on occasion cede the interpretive process to the judiciary: for example, a judge's interpreting a fact as a delict by applying an appropriate legal norm to the fact.[36] When that happens—when, in other words, Kelsen's notion of legal meaning manifests itself as an integral part of the judicial role—the *Pure Theory of Law* becomes markedly 'Weberian'. If the judicial role involves interpreting human behaviour or other events by reference to legal norms—the norms being 'applied' to the relevant behaviour or events—then a judge acts subjectively meaningfully in so interpreting the behaviour or events.[37] The judge's interpretive act—the subjective meaning of his or her action—contains as a component the evaluative legal meaning that he or she confers upon the events that are the object of the proceedings before the court. In that setting—and on a less literal reading of Kelsen—the Reconstructed Legal Norm holds out the possibility of embodying, albeit as a 'hypothesis', the interpretive judicial *activity* of conferring legal meaning on legally relevant facts and events. In short, a conclusion or judgment of the type 'If A commits an unlawful act, A ought to be punished'—which the Reconstructed Legal Norm could exemplify in any hypothetical case—necessarily involves an ascription of legal meaning in the Kelsenian sense of *rechtliche Bedeutung* because the relevant unlawful act *means* (in law, and in the perception of the judge) that a punishment ought to be exacted against A.

By that account Kelsen's concept of the Reconstructed Legal Norm or *Rechtssatz* implies not only the *activity* of 'judging' or rendering a judgment—social action in Weberian sociology[38]—but hints at the presence of the *human being* lying behind

[35] See n.32 above. [36] PTL, 11.

[37] A judge acts 'subjectively meaningfully' in rendering a judgment and in carrying out the other duties and responsibilities entailed in the judicial role. The fact that the judge is subject to a range of institutional demands and constraints, necessitated by judicial office, that require him or her to act in conformity with the norms and conventions of established judicial practice qualifies the judge's (judicial) behaviour no less as *subjectively* meaningful behaviour, and something that may be the subject of the techniques of 'understanding' applied by interpretive sociology. However, not only is the judge an actor within the collectivity that is the judiciary; the judiciary is itself an organ of the collectivity that is government (in the widest sense). The behavioural patterning, and regularities, to be found within these collectivities suggests the need for sociological analysis based not *only* on the (*genuinely* 'subjective') subjectively meaningful behaviour of individual role-occupants (e.g. of any given judge) looked at in isolation—in so far as it is possible to view such behaviour in 'isolation'—but of the *inter-subjectively* meaningful behaviour patterns prevailing within the collectivity in question (e.g. characteristic of any given *judiciary*).

[38] The concept of 'social action' is integrally related to the concept of 'sociology' in Weber's thinking: 'Sociology . . . is a science which attempts the interpretive understanding of social action in order thereby to arrive at a causal explanation of its course and effects. In 'action' is included all human behaviour when and in so far as the acting individual attaches a subjective meaning to it. . . . Action is social in so far as, by virtue of the subjective meaning attached to it by the acting individual (or individuals), it takes account of the behaviour of others and is thereby oriented in its course.' See Weber, n.28, above, 88.

this activity, i.e. the *judge*. Kelsen's concept of the Reconstructed Legal Norm thereby connects strikingly with his concept of legal meaning since the conferment of legal meaning is literally part and parcel of the activity of formulating a judgment such as one framed in terms of: 'A ought to be punished'. According to Kelsen the very idea of an 'unlawful act' takes on a new significance in the pure theory. The events constituting the unlawful act 'become' the condition, defined by the Reconstructed Legal Norm, for the imposition by the state of a coercive act:

> From the standpoint of immanence, which the Pure Theory of Law supplants, the concept of the unlawful act undergoes fundamental reinterpretation. What is dispositive for the concept of the unlawful act is not the legislator's motive, not the circumstance that a material fact is undesirable to the norm-issuing authority.... Rather, what is dispositive is simply and solely the position that the material fact in question has in the reconstructed legal norm, namely, its position as the condition for the specific response of the law, for the coercive act (the action the state takes).[39]

Sociological Repositioning of the *Rechtssatz*

The scene has been set for a sociological repositioning of Kelsen's Reconstructed Legal Norm (i.e. *Rechtssatz* in its quasi-technical sense[40]) as an 'artefact' of interpretive sociology.[41] The stimulus for this repositioning is twofold.

[39] PTL, 26–7. The interpretive act involved in bringing an 'unlawful act' within the terms of the Reconstructed Legal Norm—by any common-sense account a judicial cognitive act of conferring legal meaning on, i.e. *interpreting*, the events constituting the act (assuming the matter has come before a court for judicial determination)—seems to *inhere in* the Reconstructed Legal Norm. Kelsen's pure theory thus maintains its focus on the legal norm (specifically the Reconstructed Legal Norm) whilst other phenomena equally worthy of consideration such as the nature of judicial reasoning and the interpretive mental processes involved in applying legal norms to factual situations are subordinated. The question is whether an overtly professed interest in (for example) 'mental processes' would cause the pure theory to slide inexorably towards psychology or sociology, thereby compromising its 'purity' and forcing it into 'syncretism'. Kelsen seems to think so when he maintains this: 'The Pure Theory of Law does not look to mental processes or physical events of any kind in seeking to cognize norms, in seeking to comprehend something legally. To comprehend something legally can only be to comprehend it *as* law.' (PTL, 11, emphasis added.) Yet the pure theory's manifest interest in such matters as the motivational force of legal norms, acts of legal interpretation (in the sense of legal meaning or *rechtliche Bedeutung*), human behaviour, judicial cognitive acts, and so on, surely creates difficulty for Kelsen in plausibly maintaining this 'purist' theoretical stance.

[40] See n.6 above.

[41] Some elements of the thinking underlying the idea of the Reconstructed Legal Norm are treated as pointing towards, or serving as a point of departure for, a sociological (and basically *non-Kelsenian*) analysis of legal meaning. Essentially, what is proposed is the repositioning of the Reconstructed Legal Norm within a sociological theoretical setting. In the first place, the Reconstructed Legal Norm is taken to function as a kind of theoretical reconstitution of the acts of interpretation brought to bear by a judge on facts or events established by a court in the context of legal processes (which is tolerably consonant with Kelsen's analysis in the *Pure Theory of Law*). But, in the second place, the interpretive reconstitution in question *in its theoretically repositioned form* is taken to correspond not to the interpretive acts of just *any* hypothetical judge; but to those of a hypothetical judge sitting at—and conferring conclusive legal meaning from the standpoint of—the highest hierarchical level of a legal system: in other words, a theoretical construct such as *Iudex*, discussed further here and considered at greater length in the writer's *Law as a Social Institution*, n.3, above, 103–6 and 113–15.

First, there is the connection maintainable between the Reconstructed Legal Norm and the specifically Kelsenian concept of legal meaning (*rechtliche Bedeutung*), taken with the tendency of *both* of those concepts to 'gravitate' towards interpretive sociology in ways already indicated. The Reconstructed Legal Norm operates as a link between Kelsen's somewhat behaviourally disengaged notion of legal meaning (*rechtliche Bedeutung*) and a behavioural environment in which the interpretive process inhering in the Kelsenian idea of legal meaning may be appropriately situated. Given that the Reconstructed Legal Norm represents a hypothetical judgment—that is, the outcome of the judicial interpretive process—it can be seen as the end result of an act of conferring legal meaning upon a particular factual situation. The Reconstructed Legal Norm incorporates the (ideal) form: 'if A is, then B ought to be'. So, imagining an example where 'A is'—such as a factual scenario where Max, say, drives through red traffic lights without stopping—the legal meaning of this is an act in violation of the criminal law or an offence to which a specific penalty is attached. The legal consequence, seen as the imposition of a penalty or 'coercive act', is represented by the words ' . . . then B ought to be' in Kelsen's formulation, i.e. a penalty ought to be imposed on Max. The legal norm applicable to this factual situation thus provides a means of interpreting, or conferring legal meaning upon, relevant conditioning facts, i.e. facts A ('if A is . . . '). The act of conferring legal meaning on human behaviour is also social action in the Weberian sense of action (or human behaviour) that 'takes account of the behaviour of others and is thereby oriented in its course'.[42]

Secondly, Kelsen's stance that legal norms have a *motivational* dimension perhaps self-evidently carries the Reconstructed Legal Norm (as a legal norm in 'ideal' form[43]) towards the domain of sociology given the close connection between the idea of non-causal motivation and that of subjective meaning or *Sinn* in interpretive sociology.[44] Yet a cautionary note must be sounded here. The Reconstructed Legal Norm, as we know, takes the form of a hypothetical judgment that represents the 'norm' emanating from the judicial activity of—as Kelsen sees it—'concretizing' a general norm in its application to the facts of the case in hand.[45] In this context a legal norm is seen as a judgment or order of the court; a kind of judicial command: 'Party X ought to pay compensation to Party Y' or 'Pay compensation to Party Y' [addressed to Party X]. In taking this form the legal norm is always in a sense *ex post facto*: the end result of the institutional judicial activity of passing judgment. The difficulty here, of course, is that if the legal process necessitates the 'application' of a norm to a factual situation presented to a court, a legal norm that is imagined or hypothesized to be the outcome of judicial

[42] See Weber, n.28, above, 88.

[43] See the Paulsons' observations in PTL, 132–3 (n.6).

[44] Weber allows for the possibility of a necessary causal element to the things that motivate human behaviour whilst Kelsen resolutely denies this causal element in the legal context, promoting instead an explanation based around the notion of 'imputation'. See PTL, 23–4.

[45] PTL, 67–8.

'application' would require to have had some *antecedent* existence—or to have taken some form other than that of a judgment—in order to have been 'applied' in the first place. If a legal norm taking the 'ideal' form of the Reconstructed Legal Norm is actually constituted as an outcome of judicial 'application', what ideal form does the 'legal norm' take which pre-exists that 'application'—and which 'motivates' an actor to conform with it? Looked at another way, what form does a 'legal norm' take when it is seen as the reason, justification or basis for the hypothetical judgment of the court? It cannot surely *be* the judgment of the court.[46]

The combination of the notion of legal meaning or *rechtliche Bedeutung* and that of hypothetical judgment reflected in Kelsen's Reconstructed Legal Norm together suggest the possibility of the development of a unified theoretical construct whose principal function is to facilitate the ready identification, and sociological analysis, of any legal institutional structure that serves, among other things, as a repository of final, conclusive and authoritative legal meaning in a given legal system.[47] And that possibility suggests at least one sense in which a sociologically repositioned conception of the Reconstructed Legal Norm can be formulated as a model for 'a collectivist *verstehende* sociology' of law, towards the realization of the implications of Richard Tur's observation, mentioned at the outset.

With a view to repositioning Kelsen's Reconstructed Legal Norm within a sociological frame of reference, then, a new question arises for consideration. If the Reconstructed Legal Norm represents a hypothetical judgment expressing the linking of a conditioning material fact with a conditioned legal consequence, *whose* judgment, albeit hypothesized, can it be said to represent? Kelsen is silent as to the position in the judicial hierarchy occupied by the hypothetical judge whose task is to render the hypothetical judgment corresponding to the Reconstructed Legal Norm. Indeed, the demands of theoretical 'purism'—resulting in the kind of 'reductionism' of human behaviour to legal norms that has previously been mentioned—would no doubt count against the pursuit of that line of enquiry. In Kelsen's pure theory the 'god in the machine' is always a norm—or, in the context of the present discussion, the Reconstructed Legal Norm—not a person: a human being; an occupant of judicial office; a judge. The specifically 'judgmental'[48] dimension of the Reconstructed Legal Norm is thus given no special status in the pure theory.[49] As such, the hypothetical judgment represented by the Reconstructed Legal Norm may or may not

[46] It is beyond the scope of this chapter to attempt a resolution of this conundrum.

[47] Given that the construct in question is *Iudex* (see n.41 above, and the further discussion, below), the sociological repositioning of Kelsen's Reconstructed Legal Norm attempted here serves, more accurately, to reinforce and validate the theoretical assumptions underlying that construct.

[48] In this context 'judgmental' denotes 'cognitively judgmental' as opposed to evaluatively or normatively judgmental. In other words, if the legal norm (and by extension the Reconstructed Legal Norm) is, in Kelsenian terms, 'a hypothetical judgment that expresses the specific linking of a conditioning material fact with a conditioned consequence' (PTL, 23) then it has a 'judgmental component' in so far as it represents or corresponds to the hypothetical judgment of a hypothetical judge.

[49] That is, in terms of the hierarchical position of the hypothetical judge who *ex hypothesi* renders a hypothetical judgment.

conclusively dispose of hypothetical legal proceedings. Conceivably, then, if the hypothetical judgment is taken to be that of just *any* judge, sitting in *any* court, it may not *ex hypothesi* conclusively dispose of a case. In principle, a hypothetical judge sitting in a court at (say) the lowest level of the judicial hierarchy could render a hypothetical judgment capable of formulation in terms that *appear* to equate to a Kelsenian 'Reconstructed Legal Norm': i.e. 'A ought to be punished', or 'A ought to pay £10,000 to B'. But if that hypothetical judgment were thereupon *ex hypothesi* to be appealed to a higher court it may be overruled or modified by that higher court: e.g. 'A ought to be acquitted', or 'A ought to pay £5,000 to B'. Unless the judgment represented by the Reconstructed Legal Norm is taken to correspond to the hypothetical judgment of the *highest* court of a jurisdiction—i.e. a court beyond which no appeal is legally competent—the hypothetical judgment enshrined in the Reconstructed Legal Norm will always be contingent and potentially liable, albeit *ex hypothesi*, to revision (e.g. overruling, reversal, modification, etc) by a hypothetical higher court until the highest court is reached. This argument, of course, takes for granted that the hypothetical legal system applies a principle of *res judicata* whereby a disputed issue or judgment of a court that has been appealed to a supreme or final level in the court hierarchy is exhaustive of the disputed issue and legally conclusive of any issues of law or fact in dispute.

Overall, the heuristic value of the Reconstructed Legal Norm is questionable in so far as the status of the hypothetical judgment that it represents is unspecified or is taken to be that of a court *other than* the highest court of the hypothetical legal system concerned. An acceptable conception of the Reconstructed Legal Norm, arguably, is one that hypothesizes a conditioned legal consequence that is *not* liable to judicial revision, i.e. a consequence that is, for purposes of the hypothetical legal system in question, final and conclusive. Any other hypothesis implies a situation where the legal meaning of a fact—i.e. the 'conditioning material fact' of the Reconstructed Legal Norm—is not, or is not *necessarily*, its conclusive legal meaning for purposes of the hypothetical legal system in question. And such a hypothesis, if taken to be part of the Reconstructed Legal Norm, must surely rest the Reconstructed Legal Norm on a shifting and unstable foundation. To maximize its theoretical utility, arguably, the Reconstructed Legal Norm must be taken to correspond to the hypothetical judgment of a judge sitting in the *highest* court of a given legal system—an 'ultimate judge', a '*Iudex*'—because only such a judgment conveys a *legally settled* interpretation of the matters of fact and law hypothetically at issue. That, however, introduces into the Reconstructed Legal Norm a human element (i.e. the 'ultimate judge') that, by compromising the theoretical 'purity' of the theory, places it beyond the reach of that theory. Kelsen—possibly in order to avoid such a dilemma—engages in the kind of 'reductionism' of human actors to 'norms' already noted.[50] As the 'norm' is the pre-eminent concept

[50] I have already touched on this point above, with support for this position being drawn from writings of Roger Cotterrell and Donald Galloway. See n.34 above.

in the pure theory—not human actors such as supreme court judges, hypothetical or otherwise—the pure theory's focus is fixed on 'the norm', and on normative constructs such as the Reconstructed Legal Norm. Yet despite Kelsen's insistence that the pure theory 'does not look to mental processes or physical events of any kind'[51] key concepts in the pure theory such as the Reconstructed Legal Norm do necessarily presuppose the human beings—and the human activities and attendant 'mental processes', e.g. interpreting, judging, engaging in legal reasoning, and so on—lying behind them.[52] Hence, certain of the characteristics of these human, institutional activities—and their attendant 'mental processes'—must, it is contended, be treated as part of—or, for that matter, part of a sociologically repositioned variant of—the Reconstructed Legal Norm. The fact that Kelsen predicates the Reconstructed Legal Norm upon a form of social action—the activity of judging—without literally analysing that activity[53] does not necessarily weaken the explanatory power of the Reconstructed Legal Norm. On the contrary, it furnishes a basis for the essentially different exercise of examining the implications of the idea that the embodiment of authoritative legal meaning—the final, most authoritative acts of legal interpretation in a given legal system—factually resides with a judge, or 'collectivity' of judges, sitting in the highest court of appeal of that legal system. For the purpose of the sociological repositioning of Kelsen's Reconstructed Legal Norm the conditioned legal consequence embodied in the Reconstructed Legal Norm is taken to represent the final, conclusive and authoritative legal meaning of relevant conditioning material facts and thus, in a sense, constitutes an 'emanation' from, or hypothetical judgment of, a judge, or 'collectivity' of judges, sitting in the highest court of appeal of a given hypothetical legal system.[54]

The key point to emerge from the sociological repositioning of the Reconstructed Legal Norm suggested here—which has a bearing on the broader strategy of exploring the idea that Kelsen's pure theory represents a model for a 'collectivist *verstehende* sociology' (of law)—is this. The exercise of repositioning the Reconstructed Legal Norm in a sociological context prompts, among other things, consideration of where the final, most authoritative acts of legal interpretation in a

[51] See PTL, 11, and n.39 above. [52] An essentially similar point is made above.

[53] Presumably such an analysis might, in Kelsen's judgment, have carried the pure theory 'perilously' close to a 'contaminating' discipline such as sociology or psychology.

[54] This theoretical position, though probably 'non-Kelsenian', does not derogate from the primary function of the Reconstructed Legal Norm to enable an analytical distinction to be made, on one hand, between legal norms and moral norms and, on the other, between (normative) laws of the legal world and (causal) laws of the natural world (i.e. of natural science). In fact it reinforces that function. In the first place, it emphasizes the institutional basis of legal meaning—which is taken to reside in 'judgmental' processes underlying judicial action, albeit at the supreme hierarchical level: interpreting, judging, engaging in legal reasoning, and so on. There is probably no counterpart to this in the 'moral world'. Whilst in the second place, it preserves, or at any rate does nothing to undermine, the idea of the 'normativity' of laws of the legal world when contrasted with laws of the natural world. For there is no suggestion that laws of the legal world equate in any way to the causal laws of the natural sciences. Indeed the very opposite is implied by Kelsen's view that legal science is a 'human science' or *Geisteswissenschaft*, in so far as Kelsen consistently holds to that view.

given legal system factually reside. In other words, it prompts reflection upon what can be regarded as an 'ultimate repository of legal meaning' in a legal system. Yet the idea which has been advanced that a judge, or 'collectivity' of judges, sitting in the highest court of appeal of a legal system represents the ultimate repository of legal meaning in that system is merely a point of departure for consideration of the sense in which the definitive legal interpretation or legal meaning of material facts or events might be regarded as being in some sense within the domain of a *collectivity*.

Let us begin with the assumption that in theoretical terms the judge, or 'collectivity' of judges, sitting in the highest court of appeal of a legal system—and whose interpretive acts represent an ultimate repository of legal meaning for the system in question[55]—can be personified as a single, hypothetical, ultimate judge. I have argued elsewhere that such a judge—styled '*Iudex*'—can be constructed as a Weberian ideal type.[56] In short, in acting individually and personally *Iudex* acts subjectively meaningfully in the fullest sense of 'subjective', i.e. personal to that unique individual. But in *also* acting in his or her capacity as an ultimate supreme court judge *Iudex* conforms to institutional conventions that render his or her judicial acts 'non-subjective'—or, in some sense, 'inter-subjective'. Thus, when *Iudex* has (say) an informal conversation about the weather with a newsvendor there is nothing that makes that an official or judicial act of *Iudex*.[57] Nor is there any sense in which that, or any similar, course of social action should necessarily be regarded as establishing any kind of pattern of conduct for any group of individuals constituting a 'collectivity'. Yet there are at least two particular senses in which the legal meaning conferred by *Iudex* on material facts established in legal proceedings might be regarded as being in some sense within the domain of a 'collectivity'.

First, and most obviously, a judgment may represent the collective legal opinion of a quorum of judges sitting in a legal system's highest court of appeal. For all legal purposes—regardless of the fact that each judge will normally differ in the precise terms on which his or her judgment is formulated—the judgment will represent the decision of the court and a unitary basis on which the case is to be disposed of. Secondly, and more importantly, judgments made at a supreme

[55] This is true in two senses. First, the collected judgments, opinions and decided cases in *written form* that emanate from the relevant court represent—at any given time, and to the extent not superseded—a set of definitive statements of the law on the issues of law and fact concerned. Secondly, if a matter is litigated or appealed to the highest hierarchical level of a legal system or system of courts the resulting interpretive acts of the judges at that level will represent—at least for a period of time after delivery of the judgment—the most legally definitive and conclusive resolution or disposal of the litigated or appealed issues of law and fact that the system is competent to produce.

[56] See Ross, n. 3, above, 98 ff. That a Weberian ideal type can incorporate behavioural characteristics of a *plurality* of actors—in this case, distilling the interpretive acts of (say) a quorum of judges sitting as a final court of appeal—is clear from Weber's methodological writings: 'An ideal type is formed by the one-sided *accentuation* of one or more points of view and by the synthesis of a great many diffuse, discrete, more or less present and occasionally absent *concrete individual* phenomena, which are arranged according to those one-sidedly emphasized viewpoints into a unified *analytical* construct (*Gedankenbild*).' See Weber, '"Objectivity" in Social Science and Social Policy', n. 15, above, 90 (Weber's emphasis).

[57] A similar argument is advanced at textual n.37 above.

hierarchical level of a legal system—or judgments otherwise constituting the 'best authority' in the absence of a judgment of the hierarchically supreme court—usually, or at any rate in jurisdictions applying a *stare decisis* principle, represent a precedent for the disposal of new cases arising in the future that raise the same, or similar, issues of fact or law. That has the effect of generating what might be loosely termed a 'collective mindset' around the judgments in question, which may be discernible from an examination of the subjective component of the behaviours of individuals constituting particular interest groups or 'collectivities'. Examples of the groups in question include: lower court judges, court and other government officials, lawyers, police, prison officers, court enforcement officials, teachers of law, compliance officers in financial institutions and other large commercial organizations, charities—basically any individual, or any organization, with a concern to comply with or advise on laws that affect their or others' interests or apply to their or others' areas of activity. As I have previously remarked:

> Now *because* judicial action mobilizes coercive and sanction-exacting forces in society, countless individuals in attempting to imagine the legal consequences of their action and that of others 'out of court' ... may strive to adopt the same perspective as an 'ultimate judge'. In this way an individual may attempt to visualise what the legal result would be of a given course of action, or of *any* legally relevant 'facts', based on the hypothesis of what the legal result would be *if* a dispute were to arise or criminal proceedings were to be brought following the occurrence of certain 'events' and this dispute or those proceedings were to be litigated or tried to a point in the system where a final and authoritative determination was made. In other words, what would be the rights, duties, powers and liabilities of the litigants or, as the case may be, criminal suspects?[58]

The 'hypothesis of the ultimate judgment' in the sense outlined in the quoted passage arguably comes to be incorporated in the behavioural patterns of a variety of groups of actors. (These groups, examples of which are outlined above, may be regarded as discrete 'collectivities'.) Unless the 'mental processes' used by those involved in *definitively and conclusively* interpreting or judging relevant material facts by reference to the applicable laws of a given legal system (i.e. *Iudex*) are in some sense replicated by other groups with a vested interest in potential legal outcomes, those others may act—or may advise others to act—in a way that is unduly productive of legal, commercial or other risk; or that is unlawful or illegal; or that is civilly or criminally actionable, and so on. All such groups have an interest in attempting to visualize—in some cases by taking appropriate legal advice—what a hypothetical ultimate judge might hold the legal outcome to be, whether under criminal or civil law, if a particular course of conduct were to be pursued. The modes of behaviour predicated on the hypothesis of the ultimate judgment depend in turn on the factual reality of the senior judiciary of a legal system acting consistently in the sense of conforming by and large to the conventions attending the senior judicial role, and acting within the general environment of the legal culture

[58] See Ross, n. 3, above, 102–3.

of that 'collectivity'. It is only through consistency of action through manifested, inter-subjective understandings and motivations that anything approximating to the actings of a judicial 'collectivity' can be inferred.

Empirically, the possibility of formulating 'a collectivist *verstehende* sociology' of law around the hypothetical judicial behaviour of a theoretical construct such as *Iudex* depends on whether 'collectivities'—pluralities of human actors from a variety of different interest groups—do *in fact* possess a 'collective mindset' that replicates the legal cognitive acts, and legal reasoning processes, of *Iudex*.[59] That is a task that could be undertaken by interpretive sociology. Often enough the evidence will simply lie in the fact that individuals and groups do factually seek, and act upon, legal or other professional advice that, consciously or otherwise, applies the hypothesis of the ultimate judgment: 'if I act in manner X, what would the legal consequence of that be, in the opinion of an "ultimate judge" delivering a judgment in the highest court of appeal in the jurisdiction in question?' This is not vastly different from the formula built into Kelsen's Reconstructed Legal Norm: 'if A is, then B [legally] ought to be'; or, phrased as a question, 'if A is, what ought B [legally] to be?'.

A Kelsenian Basis for Interdisciplinarity?

In this chapter I have sought to show how Kelsen's concept of the Reconstructed Legal Norm or *Rechtssatz* (as formulated in the *Pure Theory of Law*) and the

[59] From the standpoint of traditional Weberian scholarship, the very possibility of a 'collectivist'—as opposed to a conventional 'individualist'—*verstehende* sociology of law might suggest on the face of it an unwarranted departure from that tradition and also, arguably, a contradiction in terms. What is being advanced in this chapter, however, is not a departure from any conventional Weberian position. Rather, this possibility merely elaborates on the idea that certain aspects of the behaviour of a 'collectivity', such as the senior judiciary, constituted as a plurality of particular, office-holding individuals, is recognizably patterned, or oriented in consistent ways, and is in principle capable of theoretical reconstruction as an ideal type. And to that end Weberian methods are to be applied—methods that draw on the empirical data furnished by the many concrete individual phenomena derivable from the modes of behaviour characteristic of relevant pluralities of actors who constitute identifiable 'collectivities'. *Iudex* represents the beginnings of one such theoretical reconstruction and, as already indicated, this ideal type could be the product of (to use Weber's words) a synthesis of 'a great many diffuse, discrete, more or less present and occasionally absent *concrete individual* phenomena'—i.e. specifically, a distillation of the interpretive actings of each of a plurality of individual judges who constitute the 'collectivity' of the senior judiciary. Moreover, and more importantly, beyond *Iudex*, as I have hinted, there lies the possibility of developing *other* distinct ideal types that arguably incorporate a '*Iudexian* mindset'—for example, that of the practising lawyer, or of the court official, or of the tax inspector, and so on. Those actors may be found to incorporate '*Iudexian*' interpretive modes of thought in certain areas of their activity. And likewise discrete groups, or 'collectivities', of such actors could provide a basis for the construction of ideal types associated with *their* behavioural modes, and modes of thought, applying Weberian principles of type-construct formation. (So, for instance, there could be an ideal type of litigator who adopts a '*Iudexian* mindset' whilst arguing a case in court.) The idea of 'collectivism' alluded to in this chapter is thus neither collectivism in the conventional sense nor is it intended to stand, in any sense, in opposition to methodological individualism. Generally on methodological individualism, see Steven Lukes, 'Methodological Individualism Reconsidered' (1968) 19 *British Journal of Sociology* 119.

Kelsenian concept of legal meaning or *rechtliche Bedeutung* gravitate in striking ways towards (Weberian) interpretive sociology despite Kelsen's apparent use of the Reconstructed Legal Norm, and the linked idea of 'imputation', to *resist* the gravitational pull of sociology (albeit 'sociology' in its Comteian or 'positivistic' form). I attempted a sociological repositioning of the Reconstructed Legal Norm as an 'artefact' of interpretive sociology as a point of departure for a discussion of where the final, most authoritative, acts of legal interpretation in a given legal system factually reside. What, in other words, could be regarded as an 'ultimate repository of legal meaning' in a legal system? I suggested that a judge, or 'collectivity' of judges, sitting in the highest court of appeal of a legal system represented an 'ultimate repository of legal meaning' of that system. And for purposes of sociological analysis I suggested that that judge (or judges) could be personified as a Weberian ideal type—the theoretical construct, *Iudex*.

This line of argument, however, was merely part of a broader strategy to explore the sense in which Kelsen's pure theory could, in the words of Richard Tur, be regarded as a model for 'a collectivist *verstehende* sociology' of law. In its most focused form the contention here was that the Reconstructed Legal Norm—as a key concept of the *Pure Theory of Law*—assisted in the task of identifying, constructing or, for that matter, validating the theoretical strategy of constituting *Iudex* as an 'ultimate repository of legal meaning' in a hypothetical legal system. From that point of departure, it would become the task of interpretive sociology to investigate or explore whether, and the extent to which, discrete groups or 'collectivities' seek to replicate the standpoint, or some variant of the standpoint, of *Iudex* in attempting to visualize what the legal outcome might be—whether under criminal or civil law—if any particular course of conduct were to be pursued. And these 'collectivities' could provide a basis for the construction of ideal types associated with *their* behavioural modes. In theoretical terms, the task of 'visualizing' legal outcomes from a '*Iudexian*' standpoint would take the form of the hypothesis of the ultimate judgment—'if I act in manner X what would *Iudex* hold to be the legal consequence of that?'

More generally, has a basis been identified, or a case been made, for interdisciplinarity in the sense of the present discussion? If 'syncretism' (in the pejorative 'Kelsenian' sense) denotes the *uncritical mixing* of disciplines, or beliefs, or philosophies, then self-evidently no case for an attempted 'syncretism' of the theoretical part of jurisprudence (exemplified by Hans Kelsen's *Pure Theory of Law*) and interpretive sociology is a case worth making. A different proposition altogether is the development of a genuinely interdisciplinary approach to legal theory in which the insights of the theoretical part of jurisprudence and interpretive sociology can be combined in a way that better enhances the explanatory power of each of those fields of enquiry. If the outcome is an improved understanding of the social phenomenon of law then the case for that is probably too obvious to be worth making.

6

When 'Law and Sociology' is not Enough: Transdisciplinarity and the Problem of Complexity

Julian Webb

In the eyes of our critics the ozone hole above our heads, the moral law in our hearts, the autonomous text, may each be of interest, but only separately. That a delicate shuttle should have woven together the heavens, industry, texts, souls and moral law—this remains uncanny, unthinkable, unseemly.

Bruno Latour[1]

It may be that here in our provisional world of dualities and oppositional pairs ... we compulsively act out the drama of our beginning when what was whole, halved, and seeks again its wholeness.

Jeanette Winterson[2]

Introduction

The relationship between sociology and law has long been seen by both socio-legal and legal communities as practically and intellectually troubling.[3] Thus, (academic) law has been described as an 'intellectual stepchild',[4] a 'parasitic' discipline.[5] In its

[1] *We Have Never Been Modern* (Cambridge, MA, 1993), 5.

[2] *Gut Symmetries* (London, 1997), 4–5.

[3] See, e.g. R. Cotterrell, 'Law and Society: Notes on the Constitutions and Confrontations of Disciplines' (1986) 13 *Journal of Law & Society* 9, and 'Why Must Legal Ideas be Interpreted Sociologically?' (1998) 25 *Journal of Law & Society* 171; D. Nelken, 'Blinding Insights? The Limits of a Reflexive Sociology of Law' (1998) 25 *Journal of Law & Society* 407, and R. Banakar, *Merging Law and Sociology: Beyond the Dichotomies in Socio-Legal Research* (Berlin, 2003). On the many varied conceptions of the relationship between sociology and legal theory, see further Roger Cotterrell's paper in this collection. I am particularly grateful to Roger for allowing me to read this in draft.

[4] T. Parsons, 'Law as an Intellectual Stepchild', in H.M. Johnson (ed.), *Social System and Legal Process* (New York, 1978).

[5] A. Bradney, 'Law as a Parasitic Discipline' (1998) 25 *Journal of Law & Society* 71. Cf. T. Murphy and S. Roberts, who have also described law as parasitic, but in their case the emphasis is on practice

doctrinal, black-letter, form it has been increasingly criticized for being 'rigid, dogmatic, formalistic and close-minded',[6] the product of intellectual under-achievers and failed barristers.[7] Whereas socio-legal approaches have in turn been criticized, almost paradoxically, not just for marginalizing law but marginalizing the social context of law.[8] They have also been attacked for being insufficiently rigorous and undertheorized;[9] and, most damning of all, as the work of 'failed sociologists'.[10]

To be sure, today the fierceness of this debate seems to have moderated, and 'socio-legal studies' (SLS) has become increasingly accepted, some might even say dominant, within the academy. Crucially, however, even if one accepts this still somewhat questionable assertion, there is still much groundwork to be done in developing and defining, at an epistemological level, the relationship between the legal and the social.[11] Socio-legal studies has moved significantly beyond the intellectually limited ambitions of 'contextual studies'.[12] And this in itself is, somewhat ironically, a part of the problem. While contextualism arguably required no more than a crude multi-disciplinarity, that made sociology 'safe' and applied as a mere adjunct of legal studies, socio-legal scholarship today demands more. But what? And with what consequences?

These questions can conveniently be located within current debates about the significance (and signification) of interdisciplinary versus transdisciplinary approaches to 'law and sociology'.

The idea of interdisciplinarity is one with which the academy is increasingly familiar, though not necessarily comfortable. As Vick has observed, definition remains elusive;[13] perhaps the best we can achieve by way of a minimum consensus is to suggest that interdisciplinary work implies simply a lesser or greater degree of integration or synthesis between academic disciplines. Not surprisingly,

rather than other disciplines as the source of parasitism—'Introduction' (1987) 50 *Modern Law Review* 677, 680.

[6] D. Vick, 'Interdisciplinarity and the Discipline of Law' (2004) 31 *Journal of Law & Society* 163,181.

[7] See sources cited in *ibid*, 175.

[8] L. Farmer, 'Bringing Cinderella to the Ball: Teaching Criminal Law in Context' (1995) 58 *Modern Law Review* 756, 756.

[9] A. Bottomley, 'Lessons from the Classroom: Some Aspects of the "Socio" in "Legal Education"' in P. Thomas (ed.), *Socio-Legal Studies* (Aldershot, 1997), 163, 173.

[10] The comment of R. Meagher, a former president of the New South Wales Bar Association, quoted by M. Chesterman and D. Weisbrot, 'Legal Scholarship in Australia' (1987) 50 *Modern Law Review* 709, 716. Compare also the well-known attack on the declining professional utility of American legal scholarship by Judge Harry Edwards—see H.T. Edwards, 'The Growing Disjunction Between Legal Education and the Legal Profession' (1992) 91 *Michigan Law Review* 34.

[11] Particularly within the teaching of law, these alternative approaches have often failed to counter the narrow, but formally coherent internal epistemology of 'legalism', contenting themselves to 'sprinkle moral and political comment [and we might add, social theory] over the top . . . like so much icing sugar'—S. Toddington, 'The Emperor's New Skills: The Academy, The Profession and the Idea of Legal Education' in P. Birks (ed.) *What Are Law Schools For?* (Oxford, 1996), 69, 74.

[12] Cf. Banakar, op. cit. n.3, 13, 15–16; D. Nelken, 'Getting the Law "Out of Context"' (1996) *Socio-Legal Newsletter*, Issue 19, 12.

[13] Op. cit. n.6 at 164–5.

this leaves transdisciplinarity as even more of a fugitive concept, perhaps one that even resists definition.[14]

The idea of transdisciplinarity has rapidly gained ground since the early 1980s, particularly in the context of the (philosophy of the) hard sciences, from which the earliest literature seems to derive.[15] Within much of this literature, the vision of transdisciplinarity is relatively limited and contained; it is first and foremost a *research principle.* It does not necessarily imply a transcendent or trans-scientific philosophical holism (that modern equivalent of the philosopher's stone—a Grand Unifying Theory). Whether it is better seen as a strong version of interdisciplinarity, or a distinct process altogether is more debatable. For example, Mittelstrass[16] defines the contrast between interdisciplinary and transdisciplinary research around the tendency of the former to operate pragmatically in juxtaposing or integrating disciplinary tools and concepts in the context of a specific project, over a finite time, while the latter tends to generate 'deeper' systematic outcomes that have the capacity to change the epistemic structure and content of the disciplinary order itself. But this view of the relationship between inter- and trans-disciplinarity is by no means universal. Luhmann,[17] by contrast, rejects the possibility of interdisciplinarity as inconsistent with the autopoietic nature of social systems, and uses only the notion of transdisciplinarity to describe the capacity of disciplines to import concepts and methods from other disciplinary environments. In so doing the 'host' discipline retains and exercises an autonomy to determine if and how it incorporates and responds to these environmental perturbations.[18] Luhmannian systems theory thus constructs transdisciplinarity as a process of knowledge adaptation and differentiation rather than integration. Nevertheless, in both perspectives there is tendency to see transdisciplinarity as shaped or caused by some sense of reflexive praxis.[19]

Looking beyond 'pure' systems theory, Roger Cotterrell has also come to emphasize the reflexive nature of transdisciplinarity in his work on law and sociology, and I intend, albeit briefly, to use his work here as a specific vehicle for exploring further the possible significance of transdisciplinary legal thought.

Cotterrell's version of reflexivity draws substantially on Gouldner,[20] for whom reflexive sociology involves a recognition both of the situatedness of the researcher

[14] Cf. the contributions in M. Somerville and D. Rapport (eds), *Transdisciplinarity: reCreating Integrated Knowledge* (Oxford, 2000).

[15] See, e.g. M. Gibbons et al., *The New Production of Knowledge. The Dynamics of Science and Research in Contemporary Societies* (London, 1994); J. Mittelstrass, *Der Fluge der Eule. Von der Vernunft der Wissenschaft und der Aufgabe der Philosophie* (Frankfurt am Main, 1989), 60–88.

[16] *Ibid.* [17] N. Luhmann, *Observations on Modernity* (Stanford, CA, 1998).

[18] See G. Teubner, 'How the Law Thinks: Toward a Constructivist Epistemology of Law' (1989) 23 *Law & Society Review* 727, 749.

[19] Characterized chiefly in Luhmann's terms as the capacity of systems for self-description, which is both self-observation and 'the presentation of the unity of the system in the system'—see, e.g. N. Luhmann, *Law as a Social System* (Oxford, 2004), ch. 11 (quotation at 424).

[20] A. Gouldner, *The Coming Crisis in Western Sociology* (London, 1971), *seriatim*. Reflexivity is also a strong theme in the work of other leading modern sociologists, including Pierre Bourdieu and Ulrich Beck—see further references in n.61, below.

in the social world and his/her inability to construct a knowledge of that world apart from a knowledge of him/herself. Gouldner's vision of sociology is also radical insofar as it is, like Cotterrell's, transformative.[21] A reflexive sociology seeks not merely to understand but to change the world.

Cotterrell sees the potential of a transdisciplinary sociology arising out of the very weakness of sociology as a discipline: 'the extension of knowledge beyond particular fields' he suggests, 'is likely to come through the *weakening* of disciplinary claims and not through their extension'.[22] Reflexivity of itself becomes the disruptive influence that weakens disciplinary knowledge and boundaries. And yet, at the same time, this weakness is also a strength that frees sociology, unconstrained by demarcation disputes, to move beyond its limits. Herein lies its potential to transform legal discourse, despite the law's own claim to (epistemic) autonomy.[23] Law, viewed sociologically, becomes like sociology.[24] Thus, what is really at stake when we talk about transdisciplinarity seems to be the very capacity for law to engage reflexively with itself, and for social theory to become an integral part of this internal critique of law.

If my analysis thus far is correct, it seems to me that this places Cotterrell more among those who tend to view trandisciplinarity as a radically *inter*disciplinary programme. As will become apparent, while there are many points of similarity between my own view and Cotterrell's, I suggest that in this fundamental respect we disagree, with some important implications for the possibilities of a transdisciplinary programme for law. In shaping my argument I intend to start not with law or sociology, but at where it all began: hard science.

(Re-)Constituting the 'Trans' Problem: The Case of Science, Law, and Society

I intend to develop what will become an argument for transdisciplinarity in the context of our understanding of the 'inter-disciplinary' relationship between law and science. This relationship is probably one of the most fundamental and complex questions facing us in the early twenty-first century. Many of our most pressing social and regulatory problems operate on or between the boundaries of law and science—regulating the environmental risks of technologies such as nuclear power; establishing the legitimate functions of the new reproductive sciences, and

21 See Cotterrell's *Law's Community: Legal Theory in Sociological Perspective* (Oxford, 1995) in which he adopts 'a critical, analytical view of the scientific quest itself and a reflexive attitude to the faith in science on which it is founded' (15) as a starting point in formulating an essentially moral vision of the purpose of law.

22 *The Sociology of Law: An Introduction* (London, 1992), 8.

23 This somewhat simplified summary draws primarily on Cotterrell (1998) op. cit. n.3.

24 I think this circularity is both less naive and less paradoxical than it sounds: it emphasizes the inescapability of a reflexive praxis from the sociological point of view: that there is always a sociology of sociology sitting behind a sociology of law. Compare Cotterrell in this volume.

so on. But my concern is not primarily regulatory, it is epistemological. I intend to use thinking sociologically about the relationship between law and science, as a way of triggering epistemological reflection on the relationship between disciplines in general and law and sociology in particular.

I start with the natural sciences for an obvious reason. They have, historically occupied a privileged place in the disciplines, to the extent that they have become, it is often said, the 'new religion'. But at heart this is, in fact, a very old idea. Springing from the Platonic belief in a hidden mathematical order of the universe, Aristotle wrote of scientific knowledge as *episteme,* the most profound and universal true knowledge available.[25] Although, of course, Aristotle's science itself was refuted during the Western scientific revolution, Galileo and Newton, probably more than anyone else, maintained the idea of mathematics as nature's language, and the primacy of scientific method was further embedded by Descartes and Kant, and ultimately reified by the logical positivists. Natural science thus provided a foundation for a whole rationalist epistemology, that shaped both the emerging social sciences, and, by the mid-nineteenth century, the attempts to create a rational science of law as well. But the relationship between law and science (widely defined) involved more than the threads of a common rationality. Even though, as Santos observes, by the beginning of the nineteenth century 'modern science had already been converted into a supreme moral instance, itself beyond good and evil', scientific rationality could not achieve 'the reconstructive management of the excesses and deficits of modernity' by itself.[26] Hard science and law came to use each other. To achieve its management of society, science required the means for normative integration and coercion provided by law. Law too sought to legitimize its development and expansion by seeking to ground legislation in the 'scientific' study of social behaviour and institutions.

The claims to rationality grounded in scientism have themselves proven to be a double-edged sword. Scientific 'truth' rests not on faith but knowledge. As such it is, ironically, contestable in a way that claims built on faith and trust are not. As John Paterson has observed,

> When truth was understood to be the product of revelation . . . then it could be equated with certainty. In the phase of rationality, however, truth is the product of reason and as such can only be equated with knowledge. Certainty is absolute but knowledge is mutable.[27]

Hard science itself has become increasingly aware of the limitations of *episteme.* Today we understand that scientific rationality itself is the repository of no more than provisional answers. This insight can be traced back to the work of Hume, though it is often grounded in the tensions between Karl Popper's two insights: his falsification account of scientific method,[28] and his recognition, at the same time,

[25] *Nichomachean Ethics*, 1139B18ff.

[26] B. Santos, *Toward a New Legal Commonsense*, 2nd edn. (London, 2002), 5.

[27] 'Trans-Science, Trans-Law and Proceduralization' (2003) 12 *Social and Legal Studies* 525, 531.

[28] K. Popper, *Conjectures and Refutations* (London, 1963).

that science's 'natural laws' do not exist as absolute truths.[29] For example, scientific laws are actually 'true' if and only if certain conditions apply: the so-called *ceteris paribus* condition. This provisional nature of scientific knowledge is nevertheless often overlooked because we have a long history of idealizing science. As Elizabeth Anscombe has observed, Newton's mechanics was in fact an 'intellectual disaster' for science. Since it (unusually) had a highly reliable naturally occurring model in the solar system, it encouraged people to adopt an unrealistic view of the power of scientific explanation.[30] In reality science's 'facts' can only be understood in science's terms, and a scientific 'truth' is thus true only until it is shown to be otherwise. Such insights, somewhat ironically perhaps, did much to open the way to Kuhnian notions of incommensurability and the theory-ladenness of data,[31] that have supported the rise of greater scepticism and cultural relativism in both the social study of science and in the social sciences more generally.

The consequences of Anscombe's 'disaster' (such as it is) have not been limited to the natural sciences alone, and the extent to which there has been a general societal loss of faith in expertise is a point observed by Giddens and other modern sociologists. Science in turn, has become more modest in its ambitions, and has begun to recognize the extent to which many seemingly scientific problems are in fact problems of trans-science: problems created by science, but which cannot be solved by science alone.

The phrase trans-science was coined by Alvin Weinberg in 1972[32] and it seems accurately to capture many of the difficulties we currently face in understanding and regulating the 'risk society'. But the problem with Weinberg's conception of trans-science was that it continued to put its faith in law as the other discipline hard science required to resolve its problems. As Paterson has cogently argued,[33] what this in turn has overlooked is the extent to which the problems of trans-science may be trans-legal as well; many of the more pressing problems which law and politics wishes to pass over to science, are precisely the ones which science, too, is unable to answer. The crises of modern science are also the crises of modern law.

This 'trans-' problem can be explained largely by the incommensurability of rationalities, by which I mean the tendency for different (particularly expert) discourses to talk past each other.[34] At its most abstract, the problem of incommensurablity takes us back to Hume's is/ought distinction: knowing a scientific fact does not unable us seamlessly to posit a norm, despite 'the gradual colonization of

[29] K. Popper, *The Logic of Scientific Discovery* (London, 1959); see also *The Poverty of Historicism*, 2nd edn. (London, 1961) which develops the idea that it is impossible to find historical ideas that have predictive force.

[30] 'Causality and Determination' An Inaugural Lecture delivered at Cambridge University (Cambridge, 1971).

[31] T. Kuhn, *The Structure of Scientific Revolutions*, 2nd edn. (Chicago, 1970).

[32] 'Science and Trans-Science' (1972) 10 *Minerva* 209.

[33] Op. cit. n.27.

[34] Thus I am adopting a 'soft' version of incommensurability which assumes, with the later Kuhn, that there is some capacity for communication and understanding between paradigms or (as I would argue) communicative systems.

the different rationalities of modern emancipation by the cognitive-instrumental rationality of science.'[35] Shrader-Frachette offers a practical illustration of such multiple problems of incommensurability arising out of the clash of rationalities in the case of industrial risk assessments.[36] In such cases conventional scientific rationality tends to favour minimizing industry/producer as opposed to consumer risks—this is both more consistent with the conservative tendency in scientific thinking, and is backed up by Bayesian decision rules in formal risk analysis, which tend to favour pursuing relatively low-risk activities, even where the actual consequences of such risks, though unlikely, will be catastrophic if they do occur.

Societal decision-making is not analogous to the epistemological rationality of hard science; it requires 'cultural rationality' involving an assessment of the democratic justification for the risk imposition. Moreover, legal rationality is also not necessarily consistent with either scientific practice or cultural rationality—for example, the fault basis of civil law, by requiring victims to prove causation in the case of technological risk, provides no strong (systemic) reasons for risk assessors to minimize producer risks in cases of uncertainty, despite the public's greater vulnerability, than either industrial producers or immediate users of the risky technology.[37] This is precisely where law fails to address the trans-legal; although formal and substantive notions of law are not indifferent to the argumentative implications of the is/ought distinction, they assume that an underlying rationality—be it scientific, economic, or sociological will have provided the necessary justification for normative action.

Obviously such incommensurability is not just a conceptual problem, it has real world implications. Where the solution to a problem lies potentially outside its own discipline, the inability of disciplines to talk to each other is likely to impede attempts at more 'holistic' approaches to policy intervention or problem solving.

Paterson argues that the problems of trans-science/trans-law may be addressed by moving from traditional formal or substantive paradigms of law to a procedural paradigm drawing on autopoiesis theory. Such a proceduralization of law enables a decision to be made, but in such a way that it more clearly *retains* the fundamental difference between systems/discourses that we have observed, and in fact acknowledges the fictive sense in which we allow one discourse to colonize the other: it becomes a question of how far any regulatory regime 'reflects the need to hold the factual and the normative in creative... tension.'[38] So far, so good, perhaps. But, assuming for the purposes of this argument that we accept the case for a proceduralist turn, this process also seems to require a significant shift in thinking as well as acting: the adoption of what I will call a trans-disciplinary worldview to deal with trans-legal problems.

[35] Santos, op. cit. n.26, 7.

[36] 'Uncertainty and the Producer Strategy: The Case for Minimizing Type-II Errors in Rational Risk Evaluation' in R. Baldwin et al. (eds), *A Reader on Regulation* (Oxford, 1998), 270, 271–5.

[37] *Ibid.* [38] Paterson, op. cit. n.27, 542.

Reconstructing the Disciplines

In 1996 the Gulbenkian Commission on the restructuring of the social sciences proposed controversially that:

> We come from a past of conflicting certitudes, be they related to science, ethics or social systems, to a present of considerable questioning about the intrinsic possibility of certainties. Perhaps we are witnessing the end of a type of rationality that is no longer appropriate to our time. The accent we call for is one placed on the complex, the temporal and the unstable, which corresponds today to a transdisciplinary movement gaining in vigour.[39]

This challenge it seems to me is, in some respects profound, in others it has the potential to be profoundly wrong. What it does accurately trace is the perceived problem of disciplinarity; but then it seems rather to beg the question, which transdisciplinarity is the answer for the social sciences? The assumption that transdisciplinarity inevitably leads to a questioning of 'the intrinsic possibility of certainties' could be seen as a step too far, even by some proponents of transdisciplinarity. In short, the epistemological and even ontological assumptions of transdisciplinarity are by no means settled.

Nevertheless, I think we can at least agree with the Commission that there is a problem for which transdisciplinary thinking might be a solution. We can begin to address the problem, and even the solution, in the answers to two seemingly simple questions, which I will address in this chapter, which I hope will serve as a prolegemenon to the continuing, detailed work in socio-legal studies that will be needed if we are to take the claims of epistemological complexity seriously. These deceptively simple questions are: (i) are we outgrowing our existing understanding, and (ii) if so, what theory of knowledge and process of knowledge production will enable us better to understand and address the complexity and uncertainty of the social?

Disciplinary-based understanding remains, of course, a powerful framework for organizing and producing knowledge. Many of the disciplines are deeply embedded in our social and philosophical thinking, and reflect divisions which may be traced, via the medieval universities to the Ancients. Indeed the earliest recorded use of 'discipline' in the English language to describe a 'branch of education or instruction' is given by the *Oxford English Dictionary* as 1386, that is, at a point after higher learning had already become the territory of the universities. Nevertheless, these discipline boundaries remain essentially social constructions, sustained by networks and communities of practice within these same traditionally rigid and hierarchical institutions we call universities. As Paul Wiles has observed, the disciplines thus reflect first and foremost the knowledge we have had in the past;[40] they are historical

[39] Gulbenkian Commission, *Open the Social Sciences: Report of the Gulbenkian Commission on the Restructuring of the Social Sciences* (Stanford, CA, 1996), 79.

[40] 'Policy and Sociology' (2004) 55 *British Journal of Sociology* 31, 33.

as well as conceptual constructs. But disciplines do evolve, or perhaps more accurately co-evolve as new problems emerge or new theories are imported from other contexts to test the stability of their boundaries. And in essence I think Roger Cotterrell is right to suggest that the changes to a discipline's identity come primarily through an internal weakening of disciplinary claims rather than by their extension—i.e. as a process of adaptation from within—this claim seems particularly plausible in respect of disciplines like law and sociology which arguably have always possessed a weaker or more diversified epistemological structure than, say, the pure sciences—though the stability of disciplinary knowledge has arguably declined on all fronts. The effect of this attack is perhaps best summarized in Mary Douglas's memorable idea that 'knowledge is falling apart'.[41] How this has occurred is not easy to characterize in a few words. There are, I suspect, many reasons, but the following seem strong contenders.

First, there appears to be an increasingly complex interrelationship between disciplinary knowledge, specialization, and problem-solving. The knowledge explosion itself is significant, or more precisely, there are three particular strands of the knowledge explosion which are important for our purposes. Taken together, the tendency for much new knowledge to be constructed outside the universities;[42] the academy's growing intersection with the corporate-military complex in processes of research and knowledge transfer;[43] and the universities' increased focus on their own 'performativity'[44] have contributed significantly to the increase and diversification of processes of knowledge production. With this growth comes a greater problem in actually thinking in disciplinary terms. Disciplines have tended to become larger theoretical units, with more specialized sub-disciplines—a move to what we might call 'hyper-specialization'. This seems to be leading in turn to two further tendencies, both of which challenge the formal coherence of traditional discipline boundaries. First, hyper-specialization itself reduces intra-disciplinary coherence[45] and, secondly, it generates a growing interdependence between sub-disciplines, often along apparently transdisciplinary lines. At least some of the drive behind this trend is a sense in intellectual work that many of the most interesting and pressing problems can no longer be addressed exclusively from within established disciplines. Rather, what is emerging is a 'hybridization of specialities',[46] in which new fields of study evolve by re-combining the knowledge drawn from a range of disciplinary sub-specialisms.[47]

41 *Risk and Blame: Essays in Cultural Theory* (London, 1992).

42 F. Webster, *Theories of the Information Society* (London, 1995), 184.

43 D. Dickson, *The New Politics of Science* (New York, 1984).

44 I use this term here also to imply Lyotard's sense of a commodification of the knowledge produced. See J.-F. Lyotard, *Political Writings* (London, 1993), 6, 50–3. For example, the emphasis on knowledge transfer, the prescription of sectoral research priorities and the act of research assessment can all be seen as consistent with the commodification of academic knowledge.

45 M. Dogan and R. Pahre, *Creative Marginality: Innovation at the Intersections of Social Sciences* (Boulder, CO., 1990); see also R.A. Scott, 'Book Review Symposium: The Scientific Study of Society' (2004) 55 *British Journal of Sociology* 123, 130.

46 Dogan and Pahre, op. cit. n.45.

47 Examples might include areas like cognitive science, behavioural economics, and the study of complexity itself.

Secondly, the impact of organizational change flowing from these trends should also not be underestimated. New forms of association, and new demands for collaborative work can shape not only the context for research but the very character of the discipline[48]—for example, creating new genres of representation, or diffusing or fragmenting the field as differing agendas are followed by different groups and institutions. This of itself generates greater epistemological uncertainty, which impacts both on the boundaries of disciplines, and more generally on the question of what constitutes 'good' scholarship.

Thirdly, there is growing awareness within the academy itself of limitations arising from the cultural and historical specificity of (at least some) disciplinary knowledges and boundaries. We may question their applicability in non-traditional settings,[49] and raise emancipatory concerns about the kinds of knowledge privileged by traditional disciplinary accounts. More cynically, perhaps, professionalization and empire building strategies within new disciplines or sub-disciplines may also encourage strategies of challenging the relevance of traditional disciplinary knowledge.

Based on this account, I want to suggest that it is 'complexity' itself that constitutes the greatest challenge to traditional disciplinarity, and that what we need, therefore, is a theory of knowledge that takes complexity seriously.[50] By complexity I mean not just the tendency of things to become more complicated. The complicated and the complex are not the same. The claim that intellectual work today is shaped by complexity rests chiefly on the following grounds:

- First, intellectual work is characterized by a very high degree of division of labour and both cognitive and functional specialization, reflected in extensive semantic differentiation between the functional codes of different disciplines, or perhaps even sub-disciplines;
- Secondly, I suggest, that there is a strong case for defining the disciplines in complexity terms as powerful *self-organizing* systems of signification and communication. The case for so doing is based primarily on the insight of systems theory that disciplines display a combination of cognitive openness

[48] See, e.g. G. Cooper, 'Simulating Difference: Ethnography and the Relations of Intellectual Production' (1998) 49 *British Journal of Sociology* 20.

[49] For example the evolution of both 'law in context' and 'legal pluralism' were strongly influenced by the experiences of Western legal scholars seeking to teach and understand law in a range of neo- and post-colonial settings, which challenged their conventional sense of law and legality.

[50] There is already a growing body of literature looking at the application of complexity thinking to our understanding of the social, notably M. Reed and D. Harvey, 'The New Science and the Old: Complexity and Realism in the Social Sciences' (1992) 22 *Journal for the Theory of Social Behaviour* 353; D. Byrne, *Complexity Theory and the Social Sciences: An Introduction* (London, 1998); P. Stewart, 'Complexity Theories, Social Theory and the Question of Social Complexity' (2001) 31 *Philosophy of the Social Sciences* 323; A. Mol (ed.), *Complexities: Social Studies of Knowledge Practices* (Durham, NC, 2002); J. Urry, *Global Complexity* (Cambridge, 2003).

with a tendency towards operative and normative closure that differentiates them from their surrounding environment.[51]

- Thirdly, and somewhat paradoxically, intellectual work is taking place increasingly within an understanding of knowledge as an expansive and decentralized phenomenon. As we have seen, knowledge not only grows, it possesses a capacity to be created and located away from the traditional sites of knowledge production and has the ability to seep transgressively through institutions. The boundaries of the disciplines and of mono-disciplinary knowledge are thus unstable and subject to change in ways that may be unpredictable.

In some respects these features are not particularly new; they are all products of the existing essentially mono-disciplinary system, though some more than others reflect growing[52] inter-disciplinary tendencies within that system. The academic response to the challenge of complexity has involved an element of retrenchment in some cases, but in others—such as law and sociology—there has rather been a widespread embracing of interdisciplinarity as an alternative way of knowing. However, I suggest that interdisciplinarity is problematic in a number of ways. Can one really transplant concepts across disciplines in anything more than a metaphorical sense? Complexity particularly raises the spectre of catechresis—the practice by which new concepts are (mis-)named by drawing on the concepts we already know. As Gayatri Spivak's definition makes clear, such catechresis 'means that there is no literal referent for a particular word; that its definition comes apart, as it were, as soon as we begin to articulate it.'[53] The potential for meanings to change or get lost in the very process of transplantation is thus not just phenomenologically plausible, it is almost inevitable and, from a complexity perspective (as a kind of Heisenberg uncertainty effect), this raises doubts about our capacity to enjoy meaningful interdisciplinary conversation. Interdisciplinarity, moreover, is ultimately a paradoxical solution to the disciplinarity problem. Interdisciplinarity seems to assume both the permeability of discipline boundaries and the 'existence and relative resilience'[54] of those same disciplines. This paradox seems to be resolved by interdisciplinarity creating a knowledge that is always transitional and transitory. Its fate is either to be rejected, in which case it is effectively lost to the system it seeks to influence or irritate, or it will be accepted and absorbed by its host, in which case it again loses its 'inter' character. Hence I am not convinced that interdisciplinarity carries the transformative potential that 'trans'

[51] See my discussion of reflexivity below which departs in some respects from Luhmannian orthodoxy.

[52] See, e.g. Dogan and Pahre, op. cit. n.45; D. Hicks and S. Katz, 'Where is Science Going' (1996) 21 *Science, Technology & Human Values* 379.

[53] G. Spivak, 'Can the Subaltern Speak?' in C. Nelson and L. Grossberg (eds), *Marxism and the Interpretation of Culture,* (Chicago, 1988), 273.

[54] J. Moran, *Interdisciplinarity: The New Critical Idiom* (London, 2000), 17.

problems seem to require. Rather, transformation requires a transdisciplinary approach.

So, what might this look like? Gibbons et al.,[55] have identified a transition in the hard and social sciences and the humanities from what they describe as 'mode 1' to 'mode 2' knowledge production. They define conventional, mode 1, research as academic, mono-disciplinary and homogeneous, whereas mode 2 operates in a context that is applied, transdisciplinary, and heterogeneous. This move is not posited in conventional terms of a discrete paradigm shift; mode 1 has not simply been displaced by mode 2. Rather, mode 2 is presented as an emergent property of the modern research system.[56] Adopting and adapting this model, I would suggest that a 'truly' transdisciplinary system is likely to be based on a 'mode-2 epistemology', not just mode-2 knowledge production. In so doing, I offer an integrating rather than 'holistic' concept of knowing. My modest intention here remains essentially to do descriptive sociology based on an understanding of the conditions of complexity. It is not to offer a utopian vision in pursuit of that compulsive desire for wholeness, the Holy Grail of a Grand Unifying Theory of knowledge.[57] It thus differs significantly from more radical transdisciplinary writings. It does not seek to transcend science; it treats the development of science and society as co-evolutionary; it is anti-reductionist and ultimately reluctant to throw the objectivist baby out with the mono-disciplinary bathwater. It does, however, also acknowledge that 'knowing' cannot be entirely separated from the process of knowledge production.[58] Consequently, I would define 'mode-2' as involving a number of linked claims.

First, it adopts a position of phenomenological realism. That is, it does not reject the idea of an objective reality, but it also adopts a position which acknowledges our intersubjective and internalist viewpoint, and our situatedness in time and space.[59] By a combination of a subjectivist epistemology and a realist ontology[60] we can produce a particular style of 'reflexive realism'.[61] Again the underlying point is a

[55] Op. cit. n.15.

[56] In complexity theory an emergent property is one that arises as a consequence of patterns of interaction within the system. Complexity itself is an emergent property of systems.

[57] Cf. E.O. Wilson, *Consilience, the Unity of Knowledge* (New York, 1998); D. Pels, 'Karl Mannheim and the Sociology of Scientific Knowledge: Toward a New Agenda' (1996) 14 *Sociological Theory* 32.

[58] This argument can be traced etymologically to the latin *disciplina* (instruction) which emphasizes the pedagogical and processual root of the term, and is also apparent in our phenomenological understanding of the research process.

[59] See, e.g. H. Putnam, *Reason, Truth, History* (Cambridge, 1981).

[60] As Putnam *ibid,* also observes, it is conceptually quite possible to combine a subjectivist epistemology with either a realist or subjectivist ontology.

[61] The phrase is from Ulrich Beck, 'World Risk Society as Cosmopolitan Society? Ecological Questions in a Framework of Manufactured Uncertainties' (1996) 13 *Theory, Culture & Society* 1, 7. See similarly Bourdieu's emphasis on 'socio-analysis' and an understanding of 'the subjective relation to the object'—see P. Bourdieu, *Homo Academicus* (Stanford, CA, 1984), xiii, and *Science of Science and Reflexivity* (Cambridge, 2004), 88–94. Complexity theory similarly operates within what Byrne, op. cit. n.50, at 64 calls (following R. Bhaskar, *Scientific Realism and Human Emancipation*

simple one, if we are to be serious about developing a reflexive sociology of law, and a reflexive socio-legal praxis, as Cotterrell, Nelken, and others suggest we should be, we need to answer the epistemological and ontological questions about the kind of reflexivity we have in mind. Reflexivity itself is multi-faceted, some might even say ambiguous. Do we adopt simply a relatively positivistic methodological version? Or a possibly 'ultra-reflexive' deconstructive one? Or, as I propose, a more intermediate, constructionist-realist version.

A subjectivist epistemology acknowledges the extent to which words create worlds, and that any account of 'reality' is mediated by language, culture and tradition. A realist ontology nevertheless asserts, that, whatever our problems in describing reality (in Kantian terms, as phenomenal thought objects) there are nevertheless noumenal real objects which constitute reality 'out there' as a thing-in-itself. As such it is a rejection both of the (neo-)positivism of North American empiricism, characterized by the work of theorists such as Carnap, Hempel, and Nagel, which constitutes the strongest scientistic denial of reflexive 'epistemological complexity',[62] and of the radical indeterminacy (and perhaps, as I have suggested, 'ultra-reflexivity') characterizing the more extreme 'postmodernist' positions that demand a subjectivist ontology as well as a subjectivist epistemology.

Secondly, it acknowledges and also seeks to transcend the limits of traditional scientific rationality. It recognizes that it is in the nature of Cartesian dualism to force us to distinguish in a binary fashion: rational from irrational; mind from body; reason from feeling; man from nature, science from craft; truth from untruth. This in itself becomes a powerful form of closure: '[w]here a normative claim is made on rational grounds (by experts) therefore any other intervention (by other interested parties) must logically be *irrational.* ...'[63] Disciplinary reasoning thus seeks to divide and rule; it dominates the alternatives, reducing them to a status of inferior or even non-knowledge. As Luhmann shows, the binary coding of language thus needs to be understood clearly as not just a, but the, primary tool for differentiation within systems. But there is also a strong challenge from complexity theory which dares us to ignore what we might think of as the 'in-between'. This argument is cogently advanced by Mark Taylor,[64] drawing heavily on complexity theory's notion of 'strange loops'[65] and Gödel's use of paradox to establish the incompleteness of seemingly complete (logical) systems. Taylor argues that the temporality of systems creates an opening in the midst of binary

(London, 1986)) an 'emergent realist' paradigm that accommodates social construction within a realist but adequately complex ontology. Luhmannian systems theory should, arguably, also be understood in the same light—see K.A. Ziegert, 'The Thick Description of Law' in R. Banakar and M. Travers (eds), *An Introduction to Law and Social Theory* (Oxford, 2002), 56–7.

[62] D. Zolo, *Democracy and Complexity: A Realist Approach* (Cambridge, 1992), 8.

[63] Paterson, op. cit. n.27, 530.

[64] *The Moment of Complexity: Emerging Network Culture* (Chicago, IL, 2001), 93–8.

[65] Reflexivity is characterized by circularity and recurrency in complex systems. The term 'feedback loop' is commonly used to describe this tendency of interactions in systems. Such loops become strange when the circularity generates an irresolvable paradox—*ibid*, 96.

structures, a space at the edge of order in which the future is undecidable. 'Undecidables' he posits, 'haunt all systems and structures as an exteriority which is in some sense within even though it cannot be incorporated'.[66] The in-between thus leaves an opening, or the possibility of an opening within every system that appears closed; it leaves systems open to the play of chance and uncertainty and, despite the constant striving for equilibrium, makes homeostasis within the system finally impossible.

It follows that mode 2 itself is, of course, a binary concept (it exists only in contradistinction to mode-1 rationality) and a product of this process. To that extent it is also of limited truth value, but it can and should recognize this, and create space for other, perhaps even more conditional, knowledge claims. This is implicit in the very idea that mode 2 adopts a reflexive approach to its own knowledge construction, is aware of how the meaning of trans-disciplinary concepts may be transformed by the very process of transplantation. In this regard mode 2 perhaps creates an opening not simply for transdiscip-linarity but (an intermediate) and highly unstable *para*disciplinarity. As Hillis Miller observes:

> Para is a double antithetical prefix signifying at once proximity and distance, similarity and difference, interiority and exteriority . . . something this side of a boundary line . . . and also beyond it . . . A thing in 'para', moreover, is not only simultaneously on both sides of the boundary line between inside and out. It is also the boundary itself, the screen, which is a permeable membrane connecting inside and outside. It confuses them one with another, allowing the outside in, making the inside out, dividing them and joining them. It also forms an ambiguous transition between one and the other.[67]

It would seem to follow also that we must continue to think reflexively about complexity itself. In the social sciences, there is a temptation to take complexity as a given—when, rather, 'our understanding of the social world needs to be based on how the social world deals with the complexity it faces, not with assuming the complexity of the social world.'[68] Moreover, complexity is both a discourse about uncertainty and an uncertain discourse. While there are many common themes and catechreses, there is no single version of complexity.[69] We should not

[66] *Ibid*, 97.

[67] J. Hillis Miller, 'The Critic as Host' in *Deconstruction and Criticism* (New York, 1979) cited in Taylor, *ibid*, 98.

[68] W. Medd, 'Bifurcation I' in W. Medd and P. Haynes, 'Complexity and the Social', paper given at the CSTT/ESRC workshop on the 'The Language of Complexity', Keele University, 25 September 1998. Paper available at www.keele.ac.uk/depts/stt/cstt2/comp/medd.htm (last accessed 5 October 2005).

[69] For example, as Kwa has shown, scientific discourses about complexity itself have evolved into (relatively) distinct 'romantic' and 'baroque' forms, developing (inter alia) a tendency to posit systemic uncertainty as, in the one case, an epistemological, and in the other, an ontological problem—C. Kwa, 'Romantic and Baroque Conceptions of Complex Wholes in the Sciences' in Mol (ed.), op. cit. n.50.

forget that epistemology is central to theory construction and the complexity of the social itself means that the development of knowledge must be framed as a continuing object of social investigation.[70]

Thirdly, and finally, the nature of knowledge under mode 2 cannot, as I have said, be entirely separated from the mode of knowledge production. Mode 2, in contradistinction to mode 1, emphasizes applied and contextualized knowledge. While not precluding the possibility of pure and abstract disciplinary work, it recognizes the importance of applied problem-solving in the production of new knowledge that transcends old boundaries. Mode 2 also reflects the shift to the production of collaborative work, in which multiple actors bring greater heterogeneity to the research process. In this context we may also see a move away from traditional research organizations and cultures. Complexity theory itself suggests that these traditional, often strongly hierarchical, means of organizing research may be replaced by more loose networks, flat hierarchies, etc. Lastly, in this context, mode 2 opens the door to new patterns of accountability and representation. Mode 2 knowledge production, Gibbons et al. suggest,[71] acknowledges a commitment to being accountable for the knowledge we produce. More programmatically, they seem to suggest that it should be tested by processes that are far more participatory and dialogical. Their justifications for this are largely pragmatic, though also consistent with the kind of reflexive engagement with community norms and expectations advanced by theorists such as Beck and Habermas. Knowledge that is the product of such processes is more likely to satisfy conditions of what Gibbons et al. call 'social robustness', rather than just formal reliability. Perhaps we may even go so far as to suggest that such processes may be more capable of generating socially useful knowledge. For some in the academy, even to air this possibility will seem a utilitarian step too far; but equally there is a strong tradition of reform-oriented socio-legal studies for which this is already an established objective.

Conclusion

This chapter began by posing the basic question whether established versions of the law and sociology relation are conceptually adequate to capture the complexity of a socio-legal world where many of the important problems, for example, in terms of the regulation of science and technology are fundamentally transdisciplinary in nature. In exploring this question I have sought to take seriously the epistemic roots of the problem, recognizing both that the transformations in knowing that we have observed, potentially at least, have significant consequences for the content and constitution of disciplines, and that the content and constitution of disciplines in turn has implications for the knowledge that we (can) bring to bear in resolving real-world problems.

[70] Cf. N. Luhmann, *Social Systems* (Stanford, CA, 1995), ch. 12.

[71] See op. cit. n.15.

The abstract focus on epistemology in this chapter may seem a long way removed from the practicalities of real-world problem-solving, but the two are inextricably connected. Words do shape worlds, even though there is a world 'out there', somewhere, it is becoming increasingly difficult meaningfully to describe the operations of that complex world. Mono-disciplinarity has become a part of the problem, rather than the solution. An adequately complex transdisciplinarity may give us not just an access to some greater understanding of that world, but possibly some new openings in which to influence it as well.

As will have become apparent, the real problematic in my title is neither 'law' nor 'sociology', it is the 'and' with which they are joined. Transdisciplinarity, in the version presented here, becomes a resistance to mono-disciplinary epistemic closure. But at the same time, because disciplinary closure is always already immanent within the communicative systems of law, sociology and—ultimately—science too, the possibility of the kind of sustained and radical openness anticipated by Cotterrell and others is unlikely to be realized. If we are to avoid failure, I suggest we need to focus on a more modest (and yet perhaps immodest, too) epistemological programme that acknowledges the reality of epistemic differentiation and closure. A radically interdisciplinary transdisciplinarity underplays the significance of the construction of difference.[72] But even if closure is inevitable, transdisciplinarity provides an opportunity to test the boundaries; to find openings that are themselves immanent in the creative tensions that exist between the disciplinary flows and networks of information, and in the interstices and 'undecidables' that emerge within a disciplinary knowledge. The very complexity and heterogeneity of the social world means that in the face of the inevitability of closure, the possibility of a new epistemic opening can never be foreclosed. Within this context, the possibility of the emergence of what I have called *paradisciplinary* knowledge is specifically something which seems worthy of further investigation.

This is not to suggest that a wholesale move to a mode-2 epistemology and knowledge production is necessarily and without more a social 'good'. The shift to more dialogical and visible knowledge production can undoubtedly support the emancipatory and demystifying ambitions of socio-legal scholarship, but the underlying performative and often utilitarian agendas of the universities, the funding bodies, and the state itself also threaten to use mode 2 to tie research to a narrow, technocratic, and scientistic means-end rationality. In this context a strong programme of developing collective reflexivity also needs to be seen as a *sine qua non* of mode 2 socio-legal research. As Bourdieu observed, '[r]eflexivity takes on its full efficacy only when it is embodied in collectives which have so much incorporated it that they practise it as a reflex.'[73] In mode 2 as I have defined it this implies not only a reflexive awareness of the ways in which we are imbricated as agents in the research

[72] Cf. Nelken, op. cit. n.3, 423; Luhmann, op. cit. n.19, *seriatim*.

[73] Bourdieu (2004), op. cit. n.61, 114. It is axiomatic to point out therefore that it is fundamentally important that debates about research capacity and research training recognize the significance of teaching the philosophy and sociology of socio-legal research as well as its practice.

process, but an epistemological scepticism that confronts the (im)possibility of nomological explanation and acknowledges the circularity of the truth claims of law, science, and sociology—law is only law if its normative expectations can be expected normatively; science is only science within the paradigmatic claims of the 'laws' of science, and so on. But circular though these claims may be, the challenge for transdisciplinary thinking is in understanding the difference that makes a difference; this is where complexity matters.

7

Durkheim in China

Tim Murphy

In a home it is the site that matters;
In quality of mind it is depth that matters;
In an ally it is benevolence that matters;
In government it is order that matters;
In affairs it is ability that matters;
In action it is timeliness that matters.
It is because [water] does not contend that it is never at fault.[1]

Introduction

What is the purpose of a sociological engagement with law? What kind of supplement to itself can law seek to find in sociology and especially social theory? My assumptions in this chapter are that the principal general aim of sociology (including social theory) is to explain 'how society works'. It is therefore an inherently 'positive' rather than 'normative' project: it seeks to get to grips with and present the true meaning of 'the facts'. Law, by contrast, is inherently normative and is concerned with how society (or its members) should be or behave. Durkheim is selected for special scrutiny because it is not clear, despite his claims, that these generalizations apply to him; his project, in other words, seems inherently normative. If this is the case, then it is difficult to see how his perspective offers something distinctive from normatively-oriented legal theory. So the example of China is selected as a society and governmental system (and 'tradition') which has been claimed to illustrate and exemplify Durkheimianism at the level of

[1] Lao Tzu, *Tao Te Ching* [Laozi, *Dao De Jing*] (Harmondsworth, 1963) I, VIII. Where citations are to the Wade-Giles (now Taiwanese) system, I have tried where possible to cross-refer to the Pinyin (or mainland) system. The same applies to Latinized or Westernized names. Significantly, the translator's preface to Jacques Gernet, *A History of Chinese Civilization* (2nd edn., Cambridge, 1996) states that he has 'transliterated' Chinese names according to the Wade-Giles system, 'in spite of the Chinese government's recently [1981] expressed preference for Pinyin'. The choice of Pinyin or Wade-Giles remains politically charged.

social and political practices. The consequences of this practical Durkheimianism are then examined, and their implications for Western social theory and Western law are briefly explored.

Do Lawyers Need a Theory of Society?

Both practising and academic lawyers may or maybe must have an implicit theory in which they make assumptions about both the nature of society and human nature. These implicit theories may be closely entangled or fairly distinct from each other. In many cases, however, such a theory of society may well in fact be a theory of human nature. (The term 'implicit theories' simply means here at least the kind of theory people's utterances and statements imply and to which they might assent if the theory was made explicit; the latter however is not a requirement.)

To the extent that this is the case, lawyers could and may (if educated) draw support from 'classics' such as Locke or Hobbes, which effectively start with 'individuals' or hypothetical man and derive from that starting point (which itself may be imagined or historical) a range of propositions about the nature and/or role of society and/or government. What law is for, how law should work, what law should and should not or can or cannot be slots in naturally somewhere along the way.

In such theories there may or may not be a clear distinction drawn between society and government. Natural society is little more than an extended family; certainly no very thought-through distinction is drawn at this level. Each is therefore conceived as a scene in which individuals knock along with other individuals (whether or not this includes women, children, servants, and slaves, etc) and knock along well or badly. This kind of state of nature is a sort of psychological experience, infused with a range of human qualities and attributes—hope, fear, desire, love, hate, etc. Concepts like shame, imitation, duty, responsibility, also originate here.[2]

'Society' in a more modern sense already presupposes government (and law). The question is whether, and to what extent, this concept is thought and thought through as such, rather than as an extended family. We see, for example, what are probably the beginnings of this thought of society in Smith, specifically in his 'unintended consequences'. But it would hardly be correct to suggest that 'society' was the object of Smith's thought, and much of his focus is still on the problem of the individual and government, with 'society' as just a lot of individuals, albeit with different statuses, and even if we call this a 'nation'. 'Society' is not a nation although a nation is a way of glimpsing what we mean by society.[3] Economics

[2] René Descartes, *The Passions of the Soul* ([1649] trans. Indianapolis, 1989); Charles Darwin, *The Expression of the Emotions in Man and Animals*, Paul Ekman (ed.), (London, 1998); G.S. Rousseau (ed.), *The Languages of Psyche: Mind and Body in Enlightenment Thought* (Berkeley, CA, 1990); David Healy, *Images of Trauma: From Hysteria to Post-Traumatic Stress Disorder* (London, 1993) .

[3] A 'nation', before we have the idea of society, is a rather complicated idea. It refers to territory, (usually) a ruler, one or more 'races', culture/s, language/s, traditions, laws, styles of government,

investigates this society from a partial point of view. Sociology does so up to a point but is reluctant to let go of the individual.[4] Law has little to say about society—it is closer to psychology than any other social science discipline. It is perhaps a kind of amateur psychology which operates without experiments. Hence its difficulties with groups and collectivities.[5]

So does a theory of society have anything to offer lawyers? The immediate answer to this question is probably no. A social theory might disable law or at least encourage lawyers to adopt perspectives which would undermine its capacity to produce a tension in society between the law and society's more societally attuned or oriented practices: like human resources government or the economy, neither of which would perhaps be acceptable or tolerable without some counter-weight or balance, some aspect of society in which the individual still seems to live as some kind of reality.

This might be to suggest that law seems to connect individuals to society or at least has the capacity to do so, and that this capacity does not seem to be too abstract itself to make the question of solutions where law fails seem out of reach and beyond realization. New judges can be appointed. New judges, like new popes, can be invested with hopes.

Law humanizes society (what an odd claim?). With its ally the mass media (without which law could not do this) law is the scene for joy, hope, *schadenfreude*, vengeance, hate, disappointment, suffering? Law can inflict it or compensate for it.[6]

personality structures, etc. A nation is conceived usually in terms of a hierarchically organized network of networks or a family of families. Nations and/or peoples can be combined into Empires as in the First British Empire or the 'multinational' Empire of Austro-Hungary, or China especially under the Qing dynasty. For these points, see R.R. Davies, *The First British Empire: Power and Identities in the British Isles* 1093–1343 (Oxford, 2000) and compare David Armitage, *The Ideological Origins of the British Empire* (Cambridge, 2000). More generally, see Patrick J. Geary, *The Myth of Nations: The Medieval Origins of Europe* (Princeton, NJ, 2002). For further discussions, see Uday Singh Mehta, *Liberalism and Empire: A Study in Nineteenth-Century British Liberal Thought* (Chicago, 1999); Partha Chatterjee, *The Nation and Its Fragments: Colonial and Postcolonial Histories* (Princeton, NJ, 1993); Oliver MacDonagh, *States of Mind: Two Centuries of Anglo-Irish Conflict,* 1780–1980 (London, 1992). For recent scholarship on China, see especially Pamela Kyle Crossley, *A Translucent Mirror: History and Identity in Qing Imperial Ideology* (Berkeley, CA, 1999); Evelyn Rawski, *The Last Emperors: A Social History of Qing Imperial Institutions* (Berkeley, CA, 1998).

[4] Economics is often, wrongly, thought of as the apogee of individualism; the historical lineages are in fact more complex: see Philip Mirowski, *More Heat than Light: Economics as Social Physics, Physics as Nature's Economics* (Cambridge, 1989). It is Durkheim's self-styled sociology which has the problem with the individual: see W.T. Murphy, 'Reason and society: The science of society and the sciences of man' in Philip Windsor (ed.), *Reason and History: or only a History of Reason?* (Leicester, 1990), 56–88.

[5] See in particular Mark Bovens, *The Quest for Responsibility: Accountability and Citizenship in Complex Organizations* (Cambridge, 1998).

[6] The problem delineated by Luc Boltanski in his *Distant Suffering: Morality, Media and Politics* (Cambridge, 1999) needs to be taken seriously. Beamed into our homes while we have time and are interested is all manner of suffering and misfortune the horror of which we are meant to feel. Curiously, the idiom in play here is the experience or perhaps one should say encounter of suffering face to face, best articulated by Emmanuel Levinas: see e.g. his *Of God Who Comes to Mind* (Stanford, CA, 1998), 3–24; 137–51.

In humanizing society, law can be and be seen as bad as well as good. Humanizing simply means to bring into play human attributes, and to make the attribution of human attributes seem at least partially meaningful. Of course, the humanization of society occurs across a wider canvas. Evil can include McDonalds, Microsoft, George Bush, Al-Qaida, etc; good can include the same.

How does the distinction between law and morality fit in? Do these familiar features of/issues in modern law undermine what I am saying? No, because these features and themes give us a clue to what law really is, certainly in modern societies, and to some extent in most societies. They remind us that, as Luhmann puts it, it is society's law which is involved here, or, which is the same thing, the legal sub-system of the social system, much but not all of which is organized in the form of what we usually call 'The Legal System'.[7]

Impersonality, anonymity, substitutability, probability, mediatization—these are the key hallmarks of a proper theory of society.[8] These are not particularly human categories.[9] But there is also the question of the thing-ness of this society. An alternative vision of the society of the future is that humanity will evolve into a 'superorganism', with less the image of slave ants working for alien colonies in mind than the events of the Precambrian[10] in which ' "super" metazoan organisms began to take the lead in a world previously ruled by independent unicells'.[11] Hamilton prefers the term 'superorganism' to 'superbrain' because the latter

> . . . conjures the idea of computers or networks designed for a controlling function, but this is not what is imagined. The idea is rather that control will arise spontaneously out of, at first, organizations of people. People will still feel themselves to be independent but actually will be entering increasing dependence on each other, on interactions with their machines (especially those for communication, computation, and information retrieval), and on support from 'outside' (eg from still relatively healthy manual workers and traditional hardware). Ever more decisions will be taken, in effect, by computers, and supposedly controlling human elites will serve more and more like glial cells to the computers' neurones, although this will probably not be a typical perception by the humans. At all times decision and control functions will be dispersed, more nearly analogous to the nervous system of a multigangliate sedentary invertebrate than to a highly cephalized vertebrate.[12]

This is perhaps an exorbitant perspective, but one should not dismiss it out of hand through wheeling out rather empty sloganized terms like 'agency' or 'subjectivity'. An adequate analysis needs to recognize that a village even a town no doubt has a certain thing-ness—a reality extended and confined in space, a materiality exemplified by buildings, a setting, a landscape, an horizon. Society has no setting

[7] See now Niklas Luhmann, *Law as a Social System* (Oxford, 2004).

[8] Niklas Luhmann, *The Reality of the Mass Media* (Cambridge, 2000).

[9] This is one of the main themes of Tim Murphy, *The Oldest Social Science: Configurations of Law and Modernity* (Oxford, 1997).

[10] For which see Stephen Jay Gould, *Wonderful Life* (New York, NY, 1989).

[11] W.D. Hamilton, *Narrow Roads of Gene Land I: Evolution of Social Behaviour* (Basingstoke, 1996), 194.

[12] Hamilton n.11, above 195–6 n.17.

in this sense.[13] This is probably why global warming seems so remote an issue. And this is why categories like totalitarianism must be used with some circumspection.[14] This is also true of freedom, equality . . . and justice. In this same context, lawyers have contributed to the flourishing of the idea of human rights. This is not in fact paradoxical. Even if triggered in a responsive way to specific and contingent historical events—World War Two and later the Holocaust[15]—its broader trajectory and resonance is partly a response to a number of different forms of deterritorialization; partly an effect of mediatization; and its primary mode of operation is impersonal and anonymous with high substitutability of persons (the paradox is the ideological motif about the uniqueness of each human life).

Having said that, human rights focuses both on the macro level—large numbers—and on individual actors, to the extent that part of its repertoire is or is intended to show trials of responsible individuals requiring in proper legal form the individual testimony of witnesses, victims, etc. It partakes at the same time of the humanizing orientation of the law and the impersonality of modern society. (Human rights abuses are events or incidents to be measured and counted, etc; the media provide an important vehicle for raising awareness and funds. Genocide is in part a matter of counting.)

Modern theories of society also highlight why modern society is such a problem—or more precisely what the problem is. In the developed world, at least for now, old problems are usually absent (or exported elsewhere): crop failures, famine, drought, epidemics, and pandemics. These have destroyed civilizations before and no doubt western civilization is not immune. But this civilization has become adept at risk assessment and management and in general these are not 'our' problem. (I have not seen an analysis of how if at all the problem of AIDS engulfing sub-Saharan Africa will affect the West. It is difficult to know what to make of the threat in China or India.)

But in the West there is the problem of things going wrong, the problem of things not working. A power failure is perhaps the most expressive of these problems though there are many others examples, some with human causes (e.g. strikes). ICT reliance means that everything shuts down when the technology glitches.

Equally, the complexities of modern corporate structures mean that accounting practices determine the difference between success and failure. Information becomes not just costly but fragile. Much depends not so much on trust (which is usually a lazy way of conceptualizing social relations) as on the suspension of disbelief. Luhmann often emphasized the improbability of modern society—which is precisely why disbelief needs to be suspended or why, to put the point the other

[13] This distinction is perhaps most explicitly and radically drawn by Niklas Luhmann. See his *Social Systems* (Stanford, CA, 1995), ch. 10.

[14] Sheila Fitzpatrick, *Everyday Stalinism: Ordinary Life in Extraordinary Times: Soviet Russia in the 1930s* (Oxford, 2000); Yunxiang Yan, *Private Life under Socialism: Love, Intimacy, and Family Change in a Chinese Village 1949–1999* (Stanford, 2003).

[15] Peter Novick, *The Holocaust and Collective Memory* (London, 2000); Tim Cole, *Images of the Holocaust: the Myth of the* 'Shoah' *Business* (London, 1999).

way round, modern theories of society are problematic—they bring to the fore the fragile links on which the whole 'thing' depends.[16]

Law is of course one of these improbabilities, one of the phenomena which require suspension of disbelief. When things go wrong, one reaches for the law to remedy it. Or rather, one grasps the law as one mechanism for stopping something that shouldn't be allowed to happen. This is not new but, I would argue, more central.[17]

To be clear: I am not arguing that we are required to believe in the law or in auditors. Rather, that modern society basically requires an attitude of mind which is not too enquiring or critical or that looks too deeply. It requires a certain indifference to truth, even ignorance or non-knowledge. It also requires less a belief in the goodness or badness of political leaders and others so much as a belief that these human attributes are important and that we have access to knowledge of these attributes in relation to particular incumbents of the relevant positions. Weber wrote that the man who cares for the salvation of his soul should not go into politics.[18] In this sense the rule of law is mythic, i.e. it does not warrant too close inspection. Close scrutiny of the concrete practices of lawyers, judges, legislative draftsmen, and of course legal academics would undermine this myth. I am not saying that this is why this is rarely undertaken, only that it is rarely undertaken. Durkheim is a classic contributor to this myth.

And so to China . . .

I now want to switch gear. How to govern society if not by law? This is why on one reading China is so interesting. Western legal scholars writing about China tend to emphasize the problem of the deficiencies of the judiciary (lack of training until recently, lack of independence, lack of impartiality because of the importance of *guanxi* and the prevalence of corruption) although the driving force behind this 'critique' tends to be the interests and expectations of foreign investors and the problems of establishing secure joint ventures in which expectations are met. China, it is claimed, cannot 'grow up' economically unless its legal system comes closer to the Western model.[19] But what if there is another art or science of

[16] Michael Power, *The Audit Society: Rituals of Verification* (Oxford, 1999). For disasters and so on, see Mike Davis, *Late Victorian Holocausts: El Nino Famines and the making of the Third World* (London, 2002).

[17] Oliver MacDonagh, 'The nineteenth century revolution in government: a reappraisal' (1958) 1 *Historical Journal* 52–67; a valuable appraisal of the argument is to be found in the collection of essays in Roy MacLeod (ed.), *Government and Expertise: Specialists, Administrators and Professionals, 1860–1919* (Cambridge, 1988).

[18] Max Weber, 'Politics as a Vocation' in Max Weber, *Political Writings* (Cambridge, 1994).

[19] Examples are: Randall Peerenboom, *China's Long March toward Rule of Law* (Cambridge, 2002); Stanley B. Lubman, *Bird in a Cage: Legal Reform in China after Mao* (Stanford, CA, 1999). The introduction to the latter work sets up a particularly Durkheimian framework—'Understanding China Through Chinese Law'.

government in a country like China? What if there are different fictions in a 'nation'[20] which houses 20 to 25 per cent of the world's population? The question of China is of course complicated—significantly—by geo-political considerations, and these feed back inevitably into our understanding of Chinese history. The unresolved or suspended question of Taiwan is illustrative of the importance of history for grasping contemporary Chinese thought; I will not here explore the question of Tibet, which has become a rather naïve *cause célèbre* for some commentators in the West.[21]

China is intriguing to the Western eye because in terms of the size of its territory and population it is so enormous. How to govern such a country? The obvious solution would be some kind of federalism and in practice that is what happens most of the time. However, the tradition is unitary rather than federal and this means that the centre—Beijing—must have overall or ultimate authority. (What happens inside Beijing among the senior leaders is another question.[22]) But how can the centre 'rule'? This is the enigma which China presents.

One answer is by setting an example.[23] This is not a simple idea. There is a vast mainly Western literature which emphasizes the survival from the long Imperial period of Confucian values in which morality is stressed above law. This of course accords with Habermas's acute observation about Durkheim that society is a 'moral reality'.[24] This was the whole point of Durkheim's critique of the narrowness or monovision of political economy in his *Division of Labour*. It also provides

[20] Whether or not China was a 'nation' before the Qing dynasty, under the Qing, who originated from what came to be called or designated as Manchuria, Tibet was 'absorbed', Xinjiang was taken over and settled, and the Empire explicitly became a multinational one. Nationalism (i.e. the reassertion of the Han against the alien Imperial rulers) was a central organizing theme which led to the collapse of the dynasty in 1911; see especially Frank Dikötter, *The Discourse of Race in Modern China* (London, 1992). Still today, the Chinese refer to what in the West would be called 'ethnic' minorities as minority 'nationalities' (*minzu*). Also valuable are: Dru C. Gladney, *Dislocating China: Muslims, Minorities and Other Subaltern Subjects* (London, 2004); Rana Mitter, *A Bitter Revolution: China's Struggle with the Modern World* (Oxford, 2004); Peter Hays Gries, *China's New Nationalism: Pride, Politics, and Diplomacy* (Berkeley, CA, 2004); Yongnian Zheng, *Discovering Chinese Nationalism in China: Modernization, Identity, and International Relations* (Cambridge, 1999). Recently published redactions of Foucault's lectures at the Collège de France are relevant to the somewhat hit-and-miss Chinese adoption of the tenets of Social Darwinism: see Michel Foucault, *Sécurité, Territoire, Population: Cours au Collège de France. 1977–1978* (Paris, 2004); *Naissance de la biopolitique: Cours au Collège de France. 1978–1979* (Paris, 2004).

[21] See especially: Paul A. Cohen, *Discovering History in China: American Historical Writing on the Recent Chinese Past* (2nd edn., New York, NY, 1996); Paul A. Cohen, *China Unbound: Evolving Perspectives on the Chinese Past* (London, 2003); Prasenjit Duara, *Rescuing History from the Modern Nation: Questioning Narratives of Modern China* (Chicago, Ill, 1996).

[22] Cheng Li, *China's Leaders: The New Generation* (Oxford, 2001); Andrew J. Nathan and Bruce Gilley, *China's New Rulers: The Secret Files* (2nd edn., New York, NY, 2003).

[23] Central to what follows is Børge Bakken, *The Exemplary Society: Human Improvement, Social Control, and the Dangers of Modernity in China* (Oxford, 2000).

[24] Acute in the sense that it gets to the core of Durkheim's enterprise from *The Division of Labour* onwards. Whether it provides a useful framework for understanding societies (or modern societies) is another matter. On the latter, *cf.* Niklas Luhmann, *The Differentiation of Society* (New York, NY, 1982), ch. 1; Niklas Luhmann, *Observations on Modernity* (Stanford, CA, 1998), ch 5.

the basis for the Chinese–Singaporean position on 'Asian values' in the context of the globalization of human rights.[25]

All of this leads to the conclusion that in China central government largely functions by 'example'. We encounter here a *mélange* of Durkheim[26] and Tarde.[27] Examples have a moral character; but examples are intended to be imitated. 'Models' are prevalent. The assumption is that people will wish to emulate models of what is good or desirable. Of course this could be seen as a very ethnocentric observation. My interest here is simply in the question of when these points of interest might be between Western theories and Chinese realities (including, of course, their theories of law and society). The problem with this techne of government is that it is wide open to dissimulation. It invites behavioural compliance but not much else; hence, perhaps, the equally Confucian emphasis on 'sincerity'.[28] The exemplary society relies on the idea that society is a moral reality—that morality is superior to law/coercion—and secondly on the idea (best articulated by Tarde) that by developing models others will be encouraged to imitate or follow them.[29]

There are other ways of analysing China, which is to say that other forces are at work in a society like China. To the fore is the concept of *guanxi*. *Guanxi* can be seen as a critique of the exemplary society. We need to grasp the ambivalence of the concept and in particular whether it is primarily moral or economic. There is also the question of how the concept links to the literature on 'social capital'.[30]

Social capital basically refers to the non-monetary resources upon which individuals can draw in their transactions with others. Of course, such a definition would not apply in a low- or non-monetized economy, but the basic idea, presupposing monetization, is simple enough.

The *guanxi* perspective, if not inconsistent with this, is different. It sees society as a network of connections. Morality is a component here—particularly in the notion of a perhaps circumspect trust which is central to it—but not the only one.

[25] There is growing literature on this. Some examples are: Randall Peerenboom (ed.), *Asian Discourses of Rule of Law: Theories and Implementation of Rule of Law in Twelve Asian Countries, France and the US* (London, 2004); Joanne R. Bauer and Daniel A. Bell (eds), *The East Asian Challenge For Human Rights* (Cambridge, 1999); David Kelly and Anthony Reid (eds), *Asian Freedoms: The Idea of Freedom in East and Southeast Asia* (Cambridge, 1998). To the extent that the legacy of Confucius [*Kongzi*] gets drawn into this, see: Wm. Theodore de Bary and Tu Weiming, *Confucianism and Human Rights* (New York, NY, 1998); Daniel A. Bell and Hahm Chaibong (eds), *Confucianism for the Modern World* (Cambridge, 2003).

[26] *The Division of Labour in Society; The Elementary Forms of the Religious Life.*

[27] Gabriel de Tarde, *Les Lois de l'Imitation* ([1890] Paris, 1993). Also useful is the recently republished, as part of a more general rediscovery of Tarde, his *Monadologie et Sociologie* (Paris, 1999).

[28] E.g. 'President Hu's "four-point" speech shows utmost sincerity toward Taiwan' *People's Daily*, 19 March 2005.

[29] On models, see also Frank Dikötter, *Crime, Punishment and the Prison in Modern China* (London, 2002).

[30] See Thomas Gold, Doug Guthrie and David Wank (eds), *Social Connections in China: Institutions, Culture, and the Changing Nature of* Guanxi (Cambridge, 2002); Andrew B. Kipnis, *Producing Guanxi: Sentiment, Self, and Subculture in a North China Village* (Durham, NC, 1997).

Social capital is another. If you have no social capital, it may be difficult to develop *guanxi*. If you want to network you have to have something to give. *Guanxi*, one might say, is the non-contractual element in Chinese contract formation.

The core question behind all this is how society hangs together. Comparative studies may lead us to recognize that different societies hang together in different ways at different times in their history. Traditional/modern carapaces, it is now widely recognized, may not be fit for the purpose. The life of society is not so simple. And all of this should make us recognize that in most societies law is not very important. This does not mean that it is of no importance but it is not possible to calibrate this, to measure how important law is here or there.

Most societies today, including China, claim to be governed by the rule of law. What this means is not clear. It is easier to point to abuses of the rule of law than flag up exactly what its specifications are.

There is a vast debate on how different the East and the West were or are.[31] Certainly, in China at least since 'reform and opening-up' there is no shortage of law nor of courts, judges, etc.[32] There is however a shortage of legally-trained judges (though there are programmes now in place to try to rectify this by instituting a system of judicial examinations) and a shortage of lawyers (though how many lawyers per capita does a society really need?). What is somewhat curious to a Western eye is that legislation on the same substantive content occurs at several levels—the Central Government, the Provincial Governments, and at lower levels as well. Informants tell me that courts are likely to pay more heed to the lower level law and regulations in their deliberations. And at all of these levels, there are the Party committees, the 'Party Core Groups'.

It is also difficult for the courts to escape the bonds of *guanxi*. Successful lawyers are valued because of their *guanxi* with judges.[33] In the West we call this corruption, but it is easy to cast the first stone.[34]

The real question in China is the very structure of the Party-State itself.[35] This is independent of the issues of the vastness of the country and the recurrent lawlessness of its people. This structure is duplicatory. The Party sits alongside

[31] The stress on similarity and homologies has been especially pronounced in the work of Jack Goody; see, e.g. *The Oriental, The Ancient and the Primitive: Systems of Marriage and the Family in the Pre-Industrial Societies of Eurasia* (Cambridge, 1990); *The East in the West* (Cambridge, 1996); for a contrasting emphasis stressing difference, especially of an epistemological kind, see G.E.R. Lloyd, *Adversaries and Authorities: Investigations into Ancient Greek and Chinese Science* (Cambridge, 1996); Geoffrey Lloyd and Nathan Sivin, *The Way and the Word: Science and Medicine in Early China and Greece* (New Haven, Conn, 2002); Donald J. Munro, *The Concept of Man in Early China* (Ann Arbor, MI, 2001); and the remarkable François Jullien, *A Treatise on Efficacy: Between Western and Chinese Thinking* (Honolulu, 2004).

[32] Peerenboom, n.25 above.

[33] Peerenboom, n.19 above.

[34] On corruption, a provocative study of the theme is Jean-Claude Waquet, *Corruption: Ethics and Power in Florence, 1699–1770* (Cambridge, 1991); on China, see Xiaobo Lü, *Cadres and Corruption: The Organizational Involution of the Chinese Communist Party* (Stanford, CA, 2000).

[35] For discussion of whether this is an adequate concept for political science, see Shiping Zheng, *Party vs. State in Post-1949 China: The Institutional Dilemma* (Cambridge, 1997).

the State. The current Head of State, Hu Jintao, is also General Secretary of the CPC[36] (he is also, now, Chairman of the Central Military Commission now that Jiang Zemin has finally surrendered all official positions—but who knows what goes on behind the scenes, behind closed doors?). The culture of *guanxi* and of deference to elders—which may just be a matter of how social interaction is choreographed but which may be more than that—is underpinned by Confucian elements.[37] So far Deng Xiaoping could be said to rule from the grave in that the composition of the current leadership is what he planned. This is in its own way a remarkable achievement given Chinese history. Perhaps it is only the unspeakable horror of the Cultural Revolution which made the usual faction-forming and fighting give way to an orderly succession.[38]

This Party-State is not just about the difficult business of governance. It is also about preserving the effective monopoly of the Party. And this requires ongoing education in theory—more precisely 'Marxism–Leninism, Mao Zedong Thought, Deng Xiaoping Theory and the important thought of the Three Represents'.[39] Government and Party officials—if not ordinary Party members—are periodically exhorted or required to attend study sessions. The assumption seems to be that the better developed the understanding of this *mélange* (socialism with Chinese characteristics) the better the leadership which cadres will be able to provide for society. And this leadership is in some sense 'moral', but in the sense of exemplarity. It is often pointed out that this approach to government echoes with different content, of course, the mode of recruitment to the Imperial Civil Service which was based on deep knowledge of Confucian texts.[40]

This emphasis on quality extends quite explicitly more widely. Physical quality has been judged important for admission to university (not that there are not, through *guanxi*, backdoor routes). Poor physical specimens do not set a good example to others.[41] The Party-State structure also presents problems for the judiciary and the way the courts function. Judges are not independent of the local party hierarchy. In the same way, the most senior person in a university is not the President but the university Party Secretary and it is the latter who will often have the closest contacts with the Ministry of Education in Beijing.

So we have a situation in which many things are going on at the same time. Exemplarity, *guanxi*, and the monopolization of power by an all-encompassing

[36] Here I follow the usage of the Party newspaper the *People's Daily* (*renmin ribao*) rather than the more conventional CCP used in Western scholarship.

[37] See Bell and Chaibong, n.25 above; for a profound survey of the historical roots, see A.C. Graham, *Disputers of the Tao: Philosophical Argument in Ancient China* (Chicago, Ill, 1989).

[38] See, e.g. Jing Huang, *Factionalism in Chinese Communist Politics* (Cambridge, 2000). For a graphic depiction of the Cultural Revolution, see Li Zhensheng, *Red-Color News Soldier: A Chinese Photographer's Odyssey Through the Cultural Revolution* (New York, NY, 2003).

[39] This is the conventional litany. The 'Three Represents', now incorporated into the Constitution, is Jiang Zemin's contribution to this rather baffling *mélange*. Robert Lawrence Kuhn, *The Man Who Changed China: The Life and Legacy of Jiang Zemin* (New York, NY, 2004) provides extensive discussion.

[40] Miyazaki Ichisada, *China's Examination Hell: The Civil Service Examinations of Imperial China* (New Haven, Conn, 1981).

[41] Dikötter, n.29 above.

Party which it might be misleading to call political. The energies of the Party are as much oriented to controlling itself (often with difficulty the lower down you go, especially in the countryside) and preserving its monopoly as to 'governing' the country.[42] So the new Chinese leadership visits villages during festivals and shares meals with peasants. Randomly observed defects may be ordered to be put right by local officials. But things taken for granted in the West—even in America!—like nation-wide programmes for social security, education funding, as well as effective tax-collection administered centrally are barely achievable.

Since 'reform and opening-up', Chinese intellectuals (a term they use without embarrassment though at different times of post-1949 history it has had different values attached to it and today there is a general lament that intellectuals are not valued as much as entrepreneurs—financially or in terms of social status) have been preoccupied with the birth of civil society or the emergence of a public sphere in China. But this is/cannot be free from exemplarity. Education provides one important field for this. The prospensity for self-criticism can be seen in a similar light.

The argument is not that this is the only way in which China 'works'. It cannot have become the new workshop of the world without a strong dose of instrumental action. The populations of Guangdong, Fujian, and Hong Kong, which have long sourced the remarkable Chinese Diaspora, may draw heavily on *guanxi* to grow their commercial activities but it is hard to see the force of exemplarity at work here.

Conclusion: Back to the West

Durkheim's approach, which was supposed to analyse late nineteenth-century Western societies, could, in my opinion, be described as wishful thinking. Indeed, his analysis lacks both the breadth and subtlety of Adam Smith, although, of course, Smith was seeking to understand a different and less complex society suspended in a different time. Governance in the West has relied increasingly upon instrumental law and 'regulation', development of and pluralization of political parties, and 'community' and 'nation', especially since the end of the Second World War, are fading categories—or rather, mapping these concepts on to 'reality' has become increasingly problematic.[43]

We are of course no strangers to morality and moralism. But the main lesson for present purposes of reflecting on a society like China—and perhaps other East Asian societies not discussed here except in passing—is that a Durkheimian approach to understanding Western law and society is flawed but, paradoxically,

42 See especially Bruce J. Dickson, 'Dilemmas of Party Adaptation: The CCP's Strategies for Survival' in Peter Hays Gries and Stanley Rosen (eds), *State and Society in 21st Century China: Crisis, Contention and Legitimation* (London, 2004), 141–58.

43 Mark Mazower, *Dark Continent: Europe's Twentieth Century* (Harmondsworth, 1998); Richard Vinen, *A History in Fragments: Europe in the Twentieth Century* (London, 2000).

that practical Durkheimianism may shed light on East Asian societies. It may be that East Asian societies are becoming or will become more Western in the future, less dependent on exemplarity and/or *guanxi*. Superficially, this is the impression a visitor might get in a city like Shanghai (although for a long time—since the Treaty Ports era[44]—Shanghai has not been typical: many cities may now be beginning to look Western but only Shanghai has the long-established Bund which would not be out of place in the City of London).

China is an example of a society which cannot effectively be governed by law in the sense that this is understood in the West. But with its long Confucian tradition, morality provides an alternative. In the West, governing by morality is not really possible anymore. Perhaps this is due to the long legislative tradition of Christianity.[45] Morality can be embedded in families, networks, and possibly, depending on circumstances, communities. Governing by law is not so simple. Civility rather than morality is perhaps the organizing principle.[46] This depends on a certain kind of individualism[47] which was famously what Durkheim found objectionable.[48] But it is questionable how sustainable civility is in modern conditions outside extremely localized neighbourhoods. The impersonality of modern life pulls in a different direction.

And yet: our society has increasingly developed a kind of institutional morality (if that is not a contradiction in terms) in the form of codes of practice and more generally the concept of 'good practice', guidance notes emanating from agencies, and so on. The Higher Education Funding Council for England bombards universities with this kind of material.[49] Today, so does the Campaign for Racial Equality. Exemplarity is quite prominent in these materials and exhortations. 'Models' are increasingly deployed and commended for imitation. And with it is coming the Chinese problem of sincerity. The difference is that Anglo-American culture does not take sincerity seriously. And so what results is an institutional morality towards which many if not most are cynical. But this new technique of governance does highlight the limits of the technique of law.[50]

[44] An accessible overview is provided by Jack Gray, *Rebellions and Revolutions: China From the 1800s to 2000* (2nd edn., Oxford, 2002), chs. 4 and 5.

[45] *The Oldest Social Science,* n.9 above, ch. 2.

[46] This perspective is already apparent in Adam Smith.

[47] Alan MacFarlane, *The Origins of English Individualism* (Oxford, 1978).

[48] See Steven Lukes, *Emile Durkheim: His Life and Work: A Historical and Critical Study* (Harmondsworth, 1973).

[49] See, e.g. Marilyn Strathern (ed.), *Audit Cultures: Anthropological Studies in Accountability, Ethics and the Academy* (London, 2000).

[50] I should perhaps add that I do not find the literature which has burgeoned on the rather slender basis of Michel Foucault's essay on 'Governmentality' (1979) 6 *I and C* 5–22 very illuminating on this question of techne, even if some of my terminology overlaps with it. I have reviewed, somewhat critically, Mitchell Dean's *Governmentality: Power and Rule in Modern Society* (London, 1999), which sets out the emerging canon on this, in (2000) 63 *MLR* 785–88.

8

Law and Sociology: The Petrażyckian Perspective*

Krzysztof Motyka

When that worthy knight Boucicaut was passing through Genoa in the year 1401, he happened to return in courtly and elevated fashion the greeting of two ladies of easy virtue. This outraged his manservant, but the good knight declared: 'I would much prefer to show my respect to ten of these girls, than to neglect it with regards to a single genuine lady'. This story, taken from Huizinga, firstly shows how a discussion about terms should be distinguished from a discussion about concepts, and, secondly, suggests how the scientific theory is to deal with the various, more and less noble, kinds of legal phenomena.[1]

Introduction

Leon Petrażycki (1867–1931) is justly considered the author of the most coherent and the most radical psychological theory of law. There are, however, at least four reasons to discuss his contribution in the context of 'Law and Sociology'. First, although he dealt mainly with law and legal sciences, he created a system of knowledge relevant to all humanities and social sciences, including sociology. Secondly, despite the psychological nature Petrażycki ascribed to law and his programmatic one-plane psychologism, his theory of law is actually multi-plane and consists of numerous questions, hypotheses, and statements relevant to analytical as well as to sociological dimensions of this phenomenon. Thirdly, in addition to

* The present chapter is based upon the author's book *Wpływ Leona Petrażyckiego na polską teorię i socjologię prawa* [Leon Petrażycki's Influence on Polish Legal Theory and Sociology of Law] (Lublin, 1993), the revised English edition of which, entitled *Challenging Legal Orthodoxy: Petrażycki, Polish Jurisprudence and the Quest for the Nature of Law,* is currently under preparation. Parts of it have been published in his 'Beyond Malinowski: Petrażycki's Contribution to Legal Pluralism', in Keebet von Benda-Beckmann and Harold W. Finkler (eds), *Papers of the XIth International Congress 'Folk Law and Legal Pluralism: Societies in Transformation'* (1999), 330. Many thanks are due to Paul V. Smith and Delaine Swenson who made this text more readable to an English audience.

[1] Jacek Kurczewski, 'Pojęcia i teorie' [Concepts and Theories] in *idem* (ed.), *Prawo w społeczeństwie* [Law in Society] (Warsaw, 1973), 54.

discussing social origins and social aspects of law, Petrażycki outlined his own vision of sociology. And fourthly, it was Petrażycki who after coming from Russia, via Finland, to then recently revived Poland was given in 1919 the chair of sociology, the first in his country, created for him *ad personam* at his own wish in the Faculty of Law and Political Sciences of Warsaw University, and in this way contributed to institutionalization of sociology there as well as to its inclusion into the law schools' curricula.

In this light one can understand not only the fact that in the 1920s Petrażycki was the Vice-President of the International Institute of Sociology and that such scholars as Georges Gurvitch, Pitirim A. Sorokin, and Nicholas S. Timasheff considered themselves his students and developed his theory,[2] but also the interest in it by several other eminent sociologists, including Bronisław Malinowski, Norman K. Denzin, Harry M. Johnson, and Robert Merton. Malinowski, like Gurvitch, Sorokin and, more recently, Podgórecki, proposed an understanding of law that clearly follows that of Petrażycki's.[3] Johnson claimed that Petrażycki 'at least implicitly was a structural-functionalist theorist'[4] and traced some parallels between him and Talcott Parsons, while Denzin believed that his perspective 'anticipated and overlaps with the uniquely American school of thought known as pragmatism and symbolic interactionism'[5] and saw similarities between Petrażycki and George Herbert Mead, Charles Horton Cooley, and Erving Goffman.[6] Finally, Merton,

[2] See Karl B. Baum, *Leon Petrażycki und seine Schüler. Der Weg von der psychologischen zur soziologischen Rechtstheorie in der Petrażycki-gruppe* (Berlin, 1967); Barna Horvath, 'Timasheff and Lasting Merits of the Petrazhitsky School' (1971) 21 *Österreichische Zeitschrift für öffentliches Recht* 347; Jerzy Licki, 'Petrażycki's Thoughts in American Sociology (American Group of Disciples of Leon Petrażycki)', in *Polish Sociology of Law Newsletter* (Warsaw, July 1974–December 1975), 5; David Schiff, 'N. S. Timasheff's Sociology of Law' (1981) 44 *Modern Law Review* 400. Theodore Abel, student and collaborator of Florian Znaniecki, also had the good fortune to be introduced to sociology by Petrażycki in Warsaw. See *Teodor Abel o Florianie Znanieckim. Wybór z dziennika* [Theodore Abel on Florian Znaniecki. A Selection from the Journal], selected, translated and introduced by Elżbieta Hałas (Lublin, 1996), 8.

[3] See, e.g. Nicholas S. Timasheff, 'Growth and Scope of Sociological Theory', in H. Becher and A. Boskoff (eds), *Modern Sociological Theory. Continuity and Change* (New York, 1957), 446; Judith N. Shklar, *Legalism: Law, Morals, and Political Trials* (Cambridge, Mass., 1964), 59; Jacek Kurczewski, 'Ethnographic Approach', in Adam Podgórecki, *Law and Society* (London, 1973), 67; C.M. Campbell, Book Review, (1979) 19 *British Journal of Criminology* 284, 284; Csaba Varga, 'Macrosociological Theories of Law': A Survey and Appraisal' (1986) 3 *Tidskrift för Råttssociologi* 167, 170.

[4] Harry M. Johnson, 'Petrażycki's Sociology in the Perspective of Structural-Functional Theory', in Jan Gorecki (ed.), *Sociology and Jurisprudence of Leon Petrażycki* (Urbana, IL, 1975), 39–61, 46. Some claim that Petrażyckian conception of social and legal progress is very similar to that of Talcott Parsons and considered him and Podgórecki, not without irony, 'Poland's answer to Pound and Parsons' (Colin Sumner in his quite critical review of Podgórecki's *Law and Society* (1975) 2 *British Journal of Law and Society* 246–50, 247).

[5] 'Interaction, Law and Morality: The Contributions of Leon Petrażycki', in Gorecki (ed.), n.4, above, 63–82, 63.

[6] *Ibid*, 67–71, 76–8. Such parallels see, among others, Pedro R. David, *Sociología Jurídica. Perspectivas fundamentales. Conflictos y dilemmas de sociedad, persona y derecho en la época actual* (Buenos Aires, 1980), ch. II; Wacław Makarczyk, 'Studia nad aparaturą pojęciową socjologii' [Studies on the Conceptual Apparatus of Sociology] (Warsaw, 1991), 251. *Idem*, 'Social Change in Contemporary Poland in the Light of a Theory of Social Adaptation' (1982) *Polish Sociological Bulletin* Nos 1–4, 133, 136–7.

who learned about Petrażycki at a seminar conducted by Sorokin at Harvard in the 1930s, was prepared 'to draw up a bill of indictment' against those who did not include his biography in the *International Encyclopedia of the Social Sciences*.[7]

Petrażycki's contribution, made at the turn of the nineteenth century, a bit earlier than the writings of Eugen Ehrlich, is obviously recognized in Polish[8] as well as in Russian[9] legal and sociological scholarship. But despite the publication of an abridgement of his major works by Harvard University Press exactly fifty years ago,[10] his theory is still rather unknown in the West,[11] even if from time to time it is referred to by jurisprudents,[12] sociologists of law,[13] and psycholegal scholars.[14] As Professor Michael Freeman noted, while preparing the *Law and Sociology Colloquium*, this is true also with regard to Britain,[15] but it is worthwhile to note that

[7] See his Preface to *Teoria socjologiczna i struktura społeczna* [Social Theory and Social Structure], transl. Ewa Morawska and Jerzy Wertenstein Żurawski (Warsaw, 1982), 8. See also his 'Sociology of Science in Poland' (1983) 3 *Science of Science* 179, 184.

[8] Jerzy Wróblewski, 'Teaching Jurisprudence in Poland: from Petrażycki to Marxist Theory', in *L'Educatione giuridica, II-Profili storici* (Perugia, 1979), 258; Wojciech Sadurski, 'Polish Legal Theory: Past and Present' (1980–1982) 9 *Sydney Law Review* 596; Krzysztof Pałecki, 'Leon Petrażycki: Sociology and Legal Sciences', in Piotr Sztompka (ed.), *Masters of Polish Sociology* (Wrocław, 1984), 134; Andrzej Kojder and Jerzy Kwaśniewski, 'The Development of Sociology of Law in Poland' (1985) 13 *International Journal of Sociology of Law* 261; Grażyna Skąpska, 'Polish Sociology of Law. Polemics, Problems, Social Commitment' (1987) 33 *Journal of Law and Society* 353; Krzysztof Motyka, *Wpływ Leona Petrażyckiego na polską teorię i socjologię prawa* [Leon Petrażycki's Influence on Polish Theory and Sociology of Law] (Lublin, 1993); Jacek Kurczewski, 'Sociology of Law in Poland' (2001) 32 *American Sociologist* 85.

[9] E.g. Valerii D. Zorkin, *Pozitivistskaia teoriia prava v Rossii* [Positivistic Legal Theory in Russia] (Moscow, 1978); Andrzej Walicki, *Legal Philosophies of Russian Liberalism* (Oxford, 1987); Pitirim A. Sorokin, 'Russian Sociology in the Twentieth Century' (1927) 31 *American Journal of Sociology* 57; B.A. Chagin (ed.), *Sotsiologicheskaia mysl' v Rossii: Ocherki istorii nemarksistskoi. sotsiologii poslednei treti XIX—nachala XX vieka* [Sociological Thought in Russia. An Outline of the History of Non-Marxist Sociology of the Last Quarter of XIX—the Beginning of XX Century] (Leningrad, 1978).

[10] *Law and Morality*, transl. Hugh W. Babb, introd. Nicholas S. Timasheff (Cambridge, Mass, 1955).

[11] Paul Sayre, however, wrote that 'his influence is so great in the English-speaking world, although he is known to this world almost solely in second-hand ways'. Book Review (1948) 13 *Law and Contemporary Problems* 713, 713.

[12] E.g. Roscoe Pound, 'Fifty Years of Jurisprudence' (1938) 51 *Harvard Law Review* 777, 809; Julius Stone, *Province and Function of Law* (Sydney, 1946); Edgar Bodenheimer, *Jurisprudence. The Philosophy and Method of the Law* (Cambridge, Mass., 1962); Jerome Hall, *Foundations of Jurisprudence* (Indianapolis, 1973); Surya P. Sinha, *Jurisprudence: Legal Philosophy in a Nutshell* (St. Paul, MN, 1993), ch. 9; Carol Weisbrod, 'Practical Polyphony: Theories of the State and Feminist Jurisprudence' (1990) 24 *Georgia Law Review* 985.

[13] A. Javier Treviño, 'Toward a General Theoretical-Methodological Framework for the Sociology of Law: Another Look at the Eastern European Pioneers', in Jeffery T. Ulmer (ed.), *Sociology of Crime, Law, and Deviance* (Greenwich, CT, 1998), Vol. 1, 155; *idem*, *The Sociology of Law: Classical and Contemporary Perspective* (New York, 1996). See also n. 20, 22, 23 below.

[14] June Louin Tapp and Felice J. Levine, 'Legal Socialization: Strategies for Ethical Legality' (1974) 27 *Stanford Law Review* 1, 6; Gary B. Melton, 'The Significance of Law in the Everyday Lives of Children and Families' (1988) 22 *Georgia Law Review* 851, 887–9; Gary B. Melton and Michael J. Saks, 'The Law as an Instrument of Socialization and Social Structure' (1985) 33 *Nebraska Symposium on Motivation: The Law as a Behavioral Instrument* 235, 245, 268–70.

[15] The reviewer of *Modern Theories of Law* (see n.17, below) noted that 'Petrażycki was probably on very few book lists, and even Meyendorff's account of that strange figure will hardly reconcile English lecturers or students to him.' H.F.J., Book Review (1934) 57 *Journal of the Society of Public Teachers of Law* 56, 57.

some attention to Petrażycki has been paid by several legal scholars working there, including Sir Paul Vinogradoff of Oxford[16] and Baron Alexander Meyendorff of the London School of Economics,[17] who both came to England from Russia, German Hermann Kantorowicz,[18] B.E. King, Jr,[19] and, more recently, David Schiff,[20] Polish-born Zenon Bankowski,[21] Reza Banakar,[22] and Roger Cotterrell.[23] The two latter, like several other authors,[24] link Petrażycki to sociological studies of law[25] and consider him one of its 'classical modern founders'.[26]

The present chapter is an attempt at presenting Petrażycki's contribution with a focus on what justifies listing him among the classics of a sociological approach to law and considering him, to use Adam Podgorecki's phrase, the father of sociology of law.[27] It is intended to support Professor Cotterrell's call for more sensitivity of the sociolegal academy to its intellectual tradition, which is 'still too little valued in the sociolegal enterprise and considered too arbitrarily and marginally'.[28]

Methodological Foundations

As mentioned above, Petrażycki based his theory of law on his own methodological foundations of much more general relevance.[29] His methodological innovations

[16] *Outlines of Historical Jurisprudence. Vol. I—Introduction. Tribal Law* (London, 1920), 60. It seems to be the first work in English referring to Petrażycki's theory.

[17] 'The Theory of Petrazhitsky', in Ivor W. Jennings (ed.), *Modern Theories of Law* (London, 1933); *idem*, 'The Tragedy of Modern Jurisprudence', in Paul Sayre (ed.), *Interpretations of Modern Legal Philosophies. Essays in Honor of Roscoe Pound* (New York, 1947), 521.

[18] A. H. Campbell (ed.), *The Definition of Law* ([1939] Cambridge, 1958), 51, 96, 97, 107.

[19] Book Review of *Law and Morality* (1955) *Cambridge Law Journal* 233. He wrote: 'Your reviewer would have given a great deal to have had this translation available twenty years ago' (233).

[20] Schiff, n.2, above.

[21] *Living Lawfully: Love in Law and Law in Love* (Dordrecht, 2001).

[22] 'Sociological Jurisprudence', in Reza Banakar and Max Travers (eds), *An Introduction to Law and Social Theory* (Oxford-Portland, 2002), ch. 2.

[23] Passing references, e.g. in 'The Sociological Concept of Law' (1983) 10 *Journal of Law and Society* 241, 245; 'Subverting Orthodoxy, Making Law Central: A View of Sociolegal Studies' (2002) 29 *Journal of Law and Society* 632, 635, 637.

[24] Edwin W. Patterson, *Jurisprudence. Men and Ideas of the Law* (Brooklyn, 1953), 81–2; Roscoe Pound, *The Ideal Element in Law* ([1958] Indianapolis, 2002), 104, 106; Thomas Bechtler, *Der Soziologische Rechtsbegriff* (Berlin, 1977), 78–101; Podgórecki, n.4, above; *idem*, 'The Unrecognized Father of Sociology of Law: Leon Petrażycki' (1980–1981) 15 *Law and Society Review*, 183; Varga, n.3, above, 170.

[25] See nn.22 and 23, above. See also Cotterrell, 'Viewing Legal Discourses Sociologically' in *Prawo w zmieniającym się społeczeństwie* [Law in a Changing Society] (Kraków, 1992), 55, and his edited book *Sociological Perspectives on Law, vol. I: Classical Foundations* (Dartmouth, 2001), containing two chapters on Petrażycki. As to sociologists, see particularly Michalina Clifford-Vaughan and Margaret Scotford-Norton, 'Legal Norms and Social Order: Petrazycki, Pareto, Durkheim' (1967) 18 *British Journal of Sociology*, 269.

[26] Cotterrell, 'Viewing Legal Discourses Sociologically', n.25, above, 55; *idem*, 'Why Must Legal Ideas Be Interpreted Sociologically?' (1998) 25 *Journal of Law and Society* 171, 172.

[27] Podgórecki, n.24, above.

[28] 'Subverting Orthodoxy', n.23, above, 635.

[29] See Jerzy Wróblewski, 'Philosophical Positivism and Legal Antipositivism of Leo Petrazycki', in Werner Krawietz and Jerzy Wróblewski (eds), *Sprache, Performanz und Ontologie des Rechts* (Berlin, 1993), 357.

were employed by him as a guide in formation of his own conceptions and also as a tool of criticism of other theories. The idea of adequacy and of class concepts, his comments on the role of language in science, and his classification of art and sciences are of major importance here and their brief presentation is in order.

The Idea of an Adequate Theory and of a Class Concept

According to Petrażycki, theories, statements, and groups of statements could be considered adequate when 'what is stated (that is a logical predicate and its justifier) is true in relation to the class of objects in respect of which it has been stated (or thought).'[30] Theories and statements whose predicates relate to classes of subjects which are too narrowly conceived received from Petrażycki the name of 'lame' or 'limping' theories while theories and statements relating to classes of subjects too broadly conceived, he termed 'jumping' theories.'[31] To be scientific a theory must be adequate, not merely true. In consequence, one is to create a concept, such that can be a subject of an adequate theory.

Obviously, not all concepts are capable of generating an adequate theory, but only ones (and not all of them) that cover objects possessing certain attributes or traits (general or class concept) and moreover 'as logical subjects of scientifically relevant propositions, would facilitate the proper arrangement of those propositions into system'. Such concepts are 'not limited to things which actually exist: there are class concepts of things entirely imaginary, such as those of geometry, and even class concepts meant to cover real things are not limited to those actually existent but include as well things of the past and of the future possessing the relevant attributes.'[32] Thus, in Petrażycki's anti-inductive view, one is to select some characteristic and state that all objects (past, present, future, imaginary) possessing this feature constitute a class that is covered by the given concept.

Theoretical Uselessness of Practical Terminology

Petrażycki was of the opinion that class concepts could not be generated by ordinary, colloquial language and, even more, by professional terminologies, since their concepts usually covered objects possessing the same feature or value from the practical point of view, but having nothing in common from the theoretical or empirical perspective. Thus, he believed, it was important in science to divest oneself of such concepts, and especially of all professional terminology.

It is just as we find, in the culinary world, that the most diverse plants, or even parts of plants of all sorts and kinds, are placed in a single group and then given some common

[30] Leon Petrażycki, *Wstęp do nauki prawa i moralności* [Introduction to the Science of Law and Morality] ([1905] Warsaw, 1959), 124. On the idea and its ancestry see Tadeusz Kotarbiński, 'The Concept of Adequate Theories', in Gorecki, n.4, above, 1.

[31] *Ibid.* See also Petrażycki, n.10, above, 19–21.

[32] *Ibid*, 18.

name of 'vegetables', let us say, or it might be 'greens', or 'legumes', on the sole grounds that all are valued as the raw stuff for the preparation of dishes; plants not counted within this group are excluded from it and denied the name; some because they are unpalatable, others because they take too long to cook; a third group because they have bolted or are otherwise past their best . . . and so on, and so forth. Let us suppose that we now give the task of classifying a separate category of plant corresponding to the name of 'vegetable' to some learned botanist, then quite evidently his best efforts towards isolating and constructing this class of 'vegetables' will be all in vain; the very task that has been entrusted to him contains its own internal 'contradictio in adiecto', for it involves looking for something that does not exist.[33]

This same, Petrażycki claimed, is true in regard to legal theory. It would not be possible to reach a truly scientific concept of law until dependence on the professional terminology of jurists is overcome, as a proper general methodology of class concepts is created.

Classification of Statements and of Sciences

Petrażycki's views on classification of statements and of sciences continued to develop, and two separate positions can be seen in the early *Theory of Law and the State* and the posthumous *New Foundations of Logic and the Classification of Sciences*. His classification of statements corresponds closely to his division of knowledge, with the second being derived from the first. A criterion of the latter was the type of statements produced by a given science. More precisely, according to Petrażycki each branch of science was to consist of statements of a single category.

From this perspective, Petrażycki divided statements and sciences generally, and legal sciences in particular, between the theoretical (whose propositions describe objectively what is, or what is happening, just as it is) and the practical (whose propositions define desired or expected activity). Within the former he distinguished sciences and statements (1) dealing with classes of objects (class statements and sciences or theories in the narrow sense), (2) dealing with individual objects or phenomena or with a complex of such objects or phenomena. He sub-divided the last category of knowledge into (a) descriptive and (b) historical. Practical statements and sciences were divided into (a) normative and (b) teleological (purpose-oriented). This gives five groupings of sciences and statements, (1) theoretical in the narrow sense (theories), (2) descriptive, (3) historical, (4) teleological, (5) normative.

In *New Foundations of Logic*, Petrażycki rejected traditional divisions between theoretical and practical sciences such as he himself had earlier employed and premised his classification on a classification of so-called 'positions' defined as

[33] Petrażycki, n.30, above, 159. Similar criticism is traceable in American debates over the concept of privacy. See Dorothy Glancy, 'At the Intersection of Visible and Invisible Worlds: United States Privacy Law and the Internet' (2000) 16 *Santa Clara Computer & High Technology Law Journal* 357, 359, n.6.

'simple and irreducible senses or contents of judgments or propositions [...] or of other things having similar senses'.[34] These positions (the same is true of sciences) are divided into (I) objective-cognitive (objective) and (II) subjective-relative (subjective). Objective-cognitive positions are (I1) class-related or (I2) non-class-related or concrete-individual. The latter include positions that are (I2a') descriptive (inspective, referring to the present), (I2a") historical (retrospective, referring to the past) and (I2a"') prognostic (prospective, relating to the future). Subjective-relative positions and knowledge are divided into (II1) critical (evaluatory, positively or negatively) and (II2) postulatory (imposing a requirement). The latter are either (II2a) subjective (practical, concerned with behaviour) or (II2b) objective (dealing with things other than behaviour). Subjective postulatory positions are divided into (II2a') teleological (purpose-oriented) and (II2a") categoric (normative). Finally, Petrażycki divided the categorical positions into (II2a"1) positive (dogmatic) and (II2a"2) non-positive (intuitive).

These categories were referred to in Petrażycki's discussion about law, legal sciences, and sociology.

Psychological Foundations

Petrażycki's theory of law is based not only on his own methodology but also on a new psychological foundation, which he called emotional psychology, since the concept of emotions played the fundamental part in it.[35] Having found contemporary psychology's division of psychic experiences into cognition, feelings, and will unsatisfactory, he introduced to it a fourth category—emotions or impulsions, that unlike the former are bilateral, passive-active. Hunger-appetite was, for Petrażycki, a paradigmatic example of emotion.[36] The two-sidedness of emotions corresponded, in Petrażycki's view, to the inward-outward anatomical structure of the nervous system and its motor-stimulus function. This structure also accounts for emotions' fundamental role in the life of man and of animals, in which they act 'as the principal and directing psychic factor of adaptation to the conditions of life'.[37] Among various kinds of emotions he distinguished ethical emotions, possible to be experienced only by humans,[38] and these he further divided into moral and legal, which he considered 'the essential elements of moral and legal life'.[39]

[34] *Nowe podstawy logiki i klasyfikacji umiejętności.* [The New Foundations of Logic and the Classification of Arts and Sciences], Jerzy Finkelkraut (ed.) (Warsaw, 1939), 14.

[35] See particularly Robert S. Redmount, 'Psychological Views in Jurisprudential Theories' (1959) 107 *University of Pennsylvania Law Review* 472, 489–95; Andrzej Kojder, 'Leona Petrażyckiego emocjonalna teoria motywacji' [Leon Petrażycki's Emotional Theory of Motivation] (1987) No.2 *Studia Socjologiczne* 161; Wróblewski, n.29, above, 377–80.

[36] Petrażycki, n.10, above, 23. [37] *Ibid.* [38] *Ibid*, 12. [39] *Ibid*, 27.

Petrażycki's Concept of Law

Petrażycki's own concept of law can be best characterized by three headings, namely: 1. Psychologism, 2. The correlativity of rights and duties, and 3. 'Anti-statism' and legal pluralism. Although all three of the aspects that have bearing upon Petrażycki's concept of law are closely interrelated, they can be (and quite often were) discussed to some extent separately, outside their original theoretical context, usually with a sociological colouring.

Psychologism

The quintessential feature of Petrażycki's theory of law in general, and his concept of law in particular, is psychologism. This should be understood here not so much as the ascription of a psychological character to non-psychological entities, but, rather, the view that some given entity, in this case law, may best be conceived of as a psychological phenomenon. So understood, psychologism can be seen as a form of realism, and consequently of empiricism. Realist conceptions (whether they are psychological or sociological) conceive of law as a fact, as a real phenomenon. Hence, they run contrary to the normativist tendency in legal theory, according to which we should conceive of law purely as a norm or as a system of norms, and, consequently, reject all forms of investigation into the psychological or sociological reality of law.

In Petrażycki's opinion law, and likewise morality, has its real existence only in the human psyche, where it takes the form of legal experiences, while norms, rights, and duties are nothing more or less than an 'emotional phantasmata' or a 'projection', which results from the inclination of man to objectify the content of his or her psychical experiences. Law, which with morality makes up the class of ethical experiences, was the name Petrażycki gave to all experiences that contain a legal emotion or impulsion, whether or not they refer to any normative fact and whatever their contents. In this sense, perhaps, Petrażycki's theory should be termed a theory of legal phenomena rather than a theory of law.[40] According to it:

> the number of the spheres where legal phenomena are is the same as the number of living creatures capable of experiencing—and in fact experiencing—the corresponding mental states, while the number of legal phenomena is equal to the number of these experiences.[41]

Having found legal phenomena in the psyche of the individual, Petrażycki believed, quite naturally, it was to be studied by means of psychological methods, first of all by introspection, which he considered 'the proper and the only possible method of observing legal phenomena'.[42]

[40] It must be added, however, that despite his denial of the reality of law, norms, rights, duties, etc, Petrażycki quite often presented his theory from—to use his own words—'a consciously projection point of view', as norms, rights and duties were real, extra-psychical entities.

[41] Petrażycki, n.10, above, 12. [42] *Ibid*, 13.

Imperative-Attributive Structure of Law and the Correlativity of Rights and Duties

Petrażyckian definition of law/legal phenomena rests on his distinction between moral and legal impulsions and corresponding obligations: 'obligations conceived of as free with reference to others—obligations as to which nothing appertains or is due from obligor' and 'obligations which are felt as unfree with reference to others—as made secure in their behalf', which he termed moral obligations and legal ones, respectively.[43] A legal emotion, which accompanies an idea of given, actual or merely imagined, behaviour, for example paying a bill (so-called action idea), makes us conceive of that behaviour in terms of the obligation or duty of one subject owed to another subject as the latter's right. Therefore Petrażycki describes legal experience and legal norm as two-sided, imperative-attributive, and underlines a correlation between right and duty. In the case of moral experience a sense of duty is not accompanied by a belief that anyone is entitled to have it fulfilled and due to this feature [and thus] he termed it (and moral norms) one-sided, unilaterally binding, purely imperative.[44]

Although the thesis on the two-sidedness of the legal norm and the correlativity thesis, rooted in the ancient idea of justice as to render to each his due, were quite popular in Petrażycki's time, he was the first who explicitly employed it as the *differentia specifica* of law and legal phenomena as compared with moral phenomena. The scientific value of this distinction, clearly of stipulative character, has been positively verified by Petrażycki himself in his comparative description of properties and tendencies of law and morality. This was in accord with his own conviction that a scientific appraisal of any theoretical division is its cognitive and explanatory utility.[45]

Analysis of the two classes of ethical phenomena enabled Petrażycki to grasp several important features and tendencies of law resulting from its attributiveness, which in general are absent in the realm of morality in effect of its purely imperative structure. Law, for example, tends to focus on what is due to the entitled party and in consequence does not take into account the motives of fulfilment of the duty by the obligor and not only accepts coercive satisfaction of the former right, but also a satisfaction of it by third parties (by the obligor's substitute or representative). To fulfil it is not a merit and if the entitled parties get what is due to them, they do not experience a feeling of gratitude.[46] At the same time, if a right is not respected or satisfied, law, unlike morality, which is of a peaceful character, applies various measures, including threats and even physical coercion to compel the subject of

[43] *Ibid*, 45–6. *Cf.*, e.g. Samuel Pufendorf's distinction between 'perfect duties' and 'imperfect duties' in his *De jure naturae et gentium* (1672).

[44] Petrażycki, n.10, above, 47.

[45] *Ibid*, 91. *Cf.*, e.g. Brian Tamanaha, 'A Non-Essentialist Version of Legal Pluralism' (2000) 27 *Journal of Law and Society* 296, 300.

[46] *Cf.* Joel Feinberg, *Social Philosophy* (Englewood Cliffs, 1973), 58–9.

legal duty to carry out what is required and, in the last resort, punishes lawbreakers (the repressive tendency). Petrażycki discussed extensively the unifying tendency of law, that is the tendency 'to development and adaptation in the direction of bringing the legal opinions of the parties into unity, identity, and coincidence'.[47] He saw it manifested in several special tendencies: the positivation tendency—the tendency to develop a single pattern of norms (positive law), the tendency toward precision and definiteness of content and compass of legal concepts,[48] the tendency toward limiting relevant facts to facts that can be objectively verified and established, and the tendency toward subjecting disputes to the jurisdiction of a disinterested third party.[49]

This analysis sometimes seems to have a normative ring, but Petrażycki made it clear that all these propositions were psychological tendencies. He also underlined that they were related to law in its broad sense and would be inadequate if referred to law as acknowledged by jurists.[50]

'Anti-Statism' and Legal Pluralism

Imperative-attributive structure, save its reference to individual psyche, constitutes the sole element of Petrażycki's definition of legal phenomena. For him law is to be understood as every imperative-attributive experience and thus, under his so-called 'projection point of view', as each and every norm of such a two-sided structure. Having been freed from coercion, the state linkage, or any limitations with respect to the substance of respective rights and duties, in any of its interpretation (psychological, sociological or linguistic), it is a minimal definition of law, arguably the widest one ever proposed.[51] It was conceived in accord with Petrażycki's methodological directives to cover each imperative-attributive phenomenon or norm, anywhere and any time, and thus to be of universal, cross-cultural applicability. It challenged the jurisprudential orthodoxy of Petrażycki's time, particularly that of legal positivism.

Criticism of State Conceptions of Law

Petrażycki used his methodology to offer sharp criticism of traditional conceptions of law, considering them 'naive-realistic', 'naive-nihilistic', or 'naive-constructive'. He also rejected natural law theories, claiming however that they were better grounded than those of legal positivism. His legal antipositivism is

[47] Petrażycki, n.10, above, 113. [48] *Ibid*, 115. [49] *Ibid*, 118–19. [50] *Ibid*, 105.

[51] It was considered too broad to be theoretically useful. According to Maria Ossowska, in his theory 'practically nothing is left to morality' ('Moral and Legal Norms', in Gorecki, n.4, above, 112). Also Arthur Lewis Wood, 'Book Review' (1956) 21 *American Sociological Review* 238. Similarly, Boaventura de Sousa Santos, *Toward New Common Sense: Law, Science and Politics in the Paradigmatic Transition* (New York, 1995), 429, claims that very broad conceptions of law 'can easily lead to the total trivialization of law—if law is everywhere it is nowhere.'

multidimensional,[52] but here his unorthodox broadening of the scope of the concept of law is the most relevant. He claimed that the contemporary concept of law, reflecting habits of professional jurists (he called it law in the juridical sense), did not denote an appropriate class of phenomena upon which an adequate theory could be built, since it covered an eclectic and heterogeneous group consisting of intra-state law and international law as well. Despite the obvious fact, he observed, that international law (and even some norms of intra-state law) does not enjoy an element of coercion, traditional jurists used to define law as the norms issued and sanctioned by the state authority. Due to the above-mentioned eclectic character of law in juridical sense, legal theories that are based on it must be ambivalent, and also false, since they cannot be true in reference to both categories they include. They also must be limping, because what is true to these categories (that is, that they are positive law and both have imperative-attributive character) is not specific for them and refers to far broader class of phenomena.[53]

Of particular significance is Petrażycki's criticism directed at state and coercive definitions of law, which at that time usually walked hand in hand. He claimed that such definitions involve a vicious circle because

> qua phenomena, the state, organs of state power, and the state's approval are all conditioned by the existence of a complicated system of legal norms: which suggests to us that a philosophical definition of the state requires an anterior workable definition of the concept of law.[54]

Moreover, Petrażycki believed that accepting a state theory of law leads to a substantial limitation of the field of legal studies.

> The introduction into any concept of law of so incidental a circumstance as the attitude of the state towards it, let alone the elevation of such a characteristic to an essential status, must lead us to be deprived of much rich and instructive material: of all those legal phenomena, in fact, which have been produced or are in the process of being produced outside the state, independent of the state, and before the first appearance of the state. It further restricts our field of vision to that afforded by the . . . narrow-minded official-clerical perspective.[55]

In Petrażycki's opinion this narrow-minded perspective of traditional, state-centred legal theory resulted, among others, in its limiting the scope of legal subjects. For him from theoretical, but also even from historical and comparative points of view, legal capacity, both in its attributive and imperative aspect, is to be ascribed not only to human beings (including the dead) and juristic persons, but also to beings superior to humans (God or gods, angels) and to beings inferior to them, like animals, plants, or even inanimate objects. Thus he rejected the maxim *omne jus hominum*

[52] Wróblewski, n.29, above. [53] Petrażycki, n.10, above, 142 ff.

[54] *Teoria prawa i państwa w związku z teorią moralności* [Theory of Law and the State in Connection with a Theory of Morality], Vol. I (Warsaw, 1959), 368.

[55] *Ibid*, 370. *Cf.* Rodolfo Sacco, 'One Hundred Years of Comparative Law' (2001) 75 *Tulane Law Review* 1159, 1170: 'Legal science was paralyzed for a long time by legal statism.'

causa constitutum est as, for example, Christopher D. Stone, Steven M. Wise, or Paul Shiff Berman do today.[56] In his opinion, due to the tendency of widening the subjective scope of the solidarity principle, 'certain moral and legal obligations with reference to animals will become the common ethical property of all mankind.'[57]

Official and Unofficial Law

According to Petrażycki the state law occupies very limited, even if quite important, space on the legal scene. What positivist jurists called law and equated with the whole legal universe he termed 'official law' (law 'to be applied and sustained by representatives of the state authority in accordance with their duty to serve society') and distinguished from 'unofficial law', which 'does not possess this significance in the state'.[58] Being based on extra-psychological criteria, even more (the one which Petrażycki himself considered 'incidental'),[59] this distinction is evidently inconsistent with the general premises of his theory of law.[60] He was aware of this shortcoming and therefore considered the distinction much less important than another one he had proposed—that of positive and intuitive law, which will be discussed later. The former distinction, contained implicitly in the writings of several other contemporary scholars,[61] resulted from Petrażycki's negative point of reference, which can be termed legal 'etatism', legal centralism, or legal monism, and from the necessity of confronting his own concept of law with one he rejected. Besides, having found the statist concept of law too narrow and thus inadequate, he quite naturally was inclined to expose what his unofficial law had in common with its official counterpart rather than what distinguished one from another. For him, from the theoretical point of view, there are no essential differences between the state law of the Tsarist empire, normative systems of Russian 'thieves in the law', and systems, of rules governing the life of any family, or at least such differences that would make it unsound to include those systems in one class concept.

Anyway, it was Petrażycki who in his pluralistic theory of legal phenomena, conceptualized the notions of official and unofficial law, and it was his followers

[56] References to their work can be found in Krzysztof Motyka, 'Zwierzęta na ławie oskarżonych i ich prawa (człowieka?)' [Animals at Trial and Their (Human?) Rights], in *Księga Jubileuszowa Profesora Tadeusza Jasudowicza* [The Jubilee Volume for Professor Tadeusz Jasudowicz] (Toruń, 2004), 315.

[57] Petrażycki, n.10, above, 82.

[58] *Ibid*, 139. Since official law is 'better adapted to satisfy the damands of the attributive nature of law', it is 'law of higher sort than unofficial law'. *Ibid*, 139.

[59] See the quotation accompanying n.54, above.

[60] It would be profitable to redefine the distinction by removing its reference to the state and in this way making it applicable to each legal system/subsystem, including those of the mafia or the family. Such an attempt was undertaken by Roman Szydłowski, *Siła i prawo* [Force and the Law] (Kraków, 1946), 74–5, and then by Sorokin, 'The Organized Group (Institution) and Law', in Sayre, n.17, above, 697.

[61] On 'law not necessarily professional or official' one could learn from, e.g. Frederick Pollock, who observed that 'clubs and societies have their laws; there are laws of cricket and laws of whist.' 'The Nature and Meaning of Law' (1894) 10 *Law Quarterly Review* 228, 230, 234.

who attempted to improve this distinction. Strangely enough, students of legal pluralism who employ these terms seem not to know his contribution and to the knowledge of the writer his name has never appeared in the pages of the *Journal of Legal Pluralism and Unofficial Law*.

Positive and Intuitive Law

As stated above, Petrażycki attached much more significance to his distinction, based on psychological criteria, between positive and intuitive law. Positive law is represented by those legal experiences that comprise ideas of so-called normative facts (actual or otherwise), and intuitive law by experiences lacking such ideas. From the 'projection point of view' one can describe positive law as rules referring to a normative fact and intuitive law as rules lacking such a reference.[62]

The distinction being discussed was followed by comparison characteristic of both species of legal phenomena and their interactions, analogous to the characteristic of law and morality. According to one of Petrażycki's observations, rules of intuitive law, not being limited by any normative fact, are experienced as resulting from the very nature of things—natural, just, universally valid. Therefore, in the case of conflict with rules of positive law, intuitive law, which Petrażycki equated with the sense of justice, eventually wins. In Petrażycki's explanation of the phenomenon of revolution, conflict between the two species of law plays the central role.[63] He also discussed the less spectacular, unnoticeable, everyday influence of intuitive law on positive law, including official law, with an emphasis on the role of the former in what we used to call the application of law. He was, however, far from idealizing intuitive law and pointed out that it can be, and sometimes is, less progressive than positive law or, to the contrary, too progressive for a particular society at a given time, and thus, dysfunctional for it.

For Petrażycki the name of positive law applies equally both to legal experiences (or norms) relating to official normative facts: statutes, judicial verdicts, administrative decisions, and the like, as well as to experiences (norms) where the normative function was discharged by a normative fact of unofficial character, for example the command of a family member or a guardian, even in cases where such facts (he cited as an example a contract with the devil), had only psychic existence.

Petrażycki's notion of normative facts, as that of law, is purely formal—it covers anything that is referred to by an agent as the source of the norm. Moreover, this same fact can have a normative character for one person, while not for another, also aware of it, the latter not experiencing any normative judgment. It is also possible that a given fact raises a moral experience in one person and a legal experience in another, as well as that in the course of time the status of this fact

[62] Thus Petrażycki rejects the view of autonomic character of morality and of heteronomous character of law. Both species of ethical experiences, but also of other statements or judgements, can be divided into the positive and intuitive. In law, however, the positive element is of much geater significance. See Petrażycki, n.10, above, 114.

[63] Max Laserson, 'Revolution und Recht' (1929) 8 *Zeitschrift für öffentliches Recht* 533.

changes in the mind of a given person. On the other hand, due to the above-mentioned unification tendency, imperative-attributive convictions of people are, basically, in agreement.

Petrażycki exposed a variety of normative facts: statutes, court decisions, precedents, *communis opinio doctorum*, legal expertise, legal maxims, contracts, customs and—more generally—behaviours of other persons, proverbs, programmes, promises, etc.[64] All of them, including those recognized as the sources of law by contemporary legal doctrine, were conceived by Petrażycki broadly. For instance, as examples of statutes he cites 'commands of deities, directives of ecclesiastical assemblies and authorities, directives of forebears, of councils of the elders and the like in the period proceeding the emergence of the state, commands of the master, father, mother, and so forth in domestic life, orders of ... directors, managers, or other authorities relative to private enterprises ... , directives of other private associations ... learned societies, political parties, criminal organizations, and so forth.'[65]

Ascribing the status of the legal equally to the experience of, say, a woman who finds herself obliged to pay for her shopping and to a man claiming to be, given his contract with devil, the owner of Trafalgar Square, incurred strong disapproval within a large part of the legal academe. It resulted from Petrażycki's critics' failure to keep in mind his distinction between theoretical and practical or, more precisely, normative positions, and exemplified their parochial point of view.[66] Petrażycki's definition of law as imperative-attributive experiences or rules was intended by its author as a purely descriptive, value-free theoretical concept without any implication of judgment, which might be thought to follow from their being described as legal. As his follower Jerzy Lande wrote:

The dogmatic jurist is accustomed to identify law and 'valid law' as one and the same thing, and to define law itself as some particular system of law supervised by official authority ... It is impossible for him to conceive that, besides legal dogmatics, with its own closed system of official law as the basis for normative judgements (court verdicts, administrative decisions), theory can be constructed capable of investigating the entire wealth and variety of real phenomena, with no need to claim that the contents of these phenomena have any 'validity' for the courts or other organs of state. Legal theorists in this respect lag behind scholars of linguistics, who are able to distinguish between the 'compulsory' grammatical language taught in schools which may serve as a template for judgements on the 'correctness' of the pupils' speech, and the very many linguistic phenomena of each country which are 'incorrect' if referred to those same grammatical rules. After all, one can investigate children's law and

[64] Each category generates its own law, and thus we can say not only on statute, customary or judicial law but also on proverbs law, programme law, promises law, and so on.

[65] Petrażycki, n.10, above, 252–3.

[66] See, e.g. E. Adamson Hoebel, 'Fundamental Legal Concepts as Applied to the Study of Primitive Law' (1942) 51 *Yale Law Journal* 951, 951; *idem*, 'Law and Anthropology' (1946) 32 *Virginia Law Review* 835, 836; Vilhelm Aubert, 'Case Studies of Law in Western Societies', in Laura Nader (ed.), *Law in Culture and Society* (Chicago, 1997), 273, 274, where the author calls doctrinal study of law 'parochial science'.

thieves' law just as well as children's slang and thieves' argot, without there being any question in either case that these are presented as the correct model.[67]

The Family as a Micro-Legal System

Petrażycki attempted to attract legal scientists to the study of what we call today private or small-scale social ordering, semi-autonomous social fields, or micro-legal systems.[68] Particularly, he encouraged them to seek empirical insight into the family[69]—'a broad and peculiar legal world which is awaiting investigation: a legal world with innumerable legal norms, obligations, and rights independent of what is written in the statutes, and solving thousand of questions unforeseen therein.'[70] Although he did not deny that to some extent the content and development of law governing family relations are common to all systems of law and that there are also great differences between the family normative orders, conditioned for example by the class structure, he accentuated an individual character of each of such orders. For him 'each family is a unique legal world, and each of those taking part in domestic life ... has his own particular position in the legal mentality which prevails in that family.'[71]

The child's room and the playground were of special interest to Petrażycki, who considered them excellent loci to observe and study experimentally the development of legal mentality or, as we would put it, legal socialization of the child.[72] He believed that to some extent factual data provided by such a study was of more general application, due to a kinship he saw between the child's legal psyche and that of 'the less advanced peoples or the (culturally) lower strata and classes of societies'.[73]

Social Functions and Operation of Law

Petrażycki's opposition to the paradigm of legal science of his time also manifested in his focus not on textual or normative reasoning, which is usually attributed

[67] *Studia z filozofii prawa* [Studies in Legal Philosophy] (Warsaw, 1959), 599–600. *Cf.* Tamanaha's (n.44, above, 304) hint at Santos's approach: 'It is also not clear what is gained, either analytically or instrumentally, by appending the label "law" to the informal, unwritten normative relations within the family ... [T]here is a political cost. Consider the society where the culture tacitly approves wife beating, while the state law makes it illegal ... This phraseology should give discomfort to opponents of domestic violence, for the reason that the term 'law often possesses symbolic connotations of right.'

[68] See, e.g. William M. Evan, 'Public and Private Legal Systems', in *idem* (ed.), *Law and Sociology* (New York, 1961), 165; Sally F. Moore, 'Law and Social Change: The Semi-Autonomous Social Field as An Appropriate Subject of Study' (1973) 7 *Law and Society Review* 719; Michael Reisman, 'Lining Up: The Microlegal System of Queues' (1985) 54 *University of Cincinnati Law Review* 417.

[69] Krzysztof Motyka, 'Petrażycki on Rights in the Family', in Andrzej Czynczyk and Jacek Kurczewski (eds), *Family, Gender, and Body in Law and Society Today* (Warsaw, 1990), 97.

[70] Petrażycki, n.10, above, 68. [71] *Ibid.*

[72] See, e.g. Kurczewski, 'Świat prawny dziecka' [Legal World of the Child] (1986) No. 2 *Psychologia wychowawcza* 155; Motyka, n.69, above. [73] Petrażycki, n.10, above, 70.

to the lawyer's perspective, but on functions and operation of law, commonly considered the subject-matter of the sociologist. In this area, too, his perspective was an unorthodox one, since unlike, for example, that of American Realists, and of jurists in general, it was not court- or dispute resolution-centred.[74]

Criticism of the Court-Centred Approach

Petrażycki was careful to warn against understanding law as functioning only to defend the interests of one or other category of subjects, or to resolve conflicts. He always thought this outlook, the view from the bench, was conditioned by legal professionals' dogmatic attitudes. It showed a human tendency to miss seeing subjects and phenomena in their normally functioning state. This mistaken, one-sided perspective also appeared in legal terminology's habit of only ever meaning legal proceedings when speaking of 'the practice of law'. In reality, what we see there, according to Petrażycki, is not the normal, healthy functioning of the legal order and its elements, but rather the very opposite. In his opinion

> the true practice of civil or any law is not to be found in the courts, but altogether elsewhere. Its practitioners are not judges and advocates, but each individual citizen, each national economy taken singly or as a member of the world economic order, each individual nation taken singly or as part of the world community, [all the individual] units of humankind as it is, was and will be.[75]

Accordingly, the essential and basic function of law is manifested not in conflict resolution, but in the direction of human behaviour, mass and individual.[76] This shift in approaching the problem of law's functions and operation, reflected in Petrażycki's removal of any reference to the dispute resolution from his definition of law, has been appreciated particularly by Adam Podgórecki. In his words:

> This is a very significant observation. It changes the classical outlook on the functioning of law and drives us to the following declaration: the main social agent is the law which acts at any moment and in various social contexts in the most numerous human interrelations occurring all the time everywhere (like unconflicting contracts, transactions, offers, determinations of terms, conditions of payments, agreements, loans, etc.). Thus, it is not . . . the law in courts, offices and bureaux of solicitors, though the most conspicuous, which is charged with everyday but significant social tasks.[77]

[74] *Cf.* Gidon Gottlieb, 'Relationism: Legal Theory for a Relational Society' (1983) 50 *University of Chicago Law Review* 567, 569. See Maria Borucka-Arctowa, *Die gesellschaftliche Wirkung des Rechts*, transl. Michał Miedziński (Berlin, 1985).

[75] Petrażycki, *Wstęp do nauki polityki prawa* [Introduction to the Science of Legal Policy] ([1897] Warsaw, 1968), 138–39.

[76] *Cf.* Joseph Raz, 'The Functions of Law', in A.W.B. Simpson (ed.), *Oxford Essays in Jurisprudence* (Oxford, 1973).

[77] Podgórecki, n.4 , above, 219. *Cf.* Iredell Jenkins, *Social Order and the Limits of Law* (Princeton, 1980), 9: 'Law is very like an iceberg; only one-tenth of its substance appears above the social surface in the explicit form of documents, institutions and professions, while the nine-tenths of its substance

From the very beginning of his scholarly career Petrażycki pointed out that law was a psychic factor of social life and that its operation was of a motivational and pedagogic character. In his earliest German monographs[78] he proposed to interpret Roman and Civil law from the socio-economic perspective and tried to expose the interrelations of institutions of civil law and economic efficacy and the culture of society as well as to prove that the former ones, including the institution of division of income with a change of usufructaries, which was then of prime concern to him, were unconsciously and unintentionally functional for the national economy. This perspective has been applied in his critique of the drafts of the German Civil Code.[79]

Motivational Operation of Law

According to Petrażycki, the motivational operation of law[80] consists in its stimulation both of definite motivations in the human psyche inclining people to a given behaviour, while in the second, as a long-term consequence of this, it forms and perpetuates attitudes and convictions in individuals and for society as a whole. He thought the same influence could also be found in other normative systems, particularly morality. However, he stressed, law's power in this respect significantly exceeded that of moral or aesthetic norms because of its imperative-attributive character.

Petrażycki discerned a number of types of legal motivation (and consequently of legal consciousness), partly mirrored in his classification of position, presented above. He assigned the first place to what he called basic, specifically legal motivation (active, passive, and neutral), where the main role is played by awareness of one's or others' legal rights and/or duties. He also identified several types of indirect legal motivation based most often on an assessment of profit and loss. Among them he discussed the so-called free legal motivation, where law engenders a rationale for behaviour not in itself specifically commanded by its provisions. Such would be, in Petrażycki's own example, the 'selfless' motivation at work in the direction of private economic and financial enterprises within a free market economic system. While law does not prohibit consumption of the entire gain of an enterprise or prescribe a duty of optimizing economic activity, nonetheless, in specific consequence of a system of law as a whole, and its family and inheritance law in particular, the economic life of a country invariably comes to be ordered by its

that supports the visible fragment leads a sub-aquatic existence, living in the habits, attitudes, emotions and aspirations of men.'

[78] *Die Fruchtverteilung beim Wechsel der Nutzungsberechtigen* (Berlin, 1892); *Die Lehre vom Einkommen*, Vols. I–II (Berlin, 1893–1895).

[79] While discussing social action of law and legal policy, he plainly had legal norms or normative facts, not legal experiences, in mind. See, e.g. Jan Gorecki, 'Leon Petrażycki' in Gorecki, n.3, above, 13.

[80] *Cf.* Kazimierz Opałek, '*The Motivational Operation of Law*' (1969) 2 *Archivum Iuridicum Cracoviense* 34.

people in a responsible and socially useful manner, which also contributes to economic development of the country. Abolition of, for example, inheritance rights would inevitably lead at the very least to the undermining of that motivation and detrimental economic consequences all round. In this way, Petrażycki sought to emphasize how law discharges what is eminently its organizational function, premised on the organization of society (with the phenomenon of authority playing a particular role), while at the same time having a distributive function (with the phenomenon of property playing a particular role). He discussed in detail functions of law and its operation, including conflicts of motives, with reference both to the free market economy and to the centralized (socialist) system.[81]

Educative Operation of Law

Petrażycki was convinced that the cultural-educative or pedagogical role of law is more important than the motivational one, even if, as mentioned above, the former is a further effect of the latter. He discussed three psychological laws that, in his opinion, have a fundamental role to play there: the law of learning, the law of habit formation, and the law of retroaction, but of more relevance here is his exposition of the importance of raising the sense of rights, which he called also attributive or active legal consciousness. He called for a harmonious legal socialization, that is for developing both the sense of rights and the sense of duties, and warned against atrophy or hypertrophy of any of the two elements of legal mentality, but due to its focus on law and, perhaps, his own liberal political preferences,[82] he emphasized the former. Having stated that educative effects of law depend on the content of legal rules and the level of their fit to a given society and thus can be positive and negative as well, he pointed out that in one respect these effects for individuals and societies result from its very attributiveness irrespective of its content. Consciousness of one's right, he observed, not only shapes our sense of dignity and our civic culture, but also builds other virtues that promote individuals' and societies' prosperity:

> The ... proper active legal consciousness is ... important in pedagogy from the point of view of the development of occupational and economic efficiency. It communicates the firmness and the confidence, the energy, and the initiative, essential for life. A child brought up in an atmosphere of arbitrary caprice (however beneficent and gracious), with no definite assignment to him of a particular sphere of rights ..., will not be trained to construct and carry out the plans of life with assurance. In the economic field, particularly, he will be apathetic, act at random, and procrastinate in the hope of favourable 'chances', help from another, alms, gifts, and the like.[83]

[81] Summarized by Jacek Kurczewski, *O badaniu prawa w naukach społecznych* [A Study of Law by the Social Sciences] (Warsaw, 1977), 158–9.

[82] See Walicki, n.9, above.

[83] Petrażycki, n.10, above, 99.

This is why not only parents and educators, but also law-makers, or government in general, should pay attention to rights. Petrażycki continues:

The evolution, in the masses, of a 'citizen' type of a special and ideal character—possessing economic efficiency, energy, and initiative—depends upon the structure of law and the direction of legal policy, and in particular and especially upon developing the principle of legality and a system of subjective rights which are strong, stable, and guaranteed against arbitrary conduct (instead of hanging upon the exercise of a gracious discretion) .... Legality is a condition essential to the inculcation of these traits of character.[84]

Thus law, not only criminal, but also constitutional, civil, and even tax law, is the 'omnipresent teacher'[85] of individuals and of whole societies, a very good one that—let's say—intuitively, adapts his methods and instruments to ever changing mentality of successive generations of students. Petrażycki believed that legal history demonstrates the feedback between law and human character, that directs them to 'the ideal of active love'. As he wrote:

Law (together with the other factors of socio-psychic life) ... influences the development of human mind and changes human character in the direction of better adaptation to social life but is itself changed in conformity with these psychic changes and adapted thereto. [86]

This fundamental tendency of legal development, more precisely of legal progress, manifests itself in three particular tendencies: the tendency to growing demands of law, the tendency to motivate change, and the tendency to lessen motivational pressure (within a given motivation):

The most recent legal systems require from the citizens more in the sense of socially rational conduct than did earlier systems of law which were adapted to a more primitive mentality, and attain the required conduct by acting upon the loftier sides of human character. They make use of results already attained, and rest on qualities of mass character on which earlier systems of legal motivation—adjusted to a more coarse and socially less fitting mentality—could not rest. This may be illustrated by the transition ... from the system of slavery—from slave labor with its primitive and coarse motivation (the whip of overseers, the master's right to punish by death, and so forth)—to the system of free labor, economic freedom, and competition (independent free motivation). This is a symptom and a product of the cultural advance of human masses.[87]

The better the man, the milder the law for him—this is a quintessence of Petrażyckian philosophy of legal history, or even his philosophy of history in general, in which one can hear a Hegelian ring *à la* Joseph Kohler.[88] Again, it is law that

[84] *Ibid*, 99.

[85] *Per* Brandeis J in *Olmstead* v. *United States*, 277 U.S. 438, 485. *Cf.*, e.g. Harry W. Jones, 'The Creative Power and Function of Law in Historical Perspective' (1963) 17 *Vanderbilt Law Review* 135, P.S. Atiyah, 'From Principles to Pragmatism: Changes in the Function of the Judicial Process and the Law' (1980) 65 *Iowa Law Review* 1249, 1272 (on the law's 'hortatory' function).

[86] *Ibid*, 328. [87] *Ibid.*

[88] E.g. *The Philosophy of Law*, transl. Adalbert Albrecht (Boston, 1914).

operating as the main factor of Civilization (*Kultur*) stars in Petrażyckian theory of humanity's progress. This brings us to his most cherished idea of legal policy.

Legal Policy

The entire scholarly contribution of Petrażycki, especially on social evolution and causal dependencies of law, was intended above all as the basis of a new legal discipline of a teleological character—that of legal policy. The essence of legal policy, outlined in his German works, with emphasis on its sub-discipline, civil law policy (*Civilpolitik*), Petrażycki saw in

> scientifically grounded prediction of the consequences that may be anticipated or hoped for from the introduction of specific legal provisions, and [in] elaboration of principles applicable to a system of valid law to produce desired results.[89]

Thus, legal policy was meant as a kind of social engineering through the law,[90] the one, however, different from its technical, short-term oriented and axiologically neutral versions. To the contrary, it was linked to his vision of social evolution and its ultimate aim: 'the totally socialized character, total domination of active love among men.'[91] In his lofty exposition:

> the mission of future legal policy . . . is to be the conscious guidance of humanity in that very direction in which it sought hitherto to move itself through unconscious empirical adaptation, and the acceleration and improvement of the trend towards that radiant future ideal.[92]

Apparently, legal policy so understood needs the assistance of sociology and such a conviction, perhaps, was among the motives that moved Petrażycki to become, like, for example Weber, a lawyer-turned-sociologist.

Sociology

A good deal of sociology can be found in what has already been said here about Petrażycki's work. His own students, like Sorokin or Lande,[93] in their exposition of Petrażyckian sociology, discussed his theory of law which was quite legitimate, due to the fact that Petrażyckian law norms come into existence through process

[89] Petrażycki, n.30, above, 13. See, e.g. Hugh W. Babb, 'Petrazhitskii: Science of Legal Policy and Theory of Law' (1937) 17 *Boston University Law Review* 793; Andrzej Kojder, 'Legal Policy: The Contribution of Leon Petrażycki' (1994) No. 2 (106) *Polish Sociological Review* 155;. Stanisław Czepita, 'Theory of Law and Legal Policy in the Works of Leon Petrażycki,' in Peter Koller, Csaba Varga and Ota Weinberger (eds), *Theoretische Grundlagen der Rechtspolitik* (Stuttgart 1992), 117.

[90] 'Social Engineering through Law' in Gorecki, n.3, above, ch. 8.

[91] Petrażycki, n.30, above, 15. [92] *Idem*, n.75, above, 16.

[93] Sorokin, n.9, above; Lande, 'Sociology of Petrażycki' in Gorecki, n.3, above, 23. See also Maria Borucka-Arctowa, 'Poglądy socjologiczne Leona Petrażyckiego' [Sociological Views of Leon Petrazycki] (1974) No. 1 *Studia Socjologiczne* 5; Pałecki, n.8. above.

of interaction and are responsible for making social groups, the society, and the state. One could also add here his analysis of diffusion of cultures and of legal and other cultural transplants, his division of cultures into complementary and disparate[94] and so on. His standpoint was typically evolutionary, and Darwin was its main point of reference, but he took into account also theories of Marx, Tarde, Gumplowicz, and Sombart, that he found wrong due to their single-factor interpretations of social change.[95] Unfortunately, three manuscripts of his sociology were lost forever during the turmoil of the war and one has to rely on skeletal presentations by his students and their notes of his lectures.

Following his general methodology of sciences, Petrażycki questioned the vision of sociology as a concrete-individual, idiographic science. In his opinion it also cannot be a theory of society or of 'the social'. As Lande remembered it:

> The subject is 'the social process', understood as changes in individual and group experiences, and in social behaviour, which occur in the course of social adaptation. With some reservations, sociology may be called the theory of social development or the development of culture. So conceived, it will be located on the level of generality immediately higher than the theory of the origin and the development of law, morality, state, language, religion, and so on.[96]

Thus Petrażycki rejected a vision of sociology as social statics, left by him to less general theories (of law, morality, religion) and limited it to a social dynamic. Its essence he saw in the process of social adjustment, apart from which he mentioned individual (egoistic) and species' (philocentric) adjustment. According to Petrażycki, social adjustment results from interactions, so-called 'intellectual-emotional infections', that take place within any social group, and between them. Every group is an 'enormous laboratory of evaluations' where through imitation, gestures and other bodily movements, language, etc, people exchange their experiences and individual judgments:

> In the course of interactions, individual evaluations undergo a process similar to the struggle for existence and natural selection: those which are not favourable for the group are eliminated, and only evaluations 'resultant' from social experience remain . . . The adjustment is oriented toward the good of the group, within which is occurring an intellectual and impulsive exchange.[97]

This is why Petrażycki considered sociocentric adaptation, as compared with the two others more than brilliant or 'supra-congenial'. Law as well as morality are 'crystallization' of this process, or due to its progressive character 'crystallization of love'. This, for him, is the essence of the whole culture.[98]

[94] *O dopełniających prądach kultury i prawach rozwoju handlu* [On the Complementary Cultural Currents and the Laws of the Development of the Trade] (Warsaw, 1936).

[95] Andrzej Kojder, 'Petrażycki Leon' in *Encyklopedia socjologii*, Vol. 3 (Warsaw, 2000), 100, 103.

[96] Lande, n.93, above, 29.

[97] *Ibid*, 35.

[98] See Petrażycki, n.75, above, 477. This optimistic picture seemed to be destroyed by the Bolshevik Revolution and other events in contemporary Europe. Some find it one of the reasons for Petrażycki's suicide on 15 May 1931.

Conclusion

Petrażycki's approach to law embodies, on the one hand, an anti-juridical methodological outlook,[99] manifested, among other ways, in the rejection of the lawyers' concept of law as a starting point of the formation of the legal theory, and in the discrediting of juristic theory of law in general.[100] Nobody went further than he did in a breaking away from, to use Cotterrell's phrase, 'the claustrophobic world of legal scholarship.'[101] As Denzin observed, 'Petrażycki took the study of law out of the courtroom and away from lawyers and legal scholars and placed it squarely inside the province of the sociologist.'[102]

On the other hand, however, by bringing law and its study 'directly into the sphere of everyday face-to-face interaction'[103] and by proposing perhaps the broadest understanding of law ('nearly everything and anything is law'[104]), he, like nobody else, emphasized the juridical (in his own meaning) dimension of life and culture and thus exhibited what can be called juridical[105] or even pan-juridical *Weltanschauung*.[106] As exemplified by the work of his direct and indirect disciples, despite (or, perhaps, due to?) its psychological angle, Petrażycki's interdisciplinary contribution[107] is full of potential for sociological inquiry into the capitals and the much more interesting countryside of law's empire.

[99] Walicki, n.9, above, 216.

[100] Jan M. Broekman, 'Law, Anthropology and Epistemology,' in Eugenio Bulygin *et al.* (eds), *Man, Law and Modern Forms of Life* (Dordrecht, 1985), 13, 32 writes that 'it is generally accepted that a legal theoretician is a jurist who adjudicates upon theoretical and philosophical questions from the standpoint of legal dogmatics'. *Cf.* e.g. William Twining, 'Some Jobs for Jurisprudence' (1974) 1 *British Journal of Law and Society*, 149.

[101] Cotterrell, n.25, above, 633.

[102] Denzin, n.6, above, 74.

[103] *Ibid*, 78.

[104] *Ibid.*

[105] Kazimierz Opałek, 'Leon Petrażycki's Theory and the Contemporary Theory of Law' (1973) 6 *Archivum Iuridicum Cracoviense*, 78.

[106] Walicki, n.9, above, 216.

[107] Kazimierz Opałek, 'Teoria Petrażyckiego jako program integracji prawoznawstwa z innymi naukami spodecznymi' [Theory of Petrażycki as a Programme of Intergation of Law with Other Social Science] in Eli Frydman (ed.), *Problemy kultury i wychowania* [Issues of Culture and Education] (Warsaw, 1963). Recently the point has been made by Douglas W. Vick, 'Interdisciplinarity and the Discipline of Law' (2004) 31 *Journal of Law and Society* 163, 182–3.

9

Social Dynamics of Regulatory Interactions: An Exploration of Three Sociological Perspectives

Bettina Lange

This chapter argues that sociological analysis[1] of the social still matters for understanding regulation through law. Hence, it explores how new ways of imagining the social can shed further light on the social relations which are engendered when legal regulation is created and implemented. The chapter focuses on actor-network theory, sociological and cultural perspectives on economic transactions as well as sociological analysis of emotions. The first, introductory section of the chapter discusses the claim that there is an 'end to social relations' and argues that the social has been and still is crucial for understanding legal regulation. The second shows in more detail how an analysis of regulatory agency and networks can be advanced through actor-network theory's perspective. The third section of the chapter illustrates how attention to the social in economic life highlights close interconnections between law and the economy through shared normative practices. Moreover, new organizational forms of social life, such as networks question the centrality of bureaucracies in legal regulation. In the fourth and final section of the chapter, attention turns from analytical to normative issues. The discussion aims to illustrate the relevance of a sociological analysis of emotions for understanding the purposes and values which can inform legal regulation and which it may realize.

Does Sociological Analysis Still Matter for Understanding Legal Regulation?

This chapter explores social dynamics of regulatory interactions, although it has been argued that we may be witnessing an 'implosion of the social' and an 'end to

[1] For a further discussion of how the knowledge field of sociology has been constructed by jurists see Roger Cotterrell, this volume, pp.16–31.

social relations'.[2] The social[3] has been defined as the particular way in which populations think about and act upon their collective experience.[4] It comprises: 'the sum of the bonds and relations between individuals and events—economic, moral and political—within a more or less bounded territory', usually a nation-state and national economy, 'governed by its own laws'.[5] Since the mid-nineteenth century the social has been the subject of political programmes, including the management of national economies, aimed at 'social justice, rights and solidarity'.[6] The welfare state became one of its institutional expressions[7] and modernist social science knowledge contributed to constituting and stabilizing the social sphere.

The idea that there is an end to 'the social' has been contested. First, it has been suggested that the social is just undergoing significant transformation.[8] From this perspective a unified, homogenous social sphere is fragmenting into more tenuous bonds[9] which arise primarily in a local context as the particular commitments which individuals take on with regard to their families and communities.[10] Hence, heterogeneous, including imagined and virtual, communities are now the new spaces upon which advanced liberal government acts.[11] Secondly, from an ethno-methodological perspective there is no pre-given social domain, which can be declared dead or transformed. Instead, the social comes into existence through everyday practices of constructing, grasping, and naming it in which social actors, including sociologists, still engage. Hence, claims about the end of the social should be treated with caution.[12] In fact, the social is particularly important for

[2] J. Baudrillard, *In the Shadow of the Silent Majorities or the End of the Social and Other Essays*, translated by Paul Foss, Paul Patton and John Johnston (New York, 1983), 4, 82.

[3] In classical social theory, it has been distinguished from the natural and the technical world. See Barbara Herrnstein Smith and Arkady Plotnitsky, 'Introduction: Networks and Symmetries, Decidable and Undecidable' (1995) 94(2) *The South Atlantic Quarterly* 371–88. In some contemporary perspectives, however, it is considered as interactive with and even stabilized through its association with natural and technical domains. See John Law and Annemarie Mol, 'Notes on Materiality and Sociality' (1995) 43 *The Sociological Review* 276.

[4] Nikolas Rose, *Powers of Freedom: Reframing Political Thought* (Cambridge, 1999), 101.

[5] Nikolas Rose, 'The Death of the Social? Re-figuring the Territory of Government' (1996) 25(3) *Economy and Society* 328.

[6] *Ibid*, 329.

[7] Baudrillard, n.2, above, 41; Rose, n.5, above, 327.

[8] See, e.g. Rose, n.5, above, 327–56; Scott Lash and John Urry, *Economies of Signs and Space* (London, 1994), 320; George Pavlich, 'Introduction: Transforming Images: Society, Law and Critique', in G. Wickham and G. Pavlich, *Rethinking Law, Society and Governance: Foucault's Bequest* (Oxford, 2001), 4.

[9] Lash and Urry, n.8, above, 16; Niels Albertsen and Bülent Diken, *What is the Social?*, at http://www.comp.lancs.ac.uk/fss/sociolgy/papers/albertsen-diken-what-is-the-social.pdf. Site last visited 1 October 2005.

[10] Rose, n.5, above, 327. Zygmunt Bauman, 'Viewpoint: Sociology and Postmodernity' (1988) 36(4) *Sociological Review* 800.

[11] Rose, n.5, above, 333; Mike Featherstone and Scott Lash, 'Globalization, Modernity and the Spatialization of Social Theory: An Introduction', in M. Featherstone, S. Lash and R. Robertson (eds), *Global Modernities* (London, 1995), 7; Lash and Urry, n.8, above, 3; Pavlich, n.8, above, 2.

[12] Cotterrell, n.1, above, 17, suggests that the social is still meaningful as various 'fundamental types of human relations', which can find expression in different forms of community within and beyond nation states.

understanding the dynamics of legal regulation. Its analysis advances debates because it allows us to link inquiries into legal regulation to wider debates about the nature of law, its relative autonomy, and its role in social change.

The social has featured in various ways in debates on legal regulation. First, it has been an important springboard for conceptualizing law. Sometimes law has been imagined quite like the social. Once a homogeneous, centred, unified social domain had been imagined, normative orders, rules, and regulations seemed to be the natural social forms to construct and organize this ordered social space. Legal regulation has also been considered as key to the generation of social order[13] and hence has even been equated with it.[14] At other times, law has been imagined as more distinct from the social. Here, the social is a counterfoil against which the specifically legal aspects of regulation are rendered visible. This is reflected in language which strains to keep the social and the legal separate, for instance through reference to 'social factors' and 'contexts' in the creation and implementation of legal regulation.

Secondly, the social has also been important for tracing the historical origins of modern legal regulation. The construction of a social sphere in Britain in the nineteenth century engendered legal regulation which curbed and legitimized private economic activity, through public health, pollution control, competition, as well as health and safety at work regulation.[15] In the early decades of the twentieth century, legal regulation reflected even the rise of a more far-reaching social rights discourse in Britain.[16]

Thirdly, in parallel with Nikolas Rose's argument about the rise of community as a new way of conceptualizing the social, also regulatory communities increasingly feature in the literature on legal regulation. They replace the traditional terminology of regulators and regulated, state, and civil society. Regulatory communities consist of a range of governmental and non-governmental actors, sometimes including NGOs, who 'share in the state's authority to make decisions'.[17] Communities also provide new accountability structures. For instance, by incorporating private sector management techniques in the delivery of public services, public bureaucracies are meant to become more accountable to service consumers' communities.

To summarize, this chapter starts from the idea that the social still matters for analysing legal regulation. It has been described as a territory through which governmentality practices are deployed,[18] but I want to focus here on its relational

[13] Bridget Hutter, *Regulation and Risk, Occupational Health and Safety on the Railways* (Oxford, 2001), 19.

[14] *Ibid*, 20.

[15] For instance, workmens' compensation, factory inspections and restrictions on child labour were introduced in Britain during the second half of the nineteenth century. See Rose, n.4, above, 112. In the late nineteenth century the British state began to regulate the railway industry. See Hutter, n.13, above, 4.

[16] Rose, n.4, above, 120.

[17] Julia Black, 'Critical Reflections on Regulation' at http://www.lse.ac.uk/collections/CARR/pdf/Disspaper4.pdf, site last visited 1 October 2005.

[18] Rose, n.5 above, 332, 333. See also Russell Hogg and Kerry Carrington, 'Governing Rural Australia: Land, Space and Race', in Pavlich and Wickham, n.8, above, 47 who describe the

rather than spatial aspects. I use the term 'the social' to describe the processes which are generated when formal law is created and implemented. Hence, the social is not defined as a space external to and separate from law, upon which legal regulation acts, but is considered as integral to regulating through law. Legal processes are conceptualized as social relations, including their local performance.

Why this emphasis on a relational, rather than spatial analysis of the social? It helps, first, to distinguish an instrumental perspective of legal regulation where law imposes itself on the social sphere and colonizes its life worlds.[19] Secondly, a relational analysis should facilitate a critique of the social. The image of a concrete, social territory with specific boundaries may aid its reification.[20] Holding on to the space of a tangible social sphere may be justified for normative reasons. The image of a social space can affirm the social as a repository of warm, humanist ideals, in opposition to the cold Darwinian competitive struggles of capitalist economic relations. But this perspective neglects that governance through a social domain has enabled invidious forms of micro social control. Hence, the association of a social sphere with human flourishing has been questioned.[21] Thirdly, spatial analysis—the social as the doughnut around the legal hole—'law in context'—may not further advance understanding of legal regulation. Close to Durkheim, social facts are considered here as an external constraining reality with which law engages. But this can be challenged from a semiotic perspective which abandons the idea of a pre-constituted social environment and distinctions between content and context. Legal texts and discourses can also define their contexts. Hence, more may be gained by exploring the various techniques through which content and context are built up together.[22] Fourthly, an overtly spatial conception of the social may imply a static, orderly, and thus conservative conception of a unified social field.[23] The emphasis in this chapter, however, is on the dynamics of legal regulation, brought into focus through an analysis of fluid, messy, and heterogeneous social relations.

In particular I want to explore three sociological perspectives which help to imagine the social in legal regulation in new ways and should complement the

social as 'the domain, the horizons and the resources for governing populations in liberal societies'. In fact, spatial metaphors and quasi-geographical images, such as field(s), habitus and boundaries, are increasingly referred to in sociological thinking. They replace a more temporal mode of analysis and traditional sociological concepts, such as social reality and structure. Spatial dimensions are nevertheless often linked to an analysis of social relations, such as in the archaeology of knowledge, the decentring of power relations and the stretching of social relations across time and space in globalization. See Rose n.5, above 330, 333, 343, 346; Featherstone and Lash, n.11, above, 1, 23, and Ilana Friedrich Silber, 'Space, Fields, Boundaries: The Rise of Spatial Metaphors in Contemporary Sociological Theory' (1995) 62(2) *Social Research* 323–55.

[19] David Ingram, *Habermas and the Dialectic of Reason* (New Haven, 1987), ch. 8.

[20] It also seems to exclude the possibility that the social can perform various types of spaces in which legal regulation can unfold. See Annemarie Mol and John Law, 'Regions, Networks and Fluids: Anaemia and Social Topology' (1994) *Social Studies of Science* 643.

[21] M. Dean, *Governmentality, Power and Rule in Modern Society* (London, 1999); G. Burchell, C. Gordon, and P. Miller, *The Foucault Effect: Studies in Governmentality* (London, 1991).

[22] Bruno Latour, 'On Actor-Network Theory: A Few Clarifications' (1996) *Soziale Welt* 374.

[23] Silber, n.18, above, 337, 339.

legal regulation literature which has already drawn on legal-doctrinal, neo-classical economic and a range of political science perspectives.[24] The three perspectives explored here are sociological analysis of emotions, actor-network theory, as well as some writing in economic sociology. Sociological analysis of emotions and actor-network theory attempt to develop new insights into the social, also by transcending traditional distinctions between structure and agency, macro- and micro-sociological approaches.[25] They whittle away at differentiations between social action which is internal to organized social life, such as a group or formal institution—located at a micro-level—and social structure which is external to bounded social entities, located at a macro-level, and thus acting upon them. Moreover, actor-network theory (ANT) extends understandings of the social by also considering materialities:

> ... these are material practices which extend beyond human beings, subjects and their meanings, and implicate also technical, architectural, geographical and corporeal arrangements [26]

Hence, ANT imagines the social more expansively. It considers interactions between human and non-human actants, such as a whole range of legal artefacts, files, formal statements, and courtrooms. This inclusion of materialities leads to new understandings of what constitutes a legal sphere. Moreover, interactions between human and non-human actors is clearly relevant to areas of legal regulation which involve law and technology[27] or law and nature interactions. Also sociological analysis of emotions broadens conceptions of the social to include aspects of interactions which have been traditionally relegated to a 'private' realm. Moreover, sociological analysis of emotions can also respond to the linguistic turn—the focus on communication—in legal regulation. Sociological analysis of emotions in communicative interactions can provide a critical perspective on communicative rationality. The latter has been advocated as a normative framework for legal regulation. Finally, sociological and cultural perspectives on economic transactions can further develop understandings of the social in regulatory law and economy interactions. They perceive economic transactions as cultural forms embedded in social practices and hence allow us to go beyond the abstract

[24] J. Black, 'Proceduralizing Regulation: Part I' (2000) 20 *Oxford Journal of Legal Studies* 598; S. Picciotto, 'Introduction: Reconceptualising Regulation in the Era of Globalization', in D. Campbell and S. Picciotto (eds), 'New Directions in Regulatory Theory' (2002) 29 (1) Special Issue *Journal of Law and Society* 3, 11.

[25] Michel Callon, 'Techno-Economic Networks and Irreversibility', in J. Law (ed.), *A Sociology of Monsters: Essays on Power, Technology and Domination* (London, 1991), 153.

[26] John Law 'Economics as Interference', in Paul du Gay and Michael Pryke (eds), *Cultural Economy* (London, 2002), 24.

[27] Policy debates have deliberated how compliance with legal regulation can be designed into technological processes, which are, for instance, subject to health and safety or environmental regulation. Can the meaning of law be hardwired into a plant? See, for example Silvia Gherardi and Davide Nicolini, 'To Transfer is to Transform: The Circulation of Safety Knowledge' (2000) 7(2) *Organization* 336; B. Lange, 'National Environmental Regulation? A Case-Study of Waste Management in England and Germany' (1999) 11(1) *Journal of Environmental Law* 73; Black, n.17, above, 14.

assumptions of neo-classical economics. They enable to see in detail how interactions between legal and economic processes proceed and how traditional understandings of organizations in economic life are changing. Hence, these three sociological perspectives are relevant for exploring further the social in regulatory interactions. But why focus on regulatory interactions?

Interactions between actors, organizations, and social systems have been considered as central to regulating through law.[28] From a micro-sociological, symbolic-interactionist perspective, relationships between enforcement officers and managers, and sometimes other employees—have come into focus.[29] Moreover, interactions between regulated and regulatory organizations, sometimes whole industries, such as the nursing home sector,[30] the paper and pulp industry,[31] and construction companies[32] have been analysed. On a macro-level, legal regulation has been perceived as interactions between entire social systems, such as the economy and law.

Moreover, emphasis on regulatory interactions as a dynamic process also anchors the inquiry into a key perspective in sociological analysis where social processes are understood as 'in motion' and 'in the making'.[33] Flows of goods, information, and communication in global networks are replacing the structured organization as an organizing feature of social life.[34]

In addition, the term 'regulatory interactions' draws attention to the increasingly reflexive nature of social action,[35] given also diminished trust in expert governance in risk societies.[36] Individuals are encouraged to take control of the normative and material resources of social life and to 'monitor' their own 'life narrative'[37] as traditional social structures, such as the Fordist labour process, trade unions, welfare institutions, and conventional church and family structures lose importance.[38] Hence, regulatory interactions include not just those between various social actors, but also reflexive and individualized 'action of the self on the self'.[39] Finally, focusing on regulatory interactions allows understanding legal regulation as a two-way dynamic in which regulation is often accompanied by the

[28] Black, n.17 above, 6, 14, 18; K. Hawkins, *Law as Last Resort* (Oxford, 2002), 51, 429; Hutter, n.13, above, 307.

[29] K. Hawkins, *Environment and Enforcement* (Oxford, 1984); Hawkins, n.28, above; B. Hutter, *The Reasonable Arm of the Law? The Law Enforcement Procedures of Environmental Health Officers* (Oxford, 1988).

[30] J. Braithwaite and V. Braithwaite, 'The Politics of Legalism: Rules versus Standards in Nursing—Home Regulation' (1995) 4 *Social and Legal Studies* 307–41.

[31] Robert A. Kagan, Neil Gunningham and Dorothy Thornton, 'Explaining Corporate Environmental Performance: How does Regulation Matter?' (2003) 37 *Law and Society Review* 51–90.

[32] F. Haines, *Corporate Regulation: Beyond 'Punish or Persuade'* (Oxford, 1997).

[33] Lash and Urry, n.8, above, 3. Rose, n.5, above, 332; Albertsen and Diken, n.9, above, 21, 22.

[34] Lash and Urry, n.8, above, 320.; Featherstone and Lash, n.11, above, 2.

[35] Bauman, n.10, above, 790; Lash and Urry, n.8, above, 3, 4.

[36] U. Beck, *Risk Society: Towards a New Modernity* (London, 1992).

[37] Lash and Urry, n.8, above, 314.

[38] Lash and Urry, n.8, above, 5.

[39] Dean, n.21, above, 12.

regulateds' resistance.[40] Resistance matters for understanding social relations involved in regulation through law because it can encompass not just attempts to block the exercise of power but also lead to new creative social action.[41] So what can the three sociological perspectives say about the social dynamics of regulatory interactions?

Changing Perceptions of Regulatory Agency and Networks through Actor-Network Theory (ANT)

ANT can help to think differently about agents and networks in legal regulation. But what does agency mean here and how is it involved in legal regulation? Agency describes undetermined and voluntary aspects of social action. It may be distinguished from structure which describes recurring patterns of social behaviour.[42] Structure and agency are at play in regulatory interactions:

> to govern is to structure the field of possible action, to act on our own or others' capacities for action.[43]

Hence, researchers have asked whether, to what extent and under what conditions regulators are and should be agents. Do they 'row' or just 'steer'?[44] Does regulators' agency actually hinder or facilitate legal regulation? Limits to regulators' agency, for instance through 'capture' by the regulated,[45] political and economic structures in conflict with regulatory goals[46] as well as 'creative compliance'[47] may hamper effective legal regulation. But too much agency for regulators, for instance through wide discretionary powers and over-zealous law enforcement,[48] has also been criticized as undermining legitimate and thus effective legal regulation. Often at least a better understanding of agency and various actors' motivations and constraints are perceived as conducive to achieving legal regulation. For instance, in the pursuit of a more detailed, fine-grained analysis, a homogeneous bloc of agency, such as 'the regulated company', 'industry' or 'regulatory bureaucracy', has been further differentiated. Variation in the reception of legal regulation

[40] Frank Pearce and Mariana Valverde, 'Introduction' (1996) 25(3) *Economy and Society* 307; Pat O'Malley, 'Indigenous Governance' (1996) 25(3) *Economy and Society* 323; Pavlich, above, n.8, 147.

[41] David Brown, 'Governmentality and Law and Order', in Pavlich and Wickham, above, n.8, 115.

[42] Gordon Marshall, *Oxford Dictionary of Sociology* (Oxford, 1998), 10.

[43] Dean, n.21, above, 14.

[44] D. Osborne and T. Gaebler, *Reinventing Government* (Reading, Mass., 1992), 25–48.

[45] T. Makkai and J. Braithwaite, 'In and Out of the Revolving Door: Making Sense of Regulatory Capture', in R. Baldwin, C. Scott and C. Hood (eds), *A Reader on Regulation* (Oxford, 1998), 173–91.

[46] Hutter, n.13, above, ix, 23; F. Pearce and S. Tombs, 'Ideology, Hegemony and Empiricism, The Compliance Theory of Regulation' (1990) 30 *British Journal of Criminology* 423–43.

[47] D. McBarnet and C. Whelan, 'The Elusive Spirit of the Law: Formalism and the Struggle for Legal Control' (1991) 54 *Modern Law Review* 848–73.

[48] E. Bardach and A. Kagan, *Going by the Book: The Problem of Regulatory Unreasonableness* (Philadelphia, 1982).

by different occupational groups within a company, by companies of different sizes, such as small and medium-size enterprises (SMEs) and large corporations, by front line enforcement staff, on the one hand, and managers in regulatory organizations on the other hand, by independent regulatory agencies or regulators working under close government control, have all been debated.[49] The recognition of these various agencies should help to identify different interests, goals, and behaviours which shed further light on how law regulates or fails to do so.[50] Moreover, bringing more and new actors on board has also been advocated as a possible solution to democracy and efficiency deficits in legal regulation. It has been argued that third parties, such as NGOs or external consultants, as well as employees, for instance in companies subject to health and safety regulation,[51] should be empowered to become additional actors, also because new actor coalitions may promote fuller compliance with legal regulation.[52]

Discussions of agency have also involved considerations of social structure. For instance, applications of new institutionalist economic analysis to regulatory decision-making, have considered actors as rule-bound, but also as pursuing rationally self-interested preferences.[53] Sometimes structure and agency have been perceived as two separate concepts along a vertical hierarchy where macro-level social structures shape micro-level agency. Increasingly, however, sociological perspectives have sought to de-differentiate structure and agency. They explore the morphology of the social world through networks, instead of asking how agency and structure construct social action.[54]

ANT, in particular, challenges most radically distinctions between structure and agency, resources for action and action itself.[55] Drawing also on semiotics, ANT suggests that not just meaning, but any social phenomena are performed through the relations in which they exist. Hence, agency is generated through networks. It is neither an innate quality of human actors, nor the result of their 'strategic intentions'.[56] It 'comes in a variety of forms'[57] because its nature and degree vary with the network's size and shape.[58] Hence, networks are heterogeneous and decentred. They consist of both human and non-human 'actors', such as cyborgs, market forces, machines, genes, discourses, the ozone-hole and animals.[59] Actors can only 'act' by becoming part of a network.

49 Hawkins, n.28, above. 50 Hutter, n.13, above, 14. 51 *Ibid*, 177.

52 *Ibid*, 194.

53 Julia Black, 'New Institutionalism and Naturalism in Socio-Legal Analysis: Institutional Approaches to Regulatory Decision-Making' (1997) 19(1) *Law and Policy* 66.

54 Manuel Castells, *The Rise of the Network Society* (Oxford, 2000), Vol. 1, 500.

55 Michel Callon, 'Introduction: The Embeddedness of Economic Markets in Economics', in M. Callon (ed.), *The Laws of the Markets* (Oxford, 1998), 12. There are also other, different sociological perspectives which focus on the 'network society', such as Manuel Castells' work, n.54, above.

56 Michel Callon and John Law, 'Agency and the Hybrid Collectif' (1995) 94(2) *The South Atlantic Quarterly* 496. 57 *Ibid*, 495.

58 Callon and Law, n.56, above, 495; Michel Callon, 'Actor-Network Theory—The Market Test', in J. Law and J. Hassard (eds), *Actor Network Theory and After* (Oxford, 1999), 186.

59 John Hassard, John Law and Nick Lee, 'Actor-Network Theory' (1999) 6(3) *Organization* 388; Callon and Law, n.56, above, 481.

Hence, networks grant activity to them.[60] It is actors' connection with a network which provides them with consciousness and subjectivity, attributes which are considered as pre-existing in other sociological perspectives. Moreover, network elements are not pre-constituted, but are relational effects of the network configuration itself.[61] Hence, networks allow seeing social phenomena 'in the making'.[62] From an ANT perspective, there are no pre-determined, stable social structures, but only patterns in networks. They emerge from 'knots' and 'nodes' which link concentrated resources in networks.[63] For instance, a manager's agency in an organization is generated through a network which comprises her personal computer as well as the files and statistics which enable her to make judgements about productivity.

Networks, of course, are also prominent in the literature on legal regulation. 'Regulatory', 'policing', and 'governance networks', as well as 'networks of inter-organizational relations and politics'[64] have been analysed.[65] Globalization is said to accelerate the proliferation of a variety of transnational economic and intergovernmental networks.[66] Different types of networks, such as epistemic and policy alliances have been discussed. The former are 'knowledge-based networks of specialists who pursue common policy goals on the basis of shared methods and values'.[67] Policy networks, in contrast, are informed by various lobby groups' competitive struggles over resources and thus draw more explicitly on interests rather than expert opinions. In addition, while some regulation networks are inclusive, comprising both regulated and regulators, others consist exclusively of either regulators or regulated. Networks have helped to explain, for instance, the internationalization of competition law,[68] and they have been perceived as a source of regulatory approaches and norms.[69]

[60] Latour, n.22, above, 373.

[61] Michel Callon and John Law, 'After the Individual in Society: Lessons on Collectivity from Science, Technology and Society' (1997) 22(2) *Canadian Journal of Sociology* 171.

[62] Bruno Latour, *Science in Action: How to Follow Scientists and Engineers through Society* (Milton Keynes, 1987), 21.

[63] Latour, n.62, above, 180. Callon and Law, n.61, above, 179.

[64] Hawkins, n.28, above, 38.

[65] John Braithwaite, 'The New Regulatory State and the Transformation of Criminology' (2000) 40 *British Journal of Criminology* 222–38; Colin Scott, 'Accountability in the Regulatory State' (2000) 27(1), *Journal of Law and Society* 38–60; Sol Picciotto, 'The Regulatory Criss-Cross: Interaction between Jurisdictions and the Construction of Global Regulatory Networks', in W. Bratton, J. McCahery, S. Picciotto and C. Scott (eds), *International Regulatory Competition and Coordination* (Oxford, 1996), 89–123; Sol Picciotto, 'Networks in International Economic Integration: Fragmented States and the Dilemma of Neo-Liberalism' (1996–1997) *Northwestern Journal of International Law and Business* 1014–56; P. Gill, 'Policing and Regulation: What is the Difference?' (2002) 11(4) *Social and Legal Studies* 523–46; E. Meidinger, 'Regulatory Culture: A Theoretical Outline' (1987) *Law and Policy* 9(4) 355–96.

[66] Francis Snyder, 'Governing Economic Globalisation: Global Legal Pluralism and European Law' (1999) 5(4) *European Law Journal* 336; A.M. Slaughter, 'The Real New World Order' (1997) 76 *Foreign Affairs* 183–97.

[67] Imelda Maher, 'Competition Law in the International Domain: Networks as a new Form of Governance', in D. Campbell and S. Picciotto (eds), 'New Directions in Regulatory Theory' Special Issue *Journal of Law and Society* (2002) 29(1), 118, referring to Haas.

[68] *Ibid*, 111–36.

[69] See for example in the EU context: Andreas Bächer and Sabine Schlacke, 'Die Entstehung einer "Politischen Verwaltung" durch EG-Ausschüße—Rechtstatsachen und Rechtsentwicklungen',

But perceptions of legal networks seem to replicate traditional assumptions about agency and structure.[70] Strong, functional goal-oriented agency, perceived as an innate quality of human actors, is exercised within or through these regulatory networks:[71]

> This ... is very much within the frame of policy networks where actors with considerable political power (the US and the EU in the international context), can exert influence and use their power to fix the agenda.[72]

Hence, actors can use networks strategically to promote specific policy goals.[73] These networks also focus only on social relations between human actors[74] or pre-constituted social entities, such as organizations. They do not include materialities, such as office structures, files, and texts in the legal domain. Moreover, traditional distinctions resurface between agency and the structural resources facilitating it. Access to power and knowledge are said to further enhance actors' agency in networks.[75] In addition, legal regulation networks have been described as centred by having a specific 'locus of power' and a hierarchical structure.[76] Some of the legal regulation literature also sheds further light on how networks impact on regulatory law. For example, at times 'soft power and persuasion'—exercised through regulators' networks—have been an alternative to or reinforcement of formal norms.[77] Often law has been perceived as a pre-constituted, self-contained element within a network.

If ANT's different view on networks is applied to legal regulation, what new perspectives may be opened up? To begin with, ANT can provide a new approach to 'regulatory law in action', which helps to unravel further what social relations are mobilized when regulatory law is set in motion.

Rethinking Regulatory Law from an ANT Perspective

ANT can help to look differently at regulatory law in action. First, from an ANT perspective networks can become involved in the production of normativity, including law. Conventional elements in the analysis of normativity, such as social norms, actors, and structures are not presupposed. Instead ANT is interested in how these phenomena are built up, how they decline and, hence, how products of activity are made possible. This also aims to render visible those features of social life which seem to happen behind actors' backs, but which are—perhaps exactly for that reason—important in the production of situations and

in Christian Joerges and Josef Falke (eds), *Das Ausschußwesen der EU* (Baden-Baden, 2000), 161–256.

[70] But see Julia Black, 'Proceduralizing Regulation: Part II' (2001) 21(1) *Oxford Journal of Legal Studies* 47 and J. Black, 'Enrolling Actors in Regulatory Systems: Examples from UK Financial Services Regulation' [2003] *Public Law* 85.

[71] Snyder, n.66, above, 335, 340.

[72] Maher, n.67, above, 131.

[73] *Ibid*, 118.

[74] Latour, n.22, above, 369.

[75] Maher, n.67, above, 118.

[76] Snyder, n.66, above, 340.

[77] Maher, n.67, above, 111.

interactions.[78] Hence, from an ANT perspective law is generated through relations between human actors and other actors often called 'actants', such as materialities. Examples for the latter in the context of law are files, legal statements, forms, courtrooms, stories and case histories.[79] They are beyond the creative constructive power of direct interactions and may become 'co-producers' available to situations.[80] Consequently, materialities are not merely passive objects of human agency, but have a performative and productive role. Legal files are not simply perceived as documents, but as 'instruments for preparating, investing and mobilising' legal discourse.[81] A file can become an actant because it:

> calls for additional work, spells out minimal duties, sets up dates, points at gaps, and if viable, stores/accumulates trumps.[82]

Also, statements can enrol participants in legal proceedings and keep them in check. They can even turn against their author, such as legal statements which prejudice the case of a party in the proceedings.[83] Moreover, a courtroom can become a means of production for legal discourse by steering legal speech and its reception and hence legal sense-making processes.[84] Hence, for ANT the empirical materialities of a discourse matter, and in particular how they assist in the production of legal actors' connected talk and writing.

Some approaches develop a strong temporal dimension for this discourse analysis.[85] The circulation of legal artefacts over time, for instance between client, solicitor and barrister, is dissected.[86] Hence, ANT approaches allow for a detailed depiction of how legal statements become constructed, mobilized, gain and lose significance and sometimes direct the course of legal proceedings.

Secondly, while the concept of the actor-network can help to explain the generation and circulation of regulatory law in action, it can also shed light on the function of regulatory law in such networks. In some accounts, regulatory law, such as health and safety regulations, has been conceptualized as an 'intermediary'. Intermediaries pass between actors and define relationships between them.[87] Both human beings or materialities, such as texts, technical artefacts, like computer software, or money can be intermediaries in networks.[88] They 'represent delegations

[78] T. Scheffer, 'Materialities of Legal Proceedings' (2004) *International Journal for the Semiotics of Law* 4.

[79] *Ibid*, 10, 15, 23.

[80] Scheffer, n.78, above, 5, 10, 15. They can last beyond specific situations and therefore can not be just captured through an interpretative analysis. For instance, what comes after a story has to orient itself to previous stories. See Scheffer, n.78, above, 21, 24.

[81] Scheffer, n.78, above, 12, 14, 18.

[82] Thomas Scheffer, 'The Duality of Mobilisation—Following the Rise and Fall of an Alibi-Story on its way to Court' (2003) 33(3) *Journal for the Theory of Social Behaviour* 318.

[83] Scheffer refers here to attempts to minimize the importance of initial police interviews which are disadvantageous for the accused. See Scheffer, 'Die Karriere Rechtswirksamer Aussagen—Ansatzpunkte einer Historiographischen Diskursanalyse der Gerichtsverhandlung' (2003) 24(2) *Zeitschrift für Rechtssoziologie* 21, 24.

[84] Scheffer, n.78, above, 9, 23.

[85] Callon, n.25, above, 154.

[86] Scheffer, n.83, above.

[87] Callon, n.25, above, 134.

[88] M. Callon, 'The Dynamics of Techno-Economic Networks', in R. Combs, P. Saviotti and V. Walsh (eds), *Technological Change and Company Strategies: Economic and Sociological Perspectives* (London, 1992), 75.

and inscriptions of actions already initiated elsewhere'.[89] They help to transform actions from distant social worlds into significant elements in a new network. They are a translation device which can also help to pattern the heterogeneous elements which make up a network. Whether intermediaries will be successful in the task of exercising control from a distance also depends on whether they can impose on the networks one particular way of reading them and hence 'to discourage alternative interpretations'.[90] The idea of regulatory law as an intermediary may help to analyse law and technology interactions which have been discussed in the literature on legal regulation. For instance, how can the impact of law be separated out from technological factors, such as in the reduction of accidents at work?[91] ANT's notion of regulatory law as an intermediary allows going beyond a determinist perspective where technology either shapes law or vice versa. The network perspective also questions ideas where technology would be seen as autonomous and separate from law, either as a constraint or as a tool of legal regulation. Finally, by attributing agency to technology ANT provides an alternative to accounts which strongly socialize technology by focusing on how human actors handle technology in organizations. Thirdly, ANT can also help to think differently about regulatory law by considering legal texts as networks.[92] Legal texts create connections among a range of texts, such as legislation, cases or academic commentary. Texts then have a performative role. They help to construct and enrol an interested audience. Hence, actants, such as texts, are also networks.[93]

While these accounts help to look differently at regulatory law in action, they also raise further questions. For instance, the focus on the detailed, in-depth analysis of the circulation of legal statements, seems to leave unexplored the 'before' and 'after' of regulatory law, such as the substantive field of legal doctrine on which legal statements draw and the formal legal outputs into which they can translate, such as decisions in court proceedings. In some accounts reference to the materialities of discourse is used to unravel the construction and mobilization of legal statements, but beyond that an unexplored category of 'actual legal norms'[94] is invoked or the focus has been only on the formal law's functions, such as its 'local co-ordination in networks'.[95]

To summarize, 'regulatory law in action' has often been constructed from an interpretative perspective through reference to face-to-face interactions between traditional social actors, who are endowed with varying degrees of agency. ANT, however, also brings into perspective the materialities which contribute to the construction of law and hence a whole range of new actants come into view. This

[89] Silvia Gherardi and Davide Nicolini, 'To Transfer is to Transform: The Circulation of Safety Knowledge' (2000) 7(2) *Organization* 336.

[90] *Ibid*, 338.

[91] Hutter, n.13, above, 21.

[92] Callon, n.25, above, 135.

[93] *Ibid*, 142.

[94] See, e.g. Scheffer, n.82, above, 337 such as pre-constituted rules of evidence, rules of disclosure, and norms of admissibility which are conceptualized in ANT parlance as 'obligatory passage points' in the network.

[95] Callon, n.25, above, 147, 150, 155.

can also have normative consequences. ANT supports a democratic version of agency where animals or the natural environment can be network elements equal in their importance to humans.[96] Moreover, ANT assumes equality of actants and analyses unequal distributions, for instance of resources, as imposed through networks.[97] Furthermore, from an ANT perspective the emphasis shifts to law being a consequence rather than cause of action. Hence, ANT can contribute to a more comprehensive understanding of the social relations which are involved in the construction of regulatory law in action. ANT, however, cannot only open up new perspectives on the social relations which inform regulatory law in action, it can also shed new light on legal decision-making, and in particular on discretion and interests.

Discretion

Regulators' and regulateds' discretion has been an important theme in the literature on enforcing legal regulation.[98] Social and legal norms have been considered as relevant for restricting or even enhancing choices and power available for making legal decisions.[99] Some accounts of discretion also stress the importance of interactions between social actors for determining how much discretion they have.[100] But the concept of interactions employed here draws on an interpretative perspective which proceeds from the idea that social actors are endowed with innate agency and will therefore engage in negotiations. ANT, in contrast, does not presuppose the existence of agency. In fact, it reverses the relationship between agency and discretion. It suggests that removing discretion is the first step to establish an actor's agency. This can start with an actor making herself indispensable to others. Subsequently, there may be attempts to 'lock other actors into place in a network by coming between them and alternative courses of action'.[101] Finally, an actant will attempt to define roles for other actants in a network, by 'enrolling' them into tasks. Mobilization is achieved in such a network through the principal actor turning herself into a spokesperson for other passive agents in a network.[102] Hence, for ANT discretion is a strongly relational concept where agency results from network interactions. Also, various characteristics of networks can help to further explain discretion. From an ANT perspective rules themselves cannot curtail other actors' scope for action. They can only do this when they become

[96] Marilyn Strathern, 'What is Intellectual Property After?', in J. Law and J. Hassard (eds), *Actor Network Theory and After* (Oxford, 1999), 157.

[97] Callon and Law, n.56, above, 490.

[98] See for example Keith Hawkins, 'On Legal Decision-Making' (1986) 43(4) *Washington and Lee Law Review* 1161–242; Robert Baldwin and Keith Hawkins, 'Discretionary Justice: Davis Reconsidered', in C. Scott (ed.), *Regulation* (Aldershot, 2003), 221–50.

[99] Baldwin and Hawkins, n.98, above, 228.

[100] *Ibid*, 224, 236.

[101] John Law, 'Editor's Introduction', in J. Law (ed.), *Power, Action and Belief: A New Sociology of Knowledge* (London, 1986), 15, 16.

[102] *Ibid*, 16.

mobilized as part of a network which comprises other material objects and human actors. Hence, ANT questions perspectives which consider the characteristics of legal and social rules, such as how specific, clear and determinate they are, as important for explaining the scope of legal actors' discretion. For instance, networks which bridge various times or spaces represent to the network remote social worlds in order to enable action at a distance. Such representations can open up new courses of action and hence discretion. In addition, also networks' 'obligatory points of passage'—which are temporary centres through which actants have to pass—contribute to the generation of discretion.[103] For example, legal statements may have to pass through stations, such as a solicitor's office in the case of witness statements or a court in the case of formal enforcement orders. Since—from the vantage point of these 'obligatory points of passage'—it does not matter who exactly among a number of actants will pass through a passage point, discretion is generated. To summarize, lawyers have been particularly concerned with the question whether discretion in legal regulation should be restricted, for instance in order to give expression to rule of law values. ANT's perspective further supports accounts which suggest that discretion is a fact of social life because 'confining, structuring and checking' may actually lead to more not less discretion where social actors find creative ways of handling devices for the restriction of discretion.[104] Also from an ANT perspective discretion seems pervasive, by being a result of network operations. ANT, however, makes this point from a different analytical starting point which is based on an alternative understanding of agency which also recognizes the importance of materialities. Hence, ANT reinforces the idea that discretion is still an important theme for understanding the social relations inherent in legal regulation. It focuses, however, on the operation of entire networks which include the materialities of social life when considering strategies for reducing or enhancing discretion in legal regulation. ANT, however, cannot just shed new light on discretion, but also on interests as a further element in legal decision-making.

Interests in Legal Decision-Making

Interests inform interpretative practices involved in legal decision-making, since making sense of the social world involves 'to construe interest maps all the time'.[105] The interests of participants in regulatory communities may harmonize, for instance when state legal regulation becomes a form of rent seeking and thus is in some producers' interests as suggested by public choice perspectives. Often the

[103] M. Callon, 'Some Elements of a Sociology of Translation: Domestication of the Scallops and the Fishermen of St. Brieuc Bay', in J. Law (ed.), *Power, Action and Belief: A New Sociology of Knowledge?*, Sociological Review Monograph 32 (London, 1986), 196–233.

[104] Baldwin and Hawkins, n.98, above, 227.

[105] Michel Callon and John Law, 'On Interests and their Transformation: Enrolment and Counter-Enrolment' (1982) 12 *Social Studies of Science* 617.

interests of participants in regulatory communities have been perceived to be in conflict, such as in tensions between the commercial aims and social objectives of legal regulation.[106] Also economic perspectives have drawn attention to interests in regulatory processes. For instance, public choice perspectives have analysed producers' interests as rent seeking.

In such accounts, however, interests have been often understood as static and pre-given 'theoretical constructs'.[107] They flow from political and economic structures, such as utility and profit maximization, in which actors operate. ANT, however, paints a more dynamic and subtle picture of interests. They are only 'temporarily stabilized outcomes of previous processes of enrolment' in a network.[108] 'Enrolment' involves 'translation' which refers to the techniques through which actors try to impose on others their view of the world.[109] In order to generate particular views of the world actors 'simplify, construct scales as well as label and develop schematic views of the suggested reality'.[110] Translation also involves finding new interpretations of one's own and other actors' interests and thus to steer behaviour in directions which actors otherwise may have perceived as incompatible with their original interpretation of their interests.[111] ANT also reverses the usual association between interests and organized social life. Traditionally social groups and institutions are identified first and then perceived as generating and supporting the expression of particular interests. ANT, however, suggests that temporarily stabilized interests in networks help to define and enforce institutions, groups, or organizations which sometimes exist in the social world.[112] ANT's challenge to traditional understandings of interests has implications, for instance, for incentive-based legal regulation. Attempts to tailor legal regulation to political or economic interests would have to take into account the limits to defining interests abstractly. According to ANT, interests could not be derived from pre-existing organizations, but instead would be the outcome of complex network interactions which may stabilize organizations only for a limited period of time. To conclude, ANT can yield new understandings of social relations inherent in legal regulation through different perspectives on agency and networks. But the social also features in economic transactions which have formed a core reference point for legal regulation.

[106] Hutter, n.13, above, ix; 14; Pearce and Tombs, n.46, above.

[107] Callon and Law, n.105, above, 615.

[108] Callon and Law, n.105, above, 622. It is unclear, however, whether ANT completely abandons the idea that external social structures shape actors' interests. Callon and Law, n.105, above, 617, suggest that interests are 'built out of actively constructed constraints that are recognised as limiting available options'. This paints a dynamic picture of social structures as 'actively constructed constraints', but nevertheless seems to suggest that social structures can give rise to interests. Moreover, Callon and Law, n.105, above, 622, suggest that there may be 'a backcloth of prior interests which has to be taken for granted' but should not be accorded any special explanatory status.

[109] John Law, 'On Power and its Tactics: A View from the Sociology of Science' (1986) 34(1) *The Sociological Review* 6.

[110] *Ibid*, 14, 15, 16.

[111] Callon and Law, n.105, above, 619.

[112] *Ibid*, 622.

Changing Perceptions of Law and Economy Interactions in Legal Regulation through Sociological and Cultural Analysis

Interactions between law and the economy are key to understanding legal regulation. To begin with, regulation has often been defined as state intervention in economic processes.[113] Furthermore, changing state–economy relationships have given rise to new forms of regulation. For instance, the regulatory state increasingly distances itself from direct command and control regulation, and instead relies on self-regulation or enforced self-regulation.[114] Sometimes state regulation has simply been replaced by ordering through the free play of market forces. At other times state regulation has tried to respond to commercial reasoning through economic incentive-based regulation. Moreover, private sector management techniques, such as audit and performance indicators, have been used to regulate public regulators themselves.

Policies for and academic accounts of law–economy interactions have, however, often drawn on neo-classical economics. They have underpinned, for instance, public and private interest theories of legal regulation which in turn have informed explanations of rent seeking and regulatory capture. Neo-classical economics have also provided important justifications for legal regulation through the concept of market failure, exemplified in externalities, inadequate information for market actors, and imperfect competition. Finally, in the search for 'efficient' regulation neo-classical economics have provided influential normative frameworks.[115]

But neo-classical accounts are just one particular perspective on economic life. They have focused on markets as organizing economic transactions rather than networks and hierarchies. They have paid more attention to the structural dimensions of economic behaviour than to economic agency. Since markets can be considered as a price-making mechanism, central to the allocation of resources in an economy,[116] they create motivation structures for the behaviour of economic agents. Moreover, how economic agency should be conceptualized from a neo-classical perspective is not entirely clear. On the one hand, there are the autonomous actions taken by a selfish, utility maximizing 'homo economicus'. On the other hand, economic agency has remained elusive as the 'invisible hand of the market' promoting equilibrium states.[117] Further analysis of the social may

[113] See, e.g. Picciotto, n.24, above, 1.

[114] Ian Ayres and John Braithwaite, *Responsive Regulation: Transcending the Deregulation Debate* (Oxford, 1992).

[115] See, e.g. A. Ogus and C. Abbot, 'Sanctions for Pollution: Do We Have the Right Regime?' (2002) 14(3) *Journal of Environmental Law* 283–98. A. Ogus, 'Corrective Taxes and Financial Impositions as Regulatory Instruments' (1998) 61(6). *The Modern Law Review* 767–88.

[116] R. Swedberg, 'Markets as Social Structures', in N.J. Smelser and R. Swedberg (eds), *The Handbook of Economic Sociology* (Princeton, 1994), 255.

[117] *Ibid*, 258. It has also been suggested that this neglects the significance of active entrepreneurship in the functioning of markets.

shed additional light on these questions of structure and agency in economic transactions. In fact, it has been argued that economic behaviour is becoming increasingly socialized in post-industrial societies:

> A close relationship has been perceived between the social processes of creating and manipulating symbols, the culture of society, and the capacity to distribute goods and services.[118]

So, what insights do sociological and cultural perspectives offer? How may these help to understand more about the social relations which are generated when law interacts with economic processes?

Sociological and Cultural Perspectives on Economic Life

Sociological and cultural approaches allow us to perceive 'markets, products and competition' as 'lived realities' rather than formal categories.[119] Economic concepts are grounded in empirical practices, including the practical knowledges on which economic actors draw. Sociological approaches consider economic relationships as constructed and embedded in local and transnational social contexts. Hence, interactions between social actors, their involvement in groups and society matter in economic life. In contrast to this, neo-classical 'methodological individualism' implies that economic actors' choices can be analysed in isolation from each other.[120]

From a cultural perspective symbols,[121] signs and discourses are key concepts in the analysis of economic transactions. Commodities and capital become fused with signs and symbols in the global information culture.[122] The symbolic rather than material content of commodities becomes important. For instance, some forms of consumption aim at symbolic gains, rather than the satisfaction of material needs through the appropriation of use values.[123] Similarly, in the cultural economy professional work often adds value to goods and services through the manipulation of symbols, the analysis of words and data and through the production of oral and visual representations.[124] The idea that commodities and capital can be understood as signs suggests that they can be analysed similar to encounters between texts and readers.[125] This draws attention to the role of discourse in

[118] Castells, n.54, above, 18.

[119] D. Slater, 'Capturing Markets from the Economists', in Paul du Gay and Michael Pryke (eds), *Cultural Economy* (London, 2002), 76.

[120] N.J. Smelser and R. Swedberg, 'The Sociological Perspective on the Economy', in N.J. Smelser and R. Swedberg (eds), *The Handbook of Economic Sociology* (Princeton, 1994), 4.

[121] D. Miller, 'The Unintended Political Economy', in du Gay and Pryke, n.119, above, 172.

[122] J. Allen, 'Symbolic Economies: The "Culturalization" of Economic Knowledge', in du Gay and Pryke (eds), n.119, above, 42.

[123] A.Warde, 'Production, Consumption and "Cultural Economy" ', in du Gay and Pryke (eds), n.119, above, 186.

[124] Allen, n.122, above, 39, 43, referring to Reich's 'The Work of Nations'. Symbolic forms of knowledge have also been considered as central to the delivery of services in banking, accounting and law.

[125] Slater, n.119, above, 72.

enacting and performing economic interactions. For example, discourses on accounting, marketing and finance, 'format and frame' economic transactions. Accounting tools do not simply aid the measurement of economic activity, they also shape the reality they measure and thereby contribute to the construction of calculative agencies and modes of calculation.[126] But how can these sociological and cultural perspectives on economic transactions promote further understanding of social relations engendered by legal regulation?

Normativity as a Shared Form of Social Relations in Legal and Economic Processes

First, sociological and cultural accounts of economic life allow seeing that legal and economic processes work through shared forms of social relations, such as normativity. The translation of state law into social life generates and sometimes changes existing normative practices for the purposes of achieving compliance with or evasion of legal regulation. From a sociological perspective also economic transactions involve normative practices. On a macro-level economic networks have been perceived as a form of governance.[127] Moreover, economic interactions have been considered to establish 'the laws of the markets'.[128] These are regularities, drawn, for instance, from the discipline of economics. They perform behaviour but can also be subject to change.[129] In addition, also on a micro level normative practices inform economic behaviour. Interactions between economic actors generate cultural norms which in turn influence economic behaviour.[130] Also economic rationality has been considered as a system of norms.[131] In addition, both cognitive and aesthetic knowledge have been perceived as central to production and consumption in the new economy. Aesthetic knowledge draws on normative practices because it is 'grounded in conventions of taste and the everyday' as well as habits.[132] Conventions which guide behaviour also feature in the analysis of symbols in economic life. They are said to shape the system of relations between signs which produce meaning.[133] Moreover, it has been suggested that culture plays an increasing role in economic organizations' life[134] and that it can perform regulatory functions.[135] In some accounts this argument has been developed

[126] M. Callon, 'Introduction: The Embeddedness of Economic Markets in Economics', in M. Callon (ed.), *The Laws of the Markets* (Oxford, 1998), 23.

[127] Walter W. Powell and Laurel Smith-Doerr, 'Networks and Economic Life', in N.J. Smelser and R. Swedberg (eds), *The Handbook of Economic Sociology* (Princeton, 1994), 369.

[128] M. Callon (ed.), *The Laws of the Markets* (Oxford, 1998).

[129] Callon, n.126, above, 46, 47.

[130] Smelser and Swedberg, n.120, above, 6, 12.

[131] *Ibid*, 5, referring to Parsons. 'Motivation of Economic Activities', 50–68 in T. Parsons, *Essays in Sociological Theory* (New York, (1940), (1954)).

[132] Allen, n.122, above, 41, 42.

[133] *Ibid*, 49.

[134] J. van Maanen and G. Kunda, 'Real Feelings: Emotional Expression and Organizational Culture' (1989) 11 *Research in Organizational Behaviour* 50.

[135] C. Hall, C. Scott, and C. Hood, *Telecommunications Regulation, Culture, Chaos and Interdependence inside the Regulatory Process* (London, 2000), ch. 3.

through a sociological analysis of emotions. Hence, culture has been broadly defined to also include the generation and expression of emotions. It has been argued that organizational culture 'influences not only what people think, say and do, but also what they feel'.[136] For instance, sociological analysis of the work of flight attendants and debt collectors has suggested that the management of emotions in accordance with a range of intricate feeling rules is an integral part of the economic activity of service delivery.[137] Moreover, ritualized forms of emotional expression at and through work, including rituals of resistance, are shaped by normative frameworks generated in organizations:

> Ritual is a rule-governed activity of a symbolic character that draws the attention of participants to objects of thought and feeling they are expected to hold in special significance.[138]

Hence, normativity is a shared form of social relations through which internal relations between law and the economy can be generated. This has a number of implications for the analysis of regulation. First, the focus on interactions between law and the economy through shared forms of social life implies less clear-cut boundaries around law and the economy. This questions perceptions of legal regulation being subject to independent economic constraints. Secondly, key concepts on which legal regulation builds may be further developed. Cultural analysis suggests that consumer and producer identities are not static or pre-given. Instead they are informed by aesthetic reflexivity which in turn draws on normative practices, such as 'conventions of taste and the everyday' as well as habits.[139] Hence, images of consumer and producer which feature in legal discourse, for instance on product safety regulation, are not independent legal categories. Instead they may acquire meaning through their engagement also with normative economic practices, such as aesthetic reflexivity. Hence, meaning of legal discourses may not be established in an exclusively legal sphere but may also draw on the meaning and contents of small-scale norms generated in economic life. Hence, legal regulation of economic behaviour does not start from an empty discursive field into which legal regulatory concepts—such as consumer and producer—can be projected. Instead legal discourse is also informed by interactions with normativities constructed in the economic sphere. Such interactions may help to explain how economic actors construct the meaning of legal discourse and how legal regulation becomes facilitated or blocked.

To conclude, sociological and cultural perspectives on the economy enable us to see how interactions between law and the economy arise, within forms of social practice, such as normativity. These perspectives also open up further questions. Under what circumstances may legal and economic normativities complement or obstruct each other? Can shared forms of social life, such as normative practices,

[136] van Maanen and Kunda, n.134, above, 46.

[137] Arlie Hochschild, *The Managed Heart* (Berkeley, 1983), ch. 4.

[138] S. Lukes, 'Political Ritual and Social Integration' (1975) 9 *Sociology* 289–308, referred to in Maanen and Kunda, n.134, above, 49.

[139] Allen, n.122, above.

be described as a match of the procedural logics of legal and economic processes or are legal and economic normative practices irreconcilably different and hence a potential obstacle to the implementation of legal regulation?

Sociological and cultural perspectives on economic life, however, can also question whether regulators and regulated can be thought of as bureaucratic organizations with clear boundaries.

Legal Regulation through Bounded Bureaucratic Organizations?

Accounts of legal regulation have drawn attention to bureaucratic features of organizations, such as state regulators[140] and large private corporations. Bureaucracy is here a feature of bounded organizations which can be clearly differentiated from their environment. It refers to the exercise of authority through hierarchical structures and through reliance on universal and impersonal rules which are implemented with limited discretion. In relation to regulated bureaucratic organizations such characteristics can help to account for obstacles to the reception of legal regulation. Inflexible norms and cultures of bureaucratic organizations may impede social change required by regulatory law. In the case of regulators, bureaucratic structures may be seen as a prerequisite for the faithful translation of legal mandates into actual legal regulation on the ground. But also deviations from the basic image of the bureaucratic organization have featured in accounts of the implementation of legal regulation. For instance, tensions between formal and informal norms and organizational hierarchies, as well as considerable discretion for street level bureaucrats have been discussed.[141]

Sociological and cultural perspectives of regulatory and regulated organizations in economic life emphasize, however, the decline of traditional bureaucratic organizations and the rise of networks.[142] In the case of economic transactions these networks replace specific individuals, such as entrepreneurs, or economic collectivities, like a capitalist class, the state, or large corporations. The latter could be characterized through 'vertical integration', hierarchical functional management, and 'institutionalised social and technical division of labour'.[143] Firms increasingly co-operate in business networks, and hence are no longer the self-contained and self-sufficient vertical, rational bureaucracies which were suited to standardized mass production and oligopolistic markets.[144] These networks can consist of various organizations, which change according to the environments and market structures they relate to.[145] They often span traditional public–private, state–market distinctions. Moreover,

[140] See, e.g. K. Hawkins, 'On Legal Decision-Making' (1986) 43(4) *Washington and Lee Law Review* 1163, referring to R. Kagan, Book Review, *Inside Administrative Law*, (1984) 84 *Columbia Law Review* 816.

[141] Hawkins, above, nn.28 and 29.

[142] Walter W. Powell and Laurel Smith-Doerr, 'Networks and Economic Life', in N.J. Smelser and R. Swedberg (eds), *The Handbook of Economic Sociology* (Princeton, 1994), 368–402.

[143] Castells, n.54, above, 166, 168.

[144] *Ibid*, 179.

[145] *Ibid*, 214.

perceptions of alliances and strategic co-operation in economic life are changing. Firms which co-operate for one project, may be competitors in another.[146] Networks within firms lead to a hollowing out of traditional corporations:

> The actual operating unit becomes the business project, enacted by a network . . .[147]

In addition, the 'network enterprise' relies on a whole range of other economic networks, such as supplier, producer, and customer networks as well as standardization organizations and technology co-operation networks.[148] ANT even abandons the notion of a clearly bounded organization, defined as a specific system for the performance of goals. Instead it suggests that networks perform only temporarily stabilized organizations. From an ANT perspective networks are created through 'entanglement' between social actors and materialities. This is in stark contrast to the neo-classical perspective which perceives economic actors as individuals exercising autonomous choices, often in markets, according to preferences defined on the basis of their personal self-interest.

Hence, networks are different from traditional bureaucratic organizations. They involve more flexible and fluid social relations.[149] Inquiries into the implementation of legal regulation then can no longer focus on law's impact on and reception by specific organizations, but will have to take into account how legal regulation interacts with and may become part of overlapping networks. To conclude, neo-classical economics have been influential in the analysis of legal regulation. Sociological and cultural perspectives provide an alternative which points to close law and economy interactions that are generated through shared forms of social practices. Sociological and cultural approaches also question the image of clearly bounded formal bureaucratic organizations as central to the implementation of legal regulation. Finally, attention to the social can also help to develop analysis of normative frameworks for legal regulation. In particular, a sociological analysis of emotions can inform understanding of deliberative democracy.

Emotions as an Element of Normative Frameworks for Legal Regulation

Emotions in the context of sociological analysis have been understood as:

> An awareness of four elements that we usually experience at the same time: a) appraisals of a situation, b) changes in bodily sensations, c) the free or inhibited display of expressive gestures and d) a cultural label applied to specific constellations of the first three elements.[150]

146 *Ibid*, 175. 147 *Ibid*, 177. 148 *Ibid*, 207. 149 Castells, n.54, above, 161.

150 Arlie Hochschild, 'Ideology and Emotion Management: A Perspective and Path for Future Research', in T. Kemper (ed.), *Research Agendas in the Sociology of Emotions* (Albany, 1990), 118–19.

Hence, emotions are closely linked to both physiological and cognitive processes, though the extent to which the body and the mind play a role in their production is disputed.[151]

Emotions de-differentiate structure and agency because they are a common and thus connecting element in both. Social actors feel emotions in everyday, routine interaction. Indeed, 'successful' agency may require the appropriate management of emotions since social actors need to feel trust 'in the actions of enabling others' in order to act.[152] But emotions can also inform normative social structures by being an integral part of ethical reasoning. Emotions are 'intelligent responses to the perception of value'.[153] For instance, the emotional dispositions of compassion and altruism as well as self-interest inform the public culture of liberal, pluralist democracies which provide welfare services, and the specific forms of economic and social regulation which emanate from these. Hence, while emotions are generated, expressed, and managed in specific interactions, they also transcend individual agency and can inhere in normative frameworks.

Normative frameworks, in turn, have informed specific models of legal regulation. For instance, the argument for the 'thick proceduralization' of legal regulation draws on, but also modifies Habermas's ideas on deliberative democracy.[154] Habermas's vision of deliberative democracy seeks to ascertain the conditions under which rational discussion of public affairs and hence democratic decision-making can take place. His concept of communicative action is central to this. It involves the rational evaluation of the four validity claims which acts of linguistic communication raise, that statements are comprehensible, true, right, and 'a sincere expression of the speaker's feelings'.[155] For Habermas, law can be a medium through which communicative power is transformed into administrative power. A procedural conception of law is advanced which aims to bridge divisions between the rule of law of the classical liberal '*Rechtsstaat*' and the substantive law of modern welfare states.[156] The 'thick proceduralization' model of legal regulation departs, however, in some respects from Habermas's analysis. It puts greater emphasis on differences between citizens who participate in deliberation. It suggests that in contemporary heterogeneous societies people invoke 'different discourses, techniques of argument and validity claims'. Hence, deliberation needs to be mediated through 'strategies of translation, mapping and dispute resolution'.[157] This critical perspective on Habermas's ideas can be further developed through a sociological analysis of emotions. Deliberation requires actors to engage both empathy and

[151] I. Craib, 'Some Comments on the Sociology of the Emotions' (1995) 29(1) *Sociology* 151–8; S.J. Williams and G. Bendelow, 'Emotions and "Sociological Imperialism"—A Rejoinder to Craib' (1996) 30(1) *Sociology* 145–53; Martha Nussbaum, *Upheavals of Thought: The Intelligence of Emotions* (Cambridge, 2001), 306.

[152] Jack Barbalet, 'Introduction: Why Emotions are Crucial', in Jack Barbalet (ed.), *Emotions and Sociology* (Oxford, 2002), 1.

[153] Nussbaum, n.151, above, 1.

[154] Black (2001), n.70, above.

[155] William Outhwaite, *Habermas: A Critical Introduction* (Cambridge, 1994), 40, 73.

[156] *Ibid*, 144.

[157] Black (2001) n.70, above, 33.

imaginative thought and thus to draw on both cognitive and emotional resources. It involves:

> a broader understanding of those in other social locations, developing a more comprehensive social understanding than any persons or groups can have from their own location [158]

Moreover, the linguistic analysis on which the model of deliberative democracy draws can also be applied to emotions. Language does not just render thoughts but also emotions meaningful. Hence, emotions can become the subject of deliberation and can be judged as appropriate or inappropriate. Subjecting emotions to validity claims, in turn, makes them part of a public sphere.[159] Moreover, emotions can not just form the content of communications but can also be integral to the process of communicating. Language games do not just refer to emotions, but are also played emotionally.[160] Communication can be facilitated through appeals to a 'court of common sentiment', similar to appeals to shared fundamental beliefs.[161] Contesting fundamental beliefs, in turn, can generate emotional responses.[162] But also more structural aspects of communicative situations, such as imbalances of power between participants may give rise to emotions.[163] Considering emotions as an aspect of communicative action opens up critical perspectives on Habermas's vision of communicative rationality as the basis for the 'thick proceduralization' of legal regulation. It has been argued that Habermas downplays differences between deliberating citizens.[164] A sociological perspective on emotions further supports claims that contemporary societies are strongly heterogeneous, because 'emotional vocabularies' and their behavioural manifestations contribute to the differentiation of social actors.[165] Furthermore, criticisms of Habermas's clear distinction between the lifeworld and politics[166] can be developed from a new angle, because emotions have been considered as the 'missing link' between personal lives and broader 'public issues' of social structure.[167] Most fundamentally, however, attempts to govern emotions through psychological, medical, and organizational discourses are a further dimension of the 'colonization of lifeworlds' which may ultimately impede the free functioning of communicative action.[168]

158 *Ibid*, 36, 37.

159 N. Crossley, 'Emotion and Communicative Action: Habermas, Linguistic Philosophy and Existentialism', in G. Bendelow and S.J. Williams (eds), *Emotions in Social Life* (London, 1998), 30.

160 *Ibid*, 21. 161 *Ibid*, 31. 162 *Ibid*, 31.

163 T. Kemper, *A Social Interactional Theory of Emotions* (New York, 1978), 26.

164 Black (2001), n.70, above, 44.

165 Nussbaum, n.151, above, 157, 163; Arlie Hochschild, 'The Sociology of Emotion as a Way of Seeing', in G. Bendelow and Simon Williams (eds), *Emotions in Social Life* (London, 1998), 6.

166 See, e.g. Black (2001) n.70, above, 35.

167 G. Bendelow and Simon Williams, 'Introduction: Emotions in Social Life', in Bendelow, G. and Simon Williams (eds), *Emotions in Social Life* (London, 1998), xvii.

168 Crossley, n.159, above, 35.

Conclusion

This chapter has argued that the social still matters for understanding the interactions which ensue when formal law is created and implemented. Sociological analysis applied to the interconnected fields of emotions, actor-networks and economic transactions can generate new insights into how to conceptualize the social. They help to raise questions and point to new connections between what appear to be familiar building blocks for accounts of legal regulation, such as the nature of bureaucratic organizations, legal decision-making and deliberative democracy, as well as relationships between structure and agency and legal and economic normativity.

10

Law in Society: A Unifying Power or a Source of Conflict?

*Daphne Barak-Erez**

Preface: A Divided Society in a Search for a Unifying Force

At the dawn of the twenty-first century, society in modern countries is heterogeneous and split by economic, ethnic, and religious divisions. Therefore, there is an understandable aspiration to identify unifying factors that may contribute to better social cohesion. Prima facie, law presents itself as a feasible means for achieving such unity. First, law and justice enjoy universal support, at least in principle. Secondly, law purports to bridge over disputes and presumes to establish a rule for harmonious social conduct. Thirdly, in democratic discourse law often enjoys an elevated, *quasi*-religious status.[1] Fourthly, in practice, numerous problems that are not solved by other institutions find their way to the legal system. In other words, the centrality of the legal system in public life is an additional factor making it a candidate for the role of society's unifying element. In fact, thinking of law as a tool of social integration is not new. Durkheim argued that as modern society lacks the natural solidarity which characterized simple and homogenous early societies, law can serve as modern society's basis of social solidarity.[2] Another approach relevant here is that of Habermas, who pointed out that law provides a problem-solving mechanism capable of replacing social processes when the latter fail.[3]

* The author wishes to thank Yishai Blank, Roy Kreitner and Shai Lavi for their comments and the Cegla Center for the Interdisciplinary Research of the Law at Tel-Aviv University for its support.

1 Compare Lior Barshack, 'Civil Religion and the Court' (2001) 5 *Hamishpat* 35 (Hebrew).

2 Emile Durkheim, *The Division of Labour in Society* (trans by George Simpson, Glencoe, 1933).

3 Habermas writes in this context that: 'Where other regulators—for example, the coordination patterns operating through settled values, norms, and routines for reaching understanding—fail, politics and law raise these quasi-natural problem-solving processes above the threshold of consciousness, as it were. In feeling in for the social processes whose problem-solving capacities are overtaxed, the political process solves the same kind of problems as the processes it replaces'. See: Jurgen Habermas, *Between Facts and Norms—Contributions to a Discursive Theory of Law and Democracy* (trans by William Rehg, Cambridge, Mass, 1996), 318.

At the same time, there are reasons for scepticism regarding the resort to the law as a medium of social unification. Law is first and foremost an arena of conflict. The practical function of the law is to resolve disputes and any resolution of a dispute, irrespective of its benefit in terms of public order, is by nature harsh and unpleasant, at least from the perspective of one if not both litigants. In that sense, law is more naturally identified with conflict and division. Moreover, channelling serious social disputes into the legal system may jeopardize the consensual nature of the legal system itself.

This chapter proposes to evaluate the prospects of the recourse to law as a basis for social unity. It will describe the manner in which law served as a unifying force throughout history and will then evaluate normative arguments against its utilization for that purpose. In the second part, the chapter will evaluate these arguments against the background of a case study, focusing on the impact of law on the cohesion of society in Israel.

The Unifying Function of Law

Any discussion of law's potential as a unifying mechanism in society should first recognize the impact law had on the unification of societies throughout history. Law has played a constitutive role in the formation of the polity.[4] Law applies to those considered as part of the polity, or at least subject to its jurisdiction, and excludes others. Normally, its application is determined by geographical borders, within which there are people who are already interconnected by other fibres of practical communal life. There are also special cases of legal systems whose application is not limited to community within a defined territory, but these systems too are special to communities defined by other criteria (for example, religious communities). In the usual case, the law of the state or the community is expressed by the use of an official language. Therefore law's contribution to unification is also expressed in the incentive it gives to the use of a shared common language.

The current position of international law against changes in the applicable law in occupied territories can also be understood against the recognition that law can be used as a tool for unification. International law opposes the unification of the occupied territory with the occupying state, and therefore opposes the unification of their legal systems. In the past, the conquering of foreign territories by imperialist forces was invariably accompanied by introducing the conquered countries to the law of the mother country; and the application of the conqueror's law was the first step towards unification of the conquered territory with the conquering state.

[4] The complementary aspect of this proposition is that law is also the product of a community—namely of the society and its culture. See: Eugen Ehrlich, *Fundamental Principles of the Sociology of Law* (trans by Klaus A. Ziegert, New Brunswick, 2002) ('Every legal proposition is shaped out of the materials furnished by the society, but the shaping is done by the jurist').

In the Roman Empire, Roman law was applied in the provinces, although the provinces were usually allowed to maintain cultural and religious freedom. The result was that until this very day Roman law serves as a shared cultural denomination throughout Europe. A more recent historical example is the Napoleonic conquest. The French military conquest was also accompanied by the dissemination of the 'Napoleon code' which subsequently influenced the legal cultures of many states both inside and outside of Europe.

At a later stage, modern state law served as an important factor in national projects. The emergence and crystallization of nation-states was accompanied by the creation of their separate legal systems, ostensibly expressive of the nation's values.[5] In our time too, the aspiration for harmonization and unification of European law is an integral part of the project of Europe's unification. Law is once again a medium for the merging of different states into a single, unified European entity.[6]

National constitutions are generally regarded as festive expressions of the unifying role assigned to the law. The constitution is the fundamental document of the legal system. In addition, it is an educational document, expressing the 'national spirit'. In the United States, the American Constitution is the constitutive document of American society, although upon acceptance it failed to protect all of its addressees, among them racial minorities and women. The American Constitution and its tradition have been viewed by many as the foundation of the 'civil religion' of American society,[7] despite bitter disputes over its interpretation.[8] In its famous decision in *Brown* v. *Board of Education*,[9] the US Supreme Court not only abolished segregation in education, but also facilitated American society's recovery from institutionalized racism, and ultimately promoted interracial reconciliation, despite the disputes attendant to that process.

It is important to note that the concept of law as an expression of the shared values of society is also consistent with the perspective guiding the courts themselves. When courts establish norms they also tend to describe them as social norms. In the realm of private law, the concept of 'reasonableness' is interpreted in accordance with the values of each society.[10] Reference to social norms is even more prevalent in public law litigation, for example when the court has to define unjustified discrimination, in contrast to a relevant and justified distinction.

[5] Peter Fitzpatrick, *Modernism and the Grounds of Law* (Cambridge, 2001), 132–3. Regarding the connection between civil codification and the nation-state see also: Daphne Barak-Erez, 'Codification and Legal Culture: In Comparative Perspective' (1998) 13 *Tulane European and Civilian Law Forum* 125; Stephen Jacobson, 'Law and Nationalism in Nineteenth Century Europe: The Case of Catalonia in Comparative Perspective' (2002) 20 *Law and History Review* 307.

[6] See: Fitzpatrick, n.5, above, 136–7.

[7] See: Sanford Levinson, *Constitutional Faith* (Princeton, 1988); John E. Semonche, *Keeping the Faith—A Cultural History of the U.S. Supreme Court* (1998).

[8] On the phenomenon of conflicting traditions each of which regards itself as constitutionally based, see: Robert M. Cover, 'Foreword: Nomos and Narrative' (1983) 97 *Harvard Law Review* 4.

[9] 347 U.S. 483 (1954).

[10] It is precisely for this reason that criticism was levelled against the concept of the 'reasonable man', for not being sensitive to heterogeneity in society.

Critiques of the Unifying Role of Law

The aspiration to utilize law as a unifying force is based on the assumption that a united society is a prominent goal. However, this assumption is no longer consensual. The idealization of unity is now under attack, and this attack is also directed against social institutions that are associated with it, including the legal system.

Multiculturalism

A central critique of the yearning for unity originates in multiculturalism. In general, multiculturalism challenges the desirability of the melting pot ideal. It calls for respect for different cultures and customs and for ensuring their preservation. Therefore, it does not necessarily accept the desirability of shared social values. For example, multiculturalism challenges the idea of standardized education for all, and as a result opposes also its establishment by law (like the secular state education sanctioned in France). Multiculturalism also recognizes the minority's right to preserve its language and even to aspire to non-participation in frameworks that may threaten its unique character (such as military service of members of distinct religious communities).[11] More generally, law's ability to function successfully as a medium for the preservation and propagation of shared values is always contingent upon the continued predominance of the ideal of shared values. To the extent that this ideal has worn thin, a legal system attempting to establish its hegemony is liable to find itself on the defensive. Therefore, in a multicultural society in which Muslim girls are forbidden by law to wear scarves in public schools, the prohibiting legal norm serves as a tool of division and not of unification.

The Political Concept of Law

Another important critique of the values ingrained in the legal system is more specific to the legal arena and expressed by critical legal theorists, who point to the inherently ideological and political nature of legal norms. According to this critique, throughout history, law has expressed the values of the power holders in society, both economically and politically. As such it provided an ostensibly neutral cover-up for ideological and interest-related decisions.[12] This critique points, for example, to

[11] In this context it is important to remember the distinction made by Yael Tamir between 'thin' multiculturalism, representing the meeting of cultures which share underlying liberal democratic values and 'thick' multiculturalism, representing the meeting between liberal and non-liberal cultures. See: Yael Tamir, 'Two Concepts of Multiculturalism' *Multiculturalism in a Democratic and Jewish State* (Menachem Mautner et al. (eds), Tel-Aviv, 1998 (Hebrew)) 79.

[12] For representative writings, see: Roberto Mangabiera Unger, *The Critical Legal Studies Movement* (Cambridge, Mass, 1983); Duncan Kennedy, *A Critique of Adjudication (fin de siècle)* (Cambridge, Mass, 1997).

the fact that the American Constitution expressed the values and interests of white property-owners. In the same manner, the traditional offence of rape did not protect women from sexual violence committed by their legal spouses, just as criminal law in general restricted itself to interference in the public sector and therefore exposed the weaker members of the family (primarily women and children) to violence and domestic terror. The more general conclusion derived from critical legal theory is that law cannot be sanctified as the representation of shared, common values. According to this view, law is no more than a mirror reflecting hegemonic social mores and powerful interests. In other words—there are no neutral principles.[13]

Critiques on the Unifying Role of the Courts

A more specific criticism is not aimed at the idea that law is a tool in the service of social unity, but rather at the expectation that the courts (in contrast to other institutions) will serve as the agents of unity through law by declaring society's basic values.[14]

An important distinction has to be drawn between harnessing the legal system as the harbinger of social unity by way of legislative acts on the one hand and judicial actions intended to establish shared values in the context of particular judicial decisions on the other. The legislative process is far better equipped to serve as a tool for engendering social unity. It encompasses representatives of the entire public (at least in principle) and provides a platform for public dialogue.[15] In contrast, the judicial process does not involve participation of all the social groups potentially affected by it. In addition, even when it raises fundamental social questions, they are normally discussed through the prism of a particular dispute and a particular set of facts.

When the court becomes a forum for resolution of value-laden controversial questions, it generates opposition to the legitimacy of its rulings and the values expressed thereby. The result is that judicial decisions, which are aimed to give a solution to questions in social controversy, usually achieve opposite results.

[13] The term 'neutral principles' was first coined in the context of American constitutional law in the wake of Herbert Wechsler's important article, which tried to promote judicial review guided by them. See: Herbert Wechsler, 'Toward Neutral Principles of Constitutional Law' (1959) 73 *Harvard Law Review* 1.

[14] A representative writer advocating the idea of judicial decision-making based on shared principles is Ronald Dworkin. For this purpose, Dworkin assumes the existence of such common principles. He writes that: 'People are members of a genuine political community only when they accept that their fates are linked in the following strong way: they accept that they are governed by common principles, not just by rules hammered out in political compromise'. Ronald Dworkin, *Law's Empire* (London, 1986), 211.

[15] This description of legislation is close to Waldron's argument regarding the special weight that should be attached to it as the product of an overall process which recognizes and addresses existing disputes in the society. See Jeremy Waldron, *The Dignity of Legislation* (Cambridge, 1999); Jeremy Waldron, *Law and Disagreement* (Oxford, 1999).

A conspicuous example of this process is the US Supreme Court precedent on abortion,[16] a ruling that split the entire American society.

From Substance to Procedure: Agreement on the Procedure for Resolving Disputes

Given the disputed nature of society's shared values, the expectations that the legal system will be a source for social cohesion and solidarity should be redefined and diminished. If society's core values are disputed, the mere rehashing of certain values in legal texts will not eliminate the actual dispute surrounding them. Conceivably, this dictates a change of emphasis regarding the social consensus embodied in the legal system—not a consensus on substantive values but rather a consensus that it is the right forum for resolving disputes and controversies. In other words, members of society may not agree on any set of substantive norms, but they can still agree that disputes and conflicts among them should be brought to the courts and decided by them, or more generally that the legal system defines the appropriate procedures for the resolution of these disputes. The expectations from the legal system are thus diminished somewhat in terms of their ability to promote social cohesion. According to this narrower version regarding the contribution of law to social unity, court decisions do not necessarily express any collective consensus, but rather reflect an underlying agreement to be bound by them.

Unfortunately, it seems that even this limited version of law's contribution to unity may not easily command a consensus. Contemporary political debates focus also on the question of the scope of legitimate judicial decision-making, i.e. which substantive issues are legitimate topics for adjudication. More specifically, the controversial question is which conflicts should be presented for judicial resolution, and which conflicts should be left for the decision of the polit-ical system. For example, should the court only hear petitions submitted by directly affected parties, or also hear petitions filed by public petitioners? Should it eschew any adjudication of political matters, or be more lenient in this context, in order to promote the rule of law?

From Substance to Procedure: Litigation as a Basis for a Social Dialogue

An even more limited proposal regarding law's contribution to social unity focuses upon the public and political processes that invariably accompany litigation. Litigating a petition in court is never confined to the strictly professional aspects

16 *Roe* v. *Wade* 410 U.S. 113 (1973).

of 'preparing the file'. The litigation of a publicly disputed subject is invariably conducted against the backdrop of a heated public debate where each side attempts to 'win' the battle for public support. In other words, judicial litigation contributes to the development of public dialogue, which is an important pre-condition for better mutual understanding.

Ideally, questions of crucial importance to society ought to merit clarification and discussion that is unconnected with and not dependent upon their litigation in court. Democratic theories extol the importance of the vigorous public dialogue.[17] Nonetheless, in practice, the public arena is highly conducive to noisy clamour and slogans that lack the critical dimension of serious argumentation, with factual and normative support. Litigation in court over the same issues compels the parties to present their claims in an orderly manner and to confront counterclaims. The result is that the deficiencies of the dialogue conducted in the public arena are supplemented by the dialogue conducted in the shadow of the legal proceedings.

Therefore, although public discussion does not have to go hand by hand with litigation in court, the substantive confrontation dictated by judicial litigation engenders valuable incidental profits.[18] For example, the litigation in the *Brown* case forced American society to confront the tension between its ethos of equality and the tradition of segregation.

On the other hand, it is important to note that the adjudicative context may limit the substantive boundaries of the public dialogue. It may silence claims based on value judgments or social-cultural claims to the extent that these have no 'legal' expression either in terms of legislation or case law. It encourages confrontation as opposed to cooperation, emphasizing 'rights' at the expense of dialogue, reciprocity, and consideration for others. This point was made by Avi Sagi who stated that the legal discourse promotes a 'dialogue of rights' as distinct from a 'dialogue of identities' in which each party has to consider the other party, his aspirations, and his concerns.[19]

The Israeli Case Study: Law between Nation-Building and Social Conflicts

At this point, I intend to analyse the theoretical considerations presented thus far by an evaluation of one legal system in the form of a case study. The legal system

[17] The writings of Habermas may serve a representative example of these. When presenting 'procedural paradigm' of law, he explains that: 'The forces of social solidarity can be regenerated in complex societies only in the forms of communicative practices of self-determination'. Habermas, n.3, above, 445.

[18] In this context, mention should be made of the proponents of judicial minimalism, which avoids ideological decisions of broad scope, thus leaving room for continued public dialogue. See Cass R. Sunstein, *One Case at a Time—Judicial Minimalism on the Supreme Court* (Cambridge, 1999).

[19] Compare Avi Sagi, *Society and Law in Israel: Between a Rights Discourse and an Identity Discourse* (Ramat-Gan, 2001).

chosen for this purpose—that of Israel—is an ideal candidate in the present context, because of the multicultural and highly divided nature of Israeli society, usually described as a ruptured society, chequered by numerous ethnic, cultural, ideological and social schisms. These include a religious–secular split, an Arab–Jewish split, as well as socio-economic and ethnic divisions even within the Jewish population.[20] Consequently, there is a strong desire to find uniting denominators which may contribute to a better social cohesion. In the past, Zionist ideology succeeded in providing a shared and unifying ethos for the majority of the Israeli public (more accurately, the Jewish Israeli public) but today, it is no longer capable of bridging the gaps and the internal tensions within Israeli society.[21] Furthermore, since the 1980s the Israeli judiciary has become a panacea for problems that have not found a solution in other forums. Clearly, the process of 'legalization' that has engulfed Israel is indicative of Israeli society's disenchantment with the divided world of politics, and its hope to find answers by having recourse to its legal system.[22] As a result, the centrality of the legal system in Israeli social and political life makes it a worthy candidate to serve as a tool of social unification.

Israeli Legislation in the Service of Unification and Nation-Building

After the establishment of Israel in 1948, legislation served an important tool in the service of the Israeli nation-building project. Israeli law was based on the heritage of the British Mandate legal system, but the first years of the State, mainly during the 1950s, were characterized by intensive legislative activity intended to crystallize and solidify the nascent 'Israeli' society. It is interesting to note that the political system also chose to utilize legal tools in realizing the goals of unity and solidarity in addition to initiatives in other arenas. Ben-Gurion's conception of 'Statehood' (*Mamlachtiyut*)[23] assigned an important role to the law as a normative system of general application, which embodies the connection between the

[20] Over the years, the ethnic divide within the Jewish population (between European and non-European Jews) has been absorbed into the broader problem of economic stratification of Israeli society. In practice, there is a relatively large proportion of Jewish immigrants from Arab countries in the economically weaker social strata.

[21] See Baruch Kimmerling, 'The New Israelis—Cultural Plurality without Multiculturalism' (1998) 16 *Alpayim* 264 (Hebrew).

[22] In this context, Nir Kedar wrote that the 'legalization' of Israeli society is also part of the process in which certain groups in the Israeli society consciously attempt to present an alternative, which they regard as an 'objective' clean, and efficient alternative to the disappointing political system, characterized as corrupted and impotent. In this process, law and the interpretive dialogue as its agent, become both the method of proposing an alternative to politics and the alternative itself. See Nir Kedar, 'Interpretative Revolution: The Rise of Purposive Interpretation in Israeli Law' (2002) 26 *Tel-Aviv University Law Review.* 737 (Hebrew).

[23] Eliezer Don-Yehiya, 'Political Religion in a New State: Ben-Gurion's Mamlachtiyut' in *Israel—The First Decade of Independence* (S. Ilan Troen and Noah Lucas (eds), Albany, 1995), 171.

individual and society.[24] As noted by Horowitz and Lissak, the adoption of a legal system with general application also had the effect of limiting, though not eliminating, potential for factional-partisan arrangements between the central political institutions and groups or individuals.[25]

Legislation Regarding National Institutions

The establishment of the State of Israel went hand in hand with the establishment of its national institutions. Apart from their functional purposes, these institutions were also intended to serve as consolidating forces in Israeli society. Naturally, the imposition of compulsory military service fulfilled an existential need for the State of Israel. Yet, the Defense Service Law 1949 was enacted in a manner that intended to accommodate the enlistment of the largest possible portion of Israeli society in awareness of the unifying function of the army,[26] and the Kosher Food for Soldiers Ordinance, 1948 was intended to guarantee better integration of religious soldiers in military service. Similar things can be said regarding the education legislation during those years. It was intended to ensure basic education for all, but in fact purported to go beyond this purpose. The State Education Law, 1953, which was enacted as a supplement to the Compulsory Education Law, 1949, aspired to standard, non-party education, which would inculcate universal shared values.[27] In the same manner, the State Service (Appointments) Law, 1959 was intended to lay the foundation for a public service that would be open for all, as opposed to a system based on political criteria.

Indeed, the implementation of these laws has not always mirrored the statutory ideal they embodied. The public service has never been entirely non-factional; general state education was established alongside a statutory recognition of the autonomous and independent ultra-Orthodox educational streams, and the partially autonomous state-religious educational stream; the Arab citizens and

[24] See Nir Kedar, 'Ben-Gurion and the Struggle to Appoint a Sepharadi Justice to the Israeli Supreme Court' (2003) 19 *Bar-Ilan Law Studies* 515, 534 ('Law, as a normative system and as a social and cultural institution, plays an important role in Ben-Gurion's conception of republican statehood. Law is important for Ben-Gurion because like the modern state, it is general, and its purpose is not only to regulate the mutual relations in the mass modern society, but also to serve as an agent for the liberation of man and society').

[25] Dan Horowitz and Moshe Lissak, *Trouble in Utopia: The Overburdened Polity of Israel* (trans by Charles Hoffman, Albany, 1989), 155: 'the adoption of a universalistic legal system, a legacy of the British Mandate, worked to reduce the occurrence of particularistic arrangements between the political center and groups and individuals that were common under the ambiguous rules of the game of the Organized *Yishuv*'.

[26] In the Knesset deliberations devoted to the enactment of this law, Ben-Gurion stated that: 'We must not ignore the destructive and divisive forces that still operate amongst us. Our factional and ideological fragmentation is no less than that which characterizes the most inferior and depraved nations ... apart from the school which is also partially tainted by factionalism, only the Army can and must serve as a merging and elevating force in forging the new character of the nation, and its proper integration into the new culture and society that has been created in the State of Israel' (1949) 2 *Knesset Protocols* 1338.

[27] See also Eyal Kafkafy, *A Country Searching for its People* (Tel-Aviv, 1991) (Hebrew).

ultra-Orthodox Jews are usually granted de-facto exemptions from the military draft.[28] Even so, it is important to note that legislation was an important tool in the promotion of Ben-Gurion's conception of 'statehood' during the 1950s. It also defined the targets to be aspired to even when their materialization was less than total. The conception of statehood was also consistent with the establishment of a professional and autonomous judiciary, one of the features of the Israeli legal system from its early beginning.[29]

Legislation in the Symbolic Realm

The 1950s were also the years of legislation intended to decorate the State with national symbols considered crucial for identification with the collective. The choice of the State flag and emblem were anchored in the Flag and Emblem Law 1949. The national memorial days were similarly anchored in laws that dealt with the memory of fallen soldiers and the victims of the Holocaust (Heroes' Remembrance Day (War of Independence and Israel Defense Army) Law 1963 and Martyrs and Heroes' Remembrance Day Law, 1953).[30] The Labour Hours and Rest Law, 1951 instituted the Sabbath (Saturday), the traditional Jewish day of rest, as the State of Israel's principal day of rest. Similarly, the legislation prohibiting pig-raising[31] and limiting commerce in pork,[32] followed the traditional Jewish prohibitions on pig-raising and pork consumption.[33] Notably, the importance of these symbols as unifying factors was limited to the Israeli Jewish public and did not extend to the Arab minority.

Welfare Legislation

The broad welfare legislation of the 1950s also played an important role in the consolidation of Israeli society. In this context, particular importance should be attached to the comprehensive protective legislation dealing with workers' rights,

[28] At the same time, Ben-Gurion totally rejected the demand to establish separate units for religious soldiers. Relating to this demand he wrote in his diary: 'I told them: "A. Our army will be unified without any factions; B. To Keep it unified we shall make it kosher throughout"'. See Tom Segev, *1949: The First Israelis* (Arlen Neal Weinstein (ed.), New York, 1986), 252. The separate frameworks for religious soldiers in the format of *Yeshivot Hesder* (special army programs, combining religious studies and army service), and *Nachal Haredi* (separate army service for ultra-orthodox Jews) are far later developments.

[29] At the same time, the tradition of professional appointments of judges conflicted with Ben-Gurion's concept of statehood when he aspired to appoint a *Sephardi* (non-European Jewish) judge to the Supreme Court as a means of promoting social solidarity and social inclusion of Jewish immigrants from the Arab countries. See: Kedar, n.24, above.

[30] Regarding symbolic legislation see further Yifat Holzman Gazit, 'Law as a Symbol of Status: The Jewish National Fund Law of 1953 and the Struggle of the Fund to Maintain its Status after Israel's Independence' (2002) 26 *Tel-Aviv University Law Review* 601.

[31] Pig Raising Prohibition Law, 1962.

[32] Local Authorities (Special Enablement) Law, 1956.

[33] For a more extensive treatment of this issue, see: Daphne Barak-Erez, 'The Transformation of the Pig Laws: From a National Symbol to a Religious Interest?' (2003) 33 *Mishpatim* 403 (Hebrew); Daphne Barak-Erez, *Outlawed Pigs: Law, Religion and Culture in Israel* (forthcoming).

such as the Labor Hours and Rest Law 1951, already mentioned above, and the establishment of the National Insurance system by the National Insurance Law 1953. This legislation was inspired by the socialist ideology of the first Israeli governments, but in a broader perspective, it is important to recognize its seminal contribution to social cohesion in terms of establishing a society predicated on mutual help. It is a prime example of values of social solidarity poured into legal vessels, which further fortified the status of these values. At the same time, it is important to note that the welfare legislation of that time did not create social solidarity, but rather expressed it. It helped to enhance that which was in existence even without it. Furthermore, in view of the accepted norms in the employment market during those years and the powerful status of the *Histadrut*, the main workers' union, it was possible to guarantee workers' rights even without legislation.

The Declaration of Independence and the Missing Constitution

The most obvious omission in the Israeli project of unity and solidarity through law was the failure of the initiative to establish a national constitution. As mentioned above, constitutions are tools for the inculcation and propagation of a society's most cherished values. In Israel, this important document is still missing. To a limited extent, Israel's Declaration of Independence fulfilled the unifying role normally designated for a national constitution. The Declaration was considered an expression of national consensus at a rare historical moment. Indeed, in deciding hard cases, the Israeli Supreme Court repeatedly invoked the spirit of the Declaration of Independence as a document that expressed the 'national vision', and the national 'I believe' (credo).[34]

Legislation and the Price of Unity through Law

The aspiration to achieve unity by enacting laws of consensus also had its price. The realm of Israeli family law provides an example. In this area, religious law was applied to matters of marriage and divorce, primarily due to unity-based considerations. This compromise achieved with the Jewish religious sector was understood as necessary to prevent division in the Jewish nation. The compromise led to the enactment of the Rabbinical Courts' Jurisdiction (Marriage and Divorce) Law 1953. The price of this compromise is paid by all those who are aggrieved by the application of religious law in this area as the sole alternative for marriage and divorce—women (who are often discriminated against by religious law), atheists (who have to take part in a religious ceremony for the purpose of getting married) and people interested in marrying a partner of a different religion or sex (and are barred from doing so, because their religion does not recognize these possibilities. As a result, despite its enactment as a harbinger of unity, this law has become an ongoing source of foment and division in Israeli society.

[34] The source of this expression is in the Supreme Court decision HCJ 10/48 *Ziv* v. *Gubernik* 1 PD 85, 89.

Judicial Decision-Making in a Search for Unity

Judicial Perceptions Regarding Shared Values

The Israeli judiciary has always tried to function alongside the Israeli legislature as an agent of social consensus. Since its foundation, the Supreme Court has regarded itself a national institution which echoes the voice of Israeli society. On numerous occasions it noted that it dwells amongst its people,[35] and that it both recognizes and expresses the values of society.[36] In the context of public law, the court cites social values as guiding principles for the exercise of judicial review. The question of whether an administrative decision is tainted by irrelevant considerations is examined in view of these values,[37] and in the same vein, the process of assessing whether an administrative decision followed the dictates of equality (and abstained from irrelevant distinctions) also relies on the 'fundamental values of law'.[38] The Court assumes the existence of a network of shared values that its decisions should reflect and befit,[39] echoing Dworkin's writings.[40] In addition, as already indicated, the Israeli Supreme Court has always regarded the Israeli Declaration of Independence as reflecting the national credo of the Israeli polity. Its assumption has been that a national credo of this nature exists, and that the Court is its trumpet.[41]

The inclination of the Israeli Supreme Court to act as the agent of social norms has increased since the 1980s, and in this respect there has been a 'role reversal' between the legislative-political branch and the judiciary. On the one hand, the political system's ability to determine the national agenda (including its legislative

[35] See, e.g. SSA 1928/00 *State of Israel* v. *Beruchin* 54(3) PD 694, 704 ('The court dwells amongst its people, and it reads, hears and knows that the phenomenon of sexual harassment is still rife').

[36] See, e.g. HCJ 7074/93 *Swissa* v. *Attorney General* 48(2) PD 749, 784–5.

[37] Justice Aharon Barak, later to be the President of the Supreme Court of Israel, dealt at length with the function of the basic values of society in this context. He explained that: 'The assumption is that the purpose of any legislative act is to realize the fundamental values of the system and not to contravene them'. See: HCJ 953/87 *Poraz* v. *Mayor of Tel-Aviv-Jaffa* 42(2) PD 311, 329–30. As for the sources of these fundamental values, he added that: 'The judge deduces these fundamental values from the "fabric of national life" of the people ... the judge finds expressions of these in its fundamental documents, such as the Declaration of Independence, which is a legal norm that expresses the nation's proclamation of its values ... another expression of the basic values may be found in the various laws giving them normative expression. But beyond all these, the fundamental values have an extra-legislative, extra-documentary existence, and are not a closed list. They change in accordance with changes in the "fabric of the national life" of the people'. *Ibid*, 330.

[38] Judge Zamir addressed this issue in one of his judgments: 'How does one determine the parameters of the equality group in a particular case ... since the law does not provide an answer to this question, we must extrapolate the answer in this case, as in all other cases, from the purpose of the law, the nature of the case, the fundamental values of the Israeli legal system and the particular circumstances of the case in question. Based on all the above, we can determine, with reference to a particular case, whether a specific characteristic or other is a pertinent consideration or not'. See: HCJ 6086, 6051/95 *Rekanat* v. *National Labour Court* 51(3) PD 289, 347.

[39] See also: Aharon Barak, 'Foreword: A Judge on Judging: The Role of a Supreme Court in a Democracy' (2002) 116 *Harvard Law Review* 16, 86–8.

[40] See n.14, above.

[41] See n. 34, above. See also: HCJ 73/53 *Kol Ha'am* v. *Minister of the Interior* 7 PD 871, 884.

expression) has steadily declined. On the other hand, the judicial system, led by the Supreme Court, has become increasingly involved in normative decisions which claim to express shared basic values, and as a result, it is frequently criticized as too 'activist'.[42]

Problems of Resorting to the Judiciary

The growing centrality of the courts in Israeli public life has been accompanied by increasing opposition to the legitimacy of its rulings and—by extension—to the values it proclaims. In fact, the controversy around precedents of the Israeli Supreme Court is not new, but its scope and level have broadened over the years. Even in the 1950s, the Supreme Court gave expression to values that were not subject to consensus. It served as a bastion of individualistic, liberal ethos (in contrast to the collectivist spirit that dominated the political realm) and thus established an unwritten bill of rights. Occasionally, it delivered decisions that were at the centre of political and value-oriented controversies, for example, the recognition of the status of non-married cohabitants.[43] Even so, until the 1980s the Court itself (as opposed to specific issues it adjudicated) was not the focus of dispute in Israeli society, for several reasons. First, the Court underplayed the value-based dimension of its rulings, which were presented in formalistic rhetoric,[44] and wherever possible eschewed the adjudication (and resolution) of questions that were regarded as political, by invoking preliminary doctrines such as standing and justiciability.[45] Secondly, the subordination of the judiciary to the decisions of the political system was clear and undisputed in the sense that the legislature was considered sovereign and its laws were not subject to judicial review (in contrast to administrative actions). Therefore, any controversial judgment from the perspective of the political system could be overturned by legislation. A representative example for this was the controversy around the definition of the word 'Jew' for purposes of the Law of Return 1951 and the Population Registration Law 1963.[46] Thirdly, until the end of the 1970s, the hegemony of the Labour Party in the political system effectively stifled any significant controversy over the constitutive values of Israeli society.

The 1980s witnessed changes both in the format of judicial decisions and in the social-political circumstances surrounding them. It was during this period that

[42] See (1993) 17(3) *Tel-Aviv University Law Review* ('Special Issue: Judicial Activism in Israel').

[43] See: HCJ 563/65 *Yeger* v. *Palevitz* 20(3) PD 244.

[44] See: Menachem Mautner, *The Decline of Formalism and the Rise of Values in Israeli Law* (Tel-Aviv, 1993) (Hebrew).

[45] For example, the Court refused to adjudicate the question of establishing diplomatic relations with Germany. See HCJ 186/65 *Reiner* v. *Prime Minister* 19(2) PD 485.

[46] In a very disputed decision the Israeli Supreme Court allowed the registration of children born to a Jewish father and a non-Jewish mother as 'Jews' based on their parents' declaration, and against the religious doctrine, which recognizes as Jews only children born to a Jewish mother. See: HCJ 58/68 *Shalit* v. *Minister of the Interior* 23(2) PD 477. This decision was soon after followed by an amendment to the relevant legislation that defined the word 'Jew' in a way that followed the ancient Jewish tradition: 'a person who was born of a Jewish mother or has become converted to Judaism'.

the Israeli Supreme Court opened its gates to petitions that previously would have been dismissed out of hand due to lack of standing or non-justiciability. The Court was now prepared to recognize the status of public petitioners who represent a matter of concern to the public as a whole, especially if the petition raises questions with ramifications for the rule of law. In addition, only rarely would such cases now be considered non-justiciable.[47] The Court has also begun using value-laden terms such as 'good faith' and 'reasonableness'.[48] The result was that the ideological-evaluative component of judicial decisions became increasingly prominent, exposing them to criticism regarding both the values that should be endorsed by the court and the legitimacy of its value-laden decisions. In addition, judicial resort to terms such as 'the enlightened public' was considered as alienating social groups that not only opposed the new precedents of the Israeli Supreme Court, but also felt that in the Court's eyes they were the epitome of 'darkness' and archaism.[49] Another background factor that influenced these developments was the termination of the Labour Party's political hegemony following the 1977 elections.[50]

Criticism of the Israeli Supreme Court intensified due to changes that occurred during the 1990s, following the enactment of two new Basic Laws regarding the protection of human rights—Basic Law: Freedom of Occupation, and Basic Law: Human Dignity and Liberty. These Basic Laws specified a list of human rights which were granted constitutional protection against infringing legislation, and therefore threatened the omnipotence of the legislature. The Basic Laws did not include a specific provision on judicial review of legislation, but the Court has interpreted them as implying this result. The President of the Supreme Court, Aharon Barak, described the enactment of these Basic Laws as a 'constitutional revolution',[51] terminology which attracted both attention and criticism. Soon after, this interpretation also had practical results, when the courts started to review legislation which was understood as infringing on rights protected by the new Basic

[47] A landmark judgment in terms of this new approach regarding standing and justiciability concerned a public petition against the policy of non-enlisting *Yeshiva* students to the military service. See: HCJ 810/86 *Ressler* v. *Minister of Defense* 42(2) PD 441. The petition was rejected, but the Court's judgment recognized the petitioners' standing and the justiciability of the subject matter, and therefore paved the way for the petitions that were to follow.

[48] The concept of 'good faith' was adopted by the Contract Law legislation (primarily in sections 12 and 39 of the Contracts (General Part) Law, 1973), as opposed to the requirement of administrative 'reasonableness', which was the product of case law. Even so, it was case law that bestowed the principle of 'good faith' with its elevated status as a 'majestic principle', applicable to all fields of law.

[49] Ronen Shamir, 'Society, Judaism and Democratic Fundamentalism—on the Social Roots of Judicial Interpretation' (1995) 19 *Tel-Aviv University Law Review* 699, 715 (Hebrew).

[50] For a detailed description of society and politics during the 1980s, see: Menachem Mautner, 'The 1980s—Years of Anxiety' (2002) 26 *Tel-Aviv University Law Review* 645 (Hebrew).

[51] This term was ingrained in the consciousness of the legal community primarily due to the writings of the President of the Israeli Supreme Court, Aharon Barak. See: Aharon Barak, 'The Constitutional Revolution: Protected Human Rights' (1992–93) 1 *Mishpat Umimshal* 9 (Hebrew); Aharon Barak, 'The Constitutional Revolution: Scope and Limitations' (1992–93) 1 *Mishpat Umimshal* 253 (Hebrew).

Laws.[52] Another controversy aroused by the new Basic Laws was associated with the provision which declared that their purpose is to establish in a Basic Law the values of the State of Israel as a Jewish and democratic state.[53] This provision had the effect of emphasizing the ideological dimension of Court decisions.

The developments around the enactment of the Basic Laws on human rights provided further impetus for the voices of criticism on the Israeli Supreme Court. In matters pertaining to the interpretation of the 'Jewish and democratic' formula, the Court is often perceived as expressing the values of a relatively limited segment of Israeli society—elitist, Western and liberal.[54] The potential of judicial review of legislation further sharpened the criticism against the Supreme Court. The result of all these developments seems to be that despite the official view of the Court that it embodies and reflects the values of the entire Israeli society, in fact it does not function any more as the exclusive mouthpiece for commonly shared values. There are numerous communities that regard it as being the mouthpiece of one particular community in Israeli society: one of many.

The intensified controversy over the role played by the Israeli Supreme Court results also from the defective functioning of the other branches of the Israeli Government. Questions left unresolved by the political system invariably find their way to the courts. Ultimately, the result is that the court system finds itself in the eye of the storm even when the criticism should properly be directed at other authorities. There are many examples of this phenomenon. One of the Supreme Court's important and controversial decisions in the area of law and religion—regarding an administrative decision to prohibit the use of cars in a central road in Jerusalem during prayer times on Sabbath—was given only after the failure of many attempts to reach an acceptable compromise.[55] In the same manner, the question of the draft exemption granted to *Yeshiva* students (who pursue full-time traditional Jewish studies) was repeatedly brought to the Supreme Court because the political system was unable to provide a satisfactory solution, which would assuage the hostility generated by the existing arrangement among the general population. Only after the Court declared that this exemption is *ultra vires*[56] has the Knesset started to address the matter in its legislation, and even then only partially.[57] The dysfunctionality of the political system also contributes to the

[52] See: CA 6821/93 *United Mizrachi Bank* v. *Migdal Cooperative Village* 49(4) PD 221.

[53] Section 2 of Basic Law: Freedom of Occupation, and section 1A of Basic Law: Human Dignity and Liberty.

[54] In fact, the Basic Law's reference to the phrase 'Jewish and democratic' places the Court in a trap, in view of the deep division in Israeli society regarding its meaning. Accordingly, while judges are commanded by the legislature to base their rulings on these values, any decision in this matter inevitably generates controversy.

[55] HCJ 5016/96 *Horev* v. *Minister of Transport* 51(4) PD 1.

[56] HCJ 3267/97, 715/98 *Rubinstein* v. *Minister of Defense* 52(5) PD 481. In this case, the Court ruled that a general exemption on a group basis requires specific authorization in primary Knesset legislation and therefore necessitates an amendment to the Defense Service Law [Consolidated Version], 1986.

[57] The Court's decision that the exemption given to *Yeshiva* students is *ultra vires* led to the enactment of the Law on Service Deferments for Full-Time *Yeshivah* Students, 2002, which officially

criticism of the judiciary in another way. Many petitions which lead to value-based judicial decisions begin as public petitions of players in the political arena, like Knesset members, usually those who do not succeed in gaining a majority for their views.[58] In these circumstances, the judicial decisions are sometimes understood as siding with the political agenda of the petitioners. In the same manner, groups who regard themselves permanent losers in the Court are motivated to attack it in the political arena.

The Contribution to the Public Debate

The tentative conclusion so far is that in Israel, judicial enunciation of consensual values did not enhance social unity and perhaps even led to the reverse. Sometimes, it merely aggravated existing feelings of alienation felt by certain groups. Nonetheless, as indicated above, the process of litigation can contribute to social cohesion by supplying a discursive framework that would not otherwise exist. The adjudication of passionately disputed questions such as 'Who is a Jew?'[59] or 'enlistment of *Yeshiva* students'[60] is invariably accompanied by heated debates in the public arena and by attempts to 'win' the public relations battle. In other words, the judicial proceedings also catalyze public discussion of the issues outside the walls of the courts. The recurrent litigation over the question of 'Who is a Jew?' forced Israeli society to confront repressed questions regarding its understanding of Judaism and the concept of Jewish identity in our time, although the Court's decision in this matter was formalistic.[61] In the same vein, when the Supreme Court was asked to review the practice of establishing settlements for 'Jews only',[62] Israeli society was compelled to address the tension between the Zionist ethos of settlement and the democratic ethos of equality.[63] A similar social process developed following the proceedings of the Commission of Inquiry headed by Justice Orr, which investigated the events of October 2000 in the Arab sector, where thirteen Israeli Arabs were killed by the police in the course of heated demonstrations. The commission's deliberations stimulated public discussion of questions relating to the status and rights of Israel's Arab citizens. In addition, quite often judicial decisions serve as catalysts for the instigation of political decision-making. For example, following the 'Who is a Jew' decision which ordered the registration of the children of the petitioners as Jews, the Israeli Knesset passed

sanctioned the current situation, but created a mechanism enabling the students to leave their studies for a 'year of decision', during which they can examine the possibility of integration into the work market without exposing themselves to the 'danger' of enlistment.

[58] Mautner, n.50, above, 671–72.

[59] For the purposes of the Law of Return. See: n.46, above.

[60] See the text accompanying n.56, above.

[61] According to the judicial precedent in this matter, the Ministry of Interior is obligated to register as a Jew every person who presents documents which prima facie prove it.

[62] HCJ 6698/95 *Qa'adan* v. *Israel Land Authority* 54(1) PD 258.

[63] As an example for the discussions generated by these proceedings, see: (2001) 6(1) *Mishpat Umimshal* 212.

an amending law which defined the word 'Jew' for the purposes of registration and the Law of Return. Many years later, in the context of the military service of *Yeshiva* students, although the Court refrained from specifically enunciating its own preferred view, its declaration that the administrative exemption granted to them was *ultra vires* compelled the Knesset to act and pass a new law on this matter, after years of abstention.

Once again, it is important to stress the shortcomings of the dialogue triggered by legal proceedings. It is usually a dialogue influenced by the legal environment, and limited to a discourse of rights. Hence, when several organizations filed petitions against the decisions of the Israel Lands Council to grant broad rights to agricultural lessees, the litigation focused almost exclusively on questions of contractual rights. This dictated total disregard of the ethnic rift underlying the entire case (the petitioners opposing the decisions claimed to represent mainly Jews who immigrated to Israel from Arab countries and the lessees benefiting from it were identified mainly as Jews from European origins). Admittedly, the Supreme Court's judgment was based on the principle of 'distributive justice',[64] and this rhetoric only expressed the class-status-related aspect of the case and not its ethnic background.

Developing a Judicially-inspired Value System?

Is there a possibility that court rulings will also help to develop a value system with a uniting effect on Israeli society? So far, I have expressed serious reservations regarding the viability of such an enterprise. I did so with reference to two main categories of litigation relating to the 'classic' political schisms dividing Israeli society: the religious–secular split and the Arab–Jewish conflict. The powerful ideologies fuelling these conflicts appear to preclude any possibility that judicial decisions in these areas would lead to a new social consensus (although they may contribute to a social dialogue over the issues debated in court). At the same time, from time to time it is possible to point to judicial precedents which serve as catalysts for the forging of consensual values. In the United States, the *Brown* decision which abolished racial segregation in the public schools system[65] was the pillar of fire that blazed the way to the consolidation of broad social rejection of segregation, despite the controversy that ensued when this judgment was first given. In the Israeli context, a famous decision of the Supreme Court ruled that a group of youngsters who forced themselves on a young girl, without the use of physical force, had committed the offence of rape. This judgment was a consensus-rallying decision with respect to the autonomy of women.[66] When the Court defined rape as non-consensual sexual intercourse even absent physical resistance, it ushered in a new social consensus regarding women's autonomy and their rights

[64] HCJ 244/00 *New Deliberation Association for Democratic Deliberation* v. *Minister of National Infrastructure* 56(6) PD 25.

[65] See n.9, above.

[66] CrA 5612/92 *State of Israel* v. *Be'eri* 48(1) PD 302.

over their bodies. A possible conclusion is that courts have a better chance to influence social perceptions in ordinary 'civil' areas than in matters directly touching the sensitive roots of ethnic and religious disputes which Israeli society is struggling with.

Another example of a civil area in which law traditionally had a unifying role in Israel concerns the realm of social justice. At the dawn of the twenty-first century, Israeli society is a torn and ruptured society—divided not only according to the classical rifts already mentioned, but also by socio-economic gaps. Recent years have witnessed the gradual broadening of socio-economic gaps, as a result of the inability of the traditional welfare legislation of the 1950s to withstand the pressures of globalization on the one hand, and the tremendous burden imposed by Israel's grave security situation on the other. Entire sectors of the Israeli population currently lead lives of degradation and atrophy, unable to extricate themselves from the debilitating cycle of poverty; with the welfare system powerless to help, crippled by manpower and budgetary shortages. Against this background, an interesting question is whether judicial recognition and enforcement of social rights can assist in bridging the socio-economic gap and ameliorating its evils, and thus contribute to the enhancement of social cohesion. There is some ground for hope that judicial decisions in this area will create a social consensus on the protection of the dignity of the poor. It is based on the understanding that while disputes concerning matters of social justice are severe and sometimes intractable, they are unrelated to conflicts with long and bloodstained histories. At the same time, controversies over issues of globalization and privatization prove to be more bitter than in the past, and therefore scepticism should not be neglected in this context as well.

To date, judicial decisions in Israel have had an important, though restricted, contribution to the development of a public culture of social justice. In its seminal decision on the matter of the agricultural lands, the Israeli Supreme Court ruled that administrative authorities are obliged to act in accordance with the value of 'distributive justice'.[67] The Court has also progressed towards recognizing the constitutional status of social rights, such as the right to education, bestowing on them the status of basic rights.[68] Still, the courts can and must go further. Admittedly, the Supreme Court cannot 'create' budgets out of thin air, but it can ensure just allocation of resources,[69] and it can impose sanctions on administrative authorities that attempt to 'save' their budgets by the systematic harassment of

[67] See the text accompanying n.64, above.

[68] HCJ 2599/00 *Yated, Association of Parents of Children with Down's Syndrome* v. *Minister of Education* 56(5) PD 856.

[69] See: HCJ 2814/97 *Supreme Follow-up Committee for Education of Arabs in Israel* v. *Minister of Education, Culture and Sport* 54(3) PD 233 (petition against the failure to include the Arab sector in education and welfare programmes initiated by Ministry of Education); HCJ 727/00 *Committee of Heads of Arab Local Authorities* v. *Minister of Construction and Residence* 56(2) PD 79 (petition against the discrimination of the Arab sector in the framework of suburban renewal project).

welfare recipients in the form of impenetrable bureaucracy.[70] In other words, the law should play an amalgamative role in the creation of a civil society predicated on communal solidarity. The aspiration to social justice is shared by most of the segments of Israeli society and may provide a basis for a renewed social contract between populations that lack any other common denominator—Jews and Arabs, religious and secular.

Intermediate Summary: Dialogue and Civil Values

This chapter has argued that the recourse to law as a unifying force in society is not a wonder solution, particularly not when deeply rooted disputes are in the background. As long as the values underlying conflicts brought to legal resolutions are disputed, the law pertaining to them will also be disputed. However, law can still make some contribution to social reconciliation and reconstruction. First and foremost, the legislative arena can be utilized for initiating laws aimed at nation-building and reconciliation between groups. In addition, although legal proceedings cannot fulfil the same role, they can serve a stimulus to the revival of a vigorous social dialogue.

Is there any chance that the content of judicial decisions will serve as a source of inspiration for the crystallization of social consensus? The discussion so far has expressed serious reservations regarding this possibility. These reservations were based primarily on examples taken from areas shaded by historical group rivalries. The discussion pointed, however, at the possibility for such a development in the context of judicial decisions centred on matters of individual autonomy and dignity.

It is important to add that even when judicial precedents express values which have the potential for being accepted by relatively broad sectors of society, they will not contribute to the creation of social consensus unless their content is delivered to the public in an effective manner. If the law is to make a significant contribution, measures must be adopted to improve the information flow from the legal professional community to the public at large. The problem is not one of exposure per se; indeed, courts are permanently exposed to the public eye, and are probably among the most extensively covered public institutions. Media exposure as such is not sufficient, however. In fact, public exposure to current affairs is more limited than in the past, due to the 'explosion' of information and the 'clip'- or 'sound bite'-oriented nature of the news reports on court proceedings. This is not a criticism of the media, but rather recognition of the new reality of the public discourse. In addition, even when the relevant information is forthcoming, quite

[70] The erosion of welfare rights by bureaucratic methods is also dealt with in Daphne Barak-Erez, 'The Israeli Welfare State: Growing Expectations and Diminishing Returns' *The Welfare State, Globalization and International Law* (Eyal Benvenisti and Georg Nolte (eds), Berlin, 2004), 103.

often the public lacks any real understanding of the precise question that was resolved by the court and the reasons for its ruling, including the constraints surrounding it.[71] Accordingly, the potential of the judiciary to contribute to the evolution of consensual values is contingent also on the civic education given by the school system, which should provide better tools for understanding the content of court decisions and their limitations.

[71] Media coverage is usually limited to a presentation of the question being resolved by the Court and the result of its decision.

11

The Place of Legal Culture in the Sociology of Law

Lawrence M. Friedman

The study of the sociology of law, like all branches of human learning, rests on certain critical and basic assumptions. Some of these are empirical assumptions—that is, assumptions that are either in principle or in practice testable. Some, on the other hand, are not.

Scholars who study the sociology of law all start out (consciously or not) with some sort of basic feeling or assumption about the *autonomy* of the legal system (either about the legal system they happen to be studying, or about legal systems in general). By 'autonomy,' I mean the degree to which the system grows, changes, and develops, according to a kind of inner programme. An autonomous system is essentially detached from the outside world. It is 'independent of other sources of power and authority in social life'.[1] An autonomous system does not respond to pressures and influences coming from the outside world, although it is (and must be) connected in some way to that outside world. The genetic programme of an organism, for example, is a system that can be described as autonomous. This seed is programmed to become a rose, this cell is programmed to become an octopus; and, given food, sunlight, and the like—inputs from the outside world—that is exactly what will become of them.

No serious sociologist of law thinks of the law in terms as extreme as the genetic programme of a rose or an octopus.[2] No serious sociologist of law considers the legal system, in other words, as something which is totally autonomous; which is as free from social, cultural, economic, and political influences as the genetic programme. There are, however, quite a few who think the law is *relatively* autonomous,

[1] Richard Lempert and Joseph Sanders, *An Invitation to Law and Social Science* (Harlow, 1986), 402.

[2] Perhaps such scholars as Gunther Teubner and Niklas Luhmann can be described as coming fairly close. They describe law as one of the sub-systems of society which are 'operationally closed', that is, their mode of operation is not regulated by normative factors external to them. They 'function self-referentially in accordance with their own internal logic, reproducing their constituent elements by referring to themselves.' They are, however, 'cognitively open in the sense that they selectively absorb information from their environment.' Reza Banakar, *Merging Law and Sociology: Beyond the Dichotomies in Socio-Legal Research* (Berlin, 2003), 110.

or partially autonomous, or that it has autonomous features.[3] Probably the majority of law and society scholars lean toward a conclusion which is much closer to the opposite pole. They have doubts about the autonomy of any legal system. In fact, it is possible to think of law as almost completely lacking in autonomy, as almost completely subject to the outside world—as a dependent variable, plain and simple. Probably not many scholars take quite so extreme a position; but some approach it. I have to confess that I tend to fall into this category.

The law and society scholars of this sort—the ones that think law is, on the whole, less rather than more autonomous—do not, of course, agree with each other on every detail. But if we put these disagreements to one side, I think we do find a kind of consensus that the outside world, the larger society, has a powerful, formative influence on legal systems—on every legal system—and that the outside world basically shapes the legal system in its image. Indeed, there are some who think a statement of this type distorts reality; they feel the legal order is in fact so enmeshed in the processes, culture, and institutions that make up society, that it makes no sense even trying to separate 'law' from 'society'. Each helps to 'constitute' the other.[4] It makes no sense, for example, to put such concepts and institutions as marriage, property, contract, or crime into a separate box called 'the legal system;' they are simply too fundamental.

There are four other basic propositions—closely linked to each other—which are also, I think, essential to the thought and research of most sociologists of law. These are simple, almost banal propositions; but it may be worthwhile to set them out. The first proposition is this: whether a legal rule, order, or institution actually does what it claims to do or is supposed to do, whether it has any impact at all, is always an empirical question. Conventional legal scholarship is obsessed with norms and rules. Whether these norms and rules make any difference, whether they have no effect at all, some effect, or even a negative or perverse effect, is a matter that somehow does not concern the main body of jurists. But we know that some rules have a strong impact, others only a weak impact, and some seem to have no impact at all. Some are actually counterproductive. Moreover, legal interventions have both direct effects and also indirect effects, effects like the ripples that follow when we heave a stone into water. We ought to be able to say something systematic about what kinds of rules, in which societies, have what sort of impact, and when; but this would require a great deal of research—much more than we now have at our fingertips.

[3] See the discussion in Lempert and Sanders, op cit., 405–27.

[4] Robert W. Gordon puts it this way: 'in practice, it is just about impossible to describe any set of "basic" social practices without describing the legal relations among the people involved—legal relations that . . . to an important extent define the constitutive terms of the relationship, relations such as lord and peasant, master and slave, employer and employee.' 'Critical Legal Histories,' (1984) 36 *Stanford Law Review* 57, at 103. A related notion, which Efrén Rivera Ramos refers to as 'legal consciousness', is the 'awareness of law as a constitutive element of personal and social experience that, in turn, produces a tendency to view the world through juridical lenses.' *The Legal Construction of Identity: The Judicial and Social Legacy of American Colonialism in Puerto Rico* (Washington, D.C., 2001), 218.

Secondly, the norms or rules themselves do not determine their own effects or consequences; we have to look outside the legal system itself—at least, outside the legal system as narrowly defined—and into the larger society to find out why these effects occur, as well as what they are. If Italian drivers are less likely to wear seat belts than English drivers, the differences in the texts of the laws about seat belts in the two countries are not likely to give us an explanation.[5] If a line of judicial decisions narrows the meaning of a rule, or conversely expands it, you are unlikely to understand why this is happening by studying the original rule meticulously—or even by looking at what professors of law have written about the rule. Of course, the impact of a rule depends very heavily on enforcement. Rules do not administer themselves or enforce themselves. The level of enforcement, quite obviously, is itself socially determined.

Thirdly, any significant change in society—in its structure, its economy, its position in the world, its culture or politics—will invariably lead to some sort of legal reaction. To talk about 'inertia' in the legal system is anthropomorphic. There is no drag or inertia inherent in the legal system. You often hear people say that some aspect of the legal system is 'archaic', or the like; or that the law has failed to 'keep up', or that it is 'behind the times'. Or that the legal system is inherently 'conservative.' But when people say this, they are on the whole simply saying that they disapprove of this or that feature of a legal system. No aspect of the legal system of any importance survives unless some concrete interest derives some benefit from it, or wants it to survive for whatever reason, and works to keep it going. It is a myth that the common law—a system with a long, long history—has a tendency to preserve old materials and old habits, to keep them going long after they have worn out their welcome. Law is an intensely practical matter. It has no sentimental attachment to the old and obsolete. It is, in fact, quite ruthless. If some aspects of the common law survive for centuries—the mortgage, the jury, the trust come to mind—it is because they fill what some present group or groups consider a real need. And when interests, benefits, and desires change, the law changes along with them.

To say this is not to romanticize the legal system. Nor should you take this to mean that all legal systems 'work', that all are necessarily efficient, or adaptive. At some high level of abstraction, we can in fact argue that this so—if we define the legal system broadly enough. Even a corrupt, bureaucratic system, mired in red tape, and wildly unpopular, is efficient—with regard, perhaps, to some oligarchy; and adaptive, too, for that same oligarchy. From the standpoint of ordinary people in that society, of course, the system will seem extremely dysfunctional; and for

[5] Sharply focused rules, directed to a small, definite audience, are, however, much more likely to have an impact than vague rules broadcast to the general public (which is unlikely to get the message). The size of the audience matters too. A law that insists on air bags in all new cars requires compliance only from a handful of large companies that make cars. A law that tells drivers to wear seat belts is much harder to enforce, because the rule asks millions of people, on millions of separate occasions, to change their behaviour; and monitoring all those people is beyond the capacity of most enforcement systems.

them, in fact, it is. It is all too true that the courts in some societies are corrupt; that people do not trust them (for good reason); that the police in some societies are brutal or even criminal; and that the civil service in some societies does not lift a finger without a bribe. In some societies, social change comes very rapidly; different sectors of society respond in different ways, and the traditional legal system seems to be overwhelmed and unable to cope. López-Ayllón and Fix-Fierro make this point about Mexico. After 1970, state and society seemed to 'explode;' the legal system 'responded... by growing and transforming itself but apparently not at the required scale.' The result was a 'maladjustment', with possible 'dire consequences' for both law and society.[6] But any such 'maladjustment' is not due to any inherent qualities of a legal system, but to chaos and class conflicts within Mexican society; and to the stresses and strains that came about as society 'exploded'.

Fourthly, different types of society demand and produce different types of legal system. A feudal system or a socialist system or a capitalist system or a tribe of hunters and gatherers—all of these generate specific forms of law and legal process. When a feudal system evolves into a capitalist system, the law evolves right along with it. Indeed, as we said, it is almost impossible to disentangle the two. A capitalist system is a system with certain rules about private property, contract, and markets. Without these, it is not a capitalist system at all. And, to a degree, all capitalist systems come to resemble each other—precisely because they will have a certain general type of legal system; systems with rules about private property, contract, and markets. Moreover, all the developed countries today are not pure market states; they are market states, with a regulatory and welfare structure imposed on top of the market system. In spite of differences in detail, they all have this in common.

Hence, the legal system of modern Japan—which is, after all, a rich, developed, capitalist country—has a lot in common with the legal systems of countries like Australia or Belgium, precisely because these too are rich, developed, and capitalist. Indeed, the legal system of modern Japan is much more *like* the systems of Australia or Belgium, than it is like the legal system of medieval Japan, the Japan of the samurai, or of the Tokwgawa shogunate. And the legal system of modern England is more like the legal system of modern Japan than it is like the legal system of medieval England, the system of Bracton and the Yearbooks. There was nothing in the Yearbooks about land-use planning, computer software, *in vitro* fertilization, stockholders' meetings, air traffic control, building codes, women's rights, and the dozens and dozens of other subjects and problems that go to make up a modern legal system.

What place does the concept of legal culture have in the theoretical framework of the sociology of law? In some ways, it is a troublesome concept. There is a

[6] Sergio López-Ayllón and Héctor Fix-Fierro, '"Faraway, So Close!" The Rule of Law and Legal Change in Mexico, 1970–2000,' in Lawrence M. Friedman and Rogelio Pérez-Perdomo (eds), *Legal Culture in the Age of Globalization: Latin America and Latin Europe* (Stanford, 2003), 285, 287.

serious problem of definition. Many different scholars have used the term. But unfortunately, they do not by any means agree on a definition. The concept has been severely criticized, partly on that score.[7] Obviously, there is not and cannot be any 'correct' meaning to the term. If those of us who talk about legal culture had a chance to rewind the tape, so to speak, we might have chosen a different set of words. As I use the term, it refers to what people think about law, lawyers, and the legal order; it means ideas, attitudes, opinions, and expectations with regard to the legal system.[8] If you use the term this way, then clearly every person in society has a 'legal culture'; and perhaps the legal cultures of no two people are precisely the same. But there may also be patterns and tendencies that vary systematically, and allow us to make general statements about legal culture, in any particular society. We can plausibly assume that there are differences between the legal culture of old people and young people, Americans and Chinese, women and men, Muslims and Buddhists, and so on. There are certainly differences between the legal culture of doctors, and the legal culture of lawyers. There may be differences between doctors and dentists in this regard; or even between pediatricians, psychiatrists, and eye doctors.[9] Unfortunately, only in rare cases have scholars actually studied or explored these differences. Much of the research, such as it is, has been about differences in attitudes (towards courts, for example), at the national level. There is, however, substantial interest in comparative legal culture; and some interesting work on this subject has appeared in recent years.[10]

In any event, the importance of the concept seems clear to me. We all assume that social change leads to legal change. But what exactly is the mechanism? Something happens in society: a war, a plague, a revolution. Or the situation changes—somebody invents the telephone, or the computer, or discovers antibiotics, or the birth-control pill. These social or technological changes do not, of course, automatically alter the legal system in any way. Pure social forces are too 'raw' to operate directly on the legal system.[11] But they do so indirectly. They change the legal culture. Events, inventions, and new situations lead to differences in the way people think, in what they want and expect; and these changes in attitude in turn change in the pattern of demands on the legal system. The legal culture, in other words, is a crucial intervening variable; it translates social change

[7] See Roger Cotterrell, 'The Concept of Legal Culture,' in David Nelken (ed.), *Comparing Legal Cultures* (Aldershot, 1997), 13; see also, Lawrence M. Friedman, 'The Concept of Legal Culture: A Reply,' *ibid*, 33; David Nelken, 'Using the Concept of Legal Culture' (2004) 29 *Australian Journal of Legal Philosophy* 1.

[8] See Lawrence M. Friedman, *The Legal System: A Social Science Perspective* (New York, 1975), 15–16. The term was influenced by the concept of 'political culture', as used by Gabriel Almond and Sidney Verba in their book, *The Civic Culture* (Boston, 1963), 14.

[9] I also drew a distinction between 'internal' and 'external' legal culture. The 'internal' legal culture is the culture of lawyers and judges; the 'external' is the culture of everybody else. Friedman, n.8, above, 222.

[10] For example, Jeffrey Fitzgerald, 'Grievances, Disputes and Outcomes: A Comparison of Australia and the United States' (1983) 1 *Law in Context 15*; and see the essays collected in Nelken (ed.) n.7 above.

[11] Friedman, n.8, above, 195.

into legal change. The germ theory of disease (to take one out of a thousand potential examples) not only lays the foundation for modern medicine; it also makes people less likely to feel that disease is an Act of God, or to ascribe it to chance. Instead, they begin to think that they get sick because of bad water or filthy conditions; this leads them to feel that something could and should be done about disease; and they make demands for better sanitation and public health. The germ theory, in short, changes the legal culture. Public health and sanitation laws and institutions change accordingly.

The precise influence and impact of legal culture varies, of course, from society to society. There is, obviously, a huge difference between relatively open, democratic societies, and traditional societies, oligarchic societies, autocratic societies, one-party societies, dictatorships of various types. In a more or less democratic society, the vote and the voice of the ordinary person has at least some significance. There are regular channels for transmitting demands and expectations, and for translating these demands and expectations into the legal system. When 'public opinion' is aroused or inflamed, the legal culture speaks with a very loud voice; and the legal system has to listen and take note.

As we defined legal culture, 'public opinion' is obviously one of its aspects. But 'public opinion' is a complicated and slippery concept. The 'public opinion' that counts—indeed, the legal culture that counts—is public opinion that is translated into concrete demands and expectations. This is why 'public opinion' is not easy to measure, even though all modern societies (and all modern governments) spend an enormous amount of time and energy trying to measure it. Where would politics be without opinion polls, surveys, focus groups, and the like? But public opinion polls can be and often are misleading. For one thing, these polls skip over the issue of money, power, and influence. If you take the pulse of a random sample of British subjects, you are not distinguishing between a homeless man sleeping by the Thames and a wealthy and politically active stockbroker. It is obvious that the culture and opinion of the stockbroker are infinitely more important, as a practical matter, than the culture and opinion of the homeless man. Which one of these is more likely to make political noise, to contribute money to a political party, or to send a message to a Member of Parliament?

Moreover, most polls ignore the issue of salience. Polls tend to force people to answer yes or no to a question: are you in favour of the death penalty? Do you think taxes are too high? A slight, begrudging yes counts the same as a vigorous, deeply-rooted no. But these do not translate equally into behaviour; and therefore, they do not have the same potential affect on the work of the legal system. This is because, like money, power, and influence, salience gets translated into behaviour, and indifference does not. A person passionately opposed to abortion is a person who is likely to work on the issue, lobby his representative in the legislature, donate money, recruit like-minded people, and so on. This counts more than dozens of people who disagree when they are asked, but only mildly, and who therefore are unlikely to act on their beliefs. In any event, the problems of measuring legal culture, and its various aspects, are severe. But this does not alter the fact that the concept is crucial. You cannot understand the legal dynamics of any society without it.

One of the problems resides in the use of the word 'culture'. 'Culture' of course is a very slippery and complicated word. Anthropologists have fretted over its meaning for generations. Ordinary people—and scholars, too, for that matter—often think of culture as something very long term, deeply-rooted, and fundamental. The 'culture' of the French, or of Andaman Islanders, is seen as some sort of tough, durable essence, something that underlies and animates the very structure of society.[12] 'Culture' thus changes very slowly, and with great dif-ficulty. It resists manipulation. Societies like to think of themselves as unique, as having some sort of core that sets them apart from everybody else; 'culture' is thus a kind of thick coat of armour or protective skin. The Japanese, for example, like to think of themselves as unlike everybody else—people who have modernized, on the surface, but who remain defiantly and irretrievably Japanese underneath it all. Of course there *are* aspects of culture that do change very slowly. Language is one of these. A Japanese Rip van Winkle would hardly recognize the place; but he would have almost no trouble with the language. Yet I think that the point, in general, is much exaggerated. In any event, it is an empirical question whether 'culture' is in fact as tenacious and sticky as people think; and the same with regard to 'legal culture'. There are those, for example, who think that the gulf between common law and civil law cultures is simply enormous. The two families do not speak the same language. Undoubtedly, tradition, training, pedagogical methods are not the same in, say, England or Italy. This surely makes *some* difference. But exactly how much? That is the question.

In some regards, legal culture most certainly is *not* static, stubborn, resistant, at least in modern, Western countries. After all, nothing is more characteristic of modern times than ceaseless change. People *expect* change. They expect their governments, and their legal systems, to attack problems. They expect programmes. They read and listen to 'news' every day. They know, or think they know, that the world does not and cannot stand still. But, as our axioms suggest, if this is true of the world in general, then it has to be true of law as well.[13] And 'culture' in the anthropological sense, though it bends and monitors and affects change, and the direction of change, does not stand in the way of change.

What is it that produces or influences legal culture? What are the forces that lead to changes in legal culture—or which keep it from changing? These are perhaps the questions which the sociology of law must answer. It is, of course, not possible to give a single, global answer to any of these questions. What affects legal culture in a small, isolated tribe in the Brazilian jungle and what affects legal

[12] Legal culture, too, can be used in an analogous sense—as 'one way of describing relatively stable patterns of legally oriented social behaviour and attitudes,' see David Nelken, 'Using the Concept of Legal Culture,' (2004) 29 *Australian Journal of Legal Philosophy* 1.

[13] See Lawrence M. Friedman, 'Is There a Modern Legal Culture?,' (1994) 7 *Ratio Juris* 117.

culture in England may be entirely or almost entirely different. I will confine my comments to the modern, developed world.

In that world, no aspect of life is more significant than the mass media—newspapers and magazines, radio, television, the movies and now, the internet and the world-wide web. Nothing has a more powerful effect on legal culture than these modes of communication. The rise of the popular press in the nineteenth century was the first stage in a communications revolution. The other forms followed in the twentieth century. The impact has been enormous. In our societies, more and more, we find that opinions and attitudes often change rapidly, even explosively. This is particularly the case after a scandal, incident, uproar, or crisis—whatever makes for headline news. The public is, on most issues, relatively inert; on most issues, people have no opinion, or only very shallow opinions. Most people most of the time are tending their own affairs, worrying about a job, watching football on TV, obsessing over their sex lives, or wondering whether to have fish or chicken for dinner. As everybody knows, sharp, intense, focused interest groups tend to get their way on most matters. They prevail over larger but more diffuse groups. The small, intense groups are the ones that spend time, money, and effort on a cause; and these do pay off. What a scandal or incident does is upset this normal state of affairs. It turns 'public opinion' from something theoretical into a roaring reality. It releases the genie of citizen power from its bottle.

Thus legal culture is, or can be, extremely volatile. Over and over again, in the history of the law of modern nations, some sort of scandal or some dramatic event brings public concern to a boil; out of the rage and uproar comes new law. There are innumerable examples. One particularly sharp instance, in the United States, was the scandal that led to the passage of the first Food and Drug Act, in 1906. The catalyst, a rather unusual one, was the publication of a novel, *The Jungle*, by Upton Sinclair. This was a work of fiction, but it was based at least in part on the realities of life in the stockyards of Chicago. Sinclair made sensational charges about the way the companies produced and processed meat. The public was disgusted to read about rat-infested, poisonous, unsanitary products; how mouldy sausage, 'dosed with borax and glycerine', would be 'dumped into the hoppers' and then sold. The public was particularly horrified by a passage which described how a workman fell into a vat and was turned into lard. There was a fire-storm of outrage; the President appointed investigators; and in the wake of the scandal a meat inspection law and a food and drug law, which had been bottled up in Congress, sailed through.[14]

The food and drug law was strengthened greatly during the 1930s, as the result of another scandal. In this decade, the first antibiotics appeared on the market. One company marketed these antibiotics, the sulpha drugs, in liquid ('elixir') form, with a pleasing raspberry flavour. The company put the elixir on the market without testing it. It turned out to contain a deadly poison; and more than a hundred

[14] Lawrence M. Friedman, *American Law in the 20th Century* (2002), 60.

people died. This created a tremendous outburst of rage; and, as a consequence, Congress amended and strengthened the law. Before, the agency that administered the law (the Food and Drug Administration) had power to pull bad products off the market; but no right to monitor a drug in advance. Now no 'new drug' could be marketed at all, without prior approval of the FDA.[15]

Almost a hundred years after the first American food and drug scandal, the 'mad cow' crisis erupted in Europe. This too created quite a cloudburst of concern. It led to a number of emergency measures; and it also resulted in the creation of a new European regulatory agency, the European Food Safety Agency.[16] In many modern instances, horrific crimes in the United States, crimes that made headlines and evoked great outrage, were the motor force behind new (usually draconian) criminal laws. A prime example was what came to be called 'Megan's Law'. A little girl, Megan Kanka, had been raped and strangled in New Jersey by a neighbour. The neighbour was a convicted sex offender, but the Kankas had no way of knowing that fact. The horror produced by the crime led the legislature in New Jersey to enact a law, in 1994, requiring sex offenders to register with the authorities, and (in some cases) setting up a mechanism to let people in the vicinity know about their neighbour's dark and dangerous past. Other states swiftly passed similar laws.[17] The attack on the World Trade Center, in September 2001, set off a kind of panic over terrorism in the United States. Out of this witches' brew of fear and paranoia came the so-called Patriot Act, and changes in airport security, immigration law, not to mention an actual war in the Middle East. Actions by the IRA, or by ETA in Spain, have also led to harsh legal reactions in Great Britain and Spain.

All these are examples to show that legal culture can change dramatically; that it is far more volatile than many people might imagine. But long-term processes are perhaps more important and more fundamental than scandals and incidents. Not all 'revolutions' are sudden outbursts. Neither the Industrial Revolution nor the so-called sexual revolution happened overnight. Many changes in legal culture are slow, long-term affairs. They come out of a process of evolution, of imperceptible changes that cumulate over time. Take, for example, the case of family law. This is an intensely personal field of law—a field that concerns marriage and divorce, sexual relationships, children, men and women. This is the kind of law which (it is said) cannot be (successfully) transplanted.[18] A country like Saudi Arabia can and does copy and adopt laws about such matters as stock exchanges or air traffic control. But Saudi Arabia would never dream of importing the English or French

[15] On this scandal, see Charles O. Jackson, *Food and Drug Legislation in the New Deal* (1970), ch. 8.

[16] Keith Vincent, '"Mad Cows" and Eurocrats—Community Responses to the BSE Crisis,' (2004) 10 *European Law Journal* 499.

[17] 'Megan's Law' is Laws N. J. 1994, cc. 128, 133. See Lawrence M. Friedman, *American Law in the Twentieth Century* (2002), 591, for this and other examples.

[18] On the whole issue of legal transplants, see the essays collected in David Nelken and Johannes Feest (eds), *Adapting Legal Cultures* (Aldershot, 2001), especially Nelken's own essay, 'Toward a Sociology of Legal Adaptation,' *ibid*, 7.

law of marriage and divorce; or the sections of the penal code of these countries that regulate (or deregulate) sexual relations.

Yet this does not mean that family law, in the West at any rate, has been static and resistant to change. Quite the opposite. It has actually been almost totally transformed in Western countries over the last two centuries or so.[19] Traditional rules have been bent out of shape or totally replaced. This is because the family itself has undergone dramatic changes in this period. The Industrial Revolution began a process that impacted the family in a fundamental way. Work, in the urban, industrial world, was no longer organized on a family basis. A man or woman who went to work in a textile mill had a different economic role within the family, and a different kind of family life than a man or woman who were part of a farm family and a farm community. There is a large, rich literature on how the family changed, and how gender relations changed, in the nineteenth century, as the Industrial Revolution progressed. In particular, traditional marriage gave way to what was called companionate marriage. In a traditional marriage, husband and wife occupy, in a way, totally different worlds. In a companionate marriage, men and women are supposed to be friends, lovers, partners. Marriage is supposed to afford both husband and wife 'romance, sexual fulfillment, companionship, and emotional satisfaction'.[20] But this kind of marriage puts new and heavier demands on the marriage; and many marriages crack under the strain. Companionate marriage thus leads to an increase in the demand for divorce. But there were powerful forces resisting this demand—the forces of the clergy, and of traditional values. For these people, marriage was supposed to be a lifetime commitment. Divorce was either considered totally illicit, or a last resort, and ideally as rare as possible. But this flew in the face of the vast, subterranean demand for divorce. The result was, first of all, a kind of stalemate; and then a complex, twisted, malfunctioning system in the United States, dominated by collusion and fraud.[21]

In the twentieth century, family life and family law were powerfully affected by changes in sexual morality—the so-called sexual revolution. Whatever the causes, there was, by the late twentieth century, a much more permissive legal culture. The culture of the late nineteenth century had strongly endorsed 'moderation' (actually, repression) in sexual behaviour. This was reflected in codes of law that

[19] On this, see in general, Lawrence M. Friedman, *Private Lives: Families, Individuals, and the Law* (Cambridge, Mass., 2004); on the United Kingdom, see Stephen Cretney, *Family Law in the Twentieth Century: A History* (Oxford, 2003).

[20] Steven Mintz and Susan Kellogg, *Domestic Revolutions: A Social History of American Family Life* (1988), 108.

[21] 'Collusion' was legally unacceptable, according to formal law; a man and woman could not simply decide their marriage was a mistake, and get a divorce. A person who wanted a divorce had to allege and prove 'grounds'. But in fact most divorces, by 1900, *were* collusive. See, in general, Lawrence M. Friedman, 'A Dead Language: Divorce Law and Practice before No-Fault,' (2000) 86 *Virginia Law Review* 1497. In England, too, where there were severe legal obstacles to divorce, a system of fraud and collusion also developed. In many European countries—Italy and Ireland were examples—absolute divorce was simply not allowed.

made adultery and fornication crimes, not to mention same-sex behaviour. The late twentieth century altered the situation dramatically; it turned the old notions upside down. Marriage had once had a monopoly on (legitimate) sexual relations; in the late twentieth century, it lost this monopoly. In the light of new social norms, most American states and many countries got rid of laws against fornication and adultery. What used to be called 'living in sin' was redefined as 'cohabitation', and it lost most of its social stigma; and all of its legal stigma.[22] In many countries, the law gives 'domestic partners' rights very similar to married people.[23] Some of these countries extend these rights to gay couples; and in a few places, gay couples are even allowed to marry.[24] A child whose parents were not married—the harsh old term was bastard—was at one time legally 'filius nullius', that is, nobody's child; a child without rights. The disabilities of these children have now all but disappeared.[25] The changes in divorce law are perhaps the most dramatic of all. Divorce in most Western countries became much quicker, easier—and cheaper. 'No-fault' systems appeared in the United States. California's law of 1970 was the first,[26] but no-fault then spread to almost all the other states. No-fault is the rule in many countries in Europe. Under a no-fault system, divorce, at the request of either party, is basically automatic.[27]

Family law is also an example of the powerful trend toward *convergence* in legal culture—and even in the formal law. Obviously, each country has its own particular history, its own tradition, and has followed its own trajectory over time. But the *direction* of change has been more or less the same all over the Western world. This is very much the case in the law of divorce. As we said, at one time absolute divorce was unavailable in strongly Catholic countries of Europe (Italy, Ireland); and in many Latin American countries. It was rare and expensive in England. Today all European countries (except Malta) allow divorce; and the last Latin American hold-out, Chile, has finally joined the majority. The same kind of

22 For the United States, see the famous California case of *Marvin* v. *Marvin*, 18 Cal. 3d 660, 557 P. 2d 106, 134 Cal. R. 815 (1976). The defendant was the movie star, Lee Marvin. He had lived with the plaintiff, Michele Triola, for years. She claimed they had an 'oral agreement' to pool their earnings; what she contributed were 'services' as 'companion, homemaker, housekeeper and cook.' And also, though she never said so explicitly, sex. Marvin's defence was that the contract was immoral—a contract for what the law called 'meretricious' relationships. But the California Supreme Court disagreed. Many 'young couples,' said the court 'live together without the solemnization of marriage;' and the 'mores of the society' had changed 'radically'. Michele was entitled to a trial, and the right to prove her case.

23 See, e.g. Kathleen Kiernan, 'The Rise of Cohabitation and Childbearing outside Marriage in Western Europe,' (2001) 15 *International Journal of Law, Policy and the Family* 1.

24 See Lawrence M. Friedman, *Private Lives*, 178–9.

25 This is the case, for example, in England, under the Family Law Reform Act of 1987, see Stephen Cretney, *Family Law in the Twentieth Century*, 464.

26 On the background, and the subsequent history of this statute, see Herbert Jacob, *Silent Revolution: The Transformation of Divorce Law in the United States* (Chicago, 1988).

27 Interestingly, this was not the original intent: indeed, some of the proponents thought that no-fault would make divorce more difficult, not easier. But this is not what happened. The legal culture of the public overwhelmed the expectations of the experts. See James Herbie DiFonzo, 'Customized Marriage,' (2005) 75 *Indiana Law Journal* 875, 903–9.

convergence can be seen with regard to the rights of illegitimate children, the legal position of men and women who live together without bothering to get married, the law relating to same-sex partners, and so on. There is obviously a 'common developmental thread' in the family law of Europe; the convergence has been so striking that it is possible to speak of a 'European family law'.[28]

I could multiply examples of this sort of convergence; it is certainly not confined to family law. It is obvious as well in other fields: in commercial law, corporation law, copyright, bankruptcy, criminal justice. Particularly striking is the convergence in notions of human rights: the growth of a 'subjective sense of right', economic rights, rights of minorities, 'personality and privacy rights'.[29] It is part of modern legal culture to believe that law (and society) should treat people as equals—regardless of gender, race, religion, caste. This seems obvious to most people in Western societies. But there was slavery in the United States until the 1860s; and even later in Brazil. And the notion that women (for example) should vote, hold office, run business corporations—indeed, that women should have an equal say in raising children, and an equal crack at child custody—would have struck most men of the Enlightenment as absurd. The idea that women might practise law horrified the United States Supreme Court, when the issue came up in 1873.[30] Women did not vote in the United States until the time of the First World War; and some countries (Switzerland, for example), were even slower to grant voting rights. Today, feminism is a powerful and worldwide movement. Clearly, it moves in different ways, and at different speeds, in different countries. The gulf between, say, Saudi Arabia and Sweden in this regard is positively immense. And even if we confine ourselves to the developed world, we find a large gap (socially, if not legally) between Japan and Korea, on the one hand, and Norway and Denmark on the other. But everywhere the trend is in the same direction. The same is generally true of all the components of the culture of human rights—rights the public believes to be valuable, universal, inherent, and inalienable.

The United States has been a pioneer in one regard. It was the first country to have a law explicitly directed against age discrimination. Congress passed the first age discrimination law in 1967. This law made it illegal to discriminate against people over forty in hiring and firing and conditions of work. But there was an age-cap written into the law: nobody over sixty-five was protected. The law, in short, allowed companies to keep any rules they might have which insisted that workers must retire at a certain age, provided they were sixty-five or over. Later, the law was amended to push the upper limit of protection to age seventy. Finally, the cap was removed altogether. Today, no company and no major institutions (including universities)

[28] Paolo Ronfani, 'Family Law in Europe,' in David I. Kertzer and Marzio Barbagli, *Family Life in the Twentieth Century* (2003), 113.

[29] Lawrence M. Friedman, 'Is There a Modern Legal Culture?'(1994) 7 *Ratio Juris* 117, 127–8.

[30] *Bradwell* v. *Illinois*, 16 Wall. (83 U.S.) 130 (1873). Justice Bradley, for example, felt that it was the 'law of the Creator' that women were to 'fulfill the noble and benign offices of wife and mother' as their 'paramount destiny and mission'.

are allowed to fix a time when an employee *must* retire. Decisions, in short, have to be made on an individual basis.[31]

I remember some fifteen or so years ago giving a talk in England about this aspect of American law. I found the audience—lawyers and academics for the most part—frankly rather hostile. I could tell from the questions and comments from the audience that my listeners thought it was a terrible idea to ban age discrimination, and especially bad to get rid of mandatory retirement. Old people had had their day; they should make way for the young. After all, unemployment was a big problem in society. Letting old folks hang on to their jobs seemed a recipe for disaster.

That was then. This is now. The absurd idea no longer seems quite so absurd. For one thing, age discrimination laws, and the abolition of mandatory retirement, have spread: Canada, Australia, New Zealand.[32] Getting rid of mandatory retirement, as one author put it, 'reflects the view that the right to age equality is as fundamental as that to gender and race equality;' mandatory retirement puts a stigma on age 'in an arbitrary way without reference to individual circumstances.'[33] The notion that something should be done about age discrimination has also reached the European Union; Council Directive (EC) 2000/78 ordered all the members of the Union to enact legislation banning age discrimination in the job market. There had been some movement in that direction, in some EU countries, even before the directive;[34] and the directive itself is fairly vague; it seems to allow members to keep their rules about mandatory retirement, at least for now. It is likely that different countries will enact different forms of law in compliance with the EU directive. But here too the direction of change seems quite clear.

The basic change is a change in legal culture: in attitudes toward ageing, and (more generally) rights consciousness, spreading from men to women, from young to old, from whites to blacks, from straights to gays, and then even more broadly in society. There are, of course, economic issues— the cost of the welfare state, the condition of the job market; and trends in demography are also significant. Populations are ageing in all the EU countries, and the birth rate has declined very sharply. But which, if any, of these factors has been crucial is not easy to say. Clearly, though, the culture of rights is an important factor in its own right. And

[31] See Lawrence M. Friedman, 'Age Discrimination Law: Some Remarks on the American Experience,' in Sandra Fredman and Sarah Spencer (eds), *Age as an Equality Issue* (2003), 176.

[32] The Australian labour code, for example, forbids an employer from firing any employee for a long list of prohibited reasons—race, for example—but also including 'age' and 'physical or mental disability.' Industrial Relations Reform Act 1993, s 170DF(1)(f).

[33] Bob Hepple QC, 'Age Discrimination in Employment: Implementing the Framework Directive 2000/78/EC,' in Fredman and Spencer, op. cit., n,31, above, 71, 88. As Hepple points out, there are those who defend mandatory retirement as an 'impersonal' rule that 'enables individuals to leave the labour market without the stigma of incapability,' *ibid.* Of course, there is no reason why people cannot perceive an 'impersonal' rule to be unfair; and in this case, there are many who do.

[34] See Colm O'Cinneide, 'Comparative European Perspectives on Age Discrimination Legislation,' in Fredman and Spencer, op. cit., n.31, above, 195.

the history of age discrimination law is one more example of convergence. Indeed, the EU itself, with all its talk of 'harmonization' and the like, is a prime example of convergence. It is a convergence of legal culture, which has now been turned into the tough bone and metal of formal law and institutional change.

This last point needs some amplification, because it raises a fundamental issue. Analytically, we can separate legal culture from legal structure. Structure refers to the settled, durable, institutional aspects of a legal system: the way courts are organized, for example, whether there is or is not a jury, whether there is or is not judicial review, the size and composition of the bar, whether the country has a federal system, or is highly centralized, and so on. Which is more crucial to the way the legal system operates, structure or culture? Clearly, both are significant. In the law-and-society literature about Japan, there is an ongoing argument over the nature of the Japanese legal system, and the source of some of its special features. Japan has a minuscule bar—a tiny contingent of lawyers. The Japanese also (allegedly) have an aversion to litigation. The classic explanation is cultural. The Japanese dislike contention; they prefer harmony, compromise, mediation. They shy away from the courts. Other scholars, however, strongly disagree. No, they say, the Japanese are no different, culturally, in this regard, from other developed nations. The problem lies in the *structure* of the legal system. It has been deliberately crafted to discourage litigation.[35] Change the structure, and the Japanese would go to court like everybody else.

Erhard Blankenburg has also emphasized structure, in an important body of work. Blankenburg compared aspects of two legal systems: the Dutch legal system, and the system in operation just across the border in the neighbouring parts of Germany. Blankenburg found significant differences between the two regions—in litigation rates, for example. Yet culturally and economically, the two regions were very similar; structural elements, he felt, best explained the differences between the two.[36]

Structure undoubtedly makes a difference in a legal system. A federal system, for example, may work quite differently from a centralized system. If you allow local autonomy, you are sure to get results that are different from the results you would get in a system tightly run from the centre. It has been argued, for example, that the loose, disjointed, fragmentary nature of American government helps account for differences in its political history—the absence of a labour party, for example.[37] But, in general, it is very hard to disentangle structure from culture. This is true for all of the instances already discussed—Japan, the comparison

[35] See J.O. Haley, 'The Myth of the Reluctant Litigant,' (1974) 4 *Journal of Japanese Studies* 359.

[36] Erhard Blankenburg, 'Civil Litigation Rates as Indicators for Legal Culture,' in David Nelken (ed.), *Comparing Legal Cultures* (1997), 41.

[37] For this thesis see William E. Forbath, *Law and the Shaping of the American Labor Movement* (1989). Forbath's argument, to be sure, is more complex, and includes a heavy emphasis on the role of the Supreme Court, the state high courts, and their use of the weapons of judicial review to strike down certain forms of labour legislation.

between Holland and Germany, the nature of American political and legal history. This is because structures do not fall down from the sky. If you find two countries or two regions with different legal structures, you have to ask: why? Why these structures, and not something else? Often your only sensible explanation for a structural arrangement is some cultural factor underlying it. Beyond a doubt, in the long run, structure *results* from constellations of culture. And, contrariwise, in the long run, structure *impacts* culture, in significant ways. The jury is a structural element of American law. But it has long since entered into the culture—into people's expectations and attitudes. They think of the jury system as part of their package of rights—an attitude which is lacking in Spain or Japan.

It is also quite easy to show how culture affects structure. I have mentioned the growth of a culture of human rights. In modern society, human rights are considered sacred, inherent, fundamental: beyond the reach of legislatures and not subject to majority rule. They are rights which are not to be impaired or destroyed, by anybody. If so, they have to be protected through structures that are themselves independent, structures that are also beyond the reach of legislatures and of temporary majorities. This, in most cases, means a certain kind of independent court system. It means judicial review. And, indeed, since the end of the Second World War, no structural development in the developed world has been more striking than the blossoming of courts that have these powers—or which simply *assume* these powers. There are, of course, differences from country to country. The United States gives the power of judicial review to its general Supreme Court; other countries, like Germany, have a special constitutional court. Some courts are much bolder and more active than others. The Japanese High Court is much more timid than the German Constitutional Court. But, again, the direction of change is consistent and worldwide.

I have given a few examples to illustrate a few basic points. My main argument has been about the centrality of the notion of legal culture, in the social study of law. It is a matter of regret that there is so little research on the subject. A curtain of ignorance surrounds most aspects of legal culture, but perhaps this situation will change. One barrier, of course, is that legal culture is elusive, and difficult to study. Another central concept is legal structure; but the relationship of structure to culture is complex and difficult to parse. One thing seems clear—at least to me: legal cultures seem to be converging in the rich, developed societies. These cultures are moving in parallel directions. Very likely, legal structures are also converging—judicial review is an example.

It is banal to end a chapter of this sort with a plea for more research; but I cannot resist the temptation. Legal culture is an important concept, and a fertile field for investigation. It is to be hoped that it will attract more attention in the future.

12

Rethinking Legal Culture[1]

David Nelken

The term legal culture is widely used by scholars.[2] While this suggests that there is a need for some such term, use does not necessarily prove usefulness. For a start, the term is undoubtedly employed in a variety of often inconsistent ways, and its popularity may demonstrate more the lack of anything better than any intrinsic merits. For sociologists of law (including this writer) the promise of the term is the hope that it might 'help make comparisons of legal systems more sociologically meaningful'.[3] But for many commentators, the term cannot fulfil this promise. Indeed, one Dutch socio-legal scholar who originally employed it in the title of his book about law in the Netherlands has now come to reject the term.[4] Even Lawrence Friedman, who introduced the concept into the sociology of law, has himself described it as 'an abstraction and a slippery one'.[5] In this rethinking of the concept of legal culture I shall be starting from Friedman's approach, both because his is the most widely debated use of the term[6] and because this volume includes his latest discussion of his views. It is significant, however, that he too admits that legal culture is 'a troublesome concept', that 'there is a serious problem of definition', and that if he were to start over he might not use it again. Unfortunately he does not tell us how he would deal with the criticisms to which it has been exposed.

This chapter is not intended as a defence of Friedman's concept of legal culture as such. For example, I shall not be considering his theoretical assumptions; his denial of law's autonomy, his input-output model of social systems, his pluralist model of power and so on. Nor will I examine his substantive claims, such as the importance of technological change, or the inevitability of convergence of

[1] This is a revised version of a paper delivered at the Colloquium on Law and Sociology held at UCL September 2004. I would like to thank Michael Freeman for his invitation. I have also benefited from helpful comments at subsequent presentations of this paper in Mexico City, Stanford, Berkeley, Seattle, Oxford, and Groningen.

[2] Google Scholar lists over 48,000 recent uses in the scholarly literature.

[3] R. Cotterrell, 'The Concept of Legal Culture', in D. Nelken *Comparing Legal Cultures* (Aldershot, 1997) 13–32 at 14.

[4] F. Bruinsma, *Dutch Law in Action* (Nijmegen, 2000).

[5] L. Friedman, *The Republic of Choice* (Cambridge, Mass, 1999), 95.

[6] Friedman on legal culture gets 5,610 cites in Google Scholar.

national legal cultures. I shall be asking, rather, how far the term can be put to good use even by those who may not share Friedman's starting points or conclusions.[7] However, a large number of problems have been raised with respect to any attempt to use the concept of legal culture and I can deal only with some of them here.[8] In the first part of the chapter I shall review some of the general criticisms of the value of any concept that includes the word culture, and mention some of the alternatives being proposed. I shall then concentrate on one of the most serious objections that many commentators consider to be fatal to the use of legal culture for the purpose of explanation. This claims that, because the term legal culture tends to be applied both to elements within a society and to whole societies composed of these elements, it easily ends up as an explanation of itself. In my own work in the past I tried to avoid this problem by treating legal culture more as something to be *explained* than as offering any sort of explanation.[9] But in this chapter I shall seek to offer a framework for inquiry that can also include a place for legal culture as *explanation*.

Defining Legal Culture

Two such protean terms as law and culture, each of which have multiple and controversial meanings, are hardly likely to become a beacon of clarity when put together. For social scientists and lawyers the possible implications of the terms law and culture range widely and include law seen as a cultural artefact, rather than merely as a form of social engineering,[10] law as it becomes present in everyday life and experience or through the media,[11] as well as the significance of law in accommodating cultural defences or protecting cultural treasures.[12] Both law and culture are words whose interpretation and definition have illocutionary effects ('this is the law', 'that behaviour is inconsistent with our culture'). And the term legal culture is itself sometimes used by judges or others within the legal system, or

[7] Friedman's theoretical and methodological starting points do set some limits to this attempt to rethink legal culture. For present purposes I have assumed that understanding also involves explaining patterns of behaviour and ideas in society. But, as will be noted, the presuppositions of this type of endeavour have been increasingly called into question since the period when Friedman first used the term, even though there are many who still pursue it. I say more about interpretative approaches in D. Nelken, 'Using the Concept of Legal Culture' (2004) 29 *Australian Journal of Legal Philosophy* 1–28.

[8] See, e.g. D. Nelken, 'Understanding/Invoking Legal Culture', in: D. Nelken (ed.), special issue on *Legal Culture, Diversity and Globalization* (1995) 4 *Social and Legal Studies* 435–52 and D. Nelken 'Puzzling out Legal Culture', in: D. Nelken (ed.), *Comparing Legal Cultures* (1997), 58–88. In reviewing my 1997 book Mary Volcansek suggests that it showed the 'almost insurmountable difficulties of employing the concept', see M.L. Volcansek. *Law and Politics Book Review*, Vol. 8 No. 5 (May 1998) 244–6.

[9] See Nelken, op. cit. n.7.

[10] P. Kahn, *The Cultural Study of Law: Reconstructing Legal Scholarship* (Chicago, 1999).

[11] A. Sarat and T.R. Kearns (eds), *Law in Everyday Life* (Ann Arbor, 1993) and A. Sarat and T.R. Kearns (eds), *Law in the Domains of Culture* (Ann Arbor, 1998).

[12] R. Cotterrell, 'Law in Culture' (2004) 17 *Ratio Juris* 1–14.

by political actors commenting on it, when making claims about what is or is not consonant with a given body of law, practices or ideals.[13] This use, as much prescriptive as descriptive, or prescriptive through being descriptive, can 'make' the facts it purports to describe or explain.[14] More broadly, some uses of the term overlap with the notion of the 'culture of legality', the nearest, though not perfect equivalent, to which in English is 'the rule of law'. This meaning is particularly common in those jurisdictions, or parts of jurisdictions (for example, in the former Soviet Union or Latin America or the south of Italy), where state rules are systematically avoided or evaded. Here talk of 'legal culture' is intended to point to the normative goal of getting 'legality' into the culture of everyday social and political life and so reorienting the behaviour of such populations towards (state) law.

One approach we could take would therefore be to track such practical uses of the term legal culture and examine their sense, implications and effects. The study of legal culture would then be reformulated as an effort to understand actors' own attempts to describe, ascribe, or produce legal coherence in the course of their decision-making.[15] Comparative lawyers and philosophers of law have often defined the term so as to capture the activities of the various legal professionals and jurists who bear the responsibility of (re)producing such purported coherence.[16] But these writers say little about what type or measure of coherence is required in actual practice. And this way of using the term is somewhat narrow for many of the purposes of socio-legal inquiry. On the other hand, the most common uses of the term are too broad to be helpful.[17] Here, much like 'legal system' or 'legal process', the term serves merely as an indication to librarians or prospective readers that any work so described will in some way discuss legal institutions,

[13] For example, in February 2005, Rosy Bindi, a leading Centre-Left politician in Italy, welcomed the news that the Constitutional Court had found parts of the restrictive, so called 'Bossi-Fini' law on immigration to be unconstitutional, by saying that this showed that this law was inconsistent with (Italian) 'legal culture'.

[14] More generally, because culture is both object and subject, discourses about culture (even where in some ways 'mistaken' about their object) help play a part in constituting the object they describe.

[15] J. Webber, 'Culture, Legal Culture, and Legal Reasoning: A Comment on Nelken', in (2004) 29 *Australian Journal of Legal Philosophy* 25–36, argues: 'The concept of culture is not so much a way of identifying highly specified and tightly bounded units of analysis, then, as a heuristic device for suggesting how individual decision-making is conditioned by the language of normative discussion, the set of historical reference points, the range of solutions proposed in the past, the institutional norms taken for granted, given a particular context of repeated social interaction. The integrity of cultural explanations does not depend upon the "units" being exclusive, fully autonomous, or strictly bounded. Rather, it depends upon there being sufficient density of interaction to generate distinctive terms of evaluation and debate. When there is that density, any examination of decision-making in that context will want to take account of those terms'.

[16] See, e.g. the entry 'Culture Juridique' by G. Rebuffa and E. Blankenburg in A. Arnaud (ed.), *Dictionnaire encylopédique de théorie et de sociologie du droit* (1993) *LGDJ* 139–42 which speaks of the techniques of exposition and interpretation used by jurists and legal actors. In Italy there is a leading law journal which goes under the name of *Materiali per una storia della cultural giuridica* (Materials for the History of Legal Culture). For an attempt to broaden this use of the term see John Bell's *French Legal Cultures* (London, 2001).

[17] See, e.g. V. Gessner, A. Hoeland, and C. Varga (eds), *European Legal Cultures* (Aldershot, 1996); and C. Varga, *Comparative Legal Cultures* (Aldershot, 1992).

actors, rules, procedure, or practices, with reference, to their philosophical, historical, or social context.[18]

Friedman's use of the term, by contrast, has the merit of showing how the concept can serve as a tool intended to aid socio-legal inquiry. Introduced in the late 1960s as the equivalent of the idea of political culture as used in inquiries into voting patterns and types of political system,[19] legal culture is principally taken to mean 'what people think about law, lawyers and the legal order, it means ideas, attitudes, opinions and expectations with regard to the legal system.'[20] Friedman distinguishes 'internal' legal culture, which refers to the role in the law of legal professionals, from 'external' legal culture, which refers especially to those individuals or groups who bring pressure to bear on the law to produce social change. Controversially, however, he has applied the term not only to variables but also to aggregates of such variables. Though he sees legal culture as a *cause* of 'legal dynamics', he also uses it to describe the *results* of such causes, writing for example about the traits of a variety of large aggregates such as American culture, Latin American legal culture, modern legal culture, and even global legal culture.

The same variety of referent is also found in the work of other leading writers. In their book called *Dutch Legal Culture*, Blankenburg and Bruinsma, for example, define the term as including 'four components: law in the books, law in action as channelled by the institutional infrastructure, patterns of legally relevant behaviour, and legal consciousness, particularly, a distinctive attitude toward the law among legal professionals'.[21] At the same time however, in other writings, Blankenburg has singled out the second of these components as crucial. He argued that it was necessary to 'open up "the black box" of legal culture' so as to reveal structural influences on the choice to use law. Presenting a comparative 'natural experiment' between adjoining parts of the Netherlands and Germany with very different levels of litigation, he purported to demonstrate that, 'there is no legal culture outside existing legal institutions': the influence of 'folk' or general cultural mentalities may therefore be safely ignored.[22] Like Friedman therefore he too uses legal culture to talk both about aggregates as well as the variables that play a crucial role in producing them.

More recent commentators prefer to place the emphasis on either one or the other of these two referents. Susan Silbey, for example, takes up Friedman's interest in popular attitudes to law even though she prefers to talk of legal consciousness

[18] Of course it would be a mistake to underestimate even this use of the term. It implies that there *is* something that a given body of rules, procedures or practices have in common and holds them together and it thus carries a significant, even ideological, message by reproducing rather than questioning the presuppositions of legal actors.

[19] G.A. Almond and S. Verba, *Civic Culture, Political Attitudes and Democracy in Five Nations* (Boston, 1963).

[20] Friedman, in this volume.

[21] E. Blankenburg and F. Bruinsma, *Dutch Legal Culture*, 2nd edn. (Deventer/Boston, 1995), 13–14.

[22] E Blankenburg, 'Civil Litigation Rates as Indicators for Legal Culture', in Nelken (ed.) (1997) op. cit., 41–68.

rather than legal culture.[23] Nelken on the other hand, leans towards the wider definition of legal culture in the aggregate: 'Legal culture, in its most general sense,' he writes, 'is one way of describing relatively stable patterns of legally oriented social behaviour and attitudes.' But neither author really wants to exclude the other aspects of legal culture to which Friedman draws attention. Despite her focus on micro-level social action, Silbey is also interested in the larger picture that emerges once one sees how formal legal institutions and everyday social relations intersect. And Nelken goes on to encompass the different sources of legal culture when he says that 'the identifying elements of legal culture range from facts about institutions such as the number and role of lawyers or the ways judges are appointed and controlled, to various forms of behaviour such as litigation or prison rates, and, at the other extreme, more nebulous aspects of ideas, values, aspirations and mentalities'.[24]

A Troublesome Concept

As the variety of definitions suggests, there is still little agreement about what legal culture does or should mean. But we need to bear in mind that debates surrounding its use can actually be of (at least) three types. The first type of argument presupposes a shared definition of legal culture but contests the truth of a given claim about legal culture in general, or about a given legal culture. For example, those working with Friedman's type of approach to legal culture frequently discuss whether it is 'structures' (courts, lawyers and alternative methods of dealing with disputes) or 'attitudes' (expectations and values) that are most important in explaining when people turn to law. Or they may debate whether Japan really is a society which makes little use of law.[25] The second type of disagreement is more radical and has to do with how best to define legal culture. As we have already seen, there can be a variety of referents for legal culture. Some scholars include legal rules ('law in the books') in their definition, others do not, some limit legal culture to attitudes, others include behaviour; some counterpose structure to culture, others include both, some assume that only relatively 'enduring' attitudes or behaviour count as culture, others disagree, and so on, etc. Often even the same writers change their mind over time.[26] Obviously, only if (more or less) the same meaning is ascribed to the term can it be possible to have empirically testable

[23] S. Silbey, 'Legal Culture and Legal Consciousness,' in *Encyclopaedia of the Social Sciences* (2001); see also S. Silbey and P. Ewick, *The Common Place of the Law: Stories from Everyday Life* (Chicago, 1998).

[24] Nelken op. cit., n.7.

[25] See, e.g. E. Feldman, 'Patients' Rights, Citizen Movements and Japanese Legal Culture', in Nelken (ed.) (1997), 215–36, and E. Feldman, 'Blood Justice, Courts, Conflict and Compensation in Japan, France and the United States', (2001) 34 *Law and Society Review* 651–702.

[26] Friedman, for example, used to include behaviour but now restricts his definition to attitudes (though what matters to him is the pressure on the legal system which they produce.) Silbey, on the other hand, suggests that it makes no sense to separate attitudes from behaviour.

disagreements about features of the social world.[27] The third type of debate is still more basic. Here critics put forward fundamental objections to the use of legal culture as such, *however it be defined*. They propose rather to substitute it with other terms.

These critics take issue mainly with the use of the term culture. The very popularity of this term in the social sciences (where it was at one time as central as the idea of evolution in the hard sciences) has led to its downfall. A word said to have more than 150 definitions can only create confusion. Developments in the social sciences such as 'the interpretative turn' have made culture more of a *method* of inquiry than an *object* of inquiry. And changes on the ground, such as those connected to globalization, have made it implausible to speak of self-contained regional or national cultures. As argued by Sally Merry (a leading anthropologist in the US law and society movement):

> over the last two decades, anthropology has elaborated a conception of culture as unbounded, contested, and connected to relations of power. It does not consist only of beliefs and values but also practices, habits, and commonsensical ways of doing things. The contemporary anthropological understanding of culture envisions a far more fluid, contested, and changing set of values and practices than that provided by the idea of culture as tradition. Culture is the product of historical influences rather than evolutionary change. Its boundaries are fluid, meanings are contested, and meaning is produced by institutional arrangements and political economy. Culture is marked by hybridity and creolization rather than uniformity or consistency. Local systems are analysed in the context of national and transnational processes and are understood as the result of particular historical trajectories. This is a more dynamic, agentic, and historicized way of understanding culture.[28]

Read carefully, however, it becomes clear that Merry is not trying to overcome the idea of culture itself, but only a certain idea of culture. It would anyway be difficult get rid of this term entirely, given that much of the attack on older versions of 'culturalism' is carried out under the banner of a field of study named 'cultural theory'! The same applies to investigating the consequences of globalization. If we do not seek to distinguish in some way the local and the global, how are we to investigate its effects? It is all the more vital to study interrelated 'units' of legal culture once we abandon the older view of culture in favour of one which emphasizes changing, fragmented, and porous boundaries. Indeed, some argue that legal culture should be seen as one way of actually making and unmaking boundaries[29] (though this does not mean that national jurisdictions have lost all importance).[30]

[27] Some debates are made more difficult to follow because of this lack of common language. Blankenburg, for example, argues that it is the supply side 'infrastructural' factors to do with alternatives to court processes that explain resort to law, rather than factors on the demand side. He calls these alternatives 'legal culture'. But others, in similar debates about the relative importance of larger cultural or structural factors in explaining the low use of courts in Japan, use the term 'structure' to characterize the alternatives that Blankenburg calls culture.

[28] S. E. Merry, 'Human Rights Law and the Demonization of Culture (And Anthropology Along the Way)' in (2003) 26 (1) *Polar: Political and Legal Anthropology Review* 55–77.

[29] See Webber op. cit., n.15. [30] See Nelken, op. cit., n. 7.

Insofar as it is only the 'older' meaning of culture that critics want to dislodge, we need to check that specific uses of the term legal culture are in fact vulnerable to this attack. Whatever may be true of the meaning given to legal culture by some comparative lawyers or social historians, sociologists of law seem less prone to adopt naively 'culturalist' explanations. For example, much of the extensive debate about Japanese legal culture has stressed the importance of government strategy rather than so-called 'folk' culture, and even those who argue for the importance of culture do not treat it as a matter of folk values and do emphasize the changes taking place.

It is instructive to see how little the objections contained in a recent critique of legal culture advanced by Patrick Glenn, a leading comparative law scholar, can be applied to Friedman's approach. For Glenn the idea of culture is suspect both because of its origins and its consequences.[31] It came in, he claims, to replace the dirty work done by the idea of 'race', and the results of using such a term can be negative because it implies that patterns of behaviour and attitudes are static and necessarily doomed to conflict.[32] But Glenn fails to notice that just as 'culture' has its own history, so does 'legal culture'. The German word *kultur* grew up as a defensive term to be used in romantic opposition to the French universalizing idea of *civilisation* (for which today's discourses of democracy and human rights could be considered equivalents). But, curiously, Friedman's use of the word culture in legal culture is in fact much closer to the French idea, as can be seen from his claim that we are moving to a global legal culture, based round individualism, equality, and human rights.[33]

On almost every point Glenn's criticisms seem to miss the point at least as far as Friedman's way of talking about culture is concerned. Glenn insists, for example, that the term culture implies that everyone agrees.[34] Yet Friedman argues specifically that every group has its own legal culture, even going so far as to say that this is so for every individual. And Friedman's analytical distinction between external and internal legal culture also invites us to investigate the possibility of large differences between legal professionals and others. Glenn claims that those who use culture as an explanation put too much stress on the past governing the present. But Friedman's use of the term is all about change; in this volume, if anything, he goes to the other extreme, saying that his use of legal culture does not presuppose anything 'enduring'. Glenn argues that cultural analyses both unify and essentialize the notion of culture, so that scholars are tempted to orientalize behaviour as foreign and irrational and ignore or downplay the importance of economic and related political drivers of change. Culturalist accounts, he argues, also often make

[31] H. Patrick Glenn, 'Legal Cultures and Legal Traditions', in Van Mark van Hoeck (ed.), *Epistemology and Methodology of Comparative Law* (Oxford, 2004).

[32] See A. Kuper, *Culture: The Anthropologist's Account* (Cambridge, Mass, 1999).

[33] See, e.g. L. Friedman, 'Is there a Modern Legal Culture?' (1994) 7 *Ratio Juris* 117.

[34] But it is difficult to see how anyone can believe this when terms like 'Western culture' are so freely used and understood.

it seem that people are 'programmed' to act in certain ways rather being able to choose from culture as a tool kit and to use it strategically. But, again, there is little trace of the irrational in the writings of Friedman (or Blankenburg). Actors' strategic considerations are at the centre of their analyses.

Glenn is right to remind us that cultures should not be treated as 'super organic', or 'substantive, bounded entities', but rather seen as 'shreds and patches remaking themselves'. But whilst legal actors do (perhaps must?) work with some such ideas as normative presuppositions, it is hard to find sociologists of law making such assumptions.[35] At this time of export and import of legal institutions and ideas it would be implausible indeed to see cultures as closed and self-referential. Friedman, on the contrary, argues that law is necessarily converging, and has written about the development of global culture, again, if anything, underestimating the continuing importance of national boundaries. On the other hand, it is a fair criticism of Friedman's approach to legal culture to say that it does not seem to have been influenced by the 'interpretive turn' in the social sciences. He seems unconcerned as Glenn puts it, that 'culture may be an effect of our descriptions, not its precondition'.[36]

This recognition that attempts to interpret culture form part of the object itself[37] is certainly one key way in which notions of culture have changed since Friedman borrowed his term from discussions of political culture. But it is not obvious how much difference this makes to the task of explanation.[38] Whilst talk of 'culture wars' is often exaggerated, it would be equally mistaken to assume that cultures can never clash, or to deny that social actors sometimes talk and act as if particular cultures can and must be defended. The same applies to policy implications. Any assumption that long-standing historical patterns cannot easily be changed can itself be dystopic and block possible reforms.[39] But it can be equally self-fulfilling to cite current conditions or inevitable future homogenizing trends such as globalization.[40] Glenn is opposed to using the term culture because he

[35] The criticisms might apply to the work of Pierre Legrand who is conceptually and normatively committed to protecting culture's specificity. But although he entitles a collection of his essays *Fragments on Law as Culture* (Deventer, 1997), when he actually argues his points Legrand prefers the term 'legal episteme'. And he probably would not consider himself a social scientist.

[36] But it is not obvious that other terms have any stronger ontological claims.

[37] As J. Friedman, *Cultural Identity and Global Process* (London, 1994) puts it, culture is now viewed as an endless interpretation of interpretations, part of the flow of meaning, 'the enormous interplay of interpretations in and about a culture' to which the scholar herself also contributes.

[38] It would be wrong to think that the 'interpretative turn' is a licence to ignore questions about the causes and consequences of law. For example, in studying court delay it is certainly important to ask who perceives such delay, and why it is so perceived. But waiting ten years, rather than two or three, to receive damages after a road accident is something we may want not only to interpret but also to explain and change.

[39] See Krygier's discussion of the self-fulfilling idea that East European countries without a long-standing culture of liberal democracy will have difficulty in developing one, M. Krygier, 'Is There Constitutionalism After Communism? Institutional Optimism, Cultural Pessimism, and the Rule of Law' (1996–1997) 26 (4) *International Journal of Sociology* 17–47.

[40] See. L. Zedner, 'Dangers of Dystopias in Penal Theory' (2002) 22 *Oxford Journal of Legal Studies* 341–66.

wants to deny any insuperable barriers between human groups. But Friedman actually seeks to achieve much the same aim by pointing to the growth of global culture.

Alternatives to Legal Culture

Whether or not all these criticisms hit home, given the difficulties and ambiguities of talking about culture, it seems reasonable at least to consider whether there are better alternative concepts available. The one most frequently found in the scholarly literature, especially in comparative law writings, is the term legal tradition.[41] In urging the advantages of this alternative, Glenn argues that it is more natural to speak of non-traditional behaviour and innovation than to make the same point when using the term culture. Talking about traditions, he adds, suggests overlap rather than closure. Within a given tradition there are always a range of creative possibilities. The very existence of a tradition is necessarily a result of persuasive argument and interpretation. For Glenn, because tradition is a matter of information it is hard to reify it as something 'beyond us'.

The most common alternatives within sociology of law, on the other hand, are 'living law' and the 'law in action'. Bruinsma, the joint author of a book called *Dutch Legal Culture*, indeed changed the title of the third edition to Dutch 'law in action'. 'Living law' suggests the need to look for a plurality of normative systems in any national legal order. These two terms should not be confused.[42] Although it was not developed to answer Friedman's questions about why people turn to the law, it does have something important to say about why and when people turn to official law rather than rely on other normative systems. 'Law in action', on the other hand, merely tells us that what happens in practice cannot be predicted merely from legal rules. Another possibility, that Roger Cotterrell puts forward in the course of his well-known critique of Friedman's concept of legal culture,[43] is 'legal ideology'.[44] Cotterrell argues that a term focused on the ideas of legal professionals and jurists and their larger influence allows us to have a well-defined topic suitable for empirical investigation. For example, one of the main questions that interests Cotterrell is how law succeeds in being both fragmented and particularistic but also abstract, and how it pretends to be a gapless system while filling in the gaps. As opposed to Friedman's assumption of the permeability of law to social demands, the concept of ideology allows us to explain how the rules and values of law resist modification and thrive on their inconsistencies.

These examples do not of course exhaust the existing (still less the potential) range of alternatives to legal culture. Those who are most interested in what shapes

[41] Google Scholar records 56,000 uses of the term legal traditions.

[42] See D. Nelken, 'Law in Action or Living Law? Back to the Beginning in Sociology of Law' (1984) 4 *Legal Studies* 152–74.

[43] Cotterrell, op. cit., n.3.

[44] Google Scholar indicates 26,000 references to legal ideology.

the internal culture of legal professionals tend to be attracted by notions such as legal mentalities, legal epistemes, or legal formants. Those who want to emphasize the contrasts between the organization and the effects of legal institutions in different places prefer to talk of legal fields, legal style, regulatory style, or even 'path dependency'. And, insofar as the underlying issue is what (if anything) holds a legal and social system together, a challenge to the whole 'law and society' paradigm comes from autopoiesis theory, which has its own approach to why legal communications are connected to the larger social system and other differentiated sub-systems.[45]

Should we abandon the concept of legal culture in favour of one of these alternatives? There is no easy way to resolve such a second-order question about which is the ideal term to use. Certainly, whatever alternative we choose is likely to have its own limits.[46] And some of the claims made for the superiority of other concepts seem to suffer from special pleading. Glenn argues that tradition is a widely used folk concept, whereas culture is used only in the West. But this begs the question of whether and when the terms of our explanations need to be linked to those used by social actors. In general, many would argue that tradition also carries many of the troubling implications that Glenn attributes to culture. It has for example been severely criticized for its neglect of socio-economic and political influences, as well as for committing the so-called 'intentionalist' fallacy.[47] 'Living law', for its part, only gets at part of what Friedman and others seek to explain with legal culture, nor does it lend itself easily for use in comparing legal systems. The concept of ideology is itself difficult to handle, not least because it requires us to justify our privileged position in describing other people's ideas. The term is also not necessarily suitable for all the purposes of those who use legal culture; if anything, adopting this concept would change the nature of the inquiry. As far as autopoiesis is concerned, whereas one of the purposes of using the term legal culture is to examine the how and the extent of internal legal culture's autonomy, Luhmann's theory resolves this by theoretical fiat.

What is clear is that legal culture moves in a field of alternatives, and[48] it has to prove its value in relation to these. If we are interested, for example, in explaining why Italy has extensive court delays as compared to its European neighbours, we

[45] See D. Nelken, 'Beyond the Study of Law and Society' (1986) *American Bar Foundation Journal* 323–38, and D. Nelken, 'Changing Paradigms in the Sociology of Law,' in: G. Teubner (ed.), *Autopoietic Law: A New Approach to Law and Society* (Berlin, 1987), 191–217.

[46] For some critics, legal culture presupposes too much cohesion of the various levels and regions of law in society (Cotterrell, op. cit., n.3). But for others, such as those influenced by autopoiesis theory, it assumes too little, or at least the wrong sort of cohesion. (M. King 'Comparing Legal Cultures in the Quest for Law's Identity', in Nelken (1997) op. cit. n.8, 119–34. Luhmanian system-theory eschews the term culture.

[47] J. Whitman, 'A Simple Story'; Review of P. Glenn, *Legal Traditions of the World*' [2004] *Rechtsgeschichte*.

[48] Friedman himself sometimes uses the term 'legal system' when describing the feedback effects that we would otherwise expect to see discussed with respect to the relationship between external and internal legal culture.

have to show why neither tradition nor ideology are helpful as starting points. At the same time there is also no reason to assume that legal culture must be employed to the exclusion of all other terms.[49] Approaches to legal culture also need to be responsive to larger theoretical and methodological developments. Friedman's contribution in this volume seems to show some willingness to search for new ways to formulate his ideas in face of challenges to the underlying assumptions of his framework. He admits that it makes little sense in some respects to distinguish 'law' from 'society'. When emphasizing the importance of public opinion and social interests he talks more about legislatures than about courts. And, perhaps in response to the challenge from the autopoieticists, he envisages a more independent role for internal legal culture, speaking of it as 'translating'[50] demands from society because the 'social is too raw to act directly on the legal system'.[51]

If we want to make further progress, however, we need to be clear about what 'work' we are asking the term to do. And we should also recognize that many studies can be relevant to legal culture even without using this term.[52] One important role for the term could in fact be the way it allows us to bring together a variety of only loosely connected debates so as to show the crucial issues at stake. Friedman's own writings illustrate the wide range of important questions that presuppose and contribute to larger questions about how, when and why, 'law 'is imbricated in the 'social' or the 'cultural'. He suggests that the term is helpful in inquiries into why people use or do not use law, as for example the growth of what he calls 'total justice', or comparative exercises intended to account for why women do or do not turn for help to the police in Italy or France,[53] or (in this volume) why Italian drivers are less likely than the English to wear seat belts. Friedman also now recommends the term in studying how social problems are defined or redefined as legal ones, how changes in social and economic structures and developments in technology change legal systems, and how this results from and helps reinforce convergence in legal rules and institutions, such as the spread of constitutional courts and judicial review. Inquiries inspired by Friedman's approach to legal culture may seek to explain existing differences in patterns of litigation, prison rates, or

[49] See, e.g. the study of procedural traditions in criminal law as 'the site of intersections amongst four aspects of culture: traditions, institutions, intellectual formations and 'lived structures of feeling', in C. Brants, and S. Field, 'Legal Culture, Political Cultures and Procedural Traditions: Towards a Comparative Interpretation of Covert and Proactive Policing in England and Wales and the Netherlands', in D. Nelken (ed.), *Contrasting Criminal Justice* (Aldershot, 2000), 77–116.

[50] It is hard to know how much to read into Friedman's frequent resort to metaphors. But the idea of 'translation' does seem to imply a sort of internal reconstruction process similar to that suggested by the autopoiesis theorists much more than the language of cause and effect and 'impacts' which Friedman has tended to use in the past.

[51] Where Friedman used to compare law to a rope pulled on by competing interests, he now (in this volume) speaks of 'the tough bone and metal of formal law and institutional change'.

[52] Just as many of those who use the term legal culture do so in ways which add little to our understanding of the matters that interest Friedman.

[53] L. Friedman, 'The Concept of Legal Culture: A Reply', in: Nelken (ed.) (1997) op. cit., n.8, 33–40.

court delay. But the term could also be useful in clarifying disagreements where the lack of common conceptual reference points can make it difficult to see what is at stake. For example, Garland has argued that current moves to greater punitiveness in criminal justice policies reflect convergent trends in modern societies.[54] But other writers insist on the very different approaches which still characterize different jurisdictions.[55] The same applies to debates about civil justice, where again some see so-called 'adversarial justice' in the USA as merely one version of a larger trend towards 'total justice', while others claim it belongs to a class of its own.[56] These debates might be made more fruitful if the participants talked in terms of similarities and differences in legal culture.

Legal Culture and the Problem of Tautology

For the term legal culture to be of use we must avoid the danger of circular reasoning. The promise of legal culture (as of culture itself) lies in its range and its all-inclusiveness, but this is also, of course, its weakness. There is the ever present danger of falling into the trap of 'essentialism' in cultural analyses, where cultural values are argued to cause a certain response to events: to quote Keesing,[57] these kind of claims often are 'non explanations in seductive disguises'. If we speak, for example, about American or Japanese legal culture, are we offering some sort of explanation or only indicating that which needs to be explained? As Glenn puts it, legal culture's 'shortcomings come into evidence when it shifts from something to be described, interpreted, even perhaps explained, and is treated instead as a source of explanation in itself'.[58] Until a solution is found to this problem, legal culture 'risks', as Jeremy Webber has written recently, 'being a superficially attractive but ultimately obfuscating concept, insisting upon interdependency but then cloaking that interdependency under the rubric of a single concept, doing nothing to tease out the specific relations of cause and effect within any social field'.[59] And alternative terms to legal culture will be that much more attractive to the degree that they can be shown to be less likely to lead to circular arguments in which the explanation is also that which needs to be explained.[60]

54 D. Garland, *The Culture of Control* (Oxford, 2000).

55 See e.g. A. Crawford, 'Contrasts in Victim/Offender Mediation and Appeals to Community in Comparitive Cultural Contexts: France and England and Wales', in: Nelken (ed.), op. cit., n.49, 205–29. These differences have been traced a long way back in history, see J. Whitman, *Harsh Justice* (Oxford, 2003).

56 See D. Nelken, 'Beyond Compare? Criticising the American Way of Law' (2003) 28 *Law and Social Inquiry* 181–213.

57 R. Keesing, '"Culture" and Asian Studies' (1991) 15(2) *Asian Studies Review* 85–92.

58 Glenn, op. cit., n.31.

59 Webber, op. cit., n.15.

60 Though in fact alternative terms such as legal tradition or legal ideology can also be both explanations and what needs to be explained.

One way of addressing this problem could be to distinguish different uses of legal culture by their disciplinary pedigree. Thus Friedman (in this volume) describes investigations geared to characterizing large units such as American legal culture as 'the anthropological' use of legal culture. His emphasis on why people turn to the law could then perhaps be dubbed the 'sociological', or better, the 'political science', use of the term. But making distinctions only in terms of disciplines seems unsatisfactory, not only because the differences between disciplines such as sociology and anthropology are unclear and constantly changing, but also because it fails to tell us what is at stake in these differences. A second way of contrasting uses of legal culture is to distinguish speaking about legal culture either as a variable or as an aggregate. The question why people turn to law concerns a variable which purports to explain the shape of law in a given setting or society, whereas books with titles such as 'Dutch legal culture' or 'French legal cultures', on the other hand, should be seen as mere descriptions of legal culture in the aggregate. Such 'holistic signifiers' as Glenn calls them,[61] do not have the pretence to explain anything.

But this solution could be seen as just another way of posing the problem. For it is the co-existence of such different referents for legal culture that leads to misunderstanding, all the more so as often even the same authors use the term legal culture with reference both to variables and aggregates in ways that make it difficult to keep them distinct. Friedman is of course a pioneer in the use of legal culture as a discrete explanatory variable. But, as we have noted, he does not reserve it for such uses but also uses it for describing large aggregates. Although what he means by legal culture when speaking of these aggregates has again much to do with people's expectations of the law, the 'traits' he indicates as characterizing modern legal culture are not only about expectations and have as much to do with the results of such expectations as the expectations themselves.

The muddle which can result from the many referents of legal culture has been carefully dissected by Roger Cotterrell in a highly critical analysis of what he considers to be a term which lacks rigour and theoretical coherence. Cotterrell rightly notes that Friedman uses legal culture in a variety of ways ranging from the culture of the individual to that of whole societies. This means that legal culture becomes, in his words, 'an immense, multi-textured overlay of levels and regions of culture, varying in content, scope, and influence and in their relation to the institutions, practices and knowledge's of state legal systems'.[62] For Cotterrell this has crucial implications for the possibility of using legal culture in explanatory inquiry. Although, he says, such a variety of level of super- and sub-national units could in theory provide a rich terrain for inquiry we must nonetheless reject the idea that legal culture can be reflected in 'diversity and levels' whilst also having a 'unity'.[63] For him, 'if legal culture refers to so many levels and regions of culture (with the

[61] P. Glenn, e-mail 24 June 2004. [62] Cotterrell, op. cit., n.3, 16–17.

[63] But see Nelken, op. cit., n.7, for an attempt to show unity despite internal diversity with respect to the patterns of court delay in Italy as compared to other countries.

scope of each of these ultimately indeterminate because of the indeterminacy of the scope of the idea of legal culture itself) the problem of specifying how to use the concept as a theoretical component in comparative sociology for law remains'.[64]

But, partly because of his characteristic prudence, Cotterrell's critique is itself at points very debatable. He admits that there are 'no serious problems if legal culture is used as a residual category referring to the general environment of ideas, behaviour etc. in which law exists'. But it is not clear if he is suggesting here that such a residual idea of culture is a mere 'holistic signifier' and therefore has no role in explanation, or whether, as others have argued, it may also have some use as a residual explanation when alternative explanations have run out.[65] Likewise, he argues that legal culture may be used 'as a provisional characterization where the exact relation of elements is not clear or not of concern'.[66] Yet it is already some concession to say that legal culture does have some heuristic value. In addition there is also quite some difference between using the term provisionally where the relationship between elements is 'not (yet) clear', and, on the other hand, using it provisionally (but for what purpose?) where that relationship is of 'no concern'.

The part of Cotterrell's argument which is most problematic, howcvcr, is that in which he denies that legal culture can serve as an aid to the explanation of law in any society 'made up of many diverse and possibly unrelated factors'. It can, he says, be treated as an 'empirical category' only in the study of a small isolated self-enclosed setting which ethnographers are able to describe and record 'in all its richness and complexity, a cluster or aggregate of attitudes, values, customs and patterns of social action', and where 'there are no serious problems of differentiating and distinguishing cultures'.[67] But the distinction Cotterrell draws between smaller scale 'settings' suitable for ethnographic study where empirical research into culture can be carried out, and other larger, more complex aggregates, where, in his view, it is better to proceed by means of 'ideal type' categorizations,[68] seems to confuse theory and methodology. If culture is an untenable concept then the size or complexity of setting (or unit) should be irrelevant. The possibility that, as Cotterrell puts it, what we call culture is 'made up of many diverse and possibly unrelated factors', is still present even for more bounded smaller social worlds or organizations. Of course, smaller settings are easier to study and the relationships between factors more manageable than when discussing large-scale societies. But it is never possible to describe and record even the smallest setting *'in all its richness and complexity'*.[69]

[64] Cotterrell, op cit., n.3, 17.

[65] T. Prosser, 'The State, Constitutions and Implementing Economic Policy: Privatisation and Regulation in the UK, France and the USA', in: Nelken (ed.) op. cit. n.8, 507–16.

[66] Cotterrell, op. cit., n.3, 21. [67] *Ibid*, 25.

[68] Cotterrell explains elsewhere that the ideal types he has in mind are types of community. He uses the term community basically as a shorthand for Weberian forms of social connectedness (the term is otherwise highly problematic).

[69] By contrast, ethnographers who study small-scale settings in Thailand or elsewhere have no hesitation about using studies *in* Thailand as providing valuable evidence *about* Thailand. See D. Engel, 'Globalization and the Decline of Legal Consciousness: Torts, Ghosts, and Karma in Thailand' (2005) 30 *Law & Social Inquiry 469*.

Cotterrell is on more solid ground when he argues that, as currently operationalized, legal culture either explains too much that happens or fails to happen in the legal system, or else too little, so that we can never tell which are the important factors.[70] Moreover, though he takes Friedman as his main target, Cotterrell claims that the problem of tautology is unavoidable whenever we employ the concept of legal culture both as a variable and as an aggregate. Indeed Mary Volcansek, a political scientist who specializes in the study of court systems, has made the same type of criticism of the way Blankenburg uses the term. When reviewing the second edition of Blankenburg and Bruinsma's book *Dutch Legal Culture* she first summarizes what they have to say about legal culture as an aggregate:

> The Dutch legal culture is pragmatic and flexible, rather than rigid and formalistic. It favors consensus, inclusion, discussion, and negotiation (if only among all relevant elites) rather than conflict and dichotomous, legally-enforceable outcomes. The absence of judicial review of legislation coexists with wide judicial, administrative, and prosecutorial discretion. The Europeanization of legal practices, greater public concern about crime, and a reduced willingness to fund a generous welfare state, however, are eroding the distinctive aspects of Dutch legal culture.

But she then goes on to voice her misgivings about asking an aggregate to play the role of a variable. 'I agree that legal culture is not reducible merely to public opinion or attitudes of legal professionals. Institutions both reflect the broader culture and shape it. Institutions and legal culture are, as we say, mutually constitutive.' But, she complains, this way of using the term means that 'legal culture has that slippery "residual variable" quality about it—shared by the concept political culture. It is everything and nothing simultaneously. It is the totality of laws, practices, and opinions. And it somehow simultaneously stands apart from these things and effects how they work. It is both cause and effect.'[71]

Different Uses of Legal Culture in Explanatory Inquiry

Can legal culture be used without tautology? To answer this challenge we can begin by noting, as illustrated in Table 12.1, that Friedman's term 'legal culture' is by no means a simple category and refers to (at least) four different phenomena.

Table 12.1. Friedman's concept of legal culture

Variables	Aggregates
1 Internal legal culture	3 External + internal legal cultures = Legal culture
2 External legal culture	4 Distinctive relationships between external and internal culture

[70] Cotterrell, op. cit., n.3, 20.

[71] M. Volcansek, *Law and Politics Book Review* Vol. 6 No. 9 (August, 1996), 122–3.

Friedman uses the term legal culture to describe a number of variables. But it is clear from the qualifiers 'internal' and 'external' that for him legal culture as an aggregate unit represents the combination of these two types or elements of legal culture (see cell 3). Comparisons of aggregate units of legal cultures (which should not be limited to national jurisdictions) should therefore operate at this level; and it is this we should call legal culture. In addition, however, although Friedman himself does not pursue this option, Blankenburg has argued that it is of particular interest for comparative purposes to identify what is distinctive across different units in the way internal and external legal culture are expected to relate and actually do relate to each other (cell 4). As he suggests, this varies greatly even as between common law and continental societies, never mind further afield. If we do not bear this in mind we risk imposing our own cultural background in what purports to be a framework suitable for studying legal culture comparatively.

The influence of Anglo-American assumptions may, as Blankenburg suggests, help explain why Friedman is so convinced that what really matters is external legal culture, and why it is hard to tell if this is a cultural presupposition or a hypothesis open to being tested. In other ways, too, Friedman's composite concept of legal culture begs questions. Cotterrell is right to say that internal and external legal culture are not well distinguished; lawyers, for example would seem to belong on both sides, even though Friedman allocates them to internal legal culture. Any rigid separation between internal and external legal culture cannot be sustained, their division serves only as an analytic pre-requisite to examining their relationship, as Friedman himself now concedes.

On the other hand, any analytical framework geared to empirical inquiry can only be useful heuristically if it is not already to contain within itself all the answers to future inquiry. Some indication of what such empirical inquiries should concern themselves with is provided in Table 12.2.

The first type of inquiry (set out in cell 1) concerns the elements that are hypothesized to hold together internal (or, more rarely, external) legal culture. The possibilities include assuming some sort of underlying causes or influences, historical or otherwise, Damaska's idea that different forms of procedure have an 'affinity' with each other[72] or Cotterrell's suggestion that the common element

Table 12.2. Types of inquiry using the concept legal culture

Internal Coherence	External Coherence
1 That which holds together the individual elements which make up a given internal or external legal culture	2 Legal culture in relation to general culture
3 Legal culture in relation to political culture/ economic culture, etc	4 Given legal cultures as compared to other legal cultures

[72] M.R. Damaska, *The Faces of Justice and State Authority* (New Haven, 1986).

may lie only in the observer's ideal types that we impose on reality. Such coherence may transcend national boundaries. Increasingly, those who specialize in a given area of law may find they have more in common with those working on the same matters in other jurisdictions than they do with those working on different matters in their own jurisdiction.[73] Coherence is something that is constructed rather than found by legal professionals, who either feel the requirement or the advantages of acting in ways that are coherent, or at least of making this seem to be the case. On the other hand, it would be wrong to assume that social actors always seek or recognize the patterned outcomes they produce. It is the job of the observer to underline and explain such patterns.

The second type of inquiry (cell 2) seeks to explore the ways in which legal ideas and practices are rooted in larger aspects of the society. It also seeks to examine how they may or may not be homologous with those common throughout the society (for example, insistence on a high level of formalism in legal matters often presupposes less formalism in social life). The third type of investigation (cell 3) asks how legal culture relates to what could be categorized as economic culture or political culture. Considered comparatively, for example, common law countries privilege the connection between law and economics whereas continental polities focus more on law and politics. The last type of inquiry (cell 4) seeks to bring out the similarities and differences between different legal cultures and show how perceived (or imagined) differences may themselves help to reproduce the boundaries of cultures.

We are now ready to return to the vexed question of how to avoid legal culture from serving as an explanation of itself. Table 12.3 sets out four of the ways in which legal culture can figure in explanations. In two of these legal culture is what does the explaining, in the other two it is what needs to be explained.

Table 12.3 suggests that there may indeed be some occasions when we want to explain legal culture (or legal consciousness) and others when we think it can help us explain something else. But the table also shows why the difference between legal culture as a variable and as an aggregate seems so slippery. We tend to think of aggregates as large, often national, units of legal culture. But, in practice all variables could also be treated as aggregates, just as all aggregates can have a role in explanations (and not just serve as 'holistic signifiers'). For example, attitudes to law, which Friedman treats mainly as a variable, could, where appropriate, be dis-aggregated into the different elements that make them up. This is even true at the level of the individual, where a person's 'attitude' could be taken to represent the sum of opinions tested in a survey instrument. Conversely, even large aggregates—say, American legal culture—become variables when they act on or influence something else. It is therefore mistaken to assume either that variables always explain or that aggregates never do.

In studying the way in which legal culture can be used as an explanation, we can begin from Friedman's thesis that social demands shape the law. But if our interest lies in understanding aggregate legal cultures, such as patterns in nation states, or even those in different courts, we would be unwise to reduce legal culture merely

[73] Bell op. cit., n.16.

Table 12.3. Legal culture as explanation and as what is to be explained

	Legal Consciousness	Legal Culture
As Explanation	1 The choice to use law as one factor which shapes the legal system	3 The influence exerted by legal culture, i.e. given patterns of attitudes, uses and discourses about law
As Needing Explanation	2 Why people choose to use or not to use the law	4 Why given units of legal culture have different patterns

to the choice whether or not to use the law.[74] This is only one element amongst the many that would need to be considered to make sense of legal culture. As Friedman now suggests (in this volume), structure and culture are mutually related; why American legal culture has a relatively high level of court use is not to be explained as *either* a matter of public demand *or* of structural supply but is a result of how and what happens when these come together. To avoid tautology it would also be best to call the demand for law something other than legal culture and name it, for example, legal consciousness.[75]

As Susan Silbey demonstrates in her valuable encyclopaedia entry on the subject,[76] leading figures in the law and society movement in the USA have continued to take seriously the need to study individual and group expectations and attitudes to law. But they use a different, more narrative-based, methodology, and are less interested in showing how demand changes the law. Students of legal consciousness seek to understand how and how far people come to think of themselves as rights-bearing subjects, and to describe 'legality' as a structure of action and meaning. In many respects these concerns can be seen as prior questions to that of why people turn to the law. Indeed, Friedman himself has now come to acknowledge their importance saying (in his contribution to this volume) that explaining the causes of legal culture (i.e. of turning to the law) is a priority for the sociology of law. But to avoid confusion we need to remember that this is a different question from that found in the first cell of Table 12.3. It involves explaining a variable that we may afterwards also want to use in our explanations. By renaming this topic legal consciousness we can avoid the need to speak of the causes of the causes of legal culture!

The third cell is where we examine the influence of legal culture seen as an aggregate—that is, as a specific patterns of attitudes, uses, and discourses about law. It is here that we have to be most careful about not falling into tautology. But we surely can defend explanations that refer to the 'effects' of legal culture seen as an aggregate. Even Volcansek, while discussing her concerns about the problem of

[74] This is implicit when Friedman speaks about how 'types of society' demand and produce 'different types of legal system'. At times his approach also comes near to technological determinism.

[75] Though it would be fairer to say that Friedman's ideas about the demand for law and the current study of legal consciousness, are overlapping but in some respects also distinct inquiries.

[76] Silbey op. cit., n.23.

circular reasoning, admits that 'the strongest evidence of the importance of legal culture is the different outcomes produced by similar structures in two different countries.[77] For example, the Dutch and the British may both have informal tribunals for legal conflicts over social security, mental health, and labour, yet in Britain, the tribunals will operate formally and legalistically and in the Netherlands, informally and flexibly'. The empirical claim that she is making, is one which is increasingly relevant at a time when legal institutions and ideas are increasingly being transferred and imitated. It is that what actually happens in such processes will be influenced by identifiable larger patterns of legal culture. The choice to introduce or change legal rules and institutions often results from awareness of patterns of legal culture elsewhere. What we could call 'relational legal culture' involves studying the implications of such reciprocal awareness. Domestic branches of law such as copyright law may be brought into being mainly because they exist in competing jurisdictions.[78] Governing or judicial elites may either try to mark their boundaries in relation to other cultural patterns or to blur them so as to be able to qualify as 'normal'. For example, once comparative incarceration rates began to be published, countries such as Finland and Holland sought to adjust the numbers of those sent to prison so as to remain within the European average. For Finland the goal was to reduce numbers; the Dutch Minister of Justice, on the other hand, justified his prison building programme of the 1980s on the basis that his country was too far beneath the average.[79]

Finally, the last cell in Table 12.3 treats legal culture in the aggregate as something which itself needs to be explained. Identifying which are the relevant institutional, social, political, and general cultural factors, in theory unlimited, is a subject for empirical demonstration. Especially for comparative inquiries, the more, and the more unexpected, the sources of differences in legal culture we can discover between one unit and another—the better. What needs to be avoided, on the other hand, is the temptation to find some shortcut to explanation by fixing on some key legal feature such as inquisitorial versus accusatorial systems or even socio-legal characteristics, such as 'adversarialness' in the USA, 'pragmatism' in Holland, or 'formalism' in Italy.[80] Like all stereotypes there may or may not be some validity in these labels. But they are likely to miss large parts of what goes on, and may be based on wrong or incomplete information.[81] We also need to justify

[77] See now T. Ginsburg, *Judicial Review in New Democracies* (Cambridge, 2003).

[78] B. Sherman, 'Remembering and Forgetting: The Birth of Modern Copyright Law', in: Nelken (ed.) (1997) op. cit. n.8, 237–66.

[79] As with so much else that has to do with culture we need to bracket important questions such as whether these rates really allow us to compare like with like, whether they are manipulated, whether comparative incarceration rates are the genuine or only the presented reasons for prison building, etc. It is enough for present purposes to show that 'relational legal culture' has 'effects'.

[80] for a sophisticated study of regulatory culture in Thailand see F.L. Haines, *Globalization and Regulatory Culture* (Aldershot, 2005).

[81] On the media construction of (alleged) American adversarialism see W. Haltom and M. McCaan, *Distorting the Law* (Chicago, 2004).

any assumption that the aggregate to be explained is necessarily a stable or internally consistent set of ideas and practices. A recent award-winning study of law in Muslim Indonesia, well describes law there as caught 'between local custom, Islamic law, western law, self-interest, and pragmatism, while the mixings and collisions of public discourse show a robust, multi-level, and multi-sited engagement over fundamental values and principle. It is not, then, simply a struggle over outcomes, but a struggle over the very meta-narratives of public reasoning.'[82]

When we study discrete units of legal culture we must recognize that what makes them distinctive is the special (and changeable) mixture of elements from which they are formed and re-formed. Eric Feldman, for example, argues:

> Culture, likewise, ought not be treated as an incoherent mélange of undifferentiated ingredients . . . The fluidity of culture, the way it is regularly reinterpreted and redefined, makes it a particularly cumbersome analytical tool. Different components of culture change in varying ways; while some may endure for generations, others may be short-lived. It is therefore difficult to understand the link between law and culture without disaggregating the term 'culture' into its constituent parts. Doing so enables one to sidestep the apparently endless debate over how to define culture and instead to concentrate on the distinguishing characteristics of different societies that form their cultural fabric.[83]

Working with Legal Culture

I have argued in this chapter that the approach to legal culture pioneered by Lawrence Friedman, if formulated with care in terms of a lager framework of inquiry, can indeed be used to 'help make comparisons of legal systems more sociologically meaningful'. To conclude, I shall outline briefly how the explanatory framework I have outlined so far can be applied in the course of inquiry into *one specific element of legal culture.* I shall then go on to indicate how it might also be useful in reading, and learning from, relevant socio-legal studies, whether or not such inquiries make explicit use of the concept of legal culture.

Table 12.4 applies the framework set out in Table 12.3 to a specific set of behaviours and ideas which forms part of Italian legal culture taken as an aggregate (see Table 12.3 cell 4). It concerns the relatively high level of court delay in Italy as compared to other similar industrialized societies.[84]

It suggests, as we would by now expect, the need for a series of interrelated investigations. The first two of these (cells 1 and 2) are those on which Friedman would tend to focus and involve exploring the consequences and causes of the rates at which individuals, social groups, economic interests, and others turn to

[82] See Law and Society Newsletter 2004 commenting on J.R. Bowen, *Islam, Law and Equality in Indonesia* (Cambridge, 2003).

[83] E. Feldman (unpublished, first draft December 2004) 'How Culture Shapes Law: International Norms, Domestic Legal Change, and the Disappearance of the Cigarette in Contemporary Japan'.

[84] For more extended discussion see Nelken, op. cit., n.7.

Table 12.4. Legal culture and legal delay in Italy

	Legal Consciousness	Legal Culture
As Explanation	1 Attitudes to the use of law in Italy as they affect legal delay	3 The delays forming part of Italian legal culture as an influence on social and legal behaviour
As Needing Explanation	2 Causes of attitudes to the use of law in Italy	4 The causes of distinctive levels of legal delay in Italy

the law and the courts in Italy. Who is obliged to go through the courts? Who can manage without and why? We will need to understand the legal consciousness of potential litigants who keep going despite long delays (are we dealing with fatalists?), but we cannot limit our inquiry to that. We shall also have to take into account how far it is increased resort to the law, as against a much smaller rise in the number of judges or administrative assistance, which is itself a factor that has brought about delay.

A further type of inquiry (as set out in Table 12.4 cell 3) has to do with explaining the *effects* of legal culture. Here we are specifically concerned with the consequences of the delays built into the Italian legal system and the interests, practices and values which sustain them. This is the tricky case where tautology is thought to lurk. *There is certainly little point in saying that it is Italian legal culture which 'explains' court delays if court delays are one of the ingredients or traits that make up what we are calling Italian legal culture.* But this should not prevent us from looking for links between delay and other aspects of the same legal culture which may reveal an interdependence that could be said in some way to characterize the virtuous or vicious circularity of its legal culture.

Given the current level of delay in Italy, civil litigants and criminal defendants by now may actually be counting on and aiming at delay rather than at the resolution of their cases. And lawyers may have their own reasons, in terms of the way they are paid, for accepting such an apparently inefficient legal system. Court delays may therefore help explain why lawyers in Italy have a relatively low rate of out-of-court settlement on the civil side, and also make low use of the plea bargaining possibilities introduced in the 1989 reform of penal procedure. Some lawyers admit that counting on delay (during which witnesses may die or forget things, or criminal cases be 'prescribed' for running over time limits) rather than seeking any other sort of resolution is the best strategy for their clients. Thus, as opposed to the usual argument that courts are used where no quicker alternatives are available,[85] here we could hypothesize, paradoxically, that it is the availability of overstretched courts that discourages the use of alternatives.

Italian legal culture also has 'effects' by influencing what other actors or systems do. This comes about through processes of imitation or rejection. For example,

[85] See, e.g. Blankenburg, op. cit., n.22.

the strict due process penal law procedures, which are, unfortunately, especially easily manipulated for their benefit by powerful criminal defendants, have been borrowed by many Latin American countries. On the other hand, because they fear that cases will never arrive at a resolution, international business partners will rarely agree to Italy being the country where potential legal disputes must be adjudicated.

The final field of inquiry (cell 4) has to do with identifying the various social, economic, political and other causes of the pattern of court delay in Italy. This requires looking beyond the question whether or not litigants choose to turn to the courts. Legal rules, procedures, and institutional arrangements which encourage or allow delay also need to be appreciated as resources for the 'law in action' by which legal professionals and others use margins of manoeuvre to create or reduce delay. Attributing legal delay to some stereotype of how Italian 'culture' normally functions is much too simple. There are, it is true, some similar features in other spheres of public life, such as the inefficiency of public administration or the social importance placed on waiting one's turn. But we should not forget that if 'delay' was really endemic to all of social and economic life we could not explain how Italy could be a highly efficient and successful economic power with an enviable standard of living. The relationship is a different one. Because of the demands it places on the legal system, court overload and extensive delay is a feature of post-war legal culture in Italy, the Italy which arose *after* its economic miracle. In the 1920s and 1930s, judges were often getting through more cases than were arriving in front of them.

If so, what remains to be explained is why economic interests in Italy have not produced more pressure for change and why so many politicians are fearful of making the courts more efficient. In assessing the balance of forces for change we shall also need to look outside Italy. The role of the European Court of Human Rights in condemning the Italian state for delay is particularly important here. The current persistence of delay, notwithstanding various reform efforts aimed (allegedly) at improving matters, suggests that we need to see how 'cultural' and 'structural' factors are locked together. One part of the answer could be that, through delay, law in Italy is kept to a default role in subservience to a social order based more on articulated systems of cooptation than on the vindication of individual rights.[86]

As mentioned, however, the framework outlined in Table 12.3 may also be used as a means of sorting out and cumulating the findings of other studies relevant to legal culture, whether or not they explicitly use the term. This is particularly helpful if it allows us to spot possibly misleading arguments which result from oversimplifying an explanatory problem by *collapsing* into each other two or more different inquiries. When Friedman offers as an example of valuable research into legal culture the question how much women in Italy as compared to France are likely to turn to the police for assistance, he is in fact asking us to engage in (at least)

[86] Nelken, op. cit., n.7.

two different investigations. In terms of the possibilities set out in Table 12.3 we would need to ask first why women (as compared to men) *in Italy* and *in France* turn to the law, and the effects of their doing so (cells 1 and 2). Then, in addition, we need to examine what is distinctive about the form taken by legal culture in Italy and France as the aggregate context in which these choices are shaped, and which is shaped by them (see cells 3 and 4).[87]

Another example is provided by Feldman's richly documented analysis of why the Japanese have been so swift at outlawing smoking in public. In one of his key arguments he attributes this to what he calls 'the cultural trait of conformity' which, he says, 'is here further demonstrated by the willingness to change to fit international norms'.[88] But, arguably, conformity in this second sense, what Feldman calls 'the cultural tendency to be influenced by Western norms', may not be the same factor as the conformity which is so often employed to explain Japanese respect for *their own* legal and social norms. Inspecting Table 12.3 suggests that it might be better to treat this as an aspect of 'relational legal culture' connected to the influence of what are taken to be 'normal' international standards (see cell 3). Some confirmation of this is provided by the evidence that Italy is also now engaged in what appears to be an equally successful campaign to abolish public smoking, and no-one would suggest that Italy usually scores highly on conformity to its own legal norms.

On the other hand, the more usual problem with current discussions of legal culture is the artificial *separation* of the interrelated inquiries set out in Table 12.3. As indicated at the outset of this chapter, the recent literature tends to divide up into those who focus *either* on legal consciousness, *or* else on legal culture seen in the aggregate. A good example of the first type of inquiry is represented by the important series of explorations of the use of law in Thailand by the anthropologist David Engel. His research is mainly concerned with the use of the courts by those who have suffered injuries, and with how this has changed over time. In a recent study relying on interviews with thirty-five victims of injuries,[89] Engel found that over the last twenty years the effects of globalization have actually led to less resort to law. In his words, 'although globalisation may indeed have transformed legal consciousness in Thailand, the accounts provided by injury victims suggest that it has—somewhat unexpectedly—diminished the role of law in everyday life and heightened the influence of religion in a new and more universal form'. Engel explains this by arguing that 'citizens appear to view law as existing in tension with their religious convictions, and they perceive the Buddha's teachings as morally superior to the ideology of liberal legalism.' Most important, however, 'Buddhism appears increasingly to have separated from its connections to village life and is described in more abstract and universalised doctrinal terms . . . Nearly

[87] The literature on Japanese legal culture offers the best examples of such synthesis see, e.g. V. Hamilton and J. Sanders, *Everyday Justice: Responsibility and the Individual in Japan and the United States* (New Haven, 1992).

[88] Feldman op cit. n.83.

[89] See Engel, op. cit., n.69.

all of them chose Buddhism. The choice of Buddhism, separated now from the efficacious remedy systems to which it was formerly linked, means that injury victims absorb the harm that has been done to them without any aggressive attempt to obtain compensation.' There is little evidence here of the convergence predicted by Friedman. Writers such as Engel differ from Friedman, however, not only in their findings (perhaps Thailand, or this part of Thailand, is an exception to Friedman's overall story of convergence?), but in the questions they ask and the way they explore them. They are much less interested than Friedman (or Blankenburg) in causal questions such as whether to assign priority to demand ('cultural') or supply ('structural') explanations in explaining the use of law. As Engel puts it, '[d]id Buddhist doctrine cause injury victims to forgo the use of law, or did the costs and risks of the legal system cause injury victims to invoke Buddhism as an after-the-fact rationalization? This question is probably unanswerable and is perhaps beside the point. One can rarely say whether beliefs cause people to act in a certain way or merely justify actions that occur for other reasons. Certainly, the interviewees who provided these injury narratives did not consider this to be a significant question. *It is enough for us* to observe that Buddhist beliefs provide a powerful, comprehensive, and useful interpretive framework for residents of northern Thailand as they attempt to make sense of their experiences with injuries and with law' (my emphasis).

But of course what *is enough for us* in any inquiry depends on its purpose. It is one thing to argue that a given methodology does not permit us to draw conclusions about causal priority, it is another to claim that the question is unimportant. Finding the answer *would* matter if we were engaged in a larger project of seeking to understand the specificities of legal culture in Thailand, or if we had practical reason to want to know, for example, how to increase 'access to justice'.[90] In any case, there is much to be gained by inserting an investigation of legal consciousness into the larger framework of inquiries into legal culture. Only in this way, for example, is it possible to deal with the problem of who gains and who loses by encouraging or discouraging the use of the courts. And in fact Engel does move between studying consciousness and seeking to investigate larger questions of changing structures which relate to legal culture in the aggregate. In earlier research he claimed to seek understanding of 'the self that has been harmed and the community of which he or she is part.' And in explaining his latest findings he starts from the effects of globalization and raises many of the issues we have discussed in this chapter when he asks '[to] what extent the "internal coherence" of the ideology of rights and liberal legalism has been preserved or "loosened" as the cultural flows of globalisation have washed across Chiangmai's social landscape.'

Much the same can be said of discussions that concentrate on legal culture as an aggregate. Take Bob Kagan's recent thoroughgoing critique of the pathology of

[90] Engel is right that his interviewees are not in a position to answer this hypothetical question. But a comparison of different settings in Thailand where the use of law has either grown or declined could help to clarify the matter.

what he calls 'the American way of law'.[91] Kagan argues that this is the consequence of a 'fundamental mismatch' between, on the one hand, the demand for social and political justice through law together with the expectations of equal opportunities demanded by interest groups and individuals, and, on the other hand, the difficulty of supplying this need except through the courts when the role of central and local government is deliberately hamstrung.[92] He looks to European legal cultures for a sounder balance between private and public and a greater role for policy makers and experts. In terms of the framework set out in Table 12.3 Kagan's analysis thus develops Friedman's idea of the importance of the demand for 'total justice' (cells 1 and 2) and successfully adds in relevant aspects of political structure (cells 3 and 4).

But we could also say that Kagan sometimes confuses the observation that American reliance on courts is extreme in the international context (cells 3 and 4) with the somewhat different argument that this itself proves that American use of courts is excessive and needs to be changed (cells 1 and 2). Because the focus is mainly on the aggregate, we are also given less insight than we might want into why and when people or groups turn to the law. The thinness of the account here is revealed by Kagan's resort to analogies and figures of speech. Thus he veers between saying that people are tempted to over-consume law as if it were ice cream, and the somewhat different claim that tigers (lawyers?) wait in the bushes ready to propel the litigant into the processes of adversarial justice at every available opportunity. While it is certainly important not to use concepts which lead to tautology, using the framework set out here may also help us avoid mixed metaphors!

[91] R. Kagan, *Adversarial Legalism: The American Way of Law* (Cambridge, Mass, 2001).

[92] *Ibid*, 40.

13

'Pigs in Space': Geographic Separatism in Multicultural Societies

Issachar Rosen-Zvi [1]

This chapter is concerned with the normative and spatial dimensions of sovereignty in a society characterized by cultural diversity, social fragmentation, and ideological conflict. Specifically, it seeks to explore the contradiction, which typifies many liberal-democratic societies, between the need to further solidarity among members of cultural, ethnic, and religious subgroups and the need to avoid social fragmentation and inter-group antagonism. The thesis of this chapter is that in mediating these tensions, decision makers and the courts often employ the 'ethics of provincialism', a vision of ethnic, cultural, and religious pluralism managed by geographic autonomy and isolation,[2] using geography as a proxy for subgroup affiliation. But in so doing they treat space, to use Foucault's critique, 'as the dead, the fixed, the undialectical, the immobile',[3] without paying attention to the way geography itself influences and, in turn, is influenced by the legal regime in place.

For the sake of clarity, I will ground my discussion on a recent decision delivered by the Israeli Supreme Court—*Solodkin* v. *City of Beit Shemesh*[4]—that raises important questions regarding the (appropriate) place of space in legal analysis, allowing me to analyse the severe social consequences of the ethics of provincialism. After exploring the facts of the case, I will then consider how various political theories—liberalism, multiculturalism, and civic republicanism—would address the dilemma presented in it. This discussion, in turn, will serve as a springboard for analysing pervasive questions regarding the relationship between social groups and the urban spaces they inhabit in multicultural societies.

[1] I wish to thank Daphne Barak-Erez, Tammy Meisels, Ilan Saban, and the participants of the Law and Society Colloquium, for their useful comments on earlier drafts of this chapter. Special thanks go to Marianne Meisels who provided invaluable editing assistance and to Michael Birnhak who suggested the title for this chapter.

[2] R.T. Ford, 'Geography and Sovereignty: Jurisdictional Formation and Racial Segregation' (1997) 49 *Stanford Law Review* 1365, 1401.

[3] M. Foucault, 'Questions in Geography', in C. Gordon (ed.), *Power/Knowledge: Selected Interviews and Other Writings 1972–1977* (New York, 1980), 63, 70.

[4] H.C. 953/01 *Solodkin* v. *City of Beit Shemesh* (delivered 14 June 2004).

Background

The subject matter of *Solodkin* v. *City of Beit Shemesh* is the pork trade. The breeding and trading of pigs has been a controversial issue since Israel's inception. Pork consumption is strictly forbidden by Jewish law and for various reasons the pig has become an obscene symbol in Jewish culture.[5] It therefore tends to evoke strong emotions not only among observant Jews, but also in nationalist-Zionist circles. The first attempts to proscribe the trade in pork were made a few years after the establishment of the State of Israel. Following a long and heated debate in the national government between the religious and nationalist camp ('pig rejecters'), who sought to entirely forbid the sale of both pigs and pork by state law, and the socialist and the liberal-progressive camp ('pork lovers'), who fiercely objected to such a proscription, a compromise was reached. The Israeli Parliament resolved to pass the buck to its citizenry by decentralizing the power to regulate the pork trade to local governments as the representatives of local communities.[6] In accordance with their newly possessed powers, the local governments set out to regulate the sale of pork. Some local governments, swayed by the political clout of the pig rejecters, issued ordinances banning pork trading anywhere within their jurisdiction. Other localities, more attentive to pork lovers within their population, banned the sale of pork from residential areas but allowed pork to be bought and sold in areas zoned for industry. And some local governments (admittedly the minority) resolved not to ban the pork trade at all. Throughout the 1970s and 1980s the number of pork lovers within the population was rather small, and therefore the prohibition on pork sales did not cause much controversy. The situation changed dramatically during the 1990s. The last decade of the twentieth century witnessed an influx of immigration from the former USSR, which has completely altered Israel's demographic landscape. Many of the new immigrants are non-Jews and even some of the immigrants who are ethnically Jewish do not identify with its constitutive symbols. As a result, the demand for pork soared and many businesses were opened throughout the country to meet that demand. In compliance with their ordinances, many local governments enforced the regulations against pork trading by confiscating the prohibited meat and imposing high fines on the perpetrators.

This state of affairs led a few interested parties, including a Russian-Jewish member of Parliament, a large vendor of pork and a neo-liberal party, to challenge the ordinances of three different cities prohibiting or severely restricting the sale of pork in court. The petitioners argued that these ordinances infringe on the freedom of occupation of the pork vendors and on the fundamental right of the pork lovers

[5] For an in-depth analysis of the prohibition on pigs as a reflection of social and cultural transformation in Israeli society see D. Barak-Erez, *Outlawed Pigs: Law, Religion and Culture in Israel* (Madison, forthcoming, 2006).

[6] Local Government Law (Special Authorization) 1957.

among the cities' residents to be free of religious coercion, and that therefore they should be repealed.

The Decision

Instead of upholding or striking down the city ordinances, the Supreme Court chose to send the issue back to the three local governments with guidelines as to how to structure the ordinances so that they would be lawful. The Court identified two conflicting interests that must be weighed by local governments: protection of the freedom of occupation of the pork traders and the right of pork lovers to live according to their own conception of the good, which includes the freedom to decide what to eat on the one hand; and on the other hand, protection of the religious belief and respect for the ideological convictions of the pig rejecters.[7]

The Court acknowledged that these interests are in opposition to each other and therefore cannot be fully protected simultaneously. The solution it offered is one based on geography. The Court presented three hypothetical villages: in Village A all the residents, except for a negligible minority, are pig rejecters. Such a village is allowed, according to the Court, to prohibit the sale of pork within its jurisdiction. The small minority of pork lovers among its residents can obtain pork in a nearby village or exercise their right of 'exit' and move to another village where pork lovers are the majority. The same conclusion, maintained the Court, applies to cities that can be divided into discrete homogenous neighbourhoods. For this purpose the city should not be regarded as a unity, but every individual neighbourhood should be looked upon as an independent unit.

Village B is the home of the pork lovers. All but an insignificant minority of the residents are avid pork lovers. Such a village, concluded the Court, would not be allowed to prohibit pork businesses from operating within its jurisdiction. In this case the pig rejecters are the ones who can exercise their right of exit. The Court acknowledged that the mere knowledge on the part of the pig rejecters who live in Village A that in Village B pork can be found in the market might offend them, but 'such an offense', concluded the Court, 'is part and parcel of living in a democratic society and must be tolerated', it is not comparable to the offence caused by pork being displayed and sold in one's immediate environment.[8]

Village C is comprised of both pig rejecters and pork lovers who live together in mixed neighbourhoods. When residents cannot be separated geographically, the

[7] It is possible to conceptualize the harm suffered by the pig rejecters as a harm to autonomy not only as regards feelings as argued by the court. One could argue that from a liberal standpoint the pig rejecters' autonomy—their right to shape their lives as they see fit and to raise their children in a certain environment—is at stake. They cannot lead their lifestyle, which is based on the renunciation of pigs, if pork is being sold across the street. Therefore there are two central liberal values—liberty and autonomy—being weighed against one another.

[8] *Solodkin* v. *City of Beit Shemesh*, para 28.

Court was much more ambivalent and offered but a few abstract guidelines. For example, if a mixed village seeks to prohibit the pork trade, it must guarantee pork lovers access to pork vendors. In some cases the village would be able to rely on the existence of pork sellers in a nearby village; in other cases the village would have to find a place for them within its jurisdiction. The exact result in each case must be based on the size of the territorial unit, its social character, and the degree of tolerance of its residents. The Court emphasized, however, that this third solution would apply only when it is impossible to divide the two groups geographically.

The neo-liberal party Shinui, which was one of the petitioners, hailed the Supreme Court's decision and is now seeking to use its ruling as a guiding principle for every local public decision-making process. They even offer to have a referendum for each proposed public project in local governments in order to determine the will of local residents.[9]

Analysis: The Ideal of Geographic Separatism

What do we think of the Court's decision? In order to answer this question intelligently we first have to consider two vexing issues: (1) what is hidden behind the use of geography as a proxy for affiliation to a community? and (2) what are the social consequences of such a spatial regime?

The Court's decision should be understood as reading into the law an ethics of provincialism; 'a vision of ethnic, cultural and religious pluralism managed by geographic autonomy and isolation'.[10] Rather than attempting to mediate the conflict between deep-rooted and inconsistent social and cultural norms through deliberation and debate, the provincial solution attempts to isolate distinctive cultures from one another, providing each of them with autonomy in a separate jurisdictional sphere.[11] The Court's solution to the normative conflict is strikingly similar to the framework of utopia offered by philosopher Robert Nozick in his *Anarchy, State and Utopia*. Nozick, a devoted libertarian, denies the state any role in promoting a conception of the common good. He bases his ideal social formation on communities of difference rather than a single social structure. 'The first route', Nozick asserts, 'begins with the fact that people are different ... They diverge in the values they have and have different weightings for the values they share'. Therefore, he concludes, 'there is no reason to think that there is one community which will serve as ideal for all people and much reason to think that there is not'.[12] Instead, Nozick offers us 'Utopia'—a social order comprised of a multitude of geographically isolated communities, each attempting to realize its

[9] J. Lis, 'A Jerusalem Neighborhood Demands Referendum: Whether Another Synagogue Is Needed', *Ha'aretz*, 26 July 2004, 6A.

[10] Ford, n.2, above, 1401.

[11] *Ibid.*

[12] R. Nozick, *Anarchy, State and Utopia* (New York, 1974), 309–10.

own vision of the good life, to which people join voluntarily. Nozick's Utopia allows for the maximization of individual choice in the initial selection of a community, but it has no normative vision for and no restrictions on the character of the utopias once formed.[13] Since each community is permitted to place restrictions on individual liberty, which would be condemned if they were enforced by a central state apparatus, Nozick has to make a distinction between a community and the nation. He does so by distinguishing the nation from a face-to-face community:

> In a nation, one knows that there are nonconforming individuals, but one need not be directly confronted by these individuals or by the fact of their nonconformity. Even if one finds it offensive that others do not conform, even if the knowledge that there exist non-conformists rankles and makes one very unhappy, this does not constitute being harmed by the others or having one's rights violated. Whereas in a face-to-face community one cannot avoid being directly confronted with what one finds to be offensive. How one lives in one's immediate environment is affected.[14]

This kind of reasoning is precisely the one employed by the Israeli Supreme Court in order to distinguish between the type of offence to feelings that enables Village A (the home of the pig rejecters) to remove any and all pig businesses from its jurisdiction, but does not allow Village B (the home of the pork lovers) to prohibit pork vendors from operating in its territory, despite the offence caused to Village A residents who know about it.

The provincial political scheme is very tempting in today's society, which is characterized by a diversity of cultures, identities, norms, and practices, and is very suspicious towards any kind of uniformity or attempts to prescribe a common vision of the good. Indeed, why do we need multiple and distinct territorial jurisdictions if not to separate distinctive groups of people with idiosyncratic norms and cultures? But in fact, our experience, as well as that of other nations, teaches us that provincialism does not come cheap. It fosters a society fractured into many discrete and isolated subgroups and reinforces the notion of cultural incompatibility and incommensurability that justified the provincial scheme in the first place. It frustrates any attempt to foster a vision of the common good that inspires citizens and encourages them to participate in public life.

The fallacy of the provincial attitude is twofold: it is based on a mistaken notion of cultural difference and on a romanticized, yet dangerous, notion of community. The rhetoric of cultural difference, which is so prevalent in today's multicultural societies, encourages us to see social conflicts in term of inscrutable social groups. Often, however, 'conflicts filed under the label of "cultural difference" are better understood in term of the type of ideological or normative conflicts that democracies and markets routinely mediate'.[15] I do not intend to belittle actual cultural differences (by which I refer to a variety of practices based on race, ethnicity, and religion)

[13] Ford, n.2, above, 1404. [14] Nozick, n.12, above, 322.

[15] R.T. Ford, 'Cultural Rights and Civic Virtue' (November 2003) (FEEM Working Paper No. 99.2003. http://ssrn.com/abstract=478483), 9.

between nomos communities. These differences are particularly severe in societies characterized by 'thick multiculturalism', in which some communities do not share basic liberal values such as equality, liberty and the autonomy of the individual.[16] My argument is, however, that such cultural differences do not pose, in and of themselves, a threat to democratic dialogue; what poses such a threat is the belief that culture provides an excuse to opt out of political dialogue.

The ideal of community, on which the provincial political scheme is based, is equally wrongheaded. Despite its undeniable power as a critique of liberal individualism which holds on to an image of the individual as separate, self-sufficient, and self-contained, the notion of community should be rejected as an alternative political ideal. The ideal of community expresses a longing for harmony and solidarity among people, for a notion of belonging, consensus and mutual understanding. It 'denies, devalues, or represses the ontological difference of subjects, and seeks to dissolve social inexhaustibility into the comfort of a self-enclosed whole'.[17] Whether expressed as common consciousness or as mutual understanding, the ideal of community is one of transparency of the subjects to one another. In a community people cease to be other, opaque, not understood, and instead become mutually sympathetic; they understand one another as they understand themselves. As Iris Marion Young has argued, this is an understandable dream, but a dream nevertheless, and one with severe political consequences. When translated into a vision of political life, the ideal of community privileges local face-to-face direct democracy as an alternative to the impersonality and alienation that characterizes modern democracies. Such a model is both unrealistic and undesirable. Self-identification as a member of a community occurs as an oppositional differentiation from other groups, who are feared, despised and devalued. Individuals are accustomed to feel a sense of mutual identification only with some people and to fear the difference others confront them with, only because they identify with a different culture, religion, and point of view. This rejection creates, in turn, demands for autonomy from the outside world, and the logical result is the production of social fragmentation and the legitimization of defensive behaviour and exclusionary policies.[18]

The notion of cultural difference and the romanticized ideal of community are socially destructive, especially in the context of a relatively small and fragile democratic institution such as the city. The source of the city's vitality and excitement lies precisely in its multicultural nature. The multiplicity of ways of life, cultures, opinions, and experiences coming together in a fairly small-scale space. The city provides (or should provide) public places accessible to everyone, where anyone can participate in its public life. The fracturing of the city into many units, geographically isolated from one another, each housing a homogenous community,

[16] Y. Tamir, 'Two Concepts of Multiculturalism' (1995) 29 *Journal of Philosophy of Education* 161.
[17] I.M. Young, *Justice and the Politics of Difference* (Princeton, N.J., 1990).
[18] R. Sennett, *The Fall of Public Man* (Harmondsworth, 1978).

is a deathblow to the political ideal of city life; the city as an alternative to both the ideal of the romanticized community and to alienated individualism.

Political Theories: Liberalism, Multiculturalism, and Republicanism

What, then, is a viable alternative to the ethics of provincialism and the geographic separatism it engenders? In order to respond to this question we need to explore (in an admittedly simplistic way) several political theories and examine how they deal with conflict among subgroups with distinctive cultures and value systems.

Liberalism[19]

Liberalism as a structure of ideas 'posits a sharp distinction between the institutions of the state and those of civil society and argues that the state is obliged to remain impartial toward the institutions of civil society, treating each citizen solely as an individual'.[20] Liberal ideology lacks an independent normative conception of social groups as intermediate entities between the individual and the state, reducing all social groups to mere aggregations of individuals. In this account, community is a product of individual acts of voluntary associations; an outcome of individuals who have consented to join in a group. Group autonomy is perceived only as an instrument of individual autonomy. Intermediate entities such as communities get recognition only to the extent that they conform to the individual/state dualism.[21] Therefore, ideally, liberalism does not have to worry about cultural communities with different value systems since such communities do not matter, only the individuals that comprise them do. Each individual, which is seen as an autonomous and self-sufficient unity, has the same rights against the state as well as against his fellow citizens and is allowed to pursue his or her conception of the good without interference from the state, that must stay neutral toward the diverse conceptions of the good of its citizens.

Interestingly, in *On Liberty*, John Stuart Mill discusses the prohibition on pork as an example of an unwarranted transgression of society into the realm of the individual. This example enables us to explore the classical liberal argument in the context of our own discussion. In the fourth chapter of his book, Mill deals with the limits to the authority of society over the individual and puts forward the argument that society has a jurisdiction over an individual's conduct only when the conduct affects prejudicially the interest of others. There is no room for interference

[19] The liberal tradition is very complex with many strands which I will not try to unravel here. I believe, however, that all the arguments made hereinafter fit well within central strands of liberalism.

[20] Ford, n.2, above, 1419.

[21] C. Calhoun, *Critical Social Theory: Culture, History and the Challenge of Difference* (Cambridge, 1995).

by the state when a person's conduct affects no person besides himself.[22] But the question remains: what constitutes a conduct that affects prejudicially the interest of others? There are many, admits Mill, who consider as an injury to themselves any conduct which they have distaste for, and resent it as an outrage to their feelings and therefore attempts to invest their own preferences with the character of moral laws. There is no parity, however, between the feeling of a person for his own opinion, and the feeling of another who is offended at his holding it; no more than between the desire of a thief to take a purse and the desire of the rightful owner to keep it. A person's taste is as much his own peculiar concern as his opinion and his purse.[23] The evil here pointed out, Mill warns, is not one that exists only in theory, and gives the following example:

> Suppose now that in a people, of whom the majority were Mussulmans, that majority should insist upon not permitting pork to be eaten within the limits of the country. This would be nothing new in Mahomedan countries. Would it be a legitimate exercise of the moral authority of public opinion? and if not, why not? The practice is really revolting to such a public. They also sincerely think that it is forbidden and abhorred by the Deity. Neither could the prohibition be censured as religious persecution. It might be religious in its origin, but it would not be persecution for religion, since nobody's religion makes it a duty to eat pork. The only tenable ground of condemnation would be that with the personal tastes and self-regarding concerns of individuals the public has no business to interfere.[24]

Communitarianism and Multiculturalism

Communitarian critics of liberalism reject the image of people as separate and self-contained units and replace it with communities as constitutive of the identity of individuals. The individual is always already operating within the discursive form of a community that engages its members in an integrated view of their place in the world, their history, their culture, and the meaning of personal experiences. According to communitarianism, individuals are defined by communities, their history, traditions, goals, and interests. Therefore, much more emphasis should be put on community and strong group solidarity.[25] According to Michael Sandel, a prominent communitarian scholar, '"community" and "participation" may describe a form of life in which the members find themselves commonly situated "to begin with", their commonality consisting less in the relationship they have entered than in the attachment they have found'.[26] He is also quite explicit about the social transparency as to the meaning and goals of a community to its members.[27]

Communitarianism, however, is often criticized for serving as 'little more than a foil to liberal individualism'. The notion of community is left, for the most

[22] J.S. Mill, *On Liberty* (Oxford, 1946 [1859]), ch. 4. [23] *Ibid*, 75. [24] *Ibid*, 76–7.

[25] J. Handler, *Law and the Search for Community* (Philadelphia, 1994).

[26] M.J. Sandel, *Liberalism and the Limits of Justice* (Cambridge, 1982), 151–2.

[27] *Ibid*, 172–3.

part, undefined. Communitarians provide only a general account of that which constitutes a community. As a result, it runs into trouble whenever the definition of community is itself in dispute.[28] Communitarianism also lacks a meaningful response to the problem of unequal power relationships. It conflates the issues of power and the quality of participation by arguing that, since the self is defined by the social context, the process of dialogue itself is empowering. As a result, communitarianism is often accused of being utopian and unattainable.

Multiculturalism can be seen as an attempt to respond to the shortcomings of liberalism and communitarianism by combining elements of both. It is informed by an image of society divided into distinct ethnic and religious groups, each of which has its own culture that all, or at least most members share. Since the various cultural groups may have incommensurable norms, the state must remain neutral toward all these groups. The groups, however, should be free to act on their particular norms without interference from the outside. This articulation of multiculturalism is liberal in the sense that it requires a value-neutral state, but it is also communitarian, because within the boundaries of the group the multiculturalist asserts strong solidarity and common values that take precedence over individualism.[29] Multiculturalism comes in two versions—weak and strong. The strong version, which is closer to communitarianism, calls for a fundamental shift in the understanding of citizenship. Cultural communities are to be granted strong, formal, legal standing that would permit them to govern their members according to their views and customs. The weak version of multiculturalism, which is an offshoot of liberalism, offers a more complex vision of differentiated citizenship. It argues that the challenge of multiculturalism is to find a balance between the needs and interests of three entities: the group, the state, and the individual. Proponents of weak multiculturalism, such as Will Kymlicka and Charles Taylor, seek to preserve the values and primacy of the individual while also recognizing the legitimacy of a group-based demand for accommodation.[30]

Civic Republicanism

Unlike liberals, who consider the democratic process to be a strictly procedural mechanism, republicans adopt a conception of democracy as a political dialogue, whose goal is to promote a common vision of the public good to which all citizens would have to conform. Each citizen should be active in promoting the public good, knowing that by so doing she advances her own good as well as the good of others. The republican political scheme is an offspring of Rousseau's 'Social Contract'. ' "The problem", Rousseau argues, "is to find a form of association which will defend and protect with the whole common force the person and goods of

[28] Ford, n.2, above, 1421. [29] *Ibid*, 1423.

[30] For a more in depth analysis of the two versions of multiculturalism see A. Shachar, 'The Puzzle of Interlocking Power Hierarchies: Sharing the Pieces of Jurisdictional Authority', (2000) 35 *Harvard Civil Rights—Civil Liberties Law Review* 385.

each associate, and in which each, while uniting himself with all, may still obey himself alone, and remain as free as before." This is the fundamental problem to which the Social Contract provides the solution.'[31] And the solution offered by Rousseau is based on the notion of the general will: 'Each of us puts his person and all his power in common under the supreme direction of the general will, and, in our corporate capacity, we receive each member as an indivisible part of the whole'.[32] Civic republicanism rejects liberal individualism since it endangers the realization of the general will. Each individual, admits Rousseau, may have particular will that is different from, or even contrary to, the general will, which he has as a citizen. His own particular interest may suggest other things to him than the common interest does. His separate, naturally independent existence may make him imagine that what he owes to the common cause is an incidental contribution—a contribution which will cost him more to give than their failure to receive it would harm the others. This unjust attitude could cause the ruin of the body politic if it became widespread enough. So that the social pact not become meaningless words, it tacitly includes this commitment which alone gives power to the others: whoever refuses to obey the general will shall be forced to obey it by the whole body politic, which means nothing else but that he will be forced to be free.[33]

For similar reasons civic republicanism rejects group-based political processes that fragments the body politic. Lack of understanding and divergence in conceptions of the good erode public trust and encourage citizens to abandon public virtue in favour of maximizing the short-term advantages of the individual, the family, or the ethnic, religious, or cultural subgroup.

An Alternative Vision: Neo-Republicanism and Civic Pluralism

None of the discussed political theories, standing alone, can help us replace the ethics of provincialism and the geographic separatism that comes with it. Liberalism, with its insistence on the primacy of the individual, is blinded to the centrality of group affiliation and politics in modern representative democracies. The 'common good' under a liberal conception is nothing but a mere aggregation of many individual preferences which can be drawn from the marketplace. Multiculturalism is based, as we have seen, on a mistaken notion of cultural difference and on a romanticized and misguided notion of community. In fact, liberal individualism and multiculturalism share a basic common logic. Each entails a denial of difference and a desire to bring multiplicity and heterogeneity into unity, though in different ways. Liberalism denies difference by positing the self as a separate and self-contained unit bringing all such separate individuals under a common measure of right. Multiculturalism, on the other hand, denies difference by positing fusion

[31] J.J. Rousseau, *The Social Contract* (New York, 1968 [1762]), ch. 6. [32] *Ibid.*
[33] *Ibid*, ch. 7.

rather than separation as a social ideal.[34] Multiculturalism, just like liberalism, demands a value-neutral state, but whenever the liberal speaks of individual autonomy, the multiculturalist substitutes 'individual' with 'community'. Without some common vision of the public good, which is shared universally, the public sphere is threatened and is replaced by many disjointed and segregated communities of difference. Yet, the public vision fostered by civic republicanism can also be quite destructive. It ignores subgroup diversity, imposing instead a uniform vision of the good that suppresses anything that cannot be assimilated.

What is needed is an alternative political vision; one that does not ignore the salience of group affiliation to the political process and repudiates an imperialistic assimilation of all subgroups in the name of the common good, but does justify the imposition of a thin public culture of tolerance, pluralism and civic virtue. Such a vision, which combines elements from both the liberal and the republican traditions, can be found in Cass Sunstein's neo-republicanism and Richard Ford's civic pluralism. Neo-republicanism challenges conventional legal and economic analyses, arguing that modern regulatory states are often ineffective and that they are hardly models of democratic self-governance. Most regulatory efforts of the late twentieth century are driven by efficiency and efficacy alone, while democratic deliberation on central issues is discouragingly rare. Powerful interest groups exert excessive influence over regulatory policy and real participation in the public sphere is at best episodic. Political institutions, unlike markets, should function as forums for deliberation about collective values and decentralization is an indispensable part of any strategy for general democratization since the central government is simply too remote for general citizen control.[35] Similarly, civic pluralism combines the traditions of civic republicanism and liberal pluralism with the civil rights traditions of strategic integration and strategic nationalism. It is liberal in the sense that it rejects the emphasis on 'cultural difference' and assumes that difference based on culture is exaggerated in terms of both its breadth and depth. Yet civic republicanism is not 'universalist' because it does insist on the recognition of another type of difference—one based on power and subordination, maintaining that social conflict does not generally play out in the realm of culture but instead in the realm of social hierarchy and that such differences must be acknowledged before they can be eliminated.[36] Civic pluralism is republican because it adopts the republican conception of the democratic process as dialogic rather then as strictly procedural and advances substantive conceptions of the common good and the good society, although in a pluralist manner. The common good should not be imposed from above, but rather assembled from the fragments of the collective goals and aspiration of the citizenry.[37] In a like manner, the good society 'is

[34] I.M. Young, 'City Life and Difference', in P. Kasinitz (ed.), *Metropolis: Center and Symbol of Our Time* (New York, 1995), 253.

[35] C. Sunstein, *Free Markets and Social Justice* (Oxford, 1997), ch. 13.

[36] Ford, n.2, above, 1439–44.

[37] Ford, n.15, above, 5.

one governed by a citizenry under conditions of "undominated dialogue" between a variety of social, ideological, and cultural groups'.[38]

Applying these visions to local democratic entities such as the city entails that they require a belief in the common good in order to be effective. 'Cities need common enterprises and civic vision in order to be livable cities'.[39] Divergence of opinions and views of the good life among city residents is unavoidable and even welcomed, but at the same time there must be some conception, even if very thin, of the common good that is widely shared and, if necessary, imposed. Civic pluralism does not insist on any specific vision of the common good except for the narrow notion of the public good as an undominated political dialogue between the various social groups that make up the city. A pluralist civic virtue consists of willingness to engage fellow citizens in dialogue rather than an attempt to defeat them in a legal or political battle. This vision is not naïve. It does not assume that citizens will always reach consensus, but more modestly that they will agree to discuss and attempt to persuade each other rather than always fight to win.

The politics of difference that currently controls the public sphere and is the engine behind the ethics of provincialism, should be replaced by political dialogue, negotiation and compromise on a local level. Instead of a clash of incommensurable values, we should conceptualize any disagreement as a political dispute susceptible to resolution through the normal institutions of liberal societies: political dialogue, negotiation, and persuasion. Political dialogue can be an opportunity for ethnic and religious groups that make up the city to come to understand each other and foster mutual trust between them. There is always more to human beings than just 'pork lovers' and 'pig rejecters' or any other such dichotomy. People can connect to one another on countless different levels. In large cities, alliances between Muslim-Arabs and Jewish Orthodox groups, both of which are pig rejecters, can create the sought-after coalition across boundaries. It may also help the group that loses a political conflict better accept the outcome. In some cases a group that fails to convince its fellow citizens of the merits of a cultural practice may come away more receptive to a generally applicable prohibition if their members were involved in a dialogue about the prohibition.[40]

Our analysis leads to the conclusion that the Court's ruling in *Solodkin* v. *City of Beit Shemesh* is misguided on two different levels. By mandating a specific solution (any specific solution) the Court usurped the power of local decision makers to reach a compromise using their own political mechanisms. It is possible that local communities would have reached the same compromise, but in such a case it is likely that they would have experienced it as voluntarily chosen. In contrast, when the solution is mandated by the Court they feel betrayed and coerced. It is also possible, of course, that a different compromise would have been reached, one that did not involve segregation among the various communities.

[38] Ford, n.2, above, 1440.
[39] Ford, n.15, above, 5.
[40] *Cf.* Ford, n.15, above.

The specific arrangement dictated by the Court, one that is based on segregation and geographic separatism, is particularly harmful. The map of Israel is already a mosaic of segregated settlements and neighbourhoods, each having a distinct ethnic, religious, or cultural identity.[41] The Court's ruling will aggravate the situation and deepen the reality of segregation. It encourages cultural and religious groups to self-segregate themselves in ghettos in order to obtain the autonomy and other benefits conferred by the Court on geographically isolated communities. As a result, instead of having a vibrant city life based on social differentiation without exclusion, we are bound to have a society fragmented into a multitude of communities of difference living in segregated political subdivisions.

Process Failure and Free Will: Two Objections

Two objections are commonly raised to my conclusion. One is directed at the precariousness of the political process and the inability to guarantee political power to cultural minorities, and the other involves the voluntary nature of contemporary segregationist endeavours.

Failure of the Political Process

That is all well and good, argue the critics, in an ideal world where the political process works perfectly and the various cultural groups that comprise the polity engage in an undominated political dialogue about common values and come out of the dialogue sometimes as winners and other times as losers. In such a system, conflicts over values can be mediated through the political mechanisms of dialogue, negotiation and compromise. We, however, do not live in such a world. In the real world minority groups are subject to illegitimate bias and prejudice, and their values are devalued by a majority of the citizens. Indeed, jurisdictional autonomy is predicated precisely on the political powerlessness of minority groups and their chronic inability to influence the outcome of the political process on a national level. Geographic separatism is, in fact, a solution for the failure of politics. Preventing such groups from obtaining jurisdictional autonomy, argue the critics, is tantamount to their annihilation as distinct cultures. Only by providing them with separate and autonomous geographic subdivisions in which to practise their culture and live according to their conception of the good, they stand a chance of not being crushed by the majority.

Suspending for the moment my objection to the idea that cultures are opaque and cultural values are incommensurable, inherent in such an argument, I still believe that a solution to the failure of politics which is based on segregation and geographic isolation of minority groups is a bane rather than a boon for such

[41] I. Rosen-Zvi, *Taking Space Seriously* (Aldershot, 2004).

groups. The use of geographic separatism as a vehicle for the protection of minority groups with differing cultural norms and conceptions of the good is not new and has been tried many times before. In many cases, minority groups fought to establish minority enclaves in the hope of creating a safe space in which the minority group could thrive and enjoy autonomy. But 'local autonomy' has not served historically subordinated groups well.[42] Try as they might, these groups cannot control their own destiny simply by gaining political control of a locality. Since legal protection of local government autonomy is shaky at best, these political subdivisions do not provide true autonomy.[43] Minority jurisdictions bear the responsibility of autonomy but are denied the power that should come with it. As a result, jurisdictional autonomy is, in fact, no more than a euphemism for old and notorious segregation and plays the same role segregation has always played—to isolate, to impoverish, and to disempower.

Therefore, there seems to be no escape from making hard choices about when to sacrifice 'cultural' values for other pressing concerns—the prevention of political oppression and economic subordination. It is true that minority groups may have to pay a political price for an integrated polity. They may have to fight very hard and get very few results, if any, and many of their political campaigns are doomed to failure. To come back to our example—the Court's decision in *Solodkin* v. *City of Beit Shemesh*—in the case of an integrated and heterogeneous city, pork may not be as readily available as it would have been in a homogenous Russian-Jewish or Christian-Arab locality. This is indeed very frustrating. But the price they, and the collective as a whole, pay for segregation is much higher.

Self-Segregation and the Issue of Free Choice

The second objection involves the voluntary nature of contemporary geographic separatism. It is important to distinguish, the critics argue, between two types of jurisdictional separatism: one is predicated on unlawful discrimination and should be eliminated, and the other is freely chosen and should be respected. Discrimination in the allocation of state land is forbidden by law and the Court guarantees the law's implementation.[44] Any other manifestations of geographic separatism are not imposed on cultural groups by the state, but can be freely chosen by such groups. It is a natural expression of ethnic, national, or religious solidarity, for which the government is not responsible but that it has a duty to recognize and respect. According to this account, we should differentiate active imposition from

[42] R.T. Ford, 'Law's Territory (A History of Jurisdiction)' (1999) 97 *Michigan Law Review* 843, 916.

[43] S.D. Cashin, 'Middle-Class Black Suburbs and the State of Integration: A Post-Integrationist Vision for Metropolitan America' (2001) 86 *Cornell Law Review* 729.

[44] In 2001 the Israeli Supreme Court affirmed that both direct and indirect discrimination in the allocation of state land based on ethnic or national origins is forbidden. While the Court underscored both the binding character of equality and the prohibition on discrimination, the ruling nevertheless provided some leeway for state land to be allocated for settlements designated for defined communities. See H.C. 6698/95 *Qua'adan* v. *Israel Land Administration*, P.D. 54(1) 258.

passive recognition. The conceptual split between imposition (or creation) and recognition 'is a subset of a familiar split between subjectivity and objectivity in decision-making. According to this conception, creation is a subjective decision to bring into existence that which was previously not there, whereas recognition is an unavoidable decision to recognize an objective fact that would exist regardless of state action'.[45] Hence, in the case of *Solodkin* v. *City of Beit Shemesh* the Court did not force segregation on reluctant minority groups, but only recognized jurisdictional provincialism that had existed prior to any Court intervention. This is very different from cases of forced segregation such as the one imposed on blacks in the United States during the Jim Crow era. Rather than attempt to mandate or facilitate integration nobody wants, the critique concludes, the state should recognize the will of its citizens to live in ethnically, religiously and culturally homogeneous spheres.

This critique ignores, however, the responsibility of the state for the creation of the initial conditions for segregation, the important role played by political space in the reproduction of segregation and the law's influence on people's identity.

The map of Israel is a mosaic of different settlements, each having a distinct ethnic, national or religious identity. Even in the larger cities, the different neighbourhoods consist of homogeneous groups of residents.[46] This entrenched segregation was not created naturally as a result of many private choices that the state had to respect. It is, in fact, a result of deliberate historical governmental planning schemes and practices designed to separate geographically the population based on ethnic, national, and religious affiliation. Many governmental agencies that administer public housing and supervise the allocation of state land (which amounts to 93 per cent of all land in Israel) have been participating in these segregationist efforts,[47] which were justified, by and large, by the need to respect cultural difference.[48] Moreover, not only did the state create and still creates the initial conditions for segregation through its policies, it also actively facilitates segregation through a local government structure that undermines integration.[49]

Moreover, the legal system never simply recognizes or respects pre-existing preferences, but always takes an active part in constituting and shaping them. If the law encourages geographic provincialism, separatist subdivisions will emerge and identities will begin to solidify around them. On the other hand, if the legal system discourages or prohibits segregation, people will find other ways to express

[45] Ford, n.2, above, 1368.

[46] E. Benvenisti, '"Separate but Equal" in the Allocation of State Land for Housing' (1998) 21 *Tel-Aviv University Law Review* 769.

[47] *Ibid*, 770–1.

[48] A notorious example of such an oppressive production of difference disguised as respect for cultural difference can be found in a Supreme Court decision prohibiting a Jew from purchasing a house and moving to a Bedouin settlement. The Court justified the segregation of the Bedouins by appealing to their unique nomadic culture and way of life and the threat to such culture if non-Bedouin would be allowed to live among them. H.C. 528/88, *Avitan* v. *Israel Land Administration*, 43(4) P.D. 297.

[49] For a comprehensive in-depth analysis of Israel's segragationist reality and the ideological apparatus that produced and still reproduces it see Rosen-Zvi, n.41, above.

their differences, such as through political institutions or social movements. Preferences and beliefs are constructed, rather than elicited, by social practices and institutions, and these preferences have conspicuously grown up around and adapted to the segregative status quo.[50] If the legal regime restricts the expression of difference to ethnically, religiously or culturally homogenous jurisdictions, social groups will define themselves in terms of jurisdictional autonomy. If, however, the legal system encourages public articulation of differences in institutions of broader inclusiveness, social groups will define themselves as participants in an inclusive political dialogue and as members of a pluralist polity.[51]

Under such circumstances, the freely-chosen segregation critique is hard to sustain. The dichotomy between imposition and recognition cannot be taken at face value. The state, as we have shown, created the initial conditions for segregation, and it continues actively to facilitate and support segregation through policies and rulings that benefit parochialism and sanction integration. Therefore, what seems, at first glance, to be recognition of a pre-existing reality that would exist regardless of state action is, in fact, a product of past and present policies expressed in legislation and court rulings, of which the Court's decision in *Solodkin* v. *City of Beit Shemesh* is an example. The government should not respect segregation as an expression of people's choices and preferences, but attempt to alter such flawed norms as being an obstacle to human autonomy and well-being.

Conclusion

Liberal democracies constantly negotiate a contradiction between two important needs: the need for solidarity among members of the various groups that comprise the polity expressed as a demand for cultural rights and jurisdictional autonomy, and the need to avoid social fragmentation and inter-group antagonism expressed as a national unity and a demand for the common good. This negotiation is oftentimes hard and frustrating. It is all too easy to resolve this contradiction in favour of geographic separatism granting each cultural group a jurisdictional autonomy. This short chapter is an attempt to demonstrate the fallacies of the jurisdictional provincialism paradigm and to point to the urgent need to keep searching for a viable alternative—one that promotes civic virtue and political dialogue—even if sometimes this search feels like a Sisyphean task.

[50] Sunstein, n.35, above, 27.

[51] Ford, n.2, above, 1417–18.

14

Freedom and Subjectivity in Modern Society: Re-reading Hegel's *Philosophy of Right*

Robert Fine and Rolando Vázquez

Introduction

This chapter is an engagement with Hegel's *Philosophy of Right*, a founding text for the social theory of law. We shall extract and explore the contrast between Hegel's recognition of subjective freedom as the great accomplishment of modern society and his critique of subjectivism as its foremost pathology. We suggest that the historical opposition between subjective freedom and subjectivism lies at the heart of Hegel's analysis of modern forms of 'right'. Subjective freedom is the freedom of a social and historical subject, whether the subject is an individual, a group, or the state. Subjectivism is the construction of the subject into an 'ism'—that is, into a power that refuses all resistance, denies all externality and stands above all critical understanding. It is precisely the failure to observe the difference between subjective freedom and subjectivism that causes so much confusion in the appropriation of this text.[1]

If Hegel's *Philosophy of Right* were a philosophy of the state, as many of its critics have taken it to be, then there would be little point in recovering his theory of law today. It is true that some passages appear to confirm the orthodox reading that identifies the self-realization of the individual with subjection to the state. The most notorious occur at the beginning of his section on the state. It is here that Hegel characterizes the modern state as the 'march of god in the world'. He describes the state as an absolute and unmoved end 'where freedom enters into its highest right' (PR ¶ 257 and 258). By contrast, he describes individuals as mere 'moments' in relation to the power of the state, says that our existence is a matter of indifference compared with that of the state (PR ¶ 154A) and appears to conclude that we should 'venerate the state as an earthly divinity' (PR ¶ 272A). Indeed it seems that Hegel places the state far above the individual in his hierarchy of values, but this appearance is misleading.

[1] Our argument is provoked by thoughts arising out of G. Rose, *Hegel Contra Sociology* (London, 1981) as well as R. Fine, *Political Investigations: Hegel, Marx, Arendt* (London, 2001).

While this kind of quotation underpins the most common appropriation of *The Philosophy of Right*, we need to place this apparent veneration of the state alongside what Hegel took to be the crucial achievement of the modern age: the 'right of subjective freedom'. He argues that the attainment of subjective freedom marks the difference between the ancient and modern world and that its ripples spread into every sphere of social life.

> This right, in its infinity, is expressed in Christianity, and it has become the universal and actual principle of a new form of the world. Its more specific shapes include love, the romantic, the eternal salvation of the individual as an end, etc; then there are morality and conscience, followed by the other forms, some of which will come into prominence... as the principle of civil society and as moments of the political constitution, while others appear within history at large, particularly in the history of art, the sciences and philosophy. (PR ¶ 124R)

Hegel's argument is that the right of subjective freedom is not only expressed in the emotional life of individuals (as love, guilt, salvation, etc) but that it is also institutionalized in various tangible social and legal forms (as a charter of rights, trial by jury, written constitution, separation of church and state, and so forth). For him subjective freedom is not merely a concept, but provides the solid ground on which both personal identities and legal institutions are based.

The Modern Subject

Hegel sees personality as the determinate social form of the individual in modern capitalist society. Historically, the notion of a 'person' was first developed in Ancient Rome when personality was contrasted with slavery. Persons comprised the particular class of individuals who possessed subjective freedom; they were free rather than slaves. The mark of their freedom was their right to own private property and in this sense property rights became the first embodiment of freedom (PR ¶ 40). By contrast, in the modern age the right to subjective freedom belongs to all of us. We are all in principle endowed with rights of property and obliged to relate to others as persons. Hegel brings this modern form of the subject into close and critical scrutiny.

It is often argued that the ethical significance of private property for Hegel lay in its essential relation to subjective freedom. If what makes us free is our not being restricted to our natural instincts or to fixed ways of satisfying them, then private property may appear as the mark of liberation from these constraints.[2] This appearance, however, is deceptive.

Hegel argues that modern subjectivity is premised on a radical distinction between 'persons' and 'things'. The subject is conceived as a free spirit with rights over things and obligations to respect others as persons. This subjective freedom is dependent on the self-division of the subject: I both know myself to be free and I have knowledge of myself as an object. I am an 'I' who is wholly indeterminate,

[2] J. Waldron, *The Right To Private Property* (Oxford, 1990), 343–89.

and I am someone of a particular age, religion and class, located in a particular place, endowed with particular desires. Personality is at once 'sublime and ordinary'. The person has a double existence and it is the achievement of the modern subject to support this contradiction.

As a person, I stand in opposition to the world of things—an opposition expressed in Roman law in terms of that between *persona* and *res*. A thing is anything external to my freedom into which I can place my will. This includes things in the tangible sense of the term as well as intellectual accomplishments, sciences, arts, religious observances, and inventions. To the extent that I am an object of the senses and have a natural existence, I am myself a thing as well as a person. As a person, I possess my life and body like other things. In the modern world we are all persons. If nothing else, we are at least owners of our own bodies and labour power.

> The human being, in his immediate existence in himself, is a natural entity... it is only through the development of his own body and spirit... that he takes possession of himself and becomes his own property as distinct from that of others... (PR ¶ 57)

By affirming this source of subjective freedom, the modern age refutes the basis of all historical justifications of slavery. This is familiar ground, but Hegel adds that this viewpoint is one-sided inasmuch as it regards human beings as by nature free and 'takes the concept as such in its immediacy... as the truth'. It dissolves, in other words, the relation between personality and social being.

Hegel sees personality as the starting point for the long and arduous process of education (*Bildung*) required for subjective freedom to be realized. If individuality were fixated at a stage of life in which the affirmation of rights is everything, it would in Hegel's words be 'trivial' (PR ¶ 35A), 'false' (PR ¶ 41A and 57R), 'merely formal' (PR ¶ 30R), even 'contemptible' (PR ¶ 35A). The determination of right does not have to be the exclusive aspect of social relations. Indeed, if someone were interested only in his or her rights, this would be a sign of 'pure stubbornness' (PR ¶ 37A). The determination of right is one aspect of a social relationship, a crucial aspect, but it is formal compared with the relationship as a whole. If I relate to others exclusively in terms of right, then everything that depends on particularity would become a matter of indifference. Thus, in situations where property rights come into collision with personal survival, Hegel argues the 'right of necessity' must prevail (PR ¶ 127A). Hegel insists that there is nothing absolute about rights of property and it would be the mark of an 'uncultured mind' to think there were.

Hegel does not negate the modern idea of the subject. To borrow a phrase from Hannah Arendt, he defends the 'right to have rights' as the mark of subjective freedom and he describes the 'hatred of right' expressed by both ultra-conservative and radical nationalist currents as 'the chief shibboleth whereby these false friends of "the people" give themselves away' (PR ¶ 17). However, his critique of the social forms of modern subjectivity points to the ongoing conflict between the abstract 'I' and the real possibilities of exercising subjective freedom. *The Philosophy of Right* does not impose a solution. Rather, it traces in a phenomenological mode the ways in which the modern subject lives with this contradiction. Hegel's analysis of subjective freedom moves from a philosophical concept of the isolated subject to its social and historical forms of self-realization amongst others. In his terms, subjective freedom can only be understood and realized in relation to the institutions of ethical life.

Morality and Ethical Life

We find in Hegel's *Philosophy of Right* an understanding of subjective freedom that goes beyond the isolated individual in order to look more closely at the existing social and political reality. His concern was with the subject as a social being and this drew him to the relation of subjective freedom to ethical life.

Subjective freedom is exercised and realized within and in relation to social institutions. The institutions which are central to *The Philosophy of Right* are those of family (not discussed here), civil society and the state. In the concluding section of the book Hegel also addresses international society (also not discussed here). They comprise the framework of modern ethical life (*Sittlichkeit*), which Hegel depicts in contrast with that of antiquity. In Ancient Greece the relation of the individual to the *polis* was more like one of identity than even faith or trust. Modern ethical life is *modern* because it grants 'the right of individuals to their subjective determination to freedom' (PR ¶ 153). Modern ethical life is *ethical* because it has an 'objective existence' within which subjective freedom is but a 'moment'. Ethical life, as Hegel understands it, is a system of determinations which *govern* the individual. That it imposes *binding duties* on subjects remains true in modern ethical life as it was in antiquity.

Hegel writes that the difficulty of understanding ethical life is compounded by its confusion with 'morality'. Hegel's argument is that the absence of distinction between 'morality' and 'ethical life'—an absence he found in Kant's political philosophy—is a problem in terms of understanding the modern age. If we view the institutions of ethical life from the perspective of morality, they appear as if they were the self-determination of the will. Kant's mistake, as Hegel saw it, was to think of the modern constitutional and representative republic as if it was the realization of subjective freedom. Subjective freedom is a 'moment' within modern ethical life, not its principle. The more radical but also more destructive version of this standpoint is to declare all the institutions of ethical life null and void because they have an independent existence apart from our will. Both these moral perspectives neglect the 'objective existence' of ethical powers. Both enclose *Sittlichkeit* within the lens of morality.[3]

[3] Hegel comments that there are two possible viewpoints on ethical life: 'one proceeds atomistically and moves upward from the basis of individuality' (which he calls the viewpoint of *Moralität*); the other starts from 'substantiality... the unity of the individual and the universal'. This for Hegel is the perspective of *Sittlichkeit* and the 'road of science'. (PR ¶ 156A)

The making of moral judgments is one of the activities through which subjective freedom is realized. It presupposes the right of subjective freedom and expresses a consciousness on the part of subjects that their judgements depend not on any outside power but only on themselves—according to their own reasoning or conscience. It is not yet attached to the institutions and authority of the family, civil society and state. This is why in his *Philosophy of Right* Hegel places the section on 'Morality' before 'Ethical Life' and after 'Abstract Right'. Hegel argues that morality in this subjective sense only came into being with Christianity and was only fully developed in modern times. Although Hegel's analysis of morality has been widely analysed in philosophy as an *a priori* argument concerning moral imperatives, we should understand it as a determinate social form.

Hegel saw it as Kant's great achievement to articulate the moral viewpoint and to show that the determinations of the will are a matter for itself alone and not for any external power. He fully agreed that we must look inwards to determine what is right and commented that such self-determination is an expression of subjective freedom which first arises and then recurs in those periods in which existing standards of right and good are 'unable to satisfy the better will'. Socrates provides for Hegel an early example of this moral point of view. At a time when ancient democracy was falling into ruins and appearing increasingly 'hollow, spiritless and unsettled', Socrates 'evaporated' all existing rights and duties and retreated from the institutional order to search for the right and the good. A great strength of our own times, for Hegel, is that 'reverence for the existing order is in varying degrees absent' and that people seek to 'equate accepted values with their own will' (PR ¶ 138R and ¶ 138A). This spirit of critique shows that subjective freedom is able to stand against the objectivity of institutions. It contains within itself 'an essential determination and should therefore not be dismissed' (PR ¶ 5A).[4]

However, Hegel warned against the destructive consequences of elevating the moral point of view to 'supreme status' (PR ¶ 5). He argues that once subjectivity becomes the *exclusive* principle of self-determination, it may relate to all existing forms of ethical life as if they were 'null and void'. As soon as one proceeds to act on the basis of determinations deduced purely from the concept of free will itself, everything else is 'vaporised'. The belief that all determination is a limitation on my freedom gives rise to the demand that all forms of ethical life be abolished. Subjective freedom is converted into the 'freedom of the void' and in the realm of politics and religion it becomes a kind of fanaticism. It is in destroying something that the 'negative will' has a feeling of its own existence. The subject in this case may will some positive condition, such as a new world or religious order, but cannot realize it because the negative will implies the annihilation of every objective determination. If every

[4] This contrasts with Habermas's unjustified claim, in our view, that in *Philosophy of Right* 'the individual will . . . is totally bound to the institutional order and only justified at all to the extent that the institutions are one with it'. Habermas employed the concept of 'emphatic institutionalism' to support this argument (J. Habermas, *Between Facts and Norms* (Cambridge, 1996)).

positive determination of freedom appears as an alien form of representation, the actualization of freedom can only signify destruction without end.

Let us be clear. Hegel is not saying that the political project of constructing a new world order necessarily leads to destruction; he does not express a nihilistic scepticism toward all social reformation. Rather, he explores the destructive aspect of modern subjectivity when the will to a new order becomes merely a pretext for the annihilation of the old. While it is undoubtedly true that you have to break eggs to make an omelette, the making of the omelette can be no more than the excuse for breaking eggs. The less culinary example Hegel gives is that of the Terror that followed the French Revolution:

> This was a time of trembling and quaking and of intolerance towards everything particular. For fanaticism wills only what is abstract, not what is articulated, so that whenever differences emerge, it finds them incompatible with its own indeterminacy and cancels them. This is why the people, during the French revolution, destroyed once more the institutions they had themselves created, because all institutions are incompatible with the abstract self-consciousness of equality. (PR ¶ 5R and A)

The danger arises when self-determination becomes 'sheer restless activity which cannot yet arrive at something that is' (PR ¶ 108A). Hegel's critique of subjectivism is a diagnosis of the dynamics of destruction.

Civil Society

In his observations on the relation between subjective freedom and ethical life, Hegel reveals the importance of civil society. This aspect of his work is now much praised by contemporary commentators.[5] As Manfred Riedel has ably shown, Hegel was the first political theorist to employ systematically the distinction between civil society and the state.[6] Kant, by contrast, seemed to write almost interchangeably of civil society (*status civilis*) and the state (*civitas*). Hegel saw the development of civil society and its separation from the state as a specific achievement of the modern age, and he conceptualized civil society in its modern sense as a system of interdependence among otherwise isolated, self-interested, and private individuals. The rise of civil society as 'the stage of difference which intervenes between the family and the state' (PR ¶ 182A) provides the crucial social support for subjective freedom.

Civil society, as Hegel puts it, 'for the first time allows all determinations of the "Idea" to attain their rights' (PR ¶ 182A). He is referring to the feeling of independence and self-respect among individuals, to equality before the law and

5 See A. Arato, 'A Reconstruction of Hegel's Theory of Civil Society' in D. Cornell, M. Rosenfeld and D. Carlson (eds), *Hegel and Legal Theory* (London, 1991), 301–20.

6 See M. Riedel, *Between Tradition and Revolution: the Hegelian Transformation of Political Philosophy* (Cambridge, 1984).

social solidarity. He emphasizes the complexity of civil society as a system of needs, a system of rights and a field of associational life. In practice, however, Hegel sees the relation between subjective freedom and civil society as contradictory. On the one hand, members of civil society are private persons who by having their own self-interests as their end, regard the universal 'as a hostile element'. They 'keep it at a distance' and imagine that they can 'do without it' (PR ¶ 184A). On the other hand, civil society is a 'system of all-round interdependence' in which the needs of individuals are shaped in relation to and interwoven with the needs of everyone else. Civil society is a system of ethical life '*lost in extremes*'. It consists in the multiplication of needs and the means of their satisfaction, but also in an 'equally infinite increase in dependence and want' (PR ¶ 195).

As a system of needs civil society invalidates all forms of unfree labour as inimical to its principle; it contains within itself this 'aspect of liberation'. In its multiplication and differentiation of needs Hegel sees human beings as able to transcend the constraints of natural necessity:

> the strict natural necessity of need is concealed and man's relation is to his own opinion, which is universal, and to a necessity imposed by himself alone, instead of simply to an external necessity . . . (PR ¶ 194)

This is the dimension in which the right of subjective freedom becomes more than a formality. It is tied to the growth and education of the individual in relation to others. However, the system of needs is burdened with contradictions. The wealth of civil society cannot prevent an excess of poverty, while the prevailing method the system of needs has of dealing with poverty is to 'leave the poor to their fate and direct them to beg from the public' (PR ¶ 245). Hegel's critique draws on well-established themes in classical political economy: the spread of egoism; the loss of a universal moment; the spectacle of misery and social corruption; indignation and hatred in the hearts of the poor; indifference and exploitation on the part of the rich; recurring crises when whole branches of industry suddenly collapse because of a change of fashion or a new invention. It is in this context among others that Hegel, in the tradition of classical political economy, perceives the necessity of the state: 'The boundlessness of deprivation and want can only be restored to harmony through the forcible intervention of the state' (PR ¶ 185A). State intervention is required but in turn increases the risk of administrative authoritarianism within and militarism without. The state offers no final resolution—no end to history.

Alongside the system of needs, subjective freedom in civil society implies a system of rights in which the question of freedom becomes that of freedom under the law. Classical political philosophy tends to see in the rule of law an unqualified human good—an ideal antidote to the antagonisms present within civil society rather than as a social sphere within civil society. Rousseau expressed this classical view with customary eloquence. How can it be, he asked, that all should obey, yet nobody take upon him to command, and that all should serve and yet have no masters? . . . These wonders are the work of law. It is to law alone that men owe justice and liberty . . . The first of all laws is to respect the law.[7]

From this perspective, that of social contract theory, the formation of objective law appears as a product of the rational will. For Hegel, by contrast, the transformation of subjective right into objective law is a *social process*. His argument is for a *social theory of law*—one that can explain how objective law is generated out of the generalization of the social form of right, that is, out of a society in which every individual appears as a possessor of rights. In its elementary form the idea of right confers on individuals their immediate human quality as 'persons' regardless of their particular social location. The individual is split between his concrete social being and his existence as an 'I' who is wholly indeterminate. However, rights still appear as the individual's immediate quality. This self-consciousness, that I am a bearer of rights by virtue of my humanity, is expressed very well in Kant's metaphysics.

According to Hegel, however, the first social manifestation of law occurs when the unity of the subject is split between the mass of 'ordinary' legal individuals and specific individuals or groups empowered to define, adjudicate, and enforce the rights of everyone:

When what is right *in itself is posited* in its objective existence . . . it becomes law and through this determination, right becomes positive right in general . . . Only when it becomes law does what is right take on both the form of its universality and its true determinacy. (PR ¶ 211 and 211R)

This legal function may be conceived in terms of individuals whose 'word is law' or it may assume the more complex shape of a system of norms to which even those empowered to exercise the law are subjected. In any event, Hegel sees in this separation between the legal subject and the law an essential moment in the development of subjective freedom, but also the rise of a new form of domination. Law becomes a power that purports to determine what is right and relates only to abstract persons, so that the social dependence of one individual upon another remains outside its sphere: 'what and how much a person owns is a matter of indifference as far as rights are concerned'.

The system of needs and the system of rights are both elements in the composition of civil society. They are both vehicles through which the development of subjective freedom is made possible and they share in the contradictions of civil society. One is not the ideal curative for the ills of the other. The third element in Hegel's analysis of civil society is the growth of associations in which individuals participate by virtue of some common interest or common cause. This development is taken by contemporary civil society theory to be the essence of civil society

[7] See J.-J. Rousseau, *The Social Contract and other Discourses* (London, 1973), 124 and R. Fine, *Deomcracy and the Rule of Law* (Caldwell, New Jersey, 2002), 32.

and is dissociated from the other elements of civil society as the true expression of intersubjective freedom. For Hegel, it certainly marks a further opportunity for the freedom of the individual to develop intersubjectively without the mediation of either money or law. It expands the negative liberties of civil society into positive rights of participation in its mediating institutions. Indeed, Hegel may be read as inheriting the classical, republican notion of the public sphere, extending it pluralistically from a single social level, that of political society, to civil society.

However, Hegel argues that the associations of civil society should be understood as part of the whole, not in isolation. They are not only tied to the other spheres of civil society, the system of needs and rights, but also play a mediating role between civil society and the state. Hegel makes the point that the organization of social and political interests in civil society is generally arranged in such a way as to 'prevent individuals from crystallising into a powerful bloc in opposition to the organised state' (PR ¶ 302) and to keep them under the 'higher supervision of the state' (PR ¶ 255A). Indeed, the key to modern government, according to Hegel, is that everything is done to ensure that the people at no point become a 'formless mass' uncontrolled by the state. The function of association in civil society, as Hegel sees it, is to *organize* the interests of civil society so that they can embody a 'subjective moment in universal freedom' and at the same time prevent civil society crystallizing into a bloc in opposition to the state (PR ¶ 302). In this context it is understandable that, at times of political crisis, civil society or one of its constituent spheres should rise up against its subjection to the state and declare itself to be the sovereign power. Such re-affirmation of subjective right becomes a danger to freedom only when civil society is elevated to the status of a supreme principle. In extremity, as German Critical Theory acknowledged, the power of the strongest elements of civil society to rule over the state is a distinctive characteristic of fascisim.[8]

Hegel's account of the functions of civil society contrasts rather sharply with the homage often paid to civil society within normative political theory. He grasps the complexity of civil society itself and the place of civil society within the wider framework of ethical life. To understand subjective freedom, it has to be seen in relation to the formation and education of individuals within the system of needs, system of rights and field of associations which comprise civil society as a whole, as well as in relation to the state. It is to the latter that we now turn.

The State

The relationship between subjective freedom and the state in *The Philosophy of Right* poses difficulties of interpretation and it has often been misunderstood as an irreducible contradiction. Some commentators are content to say that there are two Hegels in the text, one state-centred and the other sensitive to individual rights and civil society, but this explanation is unsatisfying. Instead of a complex

[8] See H. Marcuse, *Reason and Revolution: Hegel and the Rise of Social Theory* (Boston, 1979).

mediation it assumes from the start Hegel's own inconsistency. We are simply asked to choose which Hegel we prefer.[9]

An alternative approach, adopted by members of the Frankfurt School of Critical Theory, is to say that Hegel attempted to reconcile the state and the individual but that this attempt failed because it did not adequately address the class antagonisms determining the future of bourgeois society.[10] From this perspective, developed under the shadow of fascism, Hegel's *Philosophy of Right* is seen to mirror the vulnerability of the modern state and its tendency toward administrative solutions to class inequalities. According to Critical Theory, Hegel had to turn the state into an object of divine worship if it were to achieve the necessary integration in a modern capitalist society. Adorno puts the case most strongly in *Negative Dialectics* where he depicts the world of *The Philosophy of Right* as 'an endless procession of bent figures chained to each other, no longer able to raise their heads under the burden of what is'.[11] One way to rescue subjective freedom is to locate it outside the administrative society: 'in the face of the totalitarian unison with which the eradication of difference is proclaimed as a purpose in itself ... part of the social force of liberation may have temporarily withdrawn to the individual sphere'.[12] Critical Theory expresses very well the experience of contradiction between subjective freedom and the totalizing administrative state. It strives to rescue subjective freedom from obliteration, but can only do so by severing its relation to the political state. Reading *The Philosophy of Right* as surrendering to the state, Critical Theory fails to acknowledge the intimate, conflicting relationship of the state to subjective freedom.

We need to account for the tension between subjective freedom and the state, not as a contradiction in Hegel but as a reflection of a real tension of modern society. Hegel's *Philosophy of Right* endorses the achievement of the right of subjective freedom, and at the same time presents it as an integral element within the unity of the state. This approach contrasts with those that prioritize subjective freedom over the state or dissociate it from the state. Hegel's understanding of the relation between subjective freedom and the state comes to light through the concept of 'concrete freedom', that is, a freedom which combines the liberty of individuals with the unity of the state.

> The state is the actuality of concrete freedom. But concrete freedom requires that personal individuality and its particular interests should reach their full development ... The principle of the modern states has enormous strength and depth because it allows the principle of subjectivity to attain fulfilment in the self-sufficient extreme of personal particularity ... The essence of the modern state is that the universal should be linked with the complete freedom of particularity and the well-being of individuals ... Only when both moments are present in full measure can the state be regarded as articulated and truly organised. (PR ¶ 260)

[9] *Cf.* K.H. Ilting, 'Hegel's Concept of The State and Marx's Parly Critique' in Z.A. Pelezyaski, 93–113 at 95; J. Stewart, *The Hegel Myths and Legends* (Evanston, 1996), 79 and Arato, n.5. above.

[10] See Marcuse, n.8, above, 314 and T. Adorno, *Negative Dialectics* (London, 1990), 309.

[11] *Per* Adorno, *ibid.*

[12] *Per* T. Adorno, *Minima Moralia: Reflections From A Damaged Life* (London, 1996), 18.

The conclusion Hegel draws is that subjective freedom is coeval with the historical realization of the modern state. On the one hand, the modern state is premised on the rise and development of subjective freedom; on the other, subjective freedom requires the political support of the modern state. It is in this sense that the state and individual freedom require one another.

How then are we to re-interpret Hegel's apparent veneration of the state? The key to answering this puzzle is to be found in Hegel's definition of the idea of the state as the unity of its concept and existence. If we translate this language into one more familiar to contemporary social scientists, we might say that the state is the unity of its form and content. The concept or form of the modern state, Hegel argues, is that it is the highest form of right—the embodiment of reason, an earthly divinity. The existence or content of the state lies in its actual historical realization as a complex and differentiated organism containing a constitution, sovereign, executive, and legislature. Hegel's method of inquiry is to begin with the concept of the state and then move on to its actual existence. Subjectivism arises when this duality is lost and the concept is afforded supreme status. It is expressed in the various utopias of the totally administered society and in the allegedly 'Hegelian' end of history. The enshrinement of the concept of the state occurs when the difference between the ideal concept of the state and its material 'disfigurement' (as Hegel ironically calls its material existence) is erased in the name of the concept. Of course, the state is not an earthly God, but the detachment of the concept of the state from its existence severs the relation of the state to history and gives it its semblance of divinity.

Hegel's critique of modernity is directed against a subjectivism that mutates the state into a mystical subject—divine, rational, and ideally given. Taken in isolation from its existence, he writes, the concept is 'irrational, untrue and one-sided' (PR ¶ 1). Subjectivism fractures the idea of the state and stands in opposition to subjective freedom. Hegel engages with Kant on precisely this issue. The problem in Kant, as Hegel sees it, is to identify subjective freedom too closely with obedience to the state. Kant maintains that the 'well-being of the state' refers only to that condition in which 'the constitution conforms most closely to the principles of justice' and must not be confused with 'the welfare or happiness of the citizens of the state'. Kant's critical philosophy enjoins man to obey the law 'without regard to his inclinations'.[13] Subjective freedom, from this point of view, does not lie in our capacity to choose for or against the law, but only in our 'internal legislation of reason'.[14] At one point Kant declares that it is 'the people's duty to endure even the most intolerable abuse of supreme authority'.[15] What worries Hegel is how quickly the language of right and freedom can be transmogrified into a language of coercion and necessity. The nub of Hegel's criticism of Kant is that his critical philosophy turns out not to be critical enough. While Kant thinks of a rational form of state in accord with the idea of right, Hegel wants to show that even in this rational form subjectivism compresses subjective freedom.

[13] *The Metaphysical Elements of Justice* (Indianapolis, 1985), 15. [14] *Ibid*, 28.

[15] See R. Bellamy, *Modern Italian Social Theory* (Cambridge, 1998).

A more dangerous form of subjectivism may be exemplified by the (mis)reading of *Philosophy of Right* offered by the idealist philosopher and fascist ideologue, Giovanni Gentile. He saw himself as drawing on Hegel when he coined the term 'totalitarianism' to identify the self-realization of the individual with the universality of the state. While criticizing Hegel for maintaining a residue of individual rights, he read *The Philosophy of Right* as basically offering a philosophy of the state in which the state is advanced as the one true subject and the freedom of individuals consists in their identity with the state. Gentile sought to make humanity master of its own fate by actualizing the divinity of the state (calling his philosophy 'actualism') and he perceived the 'guarantees' provided by the system of right for subjective freedom only as a limitation on the 'divine idea' and as something to be overcome.

Social Theory and the *Philosophy of Right*

Hegel's critique of subjectivism may be seen in the very way in which he conceives of a *Philosophy of Right*. He argues that it should be understood as a science of right. It ought to study its subject matter in roughly the same way as the natural sciences study laws of nature, inasmuch as it should recognize that both the laws of right and the laws of nature are 'external to us' and that our cognition 'adds nothing to them' (PR ¶ 13). Hegel acknowledged that laws of right, unlike laws of nature, are derived from human beings; that they are not absolute; that they are never valid simply because they exist, and that there is always the possibility of conflict between what they are and what we think they ought to be. Yet it is a social theory of right he seeks to develop, an observation of social reality in which concepts are in dialogue with external reality. The laws of right are not the product of our own subjectivity. The task Hegel sets for a *Philosophy of Right* is no longer to prescribe what ought to be but to understand what is. The task of political philosophy is 'the comprehension of the present and the actual, not the setting up of a world beyond, which exists God knows where' (PR ¶ 20). It is to explore the social forms which the idea of right assumes in the modern age (personality, private property, morality, civil society, the state, etc) and how in the tension between concept and existence subjective freedom is enhanced or denied. Criticism itself is an expression of subjective freedom that recognizes the tensions within which subjective freedom lives. It does not only refuse dogma, but it uncovers the ground on which dogmatism rests: namely, the suppression of the dialectic.

To understand the idea of right we must use our heads, of course, but we have to get out of our heads as well. In a famous passage in the Preface of this wonderful book Hegel famously writes:

> To recognise reason as the rose in the cross of the present and thereby to delight in the present—this rational insight is the reconciliation with actuality which philosophy grants

to those who have received the inner call to comprehend, to preserve their subjective freedom in the realm of the substantial and at the same time to stand with their subjective freedom . . . in what has being in and for itself. (PR ¶ 22)

Reason is to be found in the existing world, not in the philosopher's head. The present is a cross, a world of suffering, not the actualization of reason. What reason it contains requires the work of understanding; it is not there on the surface. The value of understanding is that it preserves the freedom of the individual while at the same time attaching it to the world. It is an antidote to the illusion of the supreme status of the subject. The activity of understanding makes of the *Philosophy of Right* itself a resistance to subjectivism.

15

Notes on the Methodology Debate in Contemporary Jurisprudence: Why Sociologists Might Be Interested

Dennis Patterson[1]

Introduction

In the Continental tradition, legal philosophy and legal sociology are closely aligned, both pedagogically and theoretically. It is not at all unusual (especially in German-speaking countries) to have the same person hold an appointment in legal philosophy and legal sociology. The Anglophone world enjoys no such joining of the conceptual and the social. In fact, I would venture to say that most analytic philosophers of law have little time, or none, for sociology.

While I do not see any grand rapprochement in the immediate future, I do think there is a brewing debate that might bring sociologists and philosophers together. I have in mind the nascent 'methodology' debate. Methodology in any field concerns the 'right way' to conduct the field. In jurisprudence, the issue is 'What questions should we ask'? As philosophers, we are interested in the *kind* of question deemed appropriate. The question is uniquely philosophical.

Philosophers have always been interested in conceptual content. But what does it mean to say that concepts have 'content'? Where does this content come from? And what sort of content is it? The Ancients believed that many concepts had 'necessary and sufficient conditions' for their application. This perceived truth held sway until the middle of the last century. Now, almost no one believes this ancient learning, at least not without substantial qualifications.[2]

The debate over the necessity of conceptual content has reached jurisprudence. Does the concept of 'law' have necessary content? What, if anything, must a system

[1] My thanks to John Oberdiek and Jefferson White for comments on a draft of this chapter and to Amanda Lanham for excellent research assistance.

[2] An excellent, brief account is found in Jerry Fodor, 'Water's Water Everywhere' (2004) 26 *London Review of Books* 17–19 (reviewing Christopher Hughes, *Kripke: Names, Necessity and Identity* (Oxford, 2004)).

of norms possess if it is to count as 'law'? This is the question at the heart of the methodology debate. In this chapter, I will describe this debate and, apropos of the present occasion, make the case that this debate should be of interest to legal sociologists. If I am right, there may yet be an Anglophone rapprochement between philosophers and sociologists of law.

The Methodology Debate

For better or worse, the last twenty-five years in analytic jurisprudence have been dominated by the so-called 'Hart–Dworkin' debate.[3] In *The Concept of Law*, H.L.A. Hart advanced the case for a 'descriptive jurisprudence'. A central feature of Hart's project was the clarification of legal practice through a perspicuous description of its principal features. Chief among these elements are the concepts of primary and secondary rules, the internal point of view, and, most importantly, the Rule of Recognition. Through the use of the Rule of Recognition, lawyers and non-lawyers alike are able to identify legal norms as such and, in that way, decide what the law is on any given question.[4]

Ronald Dworkin—the most persistent critic of legal positivism—has consistently contested the possibility of a wholly descriptive jurisprudence. Dworkin's central claim—advanced most systematically in *Law's Empire*[5]—is that 'law' is 'an interpretive concept'. Law is an interpretive concept because to understand the concept, one needs to grasp its point or purpose.[6] Because the state exercises its coercive power over citizens, any concept of law must explain and justify this important example of state action. This is the fundamental normative dimension of jurisprudence, one that is evaluative, and necessarily so.

To the degree there has been a 'methodology debate' in jurisprudence, the debate has been over the question whether descriptive jurisprudence is possible.[7] Hart, and positivists generally, made the case that description without evaluation (endorsement) was possible. *Pace* Hart, Dworkin and John Finnis have insisted that evaluation is a necessary element of jurisprudential analysis.

Since Hart's death, the methodology debate has taken a new turn, one that joins it—finally—with important developments in metaphysics and epistemology. Before I describe this turn, a little background is in order.

Since Plato, philosophers have endeavoured to develop accounts of concepts that unpack their content in terms of necessities. According to the so-called

[3] For a polemical account of the debate, see Brian Leiter, 'The End of Empire: Ronald Dworkin and Jurisprudence in the 21st Century' (2004) 36 *Rutgers Law Journal* 165.

[4] See H.L.A. Hart, *The Concept of Law* (Oxford, 1994), 94–9 (describing the Rule of Recognition).

[5] Ronald Dworkin, *Law's Empire* (London, 1986).

[6] *Ibid*, 190 ('A conception of law must explain how what it takes to be law provides a general justification for the exercise of coercive power by the state. . . . ').

[7] For a clear and concise account of the debate thus far, see Julie Dickson, 'Methodology in Jurisprudence: A Critical Survey' (2004) 10 *Legal Theory* 117–56.

'Classical Theory of Concepts', most concepts are 'structured mental representations that encode a set of necessary and sufficient conditions for their application...'.[8] While a single theory cannot be continuously identified from Plato on, it is not an overstatement to say that something like the Classical Theory was a significant element in philosophy from antiquity to the middle of the twentieth century.[9] The reason for the longevity of the Classical Theory is not hard to see: it holds the promise of tremendous explanatory power, 'offering unified accounts of concept acquisition, categorization, epistemic justification, analytic entailment and reference determination, all of which flow directly from its basic commitments'.[10]

One or another version of the Classical Theory held sway until 1951, when Willard Van Orman Quine published his paper *Two Dogmas of Empiricism*.[11] Of the several theses Quine advanced in this paper, the most important one for present purposes is his denial of the analytic/synthetic distinction.[12] Here is the famous passage that sums up Quine's position:

> The totality of our so-called knowledge or beliefs, from the most casual matters of geography and history to the profound laws of atomic physics or even of pure mathematics and logic, is a man-made fabric which impinges on experience only along the edges. Or, to change the figure, total science is like a field of force whose boundary conditions are experience. A conflict with experience at the periphery occasions readjustments in the interior of the field. Truth values have to be redistributed over some of our statements. Re-evaluation of some statements entails re-evaluation of others, because of their logical interconnections—the logical laws being in turn simply certain further statements of the system, certain further elements of the field. Having re-evaluated one statement we must re-evaluate some others, which may be statements logically connected with the first or may be the statements of logical connections themselves. But the total field is so underdetermined by its boundary conditions, experience, that there is much latitude of choice as to what statements to reevaluate in the light of any single contrary experience. No particular experiences are linked with any particular statements in the interior of the field, except indirectly through considerations of equilibrium affecting the field as a whole.
>
> If this view is right, it is misleading to speak of the empirical content of an individual statement—especially if it be a statement at all remote from the experiential periphery of the field. Furthermore it becomes folly to seek a boundary between synthetic statements,

[8] Stephen Laurence and Eric Margolis, 'Concepts and Cognitive Science', in: Eric Margolis and Stephen Laurence (eds), *Concepts: Core Readings* (Cambridge, Mass, 1999), 18.

[9] Frank Jackson is the most vigorous, contemporary defender of conceptual analysis. See Frank Jackson, *From Metaphysics to Ethics: A Defense of Conceptual Analysis* (Oxford, 1998).

[10] *Ibid.*

[11] W.V.O. Quine, 'Two Dogmas of Empiricism' (1951) 60 *The Philosophical Review* 20, reprinted in Willard Van Orman Quine, *From a Logical Point of View* (Cambridge, Mass, 1980), 20–46.

[12] Analytic propositions are true in virtue of the meaning of their constituent terms. Synthetic propositions are true in virtue of facts. For discussion, see Georges Rey, 'The Analytic Synthetic Distinction', *Stanford Encyclopedia of Philosophy*, available at http://plato.stanford.edu/entries/analytic-synthetic/.

which hold contingently on experience, and analytic statements, which hold come what may. Any statement can be held true come what may, if we make drastic enough adjustments elsewhere in the system.[13]

There is a great deal in this quotation that merits comment.[14] For our purposes, it is sufficient to note that, if Quine is correct (i.e., if the analytic/synthetic distinction cannot be maintained), then all statements are revisable in the light of experience. In other words, the demise of the analytic/synthetic distinction means that the distinction between necessary and contingent truths disappears.

Why is this important? Even if Quine is right, how does it matter to jurisprudence? Let us return to the Hart/Dworkin debate and the question that animates it, namely: whether description of the current content of law is possible without thereby evaluating (endorsing) it? As I have pointed out, Dworkin, as well as John Finnis,[15] have argued that description without evaluation is not possible. What sort of claim is this? Is it one of logical necessity? In all the debates about the meaning of the word 'law', this is what the critics of Hart (e.g. Dworkin and Finnis) seem to be saying.

But it is not only critics of positivism who have been making claims of logical necessity. Thus, Joseph Raz maintains that:

An interpretation of something is an explanation of its meaning. Many if not all legal philosophers think of themselves as explaining the essential features of legal practices, and explaining the relations between them and related phenomena such as other forms of social organization, other social practices, and morality . . . [Hart himself] was seeking to interpret the complex social institution the law is. If Hart and others did not make as extensive use of 'interpretation' as Dworkin does, this is in part because fashions dictate the use of terms, and because they may well have wished to avoid being associated with theories that, in their eyes, misconstrued the nature of interpretation.[16]

If Quine is right,[17] neither Dworkin and Finnis nor the Exclusive Positivists (such as Raz) can be right about methodology in legal theory. The reason is that claims to be describing 'the essential features of law' depend for their efficacy on the analytic/synthetic distinction. In the wake of Quine's demolition of the analytic/synthetic distinction, no project of 'conceptual analysis' gets off the ground.

[13] Quine, n.11, above, 42–3.

[14] For a detailed explication of Quine's arguments in 'Two Dogmas of Empiricism', see Scott Soames, *Philosophical Analysis in the Twentieth Century* (Princeton, New Jersey, 2003), 351–405. For real understanding of the long-term influence of Quine's position, see Peter M.S. Hacker, *Wittgenstein's Place in Twentieth Century Philosophy* (Oxford, 1996), 183–227.

[15] See John Finnis, *Natural Law and Natural Rights* (Oxford, 1980), 4.

[16] Joseph Raz, 'Two Views of the Nature of the Theory of Law: A Partial Comparison', in Jules Coleman (ed.), *Hart's Postscript* (Oxford, 2001), 1–2.

[17] A well-regarded attack on Quine's argument is that of Paul Grice and Peter Strawson, 'In Defense of a Dogma' (1956) 65 *The Philosophical Review* 141–58, reprinted in Paul Grice, *Studies in the Way of Words* (Cambridge, Mass, 1989), 196–212.

Now what? Brian Leiter wants to fill the gap that Quine creates by importing Quine's naturalism into legal theory.[18] Quine's naturalized epistemology eliminates the conceptual work of philosophy and makes philosophy continuous with science (including social science). In other words, with the demise of the analytic/synthetic distinction, science replaces philosophy[19] (and, of course, normative legal theory) as the best explanatory methodology for law.

I will forgo for another occasion a full evaluation of Quine's argument, and of Leiter's claims about the implications of Quine's analysis for legal theory. Instead, I offer a few thoughts about why sociologists should be interested in this debate, and how they might participate.

Rejection of analyticity is an invitation to sociology. Taking their lead from Quine's demolition of analytic/synthetic distinction and Wittgenstein's remarks on rule-following, 'constructivist' sociologists of knowledge[20] have made the case that 'scientific knowledge' is not a reflection/representation of nature but a communal achievement of scientific communities.[21] In its strong expression, the constructivist view of scientific knowledge replaces natural explanations with social ones. In other words, our knowledge of nature is not the product of sense perception and data but 'interests,' 'practices,' or 'forms of life'.

In his argument for naturalism in law, Leiter wants to embrace Quine while privileging 'nature' as the explanans of legal phenomena. In the context of philosophy of science, this is precisely where the constructivists have dug in and insisted that Quine cannot have it both ways.[22] The demise of the analytic/synthetic distinction means that there is no 'first philosophy': science will not replace philosophy. Rather, science will be a discourse like any other and pragmatism will be the criterion of theory choice.[23]

Conclusion

Analytic jurisprudence is slowly emerging from a long, narrow debate, one that has kept it isolated from virtually all of the interesting debates in epistemology and metaphysics. Quine's controversial naturalism poses a direct threat to projects of conceptual analysis the efficacy of which depend upon the analytic/synthetic distinction. This debate opens the way for sociologists to engage with the discourse in analytic jurisprudence in ways not previously recognized. I hope they accept the invitation.

18 See Brian Leiter, 'Beyond the Hart/Dworkin Debate: The Methodology Problem in Jurisprudence' (2003) 48 *American Journal of Jurisprudence* 17.

19 See Brian Leiter, 'Naturalism in Legal Philosophy' (2002) *Stanford Encyclopedia of Philosophy*, available at http://plato.stanford.edu/entries/lawphil-naturalism/.

20 See, e.g. David Bloor, *Knowledge and Social Imagery*, 2nd edn. (Chicago, 1992).

21 A classic example of such work is Bruno Latour and Steve Woolgar, *Laboratory Life: The Construction of Scientific Facts*, 2nd edn. (Princeton, New Jersey, 1986).

22 This point is well developed in Joseph Rouse, *How Scientific Practices Matter* (Cambridge, 2002).

23 This is Richard Rorty's reading of Quine. See Richard Rorty, *Objectivity, Relativism, and Truth* (Chicago, 1991), 1–17.

16

The Use of Law

Iain Stewart

And

The most difficult part of the expression 'law and sociology' is the word 'and'. And the most problematic thing about this word is why it should be so much of a problem. Cooperation of neighbouring disciplines is common academic fare: one can expect a gamut of mutual understanding, peppered with misunderstandings. Sociology is normal in this regard. It has its ordinary, which is to say not always comfortable, bed-fellowships with, for instance, political science and social anthropology. Likewise, 'law and' is a familiar formula: earlier colloquia in this series have been devoted to 'law and' science, literature, medicine, religion, geography and popular culture, and more are to come. Yet the combination 'law and sociology' stands out for discomfort: despite decades of attempts to bring these two disciplines together, there is still vim in the complaint by Llewellyn and Hoebel back in 1941 that law is impenetrable to sociology,[1] while the normal attitude of lawyers to sociologists remains one of dismissal. However, collaboration between lawyers and sociologists occurs frequently and it is not uncommon for individuals to spread their work across both disciplines. All the same, the more closely that an individual attempts to link the two disciplines the further they seem to move apart. What begins as intercontinental becomes next bipolar and then biplanetary. In my own experience, one ends up with two heads each asking to be taken to the other's leader. The feeling appears to continue.[2]

When was Legal Positivism?

That feeling was largely assuaged, for many, by an assumption of shared positivism. Sociology has long been a diverse discipline. Not for nothing did Benton, in the

[1] Karl N. Llewellyn and E. Adamson Hoebel, *The Cheyenne Way* (Norman, 1941), 41.

[2] Philip A. Thomas, 'Socio-Legal Studies' in his (ed.) *Socio-Legal Studies* (Brookfield, 1997), 1. Cf. Roger Cotterrell, 'Subverting Orthodoxy, Making Law Central' (2002) 29 *Journal of Law and Society* 632 and Paddy Hillyard, 'Invoking Indignation' (2002) 29 *Journal of Law and Society* 645. See also Cotterrell in this volume.

1970s, examine 'philosophical foundations of the three sociologies'.[3] He meant positivism, neo-Kantianism and Marxism—today one must add, although not separately from each other, feminism and postmodernism. Almost all of the varieties of sociology were then and still are 'positivist' in the broad sense that they eschew metaphysics and decline to infer 'ought' from 'is'. Great, have said the lawyers, for we too are nearly all positivists now. Nearly all of us think that those who still believe in natural law are preaching nonsense on rollerblades and we would not dream of looking for a norm in a packet of facts. Both the institution and the discipline of law subscribe to 'legal positivism'. Our task is to develop a non-dogmatic version of the discipline or, in more modern language, a version free from legal ideology. One of that version's tasks would be to criticize legal ideology in society.

However, the concept of ideology bogged down, although the reason was not evident.[4] Marx gave place to Foucault, following whom the question of the nature of law tended to get diluted into the general question of social normativity,[5] and deconstructionist approaches claimed to supersede positivism altogether. Nonetheless, the Marxian concept of ideology was one half of the couple ideology/critique and remains a partner, even if a quiet one, in the continuing pursuit of a sociology of law as general critique of law.[6]

Simultaneously, legal theory divided into the social-scientifically oriented and a 'philosophy of law' dominated by analytical philosophy. To analytical legal theorists, talking about 'legal ideology' will seem as old hat as flower power. 'Positive', they would say, means actually existing and so we study positive law. We know that there is no natural law, which is a metaphysical concept. We do not confuse questions of what law is with questions of what it ought to be. And, because we take these precautions, we are rarely infected with 'ideology'.

However, the concept of positive law is very old. It has been formed and has spent most of its career within the embrace first of pagan and then of Christian idealism. Even the word 'positive (Latin *positivus*)' dates from late antiquity and in that era it was ambiguous, meaning either artificial as opposed to natural (being derived from *ponere*—to put, set, lay, or lay down) or a grammatical root. Two now more familiar meanings are medieval additions—existing or affirmative, being the opposite of 'negative (*negativus*)', and materially real, as opposed to the merely thought or imputed. Even these later meanings, then, are Christian. The expression 'positive law (*ius positivum*)' is not found before the twelfth century. Until recently, it followed the first of the above senses of '*positivus*' and meant artificial law as opposed to natural law. Even for Grotius in the seventeenth

[3] Ted Benton, *Philosophical Foundations of the Three Sociologies* (London, 1977).

[4] Cf. Alan Hunt, 'The Ideology of Law' (1985) in his *Explorations in Law and Society* (London, 1993), 117.

[5] E.g. Alan Hunt and Gary Wickham, *Foucault and Law* (London, 1994).

[6] Cf. Roger Cotterrell, *The Sociology of Law*, 2nd edn. (London, 1992), 309–13.

century, law was divided first into natural and artificial; then artificial law (*ius positivum*) could be divided into that created by God and that created by a human ruler.[7]

Today's legal positivist is therefore not entitled to hang anything on the mere expression 'positive law' but has to show independently how law can be seen positivistically. Yet rigorous moderate positivism, such as that of Kelsen, has seen the concept of positive law falling apart. And radical positivism, such as that of the Scandinavian legal realists, has cast the concept and its spawn into a dungeon where there be dragons. Nonetheless, the critique effected has remained in the moment of negation. It is not enough, only to find that the concept is imbued with or has failed to escape from metaphysical superstition. One has next to show what sense it used to make. That is, one has not just to expose its irrationality but also to give a rational account of that irrationality. And that means, where the irrationality is socially prevalent, to ask whether it is ideological.

I shall now revisit the concept of law, and not only that of positive law, under a particular conception of ideology—one that has been turned around under a concept of 'closure' so that it will be adequate in a critique of law. I will do so on the level of 'philosophical foundations', and not only those of sociology. While the argument will lie mainly in philosophy of language, its conclusion may be relevant to socio-linguistics as well as being an exploration into terminology required for social science, even any modern science, of law. Most specifically, I shall address the theme: *why law cannot be defined and how to do so.*

Seeking Definition

Law is vast, violent and familiar. Vast, it rules us from before the cradle until after the grave. Violent, it dictates when we may kill and may be killed. And it is so familiar that it is made the stuff of drama. It is, furthermore, the topic of an antique intellectual tradition. Even as an academic discipline, the study of law is one and a half millennia old. One could reasonably suppose that this tradition would, at least by now, possess a firm grasp of its central concept. Certainly, there is a huge body of work on that concept. There are books, well known even if not well-read, with grand titles such as *Pure Theory of Law*.[8] I refer to that body of work which attempts to answer the question 'What is law?' Of course, there is much more to legal theory than that—but all of it presupposes that this question can have an answer. Or, at any rate, a range of answers, from which one can select

[7] For references, see Iain Stewart, 'Critical Approaches in Comparative Law', (2002) *Oxford University Comparative Law Forum* 4, 3.1.3. Those to Grotius are to *De Iure Bellis ac Pacis*, (Washington and Oxford, 1913–25), trans. II.38–9 and *The Jurisprudence of Holland* (Oxford, 1953), I.7.

[8] Hans Kelsen, *Pure Theory of Law* (Berkeley, 1967).

the answer that one prefers in general or that is most appropriate to the particular investigation. But, strangely—and I am not the first to note it—the quest for such answers has been a tale of remarkable failure. No-one has ever formulated a definition of law that could hold water for a moment.

I will ask whether that failure has been due to a blockage that the positivist toolkit could not handle. All the same, I will not try to be specially sophisticated: my aim will be to attack the central problem of legal science, using a rather diverse set of tools, and so crash through or crash. I will be able to get sophisticated from the other side once I have got there. Or, to change the metaphor, this will be a crude version of a text that it is more important to complete than to format nicely—even if I have myself already formatted some aspects of the text more nicely then I will do here. This strategy is by no means original. There is a famous book that does this sort of thing: it is called *The Concept of Law*.[9]

I will not draw very much on other disciplines than legal science, except for philosophy. That is not because I am averse to other disciplines—quite the contrary. But, if there is such a thing as legal ideology, it is likely to have entered into the structure of those disciplines and consequently they cannot be counted on to provide a royal road out of it.

Some of what I say will have parallels with postmodernist theory, yet without drawing upon it. I will adopt that strategy because, if I am right that the nature of law remains medieval, the appropriate mode in which to further develop a critique of it will be critique of ideology rather than critique of modernity. All the same, I will wind up in a position that might have been welcomed at least by Foucault. And that not in spite of, but because of, a method that might seem like merely going for the capillaries.

As to the epistemological status of what I will construct, suffice it for this occasion to suppose that I am talking 'pure theory' in the Kantian sense, adopted by Kelsen. It should be remembered that the task of pure theory is not to remain delighted with its immaculacy but to establish rational conditions of possibility of empirical knowledge.[10] The empirical focus to which it is envisaged my approach would be relevant can be epitomized simply: it is the image of oneself standing at a line before an immigration officer's desk. What sense does it make, standing there, that the immigration officer effectively embodies the whole legal order of the country one wishes to enter and is not, ever, going to take no for an answer except as may be provided within that legal order?

[9] H.L.A. Hart, *The Concept of Law*, 2nd edn. (Oxford, 1994). In his 'Postscript' to this book Hart reflects: 'I originally wrote the book with English undergraduate readers in mind' (*ibid*, 238). A negative sign pointing in this direction, in my impression, is that the book simply does not bear the analytical weight that has been placed upon it by its closest interpreters: e.g. Jules Coleman (ed.), *Hart's Postscript* (Oxford, 2001).

[10] See Iain Stewart, 'The Critical Legal Science of Hans Kelsen' (1990) 17 *Journal of Law and Society* 273, 276–8.

The Poverty Paradox

Today, the effort to define law seems to have been given up as a bad job. It was never going to be easy. What is to be meant by 'definition' is itself a vexed and inevitably rather circular question.[11] One has also to be clear what purpose the attempt at definition is intended to serve and, consequently, what type of definition is being attempted.[12] For the present purpose, I shall not assume that there is any bright line between an empirical definition of something and a concept, idea, model or theory of it. For the moment, however, my topic is the history of attempts to define law.

I will not suppose that the juristic enthusiasm for a definition of law that persisted up to the 1970s was symptomatic of something special about the study of law, in that such enthusiasm was unique to legal science. For it was not unique to legal science—Hart was wrong there.[13] A keen quest to define the subject matter of a discipline may be typical of any discipline in its early stages, as a symptom of pressure to mark out one's real estate clearly amid the turf wars of academe. All the same, as I have observed, the discipline of law is far from new. What nonetheless does seem unique to this discipline—and on that Hart and others seem to have been right—is a discrepancy between the effort and expertise that have been expended on the task of defining the central topic and the poverty of the definitions offered. It is this discrepancy that I wish to examine. I shall call it the Poverty Paradox.

This paradox is quite well known. Kant could already jibe, 'The lawyers are still looking for a definition of their concept of law.'[14] And two recent collections, containing forty-four contemporary jurists' attempts to define law, mix poverty with desperation at poverty and end with a mood of 'resignation' from the venerable Vedel.[15] More than one contributor quotes Villey: 'I presume that, after X years of work in the Faculty of Law, you are incapable of providing a definition of law'.

In 1941, William Seagle considered that currently debated definitions of law contained such simple errors that it was 'really remarkable' that they should ever have been offered.[16] Perhaps, he mused, a definition of 'law' is neither necessary nor even terribly important; an artist, after all, is perfectly able to paint without a definition of 'art'. Yet, he observed,

[11] See generally *Routledge Encyclopedia of Philosophy* (London, 1998), 'Definition'.

[12] Robert S. Summers, 'Legal Philosophy Today—an Introduction' in his (ed.) *Essays in Legal Philosophy* (Oxford, 1970), 1.

[13] Hart, n.9 above, 1. Contrast, on definitions of a 'social fact' and other concepts central to the formative period of sociology: Émile Durkheim, *The Rules of Sociological Method* (1895) (Steven Lukes (ed.), London, 1982). Also, on definitions of 'culture' in the formative period of cultural anthropology as an academic discipline: A.L. Kroeber and Clyde Kluckhohn, *Culture* (1952) (New York, 1963).

[14] 'Noch suchen die Juristen eine Definition zu ihrem Begriffe vom Recht': Immanuel Kant, *Kritik der reinen Vernunft* (1781) (Stuttgart, 1966), 748; cf. *Critique of Pure Reason* (London, 1933), 588 n *a*.

[15] (1989) 10 *Droits*, 'Définir le droit/1' and (1990) 11 *Droits*, 'Définir le droit/2'.

[16] William Seagle, *The Quest for Law* (New York, 1941), 4.

there is this important difference in talking about the nature of law. Nobody goes to jail for being unable to say why a painting by El Greco or Matisse, as well as the drawings of the cave men, are art. But it does seem somewhat strange and inappropriate that a man should suffer the inconvenience of being hanged or compelled to pay an unjust debt if we cannot say what law is.[17]

In this way, Seagle suggests, to be able to 'say what law is' is important to justification.[18] That is: one cannot justify hanging someone, which in general is an immoral thing to do, or compelling them to pay a debt if morally the debt need not be paid, if one's justification is 'Because it's the law' yet one cannot say 'what law is'. Seagle leaves unstated the possibility that law merely cannot be defined in a way that will still keep it serviceable as justification.

A decade earlier, however, Thurman Arnold had gone striding down that road. He too had noted the manifest faultiness of available definitions of law. He also noted the energy with which the task of definition was pursued. This discrepancy between outcome and investment, he attributed to wish-fulfilment:

Obviously, 'law' can never be defined. With equal obviousness, however, it should be said that the adherents of the legal institution must never give up the struggle to define law, because it is an essential part of the ideal that it is rational and capable of definition, rather than a psychological adjustment to conflicting emotional needs. Hence the verbal expenditure necessary to the upkeep of the ideal of 'law' is colossal and never ending.[19]

This account—written in the heyday of pop-Freudianism—is, however, seriously incomplete. It does not explain either why law is a wish-dream or why its being a wish-dream would produce a demand for definition. One might think, rather, that definitions would be assassins of dreams. What is there about this wish-dream that would produce a drive to define?

A drive, Hart tells us, there certainly has been. Manifestly wonky definitions, he says, have been 'urged with eloquence and passion, as if they were revelations of truths about law, long obscured by gross misrepresentations of its essential nature'.[20] The salient error, he observes, is circularity. Among his examples of faulty definitions are Llewellyn's 'What officials do about disputes ... is the law itself' and Holmes's 'The prophecies of what the courts will do ... are what I mean by the law'.[21] 'Surely', Hart says, 'law cannot just mean what officials do or courts will do, since it takes a law to make an official or a court.'[22] This error, however, is insidious—because Hart goes on to repeat it by grounding his own 'concept of law' in recognition by 'officials'.[23]

[17] Seagle, n.16 above, 5. [18] *Ibid.*

[19] Thurman W. Arnold, *The Symbols of Government* (1935) (New York, 1962), 36–7.

[20] Hart, n.9 above, 1–2.

[21] K.N. Llewellyn, *The Bramble Bush* (1930) (Dobbs Ferry, 1951), 8–9, 12; O.W. Holmes, 'The Path of the Law' (1897) 10 *Harvard Law Review* 457, 460–1.

[22] Hart, n.9 above, 2; cf Julius Stone, *Legal System and Lawyers' Reasonings* (1964) (Sydney, 1968), 176. [23] Hart, n.9 above, 90–8.

We have, then, a paradox—between the effort and expertise expended on the task of defining law and the remarkable poverty of the definitions offered. We also have a suggestion that the reason, or at least the proximate reason, is wish-fulfilment. And the possibility that there is wish-fulfilment finds an echo in the prevalence of circularity: the definition rests gladly in the arms of that which was to have been defined.

That the circularity is a product of ideological capture or surrender appears from Max Radin's very different reaction to this paradox. He proposed in 1938 that one should resort to the 'infallible test for recognizing whether an imagined course of conduct is lawful or unlawful' which is 'to submit the question to the judgment of a court'. That 'can be done in almost every system at any time', and accordingly 'we can dispense with knowing what *"law"* means'.[24] The poverty of this suggestion is staggering. It is plainly circular: only if we already know 'what "law" means' can we know what a 'court' is. It is also blatantly false: it is simply not true that courts are ordinarily willing to answer hypothetical questions. Or, if Radin is thinking of test cases, it would be as immoral as it would be expensive to parachute into some individual's legal affairs in order to resolve an intellectually intriguing point. There is here, rather, a gambit of power: Radin is asking us to accept that the organization that calls itself a 'court'—which in a common-law system at that time amounted to saying that the organization that calls itself 'the legal system'—can be allowed to define itself and to impose that definition upon us. He is closing the courthouse door, with himself inside, against the possibility of a definition independent of the legal order.

Contemporary Theories

Let us now examine[25] the principal current types of theory of positive law, to see whether they too contain remarkable error. These theories are couched in a variety of terms, but I don't think I will misrepresent any of them if I standardize them around what is conventionally identified as the elementary component of law, the 'norm': that is, a statement whose meaning is or can be expressed as 'ought'.

(1) To conceive law by reference to *force* fails to account for the socially made distinction between a tax official and a thief: both of them demand money with menaces.

(2) To conceive law by reference to the fact that a legal order is socially *recognized as binding* fails to explain the notion of 'bindingness'.

  (a) In a *subjective* 'recognition' theory, what I 'recognize' in the morning I can decline to recognize in the afternoon.

[24] Max Radin, 'A Restatement of Hohfeld' (1938) 51 *Harvard Law Review* 1141, 1145–6.

[25] Very schematically, or the analysis would take up the whole volume. Only for point (6) would I claim any degree of originality.

(b) An *objective* 'recognition' theory, where the 'recognition' must be by (e.g.) 'officials', is circular, since they will be 'officials' only by legal authorization.

(3) To conceive law by reference to the *linguistic form of a norm*, e.g. that the utterance is in the imperative mood or is expressed as an 'ought', fails when one notices that many utterances counted as legal oughts are not expressed in an imperative mood or even in a prescriptive mood—it is indeed common to find norms expressed in the indicative.[26]

(4) To conceive law by reference to *intrinsic rationality* focuses on general norms to the neglect of the business end of the legal order, which is the individual norm according to which a collar gets felt. It also assumes that the creation and application of legal norms is a wholly or at least primarily rational process, rather than the elaboration of a chain of authorization according to various descriptive, political, moral and other assumptions.

(5) To conceive law by reference to a particular *kind of social behaviour* tends either to eliminate the prescriptive element altogether and hence to wind up unable to identify law at all, or to mix up the identification of fact and norm. As a variant of this, to conceive law by reference to a particular social institution, such as 'the state' or a 'court', may only postpone the issue, since state and court are themselves already constituted by legal norms.

(6) Perturbed writers have then labelled all these conceptions of law as 'narrow' and preferred to conceive law far *more broadly*. For example, 'law' is said to include 'folk law' or is only vaguely located within a wider category such as 'social control'.

(a) This is often *fallacious*: involving the fallacy that a broad definition is better than a narrow one. Rather, the only virtues that a definition can have are exactitude and truth.[27]

(b) It may be *political*. It does bring into the bag of 'law' types of norm that are not produced by a state: both norms that exist parallel to state norms and norms that exist in the actual absence of a state. But those norms can be taken into account without dragging them into the 'law' bag. The desire to bring them in seems to be mainly political: that not to acknowledge, say, 'folk law' is to be, in varying contexts, elitist or still colonialist. One might, alternatively, congratulate the bearers of such norms on *not* having turned them into law.

[26] Use of the indicative with the meaning of 'ought' pervades, for example, the French *Code civil*. Article 1 commences: 'Les lois sont exécutoires dans tout le territoire français . . .'. Kelsen's concept of the legal norm, however, seems not to be vulnerable to this criticism: his concern seems to be with an 'ought' meaning, however signified.

[27] Alan Hunt and Gary Wickham, developing a Foucauldian theory of law, propose a definition of law that would include among 'operations of law' the 'procedures of a company concerned with proper bookkeeping': n.5 above, 102. While Margaret Davies goes for broke: 'Law is a limit' and 'any limit is a law': *Delimiting the Law* (London, 1996), 15.

(c) It is *empirically* inadequate. Where a society contains a dominant organization, particularly a state, that organization tends to claim that its norms are 'law' while other norms of social control are 'not law', and that *therefore*—simply *therefore*—its norms override the others. If the advocate of a very broad conception of law recognizes this phenomenon, they may respond by distinguishing between 'law' (in a broad sense) and 'legal law'[28]—which is less than helpful.

(7) If one tries to define law in terms of a certain *combination of norms*, one is hard put to find a combination that avoids the same problems.[29]

(8) If one abandons the attempt to accept the word 'law' as stating a truth and investigates whether, instead, there is a 'legal ideology', meaning 'ideology' in a more or less Marxian sense, one runs up against the apparent inappropriateness of the concept of 'ideology' to the study of law: that it is a concept of a type of misdescription, while 'law' in almost anybody's sense consists centrally of norms, which are prescriptions.

(9) If one then abandons the whole attempt to conceive only descriptively and goes for an *evaluative criterion*, one either displaces the problem or loses it.

(a) If one goes for an *objective* evaluative criterion, such as justice, then effectively 'justice' is referred to as natural law and the problem of conceiving law is only displaced from the level of the artificial to that of the natural.

(b) If one goes for a *subjective* evaluative criterion, such as morality, the subjectivity of morality gives rise to the same relativistic kind of difficulty as with a recognition theory.

The Can't Say Paradox

It is beginning to look as if, when we speak of law, we really don't know what we are talking about. Yet at the same time, in a second paradox that Hart notes, it is abundantly clear that we do know. I shall name this the Can't Say Paradox.

Despite the poverty within legal theory, Hart notes, most relatively educated people can accurately identify whether something is 'legal' or not, as well as the principal institutions of the legal system that applies to them.[30] I do not think he needed to restrict this to the relatively educated. It appears to me, as a matter of

[28] R.M. MacIver, *The Web of Government* (New York, 1965/[1947]), 49–50.

[29] E.g. Hart's 'law as the union of primary and secondary rules': n.9 above, ch. 5. Such a 'union' can be found in the constitution of almost any political party, which (at least in western democracies) nobody considers to be 'law'.

[30] Hart, n.9 above, 2–3. Cf. 'In law as elsewhere, we can know and yet not understand': H.L.A. Hart, 'Definition and Theory in Jurisprudence' (1953) in his *Essays in Jurisprudence and Philosophy* (Oxford, 1983), 21, at 21.

observation, that these abilities are possessed by nearly everybody. It also seems to me, as a matter of supposition, that no legal system could be effective if they were not. For that reason, it would be an advantage if the nature of law were very simple—even if it may be simple in an obscure way. However, it seems likely to be very simple in any case, since it is used to arrive (or to claim to arrive) at unconditional decisions.

For these same reasons, too, it seems mistaken to suppose, as Hart appears to do, that the line of paradox here lies between types of people. It is not that most people are content and only legal experts are confused, but rather that even the experts are content until they undertake a confusing task. The nature of law is simply not problematical in everyday life—whether that be the everyday life of a porter, a police officer or a law professor. It does not even bother the professor during teaching or research on particular branches of law: one can readily teach or write on, say, constitutional law without the slightest reflection on the nature of law as such. The line of paradox lies not between persons, but between tasks. Only when the law professor (or anyone else, such as a social anthropologist) takes up the very task of asking 'What is law?'—only when one, as Margaret Davies puts it, actually 'asks the law question'[31]—does the nature of law as such becomes problematical. And, the more vigorously that this topic is pursued, the more resistant it seems to become.

So we know what law is. Yet, somehow, we cannot say.

Legal Ideology

Law is beginning here to look like a form of repression and I do want to presume that the failure to express is involuntary. However, since that failure seems to be so common, I would prefer to think of it as ideological. Even if an ideology is a neurosis with an army.

I have already noted, however, that in principle the concept of ideology is inapplicable to law, since the concept of ideology is of a type of misdescription while law consists largely of norms and norms are prescriptions. This applies to anybody's concept of ideology and to almost anybody's concept of law.[32] One can see this barrier in Marx's critique of Hegel's philosophy of law, where Marx effects an ideology-critique of Hegel's conception of the state but does not go on into a critique of Hegel's conception of law.[33] The same is/ought barrier affects application of related concepts, found in Marx or elsewhere, such as fetishism, objectivation, personification and projection.[34]

[31] *Asking the Law Question*, 2nd edn. (Pyrmont, 2002).

[32] That is, except for behaviourist concepts of law, which are not in issue here.

[33] Karl Marx, 'Contribution to the Critique of Hegel's Philosophy of Law' (1843) and 'Introduction' (1844) in Karl Marx and Frederick Engels, *Collected Works*, III.3–129 and 175–87.

[34] Karl Marx, *Capital* Vol. 3 (1863–6) (*Collected Works*, n.33 above, xxxvii), chs 24 and 48.

Those related concepts, moreover, tempt Marx, at least, into a certain rashness. Perhaps misled by the semantic accessibility of the texts that were the objects of his critique, he continually expressed ideology as a cultural condition rather than as something that is socially encountered. One has, better, to ask: what does an ideology look like when one meets it? And I am thinking of the bearer of legal ideology less as a law professor than as a police or immigration officer.

I shall ask the ideology question first from the angle of the signified and then from the angle of the signifier.

Philosophical Tools

To do either of these things, however, I need to pick up three further philosophical tools.[35]

The first of these tools is a logical figure conventionally known as 'opposition' or 'contrariety'. It is the theme of a child's game of 'opposites'—'retreating' is the opposite or contrary of 'advancing', and so on. The relation between 'retreating' and 'advancing' is a relation of opposition. This is different from contradiction, in that 'not-advancing' would include everything that is not 'advancing'—it would include standing still, lying flat, jumping into a hole or hanging onto a handy big balloon.

My second philosophical tool is the opposition between presence and absence. And I want to extend that opposition from states to processes, to be able to speak also of 'presentation' and (to resurrect an old word) 'absentation'.[36] Then I can also use verb forms 'to present' and 'to absent'. This is, by itself, only an abstract distinction. Concretely, what is absent is not somehow 'present in being absent': what is absent is as gone as the life of a dead parrot. Or as 'never there' as a woman's perspective in a public bar.

These combined tools may seem cumbersome, but I would suggest that they are not so much cumbersome as unfamiliar. They help to overcome a limitation of the figure of contradiction in the study of ideology, that (as Hegel knew so well) the negated is preserved in the negation. There is a contradiction when one maintains both a statement 'that P' and a statement 'that not-P'. The element 'P' is preserved in the negation: '*not*-P' is always 'not-*P*'. And this does not fit the phenomenon that an ideology, in its own terms, has no outside. Critique of ideology will mortgage itself to the ideology if it relies solely on the figure of negation: it will preserve the content of the ideology in the process of negating it; it will

35 Discussed more extensively in Stewart, n.7 above, 3.2.2.

36 I admit to having been a dictionary worm for this and other rare words, as well as French equivalents, when I have written on comparative law. I have not indulged in gratuitous neologisms, as alleged by Olivier Moréteau and Jacques Vanderlinden, 'Introduction' in their (eds) *La structure des systèmes juridiques* (Brussels, 2003), 17, 28 n.26. Nor, in my own contribution to that book, have I committed the other sins of which they accuse me.

only create a mirror loaded with the image of that which was to have been removed. On the other side, an ideology does not negate that which the critic reckons to lie outside it. The ideology absents its own externality—as I will explain in a moment.

The third tool that I need is the concept of tacit knowledge. Tacit knowledge is the ordinary form of any skill. For example, I can discuss the rules of grammar explicitly, but if I tried to make them explicit all the time that I apply them I would be tongue-tied. Tacit knowledge of an intellectual skill can ordinarily be made explicit when occasion demands, as with the rules of grammar. But I will suggest that there may be tacit knowledge that cannot be made explicit without ceasing to be knowledge.

Closure

I shall now, using these three tools, approach the concept of ideology from the angle of the signified.

Absentation of a meaning may be conditional or unconditional. Unconditional absentation I shall call 'closure'. I shall distinguish two forms of closure: 'weak' and 'strong'. By 'weak closure' I will understand simple exclusion: the Other meaning is simply absented. It is not acknowledged. Its bearer is heard, but not listened to. By 'strong closure' I will understand a more subtle figure. Here, the absentative side of the closure—the exclusion and silencing of the Other—has a flip-side which is presentative. What is consistent with the closed statement is subtracted from the realm of human discussion and appears not as constructed but as merely given. This is re-presentation, but it does not appear as being such. What is inconsistent is also re-presented, although again without appearing to be such, in a flipped-over form that is consistent with the first set. In these ways, to the eye of someone who does not accept the closure the whole range of meanings appears as flipped—as an ideology.

This process is not simply an inversion, although in the English radical tradition an ideology is vividly termed 'the world turned upside down'.[37] An ideological world view is not a mirror image of the real,[38] even a distorted mirror image, but a profoundly reworked version of it. The world, as Marx variously puts it, is 'bewitched', 'enchanted' or 'mystified'.[39] Each element of this flipped world

[37] Christopher Hill, *The World Turned Upside Down* (Harmondsworth, 1972).

[38] It is more complex—in form, origins and effects—than the 'mirror stage' of personality development observed by Jacques Lacan: 'The Mirror Stage as Formative of the Function of the I as Revealed in Psychoanalytic Experience' (1949) in his *Écrits* (New York, 1977), 1.

[39] Cf. Marx's identification of objectivated economic categories—*Capital* Vol. 3, above n.34, ch. 48: there is 'an enchanted, perverted, topsy-turvy world, in which Monsieur le Capital and Madame la Terre do their ghost-walking as social characters and at the same time directly as mere things' (at 817).

appears, whether still recognizable or not, as an 'instance' or 'total part' of an overall framework about which no question arises of its being conditioned.[40]

The process of strong closure must remain tacit or what is re-presented would be revealed to have been flipped. One must not let the dark cat out of the dark bag. How, however, could knowledge that must remain tacit be communicated? Searle proposes that any tacit knowledge can be communicated through imitation of its application: there can be an osmosis in which the repetition conveys its own necessary presuppositions.[41] Legal education, for example: we do not so much explain how to 'think like a lawyer' as tell the student 'Here is an example of legal thinking—come thou and do likewise.'[42]

So far, I have considered how the concept of closure may apply to forms of description. But it is equally applicable to forms of prescription, i.e. to norms. One can then say that a strongly closed description is an element of an ideology and that a strongly closed prescription is an element of law, i.e. a legal norm.[43]

That seems intuitively right. To utter a legal norm is not just to threaten, which could involve a weak closure. Then the response 'Oo sez' would receive merely the answer 'I sez' and perhaps a smack in the mouth. Rather, a legal norm is uttered with a prior expectation that any response 'Oo sez?' will be met with 'Because it's the law' and that this will be a completely sufficient answer. It will be completely sufficient not because of anything additional, but simply because the utterer of the norm entirely absents the possibility that any contrary norm will count as a justification. And that expectation will be completely expressed in saying 'It's the law'.

I will pause to note that, if closure is intrinsically a deplorable thing, it may not be the most deplorable. For example, the most ideological-critical jurist can argue for laws against sexual discrimination or laws to ensure safety at work. Just as one would not interfere with the work of a charity simply because the charity is religious.[44]

Dark Performatives

To identify ideology is to identify a product. To identify closure is to identify the type of apparatus through which that product is produced. It is next necessary to identify the mechanism of that apparatus. I shall suggest that this mechanism lies on the plane of the signifier, in a particular form of speech. Then I shall suggest that the word 'law', when used in relation to norms, is a speech form of that kind.

40 Seeing an ideology as an 'expressive totality' each particular element of which is an 'instance' of the whole or a 'total part' in which the whole is essentially expressed: Louis Althusser and Étienne Balibar, *Reading Capital* (London, 1970), 17.

41 John R. Searle, *The Construction of Social Reality* (London, 1995), ch. 6.

42 Cf. Llewellyn, n.21 above, 96.

43 See, further, Iain Stewart, 'Closure and the Legal Norm' (1987) 50 *Modern Law Review* 908.

44 See further Stewart, n.7 above, 4.2.3.

My initial model is J.L. Austin's theory of 'performatives'.[45] Austin argues that certain locutions do not simply denote or connote, but actually *constitute*. To take his simplest example: if I say to X 'I bet you sixpence it will rain tomorrow' and X responds with acceptory words such as 'You're on', we will have *made a bet*.[46] To utter the sentence, Austin says, 'is not to *describe* my doing of what I should be said in so uttering to be doing or to state that I am doing it: it is to do it'. He calls this sort of statement a 'performative', since 'the issuing of the utterance is the performing of an action' and not 'just saying something'.

Now, in the making of a bet there is reciprocity: I can say to X 'I bet you . . .', but there is no bet unless and until X says something by way of accepting the offer. In lawmaking, however, there is no reciprocity. If A says to B 'I make a law that . . .', B might ignore what A says. But that would not prevent A's statement from having the effect of making a law. The law would be made, indeed, even if B did not hear what A said. It is the same if B hears what A says and responds: 'That's interesting—let's discuss it'. A would still say: 'We can discuss it as much as you like, but it is law and you must obey.'

At first glance this is familiar, but at second glance it is strange. Lewis Carroll thinks so when he addresses this sort of issue in 'What the Tortoise Said to Achilles'.[47] Swift Achilles cannot out-reason a creature who, whatever proposition Achilles utters, only notes it for consideration. When the wrathful warrior threatens that 'Logic would take you by the throat, and *force* you' to accept a certain proposition, the Tortoise (who has not imbibed so much Hegel) merely notes that point too.

Suppose now that A and B are norms uttered by Priam. A is a norm 'One must not take without permission' and B is a norm 'Whatever Priam says must be obeyed'. From A and B would follow Z, 'I must not take without permission'. Then let C be the hypothetical proposition 'If A and B, then Z'. But one does not have to accept C. Then let D be the hypothetical proposition 'If A and B and C, then Z'. But one does not have to accept D. And so on, potentially infinitely.

It is evident from the fate of Kelsen's *Grundnorm* that, once such a regress starts, it cannot be ended.[48] Yet no such problem arises unless the question of a reason for the bindingness of law is asked. In the operation of law, such a problem simply does not occur. The reason for that, I will suggest, is that no such regress starts.

Let us consider the effect of an expression that includes the word 'God'. I put a moral view to you. You oppose it. I then say 'but God', attributing that view to 'God' as its author. With that attribution, all possibility of your opposition being

[45] J.L. Austin, *How to Do Things with Words* (1955) (2nd edn. Oxford, 1975), 4–7.

[46] Initially, Austin states only the offer, but the need for an acceptance is implicit in his later classification of the expression 'I bet' as 'contractual'.

[47] Lewis Carroll, 'What the Tortoise Said to Achilles' (1894) in *The Penguin Complete Lewis Carroll* (Harmondsworth, 1982), 1104.

[48] I do not think that his recourse to Vaihinger's theory of fictions succeeds: see Stewart, n.10 above, 296–7.

legitimate is excluded. More, since you are opposing the morality laid down by 'God', you are (represented as being) in a 'state of sin'. This happens without my explaining the meaning of 'God'. That might be done as supplement: more likely, however, I will declare that beyond a few pointers the nature of 'God' cannot be explained. And, if you don't also accept *that*, then in the long run so much the hotter for *you*. The expression by itself already effects the closure. In the beginning is the Word and the Word is 'God'.

It seems to be the same with expressions involving the word 'faith'. I would say 'Well, I disagree but for me this is a matter of faith'. Introducing the word 'faith' makes the difference between what Kelsen would call a 'subjective' and an 'objective' meaning. The view is now 'objective' as an 'article of faith'. I do not have to explain what I mean by 'faith'—indeed, I am unlikely to be able to do so and may well declare that it is inexplicable. And, if thou dostn't also comprehend *that*, then thou art (at coolest) among those 'of little faith'.

I shall call such expressions 'dark performatives'. What Austin calls 'performatives' may then be distinguished as 'light performatives'.[49] Probably, no word always operates as an element of a dark performative or of any other kind of performative. But it does seem that some words, such as 'God' or 'faith', usually do so.

This process is not logical, if to be logical is to follow explicit rules of logic, since a key element of closure is tacit. Nor, however, is it rhetorical, if rhetoric is centrally an attempt to persuade, since here there is no attempt to persuade—it is never going to matter whether the Other agrees. At the same time, however, what is understood as logic or rhetoric may already involve closure.

Now, suppose that by the end of some conference I still have not paid my participation fee. The organizer will politely remind me that there is a contractual obligation. I may say: 'Yes, but I have just been to a most enlightening conference where I have learned that, apart from the making of an agreement, there is nothing else to a contract but a set of illusions'. The organizer will then frostily employ expressions that will probably include the word 'legal'. With that word, the organizer will be re-presenting the agreement, which Kelsen would call a subjective meaning, as an objective meaning. That is to add something: it is to locate the agreement within the legal institution 'contract'. And then, Kelsen would tell us, we have to travel up the chain of authorization to statutory provisions and then to constitutional provisions. And then: like the Indian rope trick, at the very top of the chain the professor disappears. There is nothing at all, *on the plane of the signified*, to endow any norm with legal character—that is, to make it ultimately binding.

Then does the whole chain, rope, pyramid or whatever it is come tumbling down? Not at all. Because, I want to suggest, the job has already been done. It has been done *on the plane of the signifier*, through the use of such words as 'law' and

[49] Except so far as his legal examples might, on further analysis, turn out to be dark. For Carroll, all performatives might be Snarks and dark ones Boojums: *The Annotated Snark*, Martin Gardner (ed.) (Harmondsworth, 1962).

'legal'.[50] To use such a word is to effect a dark performance, in that, when the word is attached to a normative meaning, all contrary normative meanings are excluded from the discourse of justification. Through that mechanism, the norm becomes closed.

The norm is then unconditionally binding, through complete default of alternatives. If one has to act and the action is covered by the norm, what the norm contains is now the only way in which one is allowed to act. The norm is not binding because of anything additional to it: that it is, for instance, just.[51] It is binding simply because it is exclusive. And it is just, because it is binding.[52]

From a critical point of view, whether one will conform to the norm will be a decision whether to conform, on whatever extraneous grounds. Those might be grounds consistent with the law or even inconsistent with it—for instance, one might conform only tactically. And similarly with decisions whether to engage in the making, reform, application, enforcement or teaching of law.

In comparison with a theory such as Kelsen's, I have made two radical moves. I have switched the issue of the nature of law from the plane of the signified to that of the signifier.[53] And I have shifted it from under the concept of presentation to under that of absentation.

For simplicity, I have assumed that the core element of law is the norm. Elsewhere I have suggested that, especially in a common-law system, where legal thought is highly analogical, one might also have to think of a matching process involving 'normative patterns'.[54] Whether the element in question is a norm or a normative pattern, however, its legal character is provided by its own signifier and does not depend on criteria of membership in a legal order, such as legal validity.

Legal Institutions and Ideology

At the same time, legal norms or normative patterns, and the relations among them, coalesce in autonomously conceived 'institutions' such as 'contract',

[50] J.L. Austin himself suggests that performatives have an important role in law, both in that some of his examples are legal and in his note that Hart had proposed that he call such statements 'operative' in the legal sense: Austin, n.45 above, 7.

[51] Or even some further norm that renders the primary norm exclusionary, as Joseph Raz proposes: *Practical Reason and Norms* (London, 1975).

[52] There is recognition, and recognition by officials is the most important, but it goes to the effectiveness of law and not to its identity.

[53] Let's hear it, also, for John Austin. In identifying a law as a species of command, he shifted the focus to the plane of the signifier, but (in my view) got into the wrong mood: *The Province of Jurisprudence Determined* (1832) (New York, 1970), 120. W. L. Morison, however, valuably modifies Austin's picture by proposing that the difference between what Kelsen terms a subjective and an objective meaning is effected by performatively 'operative words'—such as 'Be it enacted', 'the order of the court will be', 'now this deed witnesseth' and even 'hereby': *John Austin* (London, 1982), 193. It is a great pleasure, in a publication from the Faculty of Laws at University College London, to credit Austin with suggesting that the key lies on the plane of the signifier: right location, only wrong locution.

[54] Stewart, n.7 above, 2.1.1.

'property' or 'citizenship'. One speaks of 'real property' and 'personal property' as if they are species of a genus 'property' and can be elucidated by reference to some essence of the genus.

A meaning that has this sort of objectivity might fall within the class that Searle calls an 'institutional fact', distinct from a physical or 'brute' fact.[55] It is 'objective' in the relatively weak sense of being socially shared. For Searle, all linguistic usage is 'rule-governed'. The rules may be 'regulative' or 'constitutive': 'regulative rules regulate antecedently or independently existing forms of behavior' while 'constitutive rules do not merely regulate, they create or define new forms of behavior'. The rules of a game, for example, do not merely regulate a game when it is played but 'create the very possibility of playing' the game.[56] A system of constitutive rules is an 'institution'. An activity so constituted is not mere behaviour, a merely material or 'brute' fact, nor is it something merely subjective: it has an objective existence, as an 'institutional' fact.[57] It is 'objective' in the relatively weak sense of being socially shared.

The ideas of the performative and the institutional fact have been brought into legal theory, in the 'new institutionalism' of Weinberger and MacCormick.[58] However, their account of each legal institution is internal, in the sense that it is an account of how the game is played—how, for example, one makes a contract or a gift, given the existence of rules for doing so. It is not an account of how the game is created or, from moment to moment, re-created. It is an account of how legal norms operate but not an account of what makes those norms legal, an account of their legal character. On the other hand, institutional facts are not mere illusions but are undoubtedly real as beliefs that are followed in action.

If, as I have suggested, legal character lies in closure and closure is effected by dark performance, one would expect legal institutions to appear as objective in the relatively strong sense of appearing as merely given. And that is just what occurs: they do not appear as constructs. They appear as so objective that a reference to them can itself effect a legal closure: to say 'Get off my property' is to close, while 'Get off this land' is a mere demand and leaves space for 'Oo sez?' At the same time, a particular property item or relation appears as an instance or total part of the institution 'property'. A particular item or relation may appear as instantiating more than one legal institution: thus, when Blackacre is sold it appears as both a property-thing and a contract-thing. If it appears within legal discourse as a bearer of economic, environmental or aesthetic value, it does so exclusively so far as these values are recognized as content of legal

[55] Briefly but succinctly in *Speech Acts* (Cambridge, 1969), 50–71; then at length throughout *The Construction of Social Reality*, n.41 above. J.L. Austin quickly dropped the notion of 'performatives', unsatisfied that he could distinguish them as a class of utterances; Searle seems content, and I agree, that at least *some* utterances can be clearly so classed.

[56] Searle, *Speech Acts*, n.55 above, 33–4.

[57] *Ibid*, 50–71.

[58] Neil MacCormick and Ota Weinberger, *The Institutional Theory of Law* (Dordrecht, 1986); Ota Weinberger, *Law, Institution, and Legal Politics* (Dordrecht, 1991).

norms.[59] All instances of a legal institution, in that they are total parts—refractions of an essence—are essentially identical. Those that occur on the same level of generality are equal by definition. Thus, under the institution 'legal personality' all legal persons—personifications of bundles of personal legal rights and duties—appear as essentially identical and, to that extent and no further, as equal.

Such an explanation might be developed by identifying legal norms and the relations between them, and legal institutions with their instances, as the principal elements of legal ideology. They are, one can now reflect, the factors that have often been identified as legal ideology—without being able to explain how they got to be ideological. Since they are elements of an essentialist ideology, the appropriate ideological methods of their interpretation are exegesis and apologetics.[60] When such interpretation is raised to the power of a definition of law, because it has no room for an outside to law it ends up in circularity or in woolly affirmation of an attitude.[61]

The Drive to Define

It is now possible to suggest an explanation for the erstwhile drive to define.

I have begun to define law in terms of absentation. I have tried to show, within those terms, why it cannot be defined in terms of presentation. That conclusion, however, makes even more mysterious the quixotic drive to define. Why should generations of jurists have expended so much energy on the meaning of a word whose meaning it seems they needed to keep obscure?

The reason for this appears to be a contradiction within the type of ideology produced. It is an essentialist ideology, in which law appears to have an essence and that essence appears to be most fully instantiated in the very word 'law'. The more rigorously that law is studied, therefore, the more one must strive to understand this word. This word, however, has already absented the possibility of understanding it in terms other than of presentation—and in terms solely of presentation it cannot make sense.

[59] I have explored in these terms the ideas of 'separation of powers' and 'the rule of law': 'Men of Class: Arisotle, Montesquieu and Dicey on "Separation of Powers" and "The Rule of Law"' (2004) *Macquarie Law Journal* 187, 219–23.

[60] In this perspective, I think Hart misses the point when he complains that Dworkin is engaging in localized justification: Hart, n.9 above, 239–44. Dworkin's conception of 'theory' as depicting 'the law' in its 'best light' is apologetical: it has to find a local legal order to which to commit itself and, having done so, what is exegetically described as the content of that order is to be portrayed in its best light. Dworkin is not being a bad 'positivist' in the philosophical sense; he is not being a positivist, in that sense, at all. Nor is he being a bad legal positivist, in the sense of supposing that all law is positive law—if I am right that the concept of positive law remains essentialist.

[61] Even if that attitude is acknowledged, with surely unintentional irony, to be imperialistic: Ronald Dworkin, *Law's Empire* (London, 1986), 413.

Use, Mention and Re-use

In what terms, then, can our lost professor reappear?

To identify the word 'law' as a dark performative is to mark it as a word not to be used. Yet it contributes to constituting a rather important social institution, which one needs to be able to refer to in some way. However, for a variety of reasons, attempts to refer to that institution by any other name than 'law' seem to have generated more confusion than they may have resolved.

A means to refer to that institution as 'law' might be built upon Searle's way of distinguishing between 'use' and 'mention'.[62] According to Searle, to say 'This is a table' is to *use* the word 'table', while to say 'The word "table" has five letters' is to *mention* the word 'table'. In the latter case the word in question is 'uttered but not in its normal use'. The word itself is *presented* and then talked about, and that it is to be taken as presented and then talked about rather than used conventionally to refer is indicated by the quotes. But the word is not referred to, nor does it refer to itself.' I agree that the word does not refer to itself.[63] But it does seem to be referred to, just as much as a table is referred to when, using the word 'table', one says 'This table has three legs'. The difference between use and mention is then that, in use, a word refers to something while, when mentioned, it is itself referred to.

In the same way, then, one could mention a performative without committing oneself to its use and hence without doing anything constitutive. Yet, because performatives are constitutive, it is then economical to use the same word to refer to what has been constituted. To say 'Tennis is a ball game' is not to constitute anything. Rather, one is referring to what has already been constituted as the 'game of tennis'. This sort of use of a word might be called a 're-use'.

The re-use is a reference to the result of a previous performative use, whether that use was by myself or by someone else. Ordinarily, the re-use itself neither endorses nor criticizes that result. Nor does it suppose that one has a clear idea of what one is referring to, or even that one is aware that the previous use was performative.

Yet, a dark performative does not leave one at such liberty. This might be the point of the tale about the vicar who, when asked his opinion of sin, said that he was against it. Likewise, to refer to law seems to carry a natural implication that one is in favour of it. That is, indirectly: in that there is no space to be against it, it is of such practical importance that one cannot be neutral with regard to it, and so (by some sort of default) one must be in favour of it. One can oppose particular laws, but there is no space to oppose law as such. If a system of norms is locally called 'law' yet is morally repulsive, the ordinary response is to deny that it really is law.[64]

[62] Searle, *Speech Acts*, n.55 above, 73–6. I change Searle's example, where the word is 'Socrates', to an example about the word 'table', in order to avoid the issue, not relevant here, of proper names.

[63] More likely to the result of a cumulation of previous performative uses, but let's keep it simple.

[64] E.g. Lon L. Fuller, The *Morality of Law*, 2nd edn. (New Haven, 1969).

This position is usually accepted. In comparative law, for example, all sorts of legal systems are discussed and sometimes they are condemned—but the idea that the legal comparatist is not necessarily a supporter of law-in-general simply does not appear. If one does not wish to accept this position, one will have to declare a refusal to let one's own re-use also be a repetition of the original use. One could specify, for instance: 'When I use the word "law" I will refer to its social use'.[65] My redefinition of law here will be such a re-use of the word.

That would be a move from the angle of the signifier. From the angle of the signified, the accompanying move is familiar in social anthropology: for example, in distinguishing between a 'folk' plane which consists of the meanings being studied and the 'analytical' plane which is the framework within which those meanings are studied.[66] The point here is less to introduce a new approach than to point up the apparent difficulty of such distancing within legal science.[67] It is on the other hand to point up a usage that is already common, so that it may receive acknowledgement and commitment.

This is to re-use the word 'law' in a way that does not involve a commitment to law.[68] The word 'law' as re-used refers to its original, ongoing social usage. This is to speak of 'law' in a way that is a reference to a socially held belief. It is a further question, whether that belief is true, valuable or even rational. Hence the word 'law' as re-used can refer to beliefs that compose natural law as well as to those that compose positive law.

65 Paul Bohannan, *Social Anthropology* (New York, 1963), 10–14.

66 As for example in Coleman, n.9 above.

67 E.g. the uncompleted distancing involved in Kelsen's distinction between a legal norm (*Rechtsnorm*) and a legal proposition (*Rechtssatz*): Iain Stewart, 'Kelsen Tomorrow' (1998) 51 *Current Legal Problems* 181, 199–202.

68 A sort of 'detached restatement', Joseph Raz might say: see on 'detached statements', *The Authority of Law* (Oxford, 1979), essay 8; 'The Purity of the Pure Theory' in Richard Tur and William Twining (eds), *Essays on Kelsen* (Oxford, 1986), 79, 90–1.

17

Are Small-Town Lawyers Positivist About the Law?

James Marshall

Devising an Analytical Framework

Putting Law Back into the Sociology of Law

Lawyers are perceived as being endowed with technical and specialized knowledge, and when additionally imbued with an 'idealized' concept of law, are traditionally associated with positivist styles of legal practice. Accredited in this way, they first find then apply law to the facts of a case. Within this perspective, law is seen as independent or autonomous, and may be applied to the facts of a case with certainty and predictability. It follows that from a positivist perspective 'the law is a given',[1] and will be perceived as a 'thing' external to the observer.

In their discussion of legal knowledge Abel and Lewis advance 'the plausible hypothesis ... that practising lawyers are positivists about the law (if often un-self-consciously) and generally deny they are involved in a normative activity'.[2] In proposing this hypothesis the authors invite researchers, as and when they investigate these issues, to emphasize lawyering aspects in their socio-legal enquiries. It is an attempt by the authors to put law back into the sociology of lawyers.

For the purposes of their hypothesis Abel and Lewis define positivism and normative activity in terms of 'what the law is or ought to be',[3] the interpretation that I have adopted for the purposes of this chapter. However, before evaluating the hypothesis' plausibility, it is necessary to address the research gap identified by Abel and Lewis earlier in their argument. 'Within the large and growing literature of the legal profession, there are few studies of what lawyers actually do'. Those that do exist, they continue, though useful 'are prescriptive rather than systematically

[1] R. Cotterrell, *The Sociology of Law: An Introduction*, 2nd edn (London, 1992), 9.

[2] R.L. Abel and P.C. Lewis, 'Putting law back into the Sociology of Lawyers', in R.L. Abel and P.C. Lewis (eds,) *Lawyers in Society: Comparative Theories* (California, 1989), 478, 503.

[3] *Ibid*, 503.

empirical'.[4] Of the various empirical studies of the profession that have been conducted, those of O'Gorman,[5] Sarat and Feltsiner,[6] Cain,[7] Carlin,[8] Rosenthal,[9] and Macaulay[10] are identified by Abel and Lewis as being useful, if limited. The same may be said of others, such as the important study by Heinz and Laumann.[11] A particular failing is that they lack frameworks that are systematic, conceptual, or empirical. Even where such frameworks appear, they require further elaboration.

My chapter attempts to make a contribution to both the issues raised by Abel and Lewis. First, it seeks to design a conceptual framework to inform theoretically the hypothesis they pose: this will involve adapting Bourdieu's concepts of habitus and field conceptually to underpin the notion of positivist lawyering. Secondly, it seeks to design a systematically empirical framework to evaluate the plausibility of the hypothesis: this will involve deploying logistic regression analysis to uncover the extent, if any, of positivist lawyering in small towns.

A Conceptual Framework Derived from a Bourdieusian Perspective

From a sociological, or socio-legal perspective, viewing law solely in legalistic terms produces an incomplete and distorted picture, because such activity is only part of law's function.[12] In Bourdieu's view, law is effective or legitimate only to the extent that it is socially recognized. It follows that the law exerts a force only when viewed in a social context. In this paradigm, social agents write the law rather than the legislature; law agents apply the law rather than individual judges.

Within this view of law, formalist theory is inadequate to account for the processes and practices of the legal world because it concentrates only upon the internal dynamics of concepts and methods. By viewing law as a 'closed' system it ignores the social interaction implicit in these legal processes and practices.[13] And as Abel and Lewis emphasize, 'The role of sociology of law is the recognition that formal law never is an adequate account of behaviour, even that of legal officials' authors to put law back into the sociology of lawyers'.[14] An instrumentalist

[4] Abel and Lewis, n.2, above, 489.

[5] H. O'Gorman, *Lawyers and Matrimonial Cases: A Study of Informal Pressures in Private Practice* (New York, 1963).

[6] A. Sarat and W. Felstiner, 'Law and Strategy in the Divorce Lawyers' Office' (1986) 20 *Law and Society Review* 93.

[7] M. Cain, 'The General Practice Lawyer and the Client: Towards a Radical Conception' in R. Dingwall and P.P. Lewis (eds), *The Sociology of the Professions* (London, 1983) 106.

[8] J. Carlin, *Lawyers on their Own: A Study of Individual Practitioners in Chicago* (New York, 1962).

[9] D. Rosenthal, *Lawyer and Client: Who's in Charge* (New York, 1974).

[10] S. Macaulay, 'Lawyers and Consumer Protection Law' (1979) 14 *Law and Society Review* 115.

[11] J.P. Heinz and E.O. Laumann, *Chicago Lawyers* (New York, 1982).

[12] P. Bourdieu, 'The Force of Law: Toward a Sociology of the Juridical Field' (1987) 38 *Hastings Law Journal* 805, 814.

[13] *Ibid*, 814.

[14] Abel and Lewis, n.2, above, 513.

approach is equally inadequate. This approach treats legal processes and practices as flowing from the economic sub-system, and as a mere reflection of the policies and decisions of dominant groups. This in turn ignores juridical discourse.

Effectively, Bourdieu's characterization for each approach amounts to the absence of the features of the other. So formalism envisages an autonomous legal system lacking an external environment, instrumentalism accounts for power groups but lacks any analysis of legal discourse. To examine the existence or extent of positivist practices, such deficiencies need to be addressed. They may be addressed by devising a framework to synthesize Bourdieu's account of both approaches, by adapting his conceptual tools of habitus and field.

'Habitus is ... the strategy-generating principle enabling agents to cope with the unforeseen and ever-changing situations ... a system of lasting and transposable dispositions which, integrating past experiences, function at every moment as a matrix of perception, appreciation and action and makes possible the achievement of infinitely diversified tasks'.[15] According to Bourdieu the practices within the legal universe, as well as others, are patterned by tradition, education and daily experience of legal custom and professional usage. They operate as a learned yet deep structure of behaviour which Bourdieu terms habitus.[16]

The notion of habitus has been developed by Bourdieu and evolved over a decade. In the process he has variously emphasized and incorporated the notions of posture, disposition, and socialization. Notwithstanding these changes in emphasis, habitus is concerned, essentially, with what actors do. It is therefore a mediating rather than determining concept between structure and activity, a link that connects social structure and practical activity.[17] This linking subsumes dispositions, created through a combination of objective structures and personal history.[18]

The socialization effect of habitus materializes when examined in the context of the concept of field. This concept, specifically the juridical field, affords a means of examining structure and practices within the legal world. It is a way of examining patterns of behaviour and characteristic activities of those engaged in the field when experiencing the magnetic force or pull of the law. In Bourdieu's analysis, the juridical field is an area of norms and practices; norms and practices that constitute the legal process within which lawyers operate.

Juridical resolution of conflicts assumes that as problems become legal problems, their resolution within the legal field is determined by the application of legal norms, 'that is, according to the rules and conventions of the field itself'.[19] Within this process, the principal operating legal norms are the rules of procedure, precedent, and legislation: norms that encapsulate the positivist lawyering concept of

[15] P. Bourdieu, cited in P. Bourdieu and L.J.D. Wacquant, *An Invitation of Reflexive Sociology* (Cambridge, 1992) 18.

[16] R. Terdiman, Translator's Introduction to Bourdieu, n.12, above, 805.

[17] R. Brubaker, 'Rethinking Classical Theory. The Sociological Vision of Pierre Bourdieu' (1985) 14 *Theory and Society* 723.

[18] R. Harker, C. Mahar and C. Wilkes (eds), *An Introduction to the Work of Pierre Bourdieu. The Practice of Theory* (New York, 1990).

[19] Bourdieu, n.12, above, 831.

'what the law is'.[20] According to Bourdieu, in a common law system 'the law is jurisprudential (case law), based almost exclusively on the decisions of courts and the rule of precedent. Such a legal system gives primacy to procedures, which must be fair (a fair trial)'.[21] Together these norms constitute the means by which legal decisions are structured, problems solved, and disputes settled within the legal field. Focusing on these norms facilitates the empirical application of my concept of positivist practices, since these main determinants of legal decisions (case law, statute, and procedural rules), are deployed in my study as variables to operationalize the positivist view of the law as it is.

Placing this concept of positivist practice within an analytical framework enables my approach to treat the law as operating as a continuous process of lawyering interaction not merely as a static phenomenon of legal rules. As such, it will attempt to clarify the operation of rules, norms, and practices, especially in conflict situations, in order to examine the interaction between lawyering and power relations, particularly in relation to clients. Focused in this way, my study forms part of a shift in the study of analysis of law from a system of rules to a process of handling client problems. This shift parallels a general shift in the field to focus more on actors' strategies.[22]

My concept of positivist lawyering can accommodate this shift in emphasis, because it forms part of a post-structuralist analysis. Within a positivist conception, it is the 'rules of law . . . [that] constitute the law, the data which it is the lawyer's task to analyse and order' . . . and in which the 'law is a ' "given"—part of the data experience'.[23] Accordingly, it ignores the role of value in law and the way in which law is established in interpretation and by treating rules as the given data of law, positivism 'assumes a certainty and clarity in rules that is by no means apparent'.[24]

Conversely, my approach is derived from the conceptual framework of Bourdieu, for whom 'predictability and calculability of the law arise' not from *stare decisis* but from the 'consistency and homogeneity of the legal habitus'.[25] Incorporating Bourdieu's concept of habitus, that is socialization, within my post-structuralist perspective, guides my analysis of lawyers as 'legal interpreters',[26] and enables my research to mitigate against a separation of fact and value. A crucial consideration, since 'Law is both fact and value'. [27]

Underlying Practices

Legal scholars and lawyers are aware of the difficulty of applying law to the facts of cases with certainty and predictability. According to Bourdieu, such outcomes are

[20] W. Morrison, *Jurisprudence: From the Greeks to Post Modernism* (London, 1998), 3.

[21] Bourdieu, n.12, above, 822.

[22] Merry and Silbey (1984) in D. Trubek and J. Esser, 'Critical Empiricism in American Legal Studies: Paradox, Program or Pandora's Box?' (1989) 14 *Law and Social Enquiry* 18, 33.

[23] Cotterrell, n.1, above, 9.

[24] *Ibid*, 10.

[25] Bourdieu, n.12, above, 833.

[26] *Ibid*, 818–19.

[27] Cotterrell, n.1, above, 13.

not sustainable, because it is the abstract nature of formal rules that entails indeterminacy. 'The process of abstraction by which legal reasoning produces and elaborates formal legal rules results in norms which purport to regulate social conduct; as Bourdieu correctly points out, their abstract nature entails indeterminacy, since they can only receive substantive content by interaction with other social spheres'.[28]

Indeterminacy of the law has significant implications for the view of lawyers as positivists, since it posits them as agents dealing with an uncertain commodity: the law. A synthesis of positivism and legal uncertainty may result from an analysis of the concept of power, referred to earlier, in particular, its impact upon lawyering practices. According to McCahery and Picciotto, lawyers' source of power is derived from their ability to mediate the application of formal rules to social practices, 'by marshalling varying degrees of technical skills and social influence'.[29] In this process, as against legal scholars who pull the law in the direction of pure theory, legal practitioners are more concerned with specific outcomes, whose orientation is towards a sort of 'casuistry of concrete situations'.[30]

These concrete situations are dealt with in the urgency of practice, with lawyers employing a set of professional tools including books, digests and legal databases.[31] Their professional tool bag will include other matters including communication skills,[32] if they are to incorporate substantive issues such as psychological aspects of social needs of their clients.[33] Accordingly, factors other than the control of legal norms underlie the law's functioning. These underlying factors comprise social, economic, psychological, and linguistic practices. An investigation into positivist lawyering must include these other factors, these underlying practices. Accordingly, Abel and Lewis's exhortation to put law back into the sociology of law must not be at the expense of the law's social context. To examine law in a social context requires an approach capable of systematically and simultaneously incorporating the socialization effects of lawyering that accompany the practices and processes occurring in the juridical field.

The activities of lawyers and social practices of the legal profession revolve around the concept of power. In Bourdieu's view, this notion of power rests on the twin pillars of lawyers and the divergent interests they represent: a dichotomy that will involve internal and external dimensions. Internally, the power relations between lawyers vary according to the respective legal skills they employ. These skills will in turn vary according to the extent of legal research that lawyers undertake.

An examination of the amount of legal research undertaken, and deployment of legal skills, will begin to uncover the nature of and the extent to which lawyers

[28] J. McCahery and S. Picciotto 'Creative Lawyering and the Dynamics of Business Regulation. Professional Competition and Professional Power', in Y. Dezalay and D. Sugarman (eds), *Lawyers, Accountants and the Social Construction of Markets* (London and New York, 1995), 238, 257.

[29] *Ibid*, 252.

[30] Bourdieu, n.12, above, 824.

[31] *Ibid.*

[32] A. Sherr, 'Lawyer and Clients: The first meeting' (1986) 49 *Modern Law Review* 323.

[33] M. Rheinstein (ed.), *Max Weber on Law in Economy and Society* (New York, 1954).

engage in positivist lawyering. Externally, it is the divergent specific interests of particular clients these lawyers represent that move the power relations between lawyers. These power relations are important in determining the real and practical meaning of law. An investigation of the specific power relations between lawyers may commence with the division of labour within the legal profession. As a starting point my study investigates the differences between personal plight areas and commercial work.

An Empirical Framework to Examine Positivist Practices

Legal conceptualization is clearly a starting point for socio-legal enquiry. But questions about the impact of law are empirical. To be comprehensive, socio-legal enquiry requires inter-penetration of theory and practice.[34] It is inadequate merely to follow '... Critical scholars [who] simply study the law or worse ... *study studies* of the law'.[35] It is similarly inadequate solely to follow 'Those scholars who ... felt that it was necessary to leave the library and get "the facts" about what really goes on in areas allegedly affected by legal rules ... Scholars like Frank Remington, from the University of Wisconsin Law School, who argued that criminal law should be studied in the patrol car and ... Stewart Macaulay [who] echoed him by claiming that business contract law should be looked at in the offices of corporate purchasing agents'.[36] It is necessary to have a framework that can accommodate both theory and empiricism, a framework that can accommodate sitting in the library and in the patrol car.

Bourdieu's conceptual approach is instructive in providing a framework for research and directing the methods employed in my survey. By devising an analytical framework to induce interpenetration between theory and empiricism my post-structuralist approach goes beyond Bourdieu's conceptual perspective. In so doing, it provides a platform from which to evaluate Abel and Lewis's hypothesis, a platform from which to question the assumption that practising lawyers are positivists about the law.

I designed a set of dependent and independent variables to examine the inter-relationship between these principal legal norms and associated lawyering styles, since interaction between the variables would ensure interpenetration between theory and empiricism. In this analysis two aspects of the interpretative process were identified for examination. The first focuses upon lawyering practices that involve the construction and interpretation of legal texts. The second focuses upon practices that involve the deployment and application of this interpretation of legal texts. This focus is deliberate: for two reasons. First, it is an attempt to operationalize Bourdieu's conceptual framework, which accepts that the legal

[34] Harker, Mahar and Wilkes, n.18, above.

[35] D.M. Trubek, 'Where the Action Is: Critical Legal Studies and Empiricism' (1984) 36 *Stanford Law Review* 575, 589.

[36] *Ibid*, 583.

process is founded on the interpretation and control of legal texts. The texts, that is, of legal corpus and legal practice. Secondly, adapting the concepts of habitus and juridical field offers an approach that is sufficiently integrated and systematic to accommodate an analysis of the interrelationships necessarily involved in positivist lawyering.

Implementation of the conceptual framework is achieved by operationalizing two aspects of the interpretative process. The first concerns the extent to which lawyers interpret legal texts. This is achieved by measuring the frequency with which research into the texts is undertaken. This relates to the second perspective, which concerns the manner in which lawyers attempt to control the deployment of texts during interpretative struggles. This is achieved by measuring the importance lawyers attribute to judicial precedent and procedural rules during negotiations. Because negotiations may become contentious, this approach is to take account of the tensions that may occur between these norms and social forces. As Bourdieu suggests, there 'is constant tension between the available juridical norms, which appear universal, at least in their form, and the necessarily diverse, even conflicting and contradictory social demand'.[37]

In an attempt to ascertain what lawyers do as legal interpreters of legal texts my empirical study first operationalizes the positivist lawyering practices of procedure, case law and statute as dependent variables. Secondly, it subjects the variables to three distinct forms of analyses; separately, in combination and as counterpoints. Separately, to ascertain the relevant importance of deployment of particular legal norms; together, to investigate the intermingling of procedure and substantive law; and in opposition to each other, to analyse the legal tensions that may arise in juridical conflict when case law and statute posited as counter-acting procedure.

In the preliminary analysis, it is assumed that these positivist practices of consulting or deploying procedural rules, case law, or statutes are undertaken separately. Whilst this provides a one-dimensional picture, it does begin to offer a basis for analysis, given the lack of empirical data as referential yardsticks in this area. A more comprehensive picture emerges by analysing these dependent variables in various permutations. The first combines the pure law areas of judicial precedent, law reports and statute but excludes procedure; the second combines procedure with these pure law areas and the third examines pure law counter-acting procedure. The combined outcome is a comprehensive analysis that results in subjecting positivist behaviour to a series of fifteen logistic regression models.

Four models necessarily emerged for analysis of lawyers' positivist practices, to take account of the two contexts in which case law was examined in addition to consulting statute (see Appendix A). The models were constructed in this manner to articulate the process whereby lawyers interpret legal texts, then deploy the knowledge so gained in subsequent interpretative struggles. The models were

[37] Bourdieu, n.12, above, 841.

combined to investigate empirically the practice of legal interpretation outlined by Bourdieu[38] and Dezalay.[39]

This approach proved justified since the explanatory powers of these logistic regression models increased as the combinations and complexity of permutations increase. When the positivist areas were examined singly, excluding procedure, the explanatory power of the four models utilized averaged 67 per cent, with a high of 69 per cent. When the positivist areas were combined, whilst the explanatory power of the four models remained at 69 per cent, the high increased to 71 per cent. When procedure was added, the average for the four models increased to 77 per cent, with a high of 82 per cent. When procedure was analysed in opposition to legal purity, the average for the four models further increased to 79 per cent, with a high of 84 per cent. Confirmation, perhaps, that my study is systematically empirical.

The Findings: A Measure of Lawyering Positivism

The Role of Procedure and the Significance of Community Networks

My analysis of the interaction between lawyers' socialization and their deployment of legal norms illuminates a particular role for procedure, with lawyers born outside Lancaster or Morecambe being three times more likely to view procedural rules as important than other lawyers (.08) (See Appendix B Table 1). Lawyers originating from elsewhere who subsequently come to work in the area are less likely to have social networks at their disposal, and accordingly, they are more disposed to rely on procedural rules. These lawyers will take time to become familiar with local practice and even more time to establish working relationships with those in the legal community. Accordingly, they may choose to present themselves as having expertise as legal technicians, by 'going by the book'. Those born locally may be more predisposed to use other than positivist practices for maintaining relations and doing business. They may rely therefore, on the underlying factors explored elsewhere in my chapter.

My analysis indicates a wider ambit for these 'insider/outsider' relations than earlier research that has been narrowly focused and often only addresses one field of law. For example, the work of Sarat and Felstiner found a repeated emphasis on insider status, reputation, and local connections, with divorce lawyers (to whom the study was confined), generally presenting themselves as well-connected insiders.[40] They regarded being known and respected as more valuable than being seen as expert legal technicians. Their clients' best chance of success, given the uncertainty of the legal process, rested upon those who were familiar with local

[38] Bourdieu, n.12, above.

[39] Y. Dezalay, 'From Mediation to Pure Law: Practice and Scholarly Representation within the Legal Sphere' (1986) 14 *International Journal of the Sociology of Law* 89.

[40] A. Sarat and W. L. Felstiner, 'Law and Strategy in the Divorce Lawyers' Office' (1986) 20 *Law and Society Review* 93.

practices and who had working relationships with those who wielded local power. My study suggests that outsiders use legal expertise and legal know-how as strategies to establish a foothold in the juridical field irrespective of particular areas of law.

A foothold that may, in time, establish these lawyers as part of the local legal community. For insiders there is a strong local network of lawyers producing a 'local community spirit': a community spirit that is sustained by informality with discussions proceeding on first name terms (Lawyer (hereafter L) 12, see Appendix C). These informal relationships contribute to the informal practices that Lancaster and Morecambe lawyers engage in, including the likelihood of delays to be overlooked. These informal relationships and practices produce an environment in which 'you don't jump on colleagues if they are late' (L18). There is considerable evidence in Lancaster and Morecambe of lawyers 'helping each other out' (L4) by 'oiling the wheels' of practice (Ls4, 9, 12, and 15). These practices will include, for example, 'defence lawyers obtaining evidence from the prosecution they are not necessarily entitled to' (L7), 'defence lawyers collaborating with each other and deciding sets of questions each will put to the prosecution witnesses' (L7), 'letting the other side have keys before completion' (Ls12, 16), and 'extending completion dates' (L6).

Not all lawyers approve of this 'old boys' network'. A senior partner, though born locally and practising in the family firm, and himself sometimes involved in these practices, expressed a preference for the more detached, objective practices operating in larger cities, such as Manchester (L3). Having worked there previously he considered that the detachment offered a more business-like and efficient service. In this working environment, lawyers who make mistakes or cause delays hear nothing until the mishap is utilized by the other side. His main reservation about the 'old boys' network' concerns the calling in of favours at later dates. He was recently involved in a property matter in which the lawyer for the other side obligingly put the matter to the 'top of his pile'. He anticipates that this lawyer will expect a reciprocal favour in due course. My survey suggests that community influence is as strong in the North of England as it is in the South.[41] Or as in the USA, where Landon's study indicates that in small cities in the State of Missouri, USA, lawyers with stronger local roots are more likely to call upon social and cultural means of dealing with legal matters rather than arcane knowledge.[42]

Positivist Lawyering, Legal Purity, and Division of Labour

Professional purity is the ability to exclude non-professional issues or irrelevant professional issues from practice. Intraprofessional status, for Abbott,[43] is a function

[41] M. Blacksell, K. Economides and C. Watkins, *Justice Outside the City* (London, 1991).

[42] D.D. Landon, *Country Lawyers: The Impact of Context on Professional Practice* (New York, 1990).

[43] A. Abbott, *The System of Professions. An Essay on the Division of Expert Labor* (Chicago, 1988), 823.

of professional purity. Within a given profession, the highest status professionals deal with issues in which human complexity and difficulty have been removed. The lowest status professionals deal with problems from which human complexities are not, or cannot, be removed. In the case of lawyers this would appear to involve personal plight areas, for example, and family law and crime as against company work. In Lancaster and Morecambe family lawyers (.02) and crimnal lawyers (.03) regard concern for emotional as well as legal issues as an important job attribute, whereas lawyers undertaking commercial work do not.

Professional purity, therefore, is the ability to exclude non-professional issues, or irrelevant professional issues, from professional practice. Successive purification is the norm of professional life, with professional purity being the basis of intraprofessional status. In the early stages of purification, there is a separation of human concerns from legal concerns. Successive purification will be accompanied by a further narrowing of legal concerns. This may result in a separation of procedural and substantive issues. It is hypothesized that the separation corresponds to a graduation of legal status. Accordingly, the higher status lawyer will deal less with technical and procedural matters.

Dezalay defines pure law as 'scholarly representation of legal practice', with the road to achieve legal purity is via case law.[44] 'The royal road for this theorisation of lawyers' intervention as mediators in social relations is case law'.[45] Whilst case law is vital to the process of legality and hence for the purity of law, lawyers do not speak in the name of the law with 'the same title or credibility'.[46] Dezalay devised this concept of legal purity in terms of lawyers maintaining work for themselves in competition with other occupations. Lawyers stress and employ legal techniques in this competitive process, taking pains to distinguish legality and to purify the law. And according to Dezalay, deployment of law in this way is plausible as against competitors from other occupations, but not amongst fellow lawyers.

Interpretative struggles will occur in a whole range of fields of law. Instances of such struggles were referred to during my personal interviews in a variety of fields, including personal injury, family, crime, and corporate work. But in these combined instances, only one respondent could recall legal authorities; a criminal lawyer (L7). If the juridical field is the site of competition for the interpretation of legal texts, then whilst all lawyers in Lancaster and Morecambe may visit this site from time to time, the pattern that emerges from my analysis is one of fairly persistent absenteeism. My analysis, which indicates a pattern of replacing the interpretation of legal texts with social and other practices to resolve legal problems, questions the assumption that lawyers are positivists about the law. At the very least it suggests variability in the extent to which lawyers interpret and then deploy the law.

Qualitative data from my personal interviews provides some evidence that positivist practices operate in personal plight areas. One respondent informed me

[44] Dezalay, n.39, above, 90. [45] *Ibid*, 91.
[46] *Ibid.*

of how he had been wrong-footed by the other side (L5). He had not realized the onus of proof regarding the multiplier in substantiating special damages in personal injury cases was on the claimant (L5). Conversely, another respondent had successfully argued, in a matrimonial matter, a legal point involving the application of the *Calderbank* ruling (L1).[47]

Since lawyers in Lancaster and Morecambe are as likely to deploy case law/legal purity against fellow lawyers as against other occupations, my findings, on this point, appear at odds with those of Dezalay. The deployment of legal purity in some of these instances may be a further ramification of the tension between insiders and outsiders. Lawyers from Lancaster and Morecambe were unanimous that relations with outside lawyers were more detached and more likely to be contentious. In this detached, strained atmosphere, an absence of social networks with outside lawyers may cause positivist practices to come to the fore.

Lawyers who Know next to Nothing about Legislation

Whilst the qualitative data from my personal interviews identified positivist practices operating sporadically in personal plight areas, my Logistic Regression analysis suggested a different pattern. Negative findings consistently emerge in personal injury and family law indicating a reduced likelihood of positivist lawyering in those areas. Earlier I mentioned Abel and Lewis's reference to the empirical work of Macaulay as 'useful if limited': limited in that the work is confined to consumer law. In his study Macaulay states that: 'We found that most lawyers in Wisconsin knew next to nothing about the Magnusson-Moss Warranty Act—many had never heard of it'.[48]

My survey shows the lack of knowledge of statute law is not confined to consumer law. There are other legal areas where lawyers know 'next to nothing' about legislation; in personal injury for example, where personal injury lawyers in Lancaster and Morecambe were 73 per cent less likely to research statute law than other lawyers (.01). Personal injury lawyers are also 60 per cent less likely to consult, and therefore interpret, law reports and statute (.07) Model 1; 82 per cent less likely to consult and interpret statute, and to regard judicial precedent as important (.007) Model 3; 89 per cent less likely to consult and interpret law reports and statute and deploy judicial precedent (.007) Model 4 (Appendix B Table 2); and 75 per cent less likely to consult and interpret law reports and statute, and deploy procedural rules (.11) (Appendix B Table 3). Where personal injury lawyers determine client outcomes, it is not by virtue of a comprehensive interpretation of a series of legal texts. Personal injury lawyers do not appear to be high in the 'market of legal interpretation'.[49]

[47] Acting for a woman petitioner, he successfully pleaded that if a husband fails to make an offer in settlement, then his client is entitled to costs.

[48] S. Macaulay, 'Lawyers and Consumer Protection Laws' (1979) 14 *Law and Society Review* 115.

[49] Dezalay, n.39, above, 93.

My analysis appears to provide quantitative grounds to affirm Genn's qualitative study in 1987 of personal injury lawyers.[50] Whilst one respondent in her study indicated that to be successful in personal injury litigation the most important quality of a claimant's solicitor was an 'understanding of law and procedure', Genn's thesis suggests the extent of this understanding is neither comprehensive nor consistent.[51] Her findings appear to suggest a dearth of application of legal knowledge, especially substantive law, and particularly in cases involving road accidents.

'In motor accident cases almost no attention whatsoever is paid to law reports because each case is decided upon its own facts and there is no such thing as a binding precedent . . . it's not a matter of law, road traffic, it really isn't'.[52] In these cases, 'precedents are of little assistance and the major task facing the [lawyer] in insurance law is to determine on the basis of experience, what is often termed "common sense", and the provisions of the Highway Code, whether the negligent party falls below the standard of the reasonable driver'.[53]

Genn's study does however highlight differences according to fields of law, in particular between road accidents and employment law. According to counsel specializing in personal injury, 'Law reports play a much greater part in employers' liability, particularly in assessing breach of statutory duty or breach of the regulations'.[54] From a claimant's perspective, personal injury cases like matrimonial cases, tend to be one-offs, since the client's objects do not usually include a requirement to establish judicial precedents for future reference.[55]

For one personal injury lawyer in Lancaster and Morecambe, clients' objects may be 'condensed into four words, how long and how much' (L5). Within this framework he pursues each case on the assumption that it will go to court. Adopting this essentially practical approach increases the likelihood that defendants, normally insurance companies, will employ a lawyer. If defendants do employ a lawyer, they will necessarily increase their costs, and the respondent's expectation is that this will encourage defendants to settle, reducing the need for positivist lawyering.

Pragmatic factors such as cost will therefore have an impact upon positivist lawyering. Of particular significance is whether the client is legally aided, since having a legally aided client 'puts the other side on notice' (L5). In these circumstances, they are more likely to settle, 'aware that your client has the money to pursue the case' (L5) and so reduce positivist lawyering. Where the client is without legal aid, the defendants usually employ delaying tactics, which may include legal argument, to drain the claimant's financial resources, hoping the case will fold (L5).

[50] H. Genn, *Hard Bargaining: Out of court settlement in personal injury actions* (Oxford, 1987).
[51] *Ibid*, 45. [52] Genn, n.50, above, 73. [53] *Ibid*, 75. [54] *Ibid*, 74.
[55] R.J. Mnookin and L. Kornhauser, 'Bargaining in the Shadow of the Law: The Case of Divorce' (1979) 88 *Yale Law Journal* 950.

Positivist Lawyering as a Function of Lawyering Business

Like personal injury lawyers, family lawyers in Lancaster and Morecambe appear to attach little significance to positivist practices, since my regression analysis indicates that there are no positive associations between family lawyers and positivist practices. Conversely, my findings indicate that family lawyers are negatively associated with positivist practices. Family lawyers are 73 per cent less likely to regard procedure as important when negotiating with the other side (.08) (see Apppendix B Table 1). When lawyering style is characterized as having pure areas of law added to procedure, they are even more negatively associated with positivist practices, the significance level increasing from (.08) to (.009) (Apppendix B Table 1).

It was hypothesized that this negative association between family law and positivist lawyering was due to gender since female lawyers, as a group, eschew engagement in positivist practices. Female lawyers are 86 per cent less likely to engage in the composite set of positivist practices comprising consulting law reports, to ascertain and deploy judicial precedent, together with procedural rules (.009). However, no statistically significant association is revealed when controlling for gender.

Whilst the figures are not statistically significant, a higher proportion (77 per cent: 23 per cent) of women lawyers in Lancaster and Morecambe undertake family law work than male lawyers (65 per cent: 35 per cent). Women lawyers comprise only 19 per cent of lawyers in Lancaster and Morecambe, but are a tightly knit group. Discrimination appears to have been experienced by those women lawyers who were the first to come to work in Lancaster and Morecambe. They were relieved when other women lawyers came to work in the area because of the support their presence brought. Over time the group has become more formalized, and currently is a forum for discussing legal issues.

It may be that changing circumstances require lawyers to be more positivist; a change in circumstance that involves, for example, a risk of loss of business. A decade ago, lawyers in Lancaster and Morecambe felt their supply of divorce business would be adversely affected following the introduction of the Children Act 1989. Under the Act, such cases are to be dealt with by probation officers and welfare officers, with lawyers excluded. A reduction of business for family lawyers appeared a necessary consequence. By adopting the appropriate lawyering practices to accommodate the conciliatory mechanism established under the Act, family lawyers were able to retain public confidence at a practical level and so sustain this jurisdiction.

These positivist practices were accompanied by other non-legal practices. To foster the process of conciliation, family lawyers in Lancaster and Morecambe took up membership of professional associations such as the Childcare Group, consisting of probation officers, welfare officers, clerks of the magistrates' court, and lawyers (L13). Family lawyers used this interrelated organizational framework to ensure speedy and amicable resolution of matrimonial matters and to sustain matrimonial business. It would appear therefore, that positivist lawyering practices and non-legal practices including conciliatory behaviour in inter-professional activity, and membership of professional associations have each contributed to sustaining family lawyers' control of this jurisdiction.

Positivist Lawyering in Crime?

In Lancaster and Morecambe criminal lawyers are positively associated with positivist lawyering, being over three times more likely to consult law reports and statute and deploy judicial precedent than other lawyers (.08) (Apppendix B Table 2). This appears at odds with current criminal law research, since positivist lawyering in criminal law appears to be the preserve of barristers.[56] Articled clerks (now trainee lawyers),[57] who were interviewed in this study conducted by McConville et al., regarded dealing with the law as a task for barristers, with solicitors handling only 'mundane matters'.[58] The articled clerks also perceived that there was 'very little law involved in crime. If it needs [advice] on points of law, we don't do that, we just pass it on to a barrister'.[59] Nor does positivist lawyering appear to be an essential ingredient for survival in the criminal law process. Defence lawyers together with magistrates' courts, are concerned more with processing defendants than involvement in an adversary system, with 'criminal defence practices geared, in co-operation with other elements of the system, towards the routine production of guilty pleas'.[60]

What might account for the apparent difference, then, in Lancaster and Morecambe criminal lawyers? For sampling purposes criminal lawyers in Lancaster and Morecambe are representative of criminal lawyers nationally (see Appendix B Table 5). Whilst 8 per cent of lawyers in Lancaster and Morecambe comprise a small number, that small group may form part of that politically motivated band of lawyers who fight for their clients' cause.[61]

Do criminal lawyers in Lancaster and Morecambe fight for their clients' cause? A move toward an affirmative answer may begin with my quantitative data, which indicated that only criminal lawyers identified themselves in Lancaster and Morecambe as being concerned with remedying the injustices in society. They are almost three times more likely than other lawyers to regard remedying injustices

[56] M. McConville, J. Hodson, L. Bridges, and A. Pavlovic, *Standing Accused: The Organisation and Practices of Criminal Defence Lawyers in Britain* (Oxford, 1994).

[57] The standard route to qualification as a solicitor comprises an academic stage, usually a law degree, a professional stage, a one-year legal practice course (LPC), then a vocational stage. Presently, this vocational stage takes the form of a term as trainee solicitor and, like the barrister's pupillage, is essentially an apprenticeship. Previously, this vocational stage was termed articles, with trainees referred to as articled clerks.

[58] McConville et al., n.56, above, 51.

[59] *Ibid.*

[60] *Ibid*, 71.

[61] *Ibid*, 82.

in society as an essential attribute of their job (.05). Further evidence of such a commitment appears to emerge from my interviews. In this instance the data came not from the lawyer personally, but by proxy from two of her law colleagues. This scenario arose because unfortunately on several occasions my scheduled interview appointments with her had to be cancelled, and ultimately even my extended time-scale for interviews expired before I had an opportunity to meet with her.

Both her work colleagues, whom I did interview, referred to her as particularly committed to clients, a commitment that extended to refusing to cross-sell work on behalf of the firm. Since this practice impacted upon the firm's potential profits it was one with which both disagreed (L14). This did not affect the high regard in which she was held, particularly in view of the time and commitment they knew she devoted to out-of-office duties as member of various bodies and organizations related to criminal work. Possibly a criminal lawyer prepared to fight for her clients' causes?

Evidence of creative use of law also appears from my interviews. A respondent specializing in criminal law, whilst acknowledging the magistrates' court is a 'factual rather than legal arena', deploys law on behalf of clients (L7). He referred to two cases, both involving admissibility of evidence, in which he believed he demonstrated legal creativity. In one such case his argument, that reference by the prosecution to the wrong formula for a blood sample rendered the sample inadmissible, was upheld on appeal in the Crown Court. In this process criminal lawyers can find that criminal clients with convictions, 'jailhouse lawyers'[62] can be quite learned in the law (L7).

If they are fighting for clients' causes and making creative use of law, does the discrepancy referred to above arise because criminal lawyers in Lancaster and Morecambe act both as positivists and normativists? To pursue this broader aspect of the hypothesis of Abel and Lewis, as to the mutual exclusivity of normative and positivist lawyering, may require further analysis, possibly comparative analysis. Confined in the first instance to criminal lawyers, it could involve comparing lawyers in Lancaster and Morecambe either with lawyers drawn from another small town or from a large city.

Why does Positivist Lawyering Occur in Corporate Work?

The classical view of the legal process regarded procedure as transparent, in that it did not add to or subtract anything from the system.[63] According to Trubek, the traditional view was that procedure was neutral, and was a way to facilitate the application of legal rules to the facts of the case. It was the legal realists who set a separate agenda. 'Legal Realism ushered in a new era in legal thought. The idea of

[62] McCahery and Picciotto, n.28, above, 255.

[63] D.M. Trubek, 'The Handmaiden's Revenge: On reading and using the newer sociology of civil procedure' (1958) 51 *Law and Contemporary Problems* 111.

procedural transparency ... ceased to make sense. In its place came the forthright recognition that procedure and substance were inextricably intertwined'. [64]

Unfortunately, we know little of the nature of this intertwining between substantive law and procedure, and what we do know appears contradictory. For example, Brazil, suggests much abuse of the process of discovery by lawyers, at least in the USA.[65] Conversely, Trubek et al. suggest relatively little discovery occurs in the ordinary lawsuit.[66] No evidence of discovery was found in over half of the 1,649 cases they investigated, and it was used intensively in only a small fraction of those cases. [67]

In this uncertainty, my empirical study attempts to uncover possible consequences of combining procedure with substantive law. Lord Mackay provides support for this approach. 'Procedure does not stand in a vacuum. Rather, it is the means by which we enable the substantive law to take effect. In that sense, it is the substantive law that sets the task to be undertaken by the courts and which largely determines the procedural needs. If the substantive law is fragmented or inconsistent so, almost inevitably, will be the procedure'.[68] Accordingly, procedure was added to the same combinations of legally pure areas that comprised the four earlier models, thereby creating four further models for analysis.

In my study, an attempt was made to capture the tension, if any, between substantive law and procedure in order to establish in what way, if any, it affected lawyers as positivists. In this part of my analysis, the focus is upon the distinction between rules of procedure on the one hand, and substantive areas of pure law on the other. To maintain consistency with earlier analysis, the variables are examined in two sets of circumstances, separately and in combination. This analysis indicates that lawyers undertaking commercial work are positively associated with legal purity. When lawyers were asked to assess the importance of case law and statute, relative to procedure when advising clients, lawyers undertaking commercial work were ten times more likely to regard case law and statute as the more important (.03).

Are these then the legal purists that Dezalay has in mind? If so, why are they legal purists? Guidance may emerge from other related differences such as their specialism and participation in continuing legal education. Statistical association with these practices suggests that positivist lawyering by corporate lawyers may be motivated by their desire to develop corporate clients. A greater propensity to specialize (.008) and undertake continuing legal education (.008) may have arisen in order to meet the increased competition for corporate work. By specializing and keeping abreast of legal changes, commercial lawyers may be more able to remain

[64] Trubek, n.63, above, 116.

[65] W. Brazil, 'The Adversarial Character of Civil Discovery: A Critique and Proposals for Change' (1978) 31 *Vanderbilt. Law Review* 1295.

[66] D.M. Trubek, A. Sarat, W.L. Felstiner, H.M. Kritzer, and J.B. Grossman, 'The Costs of Ordinary Litigation' (1983–84) 31 *UCLA Law Review* 72.

[67] *Ibid*, 81, 90.

[68] Lord Mackay of Clashfern, 'Litigation in the 1990s' (1991) 54 *Modern Law Review* 171, 179.

ahead of competitors, resist competition from other professionals, retain commercial clients, and generate fresh business.

Lawyers in Lancaster and Morecambe have extended positivist lawyering practices by applying abstracted legal principles from existing practical professional knowledge to generate new jurisdictions and also to facilitate integration of various types of work. For example, one firm earmarked three areas of work in the commercial law field were for integration; employment law, financial services, and taxation. The accompanying strategy involved identifying an existing area of work to be linked or connected to new business (L14: Firm H—See Appendix D).

These lawyers identified taxation as their base area, to be extended, subsequently, to financial services then to commercial law. By extrapolating legal principles from inheritance tax law, they broadened their client base. In this positivist lawyering practice, lawyers engage in interpreting texts by 'adapting (legal) sources to new circumstances by discovering new possibilities within them'.[69]

These positivist lawyering practices are just as likely to be deployed to retain existing business. New regulations enacted under the Financial Services Act 1986 were to change in 1996, thereby preventing lawyers from recommending financial advisers to clients by way of referral. These lawyers in Lancaster and Morecambe had to decide whether or not to embark upon this business, since passing on the work to financial advisers would have to end. In deciding to become involved, these lawyers embraced a commitment to continuing education as part of their overall strategy. This required a senior partner to attend training courses on Financial Services Law. Positivist lawyering is clearly linked to the practical necessity of getting the job done,[70] and in so doing, stimulating demand in new legal areas.

Conclusion

In this chapter I sought to provide a systematic empirical framework to investigate the assumption that practising lawyers are positivist about the law. My attempt may have met with some success: for two reasons. First, findings which link procedural practices with outsiders, link a dearth of positivist lawyering with some personal plight areas, and link positivist corporate lawyering with business mentality, appear to emerge respectively from my three-pronged analytical assault on positivist lawyering practices. Therefore the findings regarding outsiders emerge from analysing procedure separately, the findings regarding personal plight lawyers emerge from analysing positivist practices in combination, and the findings regarding corporate lawyers emerge from analysing substantive law and procedure as counterpoints. Secondly, this three-pronged analytical onslaught appears to be

[69] Bourdieu, n.12, above, 826–7. [70] Abbott, n.43, above.

further vindicated since the amount of variability in the data explained increased as the analysis became more complex.

And by being theoretically informed and empirically grounded my approach strove to achieve interpenetration of concept and empiricism. In an attempt to encapsulate what lawyers do as legal interpreters, my empirical analysis distinguished between two aspects of the lawyering interpretative process, namely the frequency with which lawyers consult and interpret legal texts and the importance they attach to the deployment of these texts. By operationalizing these aspects I attempt to illuminate the interaction between the norms of the legal process and the socialization of lawyers, and may have uncovered interactive interpretative processes at work in terms of lawyers' socialization and the deployment of procedural practices by lawyers as outsiders. In particular the different practices that appear to be employed by lawyers originating from elsewhere who, being less likely to have social networks at their disposal, are more disposed to rely on rules and to present themselves as legal technicians.

Combining quantitative with qualitative analytical techniques appears to have provided a sharper, more enhanced picture of positivist lawyering. Whilst personal interview revealed sporadic deployment of positivist practices, logistic regression analysis revealed a dearth of such practices in some personal plight areas. My analysis of the various permutations of positivist practices suggests that when some personal plight lawyers achieve desired outcomes for their clients, it is not by virtue of a comprehensive interpretation of a series of texts. For family lawyers it appears that underlying psychological factors are more important than the deployment of procedural rules to determine clients' outcomes.

In contrast, corporate lawyers are legal positivists. This is especially so in terms of substantive law, where corporate lawyers extrapolate legal principles from one legal area to another and attend law courses to keep abreast of statutory change. My survey suggests that the extent of positivist practices deployed by these lawyers may be associated with the intensity of competition for corporate clientele.

In terms of positivist lawyering, criminal lawyers in Lancaster and Morecambe sit uneasily in the conventional divide between personal plight areas and corporate work. Is this because they form part of McConville et al.'s politically motivated group of lawyers identified with causes? If they do, is this a group of lawyers who combine positivist practices with normative aspirations? And if so, is this an area for further research?

Appendix A

Models deployed in positivist lawyering

Model 1 consulting law reports and statutes to increase knowledge of a particular subject area prior to advising clients, or in preparation for negotiating with the other side.

Model 2 consulting law reports to ascertain and employ judicial precedent during negotiations with the other side.

Model 3 consulting statute to augment judicial precedent from previous research during negotiations with the other side.

Model 4 consulting statute in addition to law reports when employing judicial precedent in negotiating with the other side.

Appendix B

Table 1. Reliance on procedure (best fitting logistic regression (LR) model estimating the effects of explanatory variables on the importance of procedure when negotiating with the other side)

Explanatory Variables		Sig	Exp
Family Law		.08	.27
Degree		.06	.21
Age (Lawyers – 40 years +)		.008	.11
Birth (Elsewhere)		.08	3.17
Amount of variation explained by the model	69%		
N – 62			

Table 2. Legal purity (best fitting LR models estimating the effects of explanatory variables regarding combined areas of legal purity)

Explanatory Variables	LR&Stat		JP&LR		JP&Stat		JP&LR &Stat	
	Sig	Exp	Sig	Exp	Sig	Exp	Sig	Exp
Legal Aid Work			.03	.32				
Personal Injury	.07	.40			.007	.18	.007	.11
Place of Articles	.07	2.47					.04	3.4
Crime							.08	3.3
Conveyancing							.05	5.4
Amount of variation explained by the model	68%		65%		65%		71%	
	N = 71		N = 62		N = 62		N = 62	

KEY

JP&LR	Judicial Precedent and Law Reports
LR & Stat	Law Reports and Statutes
JP & Stat	Judicial Precedent and Statutes
JP&LR&Stat	Judicial Precedent and Law Reports and Statutes

Table 3. Combining procedure and legal purity (best fitting LR model estimating the effects of explanatory variables when intermingling procedure with legally pure areas)

Explanatory Variables	Pro&LR &JP&Stat		Pro&LR &Stat		Pro&LR &JP		Pro&JP Stat	
	Sig	Exp	Sig	Exp	Sig	Exp	Sig	Exp
Repeat clients	.09	.05	.02	5.7				
First-time clients	.10	.07			.10	3.4		
Commercial work	.07	.27						
Legal aid work	.007	.13					.04	.16
Worked for another firm	.08	.28						
Working in Lancaster	.08	3.2						
Firms' size (6+ lawyers)			.06	4.1			.08	3.5
Personal injury			.11	.25				
Length of time in practice			.06	.19			.04	.15
Place of Articles			.006	9.3			.01	7.0
Family law					.009	.14		
Probate							.08	4.0
Amount of variation explained by the model	75% N = 61		71% N = 62		79% N = 61		82% N = 61	

KEY

Pro = Procedure
LR = Law reports
JP = Judicial Precedent
Stat = Statute

Table 4. Contrasting pure law and procedure (best fitting LR model estimating the effects of explanatory variables when contrasting combined areas of legal purity with procedure)

Explanatory Variables		JP&Stat v Pro	
		Sig	Exp
Firms' size (6+ lawyers)		.002	9.2
Company clients		.03	.09
Repeat clients		.07	.06
First-time clients		.12	.06
Conveyancing		.01	31.2
Commercial work		.03	10.1
Probate		.005	.03
Family		.05	.12
Personal injury		.06	.13
Crime		.03	8.9
Length of time in practice		.005	.01
Place of Articles		.04	.18
Age (Lawyers –40 years +)		.01	14.2
Working in Lancaster		.07	.20
Amount of variation explained by the model	77%		
N = 69			

KEY
JP = Judicial precedent
Stat = Statute
Pro = Procedure

Table 5. Lawyers' work

	Chambers and Harwood (1990)	My Study (1992)
Residential conveyancing	18%	24%
Commercial property	18%	11%
Commercial work	21%	8%
Probate	7%	16%
Family	11%	17%
Personal injury	7%	11%
Crime	7%	8%
Other	11%	5%
	100%	100%

Appendix C

Profiles of lawyers who participated in the personal interviews

Lawyer	Position	Legal Work	Size of Firm	Gender	Age
Lawyer 1	Assistant solicitor	Civil litigation 60% family 30% personal injury	6 plus lawyers	Male	20–39 years
Lawyer 2	Profit sharing partner	Specialist 65% personal injury	6 plus lawyers	Male	20–39 years
Lawyer 3	Profit sharing partner	Specialist 45% commercial work 25% commercial property	1–5 lawyers	Male	20–39 years
Lawyer 4	Profit sharing partner	Mainly commercial property (50%)	1–5 lawyers	Male	40 plus years
Lawyer 5	Profit sharing partner	Civil litigation 65% mainly personal injury	6 plus lawyers	Male	20–39 years
Lawyer 6	Profit sharing partner	Generalist (mainly conveyancing)	6 plus lawyers	Male	20–39 years
Lawyer 7	Profit sharing partner	Generalist 30% crime 30% civil litigation	6 plus lawyers	Male	40 plus years
Lawyer 8	Profit sharing partner	Generalist – conveyancing, probate, crime, civil litigation	1–5 lawyers	Male	40 plus years
Lawyer 9	Profit sharing partner	Specialist – conveyancing	1–5 lawyers	Female	40 plus years
Lawyer 10	Sole practitioner	Generalist – mainly conveyancing and probate	Sole practitioner	Male	20–39 years
Lawyer 11	Assistant solicitor	Specialist – family	1–5 lawyers	Female	20–39 years
Lawyer 12	Salaried partner	Generalist – mainly conveyancing, but also probate and civil litigation	6 plus lawyers	Male	20–39 years
Lawyer 13	Profit sharing partner	Specialist 75% family	6 plus lawyers	Female	20–39 years
Lawyer 14	Profit sharing partner	Specialist commercial work	6 plus lawyers	Male	40 plus years
Lawyer 15	Salaried partner	Civil litigation 40% family 40% personal injury	6 plus lawyers	Female	20–39 years
Lawyer 16	Sole practitioner	Specialist – conveyancing	Sole practitioner	Male	40 plus years
Lawyer 17	Profit sharing partner	Generalist – but mainly commercial work	6 plus lawyers	Male	20–39 years
Lawyer 18	Profit sharing partner	Civil litigation 30% family 40% personal injury	6 plus lawyers	Male	40 plus years
Lawyer 19	Assistant solicitor	Generalist – conveyancing, probate, crime, civil litigation, and commercial work	6 plus lawyers	Male	20–39 years

Appendix D

Firms of lawyers interviewed

Firms	Number of Solicitors	Number of Branches	Location of Firm or Main Branch
Firm A	Less than 6	None	Morecambe
Firm B	More than 6	One	Lancaster
Firm C	More than 6	More than 3	Morecambe
Firm D	Less than 6	None	Lancaster
Firm E	Sole practitioner	None	Morecambe
Firm F	Sole practitioner	None	Lancaster
Firm G	Less than 6	Three	Morecambe
Firm H	More than 6	Three	Lancaster
Firm I	More than 6	None	Lancaster
Firm J	Less than 6	None	Morecambe

18

Law, Norms, and Lay Tribunals

Joseph Sanders

Introduction: Lay Tribunals and Norms

In 2004 the Japanese, who had abandoned juries in both criminal and civil cases during World War II, moved back in the other direction. The Diet recently enacted a statute that will create a mixed tribunal in criminal cases.[1] In typical Japanese fashion, the new system will go into effect in 2009 after a five-year 'get-acquainted period'. At that time, most major felony cases will be decided by a panel of three professional judges and six lay people that will decide both guilt and punishment. Each member of the panel will have one vote.[2] The system is modelled in large part on the German model.[3]

Japan is not the only country that recently has introduced lay decision makers into its judicial process. In the 1990s, both Spain and Russia reintroduced trial by jury in some cases.[4] These societies join a long list of countries that have some form

[1] Reinstating a Jury System, Japan Times 29 May 2004 WL 56378342. A lay assessor system also exists in China. Di Jiang, 'Judicial Reform in China: New Regulations for a Lay Assessor System' (2000) 9 *Pacific Rim Law and Policy Journal* 569.

[2] Joseph J. Kodner, 'Re-Introducing Lay Participation to Japanese Criminal Cases: An Awkward Yet Necessary Step' (2003) 2 *Washington University Global Studies Law Review* 231, 246.

[3] In the German system this consists of one professional judge and two lay judges in misdemeanour and non-serious felony cases. In serious felony cases, the panel consists of two lay judges and two or three professional judges. In the German case, as in Japan, because convictions require a two-thirds majority, the lay judges can always force an acquittal. Volker F. Krey, 'Characteristic Features of German Criminal Proceedings—An Alternative to the Criminal Procedure Law of the United States?' (1999) 21 *Loyola Los Angeles International and Comparative Law Review* 591. Unlike the proposed Japanese lay jurors, who will be randomly selected from a pool of eligible voters, German lay jurors are selected by local committees to serve for four-year terms. Therefore, they have the experience of being repeat players, who may hear multiple cases during their term of office.

[4] Stephen Thaman, 'Europe's New Jury Systems: The Cases of Spain and Russia,' in Neil Vidmar (ed.), *World Jury Systems* (New York, 2000), 319. In Russia the jury is comprised of twelve individuals; in Spain, nine individuals. In both cases, jurors are chosen from voter registration lists. *Ibid*, 326. As in the case of the United States and England, the jury decides the case out of the presence of the judge. However, both systems restrict the power of the jury more than is the case in the United States. For example, in the Russian case, the new system moves the criminal trial in a more adversarial direction, but judges continue to play an inquisitorial role. *Ibid*, 336. Moreover, in both systems jurors are not permitted to return a general verdict of guilty or not guilty. Rather, they are asked to respond

of jury or mixed tribunal, at least in criminal cases.[5] Undoubtedly, decision-making with juries or other types of lay participation is less efficient than decisions made by judges alone. However, other benefits of lay participation are thought to more than compensate for this cost. What are those benefits? Perhaps most important with respect to criminal cases is the jury's check on state power. However, it is another, nearly as important, justification that I wish to focus on in this chapter. It is argued that juries and other tribunals that contain lay participants are a good thing because they leaven the law with community norms.[6]

The Japanese example is instructive, however, because Japan chose to introduce lay influence through the institution of a mixed tribunal rather than the traditional common law jury.[7] One might array legal tribunals on a continuum. At one end are courts comprised only of professional judges. In the middle are mixed tribunals. At the other end are lay jurors. As one moves from a professional judge only model to a jury model, presumably one increases the possibility that community norms will infuse a decision. The Japanese decision to adopt a mixed tribunal limits the extent to which the decision maker is likely to substitute its norms for a legal rule. The existence of various types of lay tribunals focuses our attention on the role of norms in society and on how norms and law interact to produce social order.

The norms justification for lay participation is particularly interesting at this time because norms are once again at centre stage in socio-legal studies. Norms, of course have never been too far from the limelight.[8] They long have been a staple of the sociology of law.[9] Norms also play a role in law and

to specific questions. See Stefan Machura, 'Fairness, Justice and Legitimacy: Experiences of People's Judges in South Russia' (2003) 25 *Law and Policy* 123.

[5] Neil Vidmar, 'A Historical and Comparative Perspective on the Common Law Jury', in Neil Vidmar (ed.), *World Jury Systems* (New York, 2000), 1.

[6] For example, the United States Supreme Court provided this justification in *Witherspoon* v. *Illinois*, 391 U.S. 510, 519 & n.15 (1968). A number of commentators have provided this explanation. See Darryl K. Brown, 'Jury Nullification Within the Rule of Law' (1997) 81 *Minnesota Law Review* 1149, 1198. ('In their interpretation of instructions, juries tilt application of general rules toward particularized justice. They know less of the law than judges but arguably more of the social norms and practices that may inform law's application.'); Steven Hetcher, 'The Jury's Out: Social Norms' Misunderstood Role in Negligence Law' (2003) 91 *Georgetown Law Journal* 633. Recently, a United States federal district court judge in an 'open letter' to fellow judges decrying the decline in the frequency of jury trials in federal courts argued, 'without juries, the pursuit of justice becomes increasingly archaic, with elite professionals talking to others, equally elite . . . Juries are the great leveling and democratizing element in the law.' William Young, An Open Letter to United States District Court Judges, https://webspace.utexas.edu/rosem3/CRN/JuryArticle.pdf. (Last visited 18 August 2004).

[7] Early proposals that Japan should create an independent jury system were squelched by hints from the Japanese Supreme Court that it would find a statute creating such a system unconstitutional. Kodner, n.3, above, 242.

[8] For example, a concern with the role of norms and customs is at the heart of Eugen Erlich's interest in the 'living law'. Eugen Ehrlich, *Fundamental Principles of the Sociology of Law* (Cambridge, Mass, 1936).

[9] See Ellen S. Cohn. and Susan O. White, *Legal Socialization: A Study of Norms and Rules* (Berlin, 1990); James Coleman, *Foundations of Social Theory* (Cambridge, Mass. 1990); David M. Engel,

psychology[10] and legal anthropology.[11] It is fair to say, however, that in recent years research on norms has not been at the forefront of any of these disciplines. The revived interest in norms comes from a field that traditionally has been nearly devoid of norms discussions. Law and economics has discovered norms. As have other disciplines before them, law and economics scholars have begun to examine norms' relationship between norms and legal rules and how norms influence an individual's decision whether to comply with or avoid a legal prescription.

Those who are not part of the mainstream of the law and economics movement may find themselves somewhat bemused or even put off by the new law and economics norms literature, for sometimes it seems that articles in this area simply are rediscovering insights achieved long ago by other disciplines.[12] However, the renewed interest in norms encourages all socio-legal scholars to revisit the relationship between norms and law and how the two interact to create the socio-legal environment within which people live their lives.

In the next section I define norms and distinguish norms and laws. In the following section I review the law and economics approach to norms. I argue that although this approach has several strengths, its rational actor focus produces an incomplete picture of how norms operate in society. I suggest a number ways in which it may be improved by incorporating sociological insights concerning norms. In the last section of the chapter I return to a discussion of juries and other lay tribunals. I demonstrate how both law and economics and sociological approaches help us understand the behaviour of operation of these lay decision-making bodies and also note how the study of lay decision makers may, in turn, help both economists and sociologists to improve our understanding of law, norms, and law-norm interactions.

'The Oven Bird's Song: Insiders, Outsiders and Personal Injuries in an American Community' (1984) 18 *Law and Society Review* 55; Stewart Macaulay, 'Non-contractual Relations in Business: A Preliminary Study' (1963) 25 *American Sociological Review* 55; Richard D. Schwartz, 'Social Factors in the Development of Legal Control: A Case Study of Two Israeli Settlements' (1954) 63 *Yale Law Journal* 471; Philip Selznick, *Law, Society and Industrial Justice* (New York, 1969).

[10] Both distributive justice and procedural justice theories frequently invoke norms of 'fairness' See Karen A. Hegtvelt and Karen S. Cook, 'Distributive Justice: Recent Theoretical Developments and Applications' in Joseph Sanders and V. Lee Hamilton (eds), *Handbook of Justice Research In Law* (New York, 2001), 93–134; Tom R. Tyler and E. Allan Lind, 'Procedural Justice' in Joseph Sanders and V. Lee Hamilton (eds), *Handbook of Justice Research In Law* (New York, 2001), 65–92.

[11] Nearly from its inception, legal anthropology has been concerned with the relationship between law and norms and the often vague line that separates them. See Max Gluckman, *The Judicial Process Among the Barotse of Northern Rhodesia* (Manchester, 1967 [c.1955]); Carol J. Greenhouse, *Praying for Justice: Faith, Order, and Community in an American Town* (Ithaca, New York, 1986); Karl N. Llewellyn and E. Adamson Hoebel, *The Cheyenne Way: Conflict and Case Law in Primitive Jurisprudence* (Norman Okla, 1941); Bronislaw Malinowski, *Crime and Custom in Savage Society* (London (1970 [c.1926]); Laura Nader, *Harmony Ideology: Justice and Control in a Zapotec Mountain Village* (Stanford University Press, 1990).

[12] Amitai Etzioni, 'Social Norms: Internalization, Persuasion, and History' (2000) 34 *Law and Society Review* 157.

What are Social Norms?

The word norm is used to cover a very wide array of action-guiding directives. Wendel[13] notes there are moral norms (be kind to others), norms of prudence (look before crossing the street), norms of etiquette (RSVP when asked to do so), norms of civility (be a good neighbour), aesthetic norms (don't paint your house an inappropriate colour), and norms embodied in legal rules (drive on the right—or left—side of the road). Like laws, norms run the gamut of potential sanctions. The violation of some norms may result in no more than a raised eyebrow, while others may lead to permanent ostracism.[14]

Most norms scholars draw a line between norms and law. Norms are not law if by law we mean, as Max Weber would have it, an order that is 'externally guaranteed by the probability that coercion, to bring about conformity or avenge violation, will be applied by a staff of people holding themselves specifically ready for that purpose.'[15] From this perspective, social norms are nonlegal rules or obligations that influence individual decisions despite the lack of formal legal sanctions.[16]

However, it is easy to overstate the difference between legal rules and norms. Like law, norms exist when a socially defined right to control an act is held, not by the actor, but by others.[17] Thus, like law, norms are a social, not an individual phenomenon. Although norms must originally arise from individual actions, 'a norm itself is a system-level property which affects the further actions of individuals, both the sanctions applied by individuals who hold the norm and the actions in conformity with the norm.'[18] Moreover, the nature of the group holding this right to control can be more or less similar to the state, and thus norms can more or less approximate law. This idea is captured in part by Moore's well-known article on semi-autonomous social fields.[19] For example, in most neighbourhoods the aesthetic norm against painting one's house an inappropriate colour is enforceable only through gossip, shunning, and verbal disapproval.

[13] W. Bradley Wendell. 'Mixed Signals: Rational Choice Theories of Social Norms and the Pragmatics of Explanation' (2002) 77 *Indiana Law Journal* 1, 28.

[14] It is interesting to speculate about the overall severity of sanctions for norm violations. My sense is that at the very time when legal sanctions, especially criminal legal sanctions, have become harsher and harsher in the United States, sanctions for many norm violations have become less and less severe. Etiquette norms, norms of civility, and aesthetic norms whose violation once constituted a social felony, now barely rise to the level of misdemeanour.

[15] Max Weber, *On Law in Economy and Society* (New York, 1954), 5. Similar definitions include Donald Black's terse statement: 'Law is governmental social control.' Donald Black, *The Behavior of Law* (New York, 1976), 2.

[16] Ann E. Carlson, 'Recycling Norms' (2001) 89 *California Law Review* 1231, 1238.

[17] Coleman, n.9, above, 243. Ellickson offers a similar definition when he says that 'a norm is a rule supported by a pattern of informal sanctions' Robert C. Ellickson, 'Law and Economics Discovers Social Norms' (1998) 27 *Journal of Legal Studies* 537, 549, n.58.

[18] Coleman, n.9, above, 244.

[19] Sally Falk Moore, 'Law and Social Change: The Semi-autonomous Social Field as an Appropriate Subject of Study' (1973) 7 *Law and Society Review* 719. For Moore, a semi-autonomous social field is a group that can generate rules and coerce compliance to them.

However, some neighbourhoods are organized into community associations with a board of directors. A house colour objection by this formally constituted group is a more substantial sanction and presumably is more likely to cause the homeowner to acquiesce to group pressure.

Moreover, in some communities each home contains deeds restrictions explicitly giving a community association board or a committee of the board a right to approve house colours and other such matters. In these neighbourhoods, proceeding in the face of disapproval on the part of the community association board of directors potentially may result in civil litigation to enforce the board's position. This example captures Bohannan's idea that law often may be understood as the 'double institutionalization' of rules and norms originally embedded in other institutions.[20] Here, the norm of the community, as expressed by its community association board of directors is reinstitutionalized into an enforceable legal rule. In such a circumstance, the line between norms and rules is quite blurred.

Blurred, but not erased. The legal rule does not give the board of directors unfettered discretion with respect to approval or disapproval of things such as house colour. If the board wishes to use the court to enforce its decision it must act reasonably, constrained by its past house colour decisions and other norms concerning the overall aesthetics of the community. A board rule against pink houses may prevail in an upper-class neighbourhood on Chicago's north shore but seems quite unreasonable and presumably unenforceable in Miami.

Moreover, norms that are reinstitutionalized in the legal form are often changed by the process. In the legal systems of developed Western societies, they are likely to become less flexible and narrower. A civility norm about being a good neighbour, designed to express general guidelines about how to live together in harmony may, if brought into the legal system, be translated into specific rules about barking dogs, loud noises late at night, and the like. This seems to be especially likely when norms are brought into the criminal law with its requirements that offences be precisely defined and with its binary decision that someone either has or has not violated a specific legal rule.[21]

Law is more formal than norms in a second way as well. State law in developed Western societies has a substantial adjective law component, i.e. rules about the proper application of substantive rules.[22] Typically these involve procedural law and the law of evidence.

[20] Paul Bohannan, 'The Differing Realms of the Law' (1965) 67(6 pt. 2) *American Anthropologist* 133, 136.

[21] Lempert and Sanders capture these ideas in their discussion of ideal types of settlement processes. 'Issue Decision' settlement processes are ones that focus on a narrow legal question and determine a winner or loser. At the other end of the spectrum, 'Relationship Settlement' processes, as the name suggests, focus on the entire situation or relationship between the parties and attempt to find a solution that is mutually acceptable. Richard Lempert and Joseph Sanders, *An Invitation to Law and Social Science* (Philadelphia, 1986), 209.

[22] Robert Cooter, 'Three Effects of Social Norms on Law: Expression, Deterrence, and Internalization' (2000) 79 *Oregon Law Review* 1, 5.

Even when a norm is not reinstitutionalized as a legal rule, it may be compatible with legal rules. However, not all norms are compatible. When this is the case, individuals may find that they can conform to either the law or to contrary norms. If enough people conform to norms, legal rules may become nullities.[23]

Within the domain of norms, one further point is worth emphasizing; norms vary in terms of the probability of enforcement by others. To return to the house colour example one more time, one's ability to avoid detection when this norm is violated is very low, limited to one's ability to skate near the line of the unacceptable. Other norms, however, may be very hard to detect, or at least hard to detect by some potential enforcers. Norms against littering often fall into this category. Even when others observe violations, such as when they observe someone throwing litter out of a moving automobile, the opportunity to express disapproval or impose any other sanction is very limited. In the absence of detection and response, the norms may collapse unless they are internalized.[24]

The New Law and Economics Interest in Norms

The commonly accepted impetus for law and economics interest in norms is Robert Ellickson's book *Order Without Law*, in which he explored how ranchers and others resolved the issue of straying cattle by means of informal social norms.[25] Ellickson explained that regardless of legal rules with respect to damage caused by trespassing livestock,[26] disputes were settled based on a consciously adopted norm of cooperation that makes the owner responsible for the acts of his animals.[27] Deviants, that is ranchers who either do not keep their animals enclosed or who fail to pay for damage caused by their animals, may be subjected to various sanctions, ranging from negative gossip to attorney-assisted claims for compensation.

In part because Ellickson devoted the second half of his book to advancing a norms-based critique of the legal centralism of existing law and economics analyses, the book ushered in a now voluminous law and economics norms literature.[28] A central reason why this interest in norms has flourished is the belief that a better

[23] This is especially likely when numerous norms in a group conflict with applicable legal rules. Indeed, when this is so we often say of the group that it has a sub-culture.

[24] Michael Hechter, *Principles of Group Solidarity* (Berkeley, 1987), 59–60.

[25] Robert C. Ellickson, *Order Without Law* (Cambridge, Mass, 1991).

[26] The English and American common law rule was one of strict liability: the owner of domestic livestock is liable, even in the absence of negligence, for property damage caused by his trespassing animals. This 'fencing in' rule, as it is sometimes called, was rejected in parts of the United States. In its place, some states adopted a 'fencing out' rule. One cannot recover for damage caused by trespassing cattle unless one has erected a fence that the livestock breached in some way.

[27] Ellickson, n.25, above, 5.

[28] See Robert Cooter, 'Do Good Laws Make Good Citizens? An Economic Analysis of Internalized Norms' (2000) 86 *Virginia Law Review* 1579; Dan M. Kahan, 'Social Influence, Social Meaning, and Deterrence' (1997) 83 *Virginia Law Review* 349; Richard H. McAdams, 'The Origin, Development, and Regulation of Norms' (1997) 96 *Michigan Law Review* 338; Richard

understanding of the role of norms will enrich traditional rational choice models in classical law and economics. These models typically posit that individuals will act to maximize their expected utility by conducting an explicit or implicit cost-benefit analysis of competing alternatives and will select the alternative that maximizes net expected benefits. As Korobkin and Ulen note, 'thicker' versions of rational choice theory typically found in law and economics writing add predictions about the nature of individual goals and preferences.[29] Most commonly these versions posit that individuals will seek to maximize what is in their self-interest. If we can figure out what course of action most profits an individual, this conception of rational action has the advantage of suggesting falsifiable predictions about specific behaviours.

Consider, for example, the simple prediction that if there is no punishment for littering, people will litter (the cost to an individual of disposing of his litter in a lawful manner exceeds the cost to him of observing his individual litter on the ground). This prediction implicitly relies on the assumption that individuals are concerned with punishments they might receive, the disutility that they will suffer from looking at their own litter, and the time and energy it takes to dispose of litter, but not with the disutility others will suffer from looking at their litter. Or consider the prediction that if punitive damages were to be abolished or capped, more defective products would be produced. This prediction relies on the assumption that product manufacturers are concerned with their own bottom line, and are concerned with the health and safety of their customers only to the extent that those issues demonstrably affect that bottom line.[30]

Norms may explain behaviour that seems to violate traditional rational choice models by placing the behaviour and the law within the larger context of social relationships. For example, with respect to littering, if the fear of legal sanction were the only deterrent to throwing trash out the window, and if individuals were simply acting to maximize their self-interest, we should observe much more litter than we already do. Assuming that people are acting to maximize self-interest, obviously something beside law is operating and norms against littering are a plausible candidate.[31] In general, the influence of norms on behaviour might help

H. McAdams, 'Signaling Discount Rates: Law, Norms, and Economic Methodology' (2000) 110 *Yale Law Journal* 625; Eric Posner, *Law and Social Norms* (Cambridge, Mass, 2000); Paul H. Robinson, 'Why Does the Criminal Law Care What the Layperson Thinks is Just? Coercive Versus Normative Crime Control' (2000) 86 *Virginia Law Review* 1839; Cass R. Sunstein, 'On the Expressive Function of Law' (1996) 144 *University of Pennsylvania Law Review* 2021; Symposium, 'The Legal Construction of Norms' (2000) 86 *Virginia Law Review* 1577; Symposium, 'Social Norms, Social Meaning, and the Economic Analysis of Law' (1998) 27 *Journal of Legal Studies* 537; Symposium, 'Law, Economics, and Norms' (1996) 144 *University of Pennsylvania Law Review* 1643.

[29] Russell B. Korobkin and Thomas S. Ulen, 'Law and Behavioral Science: Removing the Rationality Assumption from Law and Economics' (2000) 88 *California Law Review* 1051.

[30] *Ibid*, 1065.

[31] I might add here that some may choose to reject the premise that people are acting to maximize self-interest. For such individuals, the search for variables that might explain behaviour that

to explain the substantial level of cooperative behaviour in situations in which the economically rational thing to do would be to free ride.[32]

It is this concern with rational choice that most clearly distinguishes the law and economics approach to norms from traditional sociological and anthropological approaches.[33] As Chong notes, the economic study of norms focuses on individual interests whereas the sociological study of norms generally focuses on values.[34] The study of norms enriches rational choice theory by incorporating the costs and benefits individuals experience from complying with or violating norms.[35]

The central role of rational choice thought in the law and economics approach to norms is apparent when scholars in this tradition address two central questions confronted by all who study norms: how do they arise and why do people obey them? The questions are related. For example, if one posits that norms arise because of instrumental, rational choice considerations by members of a group who desire to control or at least influence the behaviour of others, one is more likely to argue that people obey norms for instrumental reasons as well. Although there are a substantial number of different theories of norm creation and compliance within the law and economics literature, I will mention the two most prominent views, those of Richard McAdams and Robert Cooter.[36]

McAdams' theory is centred around the idea of esteem. Norms may emerge if enough individuals in a group or community share an opinion about the worthiness of engaging in some type of behaviour, can detect non-compliance with some degree of frequency, and can communicate to the group or community their opinion about the esteem-worthiness of individuals who comply or fail to comply with the norm.[37] For example, if there is a social norm encouraging recycling, then individuals deciding whether to recycle will weigh the esteem they will gain from recycling and the loss of esteem they will suffer if they do not. If the norm to

apparently disconfirms the rational actor hypothesis is a uninteresting exercise. For such people, the law and economics approach to norms itself may be uninteresting and perhaps a waste of time.

[32] Carlson, n.16, above. Although norms are a partial answer to the question of why more people do not free ride by violating legal rules when it is to their advantage, as a number of law and economics scholars note, this explanation confronts a second-order free-rider problem. If norms help explain why people obey the law when the probability of detection is low, why do people follow norms when it is not in their self-interest to do so and when the probability of detection is equally low? Why don't they free ride? I discuss this point below.

[33] In this respect, it is mirrored by recent research in political science. See Dennis Chong, *Rational Lives: Norms and Values in Politics and Society* (Chicago, 2000).

[34] Dennis Chong, 'Values Versus Interests in the Explanation of Social Conflict' (1996) 144 *University of Pennsylvania Law Review* 2079.

[35] Or, to adopt Sunstein's formulation, norms may be seen as a tax on or subsidy to choice, and hence as part of the array of considerations that people face in making decisions. Cass R. Sunstein, 'Social Norms and Social Roles' (1996) 96 *Columbia Law Review* 903, 946.

[36] For valuable discussions of McAdams and Cooter see Carlson, n.16 above and Tanina Rostain, 'Educating Homo Economicus: Cautionary Notes on the New Behavioral Law and Economics Movement' (2000) 34 *Law and Society Review* 973.

[37] McAdams (1997), n.28, above, 350–8.

recycle is strong enough, the increased esteem it provides may outweigh the costs of recycling and induce the desired behaviour.[38]

What of those situations, however, where the probability of detection, and therefore the loss of esteem is low? One answer, of course, is that compliance with the norm will in fact diminish. One may choose not to recycle. Perhaps one will simply lie about one's recycling behaviour in order to gain esteem without the cost of actually recycling. However, many people apparently do recycle even when the probability of detection is low. Why? Cooter tries to answer this question by resorting to the idea of internalization.

Cooter's theory shares with many sociological theories of norms the idea that for norms to operate effectively they must be internalized. Absent this internal regulation, the costs incurred by sanctions imposed by others are too uncertain to affect behaviour in many circumstances. When a norm is internalized, the motivation to comply is not solely a matter of whether others will observe and sanction non-compliance, but guilt or shame for doing something the actor experiences as 'wrong.'[39] Part of the cost of violating norms comes not from society but from self. Why else does one tip a waitress in a strange town one will never revisit? Why else do we recycle when in many cases we could receive all the social benefits from being known as a recycler simply by lying about our behaviour to others?[40]

True to his law and economics roots, however, Cooter's theory of how norms become internalized has a rational choice flavour.

> A rational person internalizes a norm when commitment conveys an advantage relative to the original preferences and the changed preferences. I call such a commitment a 'Pareto self-improvement.'[41]

One of Cooter's examples of a Pareto self-improvement is the decision to adopt a good work ethic that may be rewarded in terms of higher income.[42] Cooter's examples and those of other law and economics scholars tend to focus on norms that have a readily available rational actor explanation and to give rational action explanations for the normative behaviour that they do observe.[43] Whether people

[38] Carlson, n.16, above, 1238.

[39] Although McAdams' theory of norm creation focuses on esteem, he agrees that norms may become internalized in the sense that their violation produces an internal cost in terms of guilt or shame. McAdams, n.28, above, 380–1.

[40] Thus when we say that a norm is internalized we are saying something more than the fact that an actor accepts the legitimacy of a norm in the sense that the actor accepts the right of others' to sanction violations. Coleman, n.9, above, 293.

[41] Robert Cooter, 'Expressive Law and Economics' (1998b) 27 *Journal of Legal Studies* 585, 586.

[42] Robert Cooter, 'Models of Morality in Law and Economics: Self-Control and Self-Improvement for the 'Bad Man' of Holmes' (1998) 78 *Boston University Law Review* 903, 924.

[43] For example, with respect to the cattle norms in Shasta County, Ellickson notes:

> In uncovering the various Shasta County norms, I was struck that they seemed consistently utilitarian. Each appeared likely to enhance the aggregate welfare of rural residents. This inductive observation, coupled with supportive data from elsewhere, inspired the hypothesis that members of a

follow norms because they have internalized them or because of a concern for social esteem, the result is a greater level of cooperative behaviour than we might expect in the absence of normative constraints.

The law and economics concern with norms in general and internalization in particular is a promising sign for those who seek a rapprochement between law and economics and the larger field of socio-legal studies for it engages each of the fields in the quest for a better understanding of normative motivations. It moves the law and economics away from a deterrence-based social control model and closer to psychological models that centre on internal values.[44] For example, Cooter would presumably have little quarrel with the following statement by the psychologist Martin Hoffman.

> The legacy of both Sigmund Freud and Emile Durkheim is the agreement among social scientists that most people do not go through life viewing society's moral norms as external, coercively imposed pressures to which they must submit. Though the norms are initially external to the individual and often in conflict with his desires, the norms eventually become part of his internal motive system and guide his behavior even in the absence of external authority. Control by others is thus replaced by self-control.[45]

Of course, law and economics' continuing commitment to rational choice explanations for why people follow norms often meets with criticism.[46] Many non-economists believe that minimalist theories of social norms, employing a restricted set of rational choice explanatory concepts are not sufficient to explain compliance with norms.[47] I tend to agree. Cooter's rational choice theory of internalization may explain some norms such as those surrounding work ethic or being a good neighbour, it is less persuasive with respect to other norms, especially those where the probability of detection is very low. Moreover, these models sometimes run contrary to our own introspections about our internalized norms. We explain our own internalized normative commitments not solely as a matter of an instrumental choice designed to serve our own self-interest but as 'the right thing to do' regardless of our own self-interest, however it might be defined.

However, I would not join those who argue that the law and economics rational choice focus is fundamentally in error. Rational choice-based models may not be

> close-knit group develop and maintain norms whose content serves to maximize the aggregate welfare that members obtain in their workaday affairs with one another.

Ellickson, n.25, above, 167.

[44] Tom R. Tyler and John M. Darley, 'Building a Law-Abiding Society: Taking Public Views About Morality and the Legitimacy of Legal Authorities into Account When Formulating Substantive Law' (2000) 28 *Hofstra Law Review* 707.

[45] Martin L. Hoffman, 'Moral Internalization' in Leonard Berkowitz (ed.), *10 Advances in Experimental Social Psychology* (New York, 1977), 85, 85–6.

[46] Jon Elster, *The Cement of Society* (Cambridge, 1989); Jefferey J. Rachlinski, Symposium on Law, Psychology, and the Emotions: The Limits of Social Norms' (2000) 74 *Chicago-Kent Law Review* 1537.

[47] Bradley Wendell, n.13 above, 12.

the entire picture, but models of norms and norm internalization that disregard individual judgements about self-interest would also be lacking. Economic and sociological understanding of norms share more than they do not share. Law and economics explanations of why people comply with norms parallel social psychology models of norm compliance.[48] To take but one example, Kelman's taxonomy of social influence distinguishes compliance, identification and internalization.[49] Compliance is motivated by fear of social reaction, a traditional deterrence explanation for following rules or norms. Identification focuses on maintenance of a relationship with the source of influence and thus parallels McAdams' esteem model. Internalization focuses on an individual's change in values and thus parallels Cooter, albeit without the rational choice gloss.

Although Cooter's theory and to a lesser extent McAdams' as well, employ the concept of internalization, they do not have a well-developed understanding of how norms come to be internalized. Cooter conceptualizes an actor who has internalized a norm as a utility maximizing individual who is subject to side constraints. However, with respect to the process of internalization he has this to say:

> The side constraints for moral actors come from internalized obligations, as do external limits that technology and wealth impose. For purposes of my analysis, the precise mechanism of commitment—whether guilt or respect—need not concern us, so long as one accepts the proposition that internalization changes behavior.[50]

McAdams offers a somewhat more complete account when he argues that individuals, whom he assumes are seeking esteem from others, are shamed when they are sanctioned for violating norms by those from whom they are seeking esteem. Over time, the shame may produce a guilt-based internalization of the norm.[51] However, even in McAdams this process is undeveloped and although both McAdams and Cooter note that much socialization occurs in childhood, they devote very little attention to this problem.

Here sociological insights are needed if we are to have a better understanding of norms and norm internalization. Although socialization and norm internalization continue throughout the life-cycle,[52] much of this happens during childhood.[53]

[48] Yuval Feldman and Robert J. MacCoun, 'Some Well-Aged Wines for the "New Norms" Bottles: Implications of Social Psychology for Law and Economics' *Center for the Study of Law and Society Working Papers* (2003).

[49] Herbert C. Kelman, 'Compliance, Identification and Internalization: Three Processes of Attitude Change' (1958) 2 *Journal of Conflict Resolution* 51.

[50] Robert Cooter, 'Normative Failure Theory of Law' (1997) 82 *Cornell Law Review* 947, 956–7.

[51] McAdams, n.28, above, 381; John Braithwaite, *Crime, Shame, and Reintegration* (Cambridge, 1989), 75–8.

[52] June Louin Tapp and Lawrence Kohlberg, 'Developing Senses of Law and Legal Justice,' in June Louin Tapp and Felice J. Levine (eds), *Law, Justice, and the Individual in Society: Psychological and Legal Issues* (New York, 1977), 89.

[53] Tyler and Darley, n.44, above, 718; Tom R. Tyler and Gregory Mitchell, 'Legitimacy and the Empowerment of Discretionary Legal Authority: The United States Supreme Court and Abortion Rights' (1994) 43 *Duke Law Journal* 703, 743.

A substantial part of childhood socialization involves the internalization of norms. Successful internalization efforts often rely upon the child's search for approval. Socializing agents do not simply try to instil specific norms, but rather attempt to get the individual to identify with the socializing agent.[54] As Coleman notes, this occurs not only with parents and children but also with other agents as well. Nor does this process cease with childhood. Other organizations, including businesses, professional schools, religious orders, the military, and the state, take steps to create individuals for whom the internalization of norms is not a matter of rote memory but rather a matter of identifying with the value of people and institutions with which they interact. Sociology is properly criticized for sometimes presenting an over-socialized view of people,[55] but in this instance it provides a useful correction for the under-socialized view of people that is present in much legal economics.

This under-socialized view is understandable given the rational actor premise of much of law and economics. However, the individualistic bias of rational actor models, models that focus on exchanges between autonomous actors, causes the law and economics approach to under-emphasize three variables that I believe are necessary if we are to develop a more complete understanding of norms, norm internalization, and the relationship of norms and law.

The first variable is power. Dau-Schmidt notes that economists have shied away from the concept of power, in part because of the modelling difficulties it poses.[56] However, childhood socialization is possible in part because of the power differences between parents and children. The same may be said about much adult socialization. Employers, professors, officers, and abbots socialize employees, students, soldiers and novitiates. Only to a limited degree does the process run in the opposite direction. Moreover, compliance with norms is related to social power. Powerful persons are less likely to obey norms, in part because they are less likely to be sanctioned by those with less power. And at the other end of the social order, those who are lowest on the social ladder are less compliant, with norms enforced only by a process of gossip or informal reputational sanctions, in part because they have little to lose.[57]

The second under-emphasized variable is social role.[58] Most norms are role related and, across roles, the internalization of norms may vary a good deal.[59]

[54] See Robert D. Hess and Judith V. Torney, *The Development of Political Attitudes in Children* (Chicago, 1967), 95–6; Cohn and White, n.9, above.

[55] Dennis Wrong, 'The Oversocialized View of Man in Sociology' (1961) 26 *American Sociological Review* 183.

[56] Kenneth Dau-Schmidt, 'Pittsburgh, City of Bridges: Developing a Rational Approach to Interdisciplinary Discourse on Law' (2004) 38 *Law and Society Review* 199, 204.

[57] Coleman, n.9, above, 286–7.

[58] An exception to this statement may be found in Sunstein, n.35, above.

[59] For example, within the realm of athletics, the internalization of norms appears to vary from sport to sport. In some sports, violations of rules are acceptable as long as one is not caught. In other sports, for example golf, self-reporting of norm or rule violation occurs with some frequency. Of course, one could say about this situation that there is no norm of self-enforcement in some sports,

Moreover, we often occupy multiple roles and these roles may lead to conflicting norms. In this situation, one is less likely to obey or internalize a norm.

A focus on roles underlines the fact that who we are, our sense of self, is not simply as an individual but as a member of a group. Whether or not we comply with or violate normative demands turns on the nature of the role and our position in the group to which the role is relevant.[60]

The third under-emphasized factor in much of the law and economics norms literature is the rule systems in formal organizations.[61] For example, McAdams makes the following observation about his study of norms:

> [N]onlegal obligations may be created and enforced in a centralized or decentralized manner. Centralized private organizations, such as a diamond bourse, enforce relatively formal, usually written, rules, while groups and entire societies often enforce highly informal rules, such as the property norms ranchers follow in Shasta County. The distinction is important because some theorists prefer to use the term norms to refer only to decentralized rules and regard organizational rules as a set of obligations falling between centralized law and decentralized norms. However the terminological matter is resolved, this article focuses on informal, decentralized obligations.[62]

As this quote suggests, most of the law and economics interest in norms has focused on those norms that are not enforceable by a formal organization. Rather, the focus has been on norms whose violation does not potentially lead to the types of sanctions associated with legal rules, e.g. loss of liberty or economic sanctions. It is understandable why this is the case, for if one starts from a rational actor premise it is with respect to norms without formal sanctions that compliance is most puzzling.

However, McAdams agrees with David Charny that norms embedded in organizations are also important and questions whether we should not have separate terms for these different situations.[63] I agree, and I think it might be helpful to call such embedded norms 'institutionalized norms'.

It is difficult to underestimate the role played by organizations in creating and enforcing norms. Over the last decade or so, sociologists have debated the advantages and disadvantages of 'old institutionalism' and 'new institutionalism' understanding of organizations. In my opinion, our understanding of norm creation and norm internalization may be enriched by both approaches.

The 'older' perspective of Philip Selznick and his associates[64] focuses on the informal structure inside organizations and naturally lends itself to an examination

but it does seem clear that athletes in those sports do not experience a sense of guilt because of their successful breach of norms or rules.

[60] V. Lee Hamilton and Joseph Sanders, *Everyday Justice* (New Haven, 1992).

[61] Again, there are exceptions. See Lisa Bernstein, 'Merchant Law in a Merchant Court: Rethinking the Code's Search for Immanent Business Norms' (1996) 144 *University of Pennsylvania Law Review* 1765.

[62] McAdams, n.28, above, 351.

[63] David Charny, 'Illusions of a Spontaneous Order: "Norms" in Contractual Relationships' (1996) 144 *University of Pennsylvania Law Review* 1841, 1845.

[64] Philip Selznick, *TVA and the Grass Roots* (Berkeley, 1949).

of the relationship between laws and organizational norms. In this tradition, organizational forms become institutionalized when bureaucratic practices and structures become 'infused with value beyond the technical requirements of the task at hand'[65] and when their members internalize organizational values. Interestingly, some law and economics scholarship fits easily within this tradition.[66]

The 'new institutionalism' offers a somewhat different perspective. It focuses less on the informal structure inside organizations and more on the symbolic role of formal structure as a legitimizing force for the organization.[67] At the individual level, new institutionalism offers a more cognitive and less normative view of actors within organizations. It focuses on taken-for-granted scripts, rules, and classifications members bring to their tasks. These scripts simultaneously help actors to organize information and constrain the options available to them.[68] Borrowing from the work of Berger and Luckmann[69] among others, the new institutionalism emphasizes the idea that shared cognitive systems come to be perceived as objective, external structures defining social reality.[70]

This view of the relationship between organizations, norms, and law is quite compatible with that part of law and economics norms scholarship that focuses on the expressive function of law.[71] It shares the idea that law and other rule systems are a central part of the belief systems that shape the meaning of organizational life.[72] What the new institutionalism adds to this understanding is the insight that

[65] Philip Selznick, *Leadership in Administration* (New York, 1957), 17.

[66] Bernstein, n.61, above.

[67] Paul J. DiMaggio and Walter W. Powell. 'Introduction' in Walter W. Powell and Paul J. DiMaggio (eds), *The New Institutionalism in Organizational Analysis* (Chicago, 1991), 1–39.

[68] Mark Suchman, 'On Beyond Interest: Rational, Normative and Cognitive Perspectives in the Social Scientific Study of Law' (1997) *Wisconsin Law Review* 475.

[69] Peter Berger and Thomas Luckmann, *The Social Construction of Reality* (New York, 1967).

[70] W. Richard Scott, 'Unpacking Institutional Arguments' in Walter W. Powell and Paul J. DiMaggio (eds), *The New Institutionalism in Organizational Analysis* (Chicago, 1991), 164–82, 165. DiMaggio and Powell summarize the differences between old and new institutionalism as follows:

> When institutions were seen as based on values and commitment, and formal organization identified with the relatively rational pursuit of goals, it made sense to ask how the 'shadow land' of informal social relations provided a counterpoint to the formal structure. By contrast, if legitimacy is derived from *post hoc* accounts or symbolic signals, it is more sensible to focus on the institutionalized quality of formal structures themselves. Indeed, it is an emphasis on such standardized cultural forms as accounts, typifications, and cognitive models that leads neoinstitutionalists to find the environment at the level of industries, professions, and nation-states rather than the local communities that the old institutionalists studied, and to view institutionalization as the diffusion of standard rules and structures rather than the adaptive custom-fitting of particular organizations to specific settings.

DiMaggio and Powell, n.67, above, 27.

[71] See Cooter, n.41, above; Lawrence Lessig, 'The Regulation of Social Meaning' (1995) 62 *University of Chicago Law Review* 943; Sunstein, n.28, above.

[72] 'Law constructs and legitimates organizational forms, inspires and shapes organizational norms and ideals, and even helps to constitute the identities and capacities of organizational actors.' Lauren Edelman and Mark Suchman, 'The Legal Environments of Organizations' (1997) 23 *Annual Review of Sociology* 479, 493.

law affects norms and norm internalization at an organizational level as well as an individual level. Insofar as law becomes a central part of the constitutive environment of organizations, it is possible to say that the institutions themselves have internalized norms by empowering various classes of organizational actors and delineating the relationship between them.[73]

To summarize, I believe there are three under-emphasized factors in the law and economics discussion of norms: power, role, and organization. In the next section I attempt to demonstrate how these factors are beneficial to our understanding of norms within the context of the decision making of lay tribunals.

Lay Tribunals, Norms, and Laws

In this section I apply some of the points made above to the process of jury and mixed tribunal decision making. My goal is to demonstrate how incorporating concepts of power, role and institution provides a more complete picture of how norms and rules operate in this and other contexts.

As I noted at the outset of this chapter, a primary justification for lay participation is that non-professional decision makers bring social norms to bear in deciding cases. From one point of view this is a rather odd undertaking, for it is a bit like playing with fire. Max Weber made this point with respect to the English jury. Recall that Weber argued that western legal systems were moving toward the ideal of formal rationality. A legal system is formal to the degree that its rules it applies are intrinsic to the legal system. The system is substantive to the degree that the norms it applies are extrinsic to the legal system because, for example, they come from religious values. A system is rational if it yields outcomes that are predictable from the facts of the case because case outcomes are determined by the reasoned analysis of action in light of a given normative structure. A legal system is irrational when outcomes are not so predictable.[74] As Weber noted, depending on their degree of independence, lay decision makers threaten the legal system along both the formal-substantive dimension and the rational-irrational dimension. This is most obvious with respect to Common Law juries. Juries may bring substantive considerations to bear when they decide a case. That is, they may use normative standards that are not intrinsic to law. Indeed, in some ways they are encouraged to do just that. Moreover, because juries typically decide a single case with no knowledge, the outcomes over a series of cases may be irrational in the Weberian sense.

From one perspective, therefore, what is surprising is not that juries occasionally arrive at manifestly incorrect results when judged by legal rules, but that they

[73] *Ibid*, 483.

[74] David Trubek, 'Max Weber on Law and the Rise of Capitalism' (1972) *Wisconsin Law Review* 720, 729.

do so very infrequently.[75] From a norms perspective, there could be several hypotheses as to why this is so. It could be that legal rules and norms overlap such that the law simply reinstitutionalizes the norms jurors would otherwise apply. Law and professional decision makers will arrive at the same result whether they follow the law or follow norms. This explanation undoubtedly does explain a good deal of jury conformity with law.[76]

Not only do norms often parallel law, some, perhaps most, legal rules are commonly understood by both legal actors and other citizens to be interpreted to some degree in light of ordinary practice. For some legal rules, practice establishes the boundary of acceptable behaviour around which both norms and legal enforcement congeal. Many traffic laws provide a good example. Citizens, police officers, judges, and juries commonly understand that speed limits are in fact means around which there is a range of acceptable speed. The same may be said for other traffic rules such as how completely one must stop at stop signs. The norms surrounding traffic laws place a gloss on the meaning of compliance and, interestingly, here the norms trump a literal interpretation of the law. That is, a police officer would herself be subjected to rebuke by judge and juror alike if the officer routinely gave speeding tickets to individuals going three to five k.p.h over the limit on highways. Margaret Raymond captures this idea with the concept of 'penumbral crimes.' As long as one stays within the penumbra of acceptable violation, there is a low level of law enforcement or public sanction. But when one steps outside the penumbral range, sanctioning and stigma resume.[77] From crime to crime, the size of the penumbra varies. Traffic laws are examples of crimes where the penumbra is relatively large. Another example of a penumbral crime may be tax evasion.

Remaining are situations where social norms and law establish different standards and the legal system attempts to follow the legal rule. This situation may not be widespread, but it does occur. As Robinson and Darley note when summarizing a group of studies comparing community views with the criminal law in the United States, 'In our investigations we discover that often the legal codes and the community standards reflect similar rules in assigning liability to a case of wrongdoing but also often they do not.'[78] Areas of disagreement in the Robinson and Darley study include the seriousness of 'statutory rape' laws, (laws making it a crime to have consensual sex with an underage individual), felony murder laws

[75] Of course, most deliberations are hidden from scrutiny and some judgments may be arrived at through an illegitimate process, e.g. by drawing straws. However, the substantial body of jury research in the United States, both in the laboratory and through observation of actual jurors suggests that it is very rare for jurors to act in this way. The one universal from jury research is that jurors take their task seriously.

[76] See Paul H. Robinson and John M. Darley, *Justice, Liability and Blame: Community Views and the Criminal Law* (New York, 1995); Peter H. Rossi and Richard A. Berk, *Just Punishments: Federal Guidelines and Public Views Compared* (The Hague, 1997).

[77] Margaret Raymond, 'Penumbral Crimes' (2002) 39 *American Criminal Law Review* 1395.

[78] Robinson and Darley, n.76, above, 2.

(declaring accidental killings committed during the commission of a felony to be murder), and the mitigating effect of justifications even when, legally, they are unavailable. The last difference includes situations such as women claiming self-defence when they kill their abusive husbands while the husband is sleeping, and the near-acquittal of Bernhard Goetz, who shot several persons whom he believed were preparing to mug him during a trip on the New York City subway.[79] Kahan offers other areas where he believes there is a discrepancy between norms and legal rules, including date rape, drug use, and drunk driving.[80] In these cases, something other than norm/law agreement is needed to explain jury behaviour when jurors follow the law. In this circumstance, what factors influence whether lay decision makers will follow the legal rule?

A critical factor, of course is whether there are any sanction for failing to do so. This suggests the obvious hypothesis that when a judge or other legal professional is in a position to observe lay decision-maker behaviour, compliance with the legal rule is more likely. Note that this prediction is premised on an assumption: there are norms or rules about what to do in the face of a conflict between legal rules and lay values.[81] In a circumstance where professional and lay judges collectively determine the outcome of a dispute, presumably the judge often will announce and enforce a norm that legal rules trump if lay decision makers indicate a desire to apply a norm contrary to the legal rule.[82]

To my knowledge, we have little systematic research on this question. What research we do have indicates that lay judges rarely disagree with a professional judge, even when the legal rule being applied is contrary to societal norms.[83] However, to my knowledge we have no systematic data on the frequency with

[79] *Ibid*, 204–10.

[80] Dan M. Kahan, 'Gentle Nudges vs. Hard Shoves: Solving the Sticky Norms Problem' (2000) 67 *University of Chicago Law Review* 607.

[81] These rules are akin to legal rules about what to do when laws conflict. A whole area of legal study involves conflict of laws, informing courts which law they should use in situations where more than one body of law might apply. For example, whose law should we use if a citizen of France and a citizen of India have an automobile accident while on vacation in Canada? What if two French citizens happen to have an automobile accident in Canada?

These conflict rules are paralleled by a sub-species of norms about what to do in the face of conflicting norms. For example, there are parental norms about what children should do when confronted with a situation in which parental norms and the norms of a child's cohort conflict, as they may with respect to such behaviour as smoking, sex, and drug use. Conflict of norms issues arise in other places as well, e.g. teacher versus student norms, employer versus employee norms, etc.

[82] One should note that sometimes professional judges also may prefer to follow a social norm rather than the law. It may be the case that the existence of lay judges increases the likelihood that this will happen, at least on the margins. Moreover, there may be a number of areas where the legal rule is intentionally indeterminate, providing a good deal of leeway to incorporate normative judgments through means such as a reduced criminal sentence.

[83] See Sanja Kutnik Ivković, 'An Inside View: Professional Judges' and Lay Judges' Support for Mixed Tribunals' (2003) 25 *Law and Policy* 93 (lay judges in Croatia); Stefan Machura, 'Interaction Between Lay Assessors and Professional Judges in German Mixed Courts' (2001) 72 *International Review of Penal Law* 451 (lay assessors in Germany); Machura, n.4, above (lay judges in Russia).

which professional and lay judges have normative disagreements or the outcome of those disagreements.

The ability of professional judges to limit the penetration of social norms into the decision making of mixed tribunals is best understood in terms of power and role. The power of the professional judge derives from several sources. In part it is built on information that the professional judge may hold that lay decision makers do not have. Obviously, the professional judge often has superior knowledge of the law. In addition, the professional judge may have superior knowledge about the case at hand[84] and about how other, similar cases were treated.[85]

The professional judge's influence also arises from his or her role status and the deference ordinarily given to the judicial role. Here, models of how norms operate may be improved by concepts from cultural studies. Hofstede's concept of 'power distance' is useful in this context.[86] Power distance reflects the degree to which people prefer an autocratic or consultative style of authority. Those low in power distance prefer consultation and discussion and view subordinate disagreement with and criticism of authorities as appropriate and desirable. Those high in power distance prefer hierarchical leadership and dislike disagreement or criticism on the part of subordinates.[87] Societies, as well as individuals, vary along this dimension and we should expect that in societies that are relatively high in power distance, variation from the professional judge's wishes will be rarer.[88]

The willingness of lay jurors to follow the professional judge may also depend on the lay judges' status. In this regard, one would anticipate that German lay assessors would be more likely to vote according to social norms because they are selected to serve four-year terms in which they hear a number of cases, sitting for several days per year and because they themselves tend to be of higher social standing. Both of these factors reduce power differences between the professional and lay judges.[89] Even in this situation, however, it is important to keep in mind that the lay jurors understand their role as that of juror and, therefore, we should

[84] For example, German lay assessors at criminal courts have little access to case files, resulting in diminished influence. Machura, n.83, above, 145.

[85] In this regard, German assessors have an advantage because they are selected to serve four-year terms in which they hear a number of cases, sitting for several days per year. John H. Langbein, 'Mixed Court and Jury Court: Could the Continental Alternative Fill the American Need?' (1981) *American Bar Foundation Research Journal* 195, 206; Douglas G. Smith, 'Structural and Functional Aspects of the Jury: Comparative Analysis and Proposals for Reform' (1997) 48 *Alabama Law Review* 441.

[86] Geert Hofstede, *Culture's Consequences: Comparing Values, Behaviors, Institutions and Organizations Across Nations*, 2nd edn. (London, 2001).

[87] Joseph Sanders, V. Lee Hamilton and Toshiyuki Yuasa, 'The Institutionalization of Sanctions for Wrongdoing Inside Organizations: Public Judgments in Japan, Russia, and the United States' (1998) 32 *Law and Society Review* 871; Tom R. Tyler, E. Allan Lind and Yuen J. Huo, 'Cultural Values and Authority Relations: The Psychology of Conflict Resolution Across Cultures' (2000) 6 *Psychology, Public Policy and Law* 1138.

[88] A concern expressed by those who preferred a jury for Japan is that because Japanese culture is relatively high in power distance, the professional judge will have overwhelming influence on lay judges.

[89] Smith, n.85, above.

expect that they accept the legitimacy of the norms that attach to that role, including the norms concerning legal supremacy.

The idea that norms are tied to roles is a starting place to consider the nature of role influences in situations where the jury performs outside the observation of other court personnel, as is the case in societies that have traditional juries. Control of these juries, that is ensuring that they obey the norms of jury service, including the legal rule supremacy norm, is much more difficult. Absent a clear signal from the jury that it has failed to perform its task in an acceptable manner, intervention by the court is nearly impossible, especially in criminal cases.

If jurors are to follow norms, including the norm, embodied in judicial instructions, that requires them to follow the law as the judge states it, then by and large this must be because they have internalized the norm.[90] In American courts, lawyers are asked to inquire about this internalization during the voir dire, i.e. the preliminary examination of potential jurors. Jurors are asked if they can follow the law as given by the judges and the few that say no are very likely to be challenged for cause.

There are two points worth making here. First, it is remarkable how few prospective jurors do express any reluctance during voir dire about being guided by the judge with respect to the law.[91] This pattern may be due to a misunderstanding of what is required of the prospective juror. Many jurors may believe that if they do express an unwillingness to follow a law, this in itself will open them to some type of sanction. Judges do not routinely go out of their way to disabuse prospective jurors of this belief.

Juror behaviour also may be explained, at least in part, by esteem considerations such as those captured in McAdams' theory of norms. Jurors want judges and other legal actors to think well of them. However, it is important to keep in mind that jurors are one-shot players who most likely will never again see the judge or the lawyers in the case. They do not enjoy any long-term benefits from a rise in esteem.

This leads to the second point, which is that answers during voir dire do not necessarily reflect actual behaviour during subsequent deliberations. Insofar as jurors follow the law during deliberations, they are doing so for reasons other than a fear of judicial sanctions or seeking esteem from the judge or lawyers.[92] Compliance with legal rules during deliberations might be explained in two ways: because jurors are sanctioned by fellow jurors if they fail to follow the norms of proper jury behaviour or because they have internalized the norms themselves.

[90] It is an interesting question whether the obligation of jurors to follow the law is itself a law or a norm. In the American context, at least, I believe it is best understood as a norm. Jurors are not legally accountable for their verdicts, even when the verdict is manifestly contrary to the law. Randolph N. Jonakait, *The American Jury System* (New Haven, N.J., 2003), 249.

[91] The jury's willingness to be guided is a separate question from whether in fact they can sufficiently understand the instructions so as to follow them. There is some experimental work in the United States that suggests jurors are not very good at this task. Phoebe Ellsworth, 'Are Twelve Heads Better Than One?' (1989) 52(4) *Law and Contemporary Problems* 205.

[92] If there are any esteem gains from these sources, they are collective in nature, directed at the entire jury.

Recent studies in the United States that involved recording actual jury deliberations indicates that jurors do admonish each other to do as the judge has instructed and that these admonishments have their intended effect.[93] Why? Again, it is plausible that jurors attempt to follow judicial instructions, including instructions to apply the legal rules as they are given because of a desire to earn the esteem of fellow jurors. But, as is the case with the judge and the lawyers, jurors know that once the trial is over they will not have any future dealings with their fellow jurors.[94]

A more plausible explanation is that both the admonishing jurors and the jurors who are admonished have internalized the norms of what it is to be a good juror. If this is the case, we are left with the question of how this internalization comes about. Cooter's theory of Pareto self-improvement is a possible explanation, but again, it is an improvement for an activity that is engaged in very infrequently. I believe a more sociological explanation provides a preferable set of hypotheses about citizen behaviour when on jury duty. Jurors are role actors within an institutional context and within that context there are a set of ordinary scripts about how to perform the role.[95] As Etzioni puts it, jurors follow instructions because that is 'how things are done here'.[96] In addition, many citizens internalize a set of role norms as the 'right' thing to do when asked to serve on a jury. The jury task is value laden and these values are important in understanding juror internalization of the norms of jury service.

I do not want to overemphasize the level of jury compliance, however. In fact, we do not have very good data on the frequency with which jurors follow the norm that requires them to apply legal rules in deciding a case. In part, this is because the nature of judicial instructions is such that it is often very difficult for a jury to understand the legal rule.[97] Failure to follow a legal rule because the instructions fail to make the rule clear is not obviously an occasion where a jury has followed a norm rather than the legal rule. In addition, statutes themselves may be unclear or may be of questionable application on a given set of facts. In these cases, judges as well as juries might conclude that the statute should not apply and therefore a jury refusal to apply the legal rule is not an occasion where a norm trumped a rule.[98] Finally, as I noted above, we do not know how frequently jurors hold normative views contrary to the legal rule, and therefore how frequently jurors make a principled commitment either to follow the law or their normative judgment.

[93] Shari Seidman Diamond, Neil Vidmar, Mary Rose, Leslie Ellis, and Beth Murphy, 'Juror Discussions During Civil Trials: Studying an Arizona Innovation' (2003) 44 *Arizona Law Review* 1.

[94] Similar objections may be made to Posner's signalling theory of norms which, like McAdams' theory, is contingent in part on the parties having future dealings with each other.

[95] Edelman and Suchman, n.72, above, 493.

[96] Etzioni, n.12, above.

[97] See Phoebe Ellsworth and Alan Reifman, 'Juror Comprehension and Public Policy' (2000) 6 *Psychology, Public Policy and Law* 788 for a review of the literature on jury comprehension.

[98] See Darryl K. Brown, 'Plain Meaning, Practical Reason, and Culpability: Toward a Theory of Jury Interpretation of Criminal Statutes' (1998) 96 *Michigan Law Review* 1199; Lawrence M. Solan, 'Jurors as Statutory Interpreters' (2003) 78 *Chicago-Kent Law Review* 1281.

With these caveats in mind, one must nevertheless, presume that jury refusal to follow the law occurs more frequently than similar behaviour by lay judges in mixed tribunals. Certainly the economists are correct that external sanctions from others are a surer guarantee of normative obedience than internalization alone. It is this consideration that causes some jurisdictions that contemplated a jury system to opt instead for a mixed tribunal.[99]

Criminal juries do fail to follow the law in some cases.[100] They engage in what is usually called jury nullification.[101] When are they more likely to do so? One important influence that is particularly relevant to this chapter is the juror's trust in legal institutions, especially their trust in the courts. When trust is higher, so is apparent compliance with instructions.[102] This finding is consistent with research that indicates the legitimacy of courts does not turn on particular rulings, but upon diffuse support for courts as institutions.[103] When this support is not present, the possibility of nullification increases. The result is also consistent with the general sociological finding that the internalization of norms often is accomplished by getting individuals to identify with the socializing agent.[104]

Conclusion

The recent law and economics interest in norms has reinvigorated what had become a somewhat dormant corner of socio-legal studies. It has caused us to rethink the relationship between legal rules and other social norms that sometimes supplement and sometimes compete with the law. As a result, they cause us to revisit the relationship of the state and society and to ask once again that central socio-legal question of why people obey the law.

The law and economics approach is premised on a rational actor model and most frequently is directed at explaining law-abiding behaviour when self-interest

[99] Lester W. Kiss, 'Reviving the Criminal Jury in Japan' (1999) 62(2) *Law and Contemporary Problems* 261.

[100] In the United States, both the appropriateness and the extent of nullification is hotly contested. See Paul Butler, 'Racially Based Jury Nullification: Black Power in the Criminal Justice System' (1995) 105 *Yale Law Journal* 677 (arguing for racially based jury nullification in some criminal cases); Jonakait, n.90, above (assessing the frequency of nullification, especially nullification tied to the ethnicity of jurors).

[101] Nancy S. Marder, 'The Myth of the Nullifying Jury' (1999) 93 *Northwestern University Law Review* 877, 890. Laboratory research indicates that nullification is more likely when jurors are reminded that they have this power. Dennis J. Devine, Laura D. Clayton, Benjamin B. Dunford, Rasmy Seying, and Jennifer Pryce, 'Jury Decision Making' (2001) 7 *Psychology, Public Policy, and Law* 622, 666.

[102] Paula Hannaford-Agor and Valerie P. Hans, 'Nullification at Work? A Glimpse from the National Center for State Courts Study of Hung Juries' (2003) 78 *Chicago-Kent Law Review* 1249, 1270.

[103] Gregory A. Caldeira and James L. Gibson, 'The Etiology of Public Support for the Supreme Court' (1992) *American Journal of Political Science* 635; James L. Gibson et al., 'On the Legitimacy of National High Courts' (1998) 92 *American Political Science Review* 343.

[104] Coleman, n.9, above, 295.

might otherwise dictate that the individual disobey a legal rule. Perhaps because of this starting place, the law and economics literature on norms has focused on certain types of norms. It has focused on norms that help to solve collective goods-type problems, often those found in prisoners' dilemma-type situations. It looks, therefore, at norms that might rationally emerge as people enter into interactions over an extended period of time.[105] And it tends to focus on norms that exist outside formal organizations.

As a result, the law and economics analysis of norms frequently underemphasizes key variables that inform a sociological approach to norms. I have highlighted three such variables: power, role, and formal organization. The importance of these variables is easiest to see in situations where norms are embedded in organizations, occur between people of unequal power, and involve situations where the parties do not engage in repeated interactions. The norms governing the behaviour of lay judges and jurors provide a useful example.

I do not wish to conclude on a divisive note, however, or to suggest that sociology always has the best of it in explaining norms and obedience to norms. Rather, I wish to emphasize that the law and economics interest in norms opens up a new set of opportunities for two disciplines, too long estranged from each other, to renew a dialogue about law. Legal economists are largely committed to the idea of internalization and, as McAdams puts it, to understanding the normative motivations that underlie this process. If they have not as yet presented a fully compelling explanation of these motivations, neither has sociology. Moreover, the law and economics focus on rational action and adult acceptance of norms offers to enrich a sociological discussion of norms that often focuses most of its energy on largely irrational childhood socialization processes. Similarly, the law and economics emphasis on an interests explanation for norms may enrich the sociological emphasis on a values explanation of norms.[106] The proper conclusion from a review of the renewed interest in norms is not that one discipline has a better explanation than the other, but that both disciplines, once again communicating, may develop a better explanation than either alone might achieve.

[105] 'The economic analysis of social norms draws upon a fundamental result in game theory: One shot games with inefficient solutions ... often have efficient solutions when repeated between the same players. This generalization grounds the "utilitarianism of small groups" by which I mean the tendency of small groups to develop efficient rues for cooperation among members.' Cooter, n.50, above, 950–1.

[106] For example, in areas of norm/legal rule disagreement such as rape, do values alone explain why some jurors disobey their oath and choose to apply a norm that is contrary to a legal rule, or do we also need to introduce the idea of interests in the sense that jurors can imagine themselves in the position of the parties and in that circumstance would prefer that the norm rather than the rule were used to decide their case?

19

The Regulation of Computer-Implemented Inventions by Patent Law: A Critique of Decentralized Governance Techniques

Katerina Sideri

Introduction

As the state has become more complex, heterogeneous, and fragmented, the institutions of democracy and political representation have been challenged as to their capacity to correspond to the need to advance fairness, regulate markets, and secure participation of interested parties in decision-making. According to this line of thinking, the role of law is also challenged, since it is viewed as having failed to deliver social justice. In response to this criticism it has been suggested that the democratic character of governance structures should be deepened, by employing new techniques seeking to enhance participation and reduce the scope and depth of the inefficient state. In this framework, the role of law should be confined to putting in place fair procedures to enable the participation of communities in the making of rules affecting them. Hence, neutral procedures, understood as in flexible regulatory instruments and decentralized governance structures, are conceived to be the way to escape the gripping effect of command and control rules.

Instances of decentralized regulation are presented in the introduction of self-regulatory measures by the industry, as in architectural solutions (software), in DVDs (Digital Versatile Discs) to prevent unauthorized copying, or in the development of Internet filters to combat harmful material on the web. Similarly, the inclusion of interested parties in consultations in the course of developing legislative proposals, and the participation of various committees in both the development and implementation of legislation, also count as examples of decentralized regulation.

In the light of the above, the focus of this chapter is on revisiting the proposition that modern governance techniques can empower communities to participate in decision-making processes, and mediate neutrally to steer activity by means of decentralized and reflexive instruments. In formulating a critique, the empirical part of this chapter looks at the example of the proposal for a Directive on the patentability of computer-implemented inventions in the EU. The theoretical part of the argument concentrates on the concept of *communication,* as the position in favour of decentralized regulation assumes that objective legal structures can assist the effective transmission of local knowledge, as articulated by a variety of rational actors, networks, and social systems. Subsequently, the information conveyed by such communication feeds into legal structures, enabling the formation of informed laws. However, it appears that governance techniques seeking to enhance participation of interested parties in the decision-making process often fail as a result of problematic communication and co-operation.

The question then here is: Why is communication of meaning problematic? In articulating a critique, the following will engage in an exploration of the Aristotelian notion of *phronesis,* which points to accumulated experience, and tacit and practical knowledge guiding action. In particular, a *phronetic* approach may help us articulate useful insights by focusing the enquiry on uncovering the different kinds of unspoken practical knowledge encapsulated in legal documents aiming at promoting participation, and in the taxonomies carried over by interested parties involved in decentred governance structures. In a nutshell, the thesis advanced here is that legal texts and principles, and agents applying them or debating them, present the crystallization of experience. This implies that law can never be neutral, as it always promotes tacit understandings about the social world, as for example in attributing a central importance to property and technological innovation. Moreover, when agents apply legal principles, most of the time they do so by taking for granted the uncontested meaning of legal concepts. Alternatively, they apply these in the light of tacit understandings, accumulated experience, owing its existence, for example, to professional training or educational background. Finally, uncontested tacit knowledge and stereotypes embedded in legal documents can be brought onto the conscious level and challenged. In this instance, embedded 'commonsensical' taxonomies open to embrace different forms of experience, different types of culturally informed understandings about what counts as justice.

However, this is not meant to argue that communication is impossible or that law collapses in the political or social realm. For one thing, law has its own internal logic shaping how any communication between agency and legal structures is channelled. For another, communication as in the alteration of dominant definitions is possible as a result of an increase in power, an increase in the will and capacity of social groups to change the world, supported by external conditions that create the need to disrupt routine.

The following will engage in a definition of the terms governance, regulation, and information society, will then move onto a theoretical articulation of the notion of phronesis and how it can assist the understanding of the function of modern governance techniques, and finally anchor the analysis in the context of a case study: the consultation that followed the failed proposal for a Council Directive to introduce patent protection in computer-implemented inventions.

Decentralized Regulation, Modern Governance Techniques and the Information Society in Europe

I will here engage in building a definition of the terms '*regulation*', '*decentralized regulation*', and '*governance*', and in looking at how these abstract definitions acquire life in the context of the information society in Europe. Black's work[1] is a good starting point, as it draws attention to the fact that there is no clear distinction between the public and private sphere, in view of the complexity and fragmentation characteristic of modern societies, being the result of a variety of legal norms, actors, networks, or differentiated systems, all being interconnected within the European polity.[2] Information about the function and needs of networks is necessary when governments engage in providing some form of hierarchical co-ordination or assistance in the stages of policy formation and implementation. In other words, in a fragmented world, consisting of communities and networks on a global level, modern governance has to rely more than ever on information about local needs.

Moreover, interdependencies exist as no single actor has enough information to effectively pursue its interest. Similarly, no regulatory law can effectively intrude into other autonomous social systems in a direct way, as it cannot fully comprehend systems' internal mode of functioning. In addition, networks have their own understanding of what a regulatory problem is, and what solution is required, based upon shared classificatory schemes constructing a culturally informed point of view. Therefore, regulatory law should be engaged with steering activity rather than imposing goals, as this is crucial in a world characterized by increased scientific uncertainty requiring the co-operation of the administration with private forces, in order to come up with decisions informing regulatory policy and implementation. In this way, unforeseeable risks are quickly identified, and information as to possible ways to come up with solutions is furnished swiftly.[3]

What is then the role of state law in such a fragmented world inhabited by autonomous systems, networks, and groups having their own codes of conduct regulating their behaviour? *Proceduralization* is directly related to the above

[1] J. Black, 'Critical Reflections on Regulation' *Centre for the Analysis of Risk and Regulation LSE* (*CARR*) (2002) *Discussion Paper 4/2002.*

[2] J. Black, 'Proceduralizing Regulation-Part II' (2001) 21 *Oxford Journal of Legal Studies* 33; P. N. Grabosky, 'Using Non-Governmental Resources to Foster Regulatory Compliance' (1995) 8 *Governance* 527; N. Gunningham and P.N. Grabosky, *Smart Regulation: Designing Environmental Policy* (Oxford, 1998).

[3] H.K. Ladeur, 'The Integration of Scientific and Technological Expertise into the Process of Standard Setting According to German Law' in C. Joerges, K.-H. Ladeur and E. Vos (eds), *Integrating Scientific Expertise into Regulatory Decision-Making* (Baden-Baden, 1997).

processes, and in this instance law loses its normative character. As such it denotes the relocation of governmental functions, for example, to the market or the civil society. It may also denote the partnership between the state and private actors with the aim of achieving public ends, or alternatively may indicate the shift from state regulation to community self-regulation, with state law retaining the role of establishing the general conditions of negotiation. Lastly, it may point to the inclusion by governments of interest groups in the decision-making process.[4]

It appears that such a view is in certain cases adopted in the EU, as there is a tendency to promote the proceduralization of legal rules. According to the *White Paper on Governance*, regulatory law should facilitate the inclusion of interest groups and should be concerned with rules, procedures, and practices affecting the participation of European citizens, the improvement of the quality of European legislation, and the creation of a thriving civil society, promoting networks and forums for discussion. In this instance, the European Commission promotes itself as offering the hierarchical assistance required in the monitoring and enforcement stage, by means of assisting the drafting of codes of conduct for example. A culture of discussion based on the ethos of consensus building is emerging, and is being supported by neutral mediation and expertise provision, as there are multiple interests to be balanced. In such forums of discussion, each stakeholder will come to understand the concerns of the other, as long as the others are positively engaged in taking her interests into account.[5]

As for the regulation of the information society in particular, the Internet is positioned at the heart of efforts to promote it in Europe, hence issues relating to its governance, content, and privacy, intellectual property rights, and the creation of global networks, are of prime importance, often presenting us with an example

[4] J. Black 'Proceduralizing Regulation-Part I' (2000) 20 *Oxford Journal of Legal Studies* 597. However, Freeman argues that what exactly is included in such '*reinvention*' of regulatory mechanisms is quite ambiguous, but the author is also calling for the inclusion of interested parties, J. Freeman, 'Collaborative Governance in the Administrative State' (1996) 45 *UCLA Law Review* 1. Also see S. Breyer, *Regulation and its Reform* (Cambridge, Mass., 1982); B. Ackerman and R. Stewart, 'Reforming Environmental Law' (1985) 37 *Stanford Law Review* 1333.

[5] J. Dunlop, *Dispute Resolution: Negotiation and Consensus Building* (Dover, Mass., 1984); Freeman n.4 above; P. Harter, 'Fear of Commitment: An Affliction of Adolescents' (1997) 46 *Duke Law Journal* 1389–1423; C. Shearing, 'A Constitutive Conception of Regulation' in P. Grabosky, and J. Braithwaite (eds), *Business Regulation and Australia's Future* (Canberra, 1993). Various commentators touch on the normative aspect of this process from the point of view of administrative law, see M. Everson, 'Administering Europe?' (1998) 36 *Journal of Common Market Studies* 195, 203 and C. Harlow, 'Codification of EC Administrative Procedures? Fitting Foot to the Shoe or the Shoe to the Foot' (1996) 2 *European Law Journal* 3. According to Everson in particular, the problem is that the administration has little '*Constitutional*' guidance from primary legislation (the EU Treaties), as to what the European public interest is in view of the increased politicization of the European Union after Maastricht. In other words, there are competing interests to be balanced in the course of administering Europe, but how these should be balanced is not clearly provided in the Treaties. Everson notes that although Article 36 EC states the interest of Member States in social regulation, the '*four freedoms*' direct economic integration, Article F (TEU) indirectly addresses the human right of fair administration, subsidiarity suggests that decisions should be made closer to the citizen and Articles 190 and 191 (EC) state that decisions should be well reasoned, these do not provide enough legal basis to direct administrative decision-making, thus leaving considerable space for discretion.

of decentralized organization and regulation.[6] Although it is a global network, co-ordination of local centres is required, as in the creation of accepted global standards. Yet, decentralized, '*soft*' instruments, such as self-regulation and co-regulation are employed alongside more traditional hierarchical regulatory instruments, such as competition law, a process which nonetheless shows a tendency to promote ways to involve governments and various other interested parties acting in networks, manifesting a novel role for the state and the nature of its interaction with society.[7] Examples of the way such processes are institutionalized can be found in the context of industry self-regulation, as in architectural solutions introduced by the industry to DVDs to prevent copying. This is a good example of an instance when a self-regulatory measure was assisted by hierarchical rules such as the Information Society Directive, to ensure enforcement, since software code can always be decrypted or broken.

Other examples include domain name dispute resolution by the Internet Corporation for Assigned Names and Numbers (ICANN), where the European Commission plays a major role in the coordination of Internet management, and in initiating consultations between itself, the private sector, and civil society. To this effect, the European Commission develops, in conjunction with ICANN, effective codes of conduct (supported by legislation as appropriate), to cover the allocation and protection of domain names, and to combat fraud and cybersquatting, and access to personal data. Internet filters used to block harmful material on the net present another instance of industry self-regulation, while the consultation that followed the proposal for a Directive introducing patent protection in computer-implemented inventions in the EU, and the comitology and other advisory committees, which play an important role in the implementation of the European Union's Research and Technological Development (RTD) Framework Programme,

[6] Note that Boyle makes the point that the information society is not only characterized by electronic information and the Internet, but also genetic information and biotechnology, see J. Boyle, *Shamans, Software, and Spleens. Law and the Construction of Information Society* (Cambridge, Mass., 1996). In this chapter I limit my analysis on electronic information as I look at the official definitions produced by the European Commission and how these are debated. For early references to the notion of 'information society' see Recommendations of the Bangemann Group to the European Council: Europe and the Global Information Society, 26 May 1994, available at http://sirio.deusto.es/abaitua/konzeptu/w3c%5Cbange.htm (web page visited on 15 May 2003); See also European Commission Green Paper COM (87) final of 30 June 1987 on the Development of a Common Market for Telecommunication Services and Equipment: Towards a Dynamic European Economy, especially see the Introduction. Both papers advocated the need to liberalize the telecommunications sector so as to create incentives for the private sector to invest in the information society.

[7] D. Dana, 'The New "Contractarian" Paradigm in Environmental Regulation' (2000) *University of Illinois Law Review* 35; K. Harrison, 'Talking with the Donkey: Cooperative Approaches to Environmental Protection' (1998) 2 *Journal of Industrial Ecology* 51; C. Coglianese, 'Assessing Consensus: The Promise and Performance of Negotiated Rulemaking' (1997) 46 *Duke Law Journal* 255; C. Coglianese, 'Is Consensus an Appropriate Basis for Regulatory Policy?' in E. Orts and K. Deketelaere (eds), *Environmental Contracts: Comparative Approaches to Regulatory Innovation in the United States and Europe* (The Hague, 2000); S. Ackerman and N. Rose, 'Consensus versus Incentives: A Skeptical Look at Regulatory Negotiation' (1994) 43 *Duke Law Journal* 1206; J. Rossi, 'Participation Run Amok: The Costs of Mass Participation for Deliberative Agency Decisionmaking' (1997) 9 *Northwestern University Law Review* 173.

both present instances when the policy-making process opens up to include multiple interests and ensure that regional and local knowledge are taken into account when developing policy proposals and implementing legislation. The following sections of this chapter will look at some of the above-mentioned examples in detail, but first it is important to engage in some brief observations.

It follows from the above that this movement away from command and control rules, empowering people to participate in forums of discussion and relying on information to steer conduct, implies that the stages of formation of legislative proposals and implementation acquire considerable importance, more than ever before, and the European Commission assumes an important role in providing expertise, hierarchical assistance (when required), and support for forums of discussion. Against this background, the questions addressed are: What is the effect of decentralized regulation? How does it work in practice? Does it really fulfil its promise to promote deliberation and participation? What is the role of the European Commission in the process?

In answering these questions, for the purpose of this chapter, the term regulation is neither understood in the context of constitutional provisions that inform the separation of powers between the executive body, the legislature and courts, nor as in delegated legislation, or as a policy instrument or as being concerned with risk management.[8] It is understood in its broadest sense as governance. Hence, it is conceived as the sum of ways in which public purposes are authoritatively decided on and implemented[9] with various actors being active in the shaping of their content, and a variety of bodies involved in the process.[10]

[8] S. Breyer, *Regulation and its Reform* (Cambridge, Mass., 1982); B. Doern, and S. Wilks (eds), *Changing Regulatory Institutions in Britain and North America* (Toronto, 1998), 4–6.

[9] R. Pildes, and C.R. Sunstein, 'Reinventing the Regulatory State' (1995) 62 *University of Chicago Law Review* 7; Doern and Wilks n.8 above, offer four definitions of regulation. It can be viewed in the context of *Constitutional provisions* that inform the division of powers between levels of government and the separation of powers between the executive body, the legislature and courts. Regulation may also be defined in a narrow way as *delegated legislation*. In this form it may include guidelines, rules of procedures, and voluntary codes. Alternatively, regulation may be conceived as a *policy instrument*, and as such is distinguished from other instruments such as exhortation, spending, taxation, or the direct delivery of services. *Governing*, though, should be viewed in an overall sense (including Constitutions, statutes, regimes) so as to be able to address questions as to the *impact* of regulation, and in particular as to how difficult it is to tell whether regulation is expanding or being reconfigured. Furthermore, the *normative theory of market failure*, premised on the assumptions of economic analysis, understands society and economy as being separate phenomena, and prescribes that regulation is required to improve economic efficiency and correct market imperfections. In this instance, regulation encapsulates a new form of governance (*regulatory state*) as opposed to the redistribution functions of the positive state and is legitimized when market failures occur. These are: natural monopolies, externalities, public goods, asymmetric information, moral hazards, and transaction costs. Any one of these six failures legitimizes regulation, see T.C. Daintith, *Regulation* (Tübingen, 1979); G. Majone, 'From the Positive to the Regulatory State: Causes and Consequences of Changes in the Mode of Governance' (1997) 17 *Journal of Public Policy* 139; A. Ogus, *Legal Form and Economic Theory* (Oxford, 1994); B.M. Mitnick, *The Political Economy of Regulation: Creating, Designing and Removing Regulatory Forms* (New York, 1980). Finally, regulation may be concerned with risk management.

[10] As such, my approach comes close to the extensive literature on the possibility to conceptualize formal law as co-existing with autonomous normative orders emerging from codes of conduct

However, I propose to conceptualize regulation as not being the crystallization of the concerted effort of knowledgeable agents engaging in problem solving activity, as institutionalists would argue,[11] or the construct of powerful interests,[12] or a reflexive instrument aiming at promoting participation and deliberation,[13] or a technical administrative project[14] or a policy instrument in the hands of governments,[15] or the result of the non-hierarchical co-ordination of actors acting to pursue common interests,[16] or transfer of national loyalties from the national to the supranational

existing in parallel with state law, which can potentially be used as a source of resistance to the dominant ideology, see A. Hunt, 'The Ideology of Law: Advances and Problems in Recent Applications of the Concept of Ideology to the Analysis of Law' (1985) 19 *Law and Society Review* 11; J. Comaroff and J. Comaroff, *Of Revelation and Revolution: Christianity, Colonialism and Consciousness in South Africa* (Chicago, 1991); S.F. Hirsch and M. Lazarus-Black, 'Introduction/Performance and Paradox: Exploring Law's Role in Hegemony and Resistance' in S.F. Hirsch and M. Lazarus-Black, *Contested States: Law, Hegemony and Resistance* (New York, 1994). Contrary to Hart and Kelsen, anthropologists and sociologists have long ago pointed out that rules governing conduct need not emanate from the state, see E. Durkheim, *The Division of Labor in Society* (New York, 1933 orig. 1893); G. Gurvitch, *Sociology of Law* (Butler and Tanner, 1947); C. Lévi-Strauss, *Structural Anthropology* (New York, 1963 orig. 1958); P.H. Gulliver, *Disputes and Negotiations: A Cross-Cultural Perspective* (New York, 1979); A. Gramsci, *Selections from the Prison Notebooks* (London, 1971), while the extensive literature on the constitutive role of law is also relevant here as I am concerned not with *formal law*, but with the constitutive quality of instruments embracing a heterarchical understanding of law, see J. Simon, 'Ideological Effects of Actuarial Practices' (1988) 22 *Law and Society Review* 771; B. Yngvesson, 'Making Law at the Doorway: The Clerk, the Court and the Construction of Community in a New England Town' (1988) 22 *Law and Society Review* 409; J. Starr and J.F. Collier (eds), *History and Power in the Study of Law: New Directions in the Study of Legal Anthropology* (Ithaca, NY, 1989); W.T. Murphy, *The Oldest Social Science? Configurations of Law and Modernity* (Oxford, 1997); P. Fitzpatrick, *The Mythology of Modern Law* (London, 1992) and *Modernism and the Grounds of Law* (Cambridge, 2001).

11 D. Goldberg, T. Prosser and S. Verhulst (eds), *Regulating the Changing Media: A Comparative Study* (Oxford, 1989); C. Graham and T. Prosser, *Privatising Public Enterprises: Constitutions, the State and Regulation in Comparative Perspective* (Oxford, 1991); C. Scott, 'The Governance of the European Union: The Potential for Multi-Level Control' (2002) 8 *European Law Journal* 59. J. Reidenberg, 'The Formulation of Information Policy Rules through Technology' (1998) 76 *Texas Law Review* 553; D.R. Johnson, and D. Post, (1996) 'Law and Borders: The Rise of Law in Cyberspace' 48 *Stanford Law Review* 1367; T. Gibbons, *Regulating the Media,* 2nd edn. (London, 1998); L. Lessig, *Code and Other Laws in Cyberspace* (New York, NY, 1999); T. Prosser, 'Theorising Utility Regulation' (1999) 62 *Modern Law Review* 196.

12 I. Wallertsein, *The Capitalist World-Economy* (Cambridge, 1979).

13 G. Teubner, 'Substantive and Reflexive Elements of Modern Law' (1983) 17 *Law and Society Review* 239; G. Teubner, *Law as an Autopoietic System* (Oxford, 1993); I. Ayres and J. Braithwaite, *Responsive Regulation: Transcending the Deregulation Debate* (New York, 1992). Although Teubner's rich arguments in favour of reflexive law, and the important differences between his approach and other positions in favour of the proceduralist paradigm would require an extensive analysis, this cannot be taken here due to limits of space. A lengthier analysis can be found in K. Sideri, 'Questioning the Neutrality of Procedural Law: Internet Regulation in Europe through the Lenses of Bourdieu's Notion of Symbolic Capital' (2004) 10 *European Law Journal* 61 and in K. Sideri, *Law's Practical Wisdom: A Critique of Participatory Governance and Decentralized Law Making* (Aldershot, forthcoming).

14 B.M. Mitnick, *The Political Economy of Regulation: Creating, Designing and Removing Regulatory Forms* (New York, 1980); Daintith n.9 above; Ogus n.9 above; Majone n.9 above.

15 Daintith n.9 above.

16 R. Putnam, 'Diplomacy and Domestic Politics: The Logic of Two-Level-Games' (1988) 42 *International Organisation* 427; D. Knoke, *Political Networks. The Structural Perspective* (Cambridge,

level as neo-functionalists would assert,[17] but to come to grips with it as, most of the time, entailing the reproduction of common ways of thinking about the social world, which often go without saying, reproduced in the course of action beyond the conscious level and involving power relations, which ultimately may be resisted.[18] This implies the adoption of a cognitive approach by directing the present enquiry to discussing the construction of mental taxonomies of agents who participate in the making of decentralized regulation, when discussing the feasibility of strengthening democratic participation by means of modern governance structures.

Nevertheless, the approach that I propose to adopt substantially differs from Habermas's and Rawls's theoretical positions, although the level of analysis of these authors also concentrates on human minds. This is because the present analysis is sceptical to a rational understanding of the legal and political discourse, a position that is close to Foucault's devotion to a historical analysis of the relationship between truth and power and any systemic *grand* theory, drawing from Nietzsche's critique of reason as disguising power.[19] Kelly argues that there are striking similarities between Habermas's rational reconstruction organizing the elements of the ideal speech situation and Rawls's methodology identifying

1990); O. Singer, 'Policy Communities and Discourse Coalitions. The Role of Policy Analysis in Economic Policy Making' (1990) 11 *Knowledge: Creation, Diffusion, Utilization* 428; P. Kenis and V. Schneider 'Policy Networks and Policy Analysis: Scrutinising a New Analytical Toolbox' in B. Marin and R. Mayntz (eds), *Policy Networks—Empirical Evidence and Theoretical Considerations* (Frankfurt/M., 1991); D. Marsh, and R.A.W. Rhodes (eds), *Policy Networks in British Government* (Oxford, 1992); P. Sabatier and C. Hank (eds), *Policy Change and Learning: An Advocacy Coalition Approach* (Boulder; Colo, 1993).

[17] B.E. Haas, *The Uniting of Europe: Political, Economic and Social Forces, 1950–1957* (London, 1958).

[18] By taking on board the effects of power, my approach comes close to the work on legal informalism. *Informal or popular justice* is the idea that mechanisms for dispute resolution in general can be developed outside formal legal procedures and litigation, see P. Fitzpatrick, 'The Rise of Informalism' in R. Matthews (ed.), *Informal Justice?* (London, 1988); P. Fitzpatrick 'The Impossibility of Popular Justice' (1992) 1 *Social & Legal Studies* 199; C.B. Harrington and S.E. Merry, 'Ideological Production: The Making of Community Mediation' (1988) 22 *Law and Society Review* 709; R.L. Abel, 'The Contradictions of Informal Justice' in R.L. Abel (ed.), *The Politics of Informal Justice Vol 1: The American Experience* (New York, 1982); R. Matthews, 'Reassessing Informal Justice' in R. Matthews (ed.), *Informal Justice?* (London, 1988); G. Pavlich, 'The Power of Community Mediation: Government and Formation of Self-Identity' (1996) 30 *Law & Society Review* 707. However, I here look not only at dispute resolution, but also more broadly at processes underlining the formation of regulatory policy and implementation, dispute resolution being one possible facet of such processes. Finally, this chapter takes on board the critique addressed by conflict theorists, who see informal justice as existing '*in the shadow of the law*' reinforcing the legitimacy of existing power relations, see L. Nader, *Harmony Ideology* (Stanford, Conn., 1990); similarly, feminist critics of mediation argue that there may be imbalances of power between men and women participating in mediation.

[19] For the well-known intellectual debate between Gadamer and Habermas, and Foucault and Habermas see M. Kelly (ed.), *Critique and Power. Recasting the Foucault/Habermas Debate* (Cambridge, Mass., 1994), 1–13; D. Teigas, *Knowledge and Hermeneutic Understanding: A Study of the Habermas-Gadamer Debate* (Cranbury, NJ, 1995); C.H. Zuckert, *Postmodern Platos: Nietzsche, Heidegger, Gadamer, Strauss, Derrida* (Chicago, 1996).

elements of democratic common sense. They both require the identification of intuitions, then the formation of ideal categories, to finally arrive at the proceduralist conception of rules, which '... apply the idea of justification by appeal to generally acceptable reasons to the deliberations of free and equal citizens in a constitutional democracy'.[20]

However, there are still important methodological differences between the two thinkers. Rawls has been criticized as exhibiting a relativistic approach, since his reconstruction is based on the United States, and as not containing rigorous empirical research aiming at identifying embedded intuitions, given that his results are mainly based upon representative writings of the liberal democratic tradition and on the output of leading institutions of constitutional democracy, such as the US Supreme Court.[21] As Kelly argues, rigorous empirical substantiation of Rawls's claims is required, as there are certainly groups of citizens who do not adhere to the basic principles of the model presented by the original position. For example, the culture of 'gangsta rap' and other marginal social groups certainly do not follow Rawls's idealized common-sense intuitions about liberal justice, as feminists, gender, and race theorists have argued.

This links to the problem of 'coherence' in Rawls's framework, as he promotes a conception of justice as fairness that is acceptable to all citizens in a liberal society. This is because it is assumed to be capable of reflecting an overlapping consensus amongst individuals with diverse views. An implication of this is that, as Dworkin argues, when organizing intuitions in a coherent set, some would have to be rejected as not being consistent with the majority of intuitions, while in Habermas's methodology of rational reconstruction, it is assumed that all relevant intuitions, of competent speakers must be accepted as true and accounted for in a theory of communication.[22] But, what are the ramifications of this for building consensus? What are the implications for coming to grips with the concept of 'democratic common sense'? What if an interested party holds a view deeply challenging embedded and generally accepted beliefs about the social world? Should it be included? Or should it be discarded as outrageous?

Moreover, Rawls's *Political Liberalism* has been criticized as confining justice to the political sphere. The proceduralization of the public use of reason is concerned with the governmental liberal structure, such as parliamentary debates, administrative acts, and the working of courts. However, Habermas's understanding of public reason includes independent public forums of

[20] T. Kelly, 'Sociological Not Political. Rawl and the Reconstructive Social Science' (2001) 31 *Philosophy of the Social Sciences* 1.

[21] *Ibid.* Also see R. Rorty, 'The Priority of Democracy to Philosophy' in R. Rorty (ed.), *Objectivity, Relativism and Truth* (Cambridge, Mass., 1991), 175–96.

[22] Kelly n.20 above, citing R. Dworkin, *Taking Rights Seriously* (London, 1977).

discussion, and networks of citizens, hence advancing a view of participatory democracy.[23]

Taylor and Sandel are two of the most prominent critics of Rawls. Taylor reminds us that we do not only exist as autonomous subjects, but also carry the history of our socialization in communities. For Taylor, 'the subject himself cannot be the final authority on the question of whether he is free; for he cannot be the final authority on the question of whether his desires are authentic.'[24] Sandel's *Liberalism and the Limits of Justice* also makes the point that Rawls's procedural model rests on an understanding of human beings as 'freely choosing, autonomous beings'.[25] Rawls responded to this critique in his 1985 essay 'Justice as Fairness: Political not Metaphysical', rejecting this accusation. Although human beings have self-understandings such as religious convictions, these are part of their non-public identity. Rawls then reiterates that such truths can be put aside, and should not be relevant to political theory.[26] Taylor insists that this view still understands human agency as autonomous.[27] He attacks the Rawlsian conceptualization of common sense, by criticizing the assertion that political arrangements and legal rules should avoid substantive claims about the 'good'. Rawls's proceduralist position relegates discussions of the 'good' to the private realm, however, Taylor argues that it is not possible to separate substantial from procedural issues.

Of particular importance for the purpose of the present analysis is Taylor's claim that human agency should be understood in the light of historically and culturally formed intuitions developed in the course of socialization.[28] Intuitions can be made intelligible only on the basis of the contextual background, evaluative framework or horizons of significance, attributing meaning to them. Taylor draws upon Gadamer's notion of horizons to argue that we define ourselves in accordance with a social and historical background that makes the social world

[23] T. McCarthy, 'Kantian Constructivism and Reconstructivism: Rawls and Habermas in Dialogue' (1994) 105 *Ethics* 1.

[24] C. Taylor, 'What's Wrong with Negative Liberty' in C. Taylor, *Philosophical Papers II: Philosophy and the Human Sciences* (Cambridge, Mass., 1985), 216.

[25] M. Sandel, *Liberalism and the Limits of Justice* (Cambridge, 1982), 9.

[26] J. Rawls, 'Justice as Fairness: Political not Metaphysical' (1985) 14 *Philosophy and Public Affairs* 3.

[27] C. Taylor, 'Précis of The Sources of the Self' (1994) 54 *Philosophy and Phenomenological Research* 185.

[28] Kymlicka's analysis is also attentive to the cultural bonds of individuals, as it through these that individuals make sense of the world. To understand this process it is necessary to use the tools of psychology, sociology, linguistics, the philosophy of mind, and neurology, Therefore, he argues, 'for meaningful individual choice to be possible, individuals need not only access to information, the capacity to reflectively evaluate it, and freedom of expression and association. They also need access to a societal culture. Group differentiated measures that secure and promote this access may, therefore, have a legitimate role to play in a liberal theory of justice.' W. Kymlicka, *Multicultural Citizenship* (Oxford, 1995), 84.

intelligible.[29] In his essay 'The Politics of Recognition' Taylor claims that in order to undertake the moral task of recognition of the others, we must both discard the simple understanding of the self as a social construction and as individualistic. Instead, we need to recognize the dialogical nature of the self, intertwining with the notion of the other, hence the importance of *recognizing* the difference in others, and at the same time recognize our own horizons of significance, a process allowing self-development.

Habermas, in his commentary on Taylor's views on multiculturalism and the politics of recognition argues that this position negates the modern conception of freedom, by opposing a politics of universalism to a politics of difference.[30] According to Habermas, if we accept a 'proceduralist' understanding of rights, there's no need to appeal to a communitarian conception of 'collective rights' opposing the rights of individuals. However, this view begs a chain of difficult questions. For some commentators the assumption that political discourse can be truly neutral and disinterested, having been liberated from political and economic calculation, is highly problematic.[31] The problem here is the assumption that all parties have equal amounts of power in the course of deliberations.

Close to this line of criticism is the problem of institutional design that would allow the fair participation in discursive communication.[32] Moreover, research in different empirical contexts has shown that peer pressure in forums of discussion may result in parties not raising issues that they consider important, but are controversial.[33] Finally, commentators point to problems of collective action, consensus building, and even questions as to whether it is actually desirable that all issues are subject to deliberation, and that all actions are justified according to the requirements of ideal speech situation.[34]

However, the present analysis is not only attentive to the problems stemming from a conceptualization of individuals as autonomous subjects. As the analysis here focuses on the role of law in modern decentralized structures, it is important

[29] C. Taylor, *Philosophical Arguments* (Cambridge, Mass., 1995), especially see 'The Politics of Recognition', 225.

[30] J. Habermas, 'Struggle for Recognition in the Democratic Constitutional State' in A. Gutmann (ed.), *Multiculturalism and the Politics of Recognition* (Princeton, 1994), 109.

[31] J. Meehan (ed.), *Feminists Reading Habermas: Gendering the Subject of Discourse* (New York, 1995).

[32] J. Bohman. 'Deliberative Democracy and Effective Social Freedom' in J. Bohman and W. Rehg (eds), *Deliberative Democracy: Essays on Reason and Politics* (Cambridge, Mass., 1997); J. Knight and J. Johnson, 'What Sort of Equality Does Deliberative Democracy Require' in J. Bohman and W. Rehg, *Deliberative Democracy: Essays on Reason and Politics* (Cambridge, Mass., 1997).

[33] C. Coglianese, 'Assessing Consensus: The Promise and Performance of Negotiated Rulemaking' (1997) 46 *Duke Law Journal*. 255.

[34] For a review of theses issues see J. Black, 'Proceduralizing Regulation-Part II' (2001) 21 *Oxford Journal of Legal Studies* 1.

to point out that Habermas's framework also rests on the assumption that the administration can play an impartial role in coordinating engagement and discussion of interested parties during the stages of forming a legislative proposal and implementation, and that, finally, law is viewed as being a suitable medium to neutrally mediate and embrace universal principles.

All these points require discussing the problem of rationality, universality and the social function of law. Habermas's and Rawls's analyses reflect the view that there is a need for a theory that allows the articulation of universal principles, as without it the result would be contextualism and relativism. Still, the view taken here is that human activity cannot be reduced to universal rules.[35] Taylor takes on board the importance of context, as in loyalties and affiliations providing the tacit background of assumptions, practices and abilities stemming from group membership. Gadamer proposes that although our experience is anchored in different social settings, dialogue and communication between different views of the world is still possible by means of successful 'translation' of experience resulting in the fusion of our own horizon within the horizon of the 'other'. These ideas link to Aristotle's elaboration of the notion of *phronesis*, which points to the importance of context and pratical knowledge as explanatory tools. Yet, a sociological translation is required explaining these processes. In other words, the aim here is to employ the tools of social theory to articulate a critique of proceduralization of legal rules and participation, while taking on board the importance of common-sense intuitions, context and difference, power relations, and the difficulty in separating substantive from procedural issues.

Phronesis

Aristotle distinguishes between three different ways of arriving at truth: *episteme, techne,* and *phronesis*. Episteme concerns the possibility of developing universal explanatory frameworks. Techne is attentive to technical know-how. Finally, phronesis calls attention to practical knowledge and practical ethics. The notion of phronesis is particularly important, as we can address questions such as: How rational are human beings such as judges, administrators, and participants in forums of discussion? What are the social factors that limit their rationality? How feasible is it to endeavour to explain social phenomena, such as the genesis of legal norms and structures, on the basis of general and abstract rules providing universal truth claims? For instance, should we consider the truth of human rights to be invariable in time or the product of specific socio-historical circumstances? Do judges decide on the basis of shared first principles, or is this problematic in view of the moral fragmentation of modern society?

[35] B. Flyvbjerg, *Making Social Science Matter. Why Social Inquiry Fails and How It Can Succeed Again* (Cambridge, 2001).

Phronesis according to Aristotle is a virtue of those who manage households or states. Such individuals advance their own good and the good of a tradition on the basis of stocks of practical knowledge as to how a particular situation should be handled. Phronesis is a tacit skill, common sense, practical wisdom, such as the one possessed by a housewife in respect to everyday activities in the household. The latter knowledge results from the accumulation of experience in a particular social setting. In other words, it presents us with practical understandings held by a layman ('honey helps wounds and burns heal'), contrasted with the knowledge of universal rules by a doctor ('a healthy wound bed assists the regrowth of tissue'). Similarly, this type of common-sense reasoning is different from knowledge of general principles about politics, law and economy. It is a process of learning and acting by experience, going beyond rationality.[36]

For instance, according to the Dreyfus model of learning experts, that is proficient performers of particular activities such as chess and football players, paramedics and ordinary drivers, accumulate and organize experience most of the time, intuitively and not consciously used.[37] If we follow the rationale of this example in the field of legal studies and in respet to participatory governance and procedural law in particular, the research agenda should include questions aiming at uncovering unspoken understandings about the role of law, what counts as a good legal argument, who should be included in the making of laws and what makes dialogue fruitful in forums of discussion.

In other words, phronesis implies that for one thing agents are not always rational. The action of judges, administrators, and interested parties are driven by often unspoken conceptions of 'good' or 'bad', denoting the practical administration of everyday activities. According to Bourdieu, judges' and administrators' action is driven by practices reproducing the neutrality of legal rules, for instance, by means of the grammatical persistence of passive and impersonal constructions in legal texts. A person trained in law believes in the power of words inscribed in books, cases, and legal texts, and in their ability to help society progress, while most of the time, fails to see their role in reproducing the social world by means of reproducing socially constructed assumptions, such as the centrality of property and contract.[38]

In short, for one thing, phronesis points to experience, operating beyond the conscious level towards the initiation of activity according to unspoken conceptions of what counts as 'good' action. For another, it points to the importance

[36] Aristotle, *The Nicomachean Ethics* (Harmondsworth, 1976).

[37] Flyvbjerg, n.35 above citing S.E. Dreyfus and H.L. Dreyfus, *Mind over Machine: The Power of Human Intuition and Expertise in the Era of the Computer* (New York, 1998).

[38] P. Bourdieu, 'La Force du Droit: Eléments pour une Sociologie du Champ Juridique' (1986) 64 *Actes de la Recherche en Sciences Sociales* 9; P. Bourdieu, 'Habitus, Code et Codification' (1986) 64 *Actes de la Recherche en Sciences Sociales* 9.

of examining the *particular*, as opposed to the *universal*. Philosophers and sociologists such as Foucault, Nietzsche and Bourdieu adopted the 'phronetic approach' to their analysis. Very importantly, they also incorporated the notion of power in their analysis of the practical and the particular.[39] In the light of such an analysis, the questions asked do not only concern the rationality of judges, administrators and participants in forums of discussion. They also direct attention to the importance of including questions relating to power relations amongst participants in a forum of discussion, or between the administration and interested parties.

Goffman's symbolic interactionism, Garfinkel's ethnomethodological approach to courtroom inquiries, and Bourdieu's *Theory of Practice* are all concerned with the practical use of common-sense typifications, but the latter author's work is particularly attentive to the effects of power. In Bourdieu's work, a cognitive approach is adopted to come to grips with social reality, with minds being assumed to be bound by patterns of praxis, unspoken cognitive schemas, which he terms *habitus*. Habitus is 'the feel for the game (sens pratique), intentionality without intention, which functions as the principle of strategies devoid of strategic design, without rational computation and without the conscious positing ends.'[40] In this sense, while recourse to rational pursuit of interests is a possibility, as utilitarian theorists would argue, it is not the rule governing action, as 'we are empiricial'. Hence, this approach differs substantially from utilitarianism, with which the concept of interest is commonly associated, as the human mind is socially bounded, socially structured.

The above points to the fact that socialization results in learning to behave according to the standards and stereotypes characteristic to a particular society or communities, being most of the time reproduced in the course of action. A way to illustrate this is by using Coleman's famous example as to the structure of the Jewish diamond wholesale community. In this market, Jewish traders (with strong family ties) would hand diamonds for inspection to the potential buyer with no formal insurance required. Coleman explains that this is an example of a case where a norm constitutes an effective regulator, as sanctions are guaranteed, while on the basis of trust relations and information flows, individuals may discover that it is in their joint interest to cooperate.[41]

If we take this example to view it from a '*phronetic*' point of view, agents neither consciously engage in a cost-benefit analysis, nor rationally embrace

[39] For instance, in Bourdieu's framework the notion of habitus derives its meaning only when understood in respect to a particular field of study emerging under specific socio-historical circumstances, P. Bourdieu, *The Logic of Practice* (Cambridge, 1990).

[40] P. Bourdieu, *In Other Words. Essay Towards a Reflexive Sociology* (Cambridge, 1990), 107.

[41] J. Coleman, 'The Rational Reconstruction of Society' (1993) 58 *American Sociological Review* 1.

a value system organizing relationships in a community, but do what they have always been doing without questioning the belief system underlying the formation of certain practices. Therefore, understanding the practice that points to the non-requirement of insurance (which for most of us seems absurd) would direct the enquiry on cognitive schemas, phronesis, *allowing* the reproduction of particular social relations, as nurtured in hierarchial relations in families structuring sentiments, such as respect, obedience and religiosity. The above are reproduced in everyday practices, which are so '*normal*' that are beyond question or rational computation, as people act like a '*fish in the water*' to use Bourdieu's words.

However, this approach is often criticized as introducing constraints trapping free agents and rendering impossible the conceptualization of creative change. In reply to this criticism, I here seek to introduce an understanding of phronesis that comes to grips with social reality as experienced reality, fluid, relative, and immanent, encapsulated in flexible concepts. In other words, reality is being reinterpreted all the time, hence the focus on processes, on the constant communication between minds and structures, between agents' common sense and law's 'common sense' and amongst different modes of experience. In this way a path is proposed that leads to a dynamic perception of the real, as today's social reality is being described as the construction of yesterday's reality, a process that involves perpetual interaction of objective and subjective forces, with knowledge revealing its plural character. Such an understanding of cognitive schemas conforms to DiMaggio's claim that the challenge to cognitive approaches is to conceptualize the interaction between minds and structures.[42]

In the light of the above, the study of decentralized governance techniques should then be directed to seeking to uncover the '*common sense*', '*practical wisdom*' of decentralized regulation. This will be conducted by means of looking at common-sense understandings embedded in legal documents and in the phronetic knowledge of the agents involved in such forms of governance, for example, the different Directorates General of the European Commission and interested parties. If one accepts this, then understanding conflicts and problematic cooperation amongst interested parties may be attributed to differences in deeply embedded views of the world, or in law's 'common sense' and alternative ways to view a social problem. Research in such well-embedded models of conceiving the world is crucial in order to interpret the processes underlining decentralized regulation, as the ways the social world is perceived may outrun perception.

[42] P. DiMaggio, 'Culture and Cognition' (1997) 23 *Annual Review of Sociology* 263; P. DiMaggio, 'Why Cognitive (and Cultural) Sociology Needs Cognitive Psychology' in C. Karen (ed.), *Culture in Mind: Toward a Sociology of Culture and Cognition* (New York, 2002); R.W. Casson. 'Schemata in Cognitive Anthropology' (1983) 12 *Annual Review of Anthropology* 2.

Such common assumptions have a double function of acting both as frames of interpretation, and promoting images of authority and power as to how a legal proposal should look, and who should be involved in its making. They may manifest themselves in turn takings and new paragraphs added in texts, and in repetitions during interviews. This approach is inspired by the ethnomethodological research agenda that contends that documentary interpretation of official and unofficial documents can be used to interpret behaviour.[43] Moreover, fieldwork should consist of closely observing situated activities in their natural settings, and discussing them in the course of interviews with officials. The present analysis of data collected in the course of interviews with officials at various levels in the hierarchy, concentrated on identifying repetitions, themes occurring and re-occurring in the interviews,[44] and on searching 'indigenous categories', contrasted with analytical categories.[45]

However, humans are complex and fragmented beings, and have multiple identities. On the basis of this, the argument here is that a more dynamic reading of the operation of *phronesis* would require to first, anchor experience in many different settings, and second to come to grips with the conditions under which knowledge encapsulated in experience may be challenged. The following will take up these two points.

Phronesis as Subject to Experience: Emergence on the Conscious Level

The very emergence of the object of this study, alternative regulation, illustrates the possibility of well-embedded, unspoken understandings about the role and function of law in modern society emerging on the conscious level, as interest groups demanded their inclusion in the making of laws affecting their affairs, thus challenging the symbolic violence of centralized law making and enforcement. Moreover, the hot debate surrounding the way in which the Internet should be regulated may be attributed to different conceptualizations of the role of property and information in the emerging information society, as the following sections of this chapter will engage in showing.[46] The argument here is that it is antagonisms between different conceptualizations of what is '*honourable*' and '*pleasant*' that underline the evolution of the political and legal spheres.[47] Such antagonisms indicate an increase in the will and capacity

[43] H. Garfinkel, *Studies in Ethnomethodology* (Englewood Cliffs, NJ, 1967).

[44] G.R. D'Andrade, 'The Cultural Part of Cognition' (1981) 5 *Cognitive Science* 3.

[45] R. Bogdan and S.J. Taylor, *Introduction to Qualitative Research Methods. The Search for Meaning* (New York, 1984).

[46] D. Bohm, D. Factor and P. Garrett 'Dialogue—a Proposal' available at http://www.muc.de/~heuvel/dialogue/dialogue_proposal.html (page visited on 6 November 2004).

[47] F. Nietzsche, *The Will to Power* (Levy, 1910, orig. 1901), Fall 1887 9 [8] [60] in D. Breazeale, *Philosophy and Truth: Selections from Nietzsche's Notebooks of the Early 1870's* (London, 1979).

to change the world, often supported by external conditions that create the need to disrupt routine.[48]

In the light of the above, in the following sections the argument will be that external conditions, such as the continuous technological experimentation currently taking place on the net, and the mushrooming of Internet communities, have opened the way to challenge the conventional way to think about the role of law and property. The increasing support of such different understandings by academics and business organizations has started a debate on the meaning of legal concepts that were beyond controversy, and thus reproduced in legal documents, as if their connotation was to be taken for granted. This can be further attributed to the new approach in the EU, which supports the effective engagement of various interested parties in the making of decisions, in an attempt to strengthen the democratic face of the Union. Moreover, groups challenging established definitions possess expert technical knowledge (e.g. how software works), which adds weight to their opinion, since this is the kind of information that the European Commission *needs* in order to come up with informed legislative proposals, and avoid conflicts when a proposal for a Directive, for example, is read by the Council or the Parliament. In a nutshell, it is ruptures in the normal flow of events which leads us to *have to* change or reconsider established practice by bringing it onto the conscious level, and in this way phronesis is potentially being opened up to experience. I say potentially, as alternatively, ruptures may result in clinging upon and supporting on the ideological level the established, by refusing to change it. However, even if phronesis opens up to experience, new, revolutionary visions will always comfortably settle in categories of thought, presenting us with new attempts to control conduct, and impose the '*right*' way to conceptualize regulation.

Multiple Phronesis

As for the possibility to introduce the operation of *multiple phronesis*, the argument here is that another way to overcome rigidities in the phronetic approach of analysis, is by attributing to agents *multiple patterns of perception.* In simple words, the proposition here is that agents have a multiplicity of roles available to them, as a result of socialization in many different settings. This understanding assumes the mobility of individuals and the formation of a new fluid concept of community encompassing people who are at the same time members of various different communities.[49]

In other words, an analysis is proposed that takes on board the plurality of identities and the importance of interaction. As such, structural patterns of thinking

[48] Bourdieu n.40 above.

[49] D. Boden and R. Friedland, 'Now/Here. An Introduction to Space, Time and Modernity' in D. Boden and R. Friedland (eds), *Now/Here. Space, Time and Modernity* (Berkeley, 1994); J. Urry, *Sociology Beyond Societies: Mobilities for the Twenty-First Century* (New York, 2000).

about the social world may be derived from diverse professional, national, and educational backgrounds, hence the recognition of a multiplicity of drives within us. The following will anchor the present theoretical discussion in the context of the proposal for a Directive introducing patent protection in computer-implemented inventions.

The Proposal for a Directive to Introduce Patent Protection in Computer-Implemented Inventions: The Consultation

Patents are protected by the Paris Convention and the Trade-Related Intellectual Property (TRIPs) Agreement. For a patent to be granted, an invention must be new, involve an inventive step, and be capable of industrial application. Moreover, TRIPs Article 27(1) provides that patent protection can be granted to products and processes in all '*fields of technology*', and in the same spirit Article 52(1) of the European Patent Convention (EPC), which is a non-EU agreement signed by all Member States (MS) and other countries, has been interpreted as requiring that patents can be granted for inventions, which have *a technical character,* and are thus industrially applicable. Technical character can be interpreted as requiring, first, that an invention belongs *to a field of technology* and, secondly, that the invention makes a *technical contribution* to the technological state of the art.[50]

In Article 52(2) and (3) of the EPC computer programs are defined as not being *inventions*, and thus fall outside patentable subject matter. This is because a computer program is considered as being a solution to a mathematical problem, not having a technical character. For the same reasons, '*methods for doing business*', '*presentations of information*', and '*aesthetic creations*' are not patentable.

In particular, the EPO, Article 52(2) excludes from patentability:

1. discoveries, scientific theories and mathematical methods;
2. aesthetic creations;
3. schemes, rules and methods for performing mental acts, playing games or doing business, and programs for computers;
4. presentations of information.

However, para (3) provides:

> (3) The provisions of paragraph 2 shall exclude patentability of the subject-matter or activities referred to in that provision only to the extent to which a European patent application or European patent relates to such subject-matter or activities *as such*. (emphasis added)

[50] EPO T 854/90 (IBM).

This is where problems begin, as definitions as to what constitutes a computer program *as such* diverge, as a result of the different interpretations that may be given to terms such as *technical contribution* and *field of technology*, while at the heart of the debate is whether *computer-implemented inventions* should be treated differently than computer programs '*as such*', and thus be patentable.

The approach endorsed by the European Patent Office (EPO), which is the executive body of the European Patent Organization established by the EPC, is that, although Article 52(2) of the EPC provides that computer programs '*as such*' are excluded from patentability, '*computer-implemented inventions*' are intended to be covered. According to the recent case law of the EPO, a technical contribution is performed when an invention solves an objective technical problem. For example, 'ensuring optimum exposure with sufficient protection against overloading of the X-ray tube by an X-ray apparatus incorporating a data processing unit' can be patented.[51] Moreover, 'the co-ordination and control by software of the internal communication between programs and data files held at different processors in a data processing system' has also been patented.[52] This approach has been criticized heavily, as commentators have noted that there is hardly a computer program which cannot be patented, thus in practice this interpretation brings Europe close to the US position, which allows software patents, as the rather simple test of '*usefulness*' is applied, according to which business methods, algorithms, and methods for doing business, can be patented as long as they have a useful, concrete, and tangible result.[53]

Nevertheless, the European Commission adopted a Proposal for a Directive on the Protection by Patents of Computer-Implemented Inventions in February 2002, in view of the fact that inventions using software can already be patented through the EPO or national patent offices, which has resulted in considerable legal uncertainty. The Directive was meant to harmonize the way in which national patent laws deal with software inventions. Some organizations representing European businesses, lawyers, established industry players, and government agencies welcomed the proposal in view of the ambiguity and legal uncertainty surrounding the patentability of software related inventions.

However, Both EuroLinux and the Economic and Social Council of the European Community (ESC) have expressed concerns that patents on computer-implemented inventions might impede the progress of innovation in the software field.[54] The latter produced in 2002 a report critical to software patentability and

[51] PbT Consultants, 'The Results of the European Commission Exercise on the Patentability of Computer Implemented Inventions' (2000) available at http://europa.eu.int/comm/internal_market/en/indprop/comp/softanalyse.pdf; EPO Board of Appeal T26/86 [1988] OJ EPO 19.

[52] EPO Board of Appeal, T6/83 [1990] OJ EPO 5.

[53] P. Aigrain, '11 Questions on Software Patentability in Europe and the US' paper prepared for the Software and Business Method Patents: Policy Development in the US and Europe Meeting, organized by The Center for Information Policy, University of Maryland on 10 December 2001, available at http://cip.umd.edu/Aigrain.htm (web page visited on 19 May 2003).

[54] Opinion of the Economic and Social Committee on the Proposal for a Directive of the European Parliament and of the Council on the patentability of computer-implemented inventions

proposed taking into consideration the interests of small and medium enterprises (SMEs), and free/open source software companies.[55] As for the EuroLinux Alliance for a Free Information Infrastructure, this is an open coalition of commercial companies (over 200) and non-profit associations united to promote a European software culture based on copyright, open standards, open competition, and open source software such as Linux. Corporate members or sponsors of EuroLinux develop or sell software under free, semi-free, and non-free licences for operating systems such as GNU/Linux, MacOS or MS Windows.[56]

To this effect the EuroLinux Alliance organized a petition against software patents in Europe, which had an overwhelming response, as 1,161 valid responses were forwarded to DG Internal Market.[57] Interestingly, the consultation showed that the group opposing software patents (91 per cent) was numerically dominant. Nevertheless, the report prepared for the European Commission analysing the results of the consultation referred to the 9 per cent who supported software

(COM(2002) 92 final/2002/0047(COD)). The ESC is a consultative organ, which unites experts and scientists from various fields and drafts working papers or opinions for the co-deciding organs of the European Union, such as the European Parliament and the Council of the European Union.

[55] *Libre software* or *free software* refers to the freedom to 'redistribute copies, either with or without modifications, either gratis or charging a fee for distribution, to anyone anywhere. Being free to do these things means (among other things) that you do not have to ask or pay for permission,' http://www.gnu.org/philosophy/free-sw.html, http://www.gnu.org/philosophy/free-software-for-freedom.html (web pages visited on 19 May 2003). With open source software, although the source code is open, it may be that it includes programs that one can redistribute and copy only for non-profit purposes (semi-free software) or can even be prohibited from doing so without permission (proprietary).

[56] http://www.eurolinux.org/about/index.en.html, (web page visited on 19 May 2003).

[57] EuroLinux argued that software patents have caused a lot of problems, as developers find it difficult to create an innovative product without infringing some patent, due to the number of features required to be implemented. Hence, the argument is that due to the peculiarities of software, it is as if the letters of the English language have been patented. This results in more and more software patent litigation cases and many software companies and software developers being threatened outside courts to settle informally, as they cannot afford litigation costs. Moreover, start-up costs increase, as new firms have to take into account that they need an in-house lawyer or constant coordination with a lawyer/law firm, who would be able to find out whether a computer program with a technical effect is already patented, see European Commission, DG Enterprise, *Enforcing Small Firms' Patent Rights. A Publication from the Innovation/SMEs Programme Part of the Fifth Research Programme* (Luxemburg, 2003); N. Gallini, 'How Well is the US Patent System Working? (2001) *Working Paper University of Toronto* 3/2001. Commentators have also argued that big companies build large portfolios of software patents, which in fact serve the purposes of maximizing their bargaining power when striking deals, see C. Shapiro, 'Navigating the Patent Thicket: Cross Licences, Patent Tools and Standard Setting' in A. Jaffe, J. Lerner and S. Stern, *Innovation Policy and the Economy* (National Bureau of Economic Research, 2001); J. Bessen, 'Patent Thickets: Strategic Patenting of Complex Technologies' *Research on Innovation Working Paper* 8 (2002) available at http://www.researchoninnovation.org/ (web page visited on 19 May 2003). Finally, the findings of economic studies suggest that the impact of patents for computer-implemented inventions on the economy is ambiguous, see J. Bessen, and E. Maskin, 'Sequential Innovation, Patents and Imitation' *MIT and Harvard Working Paper Series 00–01*, (2000) available at http://www.researchoninnovation.org/patent.pdf, while Konqueror and iCab (which are shareware companies) and Opera (which is an open source company) are the only competitors of Microsoft in the market for browsers, PbT Consultants n.51 above.

patents, as an economic majority.[58] The directive text as amended by the European Parliament followed to a certain extent the spirit of the proposals of groups opposing the patentability of computer-implemented inventions. For example, Article 4a.1 concerning exclusions from patentability, as amended, stipulates that 'computer-implemented invention shall not be regarded as making a technical contribution merely because it involves the use of the computer, network or other programmable apparatus. Accordingly, inventions involving computer programs which implemented business, mathematical or other methods and do not produce any technical effects beyond the normal physical interactions between a program and the computer, network or other programmable apparatus in which it is run shall not be patentable'. Similarly, Article 4a.2 provides that 'Member States shall ensure that computer-implemented solutions to technical problems are not considered to be patentable inventions merely because they improve efficiency in the use of resources within the data processing system.' When the proposed Directive went back to the Council, initially it appeared that there would be no disagreement as to adopting the Irish Presidency's compromise on the Directive. However, due to the Polish intervention, the vote was delayed, but finally the Council reached agreement. Nevertheless, this was subject to criticism from campaigners and members of the European Parliament, as not all the amendments introduced by Parliament in its first reading were taken on board. When the proposal went back to the Parliament, it rejected the Council's common position in July 2005, as it considered that its views were not given sufficient weight. As a result, the Directive was not adopted.

The question here is, why could not the various interested parties reach agreement? Why did cooperation fail? The following will look into this, the suggestion being that an enquiry into actors' cognitive schemas would help solve the puzzle.

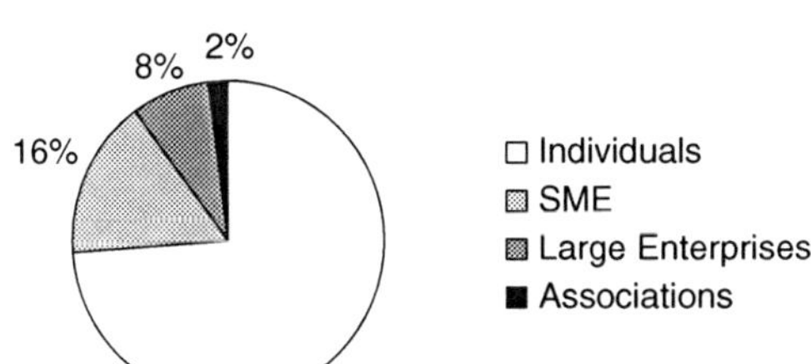

Graph 1 Opponents and supporters of software patents: Some statistics

[58] PbT Consultants n.51 above, 14.

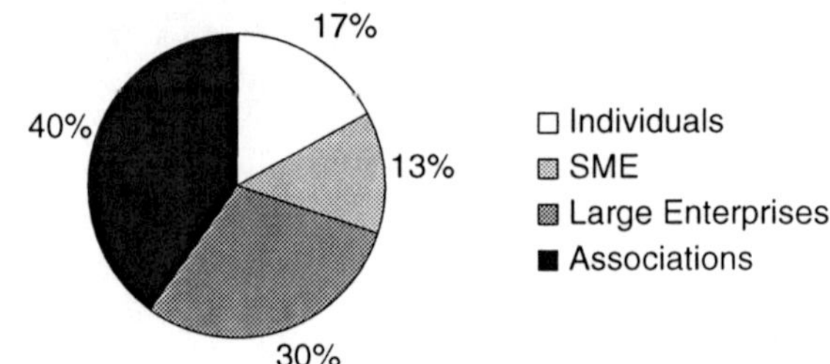

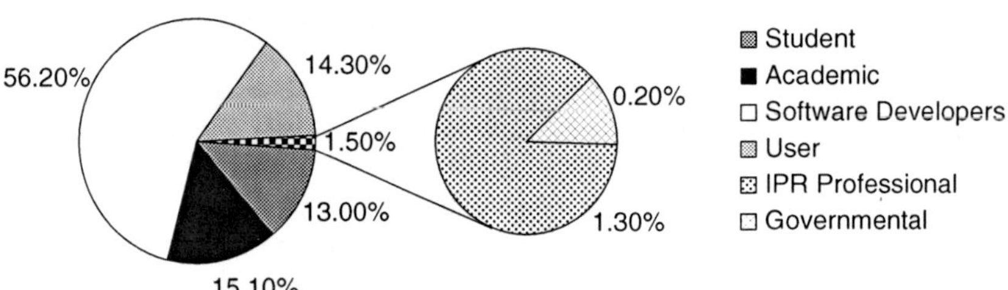

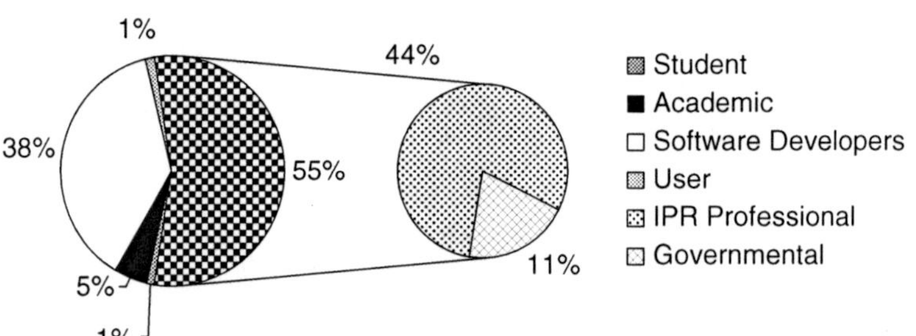

Graph 1 *Continued*

Source: PbT Consultants, 'The Results of the European Commission Exercise on the Patentability of Computer Implemented Inventions' (2000) available at http://europa.eu.int/comm/internal_market/en/indprop/comp/softanalyse.pdf, section 4, see particularly section 4.1 at 35.

Patterns of Thinking about Intellectual Property: The European Commission

Hobbes and Locke in the seventeenth century asserted that people have a '*natural right*' to own their creation. In the same spirit, intellectual property rights are premised on the romantic notion of inventor and author, who has a moral right in her works. Alternatively, economic theory offers a utilitarian perspective by drawing attention to the economic incentives that should be provided to inventors.[59] I do not seek here to engage in a discussion of the contingent character of notions such as *author* and *creator.*[60] I am concerned with the ways in which tacit understandings about the role of information, innovation, and regulatory law influence action. In short, the proposition in the following paragraphs is that, for DG Internal Market (which was the DG primarily responsible for the preparation of the proposed Directive), intellectual property rights and innovation are understood through the lenses of harmonization and market integration, when focusing on the '*knowledge-based*' aspects of the economy in Europe.

To illustrate this point requires studying the aesthetics of the language of the various legal documents produced by the European Commission and concerning in general the information society, so as to discover patterns of words that are repeated and carried over from one document to the other, to finally find their way to the one at issue, the draft directive. Such patterns of words, like rituals, are reproduced, most of the time without being questioned, being symbols of authority and continuity, by means of their mere incorporation in legal texts, such as Green and White Papers, action plans, directives, and annual reports. This would happen although the meaning of words and patterns of words, such as '*international competitiveness*', '*innovation*', or '*software as such*', have been subject to debate before being incorporated in a legal text in the first place.

For example, the 1993 Commission's *White Paper on Growth, Competitiveness, Employment* stresses that information, communication technologies, and related services have the potential to '*promote steady and sustainable growth*', to increase '*competitiveness*', to open '*new job opportunities*' and to improve the quality of life of all Europeans. Then the 1994 Bangemann Report builds on the White Paper's analysis to promote the argument for liberalizing quickly telecommunications for the virtue of '*competing on a global level with the US and Japan*'. Liberalization should be a priority, since being the first player to set technological standards for those who follow is crucial in the IT industry, where innovation runs fast. For this

59 E.C. Hettinger, 'Justifying Intellectual Property' (1989) 18 *Philosophy and Public Affairs* 31; T.G. Palmer, 'Are Patents and Copyrights Morally Justified?: The Philosophy of Property Rights and Ideal Objects' (1990) 3 *Harvard Journal of Law and Public Policy* 817; T.G. Palmer, 'Intellectual Property: A Non-Posnerian Law and Economics Approach' (1989) *Hamline Law Review* 261.

60 M. Foucault, 'What is an Author?' in P. Rabinow (ed.), *The Foucault Reader* (Harmondsworth, 1986). M. Rose, *Authors and Owners: The Invention Of Copyright* (Cambridge, Mass., 1993); B. Sherman and A. Strowel, *Authors and Origins: Essays on Copyright Law* (Oxford, 1994).

reason, global coordination mechanisms are required. Finally, the 1994 Action Plan with the title '*Europe's way to the Information Society*', in section III repeats that the information society promises to '*create new jobs and to promote Europe's linguistic and cultural diversity*'.

The introduction of the *Green Paper on Innovation* deserves a direct quotation, in order to demonstrate the particular patterns of words that are being reproduced in all these documents:

> Innovation is vital for the viability and success of a modern economy. In this regard, Europe seems less well placed than its main competitors. It has an excellent scientific base but is less successful than other regions of the world at converting its skills into new products and market share, especially in high-technology sectors. Despite certain notable success stories, such as the French high-speed train (TGV) and the GSM mobile phone system, Europe is lagging behind in many of the new technical fields, especially information and communications technology. Concern has been voiced about the extent to which European industry is taking part in the development of the information society and electronic commerce; a special effort needs to be made to improve the situation . . .
>
> It is vital to protect the fruits of innovation. In economic terms, it has been clearly established that companies with specialized know-how which sell branded products and patented products or processes have a competitive advantage when it comes to maintaining or expanding their market share. We are now witnessing the globalization of our economies. At the same time, the value of what is produced lies more in the intangible investment component . . . However, the patent system must under no circumstances act as a further brake on the competitiveness of European companies. Ease of obtaining patents, legal certainty, appropriate geographic coverage: these are all essential criteria for the effective protection of innovation in the European Union.

The Bangemann Report uses the same language, with '*developing a competitive European industry*', promoting '*common rules*' and '*international action to protect intellectual property*', being the highlights:

> While there is a great deal of information that is in the public domain, there is also information containing added value which is proprietary and needs protection via the enforcement of intellectual property rights. IPRs are an important factor in developing a competitive European industry, both in the area of information technology and more generally across a wide variety of industrial and cultural sectors . . .
>
> The global nature of the services that will be provided through the information networks means that the Union will have to be party to international action to protect intellectual property. Otherwise, serious difficulties will arise if regulatory systems in different areas of the world are operating on incompatible principles, which permit circumvention or create jurisdictional uncertainties. In this global information market-place, common rules must be agreed and enforced by everyone.

In the same spirit, Frits Bolkestein, the Commissioner of DG Internal Market, repeated the position of the European Commission, when the Council voted for the Irish Presidency's compromise position, after the European Parliament's first reading of the Directive:

> The Council's agreement is a big step towards getting this Directive adopted in a form, which will provide a major contribution to European competitiveness and assist the proper functioning of the Internal Market. We must reward investment in innovation if a real knowledge-based economy is to flourish in Europe. It is nothing more than basic common sense to make sure that inventions are not excluded from patent protection simply because they use computer software . . .
>
> The proposed Directive seeks to harmonise the way in which national patent laws deal with computer-implemented inventions. Such inventions can already be patented by applying to either the European Patent Office (EPO) or the national patent offices of the Member States. However enforcement of patents is dealt with by national courts and, as the law may differ between Member States, the level of protection may, in practice, vary. This can represent a significant barrier to trade in patented products within the Internal Market.[61]

All of these statements are underlined by one basic understanding: the commodification of information, and the centrality of property rights in safeguarding the way investment is returned and innovation is promoted (although balanced by competition law). As Boyle puts it, consciously or unconsciously, we are already developing the language of entitlement for a world in which information—genetic, electronic, proprietary—is one of the main sources and forms of wealth.[62]

The mission of DG Internal Market is to draft 'traditional instruments regulating the market, such as harmonising the laws of the Member States relating to industrial property rights to avoid barriers to trade. The aim is also to create unitary systems for the protection of such rights with Community-wide effect through the filing of one single application for protection (Community trade marks, designs and patents). The Internal Market DG is also increasingly concerned with ensuring that the Single Market functions properly in the Information Society and the fight against counterfeiting.'[63]

In other words, the aim of the European administration is to harmonize, integrate markets, and objectively put notions such as *economy* and *property* in legal categories. The tools to achieve these are, codification and objectification of practices by means of textual analysis, reliance on precedence, invention of new legal categories, and trust in legal institutions.[64] The operating parameters of the above are formality, rule of law, and an increase in legal certainty by means of providing

[61] Press Release: Patents: Commission welcomes Council agreement on Directive on computer-implemented inventions Reference: IP/04/659 Date: 19 May 2004.

[62] J. Boyle, *Shamans, Software, and Spleens. Law and the Construction of Information Society* (Cambridge, Mass, 1996).

[63] http://europa.eu.int/comm/internal_market/en/indprop/overview.htm (web page visited on 19 May 2003).

[64] P. Bourdieu,'La Force du Droit: Eléments pour une Sociologie du Champ Juridique' (1986) 64 *Actes de la Recherche en Sciences Sociales* 3.

the tools for rational predictions of outcomes. Nevertheless, by virtue of providing for certainty, objectivity, rationality, and continuity, a set of assumptions are reproduced simultaneously, which are taken for granted such as the ones regenerating the centrality of property rights. The administrator, in the course of producing a legal document, views herself as disinterested and neutrally interpreting the law, failing to acknowledge assumptions about the social world reproduced therein. In this way, notions such as property and competition, for example, are conceived to be unproblematic, and law is thought to be an effective tool to successfully order social relations.

Taken for granted conceptions concern not only the concept of romantic inventor, not only the utilitarian logic of economic analysis, but also other basic assumptions such as the one that stipulates that innovation is a good thing and that in high evolving markets firms invest heavily and need to have a return to their investment, as they undertake considerable risks. Uniform standards are important for this purpose, since the system has become increasingly international, and firms have to exploit their rights on a global scale.[65]

In a nutshell, it is normal for a person trained in law, and having to deal with the problem of different treatment of software between the EPO and MS, to seek to develop a solution that promotes harmonization, market integration, and innovation by means of established practice, and on the basis of the mainstream authoritative rhetoric promoting IP rights and innovation, already reproduced in a sequence of legal texts. It is then that a legal text appears objective, and the agent creating it seems disinterested, losing sight of the assumptions reproduced therein, while simultaneously regenerating its basic conventions, continuity, and trust in legal institutions.

In simple words, it is not easy for a civil servant working for DG Internal Market to see that protecting proprietary information may not be the only way to promote the information society. When DG Information Society was consulted by DG Internal Market, the former DG sought to include specific provisions covering interoperability, a concept that is fundamental in the IT industry[66] (so that software developers are not required to license a patent for the purpose of,

[65] European Commission Green Paper COM (87); European Commission White Paper COM (93) 700; Recommendations of the Bangemann Group, 1994; European Commission Green Paper COM (97) 314; European Commission Communication COM(2003) 226 final. Between 1987 and 1997 the American copyright and patent industries increased their output at the rate of 5.8 per cent a year compared to 2.8 per cent a year for other industries, and increased the number of jobs at 4.0 per cent a year compared to 1.6 per cent in the ordinary economy. Through the 1990s knowledge-based industry grew twice as fast as service industries overall and four times as fast as manufacturing (Maskus, 2000). A full discussion on the history of the idea that innovation is an important driving force of the economy cannot be elaborated here due to limits of space. For an excellent introduction to the works of thinkers such as Babbage see N. Rosenberg, *Exploring the Black Box: Technology, Economics and History* (Cambridge, 1994).

[66] The IT industry is characterized by product interoperability. Product interoperability underlies the fact that a computer must be compatible with the microprocessor and any necessary peripheral hardware (such as printers, keyboards, monitors, and modems). The operating system must be

for example, creating a device that can play a patented media format). However, one of the negotiators from DG Internal Market strongly disagreed, the argument being that introducing such a concept would be 'contrary to the rationale of patent law', while another point of disagreement concerned the need to have strong patent protection so that 'European companies would effectively compete with US companies'.[67]

The rationale of patent law is that a monopoly period is granted to the inventor, so that she secures a return on her investment for a limited period. In return for the monopoly the inventor must disclose her invention, so that others may utilize the embedded knowledge. True, the rationale of patent law requires that no unnecessary restrictions are imposed, thus if a provision concerning interoperability is included, according to Article 30 of TRIPs this would have to not unreasonably conflict with the normal exploitation of the patent and unreasonably prejudice the legitimate interests of the right holder, taking account of the legitimate interests of third parties. Moreover, we are reminded that patents are for technological inventions, and software should only be patented where it can be shown that it is a non-obvious invention, involves an inventive step, and can be applied in the industry. In interviews with civil servants working for DG Internal Market, the legal requirements of patentability of software were explained meticulously to me. An official from DG Internal Market complained that it is exactly because interest groups do not understand legal texts that they came up with poor proposals.[68]

It appears that the same line of argumentation was adopted in the course of the consultation amongst DGs of the European Commission. In an interview with one of the fonctionnaires working for DG Information Society[69] who has been directly involved in the negotiations between DG Internal Market and DG Information Society as to the aims and scope of the proposal, he described the extent to which and the reasons why the two services disagreed when seeking to strike the right balance between promoting innovation through the proprietary component of the patent system, and safeguarding competition, interoperability, and the interest of society in ensuring that the Internet remains an open space. It is important to note here that there is one unit in DG Information Society whose mission is to 'foster the deployment of Open Source Software, improve competition,

compatible with the microprocessor, and the application programs must be compatible with the operating system. Only if these compatibility requirements are fulfilled will the consumer be able to use the computer. Thus, hardware and software developers' choices are driven by compatibility requirements if they want to develop a commercially successful product. As a result, consumers are more likely to buy a Microsoft computer system, since they know that most current and future applications are likely to work on that system, rather than on a competing system. It follows from that point that the effect described is cyclical, and economists refer to this as the '*tipping effect*'; on these issues see M.A. Lemley, 'Antitrust and the Internet Standardisation Problem' (1996) 28 *Connecticut Law Review* 1041.

[67] Interview with an A4 official, DG Information Society, conducted on 5 June 2004.

[68] Interview with an A5 official DG Internal Market, conducted on 25 January 2002. The same view is expressed in the Consultation Report n.51 above.

[69] Interview with an A4 official, DG Information Society, conducted on 5 June 2004.

and choice.' To this effect, a working group on *libre software* was created in 1998.[70] Moreover, fostering the development and use of open source software may attract funding under the Information Society Technologies Programme (IST). Research and technology development projects aiming at free/open source software can be submitted to any action line of the IST programme.

Q: DG Internal Market had prime responsibility in preparing the text of the proposed Directive and DG Information Society was consulted. How can you describe the course of the negotiations between the two services? Was it smooth or not?
A. DG Internal Market and DG Information Society had totally different points of view. The negotiations were very difficult. It was a battle between Intellectual Property Rights people and software people. Two people from the initial team from DG Information Society left the Commission. Some people from DG Internal Market were reasonable, yet looked at the legalistic picture and missed an appreciation of the social outcome and economic impact of law. In my view, we need a balance between competition and property/monopoly rights, but nowadays patent protection is really expanding. I see the expansion of IPR as hampering innovation, as there has not been a proper evaluation of the economic data we have.

Q: DG Information Society wanted the Directive to include specific provisions safeguarding interoperability and argued that the term 'computer programs as such' should not be used. Is this true?
A: The position of the European Commission [in the proposed Directive] is normally the compromise position of transdepartmental consultation. But, the provision on interoperability was not there. After XXX [one of the chief negotiators from DG Information Society] left, I wanted to include the provision on interoperability; and that was finally accepted by DG Market.

Q: Why do you think people from DG Internal Market were promoting the particular version of the proposed Directive?
A: It is important for the regulatory output of DG Internal Market: the more legal instruments are issued, the better a DG's performance is valued. Moreover, it is the people working in DG Internal Market: I think that it boils down to that they truly believe that an expansion of IPR is good for innovation. However, we know that IPRs are abused. In DG Competition they also know it, with all these cross-licensing agreements, firms behave like cartels. But people from DG Competition are isolated. I cannot pick up the phone and call people there. They see themselves as people who have to maintain their independency and should not talk to interested parties, as others should not interfere with their files.

This last point links well to a discussion in the context of a different interview with a senior official at DG Competition concerning the importance of working with people with common sense: 'It is important to work with people with

[70] http://eu.conecta.it/ (web page visited on 10 May 2003).

common sense, and they are not many. Many times, people present perfectly drafted and justified legal arguments, which are nonetheless politically impossible. People with common sense can see the implications of the legal arguments.'[71]

This is because legal terms, such as the term '*technical contribution*', which, as the following will show, is at the heart of patent law, acquire divergent meanings in accordance with how interested parties understand the role of innovation, competitiveness, and how these can be fostered. A good legal argument is not enough to make a good proposal. The following will take this point further.

Framing with Legal Language

At the heart of patent law in general and the proposal to introduce patent protection in *computer implemented inventions* in particular (interestingly, an invented term that recently enriched the vocabulary of software developers) is the concept of *technical contribution.* It denotes that a computer-implemented invention, which makes a technical contribution to the state of the art, and which is not obvious to a person of normal skill in the field concerned, is more than just a computer program, and can therefore be patented. Hence, the position of the European Commission is that the proposed Directive, by creating transparency and legal certainty, would create an environment in which innovation could be most effectively protected and fostered.

Kennedy's thesis is relevant here, as he argued that the legal system, built upon the notions of property and contract, cannot regenerate itself internally in order to come up with new concepts that would apply to new cases. This is why, according to the author, legal principles are like commodities. When new cases emerge, legal practitioners are, erroneously, expected to have to draft legal arguments by means of interpreting precedent and first principles. According to this line of thinking, the argument presented has to be 'legally correct', otherwise a 'legal mistake' may occur due to the law-maker's incompetence or bad faith. However, Kennedy argues, in these problematic cases, the source of the error should be found in that the rules of precedent and first principles point to multiple interpretations, which may very well be contradictory. If one accepts this, it is easy to see that in reality it is law-makers, judges, and administrators who decide what the right interpretation of legal rules should be, deriving inspiration from 'legal, ethical, and political factors, including class interests and historical and social stereotypes, that contribute to any decision of a matter of importance in their particular culture'.[72]

The proposed Directive is a good example of how legal concepts are given divergent interpretations in the light of accepted social stereotypes. Not only DG

[71] Interview with an A3 official, DG Competition, conducted on 7 June 2004.

[72] D. Kennedy, 'The Role of Law in Economic Thought: Essays on the Fetishism of Commodities' [1985] *American University Law Review*, 37.

Information Society disagreed with DG Internal Market, but also the Parliament disagreed with the Commission as to what the right definitions are. The Parliament wanted wide exclusions covering the use of patented technology for interoperability and data handling. However, the Commission and Council said that these went beyond what was required to set the right balance between rewarding inventors for their efforts and allowing competitors to build on these inventions, and could ultimately harm EU competitiveness. It appears that there is not one way to promote competitiveness, harmonization, integration, and innovation. And legal concepts relevant to patent law can be given various interpretations according to socially accepted understandings about what, for example, the importance of proprietary standards and the meaning of innovation and competitiveness are.

In particular, according to the Opinion of the Economic and Social Committee of the European Parliament,[73] with the development of the open and interoperable networks such as the Internet, it is important that we promote interoperability and open standards, so that freedom of expression, communication trade, capital flows, and education are encouraged. The Opinion then addresses the question of whether the patent system is really suitable to foster the above. We see that according to this view, which comes very close to the arguments presented by EuroLinux and DG Information Society, a proprietary system will not necessarily guarantee the evolution of new technologies. Subsequently, in paragraph 3.1. the opinion goes on to criticize the legal interpretation of the notion of '*field of technology*', which has been adopted in the proposal of the European Commission, as making it possible to

> patent a programmed computer or programmed network or a process implemented through the execution of a programme. Any innovation made in this way is automatically considered 'to belong to a field of technology', even if the result is derived entirely from software operations. The door thus seems wide open to a software patent, as no programmable electronic hardware can operate without software and as the distinction between software 'by itself' and 'software producing technical results', the product of legal casuistry, is indefinable in practice as all software is made to run on a computer or an electronic component, either as a system or as an application. This extension of the scope of application of patentability could thereafter be extended without limit to software programmes and intellectual methods at successive legal rulings of the technical chambers of the EPO, irrespective of the exclusion provided for in Article 52 of the EPC.

In the same spirit, in paragraph 3.1.1 the Opinion criticizes the European Commission by arguing that the text of the proposed Directive justifies the drift of EPO's jusriprudence, when it admits that the '*technical effect*' can amount to the simple fact of a program running on a standard computer. In paragraph 3.1.2 the Opinion warns that the door may open to patenting business methods, as the

[73] 2002/0047 (COD).

EPO may in the future consider drawing an analogy between software and business methods (although currently Appendix 6 of the internal rules for examiners does not allow this). The Opinion further stresses in paragraph 3.7 that the European Commission should seriously take into account the fact that software is a very complex product, requiring the building on previously acquired scientific knowledge, hence the importance of cooperation and dissemination. Therefore, the problem with patents is exactly that cooperation and free circulation of free or open source software may be hindered.

It appears that the draft Directive did not seriously take into account the considerations of the free/open source community. It may be because, as explained earlier, patent lawyers cannot doubt the virtues of the proprietary model upon which patent law is built, feeding into the uncontested belief that the patent system will bring economic prosperity, employment, and global competitiveness, a belief that underlines any relevant legal interpretation, according to paragraph 3.9 of the Opinion. This is why, in the same paragraph, the Opinion attacks the European Commission as providing no adequate explanation as to how the patent system would provide better legal protection than copyright, reminding that there are conflicting economic analyses on the feasibility of patent protection in the software industry. After all, as an interviewee working for DG Information Society[74] pointed out, the European Commission has not so far taken open source/free software developers seriously, as 'they are considered to be '"hippies" or something', promoting arguments about 'sharing' and 'building on top of past knowledge', which certainly do not make sense to lawyers who strongly adhere to the importance of property.

This last point is a valuable one. Developers of open source/*libre* software challenge one of the most important notions underpinning the legal system, that is property, and the orthodox way to view '*innovation*' and '*international competitiveness*'. It is not at all surprising that their views are not considered '*serious*', and it is equally not at all surprising that *fonctionnaires* working for DG Internal Market adopt a view that presents the orthodoxy, being followed by countries such as the USA and Japan, promoting legal certainty and the production of more regulatory measures, the latter bolstering the image of a DG as being *powerful*. And it is normal that such regulatory measures would be produced bearing the symbols of authority and continuity, by means of the way patterns of words are repeated, based on prior texts and precedent, making a legal argument acquire the form it *should* have.

Divergent Voices and Phronetic Ruptures

It appears that different Directorates General seem to have diverse views as to what the '*correct*' and '*authorized*' interpretation of legal texts are, thus revealing a

[74] Interview with an A5 official, DG Information Society, conducted on 5 June 2004.

picture different from the one propagated by the principle of collegiality. A confrontation occurs amongst these actors, with regard to the technical competence to *interpret* a corpus of legal texts and collect the information necessary to conduct reliable assessments, as to what kind of legislation is required, and what would be the right execution of the mandate of law. For example, DG Information Society and DG Research are viewed as being the most collusive with big business, in contrast to other DGs considered as more '*liberal*'. This may be attributed to the fact that a large number of the officials working for these DGs have a scientific background, as they have been trained as electronic or telecommunication engineers. Moreover, many of them have worked both in the industry and in national administrative systems. Therefore, they feel that they are close to lobbyists and consider themselves as mediators, as they speak the same '*scientific language*' with national groups affected by the policies of the European Commission.[75] This is a good example of the simultaneous operation of the juridico-administrative mode of thinking alongside the more pragmatic industry-oriented mindset for *fonctionnaires* of DG Information Society.

Moreover, the open source and *libre* software developers have a different understanding about the role of Intellectual Property Rights. According to this, innovation and information should be shared, allowing for technological experimentation and public discussion, especially in the case of technologies running as fast as software. They promote a vision of knowledge as being built on top of past knowledge, hence, sharing is the prerequisite for truly innovative projects. As such, they promote a different understanding of the role of Intellectual Property Rights in modern economies. If one accepts this, then by means of promoting the *creator/inventor* dominant conceptualization we may undervalue the public domain. And by giving monopoly rights to established powerful firms, we do not necessarily benefit innovation, especially in fast-evolving industries.[76] For them, innovation is not only conceived as being the product of scientific research produced in laboratories, but also as the result of minor modifications introduced in the course of everyday activity, with collaboration, exchange, and experimentation being crucial to this effect. Openness and communication are the foundations of the Internet, which inherited the rationale that underlined the efforts by the military to create a decentralized network, the ethos of academic research, and the

[75] L. Jourdain, 'La Commission Européenne et la Construction d'un Nouveau Modèle d'Intervention Publique' (1996) 43 *Revue Française des Sciences Sociales* 492, 500.

[76] J.H. Reichman and P. Samuelson, 'Intellectual Property Rights in Data?' (1997) 50 *Vanderbilt Law Review* 72; P.A. David, 'Tragedy of the Public Knowledge "Commons"? Global Science, Intellectual Property and the Digital Technology Boomerang' Oxford IP Research Institute Working Paper (2000) WP 04/00A, available at http://www.oiprc.ox.ac.uk/EJWP0400.pdf; P. Samuelson, 'Digital Information, Digital Networks, and the Public Domain' (2003) 66 *Law and Contemporary Problems* 147. A very interesting conference on Public Domain was held by the Duke Law School resulting in a series of sceptical articles being published in (2003) 66 *Law and Contemporary Problems* Volumes 1 and 2.

counter-culture of hackers that viewed it as a unique medium of expression and technological innovation.[77]

Yet again, not all open source developers agreed with the common position advanced by the EuroLinux Alliance. In a *Joint Statement of the Industry* directed to the Members of the European Parliament, Graham Taylor, director of the Open Forum Europe, which seeks to promote open source, signed it acting as a representative of the Linux/Opensource world. This joint statement asked legislators to ensure that computer programs are treated as patentable inventions, taking the view that such a legislative measure would promote innovation and safeguard the interests of the open source/software *libre* community.

Interestingly, the reaction on the part of other organizations such as the Free Software Foundation, the Open Source Initiative, and Software in the Public Interest has been strong. He was accused of not having the credentials to represent Linux, Open Source, and Free Software developer communities, in view of the fact that he is in sharp opposition to the stance taken by the overwhelming majority of developers. Moreover, he was blamed as being a 'false' or 'misled' representative of the community.

The following will consolidate the basic points of this chapter.

Conclusions

Decentralized regulation and procedural law is meant to steer the activity of networks of actors, which in turn generate the raw material upon which negotiation and discussion is based. The problem in this understanding is twofold: for one thing, the steering of activity is not a neutral exercise, as the process of identifying a social problem as a legal problem is loaded with options dictated by the various disciplines feeding into it. To give an example, patent protection of computer-implemented inventions assumes that patents are good for innovation and that innovation is good for modern economies. These beliefs are not uncontested, but certainly present the orthodoxy.

For another, if one accepts the proposition that minds are socially constructed, then understanding conflicts and problems of cooperation in forums of discussion requires directing our attention to embedded patterns of perception. Having said this, in the analysis of the case study of this chapter, the proposed Directive on the patentability of computer-implemented inventions, which failed to be adopted, it was argued that there is not a single pattern of perception for all agents

[77] M. Castells, *The Rise of the Network Society*, 2nd edn. (Oxford, 2000), 353–4; Vaidhyanathan, *Copyrights and Copywrongs. The Rise of Intellectual Property and How it Threatens Creativity* (New York, 2001).

in the European Commission. Structural patterns of thinking about the social world may be derived from '*lawyer thinking*' and as such promote harmonization, legal certainty, and continuity. Alternatively, they may be based on professional background, and as such reproduce different understandings with regard to the legal/illegal taxonomy, closer to the needs of the industry. Moreover, it may be that a vision of free information and non-proprietary standards is promoted, which can be understood if reference is made to the first steps of the development of the Internet, to see that it was actually built on the need to have free flows of information and speech. In the light of the above, engaging interested parties in a discussion on the basis of common shared beliefs is certainly not an easy task, in view of conflicts amongst unspoken worldviews being the product of history. In other words, cooperation is certainly not easy in the face of conflicts between law's '*common sense*', promoting continuity and certainty, and other views challenging uncontested beliefs tacitly reproduced in legal documents.

However, this does not mean that any communication is impossible, as phronesis, and the embedded beliefs that it embraces, are subject to experience. For example, we saw that interest groups managed to have the interoperability provisions incorporated in the proposed Directive, and in general achieved the spurring of academic and policy debate as to the nature and economic function of open source/*libre* software. This accomplishment can be attributed to structural reasons, such as the new approach in the EU, which supports the effective engagement of NGOs in the policy process, in order to create a European civil society. It is also important that such groups have expert knowledge adding weight to their opinion, which the European Commission *needs* in order to form informed decisions and avoid conflicts in the Parliament and Council.

Another point that implicitly emerged from the previous discussion and which deserves the attention of future research concerns the need for an individual or an organization to be a member in networks in order to promote its interests. Belonging to networks is crucial in order to participate in any discussion. The EuroLinux Alliance is very well organized, and managed to promote a petition against the proposed Directive, and find supporters in the European Parliament, despite being an economic minority in comparison with the other networks of actors that participated in the consultation. However, to be able to support their views, software developers would have to be organized in an alliance, which would promote a unified response to the proposal. In other words, participation requires belonging to networks, which in turn advance common goals. But how 'common' are these goals? Is it possible that a 'unified' response normalizes divergent opinions even inside networks? Peer pressure, preserving prestige, and asymmetries of power, they all underline the process of presenting a cohesive response to externally imposed challenges. Although action based on consensus built in such networks is important, as the opposite would result in oppressive action, can we discard the possibility that it results in political normalization? This is why the important thing is to invent modes for political participation, safeguarding difference.[78]

I hope the analysis of this chapter succeeded in stimulating some thoughts in this direction.

[78] H.F. Haber, *Beyond Postmodern Politics: Lyotard, Rorty, Foucault* (New York, 1994).

20

Cultural Globalization and Public Policy: Exclusion of Foreign Law in the Global Village

Mohamed S. Abdel Wahab

Law has been an essential institution for all societies since the dawn of history and throughout the evolutionary process of all human societies. It represents the mirror image of the society, a product of the social processes that determine its common interests, and reflects the culture and deep-rooted traditions of the society.

In the age of globalization, cultural barriers have been breached through contemporary flows of commodities, capital, people, and values.[1] This was facilitated by rapid development in the technological field, which resulted in the neutralization of space and compression of time, easy movement of citizens of the information society, and economic globalization. Accordingly, an intensified process of cultural interaction is taking place, where foreign and domestic legal institutions as carriers of cultural patterns have thus become increasingly interactive, and societies are becoming more and more susceptible to foreign legal practices and institutions.

This new global order powered by the prevailing globalization trends has induced supervening changes in the functions of states and markets, brought about a new realism regarding the role of the rule of law in societies, and challenged the existing legal distinctiveness and classical perceptions of established legal institutions in a world that is increasingly becoming a global village. Accordingly, this contemporary state of affairs has impacted on the fundamental socio-legal notion of public policy.

Although public policy remains a classical method of rejection of a foreign law and a filtering device that acts as a last line of defence safeguarding the forum's

[1] I. Wallerstein, 'The National and the Universal: Can There Be Such a Thing as World Culture?', in: A.D. King (ed.), *Culture, Globalisation and the World-System, Contemporary Conditions for the Representation of Identity* (Minneapolis, 1997), 94; T. Spybey, *Globalization and World Society* (Cambridge, 1996), 5–6; H. Mackay, 'The Globalization of Culture', in D. Held (ed.) *A Globalizing World? Culture, Economics, Politics* (London, 2000), 49–54.

deep-rooted values and fundamental basic principles, it is no longer an inherently exclusive national conception. Under the impact of globalization it has acquired transnational dimensions (regional and global) that are increasingly constituting an integral part of the concept, hence challenging the classical model of pure nationalism. Similarly, the scope of public policy has been affected by increasing trends of cultural and economic interaction that open the door to foreign legal practices, and lead eventually to more tolerance either on a conscious or a subconscious level. Thus, with an increased level of tolerance towards foreign legal institutions and practices the frequency of operation of public policy declines, hence narrowing the scope of the concept.

Nevertheless, it should be noted that narrowing the scope of the concept does not entail an eventual erosion or demise of public policy, as there will always be cases where the application of certain foreign legal principles remains a serious threat and is repugnant to the forum's fundamental basic notions.

By and large, even though the increased exposure to globalization trends, especially cultural interaction, affects cultural and legal distinctiveness of societies, this does not result in a total transformation or erosion of distinct cultural and legal patterns due to the existence of counter trends of localization that attempt to neutralize to some extent the sweeping waves of globalization. Thus, there will remain a margin of fundamental differences between some societies that allows public policy to surface each time a foreign legal rule represents a threat to such distinct basic notions of the forum.

On such bases, this chapter aims to examine the impact of cultural globalization on the notion of public policy as a fundamental legal conception precluding the application of foreign law. Thus it will be divided into two main parts. In the first part I will attempt to scrutinize the phenomenon of globalization and cultural interaction. In the second part I will address the impact of the globalization of culture on the nature and scope of public policy.

Globalization and Postmodernization of Culture

Globalization has been a fashionable 'buzzword' that has caught the attention and interest of scholars and people across the globe and has become a central topic for commentaries on contemporary social, economic, political, legal, and cultural transformations.

As one of the fundamental forces shaping our contemporary world, globalization exerts a profound impact on economic, political, social, and legal institutions. Whether classified as an evolutionary process that commenced a long time ago or a much more contemporary phenomenon, globalization certainly has influenced our understanding of the world as a whole and challenged some classical perceptions pertaining to the socio-cultural and legal edifice of societies. It is widely viewed as one of the most powerful forces shaping the modern world and a key idea explaining the transition of the human society into the third millennium.[2]

Despite the inherent difficulty associated with defining globalization, due to the complexity of the global paradigm, many scholars across various disciplines have offered diverse definitions. Snyder defines it as 'an aggregate of multifaceted, uneven, often contradictory economic, political, social and cultural processes which are characteristic of our time.'[3] Cochrane, Allan, and Pain define it as a process that 'involves an intensification of flows and networks of interaction that transcend the nation-state as well as increasing interpenetration of economic and social practices, which in turn promote cultural interaction at the local and global levels.'[4] Robertson refers to globalization as 'the processes of the compression of the world and the intensification of consciousness of the world as a whole.'[5] Giddens defines it as 'the intensification of worldwide social relations which link distant localities in such a way that local happenings are shaped by events occurring many miles away and vice versa.'[6]

A scrupulous survey of these definitions reflects that all of them revolve around a central axial idea that is: globalization is a multifaceted phenomenon producing social, political, economic, legal, and cultural projections. On such a basis, it is submitted that globalization is a non-linear, asymmetric, and highly differentiated phenomenon, which under the influence of technology (its driving force) has intensified socio-cultural, political, economic, and legal interaction between diverse societies and systems, and induced profound transmogrification in the spatial-temporal continuum in an unprecedented manner.

Culture and cross-border inter-societal relations represent one of the main thrusts of globalization. Culture has interacted with all other globalization trends

[2] M. Waters, *Globalization* (London, 1995), 1; L. Brittan, *Globalisation vs. Sovereignty? The European Response, The 1997 Rede Lecture and Related Speeches* (Cambridge, 1997), 1. Many writers and futurologists expressed the profound change occurring across the world in all disciplines. We saw McLuhan's optimistic concept of the 'global village' as an expression of the fundamental revolution in media and communication. M. McLuhan, *Explorations in Communication* (Boston, 1960). Similarly, Alvin Toffler spoke of a new technological revolution in this era, resulting in the demassification of mass production. He argued that this revolution represents the third wave in the history of human society evolution. The first two waves were the agricultural and industrial revolutions. See A. Toffler, *The Third Wave* (London, 1981).

[3] F. Snyder, 'Governing Economic Globalisation: Global Legal Pluralism and European Law' (1999) 5(4) *European Law Journal* 335; F. Snyder, 'Europeanisation and Globalisation as Friends and Rivals: European Union Law in Global Economic Networks', in F. Snyder (ed.), *The Europeanisation of Law: The Legal Effects of the European Integration* (Oxford, 2000), 295.

[4] A. Cochrane and K. Pain, 'A Globalizing Society?', in Held, n.1, above, 16.

[5] R. Robertson, *Globalisation, Social Theory and Global Culture* (London, 1992), 8.

[6] A. Giddens, *The Consequences of Modernity* (Stanford, 1990), 64. Giddens argues that globalization is a consequence of modernity, which is inherently globalizing. It involves time-space distanciation. According to him this constitutes the prime condition for the processes of disembedding, which involves the lifting out of social relations from the local contexts of interaction and their restructuring across indefinite spans of time-space. See 3, 20–1, 63. However, Robertson is opposed to such a view as he is of the opinion that globalization should not be equated or viewed as a direct ramification of an amorphously conceived modernity. See Robertson, n.5, above, 8.

and reacted to globalization in two contrasting ways: (a) acceptance of a new global culture, and (b) rejection of a total loss of cultural identity as an expression of a distinctive group of individuals which thus strengthens localization.

Culture represents the set of practices, values, beliefs, and customs acquired by individuals as members of a distinctive society, and those resulting from interaction between people, which have accumulated, assimilated, and passed on to following generations.[7] Thus, each individual learns, interacts, and communicates with the society and through such a process s/he is being culturally shaped. This process of cultural acquisition is referred to as 'Enculturation'.[8]

Enculturation takes place over three levels:[9] (a) the level of unconsciousness where our shaping by a particular set of social practices and values acclimatize us to how we comprehend self and the world; (b) the level of consciousness but beyond our control where human behaviour is founded on the reaction and compliance to the pressure exerted by the surrounding social forces. Under this level, some people are forced to comply with the same values adopted by the majority of people in their society and which may differ from the formers' own;[10] (c) the cultural supermarket level where people are free to pick and choose the values and ideas they want. This is a level of both consciousness and control. This last level is further facilitated by the forces of globalization, which sustain an ever-increasing chain reaction of cultural interaction.

Nevertheless, one could argue that the cultural supermarket level may not be totally a level of consciousness and control because all three levels co-exist and occur simultaneously to a great extent. Thus, communicating and interacting with diverse people representing different cultural traditions and practices,

[7] Renteln defines culture as 'a dynamic value system of learned elements, with assumptions, conventions, beliefs and rules permitting members of group to relate to each other and to the world, to communicate and to develop their creative potential.' A.D. Renteln, 'Clash of Civilizations? Cultural Differences in the Development and Interpretation of International Law, Cultural Bias in International Law' (1998) 92 *American Society of International Law Proceedings* 233; C. Kerr, J.T. Dunlop, F.H. Harbison and C.A. Myers, define it as 'that complex whole which includes knowledge, belief, art, law, morals, custom, and any other capabilities and habits acquired by man as a member of a society'. C. Kerr, J.T. Dunlop, F.H. Harbison, and C.A. Myers, *Industrialism and the Industrial Man* (Harmondsworth, 1973), 94; Wallerstein defines it as 'the set of values or practices of some part smaller than some whole'. Wallerstein, n.1, above, 91; Holton refers to culture as 'both ideas and practices that have in common the function of providing meaning and identity for social actors and which combine cognitive, expressive, and evaluative elements'. R. Holton, *Globalization and the Nation-State* (Aldershot, 1998), 162; Burns defines it as 'the interaction of people and results in learning and that such learning can be accumulated, assimilated and passed on ... culture consists of behavioural patterns, knowledge and values which have been acquired and transmitted through generations, an organised body of conventional understandings manifest in art and artefact, which, persisting through tradition, characterises a human group'. P. Burns, 'Brief Encounters, Culture, Tourism and the Local-Global Nexus', in S. Wahab and C. Cooper (eds), *Tourism in the Age of Globalisation* (London, 2001), 293–4.

[8] Renteln, n.7, above, 233.

[9] G. Mathews, *Global Culture/Individual Identity, Searching for Home in the Cultural Supermarket* (London, 2000), 12–16.

[10] Usage of the word force here denotes not only physical force represented by punishment, but the society's moral reaction towards any resistance as well. Thus, resistance and refusal of compliance is not impossible, but its costs are very high.

especially in cyberspace, contribute to the shaping of the self and one's perception of the world, other individuals, and societies consciously or unconsciously. Accordingly, enculturation on the cultural supermarket level may not always be subject to awareness and control.

On such a basis, culture and enculturation are certainly affected by globalization trends, which have opened new windows on the world: windows through which we can see both the wonder of it all and the things that make us wonder about it all.[11] Thus, the tidal wave of globalization has swept throughout the world transforming the cultural mosaic of traditional societies.

Culture is a very complex institution that is being torn—in the age of globalization—between two powerful forces: a 'Centrifugal Force' and a 'Centripetal Force'. Whilst the latter, under the influence of globalization trends, works to facilitate cultural homogenization and the formation of a true global society that has dissolved all differences, the former, under the influence of national and ethnic movements and the fear of loss of identity, works to reject or mitigate the impact of globalization by protecting and preserving local identities.

Modern social systems possess a highly complex level of differentiation,[12] and are equally characterized by progressive commodification and rationalization.[13] This view was previously advocated by Durkheim, who argued that as societies expanded and increased in complexity, the degree of social and cultural differentiation developed to the point at which, even for members of the same society, the only thing they retained in common was their humanity.[14] Postmodernization of culture involves an intensification of differentiation, rationalization, and commodification, which dissolves the regional stability of culture and reverses its priorities.[15]

By and large, we are witnessing a global cultural ecumene (a region of persistent culture interaction and transformation); a medium of interaction and interpenetration between universalism and particularism. This local-global nexus reflects

[11] J. Nisbitt, *Global Paradox* (New York, 1994), 192.

[12] A differentiated society is one, which is more advanced and better adapted to its environment because it has competed with other societies and outlived them. Differentiation could be understood as exhibiting two aspects: (a) A more differentiated system is one where the subsystems which perform the four functional imperatives of adaptation, goal attainment, integration, and latency (collectively referred to as AGIL) move apart. Thus, boundaries between economy and family or between religion and politics are more obvious than traditional societies. (b) Each subsystem undergoes a series of internal differentiation along the AGIL dimensions. S. Crook, J. Pakulski and M. Waters, *Postmodernization, Change in Advanced Society* (London, 1992), 3–5.

[13] *Ibid*, 10.

[14] Cited in M. Featherstone, 'Global Culture: An Introduction', in M. Featherstone (ed.), *Global Culture, Nationalism, Globalization and Modernity* (London, 1990), 4. This view neglects the common values, beliefs, and shared memories that exist in the inner conscience of individuals, but points to the fundamental impact of cultural interaction and society expansion on cultural evolution. It also brings to mind the concept of imagined communities advocated by Benedict Anderson. However, the latter was of the opinion that despite being separated and perhaps not coming into face-to-face contact, individuals of the same society share common beliefs, shared memories and ideas, etc.

[15] Crook, Pakulski and Waters, n.12, above, 36.

the tension between cultural homogenization (the creation of a global cosmopolitan culture) and cultural heterogenization (preserving distinctive cultural identities) and as such promotes global cultural interaction.[16]

In this context, several conflicting theses about the emergence of a unified global culture, cultural polarization, and cultural hybridization have been advocated. Thus, it is necessary to give a brief analysis of these theses before scrutinizing and assessing the true nature of cultural globalization.

Homogenization and Cultural Cosmopolitanism

Proponents of the global world culture thesis argue that the rise of supraterritoriality has given people all over the world unprecedented shared orientation under the influence of global markets, global organizations, global mass media, global monies, and global symbols.[17] This has generated a condition of 'fellow-feeling', the intensity of which is directly proportional to the propensity to perceive shared interests.[18]

Dore argues that the efficiency of an industrial world system requires cultural convergence and that the increasing density of communications is leading to an increasing fleshing out of a skeletal 'world culture', and its diffusion to larger numbers of people.[19] Similarly, Rosenau argues that cultural commitments exclusivity is not protected against external influences depicted by the tides of globalization. Thus, a medium of global culture is created.[20]

Robertson acknowledges that the cultures of particular societies are an outcome of their interaction with other societies in the global system, and by the same process of interaction between national societies distinctive global culture is partly created.[21] Other writers have been so explicit as to acknowledge the emergence of a global mass culture for a single worldwide civilization of humanity.[22] According to such views, culture is considered an inconclusive element of differentiation.[23]

[16] Featherstone, n.14, above, 6; U. Hannerz, *Cultural Complexity, Studies in Social Organisation of Meaning* (New York, 1992), 218; Robertson, n.5, above, 100, 102–3, 178.

[17] J.A. Scholte, *Globalization, A Critical Introduction* (Aldershot, 2000), 178.

[18] Fellow-feeling means the belief that the society of states requires moral commitment to certain basic rules because of its inevitable continuance as one community of mankind. R. Dore, 'Unity and Diversity in World Culture', in H. Bull and A. Watson (eds), *The Expansion of International Society* (Oxford, 1985), 407–8, 413.

[19] *Ibid*, 415, 419, 424. In his support of the idea of emergence of a world culture, Dore is optimistic about the future, as he estimates that the structure of the world order reinforced by the binding ties of the world culture might improve.

[20] Global culture is understood as a set of norms shared on a worldwide scale. J.N. Rosenau, *Turbulence in World Politics* (Princeton, 1990), 420.

[21] Robertson, n.5, above, 113–14.

[22] G.B. Madison, 'Globalization: Challenges and Opportunities' (1998) *Globalization Working Papers* 9. Available at http://www.humanities.mcmaster.ca/~global/workpapers/madison/98-1mad.html; Claude Levi-Strauss cited in Holton, n.7, above, 163.

[23] The prevalence of a global cultural supermarket has instigated recent anthropologists to get rid of the term culture because in today's world of massive global flows of people, capital, and ideas culture could not be thought of as a decisive element in differentiating between people around the globe. Mathews, n.9, above, 3–4.

It has been argued that the popular version of the homogenization thesis is that which associates globalization with Westernization or Americanization. Cultural cosmopolitanism is envisaged as the self-presentation of the dominant particular. It is the hegemonic sweep at which certain local particularities try to dominate the whole scene, to mobilize the technology and to incorporate a variety of more localized identities.[24] In a nutshell, it is a form of cultural imperialism.[25]

Despite adopting an optimistic view about the emergence of a cosmopolitan global culture, and acknowledging the profound role of cultural interaction in shaping a homogenous global culture, the homogenization thesis, especially in its popular version, is not unquestionable. Understanding cultural homogenization as erosion and eradication of all diverse cultures and the emergence of a totally unified single global culture seems far from reality and possibility, at least in the near future.

The process of cultural interaction and globalization does not mean in its true sense that the world should be dominated by a single logic or culture. Thus, it should not be considered a process of Westernization or imposition of a western cultural model, but rather a process aiming at achieving mutual respect and trust, and searching for common interests, values, and principles stemming from our common human nature. It is not a one-way process but a two-way interaction. The tidal waves of this process cause transformation of cultural patterns and practices; nonetheless, this does not entail total erosion or demise of cultures involved in the process, as there is a narrow margin of cultural preservation.

Cultural Polarization: Clash and Divergence

The polarization thesis advanced by Huntington is built on the realization that the dynamics of the contemporary world are far from being dominated by a single logic.[26] Huntington argues, 'It is my hypothesis that the fundamental source of conflict in this new world will not be primarily ideological or primarily economic. The great divisions among humankind and the dominating source of conflict will be cultural. Nation states will remain the most powerful actors in world affairs, but the principal conflicts of global politics will occur between nations and groups of different civilizations. The clash of civilizations will dominate global politics. The fault lines between civilizations will be the battle lines of the future.'[27]

He defines civilizations as distinct cultural entities each possessing common objective elements, such as language, history, religion, customs, institutions, and subjective self-identification of people.[28] His opinion is that the world is divided

[24] S. Hall, 'Old and New Identities, Old and New Ethnicities', in King, n.1, above, 67.

[25] Holton, n.7, above, 163, 166–73; Mackay, n.1, above, 60, 79–80; M. Irvin, 'Global Cyber Culture Reconsidered: Cyberspace, Identity, and the Global Informational City', available at http://www.georgetown.edu/irvinemj/articles/globalculture.html, 12–13.

[26] Holton, n.7, above, 172.

[27] S. Huntington, 'The Clash of Civilizations? The Next Pattern of Conflicts' (1993) 72(3) *Foreign Affairs* 22–50.

[28] *Ibid*, 23–4.

into seven or eight major civilizations, which will be in future conflict.[29] His argument is based on several reasons, which he believes will cause an inevitable clash:[30] (a) differences among civilizations are not only real, they are basic; (b) as the world is becoming a smaller place, interactions between diverse cultures are increasing. These increasing interactions intensify civilization-consciousness and awareness of differences between civilizations; (c) the processes of economic modernization and social change throughout the world are separating people from long-standing local identities. They also weaken the nation state as a source of identity; (d) cultural characteristics and differences are less mutable and hence less easily compromised and resolved than political and economic ones; (e) successful economic regionalism will reinforce civilization-consciousness.

Huntington ends his argument by saying, 'It will require an effort to identify elements of commonality between Western and other civilizations. For the relevant future, there will be no universal civilization, but instead a world of different civilizations, each of which will have to learn to coexist with the others.'[31]

The polarization thesis seems to have two main strengths: (a) it reflects the inherent tension between globalists and localists concerning the globalization of culture; (b) it draws attention to an irreducible divergence of cultural patterns in the new world order.[32] However, Huntington's polarization thesis is not immune from criticism. First, the notion of separate and distinctive cultures and civilizations as advocated by Huntington is vastly exaggerated and over-inflated within the global field.[33] True differences exist, but to what extent? And are there no commonalities? It is true that there are existing differences, yet commonalities stemming from the increasing shared interests, common nature of mankind, and progressive cultural interaction equally exist. Secondly, Huntington himself argues that these different civilizations would have to learn to co-exist with each other. Part of this ongoing long process of learning is the identification of certain common elements, which is an indispensable factor of co-existence. Thirdly, it is true that cultural differences are less mutable and hence less easily compromised than political and economic ones, yet this does not deny the existence of interaction and similarities (at least to a certain acceptable extent). Despite being a slow process, it is an ongoing dynamic one as well. Culture has a sharp edge that is now being mitigated.[34]

Despite being thought-provoking, Huntington's thesis is still questionable and has not been totally accepted by other scholars.[35]

[29] These include Western, Confucian, Japanese, Islamic, Hindu, Slavic-Orthodox, Latin American, and possibly African civilizations. He predicts that the clash will occur between these civilizations in general and between the West and the emergent Islamic-Confucian axis in particular. *Ibid*, 24.

[30] *Ibid*, 25–7.

[31] *Ibid*, 48.

[32] Holton, n.7, above, 174.

[33] *Ibid.*

[34] Northorp said that the East and West 'can meet, not because they are saying the same thing, but because they are expressing different yet complementary things, both of which are required for an adequate and true conception of man's self and his universe'. Cited in M.J. Mazarr, 'Culture in International Relations' (1996) *Washington Quarterly*. Available at http://www.globalpolicy.org/globaliz/cultural/cultur2.htm.

[35] Mazarr argues that of the six reasons advanced by Huntington, the fifth is an observation, not a reason. The first is probably untrue as stated. And the other four in fact support an entirely different

Cultural Hybridization

The central argument of proponents of the hybridization thesis is that the increase in intensity of cultural interaction brought about by the process of globalization promotes the dissolution of the link between culture and territory or place. Accordingly, the process of disembeddedment of cultural practices produces complex hybrid forms of culture.[36]

Hannerz argues that there is now an emergent world culture with no total homogenization, but one network of social relationships with a flow of meanings, people, and goods between its diverse regions.[37] Thus, cultures rather than being separated from one another as the hard-edged pieces in a mosaic, tend to overlap and mingle.[38]

Proponents of the hybridization thesis such as Hannerz ascertain the existence of a global cultural ecumene; a medium of persistent cultural interaction and exchange, which embraces subcultures of the whole. These subcultures are only separated by nebulous boundaries.[39] This process is called creolization.[40]

Similarly, Smith views the emergent global culture as deterritorialized and a true *mélange* of disparate components drawn from everywhere and nowhere, borne upon the modern chariots of telecommunications systems.[41]

In conclusion, the hybridization thesis is based upon the fundamental effect of cultural interaction in shaping the global culture, which does not displace or totally substitute distinctive local cultures, but affects them, mingles with them and shrinks the barriers that separate them. However, the hybridization thesis remains unclear about the extent and limits of hybridity as the chosen cultural form.[42]

hypothesis—that the real causes of conflict are socio-economic, not civilizational; that they are temporary, not permanent; and that they point the way to a unified globalism rather than a parochial culturalism. When Huntington argues that 'cultural characteristics and differences are less mutable' than others, he may be right, but he is not saying anything about the causes of war—for if those cultural differences do not cause strife, their immutability is irrelevant to the level of conflict. And although differences among civilizations certainly have contributed to causing a number of nasty conflicts, they have been irrelevant to some, served as only one among many factors causing others, and may even have helped avoid war in a few circumstances. The other four reasons—a shrinking globe, the alienating features of rapid socio-economic change, the reaction to Western democracy and consumer culture, and economic regionalism—are not primarily cultural events. They are not caused by culture. They are caused by modernization and globalism: the accelerating spread of modern science, technology, free market systems, and representative democracy throughout the world. *Ibid.* Smith also states that the emergence of cultural areas does not necessarily mean that they are at odds or in conflict with each other. See A.D. Smith, 'Towards a Global Culture?', in Featherstone, n.14, above, 185–6.

[36] J. Tomlinson, *Globalisation and Culture* (Chicago, 1999), 141; Scholte, n.17, above, 180–1.

[37] U. Hannerz, 'Cosmopolitans and Locals in a World Culture', in Featherstone, n.14, above, 237.

[38] *Ibid*, 239.

[39] Hannerz, n.16, above, 218.

[40] Creolization is a term advanced by Hannerz to refer to the 'process where meanings and meaningful forms from different historical sources, originally separated from one another in space, come to mingle extensively.' *Ibid*, 96.

[41] Smith, n.35, above, 177. Tomlinson ascertains that deterritorialization of culture results in hybridization. He defines deterritorialization of culture as the 'loss of natural relation of culture to geographical and social territories'. Tomlinson, n.36, above, 107.

[42] Holton, n.7, above, 184.

Analysis: The Globalization of Culture and Cosmopolitan Vernacularism

The world, in the age of globalization, has grown more global and more divided, more interconnected and yet partitioned, cultural boundaries are being simultaneously permeated and re-established, transcended and re-invented by complex processes of social changes.[43] At the turn of the millennium, tidal waves of cultural interaction enabled people to share cultural influences on a global scale and conduct significant parts of their lives in common.

It has been seen that several theories have been advanced as attempts at deciphering the encrypted coding of cultural globalization. However, the homogenization thesis in its most popular form of Westernization or Americanization fails to provide the true essence of global culture and does not survive critical scrutiny.

Similarly, the polarization thesis seems to exaggerate and magnify cultural differences, which overall are declining rapidly.[44] It presents a powerful model of cultural relativism. However, culture is not only about differences and the rapid and powerful pace of cultural interaction is undeniable.[45]

The hybridization thesis stands somehow in the middle and seems acceptable; nevertheless, it does not solely provide an adequate explanation. Thus, individually, all three theses fail to take into consideration all relevant factors and realities in the search for an adequate explanation of the cultural globalization process.

On such account, it is submitted that globalization with all its economic, technological, ideological, and social trends does carry the seeds of cultural convergence and homogenization, understood as openness towards different and divergent cultural experiences, to the extent that intercultural competence as well as intercultural experience ensue. This is the true essence of cosmopolitanism.[46]

Being a citizen of the world implies the possession of cultural disposition, which is not limited to constraints of locality, but recognizes global belonging, openness to the diversity of global cultures, and preparation to understand and respect cultural perspectives of others. The local and the global do not inherently exist as rivals or cultural polarities, but as mutually interpenetrating principles.[47]

The present tension between the local and the global stems from the fears of being dominated by occidental cultures because the West possesses the technology that drives the wheels of globalization. However, if we think of the cultural interaction process in the global ecumene, it would be obvious that besides being a two-way process, it takes place in all levels of enculturation (consciousness and unconsciousness). It should be noted that, in a market economy operating under the rule of law, it is in the people's own interest to respect the cultural patterns and interests of others.[48]

[43] C. Geertz, 'The World in Pieces: Culture and Politics at the End of the Century' (1998) 32 *Focaal: Tijdschrift Voor Antropologie* 107–10; Holton, n.7, above, 187.

[44] Madison, n.22, above, 8.

[45] Tomlinson, n.36, above, 68.

[46] Hannerz, n.37, above, 239. The etymology of the term 'cosmopolitan' is: '*kosmos*' which is the Latin word for 'world' and '*polis*', which is the Latin word for 'city'.

[47] Tomlinson, n.36, above, 185–6, 196.

[48] Madison, n.22, above, 14.

In the new global order, the sense of togetherness, fellow feeling, and shared interests are increasing, which facilitates homogenization and convergence. A global culture is in the making and systems are converging, but traditional local cultures will not be totally abolished; they will continue to co-exist with cosmopolitan practices. However what is threatened is the idea of exclusive and virtually self-sufficient national cultures.[49]

The world is shrinking under the influence of global economy and technological advancements. The sharp edges of culture are yielding and people will become more and more understanding and accepting of each other's cultural practices. Accordingly, more and more convergence will occur as signs of commonalities and respect transcend barriers of differences. Tensions occur when respect and mutual trust is lacking. Nevertheless, we are witnessing some common values adopted by all nations and cultures as a condition for their very survival.[50]

In conclusion, in today's open societies people are more open to each other. This should promote more respect, understanding, and search for common characteristics and shared interests that outweigh possible differences and could even assist in resolving such differences in a manner that suits all parties in the interest of one human society.

Having examined the process of cultural globalization, it is necessary to shed light on its impact on one of the fundamental conceptions of private international law that continuously threatens the normal application of foreign legal norms and is considered a triumph of nationalism over internationalism, of policy over harmony and uniformity.[51]

The Local-Global Nexus and the Public Policy Impasse

In the age of globalization, we are witnessing a great metamorphosis of the international system: the birth of a truly universal legal system that involves a tectonic shift in transnational legal relationships.[52] The magnitude of cross-border transactions has given rise to intense interaction between diverse national legal systems.

All legal systems acknowledge the necessary existence of a device that acts as a safety valve regulating the application of foreign legal provisions. This device is public policy, which acts as a defensive instrument that ensures the compatibility of the foreign applicable law with the prevailing deep-rooted cultural values and fundamental interests of the forum.

The foreign applicable law might lack 'legal commonality' with the *lex fori* to the extent that the application of some foreign provisions would amount to an

[49] P. Hirst and G. Thompson, *Globalisation in Question, The International Economy and the Possibilities of Governance* (Cambridge, 1990), 266.

[50] Madison, n.22, above, 15.

[51] O. Kahn-Freund, 'Reflections on Public Policy in the English Conflict of Laws' (1953) 39 *Transactions of the Grotius Society* 57.

[52] P. Allott, 'The Emerging Universal Legal System' (2001) 3(1) *International Law Forum du Droit International* 14.

excruciating violation of the forum's prevailing socio-cultural norms.[53] In such cases, the application of a repugnant foreign rule is considered to be transcendent over the frontiers of mutual tolerance and peaceful co-existence and thus calls for a rejection through the invocation of public policy. Thus, a device, like public policy, is required to harness and thwart the flow of such repugnant rules. This is the logical justification for the indispensability of public policy in conflict of laws.

Accordingly, public policy is classically perceived as an inherently national concept that exclusively protects national value system norms and fundamental socio-cultural principles. Nevertheless, with the progressive impact of cultural interaction and social exposure to foreign conceptions under the influence of globalization, the exclusively nationalistic nature of public policy is fading, and public policy is gradually assuming a supranational global dimension reflecting inclusive interests.

Public policy principles bear a variable relative nature that change with time. Thus, they are in a constant state of flux reflecting socio-cultural and legal transformations induced by global trends of cultural and legal interaction. This has impacted on both its nature and scope.

Under the influence of globalization, more and more respect is afforded to foreign legal institutions, the scope of common interests is increasing, as well as the will to accept and respect foreign cultural patterns as reflected in the spirit of foreign legal principles.

The close interconnectedness between distant localities and the intensification of worldwide social and economic relations has resulted in the development of common global interests that have crystallized into a set of transnational fundamental principles shared by the global community at large.

As a general principle of law,[54] public policy expresses and safeguards a shared system of moral and justice values common to the entire global legal community, serving the common interests of mankind, and aiming to protect the global cultural identity and human dignity.[55] However, the existence of a margin of globally

[53] Lack of legal commonality means that there is a profound clash of concepts between the foreign law and the *lex fori* due to the sharp differences in fundamental principles and the social, economic, political, and moral basis of both societies.

[54] On the concept of general principles of law, see F.A. Mann, 'Reflections on a Commercial Law of Nations' (1957) 33 *British Yearbook of International Law* 20–51, 36–8; G.I. Turkin, 'Co-Exsitence and international Law' (1958) 95 *Recueil des Cours* 23–6; S. Abdel-Wahab, 'Reflexions on the General Principles of Law' (1963) *Revue de la Société D'Economie Politique, De Statistique et De Legislation* 33–49; M. Virally, 'The Sources of International Law', in M. Sorensen (ed.), *Manual of Public International Law* (London, 1968), 143–8; The *Barcelona Traction* Case in the [1970] ICJ Rep. 37; D.J. Harris, *Cases and Materials on International Law* (London, 1991), 48–54; I. Detter, *The International Legal Order* (Aldershot, 1994), 199–203; H.-J. Schlochauer, 'International Court of Justice', in Bernhardt (ed.), *Encyclopedia of Public International Law* Vol. II (Amsterdam, 1995), 1092; R. Jennings and A. Watts, *Oppenheim's International Law* Vol. I (London, 1996), 36–41; R.M.M. Wallace, *International Law* (London, 1997), 22–3; T. Hiller, *Sourcebook on Public International Law* (London, 1998), 83–93.

[55] F. Mosconi, 'Exceptions to the Operation of Choice of Law Rules' (1998) 217 *Recueil des Cours* 67–8; D. McClean, '*De Conflicto Legum*: Perspectives on Private International Law at

shared interests and values does not imply that all nations and states across the globe cherish and respect such values; it only means that they are shared by the majority of the global community at large.

In such cases, it could be argued that as these principles form part of the public policy of the forum there is no practical benefit in referring to their global or universal origin; they will be protected under the forum's own conception of public policy in all cases. However, it should be noted that whilst the invocation of the forum's international principles of public policy is dependent on the existence of sufficient connections with the forum that justifies the exclusion of a foreign repugnant rule on the basis thereof, principles of public policy that are based on globally shared transnational norms warrant protection regardless of any connections with the forum, due to their universal origin.

It is also worth noting that such a global or universal conception of public policy reflects a twilight zone where the fundamental principles and *jus cogens* norms of public international law are protected in private international relationships; hence the private international law and public international law orbits tend to overlap, which clearly demonstrates the impact of globalization and international cooperation on public policy and its tendency to embrace fundamental principles derived from a common global identity.

Amongst the countries that seem to support, explicitly or implicitly, the existence of universal principles of public policy that safeguard prevailing conceptions of morality, justice, and human rights are: the United Kingdom,[56] France,[57] Germany,[58] Italy,[59] and Switzerland.[60]

Global principles of public policy could be traced in many fields of international law; however, two main categories merit further consideration: fundamental human rights and universally illicit contracts.

the Turn of the Century. General Course on Private International Law' (2000) 282 *Recueil des Cours* 209.

56 There exists an international public policy compelling English courts to assist in elimination of patent international illegality in the interest of the global community. See F.A. Mann, *Foreign Affairs in English Courts* (Oxford, 1986), 158.

57 Public policy operates to safeguard universal principles of justice. Cour de cassation, 25 May 1948; (1949) 38 *Revue Critique*, 89, Lautour. See D. Lloyd, *Public Policy, A Comparative Study in English and French Law*, (London, 1953), 78; A. Bucher, 'L'Ordre Public et le But Social Des Lois en Droit International Privé' (1993) 239 *Recueil des Cours* 24–5; B. Audit, *Droit International Privé* (Paris, 1997), 269–71.

58 According to Article 25 of the Constitution, general rules of public international law prevail over domestic laws. The German understanding of this concept is that states are obligated to protect, while applying their choice of law rules, the fundamental values recognized by international public policy such as fundamental human rights and liberties. See K.G. Weil and F. Kutscher-Puis, 'General Principles', in M.R. Sammartano and C.G.J. Morse (eds), *Public Policy in Transnational Relationships* (The Hague, 1991), Chapter I–Germany 12.

59 International public policy is considered an aggregate of those principles, which are common to many countries of similar civilization aiming at the protection of human fundamental rights. See M.R. Sammartano, *International Arbitration Law* (Deventer, 1990), 12.

60 Swiss Federal Tribunal, 30 December 1994, (1995) *Bulletin of the Swiss Arbitration Association* 217.

Fundamental Human Rights: A Global Perspective

Foreign laws generally infringing human rights and dignity would not be enforced, as human rights are powerfully protected under several international instruments such as the Universal Declaration of Human Rights (1948),[61] the European Convention on Human Rights and Fundamental Freedoms (1950), the Universal Islamic Declaration of Human Rights (1981), the EU Charter of Fundamental Rights (2000), and the Vienna Declaration and Programme of Action adopted on 25 June 1993 by the World Conference on Human Rights.[62]

Human rights comprise a large number of individual rights. Whilst the majority of rights are subject to global recognition and uniform application, some are contested, especially with respect to their scope, due to the inherent ideological, cultural, and religious diversities in our global village.[63]

Amongst the fundamental rights that are uniformly shared by all mankind, regardless of race and religion are: the right of self-defence, non-discrimination, protection of private property, and the right to a fair hearing.

Accordingly, judgments obtained under a foreign law that did not permit the defendant to present his/her case or defend him/herself will not be enforced as being contrary to principles of justice.

Similarly, where a foreign law is discriminatory on the basis of race, colour, or gender, it will be excluded on the basis of public policy. Thus, laws discriminating against a distinct group of people as a means of oppression will not be enforced or recognized. In *Oppenheimer* v. *Cattermole*,[64] the Nazi discriminatory decrees fell within this category. Lord Cross stated that these laws constituted such a grave infringement of human rights that they ought not to be recognized as laws at all. He added that English courts should give effect to established norms of public international law.

[61] Article 16 entails that all courts should consider contrary to public policy laws prohibiting marriage on grounds of different race, citizenship, etc, or enabling the celebration of marriages without the consent of either spouse.

[62] The Declaration ascertains the universal nature of these rights and freedoms and considers them the birthright of all human beings. However, because every human society is universal because it is human, particularly because it is a society the application of these rights is influenced by cultural, religious, economical and political factors, which may result in diversity. Nonetheless, there exist striking similarities in many basic values of various cultures and still more and more cultural interaction would contribute to the dissolution of barriers and acceptance of principles that do not shock or frustrate the fundamentals of the society. For a detailed discussion of human rights and cultural diversity, see R. Mullerson, 'On Cultural Differences, Levels of Societal Development and Universal Human Rights', in J. Makarczyk (ed.), *Theory of International Law at the Threshold of the 21st Century* (The Hague, 1996), 927–42.

[63] For example, freedom of religion is understood in Islam from a religious perspective: that people are free to choose their faith initially. However, once a person becomes a Moslem he/she is not allowed to change his faith. Similarly, gender equality is a fundamental Islamic principle. However, it is subject to some religious constraints related to the possibility of polygamy for men only and the prohibition of marrying a non-Moslem for Moslem women.

[64] (1976) AC 249. See also *Wolff* v. *Oxholm* (1817) 6 M & S 92.

Equally, confiscation of private property without compensation is clearly against established norms of public international law and universal principles of justice.

Universally Condemned Contracts

Global public policy principles necessitate the exclusion of foreign laws, and invalidation of contracts that support activities condemned by the international community at large.

Examples include: contracts for the sale or smuggling of cultural objects,[65] contracts in promotion of governmental corruption, contracts facilitating money-laundering activities, drug trafficking, smuggling, traffic of arms between private entities, sale of weapons of mass destruction or nuclear components, and trading in human organs.

Thus, the facilitation of cultural interaction between distinctive local cultures and the emergence of global cosmopolitan cultural patterns contribute to the narrowing of the scope of public policy and rejection of the application of foreign law.

Nevertheless, it is submitted that globalization and the intensification of cross-border cultural interaction has also generated anti-global responses reflected in the four Rs (reflection, refraction, resistance, and rejection).[66] These anti-global responses aim to protect the distinctive fundamental socio-cultural foundations of the society, which constitute the essence of the society's identity and thus a rich source for public policy principles. Accordingly, there will always remain a thin red line which tolerance cannot cross. This line is composed of those fundamental public policy principles that cannot be sacrificed on the basis of tolerance, comity, or globalization. However, the local and the global are not inherently rivals or cultural polarities, but they co-exist as mutually interpenetrating principles.[67]

The present reality of this global paradox is based on a composite of dynamic patterns that have covered the world with complex processes of social changes. Whilst the openness of societies brought about by globalization has softened the forum's response and attitude towards foreign legal institutions and resulted in more respect, cooperation, and acceptance, on a different note there remain national trends of localization that aim at safeguarding those sacrosanct principles of social and cultural distinctiveness which cannot be sacrificed or overlooked.

In conclusion, in a world of increasing contacts between different people, the trend towards harmonization and accommodation of legal differences is likely to continue and the scope of public policy will become narrower and narrower. Nevertheless, there remain certain areas, especially in the family law domain

[65] Protection of cultural heritage is established as a global principle that is widely shared by the vast majority of states. L.V. Prott, 'Problems of Private International Law for the Protection of the Cultural Heritage' (1989) 217 *Recueil des Cours* 288–9.

[66] M. Archer, 'Sociology for One World: Unity and Diversity' (1991) 6(2) *International Sociology* 139.

[67] Tomlinson, n.36, above, 185–6, 196.

where public policy will continue to enjoy a flourishing presence due to the existence of some fundamental differences between occidental and oriental societies which reflect indispensable values of cultural distinctiveness and religious beliefs, and a social gap that is not easily bridged by the process of globalization whose impact in this context is slow and gradual due to the existence of opposing local responses that intervene to maintain a certain level of distinctiveness and tolerance.[68]

Conclusion

Globalization is one of the most powerful forces shaping our contemporary world. It is not a linear or a singular phenomenon, but a composite of dynamic patterns sweeping the globe and transforming all aspects of social, economic, legal, and political activities.

This ongoing process of cultural interaction and information exchange facilitated and accelerated by contemporary trends of globalization has rendered culture and enculturation in a continuous state of flux. Traditional and existing cultural patterns and practices are being transformed, interpenetrated, and reshaped by internal and external trends of change and interaction. However, as any form of change involves resistance to that change, cultural transformation in the global age has necessarily generated regional and local pockets of resistance, which aim at preserving local identities and indigenous cultures. This global-local paradox is inherently embedded in structure of the cultural globalization process.

The focal point of our contemporary and future cultural reality rests on the concepts of 'co-existence' and 'tolerance'. The emergence of a new cosmopolitan culture as the offspring of cultural interaction and mutual interpenetration co-exists with locally influenced cultures. A global culture is in the making and systems are converging, but traditional local cultures will not be totally extinct, they will continue to co-exist with cosmopolitan practices.

On such a basis, the Mahatma Ghandi was right when he said, 'I do not want my house to be walled in on all sides and my windows to be barricaded. I want the culture of all the lands to be blown about my house as freely as possible. But I refuse to be blown off my feet by any.'

This complexity of globalization trends, especially from a cultural perspective has impacted on and transformed traditional legal conceptions, especially public policy principles, which have been struck by waves of global transformations and interaction.

As a manifestation of the forum's prevailing value system norms and fundamental principles, public policy considerations have been influenced by economic

68 However, it is worth noting that other areas, such as commercial relations and contracts where harmonization and unification have proved a great success, are more interactive and sensitive to the process of globalization, which equally contributes to narrowing the scope of public policy.

and cultural globalization patterns. Universally shared values and principles have emerged as a result of harmonization of national policies and development of supranational standards that serve the common interests of humanity. Furthermore, the classical national conception of public policy reflecting idiosyncratic values and principles is not immune to contemporary globalization trends, which contribute to the mitigation of chauvinistic diversities between legal systems, and promote the recognition of foreign public policy principles that are based on alien cultural patterns under the influence of co-existence and tolerance.

By and large, although complete harmonization between states or tolerance towards foreign rules will not ensue, especially in family law where distinctive cultural patterns are deeply rooted in the society's conscience, yet the facilitation of global interaction and the emergence of a global cosmopolitan cultural practices in the new global ecumene contribute to changing the nature and narrowing of the scope of public policy, hence increasing the scope of application of foreign law.

In a world of intensified process of interaction, convergence and divergence are likely to co-exist. Legal systems will certainly develop elements of commonality, yet differences will remain. Such differences reflect the existing cultural, legal, and religious diversity between societies, which in turn are reflected in their principles of public policy. This form of inter-societal interaction not only helps mitigate differences between diverse societies without annihilating cultural distinctiveness, but also acts as a catalyst for tolerance, respect, and co-existence. Thus, as globalization advances and cultural interaction progresses and intensifies, tolerance will gain momentum and the scope of public policy will become narrower and narrower.

21

Cosmopolitan Law, Agency, and Narrative

David Hirsh

Introduction

In this chapter I argue that it is appropriate to use the term 'cosmopolitan law' to refer to a new form of law that can develop, has developed, is developing, out of international law. It is clear from the way that I have formulated this proposition that there is some degree of ambiguity or tension in the relationship between the idea of emergence on the one hand and the idea of human agency on the other. Some theorists discuss cosmopolitanism as though it were a stage of history that is superseding a previous, discredited stage of international relations between nation states. I am critical of understanding cosmopolitanism within the framework of a historical narrative of progress. I prefer to understand cosmopolitanism as a framework for human agency, as a guide for action. Yet it is true that my argument also relies on emergence, on showing ways in which international law has, partially and tentatively, developed into something new. The law that classically regulated the relationships between states began, after the Nuremberg tribunals, to hold individuals criminally accountable for their actions and to attempt to enforce the rights of individuals and groups against their own states. This shift in the scope and subject of international law is what potentially makes it into a new form of law.

By looking at legal processes that address the most serious violations of human rights and humanitarian law, I theorize the actuality and potentialities of cosmopolitan law. I also look at the ways in which these processes necessarily employ the developing norms and rules of law to produce narratives of the huge conflicts into which they intervene; narratives that aim to be free from national particularities and that aim to rise above conflict and to offer a neutral and authoritative picture of events.

Against the background of the war against terror, theories of cosmopolitan law that rely on a grand sweep of historical progress look particularly problematic. For example, the way that the decision was made to go to war against the Saddam regime and the way that the coalition chose to treat prisoners fell far short of cosmopolitan hopes. If cosmopolitan law is understood as a manifestation of human progress, then the disdain with which the great powers have sometimes related to it recently, could only be understood as a temporary 'blip' in the sweep of history. If, on the other hand, it is understood as a framework for human agency, then the methods of the war against terror can be understood as a competing framework for agency; one that threatens to take precedence over a cosmopolitan perspective. It can be seen that my conception of cosmopolitanism is as a normative project. It is an argument for a way of fighting against totalitarianism that does not replicate that which it is fighting against. Yet it is a normative project that starts with an analysis of actual events and processes, not only with abstract principles or with utopian yearnings. One lesson of the war against terror is that cosmopolitanism and human rights, when allowed to float free from a conception or an actuality of cosmopolitan law, may be employed as a language with which to make any kind of political claim. The war against terror relies partly on human rights rhetoric, but it manifests a disdain for and an opposition to a cosmopolitan law that can act as a measure of the legitimacy of particular claims.

The ICTY: An Institution built by Committed Human Beings, not simply a Manifestation of American Power

Franz Neumann, Otto Kirchheimer, and Herbert Marcuse, some of the stars of twentieth-century anti-totalitarian critical philosophy, were members of the prosecution team at Nuremberg.[1] These theorists came out of their libraries and universities in order to throw their weight behind an institution that was actualizing a new type of cosmopolitan legal process, but that was also a manifestation of the power of the victorious states of the Second World War. An alliance of the two emergent super-powers backed a cosmopolitan legal process. The powerful states accepted and legitimized the principles of 'crimes against humanity' and of universal jurisdiction for such crimes. The victors put into place a new legal framework that understood genocide to be the business of humanity as a whole, and not just of particular states; a framework that held even heads of states accountable to international criminal law. By 1946 the new institution was already breaking down under the pressures of the Cold War, but in the immediate post-war period, the Nuremberg tribunal was felt by the philosophers of the Frankfurt School to be something worth building, in spite of its compromised position at the nexus of worldly power and before it was crushed by the new struggle for global hegemony. These philosophers took their place among a cohort of idealistic lawyers to build something new, to formulate a new kind of response to totalitarianism.

Cosmopolitan law is a project, a framework for human agency, rather than a global structure that emerges out of some conception of historical progress. We are not discussing a utopian plan for world government. Rather we are looking at

[1] M. Salter, 'The Visibility of the Holocaust: Franz Neumann and the Nuremberg Trials', in: R. Fine and C. Turner (eds), *Social Theory after the Holocaust* (Liverpool, 2000), ch. 10.

instances where cosmopolitan law has had particular successes, which may point towards one kind of effective response to huge anti-human crimes. The International Criminal Tribunal for the former Yugoslavia (ICTY), which emerged at the death of the Cold War, similarly, was an institution that people struggled to build, rather than a straightforward manifestation of the will of powerful states. People involved seized the opportunity that was given by the great powers to build the ICTY and with some good fortune, were able to create a much more alive and independent institution than the Security Council of the UN had intended.

Today, as we watch the trial of Slobodan Milošević himself unfold, the tribunal can appear as a successful manifestation of 'Western', or American, power and resolve. It is not true, however, that there was a policy decision early on by the 'Western' leadership to create such a tribunal. When the tribunal was first constituted by the Security Council it was done so ambivalently.

The policy of the 'international community' swung wildly from humiliation in Sudan, to timidity in Bosnia and Rwanda, to the thunderous and blunt response in Kosovo; the uses the great powers wished to make of the ICTY must also have swung during this period, a period also of transition from Bush to Clinton to Bush, and from Major to Blair. Policy toward the court also became more favourable when Yugoslavia became more stable and when the possible threat to the fragile equilibrium held in place by NATO troops decreased; in other words, when the risk to stability and to the lives of NATO soldiers decreased. One thing is clear: that the ICTY was first established without the resources or the power necessary to succeed in bringing to justice those primarily responsible for ethnic cleansing in the former Yugoslavia.

Its growth into such a body was the result of a combination of factors. There was the work and vision of the prosecutors and judges who built the institution because they believed in it. There were the developments in the former Yugoslavia, such as fall of the Milošević regime and the liberalization of the Tudjman regime after his death. There was the increasing reliance by NATO on human rights rhetoric during the Kosovo conflict. There was the good luck of the ICTY in obtaining defendants, from the chance arrest of Tadić in Germany to the extradition of Milošević, following his overthrow, encouraged by the promise of dollars to the new Serbian regime.

In November 1993 the eleven judges took office in The Hague. Antonio Cassese later said that the Security Council had thought that they would never become operational. 'We had no budget, we had nothing. Zero.'[2] The selection of a prosecutor was a protracted and politicized process, since the prosecutor would have control over the indictments of the court. In July 1994, the Security Council appointed Richard Goldstone. In 1993–4 the UN proposed a budget of $562,300 for investigations, including witness travel, interviews with refugees,

[2] Quoted in G.J. Bass, *Stay the Hand of Vengeance* (Princeton, 2000), 217.

forensic experts, translators and protection,[3] although in the end the General Assembly gave the tribunal $5.6 million for the first half of 1994 and $5.4 million for the second half. By 1999, for comparison, the budget had risen to $94 million.[4] In those early days the morale and the confidence at the ICTY was low and there was a danger that the whole process might fold. A member of Goldstone's staff is quoted by Bass as saying 'A, you can indict Milošević and be shut down. B, or you can do low-level [indictments] and do a few trials'.[5] Even the indictments of Mladić and Karadžić, issued on 25 July 1995, were bold moves by Goldstone. Goldstone said, '... it was really done as, if you like, an academic exercise. Because our duty was clear. We weren't going to be dissuaded from doing it by any prognostications—good or bad—as to what effect it would have.'[6] The autonomy of the prosecutor and of the court was, perhaps, not seen as a problem by the powers, since its possibility for action appeared extremely limited.

The morale and sense of purpose at the ICTY strengthened greatly. It developed from a body whose central actors felt that it existed only to fail in 1993, to a body capable of indicting the (almost) top perpetrators of ethnic cleansing as an academic exercise in 1995, to a body capable of convicting Duško Tadić[7] in 1997. After the Tadić conviction there was a different feeling around the court. There were three courtrooms trying cases and a queue of defendants waiting in the cells. By 1999 the court was ready to indict Milošević himself, and by June 2001 it held him prisoner. This is a trajectory of development that would have astounded everyone in 1992 when the Security Council constituted the court. The relentless increase in leadership, competence, and self-confidence within the institution was mirrored by a gradual change in policy by the American and European powers in its favour.

The ICTY is not simply a manifestation of 'Western' power—it is an institution that came into being, as policy swung from one way to another, as outside circumstances changed, as people worked to develop it. American power is not such that it controls and regulates the minutiae of all and every institution. The first genuinely international trials happened because people took the opportunity to build the institution into one that was able to organize such trials.

Cosmopolitan Law and Narratives of Progress

Classically, international law is the system that protects the right of sovereign states to be free from external aggression and sets out a framework by which the relationships between states may be regulated. Following the experience of Nazism, a need was felt to extend the scope of international law so that it could

[3] Bass, n.2, above, 221. [4] *Ibid.* [5] *Ibid*, 229. [6] *Ibid*, 230.

[7] *Prosecutor* v. *Duško Tadić*, Case No. IT-94-1, ICTY, Judgment, 7 May 1997, www.un.org/icty/tadic/trialc2/judgement/index.htm.

protect the rights not only of states but of individuals, and also so that it could hold individuals criminally responsible for the actions of states. It was recognized that states could not always be relied upon to guarantee the most basic rights of their citizens, and neither could they be relied upon to hold those individuals committing the greatest crimes to account. Some crimes are so huge and some rights so fundamental that they become the business of humanity as a whole and not just the citizens of particular states. In this way, a new form of law began to emerge out of international law, a form of law that has a logic that transcends international law and is in some respects in contradiction with it. It seeks to limit state sovereignty and it lays down minimum standards for the treatment of human beings by states. It claims the right to put individuals on trial for certain crimes even against the will of their state and the state in whose territory and in whose name the crime was committed. I argue that, even though this new form of law can be understood simply as a development in international law, it is more appropriately recognized as *cosmopolitan* law. Cosmopolitan law represents a break from international law because it does not put the rights of states above the rights of people. Its emergence is tentative and radically incomplete; it emerges into a world dominated by forms of power that threaten to extinguish it or to strip it of its radical content. But cosmopolitan law exists as an empirical fact, in institutions such as the ICTY as well as in treaties, conventions, and charters that give ammunition and courage to those struggling against state tyranny.

The aftermath of the Second World War and the Nazi genocide of the Jews saw one of the foundational acts of cosmopolitan law: the creation of a tribunal that was able to bring together the *power* to call witnesses and punish criminals on the one hand, with the *authority* of international law on the other. The Nuremberg Trials established the precedent of international criminal tribunals and for the first time explicitly recognized and prosecuted the new offence of crimes against humanity. The Genocide Convention was agreed in 1948 and codified the crime of genocide. Both of these crimes were subject to universal jurisdiction, meaning that any state had the right to arrest and try suspects irrespective of where the crimes were committed. This brief but vigorous bloom of cosmopolitan law, however, was short lived, and quickly withered under the freeze of the Cold War. Yet immediately at the end of the Cold War it re-emerged. There was no continuous path of historical progress between Nuremberg and the ad hoc tribunals for Yugoslavia and Rwanda: the two significant successes for cosmopolitan law were separated by decades in which it struggled for any kind of recognition. But even across that separation, the ad hoc tribunals were able to build from a foundation that had previously been established. In the United States, President Harry S. Truman had requested the Senate's advice on and consent to the ratification of the Genocide Convention in 1949, but it was not until February 1989 that ratification was completed and it became binding upon the USA.[8] The Senate spent forty years

[8] L.J. Le Blanc, *The United States and the Genocide Convention* (Durham, NC, 1991), 2.

debating the issue, asserting the primacy of US sovereignty and the Constitution over international law and the International Court of Justice, and putting forward possible 'reservations' and 'understandings' that would accompany and clarify ratification. The USA was reluctant to allow its sovereignty to be limited, even in the case of genocide. Passed immediately before the start of the Cold War, the Genocide Convention was only finally ratified by the USA at its very death.

The end of the Cold War saw the concept of 'cosmopolitanism' rescued from its service as a totalitarian term of abuse by a wave of social theorists and philosophers who began to use it as a resource with which to come to terms with a rapidly changing world. Many of them picked up the thread of cosmopolitan argument from Immanuel Kant who had in turn rediscovered the concept from the Greek Stoics and Cynics,[9] and had set out a theory of cosmopolitan law in his 1795 essay, *Perpetual Peace*. He saw that the creation of democratic republics both required and made possible a supranational structure that could prevent war and that could protect the rights of the traveller in a foreign country.

> Cosmopolitan law, thus understood, transcends the particular claims of nations and states and extends to all in the 'universal community'. It connotes a right and duty which must be accepted if people are to learn to tolerate one another's company and to coexist peacefully.[10]

Central to Kant's conception of cosmopolitan law was a democratic, universal content. Cosmopolitan law could only be a framework that enshrined the principles of mutual recognition and tolerance. Kant's vision was of an international confederation of democratic republics: an international order that regulated more than just the relationships between the republics but that also set down minimum standards of human rights, not just for citizens of states, but also simply for citizens of the cosmopolis. Kant specifically attacked the 'depravity' of the Westphalian international order in which 'each state sees its own majesty ... precisely in not having to submit to any external legal constraint' and in which the glory of a state's ruler 'consists in his power to order thousands of people to immolate themselves for a cause which does not truly concern them, while he need not himself incur any danger whatsoever'.[11]

David Held[12] is typical of this new wave of cosmopolitan thinkers who have forcefully argued for a new way of thinking about international relations that puts human rights above state rights and argues for a new set of supranational institutions that can provide a democratic authoritative framework capable of addressing pressing global problems. He presents cosmopolitanism as a set of ideas and practices that are replacing the Westphalian system, both because that outdated system is no longer capable of creating a stable framework for a changed world, and also

[9] M. Nussbaum, 'Kant and Cosmopolitanism', in: J. Bohman and M. Lutz-Bachmann (eds), *Perpetual Peace: Essays on Kant's Cosmopolitan Ideal* (Cambridge, MA, 1997).

[10] D. Held, *Democracy and the Global Order* (Cambridge, 1995), 228.

[11] I. Kant, 'Perpetual Peace', in H. Reiss (ed.), *Kant: Political Writings* (Cambridge, 1991), 103.

[12] Held, n.10 above.

because it is a better, more open and more democratic paradigm. The rapid growth and importance of aspects of life that transcend national borders raise a problem of democratic accountability. The world is changing such that it is increasingly diverging, both theoretically and structurally, from existing politics that aim to keep democratic accountability over it. People are increasingly finding that the key networks of power that influence their lives have escaped from their control and that the powerful have liberated themselves from outdated political arrangements that are increasingly ineffective. Held re-works the concept of sovereignty, arguing for a layered theory in which sovereignty is sited on different levels, local, regional, national, global. What is necessary, he argues, to bind the disparate sites of power and sovereignty into a democratic framework is an agreed set of minimum principles, a system of cosmopolitan democratic law.

He sees the first step in this journey as the reform of the United Nations. This process could begin by the UN taking measures to implement, extend and enforce the UN Rights Conventions. The UN could increase its role in the settlement and prevention of inter-state conflict by requiring states to submit to compulsory jurisdiction in the case of disputes falling within the ambit covered by international law and UN resolutions. The institution of the International Criminal Court could play a central role in policing serious violations of humanitarian law. The General Assembly could play a more legislative role if a (near) consensus in that forum was recognized as a legitimate source of international law. The veto arrangements in the Security Council could be modified.

A key question is the degree to which a cosmopolitan global order is becoming a reality, or whether, on the other hand, Held's principles of cosmopolitan democracy in fact constitute little more than a utopian yearning. It is increasingly dubious that these kinds of solutions are indeed emerging out of the existing situation. Voices calling for cosmopolitan democratic reform are increasingly drowned out by the demands of the American regime and great power politics. Indeed, perhaps those liberal voices are simply being incorporated by the great power(s) as a democratic cover for the usual business of pursuing 'national' interest with all the force that can be mustered.

Cosmopolitan-*ism* is open to the charge that it may turn out to herald the appearance of a new grand narrative of emancipation to be followed, perhaps, by a new disillusionment with its inability to deliver.[13] Cosmopolitan law, in contrast, is a set of particular ideas and practices that have achieved a limited but real institutional existence. The project for cosmopolitan law has had successes and failures.

Much contemporary cosmopolitan theory is presented as a narrative, sometimes very schematically and sometimes with more sophistication. It begins with a nostalgia for a pre-modern idea of natural law that imposed ethical restrictions on anyone powerful enough to wage war. It understands modernity as the epoch of

[13] R. Fine, 'Taking the 'Ism' out of Cosmopolitanism' (2003) 6(4) *European Journal of Social Theory* 451–470.

absolute state sovereignty and of inter-state anarchy. And it understands the period following the Second World War as one in which the rupture between ethics and power is gradually being bridged. There is a growth of structural changes that decay and by-pass the system of independent states both from below and from above, creating significant networks of power that are no longer subjected to state authority. Armed groups mix organized crime and political or ethnic power struggles to undermine the classical authority of the civic state from below, as in Yugoslavia, reflecting a fundamental change in the nature of armed conflict.[14] The capitalist market organizes on a global level that is ungovernable by individual states and necessitates a supranational authority that can extend a democratic authoritative framework to the new situation. Cosmopolitanism is both 'happening', as the historical response to *globalization*, and it is also normatively desirable, as the solution to the most striking problems of our time.

If, however, the quest for this historical narrative is abandoned, then a different picture is allowed to emerge. Typically of contemporary cosmopolitan theorists, Mary Kaldor's notion of cosmopolitanism understands it as a response to specifically contemporary problems and as an analysis that supersedes those that were appropriate to the world as it used to be, but not to the world as it is now.

> [I]n the context of globalization, ideological and/or territorial cleavages of an earlier era have increasingly been supplanted by an emerging political cleavage between what I call cosmopolitanism, based on inclusive universalist multicultural values, and the politics of particularist identities.[15]

But if the cleavage between the univeralist values of cosmopolitanism and the politics of more particularist identities is not understood as a product specifically of the post-modern 'now', which supplants previous political cleavages, but is instead understood as a thread that runs throughout the time frame of the narrative, then we develop a clearer and less apocalyptic picture. Cosmopolitanism is not a historical stage that arrives after and as a result of the increasing perception of the deficiencies of the old order. The idea of cosmopolitan law does not follow nationalism, but runs parallel to it. The narrative is more appropriately understood both as one of intertwined development and also one of acute competition. Immanuel Kant did not develop his theory of cosmopolitan law after and as a result of the generalization of absolute state sovereignty. The Genocide Convention was passed simultaneously to the UN being founded as a conference of independent states. The Nuremberg Trials did not take place as a response to the failures of Israeli nationalism or against its interests or sensibilities. The tribunals for Rwanda and Yugoslavia did not come into existence because the Security Council became convinced that absolute state sovereignty was no longer a principle worth defending. Many of the events that we can understand as landmarks in the development of

[14] M. Kaldor, *New and Old War: Organized Violence in a Global Era* (London, 1999).
[15] *Ibid*, 6.

cosmopolitan law took place within, and not in opposition to, the existing order of power and law. Part of what is at stake therefore, in the argument for the recognition of cosmopolitan law, is the degree to which its principles and institutions are able to be brought to life as independent entities. Can they attain sufficient authority, independence and power to threaten some of the interests that brought them into being? If they can, then cosmopolitan law attains an existence as more than a set of ideas, but also as a new form of law.

We are concerned here with tracing a thread of law, politics, and philosophy that challenges the idea that community must necessarily be defined in an exclusive way. It is a thread that opposes tyranny while remaining vigilant to the danger of creating new exclusions. It is a thread that has always challenged that side of the dialectic of modernity that threatens its own particularly menacing and characteristically modern form of barbarism. Cosmopolitan law is not a sequel to modernity but rather an element deeply imbedded within it. It is also a characteristically modern form, based on the extension of the project of the universalization of right. And neither is it a panacea, a cure for all ills, a new ideology for a new world order; it is simply a new form of law.

Costas Douzinas: The World is so Compromised by Power that apparently Interesting Developments Turn Out, on Analysis, only to Confirm the Complete Corruption of What Exists

Costas Douzinas argues that human rights and cosmopolitanism are ideological instruments whose primary function is the legitimation of the imperialist domination of the great powers, centrally the United States.

Douzinas[16] recounts that Spanish soldiers unfurled banners in response to the Napoleonic invasion that read 'Down With Freedom'. He suggests that the oppressed may soon be ready to raise the slogan 'Down With Human Rights'. He understands the current supremacy of the rhetoric of universal rights to signify their weakness as a means by which ordinary people can seek to limit the power of state sovereignty. For Douzinas, the concept of human rights is at its strongest when it is understood as a contemporary form of natural law. In this conception its utopian element is to be cherished. The most positive function of human rights is to act as an ideal against which to measure the actuality of existing conditions. 'Human rights are the necessary and impossible claim of law to justice.'[17]

Human rights may be useful for fighting tyranny and for conceiving of a better world, but for Douzinas, those positives are far outweighed by the negative and destructive forces that are mobilized under their banner. The more that human

[16] C. Douzinas, *The End of Human Rights* (Oxford, 2000). [17] *Ibid*, 380.

rights gain an institutional and worldly existence, the less he likes them, since in that case they move away from their utopian form as a measure of the existing world and into the compromised terrain of actuality. The major powers, in the period of the post-war codification of human rights, he tells us, 'unanimously agreed that these rights could not be used to pierce the shield of national sovereignty'. The new body of human rights and humanitarian law and the possibility of its institutional actualization was a promise made by the victorious powers not to replicate the crimes of the Nazis. It was a statement that they accepted that there was at least a basic minimum of human community. They needed to make that promise for purposes of legitimization, to draw a line under the old regime. Again, after 1989, the major powers renewed their commitment to the rhetoric of human rights in order to legitimize their victory over 'Communism'. For Douzinas, the use to which the great powers put the concept of human rights expresses the central truth of human rights. Their existence as cover for the ambitions of the powerful carries more weight than any other; their existence as an updated form of natural law is important but only to the extent that it is kept clean, out of the compromised actuality of international law and international relations. Human rights, according to this conception, have become a central mechanism for the denial of human rights. Human rights rhetoric covers, excuses, and legitimizes anti-human rights action.

My argument is rather different. It is that the great powers, for purposes of legitimization, have allowed cosmopolitan law to emerge and have allowed it a certain institutional existence; they have always attempted to keep control of it and prevent it from attaining an independent existence; they will not always succeed in thus controlling it because that to which they are forced to agree for purposes of legitimization is precisely that which makes it possible for cosmopolitan law and its institutions to gain a life of their own.

The concept of crimes against humanity is powerful. The acceptance of it by the major powers as a central part of international humanitarian law constitutes an acceptance that such crimes are the business of humanity as a whole. It is a recognition that there is no sovereign right to commit such crimes and that the claim made by cosmopolitan law, that it has jurisdiction within all sovereign states in relation to such crimes, is legitimate. The actuality of international tribunals competent to prosecute crimes against humanity underlines the validity and legitimacy of the concept.

The reason that cosmopolitan law cannot simply be wheeled out for purposes of legitimization and then pushed back when it interferes with the business of government is that it attains an independent existence from the powers that allow it to develop. The need for legitimization is enduring; legitimization is not a project that is achieved, but one that is continually in need of renewal. Douzinas is right to say that the principles of human rights and sovereignty are contradictory; he is also right to say that they are both paramount in post-war international law and that they are contradictory but intertwined principles that develop together. Yet his conclusion suggests that one is somehow more real, more enduring, more powerful, than the other. He is not right to suggest that sovereign power is real while human rights exist only as epiphenomena, as tools that have the function of entrenching it. Legitimization is not just a trick; people are not so easily fooled.

The rights of man developed alongside the national state, which excluded non-citizens from rights; human rights developed alongside the principle of national sovereignty, which allowed states to ignore them. These are not questions of form and content or of phenomena and epiphenomena but of the dialectic that runs, in many different forms, throughout the heart of modernity. Both have a real and embattled existence. Cosmopolitan criminal law and human rights cannot be reduced to state power and sovereignty, since they have emergent properties. They have the possibility to emerge as structures in a social reality with a certain independence of their own. There is a struggle between the powerful states, which have an interest in allowing them a *limited but controllable independence*, and the immense power that is immanent within the concept and actuality of cosmopolitan law.

I am interested in exactly the process that compromises universal values. Their actualization in the world as it exists plunges them into arenas of competing power and interest which often overwhelms them. I do not attempt a general defence of universal values but am interested in tracing one set of their particularizations. I argue that in cosmopolitan criminal law it is possible for universal values to find a wordly existence that is not wholly subverted by power and interest.

It is not enough to set out a list of conditions for humanitarian intervention or for humanitarian law which can never be met but which would, in an imaginary world, allow us to support them. It is necessary to find ways of intervening to prevent genocide and ethnic cleansing in the world as it exists and not in the world as we would like it to exist. It is necessary to find ways of holding criminals like Milošević to account in this world and not in the next. It is also necessary to find ways of holding to account individuals like Saddam and Sharon, Putin and Kissinger, Xiang Zemin and Pinochet. But principled opposition to all existing possibilities is not a serious way to relate to actual developments. We cannot stand aside from the world as it is in order to keep ourselves and our ideas pure.

There is an old joke. An old lady comes back from a week at a hotel in the Catskills. 'How was the food?' she is asked. 'Terrible—and such small portions,' she answers bitterly.

I am interested in tracing the trajectory of the development of cosmopolitan criminal law as it exists. Cosmopolitan law is hypocritical and unfair; it is saturated with *realpolitik* and the fear of the great powers; it is compromised by its partiality; it is crippled by its lack of money, resources, publicity, and political support. And it is served in such small portions.

The Legal Construction of Cosmopolitan Social Memory

If the cosmopolitan project is to have successes then some of the mythology that underpins the ideologies of nationalism must be undercut. These mythologies of nationalism are produced and re-produced through the telling and re-telling of particular national narratives and through the suppression of others. One sphere of the nation state that plays a part in producing and re-producing myths of nationhood is the legal system. Courts play a significant role in the production of narratives that define nation. The narratives that they produce are official narratives; they carry extra weight because they have at their disposal certain state resources and powers. So what kind of narratives do cosmopolitan courts produce and reproduce? An important part of their function must be to produce cosmopolitan narratives; narratives of the type that can play their part in undercutting myths of nationhood. There are, of course, many other sources of cosmopolitan narrative as there are other sources of myths of nation; yet cosmopolitan courts also speak with a particular authority. It is an authority that is derived from their foundations in the discourse of human rights and in internationally agreed legal rules and norms. Cosmopolitan courts have a role in mediating between the claims of competing nationalisms that renders them well suited to the production of authoritative cosmopolitan narrative.

Given that nation states are the ubiquitous form of political community in our time and that nationalism relies heavily on the creation of myths of nationhood, then much of the writing about social memory focuses on its nationalistic character. Narratives of nationhood are one of the pillars upon which nation states are built and maintained. While the narratives speak of timeless community, stretching back into the mists of history, the narratives themselves, like the nations they constitute, are much more flexible than they appear.

Norman Cigar[18] argues that the processes of narrative creation occurred very quickly in the former Yugoslavia at the end of the 1980s. It was the conscious strategy of the nationalists to create and re-create ancient myths of nationhood, to re-write and re-tell the glorious history of Serbia or of Croatia. The wars in the former Yugoslavia have often been presented in the media as the result of age-old conflict in the Balkans. Yet, as Cigar shows, it was in fact a conscious re-configuration and re-popularization of the narratives of age-old conflict in the late 1980s by the nationalists that helped to energize the people for the wars of conquest and ethnic cleansing. Timeless myth can be changed very quickly by purposive political action. The project of imbuing particular social memories with a sacred and eternal quality is central to the political work of nationalists.

Crimes against humanity, ethnic cleansing, and genocide are inevitably preceded by this political work of creating and consolidating timeless narratives. How can these genocidal and mythical social memories be replaced, fought against, or superseded?

There is emerging a body of law and a set of institutions that is becoming able to try those responsible for violations of international humanitarian law, crimes against humanity, ethnic cleansing and genocide. Such trials are important in

[18] N. Cigar, *Genocide in Bosnia: The Policy of 'Ethnic Cleansing'* (College Station, TX, 1995).

themselves, in order to hold to account those who commit such crimes, and to deter others from committing them. But in order to do this, a trial has first to establish a true picture of the events under investigation. This function of finding truth is a particularly important one in the field of crimes against humanity trials. One of the central purpozes of the Nuremberg tribunals was, particularly within Germany, to publicize the truth about what the Nazis had done;[19] similarly the ICTY aims to show clearly what the nature of genocide and ethnic cleansing was. The Tadić judgment is a long and closely argued document showing how the war started in Bosnia, how the politics of the communities evolved, how ethnic cleansing and genocide was possible, how it was carried out, and who was responsible. The trial was about more than Tadić. It was about producing a version of the truth of what happened; a version that claims authority because it is produced by an impartial, cosmopolitan court according to the rules, methods, and traditions of international law. Legal processes of finding truth claim a particular authority since they have the right to impose sanctions on those who are found guilty. Their decisions are implemented by the use or threat of legally legitimate violence. The process that we can see happening in the emergence of cosmopolitan law is also in part a process of the development of a cosmopolitan social collective memory. Courts receive particular and contradictory testimony; they act upon this according to their own rules and produce a single narrative. Cosmopolitan courts receive nationally particularistic narratives as testimony that they transform into an authoritative cosmopolitan social memory.

The Sawoniuk trial[20] demonstrates this process very clearly. Andrei Sawoniuk was found guilty at his trial in London in 1999 of crimes that were committed as part of the Holocaust in Belarus. The narratives that the witnesses brought to the court from different countries were all heavily influenced by their own national social memories. The subject matter that was under investigation by the court, the Holocaust and the Second World War, are centrally important to the national myths of Israel, Belarus, Poland, Britain, Germany, the former USSR, and Russia. All the nation states involved in the trial have different tellings of the story of the War and the Holocaust and these tellings are central to the ways in which they produce and re-produce their national identities. To have an identity is to have a story; a story

[19] Elie Wiesel : '[At Nuremberg] Justice was served, but, above everything else, in a strange way, in a dark poetic way, it was memory that was confronted and celebrated at Nuremberg. When hundreds and hundreds of witnesses emerged to piece together a story—a story that we all must remember, although our memory and our mind and our soul are too small to comprehend it, to take it all in. Our sanity was at stake. If we remembered everything, we would lose our minds. But then, if we don't remember everything, we also lose our minds. Nuremberg, therefore, was the repository of testimony. Hundreds, thousands, hundreds of thousands of documents were introduced in evidence in Nuremberg. Thus, it was an important and meaningful event. For the first time, I think, it gave memory such an exposure. Now we know that if there is one word among others that also symbolised the dark years of that tragedy that has no pertinent name, it is *Memory.*' E. Wiesel, 'Inaugural Raoul Wallenberg Lecture', in I. Cotler (ed.), *Nuremberg Forty Years Later: The Struggle against Injustice in Our Time* (Montreal, 1995).

[20] *R* v. *Sawoniuk* (2000) Cr App R 220.

that gives a sense of direction and a sense of continuity. The way a nation that was involved in these events understands its role in the Second World War and the Holocaust is one of the crucial determinants of its national identity. These stories have been told and developed for fifty six years before the trial; and then the witnesses, imbued with their own national versions of the big picture, came to court to give evidence on matters intimately connected to central myths of their own nationhood.

It was the task of the court to hear testimony that was necessarily informed by these differing narratives, to process it and work on it according to its own legal rules and norms, and to produce a judgment that was free of these contradictory nationalist influences. It is as if a cosmopolitan court is a machine whose inputs are national narratives, but whose output is a single cosmopolitan one. The hardware of the machine is a set of developing cosmopolitan institutions; the software is the developing body of cosmopolitan law and the increasingly clear and precise body of rules, procedures, and precedent that is being produced by the institutions.

Crimes against humanity are exactly the kind of events of which national social memories make and are made. In order for them to occur in the first place, there are inevitably sophisticated and widely held narratives that tell why the other group needs to be disposed of. The Jews have, through the ages, been the cause of Germany's defeats and problems; the Muslims in Bosnia have, through the ages, been collaborators with the invaders against Serbs; the Tutsi in Rwanda have been, through the ages, the oppressors of the Hutu. This is one of the central reasons why international courts are necessary. It is necessary to create institutions to deal with these crimes that have some chance of raising themselves outside of myths of nationhood and of ethnic superiority. When a group or a nation has survived such severe disasters as genocide and ethnic cleansing, it weaves the narratives of these disasters into its own tapestry of identity. When a court comes to address these events then, it is forced to attempt to abstract the story of what happened from its powerful embededness in narratives that are central to conflicting national identities.

A central task of the ICTY is to carry out this work. It hears evidence wrapped up in Croatian, Bosnian, and Serbian narratives; it also hears academic evidence. It is also able to hear evidence from organizations that are self-consciously trying to be cosmopolitan, to differing extents, such as NGOs and UN peacekeeping forces. The rules and norms by which it constructs a cosmopolitan narrative are those of cosmopolitan law. The ICTY is engaged in the task of creating and building those rules and norms. It is borrowing principles and procedures from different legal traditions and binding them into a body of law and precedent. It produces judgments that are, literally, in the form of narratives.

The *Krstić* judgment,[21] for example, finding him guilty of genocide in Srebrenića, is another remarkable document. In a little over a hundred pages of

[21] *Prosecutor* v. *Krstić*, Case No. IT-98-33, ICTY, Judgment, 2 August 2001, www.un.org/icty/krstic/TrialC1/judgement/index.htm.

text, it contains 1,519 footnotes. Every assertion is backed up by evidence from the trial or other sources. It outlines the origins of the war in Bosnia; it tells the story of the siege and the cleansing of the town; it focuses on the Drina Corps, of which Krstić was the Chief of Staff, and its role in the genocide; it focuses on Krstić himself, and his role in the Corps. A court is not a bad place to produce an authoritative narrative. It has time, it is relatively well resourced, it has the expertise of defence and prosecution lawyers and investigators, a panel of judges, translators, and transcriptors, the power to call witnesses and experts.

The judgment in the *Irving* case[22] could also be understood as a remarkable cosmopolitan narrative. Irving often attempted to present himself as an English nationalist rather than a neo-Nazi but the narrative of Englishness that he attempted to present was an unusual one. In court, and also in a television interview with Jeremy Paxman on the night of the verdict, he presented his racism as nothing more than a genuine expression of English patriotism.[23]

Irving portrays his version of English nationalism as *genuine*, the view of the silent 95 per cent, rather than the *official* post-Second World War version of the 'traitors' like Lord Hailsham, whose treachery consisted in advising the British cabinet in 1958 not to bring in immigration controls. The *official* version is the multi-culturalist one that emerged after the (mistaken) war against Hitler, (who, incidentally, knew nothing about the Final Solution). Events during that war, such as the mass campaign of aerial bombing of German cities, were presented by the *official* narrative of Englishness as heroic military victories. It required Irving's *genuine* history to be written of the bombing of Dresden, which showed that when England was run by the 'traitors' it committed atrocities far greater than those committed by England's *genuine* friends. It only requires David Irving to show the 95 per cent of honest English racists the true history of the Second World War for them to see through the official nonsense and revert to their instinctual racism. Thus, if only Irving could explain the truth clearly enough, everything would revert to its natural state. He told Paxman:

> [T]hose who were in the courtroom will remember today that at the end of the trial I said to the judge that I have to apologise for the fact that I have failed to express myself with sufficiently articulate language so that you have understood the historical problems with which you are confronted in this case.[24]

In court Irving's strange narrative of English and German nationalism, and of the nationalism of the white race, was being judged against an academic historiographical narrative; one that the Nazis might have called a Jewish cosmopolitan narrative.

It could be argued that the court was not a cosmopolitan one, but rather was one that represented the official history of Englishness against Irving's dissident version.

[22] *Irving* v. *Penguin Books Limited, Deborah E. Lipstadt* [2000] EWCH QB 115.

[23] *Newsnight*, BBC Television, 12 April 2000.

[24] *Ibid.*

But it was the nature of the subject matter and the nature of the evidence presented by the Lipstadt legal team that pushed the British court onto a cosmopolitan terrain. The crimes of the Nazi regime were committed throughout Europe; they had already been the subject of the Nuremberg tribunals; the claims of the Holocaust deniers are not bounded by any national boundaries; Irving's commentary was put daily on his web site and accessed globally; trials similar to this had occurred in other jurisdictions, such as criminal trials for the crime of Holocaust denial in Germany or the *Zundel* case[25] in Canada. Lipstadt is an American whose book had been published all over the world. She had been sued in England because that was where Irving thought he had the greatest chance of success. The expert witnesses were American, Dutch, English, and German. Many factors, therefore, contributed to the British court taking on some of the characteristics of a supra-national one.

But we are left with a paradox. Is not legal discourse itself, and the narratives that it produces, equally susceptible to de-construction? The charge is that the legal discourse and the rules that govern trials create only a different method of producing narrative, not necessarily a better one. Law is not outside of or above society, even if its own rhetoric requires that it appears to be. Legal language, argues Peter Goodrich, 'like any other language usage, is a social practice and . . . its texts will necessarily bear the imprint of such practice or organisational background.' He goes on to say that we should treat legal discourse as an 'accessible and answerable discourse, as a discourse that is inevitably responsible for its place and role within the ethical, political and sexual commitments of its times.'[26] Certainly the narratives produced by cosmopolitan courts are not, in some absolute sense, *the truth*. But in fact, neither do they claim to be. They claim to be *judgments*.

There are many ways of producing truth; law, fiction, journalism, art, memoir, historiography, religion, science, astrology. All have their own rules, methods, and norms but also their own claims and purposes. If we understand these different approaches to truth-finding as social processes, then we neither have to judge that one is authentic and the others are fake, but nor do we have to judge that they are all equally valid. While they overlap, they all have distinct objectives and ways of operating.

Reiko Tachibana makes use of Michel Foucault's concept of 'counter-memory', which Foucault puts forward as an alternative to '[t]he traditional devices for constructing a comprehensive view of history and for retracing the past as a patient and continuous development', a view that he argues, 'must be systematically dismantled'.[27] Tachibana focuses on the work of post-war German and Japanese writers who write 'counter-memory': who do not seek to create all-embracing historical narratives, but who instead write de-centred and incomplete accounts that

[25] *Zundel* [1992] 2 SCR 731. [26] P. Goodrich, *Legal Discourse* (London, 1987), 2.

[27] R. Tachibana, *Narrative as Counter-Memory* (Albany, NY, 1998), 1.

'emphasise the subjectivity and selective nature of any record of events'. Such writing, continues Tachibana, 'seeks a liberation of the reader from a dogmatic perspective on, or blindness toward, the legacies of World War II, aiming instead at provocation toward an active participation in history'.[28] Tachibana is interested in the ways in which authors such as Günter Grass and Ōe Kenzaburō have produced work that seeks to tell truths of histories of mass brutality in micro rather than macro voices. Tachibana tells how, in a letter Grass wrote to Ōe in 1995, he recollects the fact that twenty thousand deserters from Hitler's armies were executed during the war. They were hanged from trees with boards around their necks reading 'I am a coward'. These men, for Grass, should be remembered as the truly courageous heroes of Germany.[29] Ōe praised the Japanese writers who had been producing 'counter-memory' in the post-war period:

> In the history of modern Japanese literature, the writers most sincere in their awareness of a mission were the 'postwar school' of writers who came onto the literary scene deeply wounded by the catastrophe of war yet full of hope for a rebirth. They tried with great pain to make up for the atrocities committed by Japanese military forces in Asia, as well as to bridge the profound gaps that existed not only between the developed nations of the West and Japan but also between African and Latin American countries and Japan. Only by doing so did they think that they could seek with some humility reconciliation with the rest of the world.[30]

Memoir, fiction, and historiography are three irreplaceable methods of telling truthful stories about totalitarianism. Cosmopolitan law is another. Law does not produce *the* truth, it produces *a* truth; it is not *the* antidote to totalitarianism, but it is *a* method of fighting against it. If you want to know what happened at Srebrenica, and how many Muslim men were murdered when the town fell, then a good way of finding out is by reading the *Krstić* judgment;[31] if you want to know how many people were killed during the Holocaust, read the *Irving* judgment.[32] Different forms of representation have different strengths and tell different kinds of stories. Primo Levi[33] or Elie Wiesel[34] can communicate with an immediacy which gives us an idea of what it was like for them to be taken from their home to Auschwitz. Lanzmann's film, *Shoah*,[35] which begins by showing Simon Srebnik revisiting Chelmno where he had been forced to sing folk songs to Nazis as a young boy, as well as burning the remains of those gassed in their vans, communicates with a different sort of immediacy. None of these can show definitive truth, but they show different aspects of the whole. All such forms of representation demand to be read critically, with a focus on what they are, where they come from and what kind of truth they aim to tell.

[28] *Ibid*, 2. [29] *Ibid*, 6.

[30] Ōe Kenzaburō in his Nobel Prize acceptance speech in Stockholm in 1994, quoted in Tachibana, n.27 above.

[31] *Prosecutor* v. *Krstić*, n.21 above.

[32] *Irving*, n.22 above.

[33] P. Levi, *If This is a Man* (London, 1987).

[34] E. Wiesel, *Night* (Harmondsworth, 1981).

[35] C. Lanzmann, *Shoah* (Paris, 1985).

During the Sawoniuk trial, Ben-Zion Blustein, the only Jewish witness, wanted to give his testimony. He wanted to tell what it was like when nearly everyone he knew was killed one day; he wanted to tell what it was like to see his family try to commit suicide; he wanted to tell us that we must believe that such things really happened. The court had a different aim; it needed to judge whether Sawoniuk was guilty of particular crimes, beyond reasonable doubt. Blustein certainly knows better than any of us what it was like for him. The strength of the legal process is that it aims to bring together different forms of evidence for a particular purpose: to guard against the danger of convicting an innocent person. Because the legal process has such severe safeguards built in, it produces, as a by-product, its distinctive from of authoritative narrative.

Lawrence Douglas[36] is critical of Hannah Arendt[37] for arguing that the main business of the Eichmann[38] trial, the weighing of charges brought against the accused, the rendering of judgment and the meting out of due punishment, was in danger of being undermined by the court's wish to accomplish other purposes as well, such as education, the writing of history, and the creation of a forum to host survivor testimony. [39] Douglas argues that Holocaust trials have rightly been concerned with these broader issues as well as focusing on the particular guilt or innocence of the accused. This dispute is apparently about the weight that the two writers assign to the different functions of the trials. But in fact, Arendt certainly did appreciate the Eichmann trial as a forum for setting out an authoritative narrative of the events of the Final Solution: most of her book on the trial is taken up with a re-presentation of the evidence presented in Jerusalem of the detailed picture of the genocide across Europe. And Douglas certainly does admit that 'the primary responsibility of a criminal trial is to resolve questions of guilt in a procedurally fair manner'.[40] For Arendt, it is the foundation of the fair procedure designed to resolve questions of guilt upon which the value of the narrative produced is based. For Douglas, the aim of doing justice to the defendant seems to be parallel to the other aims, rather than one upon which the subsidiary functions rest. 'The Eichmann trial,' he says, 'even more explicitly than Nuremberg, was staged to teach history and shape collective memory ... This mindfulness of the past was meant, in turn, to support the Zionist politics of the present.'[41]

The question becomes not whether it is a legitimate function for a trial to have a role in shaping collective memory, but what kind of collective memory does it shape? Arendt's disquiet about the Eichmann trial was not about whether or not it had a function in educating people about the Holocaust. Rather, it was about the tension than ran throughout the trial due to the court's constitution as a hybrid or transitional

[36] L. Douglas, *The Memory of Judgment: Making Law and History in the Trials of the Holocaust* (New Haven, CT, 2001), 2.

[37] H. Arendt, *Eichmann in Jerusalem: A Report on the Banality of Evil* (Harmondsworth, 1994).

[38] *Attorney General of the Government of Israel* v. *Eichmann* (1961) 36 ILR 5.

[39] This discussion of the Eichmann trial is indebted to Robert Fine's conference paper, R. Fine, 'Holocaust trials and the origins of cosmopolitan law' *Critical Legal Conference* (London, 2002).

[40] Douglas, n.36 above, 2. [41] *Ibid*, 3.

form between national and cosmopolitan law. She defends Israel's right to kidnap and try Eichmann because a trial based on more cosmopolitan principles and institutions was not on the agenda. She criticizes the prosecutor, Gideon Hausner and the Prime Minister, David Ben Gurion, for trying to build the trial into the foundation of the nationalist collective memory of the State of Israel. She praises the judges for standing against that project and for limiting the court to the task of trying Adolf Eichmann. The methods which cosmopolitan trials use to come to their judgments are ones which seek to produce a narrative free from national particularity. But the Eichmann trial was also a national trial, dealing with a subject matter that was central to Israeli national identity. Arendt was not critical of the trial's function of producing authoritative narrative of the Holocaust; she was critical when Hausner tried to use it to tell an Israeli nationalist narrative about the foundations of the state.

By 1987, the Israeli legal system was ready to subordinate entirely the requirements of a fair trial to the requirements of re-staging national drama. John Demjanjuk was accused of being 'Ivan the Terrible', a gas chamber operator at Treblinka.[42] The trial 'turned into a drama of collective unburdening, a public rehashing of both the history of the Holocaust and the horrific tales of the survivors'.[43] But they had the wrong man. Demjanjuk was accused on the basis of a questionable identity card[44] which allegedly linked him to Sobibor; it was Treblinka survivors, however, who identified him as 'Ivan' on the basis of photo spread identification procedures on which his photograph was about twice as large as the others and significantly clearer.[45] Willem Wagenaar a Dutch psychologist, who had previously testified as an expert witness on the subject of memory at forty trials, gave evidence for the defence, telling the court that the photo spreads conducted in Demjanjuk's case lacked any evidential value.[46] Later he wrote that he knows of 'no other case in which so many deviations from procedures internationally accepted as desirable occurred'.[47] The court allowed spectators in the theatre where the trial was held to shout abuse at the defence lawyers and the defendant. Demjanjuk was convicted and sentenced to hang, but on appeal the conviction was overturned. Evidence from the crumbling Eastern Bloc, which the US Justice Department's Office of Special Investigations had known about at the time of the trial, showed that 'Ivan the Terrible' was indeed, another man. The production of authoritative narrative is a by-product of procedurally and substantially fair trials; if the production of narrative is the central goal of a trial and justice is subordinated to it, then there can be no authoritative narrative.

[42] *Ivan (John) Demjanjuk* v. *State of Israel*, Criminal Appeal 347/88 (special issue) at 395396, summarized in English in (1994) 24 *Israel Yearbook of Human Rights* 323.

[43] Douglas, n.36, above 98.

[44] 'The judges ignored the clearest evidence that the crucial documents (delivered to Israel from the Kremlin by the corrupt Dr Armand Hammer) were forgeries . . .', G. Robertson, *Crimes against Humanity* (London, 1999), 223.

[45] Y. Sheftel, *The Conspiracy to Convict John Demjanjuk as 'Ivan the Terrible'* (London, 1998).

[46] *Ibid*, 164.

[47] W. Wagenaar, *Identifying Ivan: A Case Study in Legal Psychology* (London, 1998).

There are two cosmopolitan tribunals, for Yugoslavia and Rwanda; the ICC is making a start at investigating its first cases but is facing substantial opposition from the United States. In contrast, national legal systems are well developed across the world. There can be no question of waiting until some point in the future when and if cosmopolitan courts become institutionally mature before proceeding with the business of conducting cosmopolitan trials. In this chapter I have discussed a number examples of cosmopolitan trials being organized under national legal systems: the cases of Irving, Sawoniuk, Eichmann, and Demjanjuk. Many other significant cosmopolitan cases[48] have also been tried in national courts. The key aspect of cosmopolitan trials is not the particular institutional shape that they take but the fact that they happen and they happen fairly; that they actualize the principles of cosmopolitan law. In the *Eichmann* case, the court successfully resisted pressure to bend towards the needs of Israeli nationalism; in the *Demjanjuk* case it did not. A supra-national cosmopolitan court is necessary to try cases where national legal systems are unable or unwilling to hold fair trials.

Whether actualized within the framework of a national or an international court, cosmopolitan law has the particular advantage of containing within itself mechanisms that aim to rid judgments of national particularity; it also has a particularly concrete connection to the discourse of human rights. It contains within itself mechanisms that aim to make it more reliable for its purposes than raw witness testimony or memoir. None of these mechanisms are perfect, none produce a result that can be regarded as absolute. But we do not expect law to be able to produce some sort of extra-social absolute. The narratives that it does produce are imbued with a certain further social power; perhaps they contain enough of the sacred to shake the certainty of eternal myths of nationhood and ethnic superiority.

Cosmopolitan Law, Human Rights, and the War Against Terror

While the leadership of the war against terror is currently placing significant reliance on human rights and cosmopolitan rhetoric to legitimize its actions, it shows a marked antipathy to the idea that there can be any supra-national legal practice of judging the validity of claims that are made. The tentative and emergent actuality of cosmopolitan legal institutions are written off as political bodies. The fear of the Bush regime is that the ICC, for example, will function as a forum for malicious and politically motivated prosecutions of Americans. Yet at the same time, even the principle of the possibility of measuring practice against an external standard is rejected.

[48] Such as the trial of Klaus Barbie in France; the trial of Ernst Zundel for Holocaust denial in Canada; the attempts to force Pinochet to stand trial; the whole host of national Nuremberg successor trials in Germany, Poland, and other countries which had been occupied during the Second World War.

The decision to go to war in Iraq was justified by a succession of contradictory motives, each emerging as the last was discredited. The treatment of prisoners throughout the war against terror has fallen short of established international standards. Saddam himself looks likely to go on trial only now, in late 2005, and will stand before a makeshift trial process in Iraq rather than an open international tribunal. The Bush regime is going to great lengths to prevent the International Criminal Court (ICC) from developing into a significant institution. The leadership of the war against terror refuses to subject itself, either conceptually or institutionally, to any external legal constraint.

It is not accidental that when Kant presented his theory of cosmopolitanism he did so within the framework of cosmopolitan law. The concept of human rights, when anchored to such a legal framework, can constitute the heart of a social theory that moves beyond the nation state and beyond utopian critique; it can constitute the heart of a politics that affirms the fundamental equality of human beings and refuses to replicate elements of the totalitarianisms that it fights against. It can constitute a framework for the struggle to limit the freedom of action of the powerful and to reject their claims to the sovereign right to behave in a criminal way. Cosmopolitan legal processes also produce cosmopolitan narratives of events that are likely to be able to play a part in the undercutting of nationalist and racist communal identities.

The language of human rights, however, when set free from legal standards can all too easily become an empty discourse. Without a conceptual or institutional anchor to cosmopolitan law, cosmopolitanism and human rights may indeed remain little more than the abstract universals that the critics claim is their only possible existence.

22

The Case for a Sociology of Roman Law

*Janne Pölönen**

Ancient Rome and its law inspired many of the founding fathers of socio-legal scholarship, such as Charles de Montesquieu (1689–1755), Friedrich Karl von Savigny (1779–1861), Karl Marx (1818–1883), Henry Sumner Maine (1822–1888), Numa Foustel de Coulanges (1830–1889), Rudolf von Jhering (1818–1892), Max Weber (1864–1920), and Eugen Ehrlich (1862–1922).[1] The research fields of Roman studies and sociology of law have since become widely separated and highly specialized.[2] Consequently, Roman law and society no longer have such a central place in contemporary socio-legal literature.

While the importance of the study of Roman law doctrine is still debated in law schools,[3] at least in continental Europe, learning about the relationship between an ancient law and society is not considered as significant since it is unlikely to serve the practical purpose of improving modern legal systems.[4] Even sociologists of law with historical and comparative interests have better documented and more easily approachable societies to study. But scholars who specialize in Roman studies, and Roman law and society in particular, have also

* I would like to thank Professors Jean Andreau and Yan Thomas for their advice. This chapter has been prepared as a part of a larger research project concerning the social representativeness of Justinian's Digest funded by the Academy of Finland.

[1] Later scholarship has been much more hesitant to generalize about all societies and all human history. On general theories of socio-legal development see L. Pospíšil, *Anthropology of Law: A Comparative Theory* (New York, 1971), 127–92; R.M. Unger, *Law in Modern Society: Toward a Criticism of Social Theory* (London, 1976); S.F. Moore, 'Legal Systems of the World', in L. Lipson and S. Wheeler (eds), *Law and the Social Sciences* (New York, 1986), 11–62.

[2] Eighteenth- and ninteenth-century scholars did not clearly distinguish between legal, historical, or sociological approaches: P. Burke, *History and Social Theory* (Cambridge, 1992), 4–14.

[3] E.g. G. Ferrini, 'Lotte antiche e recenti contro il diritto romano' in *Opere*, IV, 413; P. Koschaker, 'Die Krise des römischen Rechts und die romanistiche Rechtswissenschaft' in *Schriften der Akademie f. Deutches Rechts* (Munich and Berlin, 1938); R. Knütel, 'Rechtseinheit und Römisches Recht' (1994) 2 *Zeitschrift für Europäisches Privatrecht* 244; R. Zimmermann, *The Law of Obligations: Roman Foundations of the Civilian Tradition* (Oxford, 1996); R. Zimmermann, 'Roman Law and European Legal Unity', in A. Hartkamp et al. (eds), *Towards a European Civil Code* (Nijmegen, 1998), 21–39.

[4] On practical and theoretical directions in sociology of law: D. Nelken, 'Law in Action or Living Law' (1984) 4 *Legal Studies* 157; R. Cotterrell (ed.), *Sociological Perspectives on Law*, Vol. I (Aldershot, 2001), 197–214; R. Cotterrell, *Law's Community: Legal Theory in Sociological Perspective* (Oxford, 1995), 23–8.

not paid much attention to modern sociological theories of law, or empirical findings from other societies.

At least from the historian's point of view, a sociological study of law can improve—besides doctrinal study—the understanding of the Roman legal system as it developed and operated in the limited context of ancient society.[5] Nevertheless, difficulties relative to quantitative and comparative analysis of Roman sources, in the context of Rome's steeply hierarchical society, made John Crook, the author of a deservedly admired book on Roman society in light of its law and legal institutions, declare that 'it is simply not possible to do a proper sociology of Roman law'.[6]

Proper sociology or not, a thousand years of law from the Twelve Tables to Justinian's codification is subject to study in the context of political, social and economic developments. Indeed, Roman socio-legal history is a growing industry,[7] which means that new findings which may be of interest to sociologists of law also are available, and that students of Roman law and society should start taking the sociology of law more seriously. It is the purpose of this chapter to take a look at the history and the present state of the Roman law and society studies, and then to consider some of the problems of and prospects for sociology of Roman law.

Historically, two distinct groups of scholars, lawyers, and historians have taken an interest in Roman law, although their motives have been very different. The study of Roman law and its sources has been, and still is, dominated by the legal scholarship and particularly its distinguished civil law tradition, development of which has largely determined the way the law's relation to Roman society has been approached. The earliest students of civil law in medieval Europe, who began to systematize and abstract Roman legal concepts and principles, treated Justinian's law as an uncontestable and timeless authority.[8]

A consciousness of the historical context of Roman law was a product of the sixteenth-century humanist scholarship whose critical approach to sources revealed the textual strata in the *Corpus Iuris Civilis*, and so made evident the historical stages of Roman law. Law was now understood also as an historical and cultural achievement, and its state relative to particular conditions of society.[9] Nevertheless, this early emergence of the socio-historical background of Roman

[5] There are numerous introductions to sociology of law: R. Cotterrell, *The Sociology of Law: An Introduction* (London, 1984); R. Treves, *Sociologia del diritto: origini, ricerche, problemi*, 3rd edn. (Torino, 1987); N. Luhmann, *Rechtssoziologie*, 3rd edn. (Opladen, 1987); A.-J. Arnaud and M. J. Fariñas Dulce, *Introduction à l'analyse sociologique des systèmes juridiques* (Bruxelles, 1998). For a bibliography: A.J. Treviño, *The Sociology of Law: A Bibliography of Theoretical Literature* (Rochester, 1994).

[6] J. Crook, *Law and Life of Rome* (London, 1967), 9.

[7] This tendency coincides with the appearance of new guidebooks such as O.F. Robinson, *The Sources of Roman Law: Problems and Methods for Ancient Historians* (London, 1997); D. Johnston, *Roman Law in Context* (Cambridge, 1999); See also A. Bürge, *Römisches Privatrecht* (Darmstadt, 1999).

[8] R. Orestano, *Introduzione allo studio storico del diritto romano* (Bologna, 1987), 186–93, 599–606; P. Stein, *Roman Law in European History* (Cambridge, 1999), 38–71.

[9] D.R. Kelley, *Foundations of Modern Historical Scholarship: Language, Law, and History in the French Renaissance* (New York and London, 1970); Orestano, n.8, above, 193–219, 606–42.

law inspired attacks mainly against its authority.[10] The study of social context remained for centuries overshadowed by interests in the abstraction and construction of Roman law doctrine, and its *usus modernus*, not least by the nineteenth-century pandectist scientists.[11]

Humanist scholarship also made Roman history a subject of study in its own right, and the idea that ancient law can be studied to learn about ancient society—already present in the writings of Cicero[12]—was awakened.[13] But although historians like Louis Le Roy (1510?–1577) and Edward Gibbon (1737–1794) paid attention to law in their histories of civilization and the Roman Empire,[14] this approach was not prevalent. Whereas political history dominated historical writing until the early twentieth century, the academic historians remained hostile even to sociological history, [15] let alone socio-legal history.

The rise of sociological thought has, however, changed the perspectives of both lawyers and historians. Although the legal experts of Roman law have not embraced sociology of law as a discipline, they have adopted during the twentieth century a predominantly historical approach to Roman law, and also to society as the context of its development.[16] At the same time, the research field of social history has exploded to cover all aspects of human life, social structures, ideas, etc. Consequently, Roman historians have also started to ask new questions and search for answers from all kinds of sources, including legal texts. Today, Roman law and

[10] François Hotman (1524–1590) argued that ancient Roman law had in the contemporary world little more than antiquarian value: D.R. Kelley, *François Hotman: A Revolutionary's Ordeal* (Princeton, 1973), 195. Roman law has been frequently attacked by the protagonists of natural and national law, as well as political, legal, and social reform: e.g. H.F. Jolowicz, 'Political Implications of Roman Law' (1947) 22 *Tulane Law Review* 62; J.Q. Whitman, 'Long Live the Hatred of Roman Law!' [2003] *Rechtsgeschichte* 40.

[11] Orestano, n.8, above, 221–90. Orestano's book, together with G. Crifò, *Materiali di storiografia romanistica* (Torino, 1998), provides a rich and critical account of the romanistic tradition. See also J.Q. Whitman, *The Legacy of Roman Law in the German Romantic Era* (Princeton, 1990).

[12] Marcus Tullius Cicero, *De oratore*, 1.63.193: *Plurima est, et in omni iure civili, et in pontificum libris, et in Duodecim Tabulis, antiquitatis effigies, quod et verborum prisca vetustas cognoscitur, et actionum genera quaedam maiorum consuetudinem vitamque declarant.* 'There is throughout the civil law, in the priestly books and the Twelve Tables a complete picture of the olden time, since a primitive antiquity of language can be studied there, and certain forms of pleadings reveal the manners and the way of life of our forerunners' (transl. E.W. Sutton and H. Rackham, *Cicero: De Oratore* I, II (London, 1959), 135).

[13] This approach to Roman law sources was pioneered by Guilaume Budé (1468–1540) in his *Annotationes in Pandectas*, in which the Justinian Digest was cited not as a legal authority but, borrowing Cicero's words, as a mirror-image of antiquity (*effigies antiquitatis*). Kelley, n.9, above, 68. See also D. Osler, 'Budaeus and Roman Law' (1985) 13 *Ius Commune* 195.

[14] Louis le Roy, *La Vicissitude des choses* (Paris, 1584); E. Gibbon, *The History of the Decline and Fall of the Roman Empire*, II (London, [1788] 1994), 779: 'the laws of a nation form the most instructive portion of its history'.

[15] Burke, n.2, above, 14–21.

[16] Orestano, n.8, above, 301–4, 406–9, 565–6. After the codification of national laws in Continental Europe the Roman law's actuality as a legal source was eclipsed: Stein, n.8, above, 128–30. On sociological perspectives to Roman law: R. Orestano, 'Sociologia e studio storico del diritto', in *Methode sociologique et droit* (Strasbourg, 1958), 149–82; H. Lévy-Bruhl, *Sociologie du droit*, 6th edn. (Paris, 1981); R. Orestano, 'Idea di progresso, esperienza giuridica romana e paleoromanistica' (1982) 9 *Sociologia del diritto* 15.

legal writings are considered vitally important sources for the reconstruction not only of Roman law doctrine, but also of Roman society.[17]

This development has brought the Roman lawyers and historians to ever closer dialogue,[18] inviting scholars of both disciplines to address questions of overlapping legal and sociological interest. Yet the distinction between internal—doctrinal—legal history and external socio-legal history still characterizes in many respects the difference between lawyer's history and historian's history.[19] *Most of the time*, legal experts treat society as marginal to their main task of reconstructing Roman law from a doctrinal perspective, while historians use the law and legal sources to learn about Roman society from a practical point of view of law's functioning in real life.[20]

Many scholars—jurists and historians—have used society as a *means* to understand Roman law, and law as a *means* to understand the Roman society.[21] and many studies are called 'social', 'sociological', 'law and society', or 'legal'.[22] This scholarship has addressed many important questions concerning the relationship between Roman law and society, such as the social motives and effects of individual statutes,

[17] S. Treggiari, *Roman Social History* (London and New York, 2002), 33; B. Frier, 'Roman Law's Descent into History' (2000) 13 *American Journal of Archaeology* 447.

[18] See, e.g. the discussions on the relationship between legal history and general history in *La storia del diritto nel quadro delle scienze storiche* (Florence, 1966), 3–192.

[19] L.M. Friedman, 'Sociology of Law and Legal History', in V. Ferrari (ed.), *Laws and Rights: Proceedings of the International Congress of Sociology of Law for the Ninth Centenary of the University of Bologna (May 30–June 3, 1988)* (Milan, 1991), 123–35.

[20] Arnaldo Momigliano declared as long ago as the 1960s 'the end of history of [Roman] law as an autonomous branch of historical research', continuing that 'we can no longer maintain a distinction between historians' history and jurists' history': A. Momigliano, 'The Consequences of New Trends in the History of Ancient Law' (1964) 76 *Rivista Storica Italiana* 133. However, cf. J. Crook, 'Legal History and General History' (1996) 41 *Bulletin of the Institute of Classical Studies* 31–6.

[21] E.g. L. Boyer, 'La fonction sociale des legs d'après la jurisprudence classique' (1965) 43 *Revue Historique de Droit Française et Étranger* 333; D. Daube, *Roman Law: Linguistic, Social and Philosophical Aspects* (Edinburgh, 1969); M. Humbert, *Le remariage à Rome. Étude d'histoire juridique et sociale* (Milan, 1972); M. Morabito, *Les réalités de l'esclavage d'après le Digeste* (Paris, 1981); A. Di Porto, *Impresa collettiva e schiavo 'manager' in Roma antica* (Milan, 1984); S. Martin, *The Roman Jurists and the Organization of Private Building* (Princeton, 1985); J. Gardner, *Women in Roman Law and Society* (London, 1986); J. Andreau, *La vie financière dans le monde romain, Les métiers de manieurs d'argent (IVe siècle av. J.-C.-IIIe siècle ap. J.-C.)* (Rome, 1987); D. Grodzynski, 'Pauvres et indigents, vils et plebeiens' (1987) 57 *Studia et Documenta Historia et Iuris* 140; S. Dixon, *The Roman Mother* (London, 1988); S. Treggiari, *The Roman Marriage: Iusti coniuges from the time of Cicero to the time of Ulpian* (Oxford, 1991); E. Champlin, *Final Judgments: Duty and Emotion in Roman Wills, 200 B.C.–A.D.250* (Berkeley, 1991); S. Dixon, *The Roman Family* (Baltimore, 1992); R. P. Saller, *Patriarchy, Property and Death in the Roman Family* (Cambridge, 1994); A. Arjava, *Women and Law in Late Antiquity* (Oxford, 1996); M. A. Ligios, *Interpretazione giuridica e realità economica dell'* 'instrumentum fundi' *tra il I sec. a.C. e il III sec. d.C.* (Naples, 1996); C. Masi Moria, *Bona libetorum: Regimi giuridici e realità sociali* (Naples, 1996); D. Kehoe, *Investment, Profit and Tenancy: The Jurists and the Roman Agrarian Economy* (Ann Arbor, 1997); T. McGinn, *Prostitution, Sexuality and the Law in Ancient Rome* (New York, 1998); J. Gardner, *Family and Familia in Roman Law and Life* (Oxford, 1999); P. Veyne, *Société romaine. Edition comportant un texte liminaire intitulé 'La ville de Rome et la "plèbe moyenne"'* (Paris, 2001); R. Berg et al. (eds), *Women, Wealth and Power in the Roman Empire* (Rome, 2002); J.-J. Aubert and B. Sirks (eds), *Speculum Iuris: Roman Law as a Reflection of Social and Economic Life in Antiquity* (Ann Arbor, 2002).

[22] It is fairly common for lawyers to use 'sociological' to denote any approach that also takes account of the extra-legal context, and for social historians to use 'legal' whenever also considering law and legal sources.

how law's development reflects societal change, and how accurately legal writings describe the realities of daily life. But relatively few scholars have made this relationship their primary *object* of study. If this objective is used to define the discipline,[23] Bruce Frier, whose work draws on a wide range of contemporary socio-legal literature, is the leading author on sociology of Roman law today.[24]

The problem of Roman law's relation to society, as formulated by Frier, is discussed in terms of the current opposition between positivist and sociological ideas of law and jurisprudence. The traditional position, argued most recently by Alan Watson, is that the Roman jurists worked the law autonomously according to its own internal logic, in complete isolation from political, social, or economic considerations.[25] Frier has sought to demonstrate that the classical jurists, and the law they created, were not divorced from the social realities, as the jurists accommodated external impulses by continuously weighing competing interests in society.[26]

Although the legal imagination of Rome's aristocratic jurists[27] was guided by an ideal conception of the interests of their peers,[28] the casuistic mode of normative production ensured that the Roman legal system was to a great extent informed of interests in the society by its reach of actual disputes.[29] The problem of social

[23] Sociology of law is notoriously difficult to define as a discipline, however the relationship between law and society often emerges as the common theme: e.g. W.M. Evan, *Social Structure and Law: Theoretical and Empirical Perspectives* (Newbury Park, 1990), 19–23; B.Z. Tamanaha, *Realistic Socio-Legal Theory:Pragmatism and a Social Theory of Law* (Oxford, 1997), 1–2.

[24] 'Sociology of Roman law' makes its first appearance as a defined field of the Roman studies in the latest edition of the *Oxford Classical Dictionary*: B. Frier, 'Law, Roman, Sociology of,' in *Oxford Classical Dictionary*, 3rd edn. (Oxford, 1994), 823–5. Frier's desire to give a narrow definition of the discipline is betrayed by his bibliography, which contains none of the items mentioned in nn. 21 above and 39 below.

[25] F. Schulz, *Principles of Roman Law* (Oxford, 1936), 24–5, 38–9; G. Pugliese, 'L'autonomia del diritto rispetto agli altri phenomeni e valori sociali nella giurisprudenza romana', in *La storia del diritto nel quadro delle scienze storiche* (Florence, 1966), 161–92; A. Watson, *Society and Legal Change* (Philadelphia, 1977); A. Watson, 'Legal Change: Sources of Law and Legal Culture' (1983) 131 *University of Pennsylvania law Review* 1121; A. Watson, *The Spirit of Roman Law* (Athens, Georgia, 1995), 64–73. On autonomy of Roman law see also A. Lewis, 'The Autonomy of Roman Law', in P. Coss (ed.), *The Moral World of the Law* (Cambridge, 2000), 37.

[26] B. Frier, *The Rise of the Roman Jurists* (Princeton, 1985), 184–96, 284–7; B. Frier, 'Why did the Jurists Change the Roman Law? Bees and Lawyers Revisited' (1994) 22 *Index* 144–5. Watson's autonomy thesis is generally refuted by legal sociologists, see, e.g. L.M. Friedman, (1979) 6 *British Journal of Law and Society* 127; R. Abel, 'Law as Lag: Inertia as a Social Theory of Law' (1980) 80 *Michigan Law Review* 785; R. Cotterrell, 'Is there a Logic of legal Transplants', in D. Nelken (ed.), *Adapting Legal Cultures* (Portland, 2001), 71.

[27] F. Schulz, *History of Roman Legal Science* (Oxford, 1950); W. Kunkel, *Herkunft und soziale Stellung der römischen Juristen* (Graz, Vienna, Cologne, 1967).

[28] B. Frier, 'Law, Technology, and Social Change: The Equipping of Italian Farm Tenancies' (1979) 96 *Zeitschrift der Savigny-Stiftung für Rechtsgeschichte: Romanistische Abteilung* 204, 218; B. Frier, *Landlords and Tenants in Imperial Rome* (Princeton, 1980), 39–47, 53–5; Martin, n.21, above, 11–14, 138–40; B. Frier, 'Law, Economics, and Disasters Down on the Farm: "*Remissio mercedis*" Revisited' (1989–90) 92–3 *Bullettino dell'Istituto di Diritto Romano* 237, 261; Kehoe, n.21, above, 13, 23–5, 65–6, 116, 138–40. See also P. D. De Neeve, *Colonus: Private Farm-Tenancy in Roman Italy during the Republic and the Early Principate* (Amsterdam, 1984), 25–6, 44–6, 100; W. Scheidel, *Grundpacht und Lohnarbeit in der Landwirtschaft des römischen Italien* (Frankfurt, 1994), 27–117.

[29] Frier (1985), n.26, above, 77–8. On casuistic normative production in Rome: L. Vacca, *Contributo allo studio del metodo casistico nel diritto romano* (Milan, 1976); T. Giaro, 'Über methodologische

reach of Roman courts, and more generally the question of litigation among the lower classes, raises important ideological and practical questions about Roman law, such as the impact of Rome's social structure on ideas of justice and quality of legal administration, as well as popular perceptions of the legal system and patterns of legal behaviour towards it.

As far as the courts were the daily meeting places of law and society, an important aspect of the discussion has been the standards used in weighing the competing interests, and the difference between the law in books and the law in action. As legal specialists, the jurists promoted technical standards of legal decision-making, but Rome's lay officialdom and public were guided by community standards and equity argued for by the orators.[30] Although law attained, due to rise of the Roman jurists in the Late Republic, a greater degree of autonomy, Frier argues that its differentiation from social context remained seriously limited.

Although the problems of writing sociology of Roman law are still present, Crook's and Frier's studies have provided a rich starting point for further research. In absence of a large documentary base of evidence, it is difficult to establish behavioural patterns by means of quantitative analysis. Yet the constantly growing *corpora* of legal *papyri* and inscriptions with the existing literary and legal texts provide information on thousands of legal cases and law issues, not to mention relatively plentiful, if piecemeal and often socially biased, material for qualitative study.[31] The law provides one of the most comprehensive images of Roman society,[32] yet it would be a mistake to deduce the game, as it was played by the Romans, from the rules of law alone. It must always be carefully considered what use, if any, are the law-books in reconstruction of social realities.

In order better to understand the legal behaviour of the Romans, comparative perspectives are open not only to other ancient societies,[33] as contemplated by

Werkmittel der Romanistik' (1988) 105 *Zeitschrift der Savigny-Stiftung für Rechtsgeschichte: Romanistische Abteilung* 180. Case-books: H. Hausmaninger, *Casebook zum römischen Sachenrecht* (Vienna, 1974); *Casebook zum römischen Vertragsrecht* (Vienna, 1978); B. Frier, *A Casebook on the Roman Law of Delict* (Atlanta, 1989); B. Frier and T.A.J. McGinn, *A Casebook on Roman Family Law* (Oxford, 2004).

30 For a recent discussion of the relationship between law and oratory in Roman courts with a bibliography see J. Crook, *Legal Advocacy in the Roman World* (London, 1995). This work, like Frier's, contains a rich apparatus of reference to modern socio-legal literature.

31 The importance of qualitative analysis of sources has been much stressed in the more recent sociological literature: e.g. P. Ewick and S. Silbey, 'Subversive Stories and Hergemonic Tales: Toward a Sociology of Narrative' (1995) 29 *Law and Society Review* 197.

32 Whereas the Romans were not interested in systematic description of their society, they produced a considerable bulk of systematic treatises on law now preserved in Justinian's Digest. It is also important to note that the positive law has been subject to centuries of doctrinal study, because of which social historians cannot afford to ignore the lawyer's perspective on Roman legal history.

33 On the legal behaviour in the Ancient Greek society see, e.g. V. Hunter, *Policing Athens: Social Control in the Attic Lawsuits* (Princeton, 1994); D. Cohen, *Law, Violence, and Community in Classical Athens* (Cambridge, 1995); D. Roebuck, *Ancient Greek Arbitration* (Oxford, 2001). See also L. Gernet, *Droit et société dans la Grèce ancienne* (Paris, 1955); R. Garner, *Law and Society in Classical Athens* (London and Sydney, 1987); V. Hunter and J. Edmondson (eds), *Law and Social Status in Classical Athens* (Oxford, 2000).

Crook, but also to better documented primitive, aristocratic and modern societies.[34] Although the classical scholarship is traditionally suspicious of foreign ideas that do not come directly out of the ancient evidence, it is reasonable to use—with due caution—today's concepts, knowledge of different societies, and sociological theory in the study of Roman society[35] and its relationship to law.

To avoid a risk of assigning modern motives and states of mind to ancient legal actors,[36] an effort must be made to study, in addition to patterns of behaviour, their motives, attitudes, beliefs, and expectations towards the legal system. The internal legal culture of jurists and officials in Rome[37] has received much more attention than the external legal culture of the general population.[38] Important

[34] For example, Donald Black's theory of law's behaviour based on a wide range of comparative evidence is interesting as an analytical tool precisely in its purport to provide universal, testable, hypotheses of how law varies in the context of different social structures and circumstances: D. Black, *The Behavior of Law* (San Diego, 1976); *The Social Structure of Right and Wrong* (San Diego, 1998). For criticism see A. Hunt, 'Behavioral Sociology of law: A Critique of Donald Black' (1983) *Journal of Law and Society* 19, however, cf. Tamanaha, n.23, above, 61–70.

[35] M.I. Finley, *Ancient History: Evidence and Models* (London, 1985); D. Kehoe, 'Comparative Approaches to the Social History of Roman Egypt' (1989) 26 *The Bulletin of the American Society of Papyrologists* 153.

[36] H.R. Hoetink, 'Les notions anachroniques dans l'historiographie du droit' (1955) 23 *Tijdschrift voor rechtsgeschiedenis* 1; E. Metzger, 'Roman Judges, Case Law, and Principles of Procedure' (2004) 22/2 *Law and History Review* 243.

[37] E.g. R. Pound, 'What is a Profession? The Rise of the Legal Profession in Antiquity' (1944) 19 *Notre Dame Lawyer* 203; A. Schiller, 'Bureaucracy and the Roman Law' (1949) 7 *Seminar* 26; Schulz, n.27, above; Kunkel, n.27, above; D. Nörr, *Rechtskritik in der Römischen Antike* (Munich, 1974); R. Casavola, 'Cultura e scienza giuridica nel secondo secolo d.C: il senso del passato', in *Aufstieg und Niedergang der Römischen Welt*, II.15 (Berlin and New York, 1976), 131–75; F. Wieacker, 'Juristen und Jurisprudenz im Prinzipat' (1977) 94 *Zeitschrift der Savigny-Stiftung für Rechtsgeschichte: Romanistische Abteilung* 319; D. Nörr, 'I giuristi romani: tradizionalismo o progresso. Riflessioni su un problema inessattamente impostato' (1981) 84 *Bullettino dell'Istituto di Diritto Romano* 9; M. Bretone, *Techniche e ideologie dei giuristi romani* (Naples, 1982); R.P. Saller, *Personal Patronage under the Early Empire* (Cambridge, 1982); M. D'Orta, 'Per una storia della cultura dei giuristi repubblicani' (1987) 90 *Bullettino dell'Istituto di Diritto Romano* 221; D. Liebs, *Die Jurisprudenz im spätantiken Italien: 260–640 n. Chr.* (Berlin, 1987); C.A. Cannata, *Histoire de la jurisprudence européenne. I, La jurisprudence romaine* (Turin, 1989); A. Schiavone, 'Il pensiero giuridico e razionalità aristocratica', in *Storia di Roma II: L'impero mediterraneo I: La repubblica imperiale* (Turin, 1990), 415–78; W. Turpin, 'Imperial Subscriptions and the Administration of Justice' (1991) 81 *Journal of Roman Studies* 101; B. Anagnostou-Cañas, *Juge et sentence dans l'Égypte romaine* (Paris, 1991); F. Millar, *The Emperor in the Roman World*, 2nd edn. (London, 1992); J.-M. David, *Le patronat judiciaire au dernier siècle de la république romaine* (Rome, 1992); A. Schiavone, 'Il pensiero giuridica fra scienza del diritto e potere imperiale', in *Storia di Roma II: L'impero mediterraneo III: La cultura et l'impero* (Torino, 1990), 7–84; A. Lintott, *Imperium Romanum: Politics and Administration* (London, 1993); T. Honoré, *Emperors and Lawyers*, 2nd edn. (Oxford, 1994); A. Schiavone, *Linee di storia del pensiero giuridico romano* (Turin, 1994); Crook, n.30, above; M. Peachin, *Iudex Vice Caesaris: Deputy Emperors and the Administration of Justice during the Principate* (Stuttgart, 1996); S. Corcoran, *The Empire of the Tetrarchs. Imperial Pronouncements and Government AD 284–324* (Oxford, 1996); J. Lendon, *The Empire of Honour* (Oxford, 1997); J. Harries, *Law and Empire in Late Antiquity* (Cambridge, 1999); L. Fanizza, *L'amministrazione della giustizia nel principato* (Rome, 1999); C. Ando, *Imperial Ideology and Provincial Loyalty in the Roman Empire* (Berkeley, 2000).

[38] 'The Roman legal culture has never been systematically studied': Frier (1985), n.26, above, 77 n.103.

pioneering work has been done,[39] but a consensus has not emerged even over such basic questions, as whether the Romans were litigiously minded or whether they sought to avoid litigation at all cost.[40] A systematic and comparative study of Roman legal culture remains an important challenge.[41]

As scholars have noted,[42] complex cultural aggregates, such as the legal culture, can be studied meaningfully, and made comparable, through Weberian ideal types. This approach may help to understand relative effects on law and legal culture of political, socio-economic, and moral aspects of society, which it is all too easy to discuss in isolation from one another. As to the impact of political authority, the passage from adversarial legal procedure of the 'free' Republic to state-controlled inquisitorial system of the Empire is considered a major factor in Roman legal history.[43] But it seems to me that the development of activist tendencies of the Roman state under the republican and imperial governments, and their influence on the internal logic and dynamics of Roman legal culture could be elaborated through Mirjan Damaska's ideal types combining state ideology, organization of officialdom, and procedural forms.[44]

[39] R. von Jhering, 'Le riche et le pauvre, dans l'ancienne procédure civile des romains', in *Etudes complémentaires de l'esprit du droit romain*, Vol. IV (Paris, 1902), 215; H. Lévy-Bruhl, *La preuve judiciaire: Étude de sociologie juridique* (Paris, 1964); J.M. Kelly, *Roman Litigation* (Oxford, 1966); P. Garnsey, *Social Status and Legal Privilege in the Roman Empire* (Oxford, 1970); G. MacGormack, 'Roman and African Litigation' (1971) 39 *Tijdschrift voor rechtsgeschiedenis* 221; J. Huchthausen, 'Herkunft und ökonomische Stellung weiblicher adressaten von Reskripten des *Codex Iustinianus*' (1974) 56 *Klio* 199; J.M. Kelly, *Studies in the Civil Judicature of the Roman Republic* (Oxford, 1976); Frier (1980), n.28, above; Y. Thomas, 'Se venger au Forum. Solidarité familiale et proces criminel à Rome' in R. Verdier and J.-P. Poly (eds), *La vengeance. Vengeance, pouvoirs et idéologies dans quelques civilisations de l'Antiquité* (Paris, 1984), 65–100; Frier (1985), n.26, above; David, n.37, above; P. Swarney, 'Social Status and Social Behaviour as Criteria in Judicial Proceedings in the Late Republic' and D. Hobson, 'The Impact of Law on Village Life in Roman Egypt', in B. Halpern and D. Hobson (eds), *Law, Politics and Society in the Ancient World* (Sheffield, 1993), 137–55, 193–219; T. Gagos and P. van Minnen, *Settling a Dispute: Toward a Legal Anthropology of Late Antique Egypt* (Ann Arbor, 1994); D. Kehoe, 'Legal Institutions and the Bargaining Power of the Tenant in Roman Egypt' (1995) 41 *Archiv für Papyrusforschung* 232; M. Humbert, 'Le procès romain: approche sociologique' (1995) 39 *Archives de philosophie du droit* 73; A.C. Scafuro, *The Forensic Stage: Settling Disputes in Graeco-Roman New Comedy* (Cambridge, 1997); E. Meyer, *Legitimacy and Law in the Roman World:* Tabulae *in Roman Belief and Practice* (Cambridge, 2004).

[40] Crook, n.30, above, 125; Kelly (1966), n.39, above, 95–111.

[41] On the concept of legal culture see L.M. Friedman, *The Legal System: A Social Science Perspective* (New York, 1975); D. Nelken (ed.), *Comparing Legal Cultures* (Aldershot, 1997).

[42] R. Cotterrell, 'The Concept of Legal Culture', in Nelken, n.41, above, 24–5.

[43] The most authoritative statement of the Roman law of civil process is M. Kaser and K. Hackl, *Das römische Zivilprozessrecht*, 2nd edn. (Munich, 1996). On the general development see W. Kunkel, *Römische Rechtsgeschichte*, 6th edn. (Cologne, Graz, 1971), English translation by J.M. Kelly, *An Introduction to Roman Legal and Constitutional History*, 2nd edn. (Oxford, 1972); H.F. Jolowitz and B. Nicholas, *Historical Introduction to the Study of Roman Law*, 3rd edn. (Cambridge, 1972); M. Talamanca (ed.), *Lineamenti di storia del diritto romano*, 2nd edn. (Milan, 1989); M. Humbert, *Institutions politiques et sociales de l'antiquité*, 8th edn. (Paris, 2003).

[44] M.R. Damaska, *The Faces of Justice and State Authority: A Comparative Approach to the Legal Process* (New Haven and London, 1986). On the development of inquisitorial procedural forms in Rome see, e.g. G.I. Luzzatto, *Il problema d'origine del processo extra ordinem* (Bologna, 1965); I. Buti, 'La "*cognitio extra ordinem*": da Augusto a Diocleziano', in *Aufstieg und Niedergang der römischen Welt*,

An increasing complexity of Rome's socio economic life is also much in the background of its legal development. Roman legal order has been seen as instrumental in legitimizing the political and economic power of the ruling classes,[45] and the emergence of formally rational law in the Late Republic has been related to the interests of the economic elites and to growing commerce.[46] Yet a consideration of the extent to which Roman legal culture was driven by economic rationalism and movement from status to contract, likewise the degree of long-term stability and predictability provided for economic operations by the Roman politico-legal order, could be given a more integral part in the discussion of the Roman economy and its degree of modernity.

The extremely liberal image of Roman private law[47] is in a striking contrast to the increasingly oppressive imperial criminal law, in which the number of capital crimes multiplied, and the punishments became harsher, especially for the lower classes.[48] Doctrinal study has covered the criminal justice system: laws, procedures,

II.14 (Berlin and New York, 1982), 29; F. Casavola, 'Gli ordinamenti giudiziari nella Roma imperiale. Princeps e procedure dalle leggi Giulie ad Adriano' (1998) 26 *Index* 89; G. Zanon, *Le strutture accusatorie della cognitio extra ordinem nel Principato* (Padua, 1998); W. Turpin, 'Formula, *cognitio*, and proceedings *extra ordinem*' (1999) 46 *Revue Internationale des Droits de l'Antiquité* 499.

[45] For the explicit statement see, e.g. Jhering, n.39, above, 233–7; P. Garnsey and R. Saller, *The Roman Empire: Economy, Society and Culture* (Berkeley and Los Angeles, 1987), 109–10.

[46] Frier (1985), n.26, above, 184–96. On the Roman law and economy: M. Weber, *Wirtschaft und Gesellschaft. Grundgriss der werstehenden Soziologie*, 4th edn., 2 vols (Tübingen, 1956), English translation G. Roth and C. Wittich (eds), *Economy and Society: An Outline of Interpretive Sociology*, 2 vols. (Berkeley, 1968); G. Tozzi, *Economisti greci e romani* (Milan, 1961); E. Volterra, 'La base economica della elaborazione sistematica del diritto romano' (1963–7) 11 *Rivista Italiana per le Scienze Giuridiche* 239; G. Grosso; *Schemi giuridici e società nella storia del diritto privato romano. Dall'epoca arcaica alla giurisprudenza classica: diritti reali e obligazioni* (Turin, 1970); F. De Martino, *Storia della costituzione romana*, 5 vols. (Naples, 1972–5); F. Serrao, *Classi, partiti e legge nella Repubblica romana* (Pisa, 1974); L. Capogrossi, A. Giardina and A. Schiavone (eds), *Analisi marxista e società antiche* (Rome, 1978); F. De Martino, *Diritto e società nell'antica Roma* (Rome, 1979); F. Serrao (ed.), *Legge e società nella Repubblica romana*, I (Naples, 1981); F. Serrao, *Diritto privato, economia e società nella storia di Roma* (Naples, 1984); G. Melillo, *Economia e giurisprudenza a Roma* (Milan, 1978); J.R. Love, *Antiquity and Capitalism: Max Weber and the Sociological Foundations of Roman Civilisation* (London and New York, 1991); L. Capogrossi-Colognesi, *Proprietà e signoria in Roma antica*, 2nd edn. (Rome, 1994); A. Schiavone, *La storia spezzata: Roma antica e Occidente moderno* (Rome, 1996); L. Capogrossi-Colognesi, *Le radici della modernità: Max Weber 1891–1909* (Rome, 1997); F. Serrao (ed.), *Legge e società nella Repubblica romana*, II (Naples, 2000); G. Melillo, *Categorie economiche nei giuristi romani* (Naples, 2000); L. Capogrossi-Colognesi, *Max Weber e le economie del mondo antico* (Rome, 2000); P. Garnsey and C. Humfress, *The Evolution of the Late Antique World* (Cambridge, 2001); J. Andreau, J. France and S. Pittia (eds), *Mentalités et choix économiques des romains* (Paris, 2004).

[47] On the individualist temper of Roman law: Schulz, n.25, above, 140–63; F. de Martino, 'Individualismo e diritto romano privato' in *Diritto e società nell'antica Roma* (Rome, 1979), 248–311; W. Simshäuser, 'Sozialbindungen des spätrepublikanisch-klassischen römischen Privateigentums', in *Melanges H. Coing*, I (Munich, 1982), 329–61.

[48] In addition to Garnsey, n.39, above, G. Cardascia, 'L'apparition dans le droit des classes d'*honestiores* et d'*humiliores*' (1950) 28 *Revue d'Histoire de Droit* 305–37, 461–85; F.M. De Robertis, *La variazione della pena nel diritto romano* (Bari, 1954); D. Grodzynski, 'Tortures mortelles et catégories sociales. Les *summa supplicia* dans le droit romain aux IIIe et IVe siècles' in *Du châtiment dans la cité. Supplices corporels et peine de morte dans le monde antique* (Rome, 1984), 361–403; R. Macmullen,

and punishments,[49] but crime and delinquent behaviour as social phenomena have been relatively little studied.[50] More attention could also be paid to the relationship of penal evolution to socio-economic conditions, ideology of punishment, and in Durkheim's terms to the movement from 'mechanical' to 'organic social' solidarity.[51] The increased harshness of criminal law is likely to have shaped the popular perception of the legal system, not least because in monopolizing the legitimate use of violence the Roman Emperors used the criminal law to personal political and fiscal ends with important private law consequences.[52]

To sum up, sociology of law provides a comprehensive, comparative and realistic perspective on socio-legal phenomena and their inter-relations in Ancient Rome which is not always evident if one pays attention only to Roman sources and Roman law doctrine. The legal-doctrinal approach has, for example, had a tendency to marginalize, because of its positivist definition of law, the importance of private conflict resolution and normative life in Rome.[53] But Roman law and

'Judicial Savagery in the Roman Empire' (1986) 16 *Chiron* 147; R. Rilinger, *Humiliores-Honestiores: Zu einer sozialen Dichotomie im Strafrecht der römischen Kaiserzeit* (Munich, 1988); J.-J. Aubert, 'A Double Standard in Roman Criminal Law? The Death Penalty and Social Structure in Late Republican and Early Imperial Rome' in Aubert and Sirks, n.21, above, 94–133.

[49] For a concise discussion and bibliography see O.F. Robinson, *The Criminal Law of Ancient Rome* (Baltimore, 1995).

[50] This argument has already been made by H. Lévy-Bruhl, 'Centre d'Etudes sociologiques' [Criminalité en droit romain] (1958) 4 *Etudes Internationales de Psycho-Sociologie Criminelle* 44. The first attempt of general discussion is J.-U. Krause, *Kriminalgeschichte der Antike* (Munich, 2004). The social aspects have been studied most notably in the case of violent crime: B. Baldwin, 'Crime and Criminals in Graeco-Roman Egypt' (1963) 3/4 *Aegyptus* 256 = *Studies on Greek and Roman History and Literature* (Amsterdam, 1985), 505; B. Frier, 'Urban Praetors and Rural Violence: The Legal Background of Cicero's *Pro Caecina*' (1983) 113 *Transactions of American Philological Association* 221; B. Shaw, 'Bandits in the Roman Empire' (1989) 105 *Past & Present* 3; K. Hopwood, 'Bandits, Elites and Rural Order', in A. Wallace-Hadrill (ed.), *Patronage in the Ancient Society* (Cambridge, 1989), 179; B. Shaw, 'Il bandito', in A. Giardina (ed.), *L'uomo romano* (Bari, 1993), 361; R.S. Bagnall, 'Official and Private Violence in Roman Egypt' (1989) 26 *The Bulletin of the Americal Society of Papyrologists* 201; K. Hopwood (ed.), *Organised Crime in Antiquity* (London, 1999); T. Grünewald, *Räuber, Rebellen, Rivalen, Rächer: Studien zu Latrones im römischen Reich* (Stuttgart, 1999); K. Hopwood, 'Aspects of Violent Crime in the Roman Empire', in P. McKechnie (ed), *Thinking Like a Lawyer: Essays on Legal History and General History for John Crook on his Eightieth Birthday* (Amsterdam, 2002), 74–9; C. Wolf, *Les brigands en Orient sous le Haut-Empire romain* (Rome, 2003).

[51] E. Durkheim, 'Two Laws of Penal Evolution' (1969 [1899–1900]) 38 *University of Cincinnati Law Review* 32; Lévy-Bruhl, n.50, above; P. Garnsey, 'Why Penalties Become Harsher: The Roman Case, Late Republic to Fourth-Century Empire' (1968) 13 *Natural Law Forum* 141; M. Humbert, 'La peine en droit romain' in *La peine, Première partie: Antiquité/Punishment — First Part: Antiquity* (Brussels, 1991), 133–83; R.A. Bauman, *Crime and Punishment in Ancient Rome* (London, 1996). For a comparative perspective see J.Q. Whitman, *Harsh Justice: Criminal Punishment and the Widening Gap between America and Europe* (Oxford, 2003).

[52] A good starting point for discussion is provided by Y. Thomas, 'Les procédures de la majesté. La torture et l'enquête depuis les Julio-Claudiens', in M. Humbert and Y. Thomas (eds), *Mélanges à la mémoire de André Magdelain* (Rome, 1998), 477–99; Y. Rivière, *Les délateurs sous l'empire romain* (Rome, 2002). But on autonomy of fiscal law: G. Boulvert, 'L'autonomie du droit fiscal: le cas des ventes', in *Aufstieg und Niedergang der römischen Welt*, II.14 (1982), 816.

[53] On arbitration: G. Broggini, *Iudex Arbiterve. Prolegomena zum Officium des römischen Privatrichters* (Cologne-Graz, 1957); M. Talamanca, *Ricerche in tema di compromissum* (Milan, 1958);

society can also provide an interesting test-case for modern sociological theories of law. Seen from the sociological perspective, Roman law appears as a far from exhausted field of research, and its relationship to Roman society becomes much more intelligible to historians, lawyers, and sociologists alike.

K.H. Ziegler, *Das private Schiedsgericht im antiken römischen Recht* (Munich, 1971); P. Martino, *Arbiter* (Rome, 1986); M. Humbert, 'Arbitrage et jugement à Rome' (1994) 28 *Droits et cultures* 47; Gagos and van Minnen, n.39, above. On 'laws' of the private associations: A. Magdelain, *La loi à Rome. Histoire d'un concept* (Paris, 1978), 46–9; J.-M. Flambard, 'Eléments pour une approche financière de la mort dans les classes populaires du Haut-Empire. Analyse du budget de quelques collèges funéraires de Rome et d'Italie', in F. Hinard (ed.), *La mort. Les morts et l'au-delà dans le monde romain. Actes du colloque de Caen (20–22 novembre 1985)* (Caen, 1987); N. Tran, 'Les procédures d'exclusion des collèges professionnels et funéraires sous le Haut-Empire : pratiques épigraphiques, norme collective et non-dits', in C. Wolff (ed.), *Les exclus dans l'Antiquité. Actes du colloque, Université Jean-Moulin Lyon 3, 23–24 septembre 2004* (forthcoming).

23

'Social Perceptions of Law after Communism': A Polish Case Study

Bogusia Puchalska

Introduction

From the earliest days of systemic reforms one of the most important aspirations of the transition countries has been the effective and lasting establishment of respect for the law and law-abiding behaviour in society. Yet, what we are now witnessing in Poland can be described as a growing de-legitimization of the political system,[1] driven by low levels of trust in state institutions and in the rule of law. Fifty per cent of Poles do not believe that the rule of law exists in Poland and more than half do not feel bound by law.[2] I think it is important to ask, what are the implications of the Polish society's low acceptance of state and law? And, why is the new Polish state incapable of fostering loyalty and support for the formal rules? Moreover, if the official law is no longer capable of providing a framework of legality, what kind of rules, norms, and practices fulfil this function? And finally, what are the emerging patters of legality, and how can we grasp their implications for society based on them?

To discuss the above issues I refer to two broad understandings of law. First, as the totality of legislative and regulatory norms produced by the state and secondly, as the cultural and social practices, habits, and traditions which determine how law functions in society. I also use the paradigm defined by the relation between the political and the legal, since it seems to offer a particularly promising explanatory potential in analysing Poland's socio-legal history during modernity and the post-1989 era. That is because the popular perception of law and legality in Poland had been influenced, to a greater degree than in the majority of other countries, by the polity, that is, the historical relationship of the Poles with the

[1] B. Misztal, *Informality* (London and New York, 2000), 220; L. Kolarska-Bobińska, 'Korupcja nasza powszednia' [*Our common corruption*] *Gazeta Wyborcza, www.Gazeta.pl;* (27 February 2004), 1.

[2] *Ibid,* 1.

state and state institutions.[3] For the best part of Polish modern history this relationship has been, to say the least, problematic. One of its most pervasive traits has been a paradigm of an alien, hostile state against the people. There is evidence to suggest that this paradigm is still playing a role in shaping attitudes to law and social perception of law in Poland, even among the younger generation.[4] Hence, I am arguing that the most promising way of establishing respect for the law in Polish society must lead through a genuine democratization of politics away from the elitist and self-serving style which currently dominates: only through a genuine transformation of the Polish political process and a dramatic change in the state-society dynamics can the legitimacy of law begin to establish itself.

There are two inter-related parts in my discussion. First, I will focus on historically shaped socio-cultural and political factors which still have an impact on attitudes to law in Poland today; secondly, I will discuss the impact of political and legal reforms on emerging patterns of legality as well as the general condition of Polish law.

Attitudes to Law in Historical Perspective

The assumption that the Poles are historically conditioned to by-pass law has become common currency in Poland today. This alleged historic inclination to lawlessness serves to explain all manners of socially problematic behaviour—from dangerous driving[5] to ethnic, racial, or cultural intolerance.[6] Even if such correlations can be contested, it surely will be difficult to reject them entirely. One reason is that there exists in Poland a long tradition of low respect for law and widespread distrust of the state. This tradition is related to centuries-long antagonism between the state, its laws, and society, which came sharply into existence during the Partitions (1795–1918). The German occupation, and following it the semi-independent regime of the Polish Peoples Republic, further entrenched the perception of the state and law as alien and hostile.[7]

Other historic traits relevant in explaining the relationship between the Poles and their official laws are the patterns of socialization which largely determined the nature of the state-nation or state-society dichotomy. Historically, 'collective

[3] This is an accepted thesis. See for instance: L. Krzywicki, *Studia Socjologiczne* [*Sociological Studies*] (Warsaw, 1951), 131; J. Kurczewska 'Democracy in Poland: Traditions and Contexts' in G.A. Bryant and E. Mokrzycki (eds), *Democracy, Civil Society and Pluralism* (Warsaw, 1995).

[4] See M. Borucka-Arctowa, M. Magoska, U. Moś and G. Skapska, 'Knowledge and Representations of Law by Children and Adolescents in Poland' in M. Borucka-Arctowa and Ch. Kourilsky, *Socializacja Prawna* [*Legal Socialisation*] (Warsaw, 1993), 77.

[5] E. Winnicka, 'Szybcy i Wściekli' [*Those fast and mad*], *Polityka*, nr. 32, 7 August 2004, 76.

[6] W. Osiatynski, 'Nienawidzę, bo sie boję' [*I hate, because I am afraid*] *Gazeta Wyborcza*, 31 July—1 August 2004, 16.

[7] See: A. Podgórecki, *Polish Society* (Westport, Conn., 1994). See also J. Szacki, *Liberalizm po kommunizmie* [*Liberalism after Communism*] (Warsaw, 1994); M. Marody, 'On Polish Political

individualism' offers an important insight. This phenomenon, described by Szacki,[8] implies individuality asserted within and for the benefit of collectivity, but directed against the state. Its origins are said to be rooted in the noble Polish traditions of 'golden freedom' and *liberum veto*, both strongly anti-authoritarian and anti-statist.[9] Some academics add to this list the so-called 'uhlan's flair', i.e. suicidal carelessness and a peculiar sense of honour (both define a romantic type of masculinity still seen as atractive).[10] Such traits lead to great acts of bravery on battlefields, for which the Poles have been rightly admired, but they also foster cavalier attitudes to legal rules, particularly when these rules are perceived to be different from the informal codes of behaviour. There is a broad agreement that these cultural traits survived well into the 1980s and beyond. This trait of upholding the romantic mythology rather than focusing on the pragmatic was evident is the content of the 'Solidarity' political programme in the 1980s, and the Round Table talks in February 1989. Both were dominated by value-loaded language of justice, dignity, 'living in truth', and a respect for honour. These values took priority over economic demands.[11]

The second of the still enduring historical traits is the prominence and endurance of symbols and rituals in social, cultural, and political discourses. The modern origins of this reach back to the Partitions, when Poland ceased to exist as a physical entity and was said to survive only as an 'idea'. In those times, an enormous amount of social energy went into upholding the cultural and ethnic sense of identity which allowed Polish culture and language to survive and re-emerge in 1918. This struggle to preserve the sense of Polishness was waged using symbols, icons, and myths vital for upholding national culture and identity.

The necessity to focus on national survival imposed the dichotomy of the 'Poles versus their oppressors' on public life and public debate. This, alongside the policies of the Partitioning powers, arrested social, political, and economic development in areas outside of the political struggle.[12] Instrumental in these processes was the ethos of romanticism, which dominated throughout the next two hundred years of Polish history. At the heart of the romantic ethos was a readiness to die for one's country; more pragmatic concerns were usually dismissed as trivial.

Attitudes' (1991) 89 *Telos*. The hostile dichotomy of state-nation had diminished to some degree during the interwar period between regaining independence and the German occupation of 1939. However, as stated by Kurczewska (see n.3), 'twenty years of the independent statehood proved too brief to eliminate it', 56.

[8] *Ibid.*

[9] *Ibid.* See also: T. Lepkowski, *Uparte Trwanie Polskości* [*The Stubborn Persistence of Polishness*] (London, 1989), 16.

[10] Winnicka, n.5, above, 76. See also the very interesting discussion of Poland's cultural identity within the paradigm of gender roles in Maria Janion's address to the Polish Business Council, which confirm the importance of the romantic type of masculinity, M. Janion, 'Żegnaj Polsko' [*Good-Bye Poland*] (1 October 2004) *Gazeta Wyborcza*, available at www.gazeta.pl.

[11] Szacki, n.7, above, 103.

[12] The 'ideal' versus the 'pragmatic' had been reflected in two opposing ideologies: romanticism which called for armed struggle, and positivism which advocated liberation through economic development.

After the Second World War, the dichotomy of capitalism/socialism had been employed successfully by many Soviet-controlled countries to similar political ends within the ideological battlefield for symbolic supremacy. In Poland, it served to reinforce the paradigm of the 'Poles versus the other' and was used by the PUWP's (Polish United Workers Party) government to legitimize and sustain their hold on power. Heavy reliance on the pulling power of rituals, mass rallies, and political propaganda had become one of the defining features of the political system. The ritualization of public life reached its apogee during the post-war years, where its functions were to legitimize the new political system and to create a new sense of social and political identity.[13] Society had been forced to take part in rituals, but excluded from influencing politics. Interestingly, the political discourse of dissident groups mirrored, in its style, that of the state—it focused on values and symbols relevant for fighting the 'system', it did not allow much internal debate.[14]

From this brief résumé it appears that the Poles had missed out, in their modern history, on the experience of a political milieu conducive to public debates in the real meaning of this word. Hence, the sense of, but also the need for the participation in or influence of politics or law has traditionally been very weak. I argue that this ritualization of public life enduring after 1989 is, in a sense, more problematic than that of state socialism, as it seeks to legitimize the new systemic reality in society, yet again, through processes, which, by their very nature, reduce society's engagement in public life to following rituals and rallying around symbols.[15] Such focus, in the absence of genuine democratic debate, leads to distortions within the political process and threatens chances for forging a genuine sense of political participation and influence over the political and legal order, which is a necessary basis for establishing the legitimacy of both. It also damages the prospects of developing a civic sense of empowerment based on identification with the policies and laws among the Poles. Tichner observed:

> Being a citizen means: to consider the state law as 'our' law, and to respect it for this reason.[16]

Osiatynski[17] stated recently that he considers the lack of any serious, sustained public debate as one of the most worrying features of Polish politics. Echoing his views, many Polish academics describe Polish democracy as retaining a democratic

[13] Inevitably parallel with Weber's 'charismatic' legitimacy. See M. Weber, *Economy and Society*, 2 vols. (London, 1978).

[14] This has prevented the political movement from developing a certain 'political maturity' which led to a split of 'Solidarity' after 1989, and which exposed the serious lack of political skills among the Solidarity elite after they were elected to the Government.

[15] Compare with Weber's charismatic type of legitimate domination, in n.13, above, ch 3.

[16] J. Tichner, 'Spolecznośc, która nie wojowała myślą' [Community who did not use thought in its battles] *Tygodnik Powszechny* (Krakow, 2 March 1977).

[17] W. Osiatyński, 'O czym nie mówią politycy' [What the politicians do not talk about] *Gazeta Wyborcza* (5 March 2004), at: www.gazeta.pl.

façade—democratic institutions including free elections and independent media are in place—while its substance is becoming undemocratic.[18] Neither society nor the politicians—since the ritualistic style of politics suits them—are willing or capable to break the façade of rituals and start a political process of a different type. In consequence, as argued by Hausner and Marody, the central structures of the state cease to be a public domain and become exclusively partisan and self-serving.[19] This, in turn, 'undermines the bases of legitimisation of power and leads to decline in social trust and support for state bodies, politics and the law'.[20] Although similar charges can be levied in some degree at many established democracies—such as the UK—the Polish situation must be seen as different, particularly given the pre-1989 context of the oppressive, authoritarian, system, in which legitimacy—political and legal—has never been established.

Although I claim that in specific Polish conditions political democratization must be seen as a necessary precondition to establishing legitimacy of law, the law, its enforcement and application (but also law-making), should be seen as different from politics, at least at an empirical level. This observation is not always reflected in social perceptions of both law and politics. Law in state-socialist countries has been seen generally as an unpredictable instrument at the Communist Party's disposal. Yet, the degree of politicization of law under state socialism remains a contentious issue. Many studies agree that predominantly the loyalty of judges and lawyers in socialist countries went towards the law, and their professional ethics rather than polity.[21] Experiential studies in Hungary confirmed that, if at all, only a tiny fraction of cases were decided on political rather than legal grounds. It is only reasonable to assume that things were no different in Poland. Of course, political abuses of the legal process took place, however, their proportion in relation to cases decided on legal merit was low enough to dismiss a charge of full subservience of law to politics.

In Poland after the political backlash of 1976, the independent lawyers employed by KOR (Committee for the Defence of Workers) used the law to defend prosecuted workers. The settlement after the 'Solidarity' uprising was negotiated and concluded within a framework of domestic law. It is difficult to assess if these events had any impact on society's faith in the law, as in some degree independent from politics.

[18] E. Mokrzycki 'Demokracja Negocjacyjna' in E. Mokrzycki, A., Rychard and A. Zybertowicz, (eds), *Utracona Dynamika? O niedojrzałości Polskiej demokracji* (Warsaw, 2002); M. Marody and K. Hausner, *The Quality of Governance: Poland Closer to the European Union?* (Krakow, 2000).

[19] Mokrzycki, n.18 above, 142–3, argues that the political scene in Poland is dominated by pressure groups; Zybertowicz suggests that networks rooted in secret services hold sway over the government of the day, A. Zybertowicz, 'Demokracja jako fasada' in Mokrzycki et al. n.18 above, 176; Wedel uses concepts of 'partially appropriated state', 'clan-state' and 'captured state' to discuss the penetration of the state bodies by the informal networks, in 'Dirty Togetherness' (2003) 2 *Polish Sociological Review* 153–7.

[20] Marody and Hausner n.18 above, 149.

[21] In contrast, the dominating view in the West has been that of total politicization of legal systems. For an overview of relevant literature and a critique of the Western perspective see: B. Puchalska-Tych and M. Salter, 'Comparing Legal Cultures of Eastern Europe' (1998) 16 *Legal Studies* 157–84.

The 1993/94 opinion polls suggest that the majority of Poles declared their willingness to obey even unjust laws.[22] There is, however, evidence to suggest that such declarations correspond only weakly with actual behaviour. This might confirm that the prevailing view of law in Poland is that of a ritualistic fiction, which does not need to be upheld in practice.[23] Arguably, the dramatic weakening of state structures in the late 1980s and 1990s and the scandal of nomenklatura privatization were also instrumental in facilitating such views.

Attitudes to Law after 1989: Politics and Society

The systemic reforms of the late 1980s constituted a dramatic political breakthrough that created a unique chance to bury the rift between the state and the people and to shift the political process towards inclusiveness, representativeness, and accountability. Most of the evidence suggests that these goals have not been accomplished to any meaningful degree. On the contrary, analyses of the condition of Polish democracy and the rule of law sound alarming. Many project scenarios of the 'softening of the state'[24] and of institutionalized unaccountability becoming entrenched to the degree where normal standards of democratic governance would not even be suitable as benchmarks.

One of the most intriguing questions to ask here is why the events in 1989 of such political and social magnitude failed to feed into a process of deep political and social change. It must be said that formal, institutional change has been achieved with relative ease. However, it is by now widely accepted that such changes are only meaningful as merely a first step towards democracy and the rule of law and cannot be equated with the realization of either. More crucial, and therefore more difficult, is the change of mentality, values, practices, and aspirations which are decisive in rendering the political institutions truly 'democratic'. In the Polish context, this should translate into a more society-oriented and inclusive style of politics, where the open debate and a greater engagement in politics is grounded in the grassroots of society. Yet there is evidence to suggest that most of these indicators of democratization stayed the same or deteriorated after 1989. Academics write consistently about these failings and fret that the Poles might be losing their faith in the idea of democracy—in the Summer of 2003, 45 per cent expressed a preference for state socialism over the current system.

Part of the explanation of this social trend, arguably, relates to the authoritarian and elitist style that dominated the political process after 1989, and which led to a

[22] CBOS [*Centrum Badania Opinii Spolecznej—Centre for the Study of Public Opinion*], 1995.

[23] Kurczewska writes about 'the negligible respect for law after 1989', n.3 above, 74. She links it to the legacy of nineteenth-century Polish struggle for independence and the Second Republic. After another decade, I think it is right to assume that this low respect for law not only endured, but possibly got even worse due to the problematic style of politics in Poland after 1989.

[24] A concept introduced by Gunnar Myrdal, Swedish economist and a Nobel Prize laureate.

disempowerment of society in the vital moment of systemic change. The most important decisions on the direction of systemic changes and other matters have been taken without much debate or consultation.[25] This remained within the historical canons of politics, social traditions, and mental heritage of previous eras. During the 'constitutional moment' of the 1989 political breakthrough, society, including trade unions, had been effectively bullied into accepting the policies of reforms imposed from above.[26] The nature of governance during the last fifteen years has, broadly, stayed within this paradigm.[27] This furthered the alienation of politicians, political parties, and the unions from society[28] and created a syndrome of an abandoned society, where the prevailing perception is that nobody represents the interests of the people. This sense of society being abandoned by its leaders deepened after the scandal of nomenklatura privatization which entrenched the old networks of social domination and re-invented the old political class in the guise of new capitalists driving the reforms. Fifteen years down the line the nomenklatura started re-converting their economic power back into political influence.

Despite the very public plunder of public assets or, in other words, an enfranchisement of the party elite and their families after 1989,[29] the social support for reforms and for governments of the first years of reforms has been very high. Since 1993/4, however, this support has been declining steadily. The law cannot remain immune to these political dynamics. Even if the social perception of the levels of corruption and manipulation of law are exaggerated, their impact is sufficient to entrench the general aversion to state law,[30] that seemed not only to have survived, but also to have increased during the fifteen years of systemic change.

I suggest that the politics of the first years of reforms, as well as the subsequent failures of Polish politics over the last fifteen years, reinforced the mental heritage of the Partitions and state socialism in many ways, and most certainly, as far as the perception of law and attitudes to law are concerned. There is also evidence to

[25] This is by now a widely accepted thesis. See for instance: J. Hausner, *Populist Threat in Transformation of Socialist Society* (Warsaw, 1992); J. Hausner, 'Akt Oskarżenia' [*Indictment*] (2003) *Polityka*, 19 June, No. 25; Interview with A. Smolar, 'Kraksa polskiej polityka' [*Crash of Polish politics*] *Gazeta Wyborcza*, 9 April 2004.

[26] Similar to the political change after 1945, the programme of reforms was presented as the only and the best option for Poland, which should be accepted without any debates.

[27] The syndrome of abandoned society has become entrenched, despite attempts to engage some sections of society through the Tripartite Commission. The Tripartite Commission had been plagued by many problems and achieved relatively little, mainly because it had failed to relate to the grass-roots, becoming an elite, central institution, lacking representativeness.

[28] Łętowska observed 'Postsolidarity politicians now have the full social mandate, but the lack of bonding with society is the same as it was before' quoted in Podgórecki n.7 above, 44.

[29] See L. Ray, *Social Theory and the Crises of State Socialism* (Cheltenham, 1996), 110, where he links the position of economic advantage of the nomenklatura with a feudal type of property holding—the fiefdoms. Mączak compared the extensive use-rights of party bosses to the feudal system of use-rights. See A. Mączak, 'Vicissitudes of feudalism in Modern Poland', in P. Than and G. Crossick (eds), *The Power of the Past* (Cambridge, 1984). In lights of such arguments, the conversion of the political power of the nomenklatura into economic assets might be compared to an enfranchisement of the feudal class.

[30] Podgórecki, n.7, above, 160.

suggest that the Poles continue to treat the law as something to be negotiated and used instrumentally for one's personal gain. At the same time, they see the need to preserve the façade of lawfulness by declaring their belief in law-abiding behaviour, which is contradicted by their failure to follow the legal rules in practice. That reflects the Polish schizophrenic mind governing the way Poles relate to the public sphere—law is accepted at the symbolic level, as social ritual, but not as a guide for one's actions.

Statistical data confirmed that levels of political activity and engagement, both in the official and alternative political processes, has fallen since 1989.[31] According to the research findings of Miller, the change of regime produced a society that was *less participant* and *less satisfied with participation* than before 1989.[32] Hence, it comes as no surprise that the constitutional moment has also been missed in at least one more crucial sense—it failed to capture the social energy and sense of mobilization, and channel it into meaningful engagement in systemic change. Skapska argues that the marginalization of ordinary people from designing the post-Communist arrangements posed a threat to the 'jurisgenerative' (law-engendering) force of the 1989 events. She recalls that only 42.86 per cent of Poles took part in the constitutional referendum.[33] With the benefit of hindsight we can now conclude that indeed the marginalization of society in both implementation of reforms and in changing the law, practically annihilated social involvement in the political process and reinforced the alienation of the political elite, and its politics from society. The low profile of the change of constitution and constitutional referendum—the first of this kind of events in a free, new Poland—has been a clear demonstration of the damaging effects of the continued, top-down style of politics.

The resulting unwillingness to become involved in the political process, both mainstream and alternative, is a consequence, but also a reinforcement of the divide between the political class and society. More crucially, it contributed to the re-discovery and re-employment of the 'escape into privacy' mechanism that used to be the main coping strategy under state socialism. In the specific Polish context, social disengagement and escape into privacy also helped to re-create the once existing conditions of party-political colonization of the state,[34] fostering corruption and disregard for law not only on the level of government, but also in society

[31] The percentage of people ready to sign a petition fell from 52 per cent in the 1990s to 29 per cent in the beginning of the 2000s. J. Zakowski, 'Polak, czyli kto?' [*Pole, i.e. who*] *Polityka* (25/2004); see also W. Miller et al., *Values and Political Change in Postcommunist Europe* (New York, 1998), 100.

[32] The statistics are as follows: 63 per cent of people in the ECE took less part in political life and 70 per cent took less part in non-political organizations (civil society structures), than under the Communist regime.

[33] G. Skąpska, 'Paradigm Lost? The Constitutional Process in Poland and the Hope of a "Grass Roots Constitutionalism"' in M. Krygier and A. Czarnota (eds), *The Rule of Law After Communism* (Aldershot, 1999).

[34] Many academics accuse the politicians of acting in their own interest only; 'involvement in politics is treated by politicians, including those holding the highest offices, as an opportunity to increase their own wealth'; J. Kurczewski, 'Współczesna Obyczajowość Polska' [Contemporary

at large. That is because of the 'normalizing' effect of the behaviour of politicians on society. To break this cycle, some academics call for 'democratic precedents' in government.[35] Zakaria, too, noted that:[36]

> Modern democracies will face difficult challenges ... Perhaps most difficult of all ... [will be that] ... those with immense power in our societies embrace their responsibilities, lead and set standards that are not only legal, but moral. Without this inner stuffing, democracy will become an empty shell, not simply inadequate but potentially dangerous, bringing with it the erosion of liberty, the manipulation of freedom, and the decay of a common life.

Arguably, the serious shortage of 'democratic precedents'[37] in governmental conduct after 1989 has had an impact on social perception of law. Even though the declared social need for the rule of law has always been very high, the belief that it can actually be achieved is diminishing, as are respect for law as a guide for one's actions. According to data from the 1990s, about 80 per cent of Poles declared a high respect for law. Data from the late 1990s, based on a sample from two small Polish towns, reveals 92.5 per cent as valuing highly the rule of law. However, half of this sample was convinced that the rule of law is still a distant prospect for Poland.[38] The recent opinion poll on a much wider sample confirmed that more than half of Poles do not believe that the rule of law exists in Poland and do not feel bound by it.[39]

Such highly cynical attitudes have in some ways been facilitated by the openly illicit nomenklatura privatization after 1989[40] which can be seen as one of those events that also provided a justification, or even a licence for lax attitudes to law. The existing uncertainty as to the state's ability to provide law enforcement and protection has deepened significantly. As a result, society lost faith in the state as legislator and law enforcer, as well as a provider of impersonal, accessible institutions and public services on which people could rely in their daily lives. Consequently, people still have to use bribes and clientelist networks.[41] This, in turn, further weakens the legalizing effect of the state whose weakness renders such practices socially acceptable in the first place.

Polish Customs] in J. Mucha (ed.), *Społeczenstwo polskie w perspektywie Unii Europejskiej* [*Polish Society from the perspective of accession to EU*] (Warsaw, 1999), 195.

[35] Miller et al., n.31 above, 29–30.

[36] F. Zakaria, *The Future of Freedom* (New York and London, 2003), 256.

[37] Miller et al., n.31 above.

[38] I. Krzemiński and P. Śpiewak, *Druga rewolucja w małym mieście* [*Second revolution in a small town*] (Warsaw, 2001), 85.

[39] See nn.1 and 2 above.

[40] This means 'process by which the former political-bureaucratic elite [...] transform political capital into economic power, which has the potential to be re-converted into political influence.' Ray, n.29 above, 187. Ray also points out that the nomenklatura privatization '... erodes law and delays legislative reforms, as legal loopholes are exploited as a source of profit', at 190.

[41] Recent research into corruption in Poland concluded that the most problematic and most widespread is the mundane character of corruption, which has become a part of everyday life of many Poles. See interview with Jacek Wojciechowicz, member of the anti-corruption team with the World Bank, 'Korupcja bije w najuboższych' [Corruption affects the poorest] *Gazeta Wyborcza*, Opinie, 4 October 2004; at www.gazeta.pl. According to the latest report of the Stefan Batory Fundation—more than half a million Poles had bribed clerks and officials. *Gazeta Wyborcza* 4 October 2004.

The evidence supporting this argument is as follows: the epidemics of defaults on due payments (see below), the explosion of criminal behaviour after 1989, the 'Wóz Drzymały' (*Drzymała's Carriage*) manner of law avoidance and evasion,[42] and the high support for political parties using unlawful means in their political campaigns (*Lepper's Self-Defence*). Given the scale and nature of the law-avoidance/evasion we might be witnessing the entrenchment of a specific paradigm of legality: grounded more deeply in an individual/group sense of what is right, which often goes against or openly rejects the official law-inspired one. In the specifically Polish conditions, however, the group/community norms are highly problematic as they reflect the patterns of socialization of the 'dirty togetherness' and 'amoral familialism'. Those are highly fragmented, rooted in a closed sense of morality and 'ethical dualism', hence, hardly conducive to the establishment of a law-abiding and law-respecting society.

Social Networks and the Law

There is strong evidence to suggest that law is perceived continually more as a disabling than as an enabling mechanism in matters of personal or economic advancement. A disproportionately high number of people believe that the skills of bypassing the law or using the law instrumentally, are necessary to achieve success in life.[43] Personal connections through informal networks of clientelism and 'dirty togetherness' continue to take a high position in surveys as conditions necessary to achieve life success.[44] The prevalence of such views after 1989 can be related to a number of factors, such as mental heritage of the Poles, the nomenklatura privatization, or the style of politics after 1989. However, probably the most enduring in a sense of entrenched culture and social habits, and, therefore, the most difficult to change, are the surviving patterns of socialization described as 'amoral familism'[45] and 'dirty togetherness'. Both relate to informal particularistic networks that were helping people to cope with economic shortages and also provided emotional and other manners of support. They were based on the ethic of 'defend your own and take what

[42] Drzymała was a hero of the resistance against Germanization and the purchase of Polish land by the Germans. To avoid German law banning the Poles from building houses on new land, he bought a Circus van and lived there permanently, moving it every day by one or two metres which allowed him to argue that his was only a mobile home. The explosion of holiday properties built now in Poland in contravention of building regulations is often compared to Drzymała's way, since the owners employ similar law-evading methods. (See P. Wrabiec, 'Interes kołem się toczy' [*Business goes round*] *Polityka*, 08/2004.)

[43] The widespread belief that being successful in Poland must involve some sort of illicit dealing is recalled frequently in the media. Also, the popularity of parties on an anti-corruption and 'cleaning up' public life mission, such as Self-Defence or the Law & Justice confirm a high level of social preoccupation with dishonest conduct among politicians.

[44] *Ibid*, 81-5.

[45] M. Marody, *Polacy* (Warsaw, 1980).

you can,'[46] which is clearly damaging to social relations and social morality outside of them.

Bojar[47] described such a—still prevailing—type of socialization in Poland as 'closed', that is, based on an ethnic-corporate model of citizenship, internally exclusive and externally hostile. Its roots are related to 'collective individualism' and the legacy of socialism, where the existence of small, exclusive groups based on a division between 'us' and 'them' was necessary for preserving values which the state was trying to eradicate. The inter-group dynamic was one of hostility and competition for scarce resources, which, in turn led to 'ethical dualism' where different moral norms are applied to internal and external relations. As a result, society evolved into a 'federation of primitive groupings—cliques, societies, ethos-based groups, without any established or elaborated rules of inter-group relations'.[48] Podgórecki uses a concept of 'social instrumentality' to describe the same phenomena. According to him, social instrumentality arises in response to 'social warpedness', which in turn refers to chaotic, unpredictable patterns of social behaviour that came to exist in a cognitive and ethical chaos of state socialism, and which produced instrumentality as the most suitable survival strategy in these conditions. Podgórecki concluded that what has emerged as the patterned behaviour of Poles can be described as a 'fiddling type of instrumental subsistence'.

It is quite clear that neither the 'closed society', described by Bojar, nor the 'social warpedness' make for patterns of socialization conducive to the creation of a culture capable of supporting and underpinning social relations based on pluralistic and inclusive types of normativeness. The prevalence of such patterns of socialization has, arguably, contributed to the highly instrumental and closed uses of law. These, in turn, have a negative impact not just on entrenching perceptions of law as largely non-consequential, but, by indirectly inviting fraudulent behaviour, such as defaults on payments, also threaten many sections of the Polish economy. This is particularly serious now—Poland's switch to a free-market, contract-based economy is taking place in the context of a serious crisis in the administration of justice—the courts are overburdened and extremely slow in processing claims, and law enforcement is very weak. In such conditions, fraudulent practices threaten the survival of many businesses—even large firms are vulnerable. The number of swindles is so high that in some branches of the Polish economy this phenomenon has been named a 'new national industry', or more straightforwardly 'a nightmare scenario for Polish economy'.[49] The Polish Digital Telecom Company files between 5,000 and 7,000 court suits a month to recover losses from unpaid debts, swindles, and deceptions. The sheer scale of the problem

[46] *Ibid.*

[47] H. Bojar, 'O źrodłach słabosci etosu demokratycznego w Polsce' [The roots of the democratic ethos weaknesses in Poland], in E. Mokrzycki, A., Rychard, and A. Zybertowicz, (eds), *Utracona Dynamika? O niedojrzalości Polskiej demokracji'* (Warsaw, 2002), 99–109.

[48] *Ibid*, 106–7.

[49] *Polityka*, 28 April 2001, 60.

is such that the affected businesses have established a coalition to defend themselves. There are also a number of law firms whose main activity is assistance in tracking down and recovering losses—curiously, by extra-legal means, since legal means are mostly ineffective. They aim to intimidate the debtor by publicizing the name of the firm and personal data of the owner, or to employ a gangster cum bailiff. Both ways are akin to mafia-like dealings.[50] Yet they enjoy a degree of acquiescence and social acceptance. The extremely low percentage of court decisions which are enforced (about 36 per cent)[51] in the area of debt collection and behaviour of law firms which in conceding the impotence of law resort to illicit dealings, not only deepens the erosion of social faith in law, but, in a sense, creates and validates an antagonistic bi-polar, schizophrenic dynamics between the law, and the illicit, but effective, abuses of law.[52]

The growing realization that fraud is not likely to be punished by legal means is not likely to change the highly cynical attitudes to law that are already engraved in the historical mentality of a nation for which most laws were already seen as transitory and instrumental. Historically, disobeying such laws and its instrumental uses have been considered patriotic[53] and a demonstration of polit-ical opposition to the state, not only during the Partitions, but also under the socialist system.[54] It seems that the law disobeying behaviour outlasted its polit-ical/historical justification and continues unabated in a society that refuses to change alongside political change and legal reforms.[55]

Legal Change after 1989

Why has there been no significant change in the perception of law after fifteen years of new political reality? Why is the Polish state closer than ever to a 'legitimacy

[50] There is now new legislation to help dealing with such situations legally. Ustawa o udostepnianiu informacji gospodarczej (Dz.U. Nr 50, poz. 242, z 25 March 2004) [*Access to Business Information Act*] which established the Business Information Bureau [*Biuro Informacji Gospodarczej*], responsible for storing and making available information about financial records of economic actors. It is still too early to assess its effectiveness.

[51] This puts Poland in the 129th position out of 133 countries audited by the World Bank in the latest ranking of effectiveness in debt execution.

[52] Another set of examples involves foreign investors who first establish a company in Poland, which, in turn, employs sub-contractors, usually small Polish firms. Once the work starts, the foreign investors' company changes the conditions of contract with the intention of accusing the Polish sub-contractor of not fulfilling contractual obligations and of using this as an excuse not to pay for the completed work. Even if the sub-contractor is successful in pursuing a court case against the foreign company, in most cases this company declares bankruptcy, leaving the main investor, based abroad, beyond the reach of law. Over the past two years this type of dealing reached epidemic proportions.

[53] Podgórecki, n.7, above, 45, 77.

[54] In Poland, particularly in the 1980s, fare dodging on public transport was considered a gesture of defiance against 'the system'. A typical argument is illustrated by the following: 'I'll travel on the bus without ticket—I am not going to give money to the Reds', in E. Czarny and B. Czarny, *From Plan to the Market: the Polish Experience 1990–1991* (Warsaw, 1992), 47.

[55] Bojar, n.47, above, 110–11.

crisis'? And, assuming that state law is to some significant degree ignored, disobeyed, or used instrumentally, on what kind of rules is the functioning of society based?

After fifteen years of legal reforms it might be worth asking to what degree the systemic changes affected the nature of law-making and law application and the socio-legal mentality of people. I argued above that the package of policies and new laws introducing systemic reforms in Poland was prepared and introduced in an authoritarian, top-down manner which excluded society from playing an active role in the reforms. As a result, some of the most problematic elements of Polish political and legal history have been revived by a society trying to find normative stability in history and tradition, in the face of normative chaos of post-1989 Poland. Even the change of constitution generally failed to mobilize social involvement and interest. It is reasonable to speculate that the low priority accorded to the re-writing of the constitution and the length of time which this took (eight years had passed since the break-through of 1989 to the adoption of the new constitution in 1997) could only have added to the spreading of social apathy. The depth of social disillusion can be illustrated by a contrast between the lack of interest in a new constitution for Poland and the zealous insistence on celebrating the anniversary of another constitution, namely that of 3 May 1791, even under threat of political prosecution.[56]

The 3 May Constitution has been of exceptional importance in Polish political culture as a precursor of modern democracy. In the Polish national and social traditions it was celebrated as a symbol of aspirations to fend off the threat of foreign occupation by restoring political unity and a strong system of government. Hence, in trying to understand reasons for the lack of interest in new constitutions, we should consider the possibility that the deepening disillusionment with the current state of Polish politics started eroding social respect of even the most sacred symbols in Polish historic memory.

Discussing the legal change after 1989 it would be impossible to avoid mentioning the negative impact of governmental legislative priorities and the disregard of formal processes of law-making by the first governments of the new Poland. During the first years after 1989, vast amounts of Parliamentary time were spent on debating issues such as abortion law and sex education in public schools. The most urgent and crucial issues relating to economic reforms were given a lower priority. Yet none of these issues has been subjected to public debate or discussion. Both types of legislation had been reduced to a role of political ammunition by politicians concerned mainly with preserving their positions. The introduction of Catholic religious education in public schools was yet another instance where not

[56] The Constitution of 3 May 1791 did not have much practical significance, since it never had the chance to be implemented. Its adoption was the last, desperate, and failed attempt to save Poland from disintegration—Poland was partitioned by Prussia, Russia, and Austria in 1792. Despite its short and purely symbolic existence, for generations of Poles it had represented a free Poland, defiant in the face of looming foreign occupation.

only were the principles of debate or consultations ignored, but also the formal processes of law-making were abused. This change in law was carried out by Ministerial instruction, and there was no debate or explanation of the rationale or impact of this on taxes, or on issues related to religious tolerance and equal rights for other religions. These continuous abuses of the formal and substantive processes of law-making,[57] harking back to state socialism, not only make the law appear unpredictable and instrumental, they also undermine the democratic bases of legitimacy of law.[58] Let us recall that this legitimacy has never been very strong. Neither state socialism nor the previous systems managed to create it.

The Condition of Law in the New Poland

One of the most crucial features of legal development in Poland both before and after 1989 seems to be a phenomenon described as an excessive 'juridification' of life.[59] In essence, it means an attempt to regulate by law all areas of life. This is driven by a certain type of *legocentrism*, that is, a belief that law is the most vital mechanism of social and political order. The specifically Polish variety of legocentrism was rooted in a strong trait of *magical thinking* which dominated the mentality of Poles as well as the style of governance. Origins of this magical thinking are related to psycho-social strategies of coping with long-term occupation, or conditions of life under oppressive regimes. Poland has been subjected to both. Wyka described this phenomenon in the late 1950s:

> The ordinary man must live . . . in these superimposed circumstances at the same time as he denies these circumstances any ideological meaning or permanence. . . . All these people divide their existence into feigned and real. . . . For the defeated this fiction involves the patterns of everyday life imposed on them by the occupier—real social existence is fiction.[60]

As far as the law was concerned, this magical thinking reached quite striking proportions: the Polish Constitution of 1952 was a good example of this, as were a number of statutes. It was common knowledge that the constitutional rights were not enforceable, and the declarations about freedom and democracy were just that—declarations. The façade-like, purely symbolic meaning of the constitution was somehow acceptable in a society much more focused on symbols and gestures

[57] During a Parliamentary debate on the introduction of visas for Poland's eastern neighbours, the Minister of Foreign Affairs declared a readiness to change this legislation by his own decision. See A. Stelmachowski, in Kochanowski, W. Staskiewicz in H. Izdebski and A. Stepkowski, *Nadużycie Prawa (The Abuse of Law)* (Warsaw, 2003), 56.

[58] L. Morawski, 'Instrumentalizacja Prawa' *(Instrumentalization of law) Państwo and Prawo (The State and Law)* (1993, No. 6), 19.

[59] J. Kochanowski, 'Trzy powody czy też symptomy kryzysu prawa' *(Three symptoms or reasons for the crises of law)* in H. Izdebski and A. Stepkowşki, *Nadużycie Prawa (The Abuse of Law)* (Warsaw, 2003), 78.

[60] K. Wyka, *Życie na niby (Pretended Life)* (Warsaw, 1957), 7–9.

than pragmatics of politics or economy. Similarly, it was believed that passing a new law is the best way to ensure the achievement of specific goals such as a rise in standards of environmental protection or the improvement in quality of certain goods. All this in a situation when there was not even a prospect of creating conditions which would allow the law to be applied or enforced, both for want of implementing regulations and for lack of necessary means, financial and technical.

The proliferation of legal regulations in new Poland has reached, according to many sources, elephantine proportions. Created in this way a legal jungle is not only very 'user-unfriendly', but often lacks coherence and technical clarity as well as permanence. This has reached such levels that both in the Polish media and in academic circles one hears frequent cries about the 'crisis of law'. The situation is made worse by the persisting style of government by instruction and a habit of changing statutory provisions by bureaucratic fiat.

Other factors contributing to the Polish legal crisis are the predominant positivism in legal thinking[61] and what Łętowska calls, 'textocentrism'.[62] A positivist approach to law and legal thinking is still a main defining feature of the Polish legal system and legal education. On the one hand, it leads to the over-production of legal acts and bolsters the magical belief in the power of law, but, on the other hand, it diminishes and often destroys other systems of rules and/or socio-cultural practices, which are necessary for law to function. Similarly, 'textocentrism', which reduces the concept of law to a mere legal text, also negates the relevance of extra-legal rules and reinforces the rift between the law in the books and the social reality. One of the tenets of 'textocentrism' is a belief that only through improvement in the legal text can any improvement of the law be achieved.[63]

Both phenomena reinforce authoritarianism, inherent to a much greater degree in codified legal systems than, for instance, in the common law traditions. In this sense, the law and legal culture in Poland over the last fifteen years go hand in hand with an unchanging style of politics, and neither is capable of providing impetus for much needed change.

Conclusions

The continued disillusionment with politics and the state is one of the main reasons why the rejection of state law as a guide for one's actions holds strong in Polish society. The crises of official law and the dominating syndrome of an 'abandoned society' create a state of normative limbo. Law is once again perceived

[61] See, e.g. Stelmachowski, n.57, above, 161–8.

[62] E. Łętowska, 'The Barriers of Polish Legal Thinking in the Perspective of European Integration', in *The Yearbook of Polish European Studies* (Warsaw, 1997), 56–62.

[63] *Ibid*, 59.

as an alien ritual in which the participation of society is not even required. There is almost no attempt to engage people in political and legal processes, and there is little concern about the lack of such engagement. Internally, Polish society seems to be drifting further away from politics and state law.

The still strong influence of some historical traditions has a predominantly negative impact on the course of the legal and political change in society. The fact that these traits hold strong in Poland today suggests that these offer some normative certainty[64] in times of a growing lack of such certainty in the current political climate in Poland.

In such conditions, the rules governing networks of 'dirty togetherness' and other social networks based on inward-looking paradigms, such as the 'ethos groups' and 'amoral familialism', dominate. It seems that the erosion of most forms of normativeness[65] that could have, potentially, provided genuine foundations for a more legitimate political system based on the rule of law and supported by meaningful levels of respect for law has been progressing at a steady pace.

[64] Compare with Kurczewska, n.3, above, 39.

[65] Compare with W. Staśkiewicz, in Izdebski and Stepkowski, n.57, 166.

24

Sociology of Law for Legal Education—Italian Experiences

Vincenzo Ferrari

Two Strategies for a Newly Born Field of Study

While the idea, the name, and the very existence of sociology of law in academic institutions were not new, its birth as a formally recognized topic may be said, conventionally, to have coincided with some significant events, such as the creation of the International Sociological Association's Research Committee on Sociology of Law in 1962 or, a little later, of the Law and Society Association in 1964. It was in that period—times of social reform in the Western countries and of détente with Eastern Europe—that a study of law in its social context was perceived as a chance not to be missed. A scientific analysis of the social processes of approval and enforcement of laws, of the connections between ideologies and actual normative decisions or of the realities that legal rules often happen to conceal was seen as an urgent need. The idea that laws might produce effects in sharp contrast with formal provisions, that they might even be no more than empty boxes and play a merely symbolic function became widespread in those times and was advanced as an original and specific contribution of the newly born sociology of law to the understanding of the legal systems.

However, there was no complete coincidence between these views, which were quite universally shared, and the strategic projects that aimed at reinforcing the institutionalization of sociology of law and strengthening it in the diverse academic milieus. In short and simplified terms, there were two contrasting strategies, which can be symbolized with the figures of Jean Carbonnier and Renato Treves, both authentic protagonists of the birth of the 'sociological movement in law', as Alan Hunt[1] came to define it.

Carbonnier, a high ranking French civilist, yet no devotee of the exegetic method so common in his country's civil law doctrine, conceived of sociology of law, essentially, as a highly specialized topic, to be practised at a doctoral level only,

[1] A. Hunt, *The Sociological Movement in Law* (Basingstoke, 1978).

by people who had previously achieved profound knowledge of the concepts and methods of both legal science and sociology. Thus, as a professor at the Faculty of Law at the Sorbonne, he did not ask that sociology of law be included in the curriculum of the *licence en droit*, but created and directed for a long time a *Laboratoire de sociologie juridique*, where a number of post-graduate scholars, both French and foreign, were trained to undertake specialized research. Back home, some of them succeeded in convincing their respective institutions to open law and society courses.

As a legal philosopher who had introduced Kelsen's Pure Theory of Law to Italy and a Jew who had chosen exile, teaching sociology—and also philosophy of law—in Argentina's University of Tucumán from 1939 to 1947, Treves also brought his experiences in the empirical research field back to Italy and envisaged quite a different strategy. Though sharing Carbonnier's view of sociology of law as a specialized topic, he strove for its formal inclusion in undergraduate law curricula, highlighting its basically 'cultural' function. To a certain extent, he was obliged to do so, since at that time advanced university curricula were rather exceptional in Italy, both at the Masters and at the PhD level (the latter would not be inaugurated before 1980), so the market offered no real alternative chances. Nevertheless, Treves insisted that sociology of law should advance side by side with philosophy of law—and maybe replace it—in the first half of the law curriculum, i.e. the first or the second year, rather than in the second half, culminating with the final *laurea in giurisprudenza* (corresponding roughly to an LL.B). Maybe the motives that induced him to make this choice were more 'political', in a wide sense of the word, than scientific or methodological. Teaching sociology of law, a typically interdisciplinary subject, to students not yet exposed to the basics of either law or sociology might appear questionable and in fact has always raised some far from easy problems of communication in the initial stages of a course, as well as in the choice of the textbooks to be recommended for reading. On the other hand, not only did sociology of law become immediately popular among law students, who have been choosing it as a favourite optional course ever since, but, no less important, it also conquered a cultural space in a number of law faculties which accepted it without excessive reluctance, despite the predominantly positivistic approach of Italian legal culture.

It would now be hazardous to state which of the two strategies may have enjoyed greater success. To make sense, it would be necessary to analyse other local situations comparatively and to consider the weight of other variables, to begin with the academic systems in the different countries. It would be even more difficult to envisage a connection between the status of sociology of law in education and its scientific development. From this specific perspective, and at least on a quantitative level, the differences between France and Italy, or between these and other European countries, do not seem to be that impressive. The only visible outcome of Treves' strategy, which in fact seems to distinguish the Italian situation from the rest of Europe, is the high degree of institutionalization of sociology of law in Italian academies and, correspondingly, the high number of law graduates who have had an opportunity to come into contact with sociology of law, though not necessarily becoming fully fledged legal sociologists.

I shall now describe this landscape briefly, before speculating whether and to what extent these chances offered by sociology of law in the framework of legal education have actually been taken or still can be.

Sociology of Law in Italy

Some data will give an idea of the status of sociology of law in the field of Italian legal studies.

The topic made its first official appearance under this formal heading in 1968 at Catania University Law Faculty, with a course given by Vittorio Frosini, a legal philosopher who was especially sensitive to the effects of technological innovation. Treves, who, besides his course in philosophy of law, had read general sociology for years, with a predominant focus on socio-legal matters, followed Frosini in 1969, in Milan University Law Faculty. Within a short time, this panorama was to become much richer. In 1975, the Faculty of Political Sciences of Messina University established the first tenure in sociology of law with a public contest that was won by Vincenzo Tomeo, a senior assistant of Treves and a clear-sighted analyst of law and social conflict. Between 1975 and 1985, ten new tenures and a number of permanent associate professorships were established in various universities, such that Valerio Pocar, in his national contribution to an international documentary enquiry updated to 1987, could report that there were twenty-two official courses in sociology of law, including twelve in law faculties.[2] At that time, the Italian situation could already be described as particularly flourishing, for most countries had already faced both the crisis of reformist ideologies and economic difficulties, two things that had converged to give rise to budgetary cuts and the suppression of law and society courses that had been established only a few years before.[3]

Nor was this favourable trend reversed in the 1990s, despite the dramatic crisis, both political and economic, which brought Italy's so-called (*à la française*) 'First Republic' to a quick end. By the end of the decade, there were up to thirty-eight official courses in sociology of law, including twenty-five in law faculties.[4] A little later, a more analytical insight based on the data supplied by the deans of the same faculties on the occasion of the enforcement of the new '3+2' university

[2] V. Pocar, 'Sociology of Law in Italy', in: V. Ferrari (ed.), *Developing Sociology of Law. A world-wide documentary enquiry* (Milan, 1990), 424.

[3] E. Blankenburg, 'Sociology of Law in the 1980s Compared to the Glorious 1970s' (1983) 2 *Sociologia del diritto*, 159.

[4] V. Ferrari and P. Ronfani, 'A Deeply Rooted Scientific Discipline: Origins and Development of Sociology of Law in Italy' (2001) 32 *The American Sociologist*, 61 n.2.

system, revealed the existence there of twenty-seven courses, in some cases compulsory or semi-compulsory.[5] Finally, in 2004, whilst reporting on the matter at the congress of the *Associazione Italiana di Sociologia*, Guido Maggioni confirmed that sociology of law appeared formally in almost all the country's law faculties, with a number of credits ranging from six to nine.[6]

Coming to a more detailed analysis, it can be said that sociology of law is offered to undergraduate students in the great majority of cases as a basic course in the first or in the second year, according to Treves' original model, no longer as an alternative to philosophy of law that has once again become a compulsory subject since 1996, but as a 'strong' optional course, to be chosen in a narrow range which may include such items as History of Roman Law, Canon Law, Statistics, and others. A law and society course may then be offered again, at an advanced level, in the final stages of the law curriculum, which was extended from four to five years in 2001. There are therefore many hundreds of Italian law students who follow a sociology of law course every year and/or sit an exam in the field.

So far, quite a few students have also taken their final examination in law and been awarded their *laurea in giurisprudenza* by submitting and discussing a thesis on sociology of law—a question whose importance deserves attention *per se*. The *tesi di laurea*, a written dissertation whose purpose, according to a rule that dates back to the 1920s, is to 'give an original contribution' to a specific topic, has always been a requirement for a degree in almost all fields and will be continue to be so for the *laurea magistrale*, i.e. the higher degree (corresponding to an LL.M) envisaged by the newly established '3+2' system. This means that many thousands of theses are discussed in Italy every year in the most diverse faculties. Controlling and regulating this enormous flow of works is indeed a daunting burden shouldered by professors, lecturers and assistants at various levels, who are quite often badly paid or unpaid. A burden, moreover, that is not very amusing, since in most cases (and leaving aside the pathology, i.e. theses literally copied from various sources—especially through the Internet—or just commissioned from a hired ghostwriter) these works are no more than descriptive contributions that add not a dash to the scientific knowledge already available. However, notable exceptions are thankfully frequent. Not only top students, whose theses may easily turn into good Ph.D dissertations some years later, but also students at a middle or even lower level often submit works whose quality would never have been imagined on the basis of their previous performances.

Sociology of law has proved to be especially fertile in this respect. Since the subject is relatively marginal and its essential literature is mostly in foreign languages, especially English, students find it more difficult to go in search of external help

[5] V. Ferrari and E. de Tullio, *The Place of Philosophical and Sociological Approaches to Law vis-à-vis an Overall Reform of Legal Studies. The Italian Case.* Unpublished paper presented at the W.G. Hart Workshop, Institute for Advanced Legal Studies, London, in June 2001.

[6] G. Maggioni, *La sociologia del diritto dialoga con altre discipline.* Unpublished paper presented at the Congress of the Associazione Italiana di Sociologia, in Naples, 5–6 March, 2004.

and are therefore obliged to engage in a personal research project. Many of them also agree to do empirical work, usually on the level of small-scale pilot studies designed to establish hypotheses rather than to test them. Yet, there are cases of empirical investigations carried out by students whose scope is far wider and that contribute substantively to shedding light on actual phenomena, if not to theorizing. *Sociologia del diritto*, the Italian journal on the subject, often hosts this kind of contributions of that sort, whose authors had not planned to do research and will not continue doing research in the future.

This academic panorama affects the state of Italian research in the socio-legal field quite characteristically. The relatively wide audience of students engaged in research projects multiplies the number of the topics which can be tackled using socio-legal methods and which are—incidentally—countless, in that they cover the whole area of law, which is borderless by definition. It may occur that the opportunity to glance at new areas, perhaps merely local in scope, but potentially rich and deserving the utmost attention, comes from students rather than from their supervisors. A number of studies of traditional systems of justice, the local revival of customs and the survival of pre-bourgeois forms of collective ownership has come to light in this way in the recent past.

The number of potential scholars is also greater. There are now four ad hoc national Ph.D programmes in sociology of law, established in Milan, Macerata, Campobasso, and Urbino respectively, plus an 'International Ph.D programme in law and society', named after Renato Treves, which is established in Milan but to which seven other universities (four Italian, three from other European countries) and the historical *Centro nazionale di prevenzione e difesa sociale* actually contribute, with the formal recognition of the ISA Research Committee on Sociology of Law. A relatively wide community of socio-legal scholars—at least 200 people of various generations—has developed, every year generating dozens of books or essays, the latter appearing in *Sociologia del diritto* or other related journals.

The public image of sociology of law also derives a certain advantage from this relatively prosperous academic status. Socio-legal scholars appear on the media from time to time (some of them have also occupied high-level institutional offices) and co-operate with political institutions, both nationally and locally. One significant example is that of the large research project on the state justice system at the beginning of the twenty-first century, commissioned by the *Consiglio Superiore della Magistratura* (Supreme Council of Judicature) from the *Centro nazionale di prevenzione e difesa sociale* in 2001 and actually carried out by a team of no less than twenty socio-legal scholars, together with a smaller number of 'pure' sociologists, economists, and historians.

Even more important, however, is the chance offered by the Italian university system to disseminate a kind of knowledge of law that is not restricted to a merely linguistic analysis of legal rules, as well as, hopefully, to educate a multitude of future professionals of law—lawyers, judges, public prosecutors, notaries, and the like—to look at law from 'outside' and not only from 'inside', as Herbert Hart said, or, if one prefers, to see law not as an undisputable 'constant' element but as a variable of social life, open to discussion and criticism. They may as a result be better equipped for the transformation that our legal system is currently undergoing.

A Critical Overview

The landscape portrayed so far is certainly quite rosy, objectively speaking. After twenty years of budgetary cuts throughout Europe, Italy is possibly the place where sociology of law is in best shape, at least on the most visible institutional level, that of the academy and of the number of scholars who devote themselves to it officially and on a full-time basis. For this same reason, at all events, this local experience may be seen as an interesting benchmark for measuring the effects of the diffusion of socio-legal knowledge in the academic world and at a larger societal level. Coming back to how sociology of law was seen originally may help this to be achieved.

In his introduction to the first issue of *Sociologia del diritto*, in Spring 1974, Renato Treves described three different paths that sociology of law had taken in the past and could take in the years to come. The first was the path of sociological Grand Theorizing, to which legal sociologists could contribute by including the legal variable in the general portraits of society described by the most influential mainstreams of theoretical sociology, which at that time oscillated between the two extremes of functionalism and conflict theories. A second option was that of the general theory of law, which stood to be enriched if socio-legal experts were to add a number of non-legal variables to the most common juristic descriptions of legal systems and of their reciprocal links. The third path—he stressed—was empirical research into the life and development of specific legal institutions, to be analysed using the techniques of sociological investigation, according to a typical middle range approach. Though acknowledging, nay advocating, the connection between these three visions—which all looked at law from 'outside', as he stressed—and therefore conceding 'full validity' to the first two approaches, the author observed that the third way seemed to be the most promising and fertile, in view of the need to measure 'the distance between normative structures that are often obsolete and social contexts in endless development', to verify whether and how legal provisions are enforced or remain unenforced, as well as to understand why legal rules are issued and whether they achieve the goals aimed at by law-givers.[7] Briefly, Treves wanted to give sociology of law a critical function, to be accomplished by using the most appropriate techniques, to disclose the 'reality' of legal institutions, so often hidden behind the curtain of words and ideologies—a job (he added significantly) to be done with the spirit of such scholars as Charles Wright Mills, one of his favourite sources of inspiration. The author repeated this

[7] R. Treves, 'Tre concezioni e una proposta' (1974) 1 *Sociologia del diritto* 1.

vision of sociology of law quite often in the following years, stressing that it would provide the highest degree of autonomy to the newly born discipline, especially vis-à-vis the powerful and historically well-rooted legal science.

Thirty years later, it is legitimate to ask whether Italian sociology of law has met its founder's expectations, especially as far as the third vision is concerned, i.e. the one that he declared to prefer. As a matter of fact, it would seem that empirical sociology of law has suffered from the stringent competition of the other two visions.

Sociological Grand Theorizing was especially attractive for the new generation of the country's legal sociologists. The 1970s were largely dominated by a Marxist-like theoretical approach, focusing on a sharp criticism of capitalist institutions, yet on the grounds of an holistic epistemology that conceded the use of empirical methods only within the framework of a general *Weltanschauung* taken as axiomatically true. Such orientation was so resistant that it could survive the crisis of Marxism that began in the mid-1980s and culminated with the end of the Communist regimes in Eastern Europe by the end of the decade. At that point, a large and vocal portion of the Italian socio-legal community—much the same schools and sometimes the same protagonists—turned towards neo-functionalism *à la* Luhmann, irrespective of its political inspiration, which was quite distant from the conflict theories of the preceding decade. Luhmann's success in Italy, especially among socio-legal scholars, was overwhelming—more so, indeed, than in Germany—and is in itself a social phenomenon that would be worth analysing. Many scholars of the second and third generation of legal sociologists were won over so completely by Luhmannian conceptual schemes that those who dared to object to their foundations, though admiring their complexity, often had the feeling of being kept to the threshold of scientific debates, as they were alien to a paradigm that was taken, once again, as axiomatically true. This attitude was particularly harsh toward those who insisted on the need for empirical investigation, since Luhmann himself looked at it with more than a hint of conceit.

One might have expected that the—not total, yet visible—demise of Luhmannianism in the 1990s, especially after the scholar's untimely death in 1998, would have opened the way to a return of scholars to field research. In fact, though the general atmosphere might have favoured such a turn, in the last decade Italian socio-legal scholars again addressed their attentions to predominantly theoretical reflection, this time leaning toward general jurisprudence rather than general sociology—i.e. toward the second, rather than the first, of the three paths envisaged by Treves in 1974. The foreground came to be occupied by certain subjects, especially of middle range, such as technological revolutions, communications, privacy, human and citizenship rights, migrations from developing to developed countries, and economic and cultural globalization—a set of problems that was deemed to pave the way, in particular, for a new wave of the pluralist visions of law. No question indeed about this, in principle. Legal pluralism can hardly be opposed, especially in our times, as an historical fact, i.e. on a descriptive level, if not on the normative level of concrete legal decisions to be taken under the aegis of one legal order or another. Moreover, the renaissance of discussions inspired by theoretical pluralism, on a profound mental level, may have had a positive effect on the general atmosphere in which people came to discuss and compete.

However, even in this more friendly atmosphere, a worrying poverty of empirical knowledge, i.e. of scientific information, can unfortunately be observed. Obviously, this remark should not be taken literally. Empirical research has never ceased to exist in Italy throughout the whole period described here, especially in such areas as family law, litigation in court or out of court, the implementation of law, some aspects of welfare policies, etc. Yet by no means could it be said that it was sufficient, also for the needs of theory itself.

There are sound reasons for this, incidentally. On the one hand, there are obvious practical difficulties that hinder empirical research. Doing it is often quite boring, time-consuming, maybe deceptive and, unfortunately, increasingly expensive. Theory is more exciting and can be conducted in one's office, as was the case with the nineteenth-century's 'armchair anthropology'. On the other hand, it should also be remembered that Italian culture has traditionally leant toward French rationalism or German idealism rather than Anglo-Saxon empiricism, which has often been considered to be a second-rate philosophy by Italian academic elites, while sociology itself was banned from Italy's universities for a long time before the Second World War. However, a more serious insight into this question would lead us too far in this context. I shall therefore confine myself to pointing to the most visible shortcomings that the relative lack of empirical research has produced, or may produce, as I said before, at the academic and at a wider societal level.

First of all, the subjects most frequently tackled by socio-legal scholars in recent years would have profited considerably from a more detailed and scientifically reliable set of data. Let us take the most obvious of examples, globalization. In the legal field, this phenomenon is said to go hand in hand with certain profound changes, indeed authentic and qualitative 'revolutions' in the sense that Harold Berman, among others, has described[8]—the inextricable links between all legal systems, the crisis of parliamentary legislation as the primary source of law, the expansion or the renaissance of other sources of law, such as contract, precedent, custom, doctrinal writing, soft or hard administrative decisions and technical regulations, the restructuring of legal services both in private law firms and in the field of company lawyership, and so on and so forth. All this may well be true, but to what extent? Is it not necessary to go into more detail, so that light may be shed on more specific aspects, more accurate distinctions be drawn and clearer relationships be perceived between the diverse legal cultures and the diverse shapes taken by the phenomena under scrutiny?

[8] H.J. Berman, *Law and Revolution. The Formation of the Western Legal Tradition* (Cambridge, Mass., 1983).

To cite but one example, there is the potentially perverse relationship that connects the transnational scope of production and commercial exchanges—the latter increasingly subject to uniform regulation—and the survival of sharply distinct and separated national legal orders in the field of labour relations. Even today, though sociological thinking may profit from the macro-data collected by the International Labour Organization, there is no detailed knowledge of the social impact of such local legal peculiarities. As a consequence, hidden mechanisms of exploitation, social marginality, and oppression, at the level both of the factory and—no less significantly—the family, may not come to the surface. How are such mechanisms affected by—for example—the availability of computer facilities at increasingly lower societal levels, or the concentration of patents in increasingly fewer hands, or the international diffusion of franchising? Such links are often a matter of intuition, rather than of direct experience, on the part of Italian legal sociologists, even when they devote brilliant pages to such phenomena.

On another level of discussion, one could also complain about the lack of empirical investigations about some legal reforms of undisputable relevance for the country.

In 1989, for example, a new model of criminal trial, largely inspired by the American adversary system, was adopted in Italy and the traditional inquisitorial model was abandoned as a consequence. Some suspect that there is a connection between the adoption of the new system and the even greater duration of legal proceedings in the criminal field. On the other hand, it may be that this is rather the effect of the law which, together with the new code of criminal procedure, established that amnesties be subject to a qualified parliamentary majority, thus virtually outlawing a legal tool that had previously been used cyclically to cancel a large portion of criminal proceedings, even before any first instance decision had been made. Again, how much may all this be linked to the current high probability that even grave offences—especially political corruption—run into the statute of limitations? How much is all this connected with the changing political climate in the country?

Quite similar arguments could be advanced about a number of other prominent aspects of the country's institutional life. Such is the case of the civil justice system, which was partially modified between 1990 and 1998 and is now expected to undergo a new reform based on a private, rather than a public, view of civil proceedings; or of company law, which was recently reformed in both its substantive and its procedural aspects, special attention having been paid by the government to its criminal implications, especially to the practice of false statements in Annual Reports, which was virtually abolished as a crime; or of labour law, where two basic reforms, passed in 1997 and 2002 respectively, put the traditional set of labour relations in real jeopardy; or of constitutional law, currently being overturned by a reform bill that, rather oddly, tries to combine regional federalism with central autocracy; and, finally, of the ever increasing impact of European law upon national law.

In such a wide area, pure theorizing is not enough. Though a theory should be both the beginning and the end of all scientific endeavours, it must be grounded on a set of data which may help to build it up and reorient it, if necessary. Only a detailed knowledge of this kind can shed true light on the links between rules and actions, or between rules and the culture or the values of a population, so that public opinion may be informed more properly and accurately than through opinion polls that often happen to correspond with the interests of the more powerful and become self-fulfilling prophecies.

Needless to say, such information may even be vital for the survival of at least a hint of the rule of law, which is now seriously threatened in the Italian Republic.

Conclusion

This model of sociology of law, in which pure theoretical reflection prevails over empirical research in Italy, has, or may have, some consequences on legal education, at least in the long run.

From the beginning of their training, Italian law students—much like any other law student in the civil law countries—are literally plunged into a theory that aims to supply the tools and the general framework on which they will be expected to base their legal decisions in the future. Following historical cycles, this peculiar kind of theory may have more or less formal characters. When a formalist legal culture prevails, the future lawyer is asked to apply abstract concepts and to interpret positive rules on the basis of a logical-deductive method inspired by the 'superior' principles of completeness, consistency, and unity of a specific legal order. When a more informal legal culture takes the lead, the future lawyer is allowed to do the same exercise, i.e. applying concepts and interpreting rules, also having recourse to so-called 'extra-juridical' elements or arguments, such as the principles of justice or fairness, political goals, value judgments etc, even if these introduce some degree of disorder or inconsistency in the logical structure of the system. In both cases, anyway, the legal theory with which the future lawyer is educated is at once *dogmatic* and *prescriptive*, since (s)he is educated to take future decisions that can be justified as the consequence or the implication of higher binding principles, be they logical or axiological (most rarely, I should stress, of a 'factual' nature, e.g. based on the concrete consequences that will derive from the decisions made).

Vis-à-vis this world of pure jurists, sociology of law may behave more or less ambitiously. For example, especially when anti-formalist visions prevail, it may only seek to *integrate* the legal theory with some 'extra-juridical' elements drawn from actual social life and thus address the juristic interpretation, case by case, toward different conclusions. However, a socio-legal discourse may also be far more ambitious, seeking not so much to integrate the legal theory as to build up a different theory that may *develop alongside* it and whose content would be not legal precepts as such, but the relationship between them and social action or, more precisely, *law as a means of social action*: a theory, therefore, that would not be prescriptive and dogmatic, but *descriptive* and *critical*, in that it would be addressed to merely cognitive rather than practical ends. This conception of sociology of law, which can be traced back to the teachings of Max Weber and the other scholars who advocated the division between legal science and sociology of law, was indeed the one that those who strove for official academic recognition of this field of study, about forty years ago, actually had in mind.

To this conception, however, it could be (and often is) objected that sociology of law would in that case turn into a sort of de-sanctification of law in the eyes of law students—in brief, it would perform a 'subversive' function with respect to an enforced legal system. This objection is more serious than may appear at first sight and should therefore be countered as far as possible with sound arguments.

One argument may be based on the epistemological difference, just mentioned, between legal theory and sociology of law. Students should be led to understand that the two discourses actually go hand in hand and are not mutually incompatible. Sociology of law seeks to widen their overall panorama, to the benefit of their future professional careers. Yet knowledge of how and in which context social actors behave through law does not imply that lawyers should act in accordance with the actors' behaviour. On the contrary, they may actually be induced to go against it. A concrete example could be a case in which a judge, who may have achieved full awareness of her/his *actual freedom* to 'create' law, may then *freely* and *ethically* opt either to exploit this freedom to the utmost or to reduce it to the minimum and become a *bouche de la loi*, for the sake of the unity and the consistency of the legal system or of the certainty of law.

This argument may look quite sound in itself, but it must be admitted that it is not so easy to propound it, especially with young students. It is not surprising that both in my courses to students and in my textbook I spend considerable time discusssing this.

Another argument may be based on the tough remark that there is no reason whatever why future lawyers should not be equipped with 'factual' elements that may help them look at their own legal ordering in a less 'sacred' way, should they wish. Precisely because legal theory is dogmatic in nature, it appears to be vital to build up—as said before—a different theory that may unveil the ideological foundations on which the former is based. Suffice to think, quite simply, of totalitarian legal systems, which deserve to be 'de-sanctified' *per se*, but also of the numerous *fictiones iuris* with which all legal theories are interwoven and whose social function can often be revealed only by looking at the concrete use made of them by social actors. This also seems to be a sound argument, one that may be even easier to propound, though somewhat risky in that it may excite political passions and arouse the protest of those who have no interest in the unveiling of ideologies or devices of any kind.

At all events, these and other good arguments that can be used to counter the above-mentioned objection will be much stronger if they are advanced on the basis of scientific evidence and with a true spirit of humility. A this point, then, we can go back to the question of empirical research, which was dealt with in the last section of this chapter.

Field research, which seeks to use scientific methods (be they qualitative or quantitative, the latter obviously implying previous qualitative choices) to supply reliable data, displays both these virtues, at least potentially: it supplies observable evidence and is (or should be) inspired by humility. There is no contradiction between these two terms. Good sociologists, who observe the world around in order to describe it with an objective spirit, should know, first, that the scope of their observation is narrow, i.e. it is not that world, but rather fragments of it; secondly, that the 'reality' they observe is affected by their own subjective perspectives, perceptions, culture, and general visions of things; thirdly, that a researcher only proceeds from one hypothesis to another and through a sequence of tests that may help arouse and discard doubts, but never supplies absolute certainty; and, fourthly, that the data collected may disprove the theoretical foundations on which the hypotheses were originally laid down.

On the other hand, a sociological theory which makes no use of empirical observation, preferably carried out by a researcher directly, runs the risk of being considered arbitrary and arrogant. If proposed as a collateral theory to jurisprudence, it will easily be perceived as a sheer alternative to it and may have a negative effect on the community of lawyers and also on legal education, especially for young students, in that they may become convinced that they possess a definite, alternative truth that does not even need to be demonstrated scientifically. Moreover, some potentially good researchers may lose their way and miss the chance of offering an original contribution to the development of scientific knowledge in the future.

It must be said that Italian sociology of law has not so far succumbed to this. At least, the field has been rich in lively discussion, on an epistemological level as well. Yet a more profound commitment to field research would prevent this happening in the future.

25

The Socio-Legal Construction of the 'Best Interests of the Child': Law's Autonomy, Sociology, and Family Law

Robert van Krieken

Introduction: Law and Sociology in the Post-Separation Custody Debate

For the last few decades there has been considerable discussion across the social sciences and in socio-legal circles about the changing nature of family life, intimate adult relationships, and relationships between adults and children. Against the background of the sociological analyses of broader trends in family life—increasing divorce (and remarriage) rates, declining fertility, increasing age at marriage, increasing female workforce participation rates—a central theme in this discussion has been the question of parental separation and its impact on the character of parent-child relationships. Nested still deeper within this question has been the more particular one of the role of fathers, with important transformations taking place in the way that has been conceived, both during a marriage or relationship and beyond a separation. These transformations include an increasing tendency towards framing the 'best interests of the child' in terms of a 'right' to contact with both parents, which includes a turn away from an overt 'maternal preference' in determining post-separation custody, a shift from the notion of a 'clean break' to that of joint parenting, or what Irene Thèry has called a shift from the 'logic of substitution' to 'logic of durability' in the construction of parent-child relations.[1] All of this has in turn operated as part of a broader

[1] Irène Thèry, ' "The interests of the child" and the regulation of the post-divorce family' (1986) 14 *International Journal of the Sociology of Law* 341.

process of defining children's rights and interests independently from those of their parents.[2]

This post-separation custody debate has been organized around a particular range of recurrent themes and issues: the effects of divorce on children, especially the impact of paternal absence; the extent to which physical and sexual abuse by fathers has been adequately recognized, and whether joint custody often operates as an extension of that abuse; the fairness of the courts' approach to custody and access questions and whether parents, especially non-resident fathers, should be seen as having any sort of 'right' to access to their children; the explanations for the legislative changes which have taken place in family law since the 1970s, particularly the role of social science research and the political activity of various interest groups (e.g., fathers' rights groups); the practical problems associated with co-parenting and how it actually works for children; whether the adversarial nature of formal legal processes is itself a problem in such an emotionally complex field of disputation, including arguments for and against mediation and counselling; and the problem of relocation and the degree to which the significance of children's continuing contact with both parents should restrict the physical movement of parents from one city, region or country to another.

One of the more interesting aspects of family law, however, is the depth of the concern to align law with a supposedly changing social reality itself, and the important role played by competing bodies of knowledge in a range of social science disciplines, including sociology, concerning and, of course, constructing, that 'reality'. This relates to the broader question of law's epistemic autonomy and authority in relation to other forms of knowledge-production, which has been discussed in other arenas but, with only a few exceptions, at a fairly abstract level, and without having been linked in great detail with these current debates around parental separation, child custody and joint parenting. This chapter works towards just such a linkage, reflecting not on the substantive concerns of the debate itself, but on the ways in which it has emerged from a particular kind of structuring of the relationship between law on the one hand, and disciplines such as sociology on the other.

(Family) Law's Autonomy

To suggest that legal reasoning concerning post-separation child custody should be responsive to the results of social scientific research into the effects of separation on childhood experience is, in principle, at odds with both law's own self-perception and with what a variety of observers have had to say about law's autonomy or 'closure'. This is a terrain that has been very well charted by a number of writers,

[2] A. James and M. Richards, 'Sociological perspectives, family policy and children: adult thinking and sociological tinkering' (1999) 21 *Journal of Social Welfare & Family Law* 23. For a more detailed discussion, see Robert van Krieken, 'The "best interests of the child" and parental separation: on the "civilizing of parents"' (2005) 68(1) *Modern Law Review* 25–48.

including Niklas Luhmann,[3] Gunther Teubner,[4] David Nelken,[5] Roger Cotterrell,[6] and Michael King,[7] so there is no need to discuss it here in any great detail, other than to identify those elements of the debate which are most significant for the question of its application to the child custody question.

In itself, the idea that law might possess greater or lesser degrees of autonomy or closure in relation to the extra-legal world is not particularly new.[8] Max Weber, for example, said of the relationship between law and economic activity:

> [T]he expectations of parties will often be disappointed by the results of a strictly professional legal logic. Such disappointments are inevitable indeed where the facts of life are juridically 'construed' in order to make them fit the abstracted propositions of law and in accordance with the maxim that nothing can exist in the realm of law unless it can be 'conceived' by the jurist in conformity with those 'principles' which are revealed to him by juristic science. The expectations of the parties are oriented towards the economic and utilitarian meaning of the legal proposition. However, from the point of view of legal logic, this meaning is an 'irrational' one ... such conflicts ... are the inevitable consequence of the incompatibility that exists between the intrinsic necessities of logically consistent formal legal thinking and the fact that the relevant agreements and activities of private parties are aimed at economic results and oriented towards economically determined expectations.[9]

The observation generally made is that law's relationship to other fields of knowledge tends to be organized around either (1) the *displacement* of alternative sources of explanatory authority,[10] or (2) the *appropriation* of the knowledge

[3] Niklas Luhmann, 'Closure and Openness: On Reality in the World of Law', in: Gunther Teubner (ed.) *Autopoietic Law: A New Approach to Law and Society* (Berlin, 1988); Niklas Luhmann, 'Operational Closure and Structural Coupling: The Differentiation of the Legal System' (1992) 13 *Cardozo Law Review* 1419.

[4] Gunther Teubner, 'How the Law Thinks: Toward a Constructivist Epistemology of Law' (1989) 23 *Law & Society Review* 727; Gunther Teubner, 'Altera Pars Audiatur: Law in the Collision of Discourses', in: Richard Rawlings (ed.), *Law, Society and Economy* (Oxford, 1997); Gunther Teubner, Richard Nobles and David Schiff, 'The Autonomy of Law: An Introduction to Legal Autopoiesis', in James Penner, David Schiff and Richard Nobles (eds), *Introduction to Jurisprudence and Legal Theory: Commentary and Materials* (London, 2002).

[5] David Nelken, 'The Truth About Law's Truth' (1993) *European Yearbook for the Sociology of Law* 87; David Nelken, 'Blinding Insights? The Limits of a Reflexive Sociology of Law' (1998) 25(3) *Journal of Law & Society* 407; David Nelken, 'A Just Measure of Science', in Michael Freeman and Helen Reece (eds) *Science in Court* (Aldershot, 1998); David Nelken, 'Can Law Learn from Social Science?' (2001) 35(2–3) *Israel Law Review* 1.

[6] Roger Cotterrell, 'Sociological Perspectives on Legal Closure', in: Alan Norrie (ed.), *Closure or Critique: New Directions in Legal Theory* (Edinburgh, 1993).

[7] Michael King, 'Child Welfare within Law: The Emergence of a Hybrid Discourse' (1991) 18 *Journal of Law & Society* 303; Michael King, 'The "Truth" About Autopoiesis' (1993) 20 *Journal of Law & Society* 218; Michael King, 'Future Uncertainty as a Challenge to Law's Programmes: The Dilemma of Parental Disputes' (2000) 63(4) *Modern Law Review* 523.

[8] Hans Kelsen, 'The Pure Theory of Law, Its Methods and Fundamental Concepts' (1934) 50 *Law Quarterly Review* 474; Roger Cotterrell, 'Sociological Perspectives on Legal Closure', in Alan Norrie (ed.) *Closure or Critique: New Directions in Legal Theory* (Edinburgh, 1993); François Ewald, 'The Law of Law', in: Gunther Teubner (ed.), *Autopoietic Law: A New Approach to Law and Society* (Berlin, 1988).

[9] Max Weber, *Economy and Society* (Berkeley, 1978), 885.

[10] At times to the irritation of the individuals and groups representing those other bodies of knowledge. Sheila Jasanoff, for instance, refers to the example of Charlie Chaplin being found liable

produced by those other fields in order to enhance that privileged position, while surrendering the minimum degree of cognitive or normative authority to those other modes of knowledge production.[11] Niklas Luhmann, in particular, suggests that it is precisely the character of law as a system of *communication* which constitutes its autonomy, and that it is useful to treat law as an 'autopoietic' or *self-reproducing* system of meaning and communication rather than as a set of institutional forms, structures or practices:

> . . . the law differentiates out within society as an autopoietic system on its own, by setting up a network of function-specific communication which in part gives words a narrower sense, in part a sense incomprehensible for non-legal communication, in part adding coinages of its own (for instance, liability, testament), in order to make the transformations needed by law communicable. Whether thallium is necessary in the production of cement and what consequences this has is not a specifically legal question. It may however be the case (or else not) that an environmental law develops that gives this question additional legal relevance.[12]

He sees the central problem of any theoretical understanding of the legal system as being the question of '*how to define the operation that differentiates the system and organizes the difference between system and environment* while maintaining reciprocity between dependence and independence'.[13] This means that the binary code of the legal/non-legal distinction is crucially significant *in itself*,[14] at an abstract level in addition to whatever substantive distinctions are represented through it. Luhmann argues that the autonomy of law is threatened only when this 'code' is challenged, when decisions are instead made in terms of other distinctions, such as benefit/harm, productive/unproductive, and so on.[15]

For Luhmann, the idea of autonomy or closure does not mean that the legal system proceeds as if there was no environment, or that it is not subject to external determination. It means that (1) *all* of its 'operations' reproduce it as a system, and (2) *only* its own operations reproduce it as a system.[16] The core problem facing any social system is that of mediating between the inside and the outside of the system, and 'the real operations which produce and reproduce such combinations are always internal operations. *Nothing else is meant by closure*'.[17] The non-legal can have no

for child support, despite the scientific evidence which appeared to establish that he was not the father: Sheila Jasanoff, *Science at the Bar: Law, Science, and Technology in America* (Cambridge, Mass., 1995), 11.

[11] Christopher Tomlins, 'Framing the Field of Law's Disciplinary Encounters: A Historical Narrative' (2000) 34(4) *Law & Society Review* 911.

[12] Luhmann, 'Closure and opennness', n.3 above, 340.

[13] Luhmann, 'Operational Closure and Structural Coupling' n.3 above, 1426.

[14] Luhmann, 'Closure and opennness', n.3 above, 346. [15] *Ibid*, 347.

[16] Niklas Luhmann, 'The Unity of the Legal System', in Gunther Teubner (ed.), *Autopoietic Law: A New Approach to Law and Society* (Berlin, 1988), 15; Klaus A. Ziegert, 'The Thick Description of Law: An Introduction to Niklas Luhmann's Theory of Operatively Closed Systems', in: Reza Banakar and Max Travers (eds), *An Introduction to Law and Social Theory* (Oxford, 2002), 60–1.

[17] Luhmann, 'Operational Closure and Structural Coupling' n.3 above, 1431.

authoritative and effective impact in relation to the legal unless and until it has been somehow 'assimilated'. For example, Luhmann refers to the lack of connection between law and broader systems of morals, something of which the courts regularly remind naïve litigants. This does not mean, Luhmann emphasizes, that the legal system does not incorporate moral restraints from outside of itself, but that 'this has to be done within the system and has to checked by the usual references to legal texts, precedents, or rulings that limit the realm of legal argument'.[18] An idea, event or process can only be effective within law, it only exists within the legal system, after it has been translated into legal terms.[19] Within the legal system, the primary considerations are its own operations, the various sources of law (statutes, the common law, the constitution, principles of international law), and if sources such as religion, politics, policy considerations, or economic concerns are referred to, this means, argues Luhmann, that they have already become 'legal norms, which *legally* legitimate block acceptance of external norms or decisions (of good morals, say, or sound management, or the majority decisions of political processes)'.[20]

There are no extra-legal 'truths' exempted from the juridical gaze and cross-examination, no facts which have any autonomous status, all knowledge is mere testimony in favour of one party or another. All science is merely 'opinion', the reliability of any area of knowledge is always open to the court's critical scrutiny, and what any expert is actually expert in is a matter for the court to decide, guarding the boundary around the territory which belongs to the 'trier of fact', either the judge or the jury. Knowledge, as Luhmann puts it, has a different 'credibility profile' within the legal system, and before they can take effect within law, facts have to be 'legally constituted':

> Legal facts are made to fit the legal framework; they have to facilitate as much as possible the deductive use of legal norms. They have to support the presentation of legal validity by conveying the impression that, given the rules, the decision follows from the facts of the case. They have to be certified facts.[21]

Experts merely *assist* the trier of fact, and this concept itself is revealing: facts are to be subject to trial, they do not simply exist. 'Interpretations' are clearly on even shakier ground, and any discipline which sees itself as essentially contested, such as sociology, anthropology or (today) history, correspondingly increases its vulnerability to judicial scrutiny.

Luhmann refers to the autonomy of the legal system in terms of both *operational* closure (only internal operations reproduce the system) and *normative* closure.

[18] *Ibid*, 1429.

[19] In relation to contract law, see Hugh Collins, *Regulating Contracts* (Oxford, 1999), 52. For a discussion of the phenomenology of this process, and especially the violence of its impact on participants, see William E. Conklin, *The Phenomenology of Modern Legal Discourse: The Juridical Production and the Disclosure of Suffering* (Aldershot, 1998).

[20] Luhmann, 'Closure and opennness', n.3 above, 345.

[21] Luhmann, 'Operational Closure and Structural Coupling' n.3 above, 1430.

This is because he defines 'norms' as the means by which greater control is achieved over the future through reduction of the range of possible actions.[22] Normativity consists of an individual, unit, or system either failing or refusing to learn from its environment: so, instead of simply observing that people murder each other and learning how that might be relevant to one's own behaviour, one refuses simply to learn, and holds to a norm that murder should not be committed. He defines 'normativity', then, as 'a clinging to expectations despite disappointments'.[23] Within any given system, norms refer to whatever constitutes the system's distinctiveness from other systems and its environment and in turn serve its self-reproduction. Norms, write Luhmann, 'are purely internal creations serving the self-generated needs of the system for decisional criteria without any corresponding "similar" items in its environment. Nothing else is meant by "autopoiesis"'.[24] This also has a particular significance for the self-understood history of any system, because it means that there can be no origin, no starting point, only a historical past (not the same as 'history') which has to be reconstructed constantly.[25] Luhmann also comments on the distinct sense of time in law, in which past, present, and future are interrelated in a very particular way. The understanding of the relation between past and present cases is driven by the fact that the present case is always understood as the past of a future case.[26] The doctrine of *stare decisis*, then, is as much as way of indicating what relationship the present decision will have to *future* cases as it is a way of exercising the influence of past cases on the present case.

The law's normative and operational closure is reflected in the nature of legal reasoning, in which the legal system 'observes itself not as a system (in an environment) but as a collection of texts referring to each other':[27] statutes, case law, authoritative legal texts, and so on. Legal practice thus constitutes argumentation preceded by and organized around the (speedy) location and (appropriate) utilization of the range of possible relevant texts, with 'relevance' being defined by the opposing team's likely strategy and an estimation of the judge's expectations. This 'invention' of the topical traditions is one of the more important competencies which Luhmann sees as specific to the legal profession and as sustaining the legal profession as a distinct field of knowledge and professional practice.[28]

At the same time, however, the legal system, like any other, also has to coordinate itself with other systems and with its environment,[29] and this raises the question of

[22] Klaus A. Ziegert, 'The Thick Description of Law: An Introduction to Niklas Luhmann's Theory of Operatively Closed Systems', in: Reza Banakar and Max Travers (eds), *An Introduction to Law and Social Theory* (Oxford, 2002), 63–4.

[23] *Ibid*, 22.

[24] Luhmann, 'Operational Closure and Structural Coupling' n.3 above, 1430.

[25] Luhmann, 'Operational Closure and Structural Coupling' n.3 above, 1428.

[26] Hugh Baxter, 'Autopoiesis and the 'Relative Autonomy' of Law' (1998) 19(6) *Cardozo Law Review* 1987, 2023.

[27] Niklas Luhmann, 'Legal Argumentation: An Analysis of Its Form' (1995) 58(3) *Modern Law Review* 285, 287.

[28] *Ibid*.

[29] As Karl Llewellyn, 'Some Realism About Realism—Responding to Dean Pound' (1931) 44 *Harvard Law Review* 1222, and the legal realists had pointed out in the 1930s.

exactly what the relationship is between the legal system's self-reproduction and the interactions between itself and its environment.[30] Luhmann suggests that this relationship produces a corresponding requirement for cognitive responsiveness, adding to the normative closure of law a second dimension or aspect of 'cognitive openness'. Every operation in the legal system—procedure, interpretation, judgment—is both normatively or operationally closed and cognitively open at the same time, each serving a different function: the first the self-referential reproduction of the system, the second its coordination with its environment, inevitably generating 'perturbations, irritations, surprises, and disappointments' for the legal system to cognitively process, reconstruct, and assimilate.[31] Luhmann refers to the parallel example of the economic system to illustrate this point:

> The economic system is also differentiated as an autopoietic system. It ties all operations to payments and is, in monetary terms, a closed system. Outside the economy there are no payments, not even as input or output of the economic. Payments serve the exclusive purpose of making other payments possible, ie they serve the autopoiesis of the system. But precisely this closure is also the basis of the wide-ranging opennness of the system, because every payment requires a motive which is ultimately related to the satisfaction of a demand.[32]

The legal system's environment is incorporated within legal communications and does produce change in the legal system (in contrast to formalist approaches), but it is not true to say that it has a determining effect, given the legal system's 'processing' of all external input.

However, Luhmann also posits a hierarchical relation between the two, in that the legal system's normative closure is never 'overpowered' by the requirement of cognitive openness. The mechanism by which this is achieved is a concern with 'relevance' and the very flexible capacity to exclude what is defined as irrelevant to the legal issues in particular cases. In other words, for the legal system to change, some internal elements of the system have to be aligned with that change, and without this factor it is highly resistant to its environment. The legal system's cognitive openness thus has to be understood as secondary to its normative closure, that is, its self-reproduction.[33] A core manifestation of the distinction between normative closure and cognitive openness is, then, the parallel distinction between 'law' and 'facts', the former being determined entirely internally according to the legal system's own rules and procedures, and the latter determined in responsiveness to the law's environment. Luhmann expresses this as the distinction between 'was a crime committed?' which requires cognitive openness, and 'is this act a crime?' which requires normative and operational closure.[34]

[30] Luhmann, 'Closure and opennness', n.3 above, 335.

[31] Luhmann, 'Operational Closure and Structural Coupling' n.3 above, 1432. See also Edward L. Rubin, 'Law and the Methodology of Law' (1997) 1997 *Wisconsin Law Review* 521. For a discussion of an example of cognitive openness as 'irritation', see Teubner, 'Altera Pars Audiatur' n.4 above.

[32] Luhmann, n.16 above, 20.

[33] Luhmann, 'Closure and Openness', n.3 above, 341.

[34] Luhmann, 'Operational Closure and Structural Coupling' n.3 above, 1427.

Luhmann uses the term 'structural coupling' to capture the way in which the legal system is structurally interlinked with other social systems, in which particular concepts, institutions, or events have at least a dual function in more than one system, and thus acts as linkage or coupling points between them. The ideas and practices surrounding property and contract thus operate as a structural coupling between the economic and law, and the idea of the state links political and legal sovereignty. Other examples are financial payments, which possess both economic and legal meaning,[35] and judicial decisions, which can play as important, sometimes more important, a role within the political system as within law.[36] Constitutions are particularly important as overall frameworks for both separating systems and structurally coupling them:

> The ultimate paradoxes and tautologies of the legal system (that law is whatever the law arranges to be legal or illegal) can be unfolded by reference to the political system (for example, the political will of the people giving itself a constitution), and the paradoxes and tautologies of the political system (the self-inclusive, binding, sovereign power) can be unfolded by reference to the positive law and by supercoding the legal system with the distinction of constitutional and unconstitutional legality.[37]

The operation of structural coupling is also reflected in the particular structuring of legal reasoning, specifically the distinction which Luhmann acquired from American political scientist, Martin Shapiro, between *redundancy* and *information*.[38]

Shapiro uses the concept of redundancy because a typical form of legal argumentation is to argue that the facts and law of a case are identical to all previous cases, based on a step-by-step layering of citations which could, in themselves, tell a skilled lawyer what the argument was: this is why the current legal argument is in fact redundant, and in law the more redundant the argument, the more powerful and persuasive it is. A 'leading' case is precisely one which has been repeated and cited in numerous other cases. Shapiro approaches the legal system 'as if' it were a large, decentralized, non-hierarchical organization faced with the problem of coordinating the actions of a widely dispersed and otherwise dissociated set of actors (lawyers and judges).[39] Because of the absence of either a directly imposed, hierarchical structure characteristic of classic organizations or a consciously structured communications network, the legal system is one with a high level of 'noise', in the sense of communications which have the capacity to lead to uncoordinated outcomes. Shapiro sees the concept of a litigational 'market' as best capturing the mechanisms of the coordination process, much like the 'invisible hand' of an economic market. Communication is the means by which this invisible hand works, specifically the systematic coding of communication, with lawyers both

[35] Luhmann, 'Closure and Openness, , n.3 above, 342.

[36] Hugh Baxter, 'Autopoiesis and the "Relative Autonomy" of Law' (1998) 19(6) *Cardozo Law Review* 1987, 2079.

[37] Luhmann, 'Operational Closure and Structural Coupling' n.3 above, 1436–7.

[38] Martin Shapiro, 'Toward a Theory of *Stare Decisis*' (1972) 1(1) *Journal of Legal Studies* 125.

[39] *Ibid*, 130.

highly trained in particularly coding rules, and constantly carrying messages to each other (via case law and citations) to coordinate those coding rules.[40] Shapiro interprets the phenomenon of 'string citations' in judicial decisions (in which the same string of citations will be cited and simply added to in most decisions in that field of law) as part of a 'flow of a very large number of *confirmation* messages between independent decision-makers, reassuring each other that the others have been agreeing with it'.[41] As Shapiro points out, the practice of citation itself serves the function of saying 'I am not saying anything new, it's already been said' (the more often the better). The central place of the doctrine of *stare decisis* within legal communication thus indicates 'an instance of communication with extremely high levels of redundancy'.[42]

In contrast, information provides the basis for a critical attack of legal positions based on redundancy, by arguing that the judgments cited actually say something different from the current case, that they should be 'distinguished', or that there are internal distinctions within the set of cases cited, so that they do in fact contain information about the issues at stake. Another way in which information is introduced into legal communications is through a recognition of changed social conditions, changed community standards, economic constraints, or external policy considerations deriving from the legislature. However, the legal system is heavily biased towards redundancy, with informational input always minimized, explained away as not 'really' major changes, and so on.[43] As Shapiro points out, there is a very clear and simple hierarchy in the chances of success enjoyed by legal communications with differing relations to redundancy and information: the argument with the best chance of success is that the court should continue doing what it has always done; next best is arguing for the same thing other courts have been doing; next is arguing for only a slight change from what it and other courts have been doing, or a 'change = continuity' argument—the court is being most faithful to preceding decisions by coming to a different one within a changed environment—and the toughest prospect is arguing for major change.[44] If redundancy = closure and information = cognitive openness, then, it is clear that the workings of *stare decisis* within legal communications provides for both, but with the heaviest emphasis on redundancy/closure, driven again primarily by the self-reproduction of the legal system Michael King has observed, for example, the way law's cognitive openness to an extra-legal body of knowledge, child welfare science, still ends up 'enslaving' the other field of knowledge production in the service of the legal system's self-reproduction.[45]

[40] *Ibid*, 131. [41] *Ibid.* [42] *Ibid*, 129.

[43] *Ibid*, 131–2; see also the Australian High Court decision in *Mabo and Ors* v. *Queensland* (1992) 175 CLR IFC 92/104.

[44] Shapiro, n.38 above, 131.

[45] King, 'Child Welfare within Law' n.7 above; for a different perspective, see S. White, 'Interdiscursivity and Child Welfare: The Ascent and Durability of Psycho-Legalism' (1998) 46(2) *Sociological Review* 264. Dingwall, Eekelaar and Murray also provide evidence which supports

It is also important to note that the same arguments are also relevant in at least two other senses *internal* to 'the legal system': first, to the operations of the various *sub*-systems of law, such as contract, tort, equity, family law, company law, discrimination and equal opportunity law, and so on, and their communications with each other.[46] Collins suggests three distinct ways in which the operational closure of legal subsystems can be identified: (1) differing interpretations, drawing different conclusions of the same events; (2) divergent approaches to the same concepts (e.g., 'reliance' in contract and negligence); and (3) 'blindness' to the implications of decisions in one subsystem for those of another.[47] Secondly, across national boundaries, in the form of legal transfers or transplants from one country's legal system and legal culture to another. Gunther Teubner's proposition, for example, that the concept of 'good faith' is extremely difficult to transplant from the German context into the body of English law, and in any case will be transformed into a completely different idea, can be read as an argument for the 'operational closure' of national legal systems and legal cultures vis-à-vis those of other countries and cultures,[48] whereas Alan Watson's[49] and William Ewald's[50] arguments for the frequency and success of legal transplants provide support for seeing national legal systems as cognitively open, to each other more than to non-legal forms of knowledge.[51]

another construction, observing that in proceedings concerning children at risk, in comparison with the modes of understanding of social workers and medical practitioners, the courts 'are making much the same sorts of judgments on much the same sorts of issues using broadly commonsensical rather than strictly legal criteria': Robert Dingwall, John Eekelaar, and Topsy Murray, *The Protection of Children: State Intervention and Family Life* (Oxford, 1983), 205. In relation to contract law, see Collins, n.19 above, and for an analysis which emphasizes both this point *and* law's colonization, if not 'enslavement', by other discourses, see Teubner, 'Altera Pars Audiatur' n.4 above.

[46] Hugh Collins, 'Legal Classifications as the Production of Knowledge Systems', in Peter Birks (ed.), *The Classification of Obligations* (Oxford, 1997); Hugh Collins, 'Productive Learning from the Collision between the Doctrinal Systems of Contract and Tort' (1997) *Acta Juridica* 55; Collins, n.19 above; Neil Andrews, 'The Inherited "Peculiarities of the English": Exploring the Culture of the Common Law Statements of Directors' Duties with Luhmann and Bourdieu', in Mads Andenas and David Sugarman (eds), *Developments in European Company Law: Volume 3/1999 Directors' Conflicts of Interest: Legal, Socio-Legal and Economic Analyses* (London, 2000), 180–1.

[47] Collins, n.19 above, 61–2.

[48] See also the strong version of this position in the culturalist arguments of Pierre Legrand, 'Comparative Legal Studies and Commitment to Theory' (1995) 58 *Modern Law Review* 262; 'The Impossibility of Legal Transplants' (1997) 4 *Maastricht Journal of European & Comparative Law* 111.

[49] Alan Watson, *Legal Transplants: An Approach to Comparative Law* (Edinburgh, 1974); Alan Watson, 'Legal Change: Sources of Law and Legal Culture' (1983) 131 *University of Pennsylvania Law Review* 1121; Alan Watson, *Legal Origins and Legal Change* (1991); Alan Watson, 'Aspects of Reception of Law' (1996) 44 *American Journal of Comparative Law* 335.

[50] William Ewald, 'Comparative Jurisprudence II: The Logic of Legal Transplants' (1995) 43 *American Journal of Comparative Law* 489.

[51] See also Nelken's discussion of Teubner's arguments—David Nelken, 'Beyond the Metaphor of Legal Transplants? Consequences of Autopoietic Theory for the Study of Cross-Cultural Legal Adaptation', in: Jiri Priban and David Nelken (eds), *Law's New Boundaries: The Consequences of Legal Autopoiesis* (Aldershot, 2001), as well as his overview of the general question of legal adaptation: David Nelken, 'Towards a Sociology of Legal Adaptation', in David Nelken and Johannes Feest (eds), *Adapting Legal Cultures* (Oxford, 2001).

Michael King provides a useful example of how this theoretical perspective can be used to approach the arguments concerning the legal construction of child 'welfare' and the 'best interests of the child', by focusing on what is specifically 'legal' about those legal decisions and what distinguishes their mode of reasoning from that of non-legal commentators attempting to establish what constitutes children's welfare.[52] The difficulty with entering into the substantive concerns of the debates around whether or not courts get children's welfare 'right', suggests King, is that the normative or operational closure of the legal system means that the 'rightness' of legal decisions is determined by law itself, by questions of 'pure' legality, and not by reference to externally-generated information or the 'reality' of the substantive issue.[53] The particularity of 'law's truth', as David Nelken refers to it,[54] is that its function is not to establish the 'truth' of the 'best interests of the child', but to stabilize the normative expectations *about* the 'best interests of the child' over time, 'and this is necessarily achieved in a blind, semiautomatic and self-referring way by determining the legality or otherwise of any situation, including its own decision-making'.[55] To the extent that what will or will not be in a child's best interests is something that cannot actually be known, the legal system 'refuses to decide' (settlement culture), directing itself, using Luhmann's terminology, at 'present futures' rather than 'future presents', and instead confining itself to operationalizing its own rules about how parental disputes are to be settled, *regardless* of the impact this actually has on children's welfare. As King points out, because children's welfare is not of functionally determinant significance for the legal system, law 'has no difficulty in managing itself in ways that appear to suspend or ignore any nested purpose-oriented programme directed at children's welfare and even accept decisions as valid, which may be to the serious detriment of those children affected by them—*just so long as it does so legally*'.[56] In its particular construction and mobilization of the 'best interests of the child', the legally-right decision is thus *as likely* to produce 'failure' as 'success' in relation to the children's welfare, and any relationship between the legally-correct decision and children's welfare should be seen as largely contingent. The fact that the 'paramount' principle in family law cases concerning children is the 'best interests of the child' should not be interpreted as meaning that law is functionally concerned with actually delivering such a 'best interest', but that this is the principle which most effectively stabilizes all the relevant normative expectations.

More recently, Carole Smith has reflected on Luhmann's arguments around law's normative closure and cognitive opennness in relation to the law concerning adoption and contact, against the background of the more general question of how law responds to 'discursive challenges to its authority',[57] to 'political and

[52] King, 'Future Uncertainty', n.7 above. [53] *Ibid*, 525.

[54] Nelken, 'The Truth About Law's Truth', n.5 above, 87. [55] King, n.57 above, 539.

[56] *Ibid*.

[57] Carole Smith, 'Autopoietic Law and the "Epistemic Trap": A Case Study of Adoption and Contact' (2004) 31(3) *Journal of Law & Society* 318, 324.

social-scientific "intereference"',[58] suggesting that it is conceptually productive to work through autopoietic theory in relation to particular case studies. She agrees with Teubner that 'science' is the cognitive system which most frequently challenges law's epistemic authority, and turns to the field of adoption and contact as a particularly interesting example of a complex set of relations linking 'politics (social policy debates), law (the rights of parties to adoption and the legal construction of new families), and science (theories and empirical evidence about the relationship between identity development and children's well-being)',[59] in which law is clearly challenged by a range of social scientific discourses.[60]

In contrasting social science with legal reasoning about adoption, Smith finds, on the one hand, clear confirmation of legal closure, observing that 'in the vast majority of cases, law refuses to incorporate social scientific knowledge into its decisions and diverts the issue of contact away from law to the realm of trust'.[61] She suggests that the response of the legal system here 'reflects Luhmann and Teubner's contention that it can circumvent epistemic entrapment by diverting social issues that it is unable or unwilling to reconstruct into legal communications'.[62] Social scientific perceptions do, however, get 'smuggled' into law if translated into what law can recognize as a legal communication,[63] and they also otherwise exist on the margins of law in fields such as mediation. On the other hand, Smith's case study also develops autopoietic theory in new directions by having more to say about the complexity of situations where the challengers to law's authority are themselves divided by internal disputes, or where there are numerous sub-systems at play, such as different aspects or sub-fields of politics and the social sciences.

The question of *how* the articulation of normative closure and cognitive openness, the structural coupling of the legal system with other systems and its environment, actually works is a *strategic* question which can only be answered 'on the ground' in relation to specific configurations of issues and the actual choices made by the relevant parties, and also depends on the ways in which different parts of what Bourdieu calls the 'juridical field' relate to each other.[64] Equally significant is the *competition* between different sources of cognitive openness, either as pursued by the representatives of those fields of knowledge production themselves, or as produced by the adversarial logic of the legal process. It is also important to examine the role of forms of knowledge-production which are both non-expert and non-legal, such as lay ('common-sense') and administrative modes of knowledge.[65]

[58] Smith, n.57 above 319. [59] *Ibid.* [60] *Ibid*, 327. [61] *Ibid*, 338.
[62] *Ibid.* [63] *Ibid*, 342.
[64] Pierre Bourdieu, 'The Force of Law: Towards a Sociology of the Juridical Field' (1987) 38(5) *Hastings Law Journal* 814.
[65] Mariana Valverde, *Law's Dream of a Common Knowledge* (Princeton, 2003); Tony Ward, 'Law, Common Sense and the Authority of Science: Expert Witnesses and Criminal Insanity in England, C. 1840–1940' (1997) 6(3) *Social & Legal Studies* 343; Tony Ward, 'Law's Truth, Lay Truth and Medical Science', in Helen Reece (ed.), *Law and Science* (Oxford, 1998).

There is also much to be gained, then, conceptually as well as empirically, from linking Luhmann's conceptual arguments to the evolution of particular bodies of law, in order to give those arguments a much firmer empirical anchorage in the operation of the legal system itself. The configuration of the relationships between legal and other forms of knowledge changes over time, and a diachronic study of its *historical development* is as important as the more synchronic analyses found in Luhmann and his followers. Again, this is an issue which will only become clearer with detailed consideration of a variety of empirical examples. Let us look more closely, then, at the recent Australian developments in the field of family law, separation, and child custody.

The Co-Parenting Project in Australia

Since the 1970s, a number of shifts have taken place in both the legislative framework and the jurisprudence of Anglo-Australian family law, centred on changes in the construction of the 'best interests of the child'. The model which arose for the construction of the best interests standard revolved around what Thèry calls the 'logic of durability', in which shared parental authority replaces the 'which parent?' choice, equal care and control by both parents is pursued as a goal, the child is seen as having two households, and both parents subordinate their own needs and desires to the requirements of the model, particularly the necessity for cooperation, agreement and negotiation between them. In the 'substitution' or 'clean break' model, the mother remains the primary, generally sole carer beyond separation, with a more or less judicially explicit 'maternal preference rule' as 'the dominant doctrine in most Western countries',[66] in conjunction with a 'tender years doctrine', that the younger a child is the more preferable it is for the mother to retain care and control.[67] The 'durability' model, in contrast, pursues gender-neutral equality between fathering with mothering, a more even spread of caring across both parents and, above all, a rejection of the 'clean break' model, constructing the parent-child relationship, for both fathers and mothers, as a permanent one which extends beyond parental separation. A number of American states, beginning with California, have been moving towards a joint custody preference since 1979, as have all Western European countries.[68] The concept of a need for a shift from

66 Jon Elster, 'Solomonic judgements: against the best interests of the child' (1987) 54 *University of Chicago Law Review* 1, 8.

67 Robert H. Mnookin, 'Child-Custody Adjudication: Judicial Functions in the Face of Indeterminacy' (1975) 39 *Law and Contemporary Problems* 226, 235.

68 Kirsti Kurki-Suonio, 'Joint custody as an interpretation of the best interests of the child in critical and comparative perspective' (2000) 14 *International Journal of Law, Policy and the Family* 183; the Council of Europe has also issued a 2003 draft *Convention on Contact Concerning Children*: Article 4—Contact between a child and his or her parents—consists of the following provisions:

1 A child and his or her parents shall have the right to obtain and maintain regular contact with each other.

the substitution to the durability model had appeared in the UK in the form of the Children Act 1989,[69] especially in its arguments for the concept of 'parental responsibility', stretching beyond parental separation.

In Australia, these developments were reflected in the Family Law Council's 1992 report to the Minister for Justice and Consumer Affairs, *Patterns of Parenting after Separation*,[70] which also argued for maintenance of contact with both parents, both for the children's welfare and in order to encourage child support payments, and a change in the culture of post-separation parenting revolving around the replacement of the concepts of 'custody/access' 'residence/contact', in order to move away from a win/lose outcome to one of co-parenting continuing despite the termination of the intimate relationship between the parents.[71] The legislative intervention which embodied all these arguments in the Australian context was the Family Law Reform Act 1995 and its changes to 'Pt VII—Children'. The objectives of the new Act are outlined in s.60B2, which declares children's 'right to know and be cared for by both their parents', as well as 'right of contact, on a regular basis, with both their parents and with other people significant to their care, welfare and development'. It also exhorts parents to 'share duties and responsibilities concerning the care, welfare and development of their children', and to 'agree about the future parenting of their children'. A key mechanism for the realization of such agreement is the parenting order, which lays out the terms and conditions of the co-parenting regime.

The field refuses to settle, however, with a continuing stand-off between those arguing that the changes have gone too far, and those who believe they still have not gone far enough.[72] As manifestations of the on-going dissonance concerning post-separation child custody, Government reports have been published in both

2 Such contact may be restricted or excluded only where necessary in the best interests of the child.
3 Where it is not in the best interests of a child to maintain unsupervised contact with one of his or her parents the possibility of supervised personal contact or other forms of contact with this parent shall be considered.

[69] J. Roche, 'The Children Act: once a parent, always a parent?' (1991) 5 *Journal of Social Welfare Law* 345; John Eekelaar, 'Parental Responsibility: State of Nature or Nature of the State?' (1991) 13 *Journal of Social Welfare & Family Law* 37.

[70] Family Law Council, *Patterns of Parenting After Separation* (1992) law.gov.au/flc/reports/patterns.html; www.ag.gov.au/flc/reports/patterns.html.

[71] Helen Rhoades, 'Child law reforms in Australia—a shifting landscape' (2000) 12(2) *Child and Family Law Quarterly* 117.

[72] Apart from on-going discussion in the media and in social scientific research, the Government reports include: Joint Select Committee on Certain Aspects of the Operation and Interpretation of the Family Law Act, *The Family Law Act 1975: Aspects of its operation and interpretation* (Canberra, 1992); Joint Select Committee on Certain Family Law Issues, *The Operation and Effectiveness of the Child Support Scheme* (Canberra, 1994); House of Representatives Standing Committee on Legal and Constitutional Affairs, *To have and to hold: Strategies to strengthen marriage and relationships* (Canberra, 1998); Family Law Pathways Advisory Group, *Out of the Maze: Pathways to the future for families experiencing separation: Report of the Family Law Pathways Advisory Group* (Canberra, 2001).

Australia[73] and the UK[74] which continue to pursue the question of how family law can be reformed in response to the criticisms from all the various quarters. I will here focus only on the Australian Report. The concept at the heart of *Every Picture Tells a Story*, the House of Representatives Standing Committee on Family and Community Affairs' 2003 'Report of the inquiry into child custody arrangements in the event of family separation' is that of shared parenting, how to encourage more of it, how to make it work 'better'.[75] Announcing the Inquiry, the Australian Prime Minister, John Howard, expressed his concern that 'far too many boys are growing up without proper role models', and the brief given to the Inquiry was specifically to explore the possibilities of restructuring family law around a rebuttable presumption that children spend equal time with each parent. The Inquiry received more than 1,700 submissions and held twenty-one public hearings, together taking it as close as it could reasonably get to a comprehensive representation of the full range of perspectives on the separation process and post-separation family life, and it is fair to say that the Report's conceptualization of the issues reflects the strong impact of the broad spectrum of social scientific research into the topic.[76]

The Report's narrative concerning shared parenting is complex and in some respects contradictory. On the one hand, there are reports of the supposed increase in the incidence of shared parenting, presenting it as a 'fact' about the 'reality' of contemporary family life which family law should take better account of. On the other hand, we are also told of evidence entirely to the contrary: declining joint residence orders, mothers still spend more time on child care, the small proportion of children (less than 3 per cent) currently in shared parenting arrangements. If one attempts to pin the Report down, it seems that it is engaged less in an argument about the ways in which family law should adjust itself to an actually altered social reality, and more in a *normative* argument about the direction that post-separation arrangements *should* go in, with the problem then becoming that of identifying and constructing an assemblage of family instances to support this shift. This is what the research informing the Report indicates, a

[73] Commonwealth of Australia, *Every Picture Tells a Story: Inquiry into Child Custody Arrangements in the Event of Family Separation* (Canberra, 2004); URL: http://www.aph.gov.au/house/committee/fca/childcustody/report.htm.

[74] Department for Constitutional Affairs, *Parental Separation: Children's Needs and Parents' Responsibilities* (London, 2004); URL: http://www.dfes.gov.uk/childrensneeds/.

[75] The title of the Report is a reference to the pictures drawn by a young boy, Jack, which the Report said told us the following story: 'Jack shares his time between mum's house and dad's house; He loves his mum and he loves his dad; He doesn't like it when his mum and dad argue; He's happy when they talk to each other; It is a tough story because dad lives in one city and mum lives somewhere else; He likes to see them both all the time but he can't because the distance makes it too hard. Jack's pictures encapsulate the most important voice of all—the voice of the children' (xi).

[76] This despite the apparent indication of the Chair, Kay Hull, that she was 'a bit of an anti-research person myself', preferring to rely instead on her own lay construction of the issues: cited in Helen Rhoades and Susan B. Boyd, 'Reforming Custody Laws: A Comparative Study' (2004) 18(2) *International Journal of Law, Policy and the Family* 119, 134–5.

desire for qualitative changes to post-separation family life. However, the Report's narrative resists such as 'fixing' of its overall direction by constantly moving fluidly between these two modes of argumentation.

The Report both decided against the concept of a rebuttable presumption of joint custody, and searched for other ways of encouraging shared parenting, largely on the basis of what Rhoades and Boyd refer to as a 'plethora of empirical studies of family life'[77] conducted since the passage of the 1995 changes to the Family Law Act. The main elements of the picture drawn by that body of research are that, on the one hand most parents and children do want to have as much sharing of care as possible. Among both separated fathers (74 per cent) and mothers (41 per cent), as well as children themselves, there appears to be dissatisfaction with current patterns of post-separation child-rearing, supporting the arguments concerning the importance of the presence of both parents in children's lives, and framed in terms of a rejection of gender as a relevant dimension of parenting roles, or any kind of explicit 'maternal preference'. On the other hand, the research has also made it clear that shared parenting is difficult, and that the question of maintaining contact with both parents needs to be seen as balanced against another, equally important concern, that of minimizing conflict. To the extent, then, that *imposed* shared parenting intensifies conflict between the parents, children will experience such an outcome as paradoxical, and this was largely what ultimately defeated the concept of a 'hard' rebuttable presumption of shared parenting, in favour of a 'soft' encouragement of 'equal shared parenting responsibility'.

The Committee, on the basis of the evidence of influential family law academics such as Patrick Parkinson, identified the legal system's rules for settling disputes (or stabilizing norms) as themselves exacerbating many of the problematic aspects of the separation process, encouraging rather than reducing parental conflict. The problematic aspects of the structure of law's mode of decision-making were seen as, first, its adversarial character—from law's point of view, essential for the correct handling of a range of conflicting rights, duties, and entitlements, but not conducive to compromise, and encouraging the problematically hybrid phenomenon of the self-represented litigant.[78] Secondly, a central problem was seen to be its determinate nature—a decision is reached that is not easy to change, which is central to law's force and effectivity, but also a barrier to flexible adaptation to changing circumstances. The Committee declared that the 'overwhelming impression' created by the evidence it had received was that 'the time is ripe for a significant reform of legal processes for parenting disputes'.[79]

The Committee thus expended considerable effort attempting to identify an alternative process for dealing with contact issues, declaring its objective to be 'to

[77] Rhoades and Boyd, n.76 above, 131.

[78] However, see Rosemary Hunter, 'Adversarial mythologies: policy assumptions and research evidence in family law' (2003) 30 *Journal of Law & Society* 156 for a critical discussion of this constructions of the supposed problems accompanying the adversarial character of legal processes.

[79] Commonwealth of Australia, n.73 above, at 76.

devise a system where the involvement of lawyers is the exception rather than the rule',[80] and it was here that the operation of the binary legal/non-legal code is most significant. The Committee sought some sort of 'non-adversarial tribunal process'[81] and 'alternative sources of authority for orders about parenting'[82] which would be understood and experienced as non-legal, with the exception of cases involving violence, abuse or 'entrenched conflict'; they would continue to be dealt with by the Family Court. The idea of a Families Tribunal was outlined as follows:

> The processes in the Tribunal are envisaged to be as informal as possible, with very little documentation, but consistent with the rules of natural justice. It is anticipated that Tribunal members would be appointed from the ranks of professionals working in the family relationships field. First, the Tribunal would attempt to conciliate the issues in dispute. This could be undertaken by a single member. If this does not resolve it, the hearing of the dispute and the decision making function of the Tribunal could be performed by a panel of members comprising a mediator, a child psychologist/other person able to address the child's needs and a third person with appropriate legal expertise.[83]

However, the immediate problem such an idea threw up was that the outcomes of such a process were also meant to have legal effect, in the sense of binding all the parties.[84] What was being sought, then, was what Teubner would call a hybrid legal discourse, but one which works in the opposite direction to the socio-legal constructs analysed by him.[85] Teubner speaks of social science concepts being reconstructed within legal communications, but with the concept of a new Family Tribunal, the Committee was pursuing the opposite, the construction of communications which are to have legal effect, but which would be reconstructed within a different communicative field, one of mediation, compromise, and conflict-reduction. Various submissions to the Committee conveyed law's position on such a creature, namely that it was abhorrent to the rule of law, in the sense that if any *power* is to be exercised in relation to family matters, it can only be exercised by a duly constituted court, and can only work within the legal framework of the Family Law Act.[86]

The Committee attempted to skirt around this problem of socio-legal hybridity by arguing that the strictly legal position concerning the exercise of judicial power related only to decisions concerning *existing* legal rights, but that 'decisions which are essentially about adjustment of rights in the future, based on what is in the best interests of the child, can be made administratively', that is, by a Families

[80] At 77. [81] At 83. [82] At 76. [83] At 93.

[84] At 93: 'The outcome of the hearing would be a binding order, confirmed by the relevant legislation'.

[85] Teubner, 'How the Law Thinks' n.4 above, 749; see also the discussion in Smith, n.57 above, 325–6.

[86] John Dewar submitted: 'If you had a tribunal that was a decision-making tribunal, it would still be part of a formal legal system. Its decisions would still have to be, to some extent, subject to review by a higher authority; it would still be operating within a framework of legal rules. If it were making decisions about where children should spend their time and with whom, it is hard to see how it would do that without doing it within the framework set by the Family Law Act' (86).

Tribunal.[87] It received considerable support for this position from the ranks of the Australian Liberal Party, including the Children's Minister, Larry Anthony. However, Chief Justice Nicholson of the Family Court indicated his strong disapproval, and both the Prime Minister, John Howard, and the Attorney-General, Philip Ruddock, have clearly had enough legal training also to understand the boundary-crossing problems it would throw up. The Government has instead announced its support for the idea promoted by Parkinson, a national network of sixty-five 'Family Relationship Centres', outsourced to agencies such as Relationships Australia, Centacare, Uniting Care and Anglicare, staffed by professionals in counselling and mediation, and accompanied by an education campaign. Although such counselling services already exist, Parkinson's proposal is that the centres will have greater impact and authority, through a common badge, high visibility, change to the Family Law Act promoting 'shared parental responsibility', an initial free consultation, and mandatory attendance before couples can file a court application. The Centres will provide three hours of counselling,[88] in which both parents would be encouraged to stay 'meaningfully involved' with their children and agree on decisions about education, religion, and residence.

It is fair to say, then, that the Australian family law system has successfully resisted the construction and institutionalization of any sort of hybrid socio-legal discourse around parental separation and child custody, and the binary distinction between the legal and the non-legal remains intact. The principle of 'not deciding' between the parents, unless a decision can be forced because of violence or abuse, has also been maintained with a continuing focus on the 'best interests of the child'. Any change is to take place entirely outside the field of law, with the establishment of the network of Family Relationship Centres constituting a turn to 'legal informalism' as the primary mode of altering the 'family law system'. In this sense these developments resonate strongly with Carole Smith's observations on the law surrounding adoption and contact, in that the concerns about the operation of the child custody regime have been almost entirely diverted away from law, to the realm of mediation and counselling, and they confirm Luhmann's and Teubner's arguments concerning law's normative/operational closure, despite the best efforts of various political and community groups, the Committee itself, and a range of members of the Liberal Party.

At the same time, however, if one places this particular episode within its broader context of the development of Australian family law over the whole period of the shift from a 'logic of substitution' to a 'logic of durability', a more nuanced picture emerges. The arguments concerning law's normative closure seem most effective in relation to the operation of law at a particular point in time, but the effects of law's cognitive opennness appear to become more significant when one looks more closely at the development of legal reasoning over time—especially the precise way in which legal rules are operationalized, and at the

[87] At 86.

[88] At no cost, more counselling time will have to be paid for!

contingency of what constitutes 'legality'. The 'maternal preference rule' and the 'tender years doctrine' did not emerge entirely independently of positions and perspectives dominating the relevant fields of scientific research, and the shifts in those dominant perspectives also seems to have been accompanied by similar shifts in the legal reasoning surrounding post-separation child custody, at a formal level at any rate.[89]

Law's normative closure is most apparent, then, in relation to particular cases or episodes in law reform, but less so for the way legal thinking evolves over time, for the development of what constitutes legality itself. Law's function may be to stabilize normative expectations, but those normative expectations change, and this change is often influenced by social science research. In this particular case, the most significant impact of the social science research drawn on by the *Every Picture Tells a Story* Inquiry was the largely passive one of blocking a particular legislative change—the introduction of a rebuttable presumption of shared parenting—rather than one of actively altering legal thinking or procedure concerning post-separation child-rearing. However, there are also a number of other features of the operation of the relationship between legal and non-legal forms of knowledge production which are important to reflect upon in some more detail, beyond the legal system's capacity, in this case, for normative closure.

Law and Sociology

The potential for challenge to law's epistemic authority is often seen as lying primarily in the field of 'science', and the picture which is most frequently drawn is that of only two 'players', law and science, as well as of a certain kind of relationship between them. However, the developments in this particular situation show, additionally, the degree to which the field of science is fragmented rather than unified; that the relationship between law and the various representatives of non-legal, 'scientific' perspectives runs through the 'filter' of a range of *mediating* agencies; the strategic significance of political, 'consumer' groups; as well as the importance of 'lay' knowledge.

If we examine the basis of the Committee's epistemic authority and legitimacy, it is organized around a number of elements. There are times when the Committee simply claims epistemic legitimacy on no particular foundation at all, merely its own authority, 'common sense', or its unique distillation of the views put in the submissions to the inquiry and aired in the public hearings. At other points it will defer to the authority of particular mediating agencies (the Institute

[89] One of the core complaints of the fathers' groups is precisely that a maternal preference rule remains in place, but has simply become implicit in judicial reasoning. Another interpretation would be that it is more significant that a 'maternal preference' is embedded in pre-separation family life, and that this in turn structures the character of post-separation family relations, what Rhoades and Boyd call the 'innocent' factors, n.76 above.

of Family Studies, the Family Law Council, etc) who have themselves conducted or processed what is presented as a comprehensive range of social scientific investigations of the relevant topics, and translated them into a form which is comprehensible to legal communication. Other sources of epistemic authority include the submissions, the authority of which is established in the first place by the sheer *volume*, indicating comprehensiveness and representativeness, as well as the public hearings, which are presented as constituting the voice of 'the people', particularly that of children, which is authoritative by virtue of being 'authentic' and based on 'experience'.[90] The submissions and hearings operate as an open field for the Committee to move across as it chooses, picking which submissions and points of view to respond to and treat as authoritative, and which to ignore or play down. Finally, political representativness is also a basis of epistemic authority: any claim to represent a particular constituency will be given a certain degree of weight, again at the discretion of the Committee.

There is no single discipline or field of study which dominates all the others, and the Committee is free to decide how to assess their authoritativeness. Rather then being confronted by the field of 'science', then, the Committee faces a whole network of scientific approaches, a disparate range of disciplinary orientations which has no particular shape to it prior to the Committee's processing of the knowledge they have produced. Often the differing orientations, methodologies and constructions of the topic—both within and across disciplines—are in competition with each, leaving it to the Committee itself to decide how to manage that competition.

The most influential forms of organized knowledge are those research forms which have been tailored either to law generally, or to the Committee's task in particular, conducted either by legal academics or in collaboration with them, and this is to a large extent a product of the lack of consistent unanimity within the social science disciplines. Research agencies like the AIFS and the research conducted or reviewed by the Family Law Council also gain in credibility by virtue of both their interdisciplinarity, their capacity to 'process' the social sciences' internal disputes, and their more direct connection with the legal system. Much of the assimilation or translation of extra-legal knowledge thus takes place before such knowledge even hits the legal system itself, these agencies are assimilation/translation 'factories'. Because a core question is the impact of parental separation on children and child development, psychologists have a high profile in the research which is utilized.[91] Internationally, the strongest direct representative of sociology as a discipline is probably Carol Smart and her team in the Centre for Research on Family, Kinship

[90] In contrast to the 'artificiality' of academic research. The Committee moves freely between these two registers, at its discretion, in accordance with what it chooses to say.

[91] For example, Judith S. Wallerstein, and Joan B. Kelly, *Surviving the Breakup, How Children and Parents Cope with Divorce* (New York, 1980); Judith S. Wallerstein, and J. Lewis, 'The Long-Term Impact of Divorce on Children: A First Report from a 25-Year Study' (1998) 36 *Family & Conciliation Courts Review* 368.

and Childhood at the University of Leeds, whose work sits on the border of sociology and social policy, although they pursue their arguments across as many disciplinary fields as possible, including philosophy and psychology. In addition to their own particular contribution, Smart and her team have functioned as a 'funnel' through which broader sociological arguments concerning family life and childhood have entered into the perceptions of family law. However, although her work has been relied upon in earlier government reports, for *Every Picture Tells a Story*, its only direct presence was in submissions of conference papers provided by the Queensland Law Society and the Western Australian Family Law Foundation, and indirectly through its influence on the submissions of Parkinson and other commentators. The social scientific research into the particular effects of the adversarial character of the legal process play an important role, as do official statistics, especially the time-use studies which map the gendered division of domestic labour.

Alongside this disparate array of research into the effects of parental separation, the operation of various forms of post-separation child-rearing regimes, and the family law system itself, a place is also given in the socio-legal construction of the whole topic to a broad range of political, welfare, and other groups and organizations: fathers' rights groups, grandparents' groups, youth welfare organizations, child protection agencies, government departments, community legal centres, domestic violence agencies, community legal centres and associations. There are two dimensions to epistemic status given to their perspectives: first, as representing the points of view of particular political *constituencies*, and as constituting the voice of particular sets of *consumers* or *clients* of family law, with an attendant set of rights to have their views play a role in the delivery of the relevant 'services'. Secondly, as constituting a valid form of lay knowledge which embodies the 'authentic' voice of experience, as eye-witness *testimony* to how particular principles, such as shared parenting, actually work in practice. Although social science research will often base its epistemic authority on precisely the same kind of testimony, the Inquiry process effectively cuts out the social scientific research 'middle man' by gathering such empirical evidence directly. In this sense, the Committee becomes its own sociologist/psychologist/social policy researcher, sitting across all the boundaries between law, various scientific disciplines, research subjects, constituents, consumers, clients.

Conclusion

Although this chapter has concentrated on the autonomy and closure of law from other sources of cognitive authority, it may be useful to conclude by reflecting on how this question might need to be seen alongside that of the closure of other communicative systems, or in terms of the limits of legal action.[92] A number of

[92] Roscoe Pound, 'The Limits of Effective Legal Action' (1916) 27 *International Journal of Ethics* 150; Niklas Luhmann, 'Limits of Steering' (1997) 14(1) *Theory, Culture & Society* 41.

observers[93] have highlighted the extent to which many aspects of the achievement of the 'best interests of the child' simply cannot be addressed through legal mechanisms, and in this sense the turn to legal informalism is an entirely appropriate way to deal with the changing complexities of post-separation child custody. The changes which have taken place in family relations are themselves more the product of social than legal transformations, and an observation consistently made about the effects of the changes accompanying the Australian 1995 Family Law Reform Act is precisely how little impact they have had on patterns of child custody, both pre- and post-separation. Rhoades and Boyd thus point to the extent to which current patterns may have little to do with legal decision-making, and are better understood in terms of the logistical, emotional and economic structure of pre- and post-separation family life.[94] It may be, then, that sociological theory and research has as significant a contribution to the entire field entirely independently of any impact it might have on family law, and that the autonomy from law of the political and social world encompassing the question of parental separation is as important as law's autonomy.

[93] J. Pearce, G. Davis, and J. Barron, 'Love in a Cold Climate—Section 8 Applications under the Children Act 1989' (1999) *Family Law* 22; King, n.7 above.

[94] Rhoades and Boyd, n.76 above, 137.

26

From Parental Responsibility to Parenting Responsibly

*Helen Reece**

Introduction

The Anti-social Behaviour Act 2003 has recently followed the Crime and Disorder Act 1998 in making parents more responsible for their children's crimes and misdemeanours, building on the foundations laid by the Criminal Justice Act 1991.[1] In this article I want to argue that this development, while most easily interpreted as an *extension* of pre-existing parental responsibility, rather represents a far more widespread change in the *meaning* of parental responsibility. After having examined how parental responsibility has changed its meaning, I will look at related developments,[2] before finally examining consequences of the change in meaning.

The Changing Meaning of Parental Responsibility: From Parental Authority to Parental Accountability

It has been suggested that:

> ... although the term 'parental responsibility' is gaining international acceptance, it is an elusive concept to define ... [i]n part ... because the concept is concerned not just with the parent-child relationship but also the parent's relationship with the state and with other individuals.[3]

* I am grateful to the participants at the Law and Sociology colloquium and to John Gillott for helpful comments on earlier versions of this chapter.

[1] See L. Gelsthorpe, 'Youth Crime and Parental Responsibility', in A. Bainham, S. Day Sclater and M. Richards (eds), *What is a Parent? A Socio-Legal Analysis* (Oxford and Portland, Oregon, 1999), 231; R. Arthur, 'Punishing Parents for the Crimes of their Children' (2005) 44 *The Howard Journal of Criminal Justice* 233, 233–7. See J.H. DiFonzo, 'Parental Responsibility for Juvenile Crime' (2001) 80 *Oregon Law Review* 1 for comparison with United States developments.

[2] I describe these as related developments because the causal connection is unclear to me.

[3] N.V. Lowe, 'The Meaning and Allocation of Parental Responsibility—A Common Lawyer's Perspective' (1997) 11 *International Journal of Law, Policy and the Family* 192, 193. See also *ibid*,

The starting point for any attempt to define the meaning of parental responsibility can only be Eekelaar's classic exposition of the concept, published in 1991.[4] His argument is that parental responsibility changed its meaning during the course of the 1980s discussions that culminated in the Children Act 1989. According to Eekelaar, when the concept of parental responsibility was first introduced into United Kingdom legal discourse, in the Law Commission Report on Illegitimacy in 1982,[5] it meant simply 'acting dutifully'.[6] But by the time the concept was enacted in the Children Act 1989, 'parental responsibility' was synonymous with 'parental authority', embodying ideas of freedom of parents from government.[7] The following year, Edwards and Halpern reached a similar conclusion to Eekelaar when they analysed parental responsibility within three contemporary pieces of legislation, namely the Children Act 1989, the Child Support Act 1991, and the Criminal Justice Act 1991. They found that at this point parental responsibility contained several 'major but not always consistent or complementary threads'.[8] One of these threads was 'a notion of responsibility which emphasizes the emotional and psychological commitment parents owe to their children',[9] which roughly corresponds to Eekelaar's first meaning of responsibility as acting dutifully. But secondly, the reforms functioned 'so as to positively promote parental responsibility in the place of state responsibility ... firmly supported by the fundamental principles of *laissez-faire* individualism and self-sufficiency',[10] coinciding with Eekelaar's second meaning of parental responsibility as embodying ideas of freedom of parents from government. They ended by endorsing Eekelaar's conclusion that within the Children Act 1989 at this juncture parental responsibility meant parental authority.[11]

Whether or not Eekelaar is correct about the original meaning, he is probably right that at the point at which parental responsibility was enacted into law at least one important strand in the meaning was that of parental authority.[12] Apart from the evidence provided by Eekelaar himself,[13] his interpretation is supported by the

210; M.G. Wyness, 'Parental Responsibilities, Social Policy and the Maintenance of Boundaries' (1997) 45 *Sociological Review* 304, 312; R. Smith, 'Parental Responsibility—and an Irresponsible State?' (1990) 71 *Childright* 7, 8.

4 J. Eekelaar, 'Parental Responsibility: State of Nature or Nature of the State?' (1991) 13 *Journal of Social Welfare and Family Law* 37.

5 Law Commission, *Family Law: Illegitimacy*, No. 118 (London, 1982).

6 See also S. Edwards and A. Halpern, 'Parental Responsibility: An Instrument of Social Policy' (1992) 22 *Family Law* 113.

7 Eekelaar, n.4, above.

8 Edwards and Halpern, n.6, above, 118. See also M.G. Wyness, *Schooling, Welfare and Parental Responsibility* (London and Washington, 1996), 1, and Wyness, n.3, above, 305 for recognition that there are inconsistent images of the 'responsible parent'.

9 Edwards and Halpern, n.6, above, 118.

10 *Ibid.*

11 *Ibid.* See also Gelsthorpe, n.1, above, 229 for a similar interpretation of the meaning of parental responsibility in the Children Act 1989.

12 Support for the view that parental responsibility no longer means 'acting dutifully' is provided by the fact that the phrase used in *The Framework for the Assessment of Children in Need* is parental capacity, not parental responsibility (London, 2000): see C. Henricson, *Government and Parenting: Is there a case for a policy review and a parents' code?* (York, 2003), 44.

13 Eekelaar, n.4, above, 40–8.

statement in the 1988 Law Commission Review of Guardianship and Custody that a 'fundamental principle which guided both the Review of Child Care law and the Government's response to it was that the primary responsibility for the upbringing of children rests with their parents'.[14] This interpretation is even more plausible given that the concept of parental responsibility developed out of the concept of parental rights. Originally, the shift was conceived of as 'largely a change of nomenclature',[15] the Law Commission assuring that it 'would make little difference in substance',[16] so parental responsibility bore the meaning closest to parental rights. The strong connection with parental rights is evident in the definition given in the Children Act itself, which provides that:

> In this Act parental responsibility means all the rights, duties, powers, responsibilities and authority which by law a parent of a child has in relation to the child and his property.[17]

This definition 'immediately throws one back to the rights and duties concept which 'responsibility' was supposed to replace',[18] the first word used to describe parental responsibility being 'rights'.[19]

Edwards and Halpern argue that although within the context of the Children Act 1989, parental responsibility means parental authority:

> . . . it can equally well be argued that the psychological device of parental responsibility is used in cases where parents fail in their responsibility as a mechanism which allows the state to exercise greater control over the individual than before by more determinedly enforcing that responsibility.[20]

It is interesting that, while 'responsibility' certainly can and often does bear the two meanings highlighted by Eekelaar, the predominant meaning given in the *Shorter Oxford English Dictionary* for 'responsible', through which 'responsibility' is defined, is 'answerable; accountable (*to* another *for* something); liable to be called to account'. Accordingly, 'parental responsibility' was able to evolve into a concept based on a completely different meaning of responsibility, which has been summed up nicely as 'the idea that the parent acts as a moral and social guarantor for their children.'[21]

[14] Law Commission, *Family Law: Review of Child Law, Guardianship and Custody*, No. 172 (London, 1988), 5.

[15] Lord Mackay, 'Perceptions of the Children Bill and Beyond' (1989) 139 *New Law Journal* 505, 505.

[16] Law Commission, n.14, above, 6. See also S.M. Cretney, J.M. Masson and R. Bailey-Harris, *Principles of Family Law*, 7th edn. (London, 2002), 522.

[17] Children Act 1989, s. 3(1).

[18] Lowe, n.3, above, 195.

[19] J. Herring, *Family Law*, 2nd edn. (Harlow, 2004), 351.

[20] Edwards and Halpern, n.6, above, 118. See also Wyness, n.3, above, for recognition that alternative trends within social policy emphasize parental responsibilities as obligations rather than boundary-setting powers.

[21] Wyness, n.3, above, 310. See also Department of Health, *An Introduction to the Children Act* (London, 1989), 1; Lord Mackay, n.15, above, 505.

This happened through the intermediate stage of an emphasis on parental powers being for the benefit of the child not the parent. This approach applied to parents' rights and long pre-dated the incorporation of parental responsibility into the law. Originally, this stance was taken to mean that parents had authority, but that this authority existed purely for their children's benefit. So a 1983 study suggested:

Perhaps, then, the best legal model for analysing the relationship between parents and children is that of a trust . . . Trustees have rights over the relevant property which they can defend against third parties but which they must use in the interests of the beneficiaries. If they fail to do this, whether out of misconduct or incompetence, the beneficiaries may call them to account before a court with a view to their appointment being terminated. In the case of parents, the object of the trust is the promotion of children's welfare. Where they prove deficient, for whatever reason, the beneficiaries have a ground for legal action in respect of the negligent discharge of their trustees' duties.[22]

This approach was entrenched in the law by the House of Lords in the celebrated case of *Gillick* v. *West Norfolk and Wisbech Area Health Authority* in the mid-1980s in relation to parents' rights.[23] Thus, according to Lord Fraser:

. . . parental rights to control a child do not exist for the benefit of the parent. They exist for the benefit of the child and they are justified only in so far as they enable the parent to perform his duties towards the child, and towards other children in the family.[24]

Accepted on all sides, this was not one of the points of contention in *Gillick*.[25] The House of Lords made quite clear that they were making explicit a long-standing principle, which they traced back to *Blackstone's Commentaries* of 1830.[26]

Despite the fact that the principle that parental powers existed for the benefit of children was settled beyond peradventure, it was concern to emphasize this principle further that provided both the initial and the main impetus for switching from parental rights to parental responsibility. The 1982 Law Commission Report on Illegitimacy stated:

. . . parental rights have become largely irrelevant in legal proceedings: the court does not usually need to ask what a parent is *entitled* to do at common law, since it will concern itself solely with the question of what course of action will best promote the welfare of the child. So far has this trend been carried that it can be cogently argued that to talk of parental 'rights' is not only inaccurate as a matter of juristic analysis but also a misleading use of ordinary language. In this view, the concept of parental rights, in the sense of conferring on

[22] R. Dingwall, J. Eekelaar and T. Murray, *The Protection of Children: State Intervention and Family Life* (Oxford, 1983), 224. See also Law Commission, n.5, above, 26; Wyness, n.3, above, 312.

[23] [1986] AC 112. See Cretney, Masson and Bailey-Harris, n.16, above, 522; Herring, n.19, above, 352.

[24] *Gillick* v. *West Norfolk and Wisbech Area Health Authority* [1986] AC 112, 170. See also Lord Scarman, *ibid*, 184.

[25] *Ibid*, 170.

[26] *Ibid*, 170, 184–5.

a parent control over the person, education and conduct of his children throughout their minority reflects an outdated view of family life which has no part to play in a modern system of law—the more so since the court will never enforce such rights against the interests of the child. We agree that the connotations of the word 'rights' are in this context unfortunate; and that it might well be more appropriate to talk of parental *powers*, parental *authority*, or even parental *responsibilities*, rather than of *rights*.[27]

Three years later, in their Working Paper on Guardianship, the Law Commission had become 'certain' that talk of parental rights was inaccurate and misleading for similar reasons and so resolved to use the term responsibility in preference to that of rights, because:

[T]o the extent that the law enables parents to decide how to bring up their children without interference from others or from the state, it does so ... in order thus to promote the welfare of their children.[28]

This shift then set the stage for the current approach, which has switched from the idea that parental authority exists purely for the benefit of children to the idea that parental authority *itself* is antithetical to children's welfare. A good example of this switch is Herring's interpretation of the shift from parental rights to parental responsibility as demonstrating that 'children are not possessions to be controlled by parents but instead children are persons to be cared for',[29] as if in living memory the former had ever been legally endorsed or the latter legally doubted.

There is a long-standing trend from authority to accountability for parents.[30] Donzelot dates this trend from the late nineteenth century,[31] and Lasch described it as contemporary in 1977.[32] But as we will see, in the years since the enactment of the Children Act 1989, and particularly since New Labour took office, the significance of this trend has been dramatically exacerbated.[33] So if, as Eekelaar plausibly suggests, 'parental responsibility' meant 'parental authority' in 1989 then there was a cataclysmic shift in meaning in the course of the 1990s. 'Parental responsibility' now means 'parental accountability'.

It is commonly argued that one reason that parents have become increasingly accountable to external agencies is that they have delegated traditional aspects of

[27] Law Commission, n.5, above, 26.

[28] Law Commission, *Family Law Review of Child Law: Guardianship*, Working Paper No. 91 (London, 1985), 9. See also Law Commission, *Family Law Review of Child Law: Custody*, Working Paper No. 96 (London, 1986), 218; Law Commission, n.14 above, 5; Department of Health, n.21, above, 9; Cretney, Masson and Bailey-Harris, n.16, above, 522; Eekelaar, n.4, above, 38; Edwards and Halpern, n.6, above, 114; Lowe, n.3, above, 210 and 211.

[29] Herring, n.19, above, 351. See also Lowe, n.3, above, 192 for the association between parental responsibility and parental care.

[30] See Wyness, n.8, above, 11.

[31] J. Donzelot, *The Policing of Families* (Baltimore and London, 1979). See also Henricson, n.12, above, 70; G. Jones and C. Wallace, *Youth, Family and Citizenship* (Buckingham and Philadelphia, 1992), 76; Wyness, n.3, above, 312.

[32] C. Lasch, *Haven in a Heartless World: The Family Besieged* (New York and London, 1977), 172.

[33] Henricson, n.12, above, 3 and 70. See also J. Bristow, 'A Sure Start for the therapeutic state', www.spiked-online.com, 22 September 2005.

parental competence to these agencies.[34] Again, although this is a long-standing trend,[35] there is no question that it gained momentum with the change of government in 1997:

For example, there has been substantial expansion in personal, social and health education in schools to the extent that there are concerns about teacher overload. Many of the functions that parents might have thought were their responsibility—such as talking about the role of marriage, the nature and responsibilities of good parenting, sex and relationship education, self-esteem, self-discipline and respect for others—are now being provided by schools through this route. Furthermore, pilots have been conducted in schools to provide health advice and contraception directly to children on a confidential basis.[36]

In essence:

Parents are thus relieved of various duties in looking after and orientating their children, which also implies decreasing rights to watch over and sanction their children's activities. These developments ... can ... be seen in terms of a new balance of social power and control. Effectively, they represent a redistribution of family and non-family spheres of influence on the course of children's lives.[37]

But there is yet another conception of responsibility, namely that of causal efficacy, for 'the term "responsible" nicely combines the notions of both causal efficacy and moral responsibility.'[38] A defining characteristic of twentieth-century family life has been the notion that parents' behaviour towards their children is decisive in forming their children's characters:

[W]hereas in the past a bad child was seen as a misfortune and the parent deserving of sympathy, it now symbolises a character defect on the part of the parent ('I don't know where we went wrong'). This perspective constitutes a 'domain assumption' of childrearing ideology which both survives the swings of fashion and affects the attitudes and behaviour of those whose approach to childrearing is unaffected by those fashions.[39]

Correspondingly, another of the strands found by Edwards and Halpern in their analysis of parental responsibility was one that 'blames parents for any failure to exercise parental responsibility which contributes to the delinquency of their children';[40] this seems to combine notions of accountability and causal efficacy.[41]

[34] P. Büchner, 'Growing Up in the 1980s: Changes in the Social Biography of Childhood in the FRG', in L. Chisholm, P. Büchner, H. Krüger and P. Brown (eds), *Childhood, Youth and Social Change: A Comparative Perspective* (London, New York and Philadelphia, 1990), 75; Donzelot, n.31, above, 91; Wyness, n.8, above, 11.

[35] Lasch, n.32, above, 172; Jones and Wallace, n.31, above, 76; Wyness, n.8, above, 11.

[36] Henricson, n.12, above, 34. See also *ibid*, 70; K. Abley, 'Passing the book', www.spiked-online.com, 5 September 2005.

[37] Büchner, n.34, above, 75.

[38] C.C. Harris, *The Family and Industrial Society* (London, Boston and Sydney, 1983), 240.

[39] *Ibid*, 240. See also Wyness, n.8, above, 11.

[40] Edwards and Halpern, n.6, above, 118.

[41] The other thread that they identified was financial responsibility, with which this chapter is not concerned.

The fact that this causal dimension of parental responsibility has gained strength in recent years, so that it would now 'seem to be deeply entrenched in social consciousness, and to affect members of all social strata',[42] further undermines parental responsibility as authority and further bolsters responsibility as accountability:

> Parents are socially regarded as responsible for their children's characters but, at the same time, are deprived of the ability to control their children which the attribution of responsibility *tacitly* assumes.[43] ... the doctrine of parental responsibility ... diminishes parental control and inhibits the exercise of authority ...[44]

Parenting Education

'[T]he Crime and Disorder Act 1998 introduced parenting education into the criminal justice system.'[45] The Act allows a court to make a parenting order in respect of the parent or guardian if the parent has been convicted of an offence relating to the child's attendance at school or the child is the subject of a child safety order, anti-social behaviour order or sex offender order, and the court is satisfied that the parenting order would be desirable in the interests of preventing the commission of a further offence or repetition of the behaviour which led to the order respectively.[46] In addition, the court must make a parenting order if a child under the age of sixteen has been convicted of an offence and the court is satisfied that the parenting order would be desirable in the interests of preventing the commission of a further offence.[47] The effect of the parenting order is that the parent must comply with the requirements in the order for up to a year and in particular must attend specified counselling or guidance sessions up to once a week for up to three months.[48]

The Anti-social Behaviour Act 2003 extends the purview of the Crime and Disorder Act 1998 in three main ways. First and most dramatically, the limitation that the parent be required to attend counselling and guidance sessions no more than once a week has been removed, paving the way for residential courses lasting up to three months.[49] It is true that there is a nod to the Human Rights Act 1998 in the proviso that a residential course may be included in a parenting order only if any likely interference with family life is proportionate.[50] However, the early judicial response to the argument that parenting orders are themselves an interference with family life does not bode well for a generous interpretation of this

[42] Harris, n.38, above, 240. See also Wyness, n.8, above, 1.

[43] Harris, n.38, above, 240.

[44] *Ibid*, 245. See also Wyness, n.8, above, 9; Wyness, n.3, above, 311. See F. Furedi, *Paranoid Parenting: Abandon Your Anxieties and be a Good Parent* (London, 2001) for further development of these themes.

[45] Henricson, n.12, above, 3.

[46] Crime and Disorder Act 1998, s. 8(1), (2), (6).

[47] Crime and Disorder Act 1998, ss. 8(1), (2), (6), 9(1).

[48] Crime and Disorder Act 1998, s. 8(4). See further Henricson, n.12, above, 70.

[49] Anti-social Behaviour Act 2003, ss. 18(1), (2), 20(4)(b).

[50] Anti-social Behaviour Act 2003, s. 18(7A)(b), 20(6), (8), 26(6), (8).

proviso: in *R (M) v Inner London Crown Court*, Henriques J unreservedly adopted the Government's contentions that there was a pressing social need to address the problems created by juvenile crime, to which the introduction of parenting orders corresponded.[51] Secondly, there are new additional grounds on which a parenting order is available.[52] Thirdly, a connection has been forged between (voluntary) parenting contracts and (compulsory) parenting orders.[53] In certain circumstances,[54] the parent may be invited to enter into a parenting contract, which is defined as a document that includes a statement by the parent that he agrees to comply with specified requirements, which may include attendance at a counselling or guidance programme.[55] When the court has to decide whether to make a parenting order in circumstances where parenting contracts are available, the court must take into account any refusal by the parent to enter into a parenting contract or any failure on the part of the parent to comply with the terms of the parenting contract.[56]

The Prime Minister has recently announced his intention to extend the use of parenting contracts and orders in two main ways. First, a wider range of authorities, such as housing officers, local anti-social behaviour teams and schools will be allowed to apply for orders, Secondly, the new powers will be available in relation to children at an earlier stage, when they are 'showing the propensity to get involved in antisocial behaviour'.[57]

When these proposals were first being mooted, it was suggested that they were almost guaranteed to undermine parents' authority in the eyes of their children and to reinforce parents' sense of failure.[58] Parenting education is perhaps the clearest example that the law provides of parents having to answer for their children. Rather than parents being given authority for disciplining their children or being assumed to be doing their utmost to exercise control over them, they are held directly accountable for their children's misdeeds.[59] Recent changes in the criminal justice system are 'quite explicit in pointing the finger at parents for not upholding their end of an implicit social contract, to produce moral upstanding young citizens'.[60]

It has been rightly recognized that the change in terminology from parental rights to parental responsibility has 'made it easier to impose legal obligations on

[51] [2003] 1 FLR 994, 1003. [52] See p. 469.

[53] See further Henricson, n.12, above, 70. [54] See p. 469.

[55] Anti-social Behaviour Act 2003, ss. 19(1)–(5), 25(1)–(4).

[56] Anti-social Behaviour Act 2003, ss. 21(1), 27(1).

[57] Tony Blair, 'Speech on improving parenting', 2 September 2005, available at www.pm.gov.uk/output/Page8123.asp.

[58] D. Boyd, 'Blaming the Parents' [1990] *Journal of Child Law* 65, 67. See also Arthur, n.1, above, 237; J. Bristow, 'Parents: we are not the law', www.spiked-online.com, 5 September 2005.

[59] But see Edwards and Halpern, n.6, above, 116; Gelsthorpe, n.1, above, 229 and 231; R. Smith, 'Contradictions in children's policy: partnering families—or policing them?' (1995) 17 *Journal of Social Welfare and Family Law* 301, 304 and 305; Eekelaar, n.4, above, 46; DiFonzo, n.1, above, 3 for various different interpretations of the meaning of parental responsibility in these statutory provisions.

[60] Wyness, n.3, above, 312, writing specifically about the Criminal Justice Act 1991.

parents whose children commit offences'.[61] In support of this thesis, it is noteworthy that it was only in the 1990s that parents became so closely identified with their children's crimes.[62] The watershed was the Criminal Justice Act 1991 which was the first law in England and Wales to hold parents directly responsible, as opposed to financially liable, for their children's wrongdoing.[63] As well as strengthening the court's powers to require parents to attend court with their children[64] and pay their children's fines,[65] the Act introduced a completely new presumption that magistrates should bind over the parents of a child under sixteen to take proper care and exercise proper control over the child;[66] if magistrates declined then they had to state their reasons for not doing so in open court,[67] and if the parents refused to be bound over then the Criminal Justice Act introduced the power to fine the parents.[68] If the child re-offended then the parents were liable to forfeit up to £1,000.[69] This was the first time that parents could be fined for their failure to control their children's behaviour, as opposed to being ordered to pay their children's fines.[70] The Criminal Justice and Public Order Act 1994 extended the provisions to include the power to bind over parents to ensure that their child complied with the requirements of a community sentence as well.[71]

Conclusion

It is interesting that 'responsibility' is able to mean its own opposite.[72] 'Authority' is the reverse of 'accountability'. While authority embodies independence and freedom, answerability implies dependence and a loss of control. I am of course not suggesting that people in authority should be unaccountable but rather that

[61] Cretney et al, n.16, above, 522. See Jones and Wallace, n.31, above, 91, and DiFonzo, n.1, above, 9, for the opposite view that by making parents liable for their children's crimes, the law has increased parents' control over their children.

[62] See Arthur, n.1, above, 234–5, for an account of the development of parental responsibility for juvenile offending. See Gelsthorpe, n.1, above, for a full account of historical trends in juvenile crime control.

[63] Arthur, n.1, above, 235.

[64] Criminal Justice Act 1991, s. 56.

[65] Criminal Justice Act 1991, s. 57, now contained in Powers of Criminal Courts (Sentencing) Act 2000, s. 137.

[66] Criminal Justice Act 1991, s. 58, now contained in Powers of Criminal Courts (Sentencing) Act 2000, s. 150.

[67] Criminal Justice Act 1991, s. 58(1)(b), now contained in Powers of Criminal Courts (Sentencing) Act 2000, s. 150(1)(b).

[68] Criminal Justice Act 1991, s. 58(2)(b), now contained in Powers of Criminal Courts (Sentencing) Act 2000, s. 150(2)(b).

[69] Criminal Justice Act 1991, s. 58(3), now contained in Powers of Criminal Courts (Sentencing) Act 2000, s. 150(3).

[70] Arthur, n.1, above, 235.

[71] Schedule 9, paragraph 50, Criminal Justice and Public Order Act 1994, now contained in Powers of Criminal Courts (Sentencing) Act 2000, s. 150(2).

[72] On different meanings of responsibility generally, see J. Lucas, *Responsibility* (Oxford, 1995), especially 5 and L. McClain, 'Rights and Irresponsibility' (1994) 43 *Duke Law Journal* 989, especially 994; R. Eckstein, 'Towards a Communitarian Theory of Responsibility: Bearing the Burden for the Unintended' (1991) 45 *University of Miami Law Review* 843, 896.

authority and accountability are at opposite ends of the spectrum. While it is desirable to be both authoritative and accountable, complete authority is the antithesis of complete accountability. In the case of parents, in recent years their responsibility *for* their children has been undermined by their responsibility *to* external agencies.[73] Currently, 'parental responsibility is used as a powerful instrument of social policy in shaping the family.'[74]

Related Developments

Prevention of Potential Harm

The last fifteen years have seen an increasing emphasis on prevention of potential harm both to and by children. Parental responsibility as parental accountability is related to this development in the following way. If someone is in authority, we take for granted that they are keeping an eye on emerging problems. In contrast, an important aspect of parents' being held to account is that external agencies are now keeping a watching brief on parents' care of their children, and part of that watching brief is making sure that problems are 'nipped in the bud', that parents are alerted to risks and dangers, that the authorities do all that they can to prevent matters escalating.

The focus on prevention of potential harm was given succour by the first Government Consultation Document on the family, *Supporting Families*, published in 1997.[75] In this paper, the Government encouraged parents to ask for help and support:

> at an early preventative stage[76] . . . to ensure that small problems in a child's behaviour or development do not grow unchecked into major difficulties for the child or the family[77] . . . to tackle problems before they become entrenched.[78]

Therefore an enhanced role for health visitors was proposed, involving 'a shift of emphasis from *dealing with* problems to *preventing* problems from arising in the first place.'[79]

This emphasis on prevention of potential harm is clearly present in the parenting education provisions. As we saw above, one of the circumstances in which a parenting order can be made is where the child is the subject of a child safety order.[80] If we look at the criteria for making a child safety order, the emphasis on prevention and potential is apparent. A child safety order may be imposed for up to a year in exceptional circumstances when a child has committed an act that

[73] See Wyness, n.3, above, 321. See also Bristow, n.58, above.
[74] Edwards and Halpern, n.6, above, 118.
[75] Home Office, *Supporting Families: A Consultation Document* (London, 1998).
[76] *Ibid*, 10. [77] *Ibid*, 7. [78] *Ibid*, 14. [79] *Ibid*, 11.
[80] See p. 465.

would have constituted an offence had he been old enough to be criminally responsible or when such an order is necessary to *prevent* the child committing such an act, when a child has breached curfew, or when a child has acted in a manner that caused or was *likely to cause harassment, alarm or distress* to anyone outside his household.[81]

We can see a similar stress on prevention and potential with regard to the grounds for parenting orders added by the Anti-social Behaviour Act 2003. A parenting order may now additionally be made where a child has been excluded from school, so long as the court is satisfied that making the order would be desirable in the interests of *improving the child's behaviour*.[82] A parenting order is also now available where a court is satisfied that a child who has been referred to a youth offending team has engaged in criminal conduct, defined to include any conduct of a child under the age of ten that would constitute a crime if the child were older, or *anti-social behaviour*, defined in terms identical to one of the criteria for making a child safety order as behaviour which causes or *is likely to cause harassment, alarm or distress* to anyone outside the child's household, and that a parenting order would be desirable to prevent the child from engaging in further such activities.[83] In relation to parenting contracts, introduced by the Anti-social Behaviour Act 2003, one of the circumstances in which a parent may be invited to enter a parenting contract is that a child has been referred to a youth offending team and a member of that team has reason to believe that the child has engaged or *is likely to* engage in criminal conduct or *anti-social behaviour*.[84] Here the focus on prevention and potential is two-fold: a parenting contract is available when the child *is likely to* engage in *anti-social behaviour*, which is defined as behaviour *likely* to cause harassment, alarm or distress.[85]

As we have seen, the Prime Minister plans to take the emphasis on prevention of potential harm still further. In a recent speech he announced:

> The new powers [for parenting orders] are also going to apply to children at a much earlier stage, and here is something that is very important. Far too often we get heavy after the problem has got incredibly serious. It might be more sensible if we intervened somewhat earlier and tried to prevent the problem arising in such a serious way. So this will apply not just where there has been a criminal offence committed, or the child has been say excluded from school, as is currently the case, but if they are showing the propensity to get involved in antisocial behaviour, if they are beginning to go off the rails, making sure that we deal with them before they do so.[86]

[81] Crime and Disorder Act 1998, s. 11(3), (4). For a critique of the identical statutory formulation in the Protection from Harassment Act 1997 see H. Reece, 'The Development of Family Law in the Twentieth Century: Informed Reform or Campaigns and Compromises?' (2000) 63 *Modern Law Review*, 608, 619–20; D. Mead, 'The Human Rights Act—A Panacea for Peaceful Public Protest?' (1998) 3 *Journal of Civil Liberties* 206; K. Kerrigan, 'Right to Freedom of Assembly' (1998) 3 *Journal of Civil Liberties* 37.

[82] Anti-social Behaviour Act 2003, s. 20(1), (2), (3).

[83] Anti-social Behaviour Act 2003, ss. 26(1)–(3), 29(1).

[84] Anti-social Behaviour Act 2003, ss. 19(1)–(5), 25(1)–(4).

[85] Anti-social Behaviour Act 2003, s. 29(1).

[86] Blair, n.57, above.

Parental Responsibility as an Attitude

I have previously argued that we are no longer judged by what we do but by how we approach our decisions; the focus has shifted from the content of the decision to the process of making the decision. In other words, responsibility has become a mode of thought.[87] In the context of parenting, this means that to a large extent there is no longer a right way to parent: good parenting is now an attitude,[88] and an important part of that attitude is being prepared to learn.[89]

It is clear that parental responsibility as an attitude is feasible only if parents are accountable rather than authoritative. If someone is in authority then he or she may fail to meet his or her authority which may consequently be removed, but he or she would not be expected to exhibit the right attitude, which smacks of someone in a subservient position. In contrast, someone who is answerable can be answerable for his or her attitude as well as his or her actions.[90]

A good illustration of the operation of parental responsibility as an attitude is Tony Blair's response to his son's arrest, coupled with the media reaction to the incident. In July 2000, the Prime Minister's sixteen-year-old son, Euan, was arrested for being drunk and incapable, after police officers found him lying on the ground in Leicester Square. Euan also gave the police a false name, age and address. Five days after the incident, Euan's headteacher told the *Sunday Telegraph* that it was the responsibility of parents to prevent teenage drinking:

> ... in the way that adults, parents and society generally exercise responsibility in these areas. That's to be aware of the fact that it's happening and to try to ensure that children don't start drinking too early and that when they do they understand the effects of alcohol and learn to use it responsibly.[91]

This isolated and oblique suggestion that Tony Blair had lacked responsibility as a father was universally condemned.[92] Tony Blair's own verdict on the incident, given in a speech at the Faith in the Future conference the day after Euan's arrest, was far more in tune with current notions of parental responsibility:

> The values you represent are the values we all share. Respect, tolerance, the family, trying to bring up children properly. ... Being a Prime Minister can be a tough job, but I always think that being a parent is probably tougher. Sometimes you don't always succeed, but to me the family is more important than anything else.[93]

[87] H. Reece, *Divorcing Responsibly* (Oxford, 2003), 209–10.

[88] *Ibid*, 230; C. Piper, 'Divorce Conciliation in the United Kingdom: How Responsible Are Parents?' (1988) 16 *International Journal of Sociology of Law* 477, 480 and 488; M. Sandel, *Democracy's Discontent: America in Search of a Public Philosophy* (Cambridge, Massachusetts, 1996), 113.

[89] Reece, n.87, above, 162.

[90] Conversely, until parental responsibility became an attitude, the absence of any definition of parental responsibility made it difficult to hold parents to account: see Smith, n.3, above, 8.

[91] John McIntosh, quoted in C. Milmo, 'Head accused of playing politics over Euan Blair', *The Independent*, 10 July 2000.

[92] See *ibid*.

[93] Tony Blair, quoted in P. Waugh, 'Honest, contrite and above all emotional, Blair faces up to the morning after the night before', *The Independent*, 7 July 2000. See also 'Blair's son says sorry after

In this passage, Tony Blair showed that he understood that being a good parent did not mean succeeding but did mean trying hard; he demonstrated that he was aware that parenting was both arduous and crucial. He revealed awareness that it was neither how he acted as a parent nor what decisions he made in his capacity as a parent that determined his level of responsibility. Rather, his success as a parent depended on his attitude. The following description from a journalist indicates that Tony Blair was successful in demonstrating that his attitude was responsible: 'Honest, contrite and above all extremely emotional, the Prime Minister gave possibly the most personal speech of his career.'[94] In the resulting media coverage, Tony Blair was universally praised for having rightly realized that the virtues of parenting were procedural not substantive, one commentator confirming that '[t]he only real skills of value are compassion, openness and emotional literacy.'[95] The stance adopted by Tony Blair and the media echoed that adopted two and a half years earlier, when William Straw, the seventeen-year-old son of Jack Straw, then Home Secretary, was cautioned for dealing cannabis. Jack Straw commented:

> William is now learning the lessons of this episode and he has of course my full support in doing so.[96]

BBC News delivered the general media verdict on the incident, which was that Jack Straw had 'won admiration for his honest approach to the family crisis'.[97]

In the final part of this chapter, I will look at a couple of worrying consequences of the development of procedural parental responsibility, but at this juncture it is worth sounding two further notes of caution in relation to parental responsibility as an attitude.

Not Asking for Advice is Irresponsible

I have just suggested that a good parent is being re-defined as one who is prepared to learn.[98] This is evident in *Supporting Families*, which stresses throughout that seeking advice is responsible behaviour:

> We want to change the culture so that seeking advice and help when it is needed is seen not as failure but the action of concerned and responsible parents[99] . . . so that asking for help and support at an early preventative stage is seen as a sign of responsible parenting.[100]

To put this more precisely, in *Divorcing Responsibly*, I suggested that the definition of a moral agent has become someone who accepts that he or she needs lessons in

'drunk and incapable' arrest', *The Guardian*, 6 July 2000; *BBC News*, 'Blair's son "drunk and incapable"', www.bbc.co.uk/news, 6 July 2000; N. Watt, 'Emotional PM talks of faith and family', *The Guardian*, 7 July 2000; M. White and N. Watt, 'Blair shows strain after son's arrest', *The Guardian*, 7 July 2000; A. Grice and P. Waugh, 'Being a Prime Minister can be tough, but being a parent is sometimes tougher', *The Independent*, 7 July 2000. See further Blair, n.57, above.

94 Waugh, n.93, above. 95 R. Coward, 'Kids and kidology', *The Observer*, 9 July 2000.

96 *BBC News*, 'Cabinet Minister's son cautioned', www.bbc.co.uk/news, 12 January 1998.

97 *BBC News*, 'A history of Christmas scandal past', www.bbc.co.uk/news, 22 December 1998.

98 See p. 470. 99 Home Office, n.75, above, 7. 100 *Ibid*, 10.

how to approach moral dilemmas, so that a moral agent who believes that he or she does not need moral instruction has become a contradiction in terms. Asking for advice is being moral.[101] But if asking for advice is a sign of responsible parenting then the more threatening corollary is that not asking for advice is a sign of irresponsible parenting.

In sounding this note of caution, I am not suggesting that people facing significant events do not want high-quality advice; certainly, the evidence shows that many divorcing couples need and value advice and information,[102] and this is quite possibly even truer of parents than divorcees.[103] However, as I have previously demonstrated with regard to divorcing couples,[104] for this Government, the purpose of providing information is not to inform but to direct decision-making.

Purpose of Information is to Direct Decision-making

> A common theme throughout the government's support for parents in health and education is to provide them with information, whether it be about child development or the education system, as we have seen. Other information systems spanning a host of issues pertinent to parenting can also be pointed to . . .[105]

The 2003 Joseph Rowntree Foundation publication, *Government and Parenting*, gives the following examples: National Family and Parenting Institute parent information publications, helplines such as Parentline Plus and NHS Direct, the Home Office information strategy to distribute government information on parenting and the Children's Information Services in the Early Years and Child Development Partnerships.[106] The publication concludes that 'these sources of support . . . undoubtedly point to a government conviction that it has a significant role to play in providing parents with information.'[107]

Nowhere is this conviction clearer than in *Supporting Families*, which first proposed such key providers of information as the National Family and Parenting Institute,[108] Parentline Plus[109] and the Sure Start programme.[110] *Supporting Families* makes clear at the outset that:

> Except in exceptional circumstances, where the well-being of family members is at stake, it must be the decision of the parents when to ask for help or advice.[111]

[101] Reece, n.87, above, 154–5. [102] *Ibid*, 168–70.

[103] For support, see Gelsthorpe, n.1, above, 231, summarizing the Save the Children (Scotland) Report: *Supporting Parents, Supporting Parenting, Positive Parenting, First Year Report* (London, 1998); Department for Constitutional Affairs, Department for Education and Skills and Department for Trade and Industry, *Parental Separation: Children's Needs and Parents' Responsibilities* (Norwich, 2004), 2 and 5; Department for Education and Skills, *The Government's Response to the Children Act Sub-Committee (CASC) Report: 'Making Contact Work'* (2004), available at www.dfes.gov.uk/childrenandfamilies/docs/CASC%20Final%20Version.doc, 22.

[104] Reece, n.87, above, ch. 5.

[105] Henricson, n.12, above, 35. See also *ibid*, 70. [106] *Ibid*, 35.

[107] *Ibid*, 35. [108] Home Office, n.75, above, 7–9. [109] *Ibid*, 10.

[110] *Ibid*, 13–15. [111] *Ibid*, 6.

True to its word, until the chapter entitled *Better Support for Serious Family Problems*,[112] there is nothing compulsory in the document. Help is consistently contrasted with interference:[113]

They [parents] do not want to be lectured or hectored,[114] . . . nagged or nannied[115] . . . least of all by politicians.[116] . . . [G]overnments have to be wary about intervening in areas of private life and intimate emotion. We in Government need to approach family policy with a strong dose of humility. We must not preach and we must not give the impression that members of the Government are any better than the rest of the population in meeting the challenge of family life. They are not.[117] . . . But [parents] do want clear advice to be available when they need it . . . [118]

However, when we look more closely, it is clear that the purpose of all this advice is to direct decision-making. Two outstanding illustrations come from recent Government activity in the area of post-separation contact. The first is *Making Contact Work*, a report from the Children Act Sub-Committee of the Advisory Board on Family Law,[119] together with the Government's response to the report.[120] In *Making Contact Work*, the Board's starting point was recognition that when the primary carer disobeys a contact order requiring him or her to allow contact between the child and another adult, generally the other parent, enforcing the contact order by fining or imprisoning the carer is both crude and ineffective.[121] The main reason is that it is hard to justify such punishment as being in the child's best interests.[122] Their conclusion was that the Government should legislate to provide the courts with a range of therapeutic remedies in such cases,[123] so that fines or imprisonment would be genuinely the last resort only when education, therapy, and persuasion had failed.[124] The Government has recently introduced legislation to this effect in the form of the Children and Adoption Bill 2005.[125]

The Report regarded better information to both parents at the earliest possible stage in the breakdown of their relationship and preferably before they had parted,[126] as of crucial importance in making contact work.[127] There were four pieces of information that the Board considered particularly necessary. The first

112 Home Office, n.75, above, ch. 5. 113 *Ibid*, 3. 114 *Ibid*, 2. 115 *Ibid*, 6.
116 *Ibid*, 2. 117 *Ibid*, 4. 118 *Ibid*, 2.

119 Lord Chancellor's Advisory Board on Family Law: Children Act Sub-Committee, *Making Contact Work: A Report to the Lord Chancellor on the Facilitation of Arrangements for Contact Between Children and their Non-Residential Parents and the Enforcement of Court Orders for Contact* (London, 2002). 120 Department for Education and Skills, n.103, above.

121 Lord Chancellor's Advisory Board on Family Law, n.119, above, 13 and 97.

122 *Ibid*, 13. 123 *Ibid.* 124 *Ibid*, 14 and 97.

125 See Department for Education and Skills, n.103, above, 37–8 and Department for Constitutional Affairs, Department for Education and Skills and Department for Trade and Industry, *Parental Separation: Children's Needs and Parents' Responsibilities. Next Steps* (Norwich, 2005), 13, 16, 36 and 38, for expressions of the intention so to legislate.

126 Lord Chancellor's Advisory Board on Family Law, n.119, above, chs. 1 and 22.

127 *Ibid*, 11 and 22.

was the importance to children of maintaining contact wherever possible with the parent with whom they are not living. Secondly, parents needed to know how difficult successful post-separation parenting is for both parents. Thirdly, they needed information about the serious harm caused to children by continuing acrimony between their parents. Finally, they needed to be aware of the services available to help resolve difficulties over contact.[128] More broadly, there was a need to promote general understanding of the importance of the involvement of both parents in the upbringing of their children.[129] The directive nature of this information is too obvious to be dwelt on, and was spelt out even more clearly in the Government response:

> Information for those experiencing relationship breakdown forms part of the Department for Constitutional Affairs' (DCA) overall objective of encouraging increased safe contact between children and their non-resident parents.[130]

The importance placed on information in the Report was also clearly founded on the assumption that if parents were fully informed then they would be inexorably driven to the right result, which was that the primary carer would allow conflict-free contact:

> Whilst it is in no sense a panacea, we are strongly of the view that if parents have ready access to high quality information about the effects of their separation on themselves and on their children; about the difficulties involved in post separation parenting; and about the effect of continuing parental hostility on their children, then their views on contact will be much better informed. An understanding of the traumatic process through which both adults and children are going is likely to help make contact easier for both adults and for children.[131]

The Report envisaged plenty of opportunities for providing information, recommending that courts should have the power to compel parents to attend a range of meetings, including information meetings, conciliation meetings, meetings with a mediator, psychological assessments, meetings with a counsellor and parenting classes designed to persuade parents to obey the contact order.[132]

The Government has recently sponsored legislation to provide for these powers.[133] The Children and Adoption Bill 2005 provides that where a court is considering a contact dispute, or making or varying a contact order in continuing proceedings, the court may require parents who are party to the proceedings, among other parties, to take part in an activity that promotes contact. The

[128] Lord Chancellor's Advisory Board on Family Law, n.119, above, 11.

[129] *Ibid*, 22.

[130] Department for Education and Skills, n.103, above, 21.

[131] Lord Chancellor's Advisory Board on Family Law, n.119, above, 22.

[132] *Ibid*, 43, 90, 98, 99.

[133] See Department for Constitutional Affairs, Department for Education and Skills and Department for Trade and Industry, n.103, above, 30, Department for Education and Skills, n.103, above, 35, and Department for Constitutional Affairs, Department for Education and Skills and Department for Trade and Industry, n.125, above, 13, 36 and 38 for expressions of the intention so to legislate.

activities that may be required include programmes, classes and sessions providing counselling, guidance, information, or advice.[134] The Report also recommended that courts should have the power to order parents to undergo psychiatric assessments,[135] but the Children and Adoption Bill has specifically excluded these, along with psychiatric treatments, medical assessments and treatments and mediation sessions, from the court's purview.[136]

For those parents in breach of an order, the Report recommended education programmes or perpetrator programmes,[137] brought into existence by recent legislation.[138] Finally, the Report recommended giving courts the power to place parents on probation, with a condition of treatment or attendance at a particular class or programme, or impose a community service order to include programmes specifically designed to address the default in contact.[139] The Government has gone a long way towards implementing these proposals in the Children and Adoption Bill: the Bill provides that if the court is satisfied beyond reasonable doubt that a person has failed to comply with a contact order without a reasonable excuse, it may make an enforcement order imposing an unpaid work requirement on the person.[140]

The Bill also implements a proposal stemming from the Government response to *Making Contact Work*, namely that family assistance orders should be more closely harnessed to information provision.[141] Specifically, the Children and Adoption Bill provides that where a family assistance order operates in conjunction with a contact order, the family assistance order may direct the officer concerned to give advice about contact. The Bill clearly envisages that this expanded role for family assistance orders will augur their greater availability: the Bill removes the requirement that the circumstances of the case must be exceptional before a family assistance order may be made, and increases their maximum length from six months to a year.[142]

Moreover, the Government is in the throes of implementing those recommendations of the Report that do not require new legislation.[143] The Government is currently developing a strategy to make it simpler for parents to access

[134] Children and Adoption Bill 2005, cl 1.

[135] Lord Chancellor's Advisory Board on Family Law, n.119, above, 98 and 99.

[136] Children and Adoption Bill 2005, cl 1.

[137] Lord Chancellor's Advisory Board on Family Law, n.119, above, 89, 90, 98 and 99.

[138] See p. 465.

[139] Lord Chancellor's Advisory Board on Family Law, n.119, above, 14, 89 and 99.

[140] Children and Adoption Bill 2005, cl 4. See Department for Constitutional Affairs, Department for Education and Skills and Department for Trade and Industry, n.125, above, 38, for the expression of the intention so to legislate.

[141] Department for Education and Skills, n.103, above, 33. See also *ibid*, 42.

[142] Children and Adoption Bill 2005, cl 6. See Department for Constitutional Affairs, Department for Education and Skills and Department for Trade and Industry, n.125, above, 13 and 16, for the expression of the intention so to legislate.

[143] Lord Chancellor's Advisory Board on Family Law, *Government's Response to the Report of the Children Act Sub-Committee of the Lord Chancellor's Advisory Board on Family Law, 'Making Contact Work'* (London, 2002); Department for Education and Skills, n.103, above, 20.

information and advice.[144] Parenting Plans and leaflets have been distributed to CAFCASS offices, courts, solicitors, Citizens Advice Bureaux, Relate services, health visitors, Directors of Social Services, educational welfare services, and other organizations working with children and parents. They are currently accessible through the Department for Constitutional Affairs web site, but the Government intends to make them available on a general parenting internet site imminently.[145] Steps are also being taken to make them more widely available to the general public by distributing them through health and educational outlets.[146] In addition, the Government is supporting a two-year media and public relations campaign called *Contact Counts*, organized by Parentline Plus, to 'raise parents' awareness'[147] of the available information. *Contact Counts* has already received coverage in *The Sun*, *The Voice*, *Woman* magazine, the *Daily Star*, and *19* among other media outlets.[148]

The second illustration of the directive nature of information provision is the Government Consultation Document, *Parental Separation: Children's Needs and Parents' Responsibilities*,[149] coupled with the subsequent White Paper, *Parental Separation: Children's Needs and Parents' Responsibilities: Next Steps*.[150] The starting point in the Consultation Document was that the ninety per cent of parents who reached agreement on contact were far more satisfied with their contact arrangements than the ten per cent whose contact was determined by court order. Despite the fact that the Document recognized that the lower level of satisfaction in those cases resolved by the courts was probably due to a previously higher level of conflict between those parents,[151] the Document immediately and without any explanation leapt from correlation to cause in declaring that a policy aim was to increase the proportion of parents reaching agreement themselves.[152] This objective was continually stressed throughout both the Consultation Document and the White Paper.

In the Consultation Document and White Paper, information and advice were considered crucial. Accordingly, the Government promised to work in partnership

[144] Department for Education and Skills, n.103, above, 41. See further Department for Constitutional Affairs, Department for Education and Skills and Department for Trade and Industry, n.125, above, 5 and 7.

[145] See www.direct.gov.uk/Parents/fs/en.

[146] Department for Education and Skills, n.103, above, 23–4. See further Department for Constitutional Affairs, Department for Education and Skills and Department for Trade and Industry, n.125, above, 21.

[147] Department for Education and Skills, n.103, above, 22.

[148] *Ibid*, 22–5.

[149] Department for Constitutional Affairs, Department for Education and Skills and Department for Trade and Industry, n.103, above.

[150] Department for Constitutional Affairs, Department for Education and Skills and Department for Trade and Industry, n.125, above.

[151] See also Department for Education and Skills, n.103, above, 4.

[152] Department for Constitutional Affairs, Department for Education and Skills and Department for Trade and Industry, n.103, above, 9 and 10. See further Department for Constitutional Affairs, Department for Education and Skills and Department for Trade and Industry, n.125, above, 5 and 7.

with existing information and advice providers, such as Parentline Plus, Sure Start, Relate, and other Marriage and Relationship Support grant recipients, to improve services so that helpful information and support would be more widely available and accessible.[153] The advice would be both legal and emotional, provided both over the telephone and via web sites.[154] The Government noted that one specific form of existing information that had been well received was the Government's 'Parenting Plan'. Accordingly, the Government promised to develop and revise these, publishing and promoting them widely by April 2005.[155] The Document also referred favourably to the Family Advice and Information Service initiative, which seeks to provide parents with tailored information and advice.[156] However, the Government recognized that some parents would need 'additional support to enable them to reach agreement';[157] these parents would be subject(ed) to the Family Resolutions Pilot Project. This project would involve a three-stage process. First of all, parents would be sent an information pack. Secondly, parents would be directed to attend two group sessions. The final stage would involve one or more parent planning sessions for both parents with a CAFCASS Family Court Adviser. Information would not stop at the courtroom door: the Government proposed to make available to those parents undertaking in-court conciliation improved information, Parenting Plans and the materials used in the Family Resolutions Pilot.[158] According to the White Paper, the findings of the pilot project will be published in April 2006, and this will inform the Government's decision about how to develop the project.[159]

> The proposals in the Green Paper are aimed at helping separating parents to make arrangements in the interests of their child. To help parents more effectively to reach these agreements, the proposals are intended to provide improved access to information, advice and mediation at the time of separation.[160]

At every mention of information provision, the Government never omits to stress that the aim of providing the information is to help parents reach

[153] Department for Constitutional Affairs, Department for Education and Skills and Department for Trade and Industry, n.103, above, 5 and 21. See further Department for Constitutional Affairs, Department for Education and Skills and Department for Trade and Industry, n.125, above, 20.

[154] Department for Constitutional Affairs, Department for Education and Skills, and Department for Trade and Industry, n.103, above, 5. See further Department for Constitutional Affairs, Department for Education and Skills and Department for Trade and Industry, n.125, above, 11, 21, and 23.

[155] Department for Constitutional Affairs, Department for Education and Skills and Department for Trade and Industry, n.103, above, 21–2. See further Department for Constitutional Affairs, Department for Education and Skills and Department for Trade and Industry, n.125, above, 10, 20–1, and 32.

[156] Department for Constitutional Affairs, Department for Education and Skills, and Department for Trade and Industry, n.103, above, 23.

[157] *Ibid*, 25.

[158] See further Department for Constitutional Affairs, Department for Education and Skills, and Department for Trade and Industry, n.125, above, 11 and 28.

[159] *Ibid*, 25.

[160] *Ibid*, 5.

agreement.[161] However, this does not mean that the Government has recoiled from the purpose of information provision envisaged by *Making Contact Work*: the aim of the group sessions in the Family Resolutions Pilot Project is to 'discuss how difficult separation and disputes about contact can be for the children and how these might be lessened',[162] and the preceding information packs will make clear that a legitimate agreement is one that provides for 'a meaningful ongoing relationship with both parents'.[163] These purposes are combined in the Government supported media campaign mentioned above, which is intended:

> . . . to raise parents' awareness of the available information on, and support for, negotiating workable contact arrangements[164] . . . to convince parents that, where it is safe, continued contact between the child and the family members who are no longer living with them is important to the child's well being[165] . . . to encourage parents to negotiate contact arrangements constructively with each other, turning to legal procedures only as a last resort.[166]

Both the Report and the Consultation Document show that classically punitive measures are seen as less necessary when information provision becomes directive.[167] However, this point should not be misunderstood as seeking to diminish the punitive nature of information provision. In this respect, it is instructive to note the difference that the Report envisaged between punitive and non-punitive remedies. The Report recommended that there should be two stages, the first being essentially non-punitive. At this non-punitive stage:

> The resident parent could, for example, be directed to attend an information meeting, or a parenting programme designed to address intractable contact disputes or required to seek psychiatric advice.[168]

At the punitive stage, the only difference would be that the court could impose an order with a penal sanction, such as community service or regular attendance at parenting classes.[169] The Government response has made the distinction between punishment and information even blurrier, referring to the 'facilitation/enforcement spectrum', because '[f]acilitation and enforcement are not properly viewed as

[161] Department for Constitutional Affairs, Department for Education and Skills, and Department for Trade and Industry, n.125, above, 5, 7, 21 and 23; Department for Constitutional Affairs, Department for Education and Skills and Department for Trade and Industry, n.103, above, 5, 21, 23 and 25.

[162] Department for Constitutional Affairs, Department for Education and Skills, and Department for Trade and Industry, n.103, above, 25.

[163] *Ibid.*

[164] Department for Education and Skills, n.103, above, 22.

[165] *Ibid*, 24.

[166] *Ibid*, 25. See further Department for Constitutional Affairs, Department for Education and Skills and Department for Trade and Industry, n.125, above, 7.

[167] See more generally J. Nolan, *The Therapeutic State: Justifying Government at Century's End* (New York, 1998), 298.

[168] Lord Chancellor's Advisory Board on Family Law, n.119, above, 98.

[169] *Ibid.*

alternatives, but rather as points on a spectrum'.[170] As we have seen, the Children and Adoption Bill follows this approach.[171]

The current approach to information has been dramatically adopted in a contact dispute, *Re H*.[172] In this case the Court of Appeal disagreed with the trial judge's view that every avenue had been explored to enable contact between the father and his child, and accordingly ordered that a consultant child psychiatrist see every member of the family. Moreover, academic writers want to take the emphasis on information still further. An outstanding example is an article focusing on child sexual abuse.[173] The author takes as the starting point that girls are at greater risk of sexual abuse after their parents' divorce. The argument is that the way to guard against this risk is through capitalizing on education programmes for divorcing families. A parent given notice of the heightened risk could then mitigate it by taking an in-depth sexual abuse prevention class for parents, designed to educate caretakers about the signs of abuse,[174] or by enrolling her daughter in a school-based prevention programme,[175] to empower a child to protect herself from abuse.[176] Unsurprisingly, in the light of the current Governmental approach to information provision examined above, the author suggests that divorce proceedings do seem to 'offer a viable opportunity to raise parental awareness' about the risk of abuse.[177]

Behaviour Modification Disguised as De-Legalization

In *Divorcing Responsibly*, I examined the twin aims pursued in Part II of the Family Law Act 1996 of first, the de-legalization of divorce but secondly, behaviour modification, and I followed Eekelaar and Dewar in suggesting that the tension between these aims is only apparent, because the Family Law Act embodied a belief that the law had a role to play in *pushing* divorcing parties towards settling matters themselves.[178] To examine the same apparent tension in relation to parental responsibility, it might seem that, while behaviour modification clearly complements parental responsibility as accountability, de-legalization pulls in the opposite direction, back towards parental responsibility as authority. In fact, the tension is resolved in the same way as in the Family Law Act but even more dramatically: an examination of de-legalization in the context of parental responsibility shows that

[170] Department for Education and Skills, n.103, above, 43.

[171] P.473. See Department for Education and Skills, n.103, above, 35, for expression of the intention so to legislate. See further Blair, n.57, above.

[172] [2001] 1 FCR 59.

[173] R. Wilson, 'Fractured Families, Fragile Children—The Sexual Vulnerability Of Girls In The Aftermath Of Divorce' (2002) 14 *Child and Family Law Quarterly* 1. See also D. Ellis and D. Anderson, 'The Impact of Participation in a Parent Education Program for Divorcing Parents on the Use of Court Resources: An Evaluation Study' (2003) 21 *Conflict Resolution Quarterly* 169.

[174] Wilson, n.173, above, 12 and 18.

[175] *Ibid*, 12.

[176] *Ibid*, 18.

[177] *Ibid*, 22.

[178] Reece, n.87 above, 11–12; J. Dewar, 'The Normal Chaos of Family Law' (1998) 61 *Modern Law Review* 467, 476; J. Dewar, 'Family Law and Its Discontents' (2000) 14 *International Journal of Law, Policy and the Family* 59, 79; J. Eekelaar, *Regulating Divorce* (Oxford, 1991), 154.

de-legalization is a further device for behaviour modification, operating alongside support, advice and information. In essence, parents are being *made* to settle matters themselves.

In a seminal article, Bailey-Harris et al. found that:

> One of the strongest principles adhered to in the [Children] Act's practical operation is one not expressly stated in section 1—the promotion of settlement, underpinned by the conviction that if parents can reach agreement, this must necessarily be preferable to any solution the court can impose. … [T]win assumptions—that mediation is 'a good thing' and that (whether or not it is achieved through the mediation process) settlement is desirable—now permeates all courts and all professionals' thinking.[179]

According to Bailey-Harris et al., while the prevailing belief is that trials are damaging, the evidence to substantiate this belief is equivocal.[180] Indeed, the authors suggested that there may well be little real substance in apparent parental agreement, which could often be more plausibly interpreted as reflecting coercion or resignation,[181] because:

> However much parental autonomy is currently valued by courts as an ideal, the reality is that if the two parents want different things, one or both of them will need to give way in some respects. It is unrealistic to believe that this is always due to a genuine change of mind (based on further reflection) rather than a resigned bowing to the power of the other parent and the court.[182]

The problems with encouraging settlement were twofold: first, in effect, court welfare officers were being given the power to decide disputes because parents were being persuaded against their better judgment to settle on the basis of the welfare report;[183] secondly, it could be easier for a parent to accept a judgment from a stranger than to concede points to his or her ex-partner.[184] This study uncovered 'many examples of judges using the *rhetoric* of parental autonomy to justify the refusal to make an order, even in proceedings where there is *real* dispute'.[185]

Nowhere is this compulsion clearer than in *Parental Separation: Children's Needs and Parents' Responsibilities*. We have already seen that the Consultation Document places huge emphasis on encouraging parental agreement: it also makes clear that refusal to agree carries penalties, specifically in relation to access to legal aid.[186] The Government confirms that:

> publicly funded parents must show they have at least explored the option [of mediation] as an alternative before turning to litigation, in order to be able to access continued funding.[187]

179 R. Bailey-Harris, J. Barron and J. Pearce, 'Settlement Culture and the Use of the "No Order" Principle under the Children Act 1989' (1999) 11 *Child and Family Law Quarterly* 53.

180 *Ibid*, 56. 181 *Ibid*, 54–5. 182 *Ibid*, 56. 183 *Ibid*. 184 *Ibid*.

185 *Ibid*, 60, emphasis added.

186 Department for Constitutional Affairs, Department for Education and Skills and Department for Trade and Industry, n.103, above, 5. See also Department for Education and Skills, n.103, above, 41.

187 Department for Constitutional Affairs, Department for Education and Skills and Department for Trade and Industry, n.103, above, 24.

Even more ominously, the Consultation Document continues:

The Government, in conjunction with the senior judiciary and rule committees, proposes to review relevant rules and Practice Directions so that the strongest possible encouragement is given to parties to agree to mediation or other forms of dispute resolution, in order to ensure that all alternative means of resolving family disputes, short of contested court hearings, are fully utilised.[188]

Those parents who 'need additional support to enable them to reach agreement'[189] will be referred to the Family Resolutions Pilot Project.[190] The White Paper states that participation in the project is not mandatory, but warns that:

there is a strong judicial expectation that parties to cases will participate. We expect that this will be quite sufficient in the vast majority of cases.[191]

Emphasis on Complexity of Parenting

If parenting were currently regarded as straightforward then perhaps parents could have retained authority; they could have been left in charge. But recent Government edicts on parenting are univocal in pronouncing that parenting is incredibly complex: this is why parents need to be helped and therefore held to account.[192] There is no better example than *Supporting Families*, which stresses the complexity of parenting throughout. We are told that parenting is 'a hard job'[193] 'a challenging job',[194] 'a difficult job',[195] 'a complex task',[196] and consequently promised 'greater emphasis in the curriculum on the responsibilities of parenthood at the first opportunity.'[197] Accordingly, the National Curriculum now states that Key Stage 4 pupils should be taught 'about the role and responsibilities of a parent, and the qualities of good parenting and its value to family life'.[198] As we have also seen, integral to Tony Blair's response to his son's arrest was his statement that an activity that millions of people carry out every day could be regarded as more difficult than being uniquely entrusted to head the nation.[199]

If parenting in an intact family is seen as hard, this is nothing compared with the difficulties after separation; as we saw above, *Making Contact Work* considered that parents needed to know how difficult successful post-separation parenting was for both parents.[200] Apparently, children need to be told how difficult post-separation

[188] Department for Constitutional Affairs, Department for Education and Skills and Department for Trade and Industry, n.103, above, 24. See further Department for Constitutional Affairs, Department for Education and Skills and Department for Trade and Industry, n.125, above, 11 and 25; J. Heartfield, 'Pitting parent against parent', www.spiked-online.com, 20 January 2005.

[189] Department for Constitutional Affairs, Department for Education and Skills and Department for Trade and Industry, n.103, above, 25.

[190] See p. 477.

[191] Department for Constitutional Affairs, Department for Education and Skills and Department for Trade and Industry, n.125, above, 28.

[192] See Bristow, n.58, above.

[193] Home Office, n.75, above, 2.

[194] *Ibid*, 7.

[195] *Ibid*, 15.

[196] *Ibid*, 9 and 10.

[197] *Ibid*, 17.

[198] www.nc.uk.net/webdav/servlet/XRM?Page/@id=6001&Session/@id=D_dTyitpHS-PwIfthUjzy86&POS[@stateId_eq_main]/@id=436&POS[@stateId_eq_note]/@id=4361.

[199] See p. 470. See further Blair, n.57, above; Bristow, n.58, above.

[200] See p. 474.

parenting is as well. A new proposal in the White Paper is that information on parental relationship breakdown should be included in the school curriculum,[201] in order to provide children with 'the opportunity to learn about and examine the issue of parental separation schools'.[202]

Consequences of Parental Responsibility as Parental Accountability

Undermining of Authority Means Loss of Confidence

The more parents are told that parenting is difficult and the more they are encouraged to seek help, the less they will believe in their own capabilities and judgments. I have previously made this point in relation to divorcing couples.[203] In relation to parents there is an objective knock-on effect on their actual capabilities: a large part of successful parenting is confidence, as anyone who has had to deal with a toddler's tantrum will instantly confirm. Ironically, *Supporting Families* expresses the desire to bolster parents' confidence, while doing more than any other Government Document to undermine it further.[204]

This phenomenon was recognized by Lasch in the late 1970s. He argued that dependence on external advice destroyed parents' confidence in their ability to perform even the most elementary functions of child-rearing. This created a vicious circle because the less confident parents felt, the more they depended on outside advice,[205] but outside advice 'weakens parents' already faltering confidence in their own judgment'.[206] The damage to confidence occurred on two levels, that of form and substance. First, outside advice *in itself* weakened parental confidence. Secondly, the *content* of expert help undermined parents' assurance 'by reminding them of the incalculable consequences of their actions':[207]

> The proliferation of medical and psychiatric advice undermines parental confidence at the same time that it encourages a vastly inflated idea of the importance of child-rearing techniques and of the parent's responsibility for their failure.[208]

This process is reinforced by the transferral of areas of expertise from parents to external agencies: because parents lack competence in specific areas, they redouble

201 Department for Constitutional Affairs, Department for Education and Skills and Department for Trade and Industry, n.125, above, 20.

202 *Ibid*, 21.

203 Reece, n.87, above, 157.

204 Home Office, n.75, above, 7.

205 C. Lasch, *The Culture of Narcisissm: American Life in An Age of Diminishing Expectations* (New York and London, 1979), 169–70.

206 Lasch, n.32, above 172.

207 *Ibid*, 172.

208 *Ibid*, 172. See further p. 464; Wyness, n.8, above, 8–9; Abley, n.36, above. See Furedi, n.44, above, for further development of these themses.

their dependence on outside experts.[209] As we have seen, although Lasch described this trend in 1977:

> ... it is undoubtedly the case that since New Labour took office there has been a rapid escalation in the range and scale of parenting interventions that is distinctive.... Looking back over five years the National Family and Parenting Institute's mapping of family services in England and Wales ... found that 40 per cent of family support services had been established within this short time frame.[210]

Responsibility as Continuum

Parental responsibility as authority was clear-cut: either the responsible parent fulfilled his or her responsibility or in extreme cases the responsibility was removed. But now that responsibility has become an attitude for which the parent is held to account, he or she is no longer able to be fully responsible or fully irresponsible, because there is no action that he or she must take or refrain from taking in order to be responsible.[211] Responsible behaviour has become a continuum: one's attitude can be more or less reflective but it can never be reflective enough.[212] It is clear that the current approach leads to more far-reaching, diverse and nebulous responsibilities. Responsibility now extends infinitely; it is therefore impossible to define, impossible to fulfil and, crucially, virtually impossible to regulate. As I discussed in *Divorcing Responsibly*, attempts by the law to do so are inevitably uniquely interventionist.[213] The shift in the meaning of parental responsibility enables the law to be uniquely intrusive and judgmental, because every parent, on being held up to scrutiny, is found lacking.[214] Accordingly, the blurry spectrum of facilitation and support that has recently replaced clear-cut punishment and enforcement can be explained by its much better fit with parental responsibility as accountability.

[209] Lasch, n.32, above, 172; Jones and Wallace, n.31, above, 76. See also Wyness, n.8 above, 8–9 and 11. See further p. 463.

[210] Henricson, n.12, above, 3. See also Bristow, n.33, above.

[211] Reece, n.87, above, 209.

[212] *Ibid*, 228.

[213] *Ibid*, 235.

[214] *Ibid*, 238. See also Bristow, n.33, above; Bristow, n.58, above.

Index

Printed in the United States
96190LV00001B/12/A

9 780199 282548